Oxford
Primary
Dictionary

Editors and Contributors:

Robert Allen

Andrew Delahunty

Mary O'Neill

Susan Rennie

OXFORD

UNIVERSITY PRESS

OXFORD
UNIVERSITY PRESS

Great Clarendon Street, Oxford OX2 6DP

Oxford University Press is a department of the University of Oxford.
It furthers the University's objective of excellence in research, scholarship,
and education by publishing worldwide in

Oxford New York

Auckland Cape Town Dar es Salaam Hong Kong Karachi
Kuala Lumpur Madrid Melbourne Mexico City Nairobi
New Delhi Shanghai Taipei Toronto

With offices in

Argentina Austria Brazil Chile Czech Republic France Greece
Guatemala Hungary Italy Japan Poland Portugal Singapore
South Korea Switzerland Thailand Turkey Ukraine Vietnam

Oxford is a registered trade mark of Oxford University Press
in the UK and in certain other countries

First published 1993
Second published 1998
Revised second edition 2001
Third edition 2007
Fourth edition 2007

This new illustrated edition 2011

All artwork by Dynamo Design

British Library Cataloguing in Publication
Data available

ISBN: 978-0-19-273263-7
20 19 18 17 16 15 14
Kingston Bookshop ISBN: 978-0-19-913921-7
10 9 8 7

Printed in China by Leo Paper Products Ltd

Paper used in the production of this book is a natural, recycleable product
made from wood grown in sustainable forests. The manufacturing process
conforms to the enviromental regulations of the country of origin.

This dictionary has been written for primary school children, especially those who are aged 9+. The Oxford Primary Dictionary is designed to address school and curriculum needs and has been checked by teachers, and the Oxford Children's Corpus, a large language database consisting of over 30 million words of texts written for children.

The words in this dictionary have been carefully chosen according to level and appropriacy, and definitions are expressed clearly and in simple language.

Most definitions are supported by example sentences or short example phrases showing words in use, including a generous selection from children's authors. Dictionaries are traditionally used to help with reading, but we hope that this dictionary will support children when they are writing too. Informative illustrations have been added to support the definitions and help children in their project work.

The illustrated headwords are aeroplane, beak, bicycle, castle, centurion, coat of arms, continent, diver, eclipse, eye, fish, flower, food chain, galleon, granny knot, heart, iceberg, insect, kayak, lens, magma, metamorphosis, Morse code, oil rig, pasta, planet, pulley, reptile, satellite, semaphore, skeleton, solstice, strait, suspension bridge, tarantula, three dimensional, trumpet, Venn diagram, water cycle, and wind turbine.

At the end there is a short reference section of spelling tips, common irregular verbs, and prefixes and suffixes as well as a short selection of words with interesting word histories.

Dictionary entries

The words are defined and arranged in alphabetical order. Words which are derived from each main word (e.g. believable from believe) are often included at the end of an entry. Words with the same spelling but with a different meaning or origin are given separate entries and are numbered with a superscript number, e.g. lean[1] (bend your body) and lean[2] (not fat).

Pronunciation

Help is given with pronouncing words when they are difficult in some way. The pronunciation is given in brackets, introduced by 'rhymes with' or 'say', followed by a simple scheme that uses ordinary letters.

> **acre** (say **ay**-ker) noun acres
>
> **draught** (rhymes with craft) noun draughts

Words are divided into syllables, and the main stress is shown by bold type **like this.** Note the following:

oo shows the sound as in soon   *th* shows the sound as in *th*is
uu shows the sound as in b**oo**k   **zh** shows the sound as in vi**s**ion
th shows the sound as in **th**in

Word classes

Word classes (e.g. noun, adjective, verb) are printed after the word. When a word has more than one word class, the entries are grouped together.

> **below** preposition
> lower than, under *We have nice neighbours in the flat below us.*
> **below** adverb
> at a lower point, or to a lower point *I'll have the top bunk, and you can sleep below.*

other forms different forms so that you can see how to spell them

illustrations give further information and vocabulary relating to the entry

headword in alphabetical order, in blue

numbered headwords show that the word has different meanings or origins

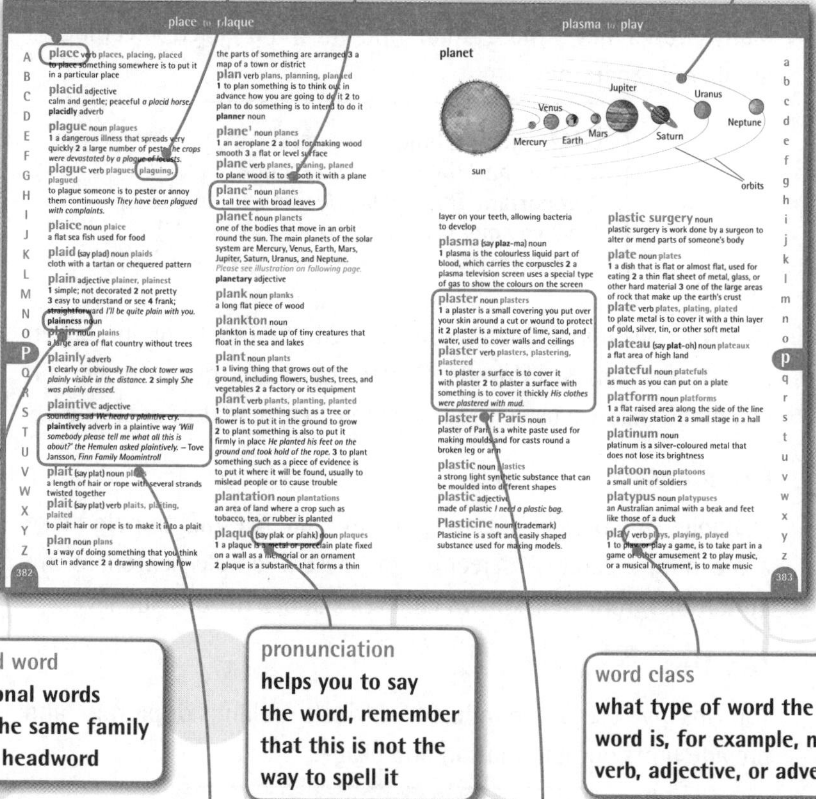
place to plaque
A B C D E F G H I J K L M N O P Q R S T U V W X Y Z
place verb places, placing, placed
to place something somewhere is to put it in a particular place
placid adjective
calm and gentle; peaceful a placid horse.
placidly adverb
plague noun plagues
1 a dangerous illness that spreads very quickly 2 a large number of pests The crops were devastated by a plague of locusts.
plague verb plagues, plaguing, plagued
to plague someone is to pester or annoy them continuously They have been plagued with complaints.
plaice noun plaice
a flat sea fish used for food
plaid (say plad) noun plaids
cloth with a tartan or chequered pattern
plain adjective plainer, plainest
1 simple; not decorated 2 not pretty 3 easy to understand or see 4 frank; straightforward I'll be quite plain with you.
plainness noun
plain noun plains
a large area of flat country without trees
plainly adverb
1 clearly or obviously The clock tower was plainly visible in the distance. 2 simply She was plainly dressed.
plaintive adjective
sounding sad We heard a plaintive cry.
plaintively adverb in a plaintive way 'Will somebody please tell me what all this is about?' the Hemulen asked plaintively. – Tove Jansson, Finn Family Moomintroll
plait (say plat) noun plaits
a length of hair or rope with several strands twisted together
plait (say plat) verb plaits, plaiting, plaited
to plait hair or rope is to make it into a plait
plan noun plans
1 a way of doing something that you think out in advance 2 a drawing showing how the parts of something are arranged 3 a map of a town or district
plan verb plans, planning, planned
1 to plan something is to think out in advance how you are going to do it 2 to plan to do something is to intend to do it
planner noun
plane1 noun planes
1 an aeroplane 2 a tool for making wood smooth 3 a flat or level surface
plane verb planes, planing, planed
to plane wood is to smooth it with a plane
plane2 noun planes
a tall tree with broad leaves
planet noun planets
one of the bodies that move in an orbit round the sun. The main planets of the solar system are Mercury, Venus, Earth, Mars, Jupiter, Saturn, Uranus, and Neptune.
Please see illustration on following page.
planetary adjective
plank noun planks
a long flat piece of wood
plankton noun
plankton is made up of tiny creatures that float in the sea and lakes
plant noun plants
1 a living thing that grows out of the ground, including flowers, bushes, trees, and vegetables 2 a factory or its equipment
plant verb plants, planting, planted
1 to plant something such as a tree or flower is to put it in the ground to grow 2 to plant something is also to put it firmly in place He planted his feet on the ground and took hold of the rope. 3 to plant something such as a piece of evidence is to put it where it will be found, usually to mislead people or to cause trouble
plantation noun plantations
an area of land where a crop such as tobacco, tea, or rubber is planted
plaque (say plak or plahk) noun plaques
1 a plaque is a metal or porcelain plate fixed on a wall as a memorial or an ornament 2 plaque is a substance that forms a thin
382
plasma to play
planet
sun
Mercury
Venus
Earth
Mars
Jupiter
Saturn
Uranus
Neptune
orbits
layer on your teeth, allowing bacteria to develop
plasma (say plaz-ma) noun
1 plasma is the colourless liquid part of blood, which carries the corpuscles 2 a plasma television screen uses a special type of gas to show the colours on the screen
plaster noun plasters
1 a plaster is a small covering you put over your skin around a cut or wound to protect it 2 plaster is a mixture of lime, sand, and water, used to cover walls and ceilings
plaster verb plasters, plastering, plastered
1 to plaster a surface is to cover it with plaster 2 to plaster a surface with something is to cover it thickly His clothes were plastered with mud.
plaster of Paris noun
plaster of Paris is a white paste used for making moulds and for casts round a broken leg or arm
plastic noun plastics
a strong light synthetic substance that can be moulded into different shapes
plastic adjective
made of plastic I need a plastic bag.
Plasticine noun (trademark)
Plasticine is a soft and easily shaped substance used for making models.
plastic surgery noun
plastic surgery is work done by a surgeon to alter or mend parts of someone's body
plate noun plates
1 a dish that is flat or almost flat, used for eating 2 a thin flat sheet of metal, glass, or other hard material 3 one of the large areas of rock that make up the earth's crust
plate verb plates, plating, plated
to plate metal is to cover it with a thin layer of gold, silver, tin, or other soft metal
plateau (say plat-oh) noun plateaux
a flat area of high land
plateful noun platefuls
as much as you can put on a plate
platform noun platforms
1 a flat raised area along the side of the line at a railway station 2 a small stage in a hall
platinum noun
platinum is a silver-coloured metal that does not lose its brightness
platoon noun platoons
a small unit of soldiers
platypus noun platypuses
an Australian animal with a beak and feet like those of a duck
play verb plays, playing, played
1 to play, or play a game, is to take part in a game or other amusement 2 to play music, or a musical instrument, is to make music
a b c d e f g h i j k l m n o p q r s t u v w x y z
383

derived word additional words from the same family as the headword

pronunciation helps you to say the word, remember that this is not the way to spell it

word class what type of word the word is, for example, noun, verb, adjective, or adverb

example sentence examples, many from children's authors, show headwords in context

definition what the word means, if a word has more than one meaning, the definitions are numbered

Inflections and plurals

The parts of verbs, plurals of nouns, and some comparatives and superlatives and adverbs are given after the word class.

> **cancel** verb cancels, cancelling, cancelled
> **camp** noun camps
> **calm** adjective calmer, calmest

Meanings

Many words have more than one meaning. Each meaning is numbered separately.

> **big** adjective bigger, biggest
> **1** more than the normal size; large
> **2** important *This is a big decision.* **3** elder *Have you met my big sister?*

Labels

Words or meanings that are only used informally or in spoken English are marked informal. Subject labels are given for certain meanings that are used in, for example, mathematics or science.

Examples

Examples of words in use are given in italic *like this* to help make a meaning clearer. A selection of these example sentences are quotations from well-known children's books for this age level.

Top Tips

Top Tips give useful reminders of difficult spellings or plurals, and provide hints on punctuation and usage.

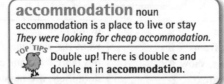

> **accommodation** noun
> accommodation is a place to live or stay
> *They were looking for cheap accommodation.*
> TOP TIPS Double up! There is double **c** and double **m** in **accommodation**.

Aa

a determiner (called the indefinite article)
1 one; any *I've bought you a present.*
2 each; every *I go swimming twice
a week.*

aardvark (say **ard**-vark) noun
aardvarks
an African animal that has a long snout and
eats ants and termites

aback adverb
to be taken aback is to be surprised and
slightly shocked by something *We were
taken aback by this silly idea.*

abacus noun abacuses
a frame with rows of sliding beads, used for
counting and doing sums

abandon verb abandons, abandoning,
abandoned
to abandon something or someone is to go
away and leave them, without intending
to go back *The lioness had abandoned her
two cubs.*

abbey noun abbeys
1 a group of buildings where monks or
nuns live and work **2** a church which is or
was part of an abbey, such as Westminster
Abbey in London

abbot noun abbots
the head of an abbey of monks

abbreviate verb abbreviates,
abbreviating, abbreviated
to abbreviate a word or phrase is to write it
with fewer letters so that it is shorter

abbreviation noun abbreviations
a word or group of letters that is a
shorter form of a word or phrase
*BBC is an abbreviation of 'British
Broadcasting Corporation'.*

ABC noun
a name for the alphabet *We know our ABC.*

abdomen noun abdomens
1 the part of your body below your chest,
which contains your stomach and intestines
2 the back part of the body of an insect
or spider

abdominal adjective
in your stomach or intestines *an
abdominal pain*

abide verb abides, abiding, abode or
abided
1 you cannot abide something or someone
when you don't like them at all *Some people
can't abide spiders.* **2** to abide by a rule or
promise is to keep to it

ability noun abilities
1 ability is the skill or talent to do
something *the ability to see in the dark*
2 an ability is a special skill or talent *a
player with many abilities*

ablaze adjective
a building is ablaze when it is on fire and
burning strongly

able adjective abler, ablest
1 having the power or skill or opportunity
to do something *No-one was able to crack
the code.* **2** having a special talent or
skill *You must be an able swimmer to join
the team.*

abnormal adjective
unusual or peculiar, not normal
abnormality noun **abnormally** adverb

aboard adverb, preposition
someone is aboard when they have got on a
train, ship, or aircraft *The passengers were all
aboard. It's time to get aboard the train.*

abode noun abodes
a formal word for the place where
someone lives

abolish verb abolishes, abolishing,
abolished
to abolish a rule or custom is to get rid of it
The class voted to abolish homework.

abolition (say ab-o-**lish**-on) noun
getting rid of something *the abolition
of slavery*

a
b
c
d
e
f
g
h
i
j
k
l
m
n
o
p
q
r
s
t
u
v
w
x
y
z

A
B
C
D
E
F
G
H
I
J
K
L
M
N
O
P
Q
R
S
T
U
V
W
X
Y
Z

abominable adjective
very shocking, dreadful *a series of abominable crimes*

Aborigines (say ab-er-ij-in-eez) plural noun
the people whose ancestors were living in Australia before European settlers arrived

abort verb aborts, aborting, aborted
to abort a plan or mission is to cancel it after it has begun

about preposition
1 to do with, connected with *The film is about a family of superheroes.* **2** approximately, roughly *The castle wall is about 10 metres high.*

about adverb
1 in various directions or places *People were running about madly.* **2** somewhere near by *There may be bears and wolves about.* **to be about to do something** is to be just going to do it *They are about to announce the winner.*

above preposition
1 higher than, over *on the shelf above the fireplace* **2** more than *The temperature was just above freezing.*

above adverb
at a higher point, overhead *Fireworks lit up the sky above.*

abracadabra interjection
a word that people say when they are doing magic tricks

abroad adverb
in a foreign country *They live abroad now.*

abrupt adjective
1 sudden and unexpected *an abrupt change in the weather* **2** rude and unfriendly *He gave an abrupt reply.* **abruptly** adverb

abscess noun abscesses
a painful swelling on the body containing pus

abseil verb abseils, abseiling, abseiled
to abseil is to lower yourself down a steep cliff or rock by sliding down a rope

absence noun absences
not being in a place where you are expected, for example school or work

absent adjective
not present; away

absentee noun absentees
someone who is away, for example not at school or work

absent–minded adjective
forgetting things easily
absent-mindedly adverb to do something absent-mindedly is to do it without thinking about it much *Lydia absent-mindedly put too much sugar in her tea.*

absolute adjective
total, complete, not restricted *I have absolute confidence in you.*

absolutely adverb
1 completely **2** (informal) definitely *'Are you going to Beth's party?' 'Absolutely!'*

absorb verb absorbs, absorbing, absorbed
1 to absorb something like liquid is to soak it up **2** to be absorbed in something is to be interested in it and give it all your attention *He was very absorbed in his book.*

absorbent adjective
an absorbent material soaks up liquid easily

abstract (say **ab**-strakt) adjective
to do with ideas and not with physical things *abstract patterns*

absurd adjective
silly or ridiculous *What an absurd idea!*

abundance noun
a large amount, plenty *an abundance of fresh air*

abundant adjective
large in amount, plentiful *an abundant supply of food*

abuse (say a-**bewz**) verb abuses, abusing, abused
1 to abuse something is to treat it badly and harm it **2** to abuse someone is to say

unpleasant things about them **3** to abuse someone also means to hurt them or treat them cruelly

abuse (say a-**bewss**) noun abuses
1 treating something badly **2** unpleasant words said about someone *She got a lot of abuse from her so-called friends.* **3** physical harm or cruelty done to someone

abusive adjective
saying unpleasant things about someone

abysmal adjective (informal)
very bad *The weather was abysmal.*

abyss noun abysses
a deep dark hole that seems to go on for ever

academic adjective
to do with learning in a school or university *an academic subject*

academy noun academies
1 a college or school **2** a society of scholars or scientists who meet to discuss their work

accelerate verb accelerates, accelerating, accelerated
to accelerate is to go faster

acceleration noun
an increase of speed, going faster

accelerator noun accelerators
a pedal that you press down to make a motor vehicle go faster

accent (say **ak**-sent) noun accents
1 an accent is the way that people from a particular area pronounce words *He has a Yorkshire accent.* **2** the accent in a word is the part you speak more strongly than the rest of it *The accent in 'dinner' is on the first syllable.* **3** an accent is a special mark put over a letter in a foreign word, to show its pronunciation *The word 'cliché' has an accent on the 'e'.*

accent (say ak-**sent**) verb accents, accenting, accented
to accent part of a word is to speak it more strongly than the rest of it

accept verb accepts, accepting, accepted
1 to accept something is to take it when someone offers it to you **2** to accept an invitation is to say 'yes' to it **3** to accept an idea or suggestion is to agree that it is true or worth thinking about

acceptable adjective
1 good enough to accept *We think it is an acceptable offer.* **2** all right, satisfactory *Their behaviour was not acceptable.*

acceptance noun
taking something that someone offers you

access noun accesses
a way to reach a place *This road is the only access to the house.*

access verb accesses, accessing, accessed
to access a computer file is to find and be able to use it

accessible adjective
easy to reach or approach

accessory noun accessories
1 an extra or spare part that goes with something bigger **2** an item like a piece of jewellery or a handbag that goes with clothes

accident noun accidents
something unexpected that happens, especially when something is broken, or someone is hurt or killed **by accident** by chance, not intentionally

accidental adjective
something is accidental when it happens by chance and not because someone wants it to happen *accidental damage* **accidentally** adverb

accommodate verb accommodates, accommodating, accommodated
1 to accommodate someone or something is to provide them with a place to stay **2** to accommodate someone also means to do what you can to please them

A

B
C
D
E
F
G
H
I
J
K
L
M
N
O
P
Q
R
S
T
U
V
W
X
Y
Z

accommodation noun
accommodation is a place to live or stay
They were looking for cheap accommodation.

TOP TIPS Double up! There is double **c** and double **m** in **accommodation**.

accompaniment noun
accompaniments
the music played on a piano or another instrument while a singer sings

accompany verb accompanies,
accompanying, accompanied
1 to accompany someone is to go somewhere with them **2** to accompany a singer is to play the piano or another instrument while they sing

accomplish verb accomplishes,
accomplishing, accomplished
to accomplish something is to do it successfully

accomplished adjective
good at doing something, skilful

accomplishment noun
accomplishments
something you do well

accord noun accords
to do something of your own accord is to do it willingly and without being told to

according to preposition
1 You say **according to someone** to show where a piece of information comes from. *According to Katie, there is a party tomorrow.* **2** You say **according to something** when you are comparing two things. *Nothing went according to our plan.*

accordion noun accordions
a portable musical instrument which you play by squeezing the sides and pressing on the keys

account noun accounts
1 a description or story about something that happened *a thrilling account of their adventures* **2** an amount of money someone has in a bank or building society **3** a statement showing how much money

someone owes, a bill **on account of something** because of it **on no account** certainly not **to take something into account** is to consider it along with other things

account verb accounts, accounting,
accounted
to account for something is to be an explanation of it *What could account for his odd behaviour?*

accountant noun accountants
a person whose job is to write and organize the money accounts of a person or organization

accumulate verb accumulates,
accumulating, accumulated
1 to accumulate things is to collect them or pile them up **2** things accumulate when they form a heap or pile

accumulation noun
1 accumulating things **2** a heap or pile, a collection *an accumulation of junk*

accuracy noun
accuracy is being exactly right or correct

accurate adjective
correct, done exactly and carefully *an accurate drawing of a skeleton*
accurately adverb

accusation noun accusations
a statement accusing someone of something

accuse verb accuses, accusing,
accused
to accuse someone is to say that they did something wrong

accustomed adjective
to be accustomed to something is to be used to it *I'm not accustomed to staying up late.*

ace noun aces
1 a playing card with an A in the corner and a large emblem of the suit in the centre **2** a very clever or skilful person *She is an ace at sudoku.* **3** in tennis, an ace is a serve that the other player cannot return

ache noun aches
a dull steady pain

ache verb aches, aching, ached
to ache is to feel a dull steady pain

achieve verb achieves, achieving, achieved
to achieve something is to succeed in doing it or getting it

achievement noun achievements
something someone has succeeded in doing *Winning the gold medal was a great achievement.*

acid noun acids
a substance that contains hydrogen and causes chemical change. Acids are the opposite of alkalis

acid adjective
sour or bitter to taste

acid rain noun
rain that contains harmful acids because it has mixed with waste gases from the air

acknowledge verb acknowledges, acknowledging, acknowledged
1 to acknowledge something is to admit that it is true 2 to acknowledge a letter is to say that you have received it 3 to acknowledge a debt or favour is to say you are grateful for it

acknowledgement noun acknowledgements
1 something that you admit or confess 2 a note to say that you have received a letter or message *This is an acknowledgement of your email.*

acne (say **ak**-ni) noun
a skin disease which causes red pimples on the face and neck and is common among teenagers

acorn noun acorns
an oval nut which grows on an oak tree and has a cup on its stem

acoustic (say a-**koo**-stik) adjective
1 to do with sound or hearing 2 an acoustic guitar or other musical instrument uses its own shape to make the sound, and does not have an electrical amplifier

acoustics (say a-**koo**-stiks) plural noun
1 the acoustics of a place are the qualities that make it good or bad for sound
2 (singular noun) the science of sound

acquaint verb acquaints, acquainting, acquainted
1 to acquaint someone with something is to tell them about it 2 to be acquainted with someone is to know them slightly

acquaintance noun acquaintances
someone you know slightly **to make someone's acquaintance** is to get to know them

acquire verb acquires, acquiring, acquired
to acquire something is to obtain it, usually with some effort or difficulty

acquit verb acquits, acquitting, acquitted
to acquit someone is to decide that they are not guilty of a crime, especially in a law trial

acre (say **ay**-ker) noun acres
an area of land measuring 4,840 square yards (about 4,047 square metres)

acrobat (say **ak**-ro-bat) noun acrobats
an entertainer who gives displays of jumping and balancing **acrobatic** adjective

acrobatics plural noun
exercises of jumping and balancing that an acrobat does.

acronym (say **ak**-ro-nim) noun acronyms
a word or name that is formed from the first letters of other words, for example *UFO* is an acronym of *unidentified flying object*

across adverb, preposition
1 from one side of something to the other *The table measures 1.5 metres across.* 2 to the other side of something *How can we get across the busy road?*

A
B
C
D
E
F
G
H
I
J
K
L
M
N
O
P
Q
R
S
T
U
V
W
X
Y
Z

act noun acts
1 something that someone does 2 an individual performance in a programme of entertainment, for example a juggling act or a comic act 3 one of the main sections of a play or opera 4 a new law that a government makes

act verb acts, acting, acted
1 to act is to do something useful or necessary *We need to act straight away.* 2 to act stupid or act clever is to behave stupidly or cleverly 3 to act in a play or film is to take part in it

action noun actions
1 an action is something that someone does 2 action is moving or doing things *The film is full of fast-paced action.* 3 action is also fighting in a battle *He was killed in action.*
out of action not working properly

activate verb activates, activating, activated
to activate a machine or device is to start it working

active adjective
1 busy, taking part in lots of activities 2 doing things, working *an active volcano* 3 (in grammar) an active verb is one where the subject does the action, for example in the sentence *We made a cake*, the subject is *We* and *made* is an active verb

activity noun activities
1 activity is doing things 2 an activity is something special that someone does *They enjoy outdoor activities.*

actor noun actors
someone who takes part in a play or film

actress noun actresses
a girl or woman who takes part in a play or film

actual adjective
really there or really happening *Is that an actual dinosaur bone?*

actually adverb
really, in fact *Actually, I think you are wrong.*

acute adjective
1 sharp or intense *an acute stomach pain* 2 severe *an acute shortage of food* 3 clever, quick to understand something 4 an acute accent is a mark (´) put over a letter, as in *cliché* 5 an acute angle is an angle of less than 90°

AD
short for *Anno Domini*, used with dates that come after the birth of Jesus Christ, for example AD 1492 is the year Columbus reached America

Adam's apple noun Adam's apples
the lump at the front of a man's neck

adapt verb adapts, adapting, adapted
1 to adapt something is to change it so you can use it for something different 2 to adapt to something is to make yourself cope with it *They adapted to life in the country very quickly.* **adaptation** noun

adaptable adjective
able to adapt to or become suitable for different things

adaptor noun adaptors
a device for connecting different pieces of equipment

add verb adds, adding, added
1 to add one number to another is to put them together to get a bigger number 2 to add one thing to another is to mix them together, for example the different things in a recipe **to add up** is what numbers do to make a bigger number, called a total

adder noun adders
a small poisonous snake

addict noun addicts
someone with a habit they can't give up **addicted** adjective

addiction noun addictions
a habit that someone can't give up

addition noun additions
1 addition is the process of adding numbers together 2 an addition is something or someone that has been added *Matt was a*

late addition to the team. **in addition** also, as well

additional adjective
extra, added on

additive noun additives
something that is added to food or to something else in small amounts

address noun addresses
1 the details of the place where someone lives *My address is 29 High Street, Newtown.* 2 (in computing) a set of letters and symbols that you use to find a website or to send an email *What's your email address?* 3 a speech

address verb addresses, addressing, addressed
1 to address a letter or parcel is to write the address on it before sending it 2 to address a group of people is to make a speech to them *A man stepped forward and addressed the crowd.*

 TOP TIPS — Double up! There is double **d** and double **s** in **address**.

adenoids plural noun
your adenoids are the spongy flesh at the back of your nose, which can become swollen making it difficult to breathe

adequate adjective
enough, sufficient **adequately** adverb

adhere verb adheres, adhering, adhered
1 something adheres to a surface when it sticks to it 2 you adhere to a promise or rule when you keep it

adhesive noun adhesives
something such as glue that you use to stick things together

adhesive adjective
causing things to stick together

Adi Granth (say ah-di **grunt**) noun
the holy book of the Sikhs

adjacent adjective
near or next to something *Her house is adjacent to the shop.*

adjective noun adjectives
a word that describes a noun or adds to its meaning, for example *big, honest, red*

adjust verb adjusts, adjusting, adjusted
1 to adjust something is to change it slightly or change its position 2 to adjust to something is to try to get used to it *They found it hard to adjust to life in the city.*

adjustment noun adjustments
a small change you make to something *She made a quick adjustment to her hair.*

administer verb administers, administering, administered
1 to administer a country is to govern it 2 to administer a medicine is to give it to someone

administrate verb administrates, administrating, administrated
to administrate a country or business is to govern it or run it **administrative** adjective

administration noun administrations
1 administration is running a business or governing a country 2 in the USA, an administration is a government that is holding office *the Obama administration*

admirable adjective
worth admiring; excellent *an admirable piece of work* **admirably** adverb

admiral noun admirals
an officer of the highest rank in the navy

admiration noun
you feel admiration for someone or something when you think they are very good or very beautiful *I'm full of admiration for her courage.*

admire verb admires, admiring, admired
1 to admire someone or something is to think they are very good or very beautiful 2 to admire something is also to look at it and enjoy it *They went to the top of the hill to admire the view.*

admirer noun admirers
someone who thinks that a particular

a
b
c
d
e
f
g
h
i
j
k
l
m
n
o
p
q
r
s
t
u
v
w
x
y
z

A

person or thing is very good or beautiful *Cleopatra had many admirers.*

admission noun admissions
1 admission is being allowed to go into a place *Admission to the show is by ticket only.*
2 an admission is something that someone admits or confesses *He is guilty by his own admission.*

admit verb admits, admitting, admitted
1 to admit someone is to let them come into a place 2 to admit something is to say that it has happened or that you have done it

admittance noun
admittance is being allowed to go into a private place

admittedly adverb
as an agreed fact; without denying it *Admittedly, it was a silly thing to do.*

ado noun
without more ado without wasting any more time

adolescent noun adolescents
a young person who is older than a child and not yet an adult, from about 15 to 18 **adolescence** noun

adopt verb adopts, adopting, adopted
1 to adopt a child is to take them into your family and bring them up as your own 2 to adopt a system or method is to start using it **adopted** adjective **adoption** noun

adorable adjective
lovely, worth adoring *an adorable new puppy*

adore verb adores, adoring, adored
to adore someone or something is to love them or admire them very much **adoration** noun

adorn verb adorns, adorning, adorned
to adorn something is to decorate it or make it pretty

adrenalin noun
a hormone that stimulates your nervous

system and makes you feel ready to do something

adrift adverb, adjective
something such as a boat is adrift when it is loose and drifting about

adult noun adults
a fully grown person or animal

advance noun advances
1 an advance is a forward movement 2 advance is improvement or progress 3 an advance of money is a loan 4 an advance warning is a warning given beforehand **in advance** beforehand

advance verb advances, advancing, advanced
1 to advance is to move forward 2 to advance is also to make progress

advanced adjective
an advanced course or exam is one at a higher level

advantage noun advantages
something useful or helpful **to take advantage of someone** is to treat them unfairly when they are not likely to complain **to take advantage of something** is to make good use of it

Advent noun
in the Christian Church, the period before Christmas

adventure noun adventures
1 an adventure is something exciting or interesting that someone does 2 adventure is doing bold and exciting things *She enjoys a bit of adventure.* **adventurous** adjective

adverb noun adverbs
a word that tells you how or when or where or why something happens. In these sentences, the words in italics are adverbs: They moved *slowly.* Come back *soon.* I *only* want a drink.

adversary (say ad-ver-sa-ri) noun adversaries
an opponent or enemy

adverse adjective
not good; harmful *The magic potion had an adverse effect.*

adversity noun **adversities**
adversity is bad things that happen to someone

advert noun **adverts** (informal)
an advertisement

advertise verb **advertises, advertising, advertised**
1 to advertise something is to praise it in a newspaper or on television so that people will want it **2** to advertise an event is to tell people when it will take place *Have you advertised the concert?*

advertisement noun **advertisements**
a public notice or short television film that tries to persuade people to buy something

advice noun
advice is something you say to someone to help them decide what to do

advisable adjective
sensible, worth doing

advise verb **advises, advising, advised**
to advise someone is to tell them what you think they should do

advocate (say **ad**-vo-kat) noun **advocates**
1 a person who speaks in favour of someone or something **2** in Scotland, an advocate is a lawyer who presents a case in court.

advocate (say **ad**-vo-kayt) verb **advocates, advocating, advocated**
to advocate something is to speak in favour of it

aerial noun **aerials**
a wire or metal rod for receiving or sending radio or television signals

aerial adjective
from or in the air, or from aircraft *an aerial view of the island*

aerobatics plural noun
an exciting display by flying aircraft
aerobatic adjective

aerobics plural noun
aerobics are energetic exercises that strengthen your heart and lungs

aeronautics plural noun
the study of aircraft and flying

aeroplane noun **aeroplanes**
a flying vehicle with fixed wings and powerful engines

a
b
c
d
e
f
g
h
i
j
k
l
m
n
o
p
q
r
s
t
u
v
w
x
y
z

aeroplane

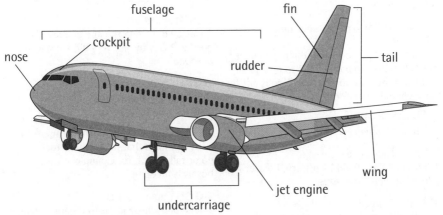

fuselage
fin
cockpit
nose
rudder
tail
wing
jet engine
undercarriage

A
B
C
D
E
F
G
H
I
J
K
L
M
N
O
P
Q
R
S
T
U
V
W
X
Y
Z

aerosol noun aerosols
a device that holds a liquid under pressure and lets it out in a fine spray

affair noun affairs
1 something interesting that happens, an event *The party was a very strange affair.* 2 someone's affairs are their private business *Why are you so interested in my affairs?*

affect verb affects, affecting, affected
to affect someone or something is to cause them to change or to harm them *The dampness might affect his health.*

affected adjective
not real, pretended *'Really, Daisy!' said Chloe, clutching her ears in an affected way. 'You practically deafened me.'* – Jacqueline Wilson, *Sleepovers*

affection noun affections
affection or an affection is love or fondness *She has a great affection for her cat.*
affectionate adjective

afflict verb afflicts, afflicting, afflicted
to be afflicted by something unpleasant, like an illness, is to suffer from it
affliction noun

affluence (say af-loo-ens) noun
having a lot of money or wealth *There is more affluence in the bigger cities.*
affluent adjective

afford verb affords, affording, afforded
1 to be able to afford something is to have enough money to pay for it 2 to be unable to afford the time to do something is not to have enough time for it

afloat adverb
floating *We managed to keep the raft afloat.*

afraid adjective
frightened **I'm afraid** I am sorry; I regret *I'm afraid I've burnt the cakes.*

afresh adverb
again; in a new way *We must start afresh.*

African adjective
coming from or to do with Africa
African noun Africans
a person from Africa

after preposition, adverb
1 later or later than, following *They set off after breakfast. We saw them again the week after.* 2 following or coming behind *They were after us in the queue.* 3 to be named after someone is to be given their name *She was named after her grandmother.*

afternoon noun afternoons
the time from midday until evening

afterwards adverb
at a later time

again adverb
1 once more; another time 2 as before *You will soon be well again.* **again and again** lots of times

against preposition
1 touching or hitting *He was leaning against the wall.* 2 opposed to, not liking *Are you against animal testing?*

age noun ages
1 your age is how old you are 2 an age is a period of history *the Elizabethan age* 3 age is the last part of someone's life *She had the wisdom that comes with age.* **ages** (informal) a long time *We've been waiting ages.*

age verb ages, ageing, aged
to age is to become old

aged adjective
1 (say ayjd) having the age of *The girl was aged 9.* 2 (say **ay**-jid) very old *We saw an aged man.*

agency noun agencies
the office or business of someone who organizes things

agenda (say a-**jen**-da) noun agendas
a list of things that people have to do or talk about, for example at a business meeting

agent noun agents
1 someone whose job is to organize things

for other people *We booked our holiday with a travel agent.* **2** a spy *He is a secret agent.*

aggravate verb aggravates, aggravating, aggravated
1 to aggravate something is to make it worse **2** (informal) to aggravate someone is to annoy them **aggravation** noun

aggression noun
starting a war or attack; being aggressive

aggressive adjective
1 an aggressive person or group is one that is likely to attack or use violence **2** an aggressive activity is done with energy and has a strong effect *They began an aggressive sales campaign.*

agile adjective
able to move quickly and easily **agility** noun

agitated adjective
feeling worried and anxious *Frank was starting to look agitated.* **agitation** noun

agnostic (say ag-nos-tik) noun agnostics
someone who believes that we cannot know if there is a God

ago adverb
in the past *She died long ago.*

agonizing adjective
1 an agonizing pain is one that hurts terribly **2** an agonizing choice or decision is one that you find very difficult to make

agony noun agonies
severe pain or suffering

agree verb agrees, agreeing, agreed
1 to agree with someone is to think the same as them **2** to agree to do something is to say that you are willing to do it *She agreed to show us the way.* **3** food does not agree with you when it upsets your stomach *Spicy food doesn't agree with me.*

agreeable adjective
1 willing to do something that someone suggests *Both sides were agreeable to the idea.* **2** pleasant *an agreeable place for a holiday*

agreement noun agreements
1 agreement is thinking the same *Are we in agreement?* **2** an agreement is an arrangement that people have agreed on

agriculture noun
agriculture is farming, or growing food on the land **agricultural** adjective

aground adverb
a ship runs aground when it gets stuck in shallow water

ah interjection
a word you shout out when you are surprised or pleased

ahead adverb
forwards, in front *Sheila went ahead to show us the way.*

ahoy interjection
a shout used by sailors to attract attention

aid noun aids
1 aid is help you give someone **2** aid is also money or food or other help that a country sends to a poorer country **3** an aid is something that helps someone to do something better *He was wearing a hearing aid.*

aid verb aids, aiding, aided
to aid someone is to help them

ailing adjective
suffering, in a bad way

ailment noun ailments
a minor illness

aim verb aims, aiming, aimed
1 to aim a gun at someone or something is to point it at them so as to shoot them **2** to aim something like a ball is to throw it or kick it in a particular direction **3** to aim to do something is to try to do it

aim noun aims
1 a person's aim is what they intend to do **2** aim is also pointing a weapon in a particular direction

aimless adjective
not having any definite aim or purpose *He led an aimless life.* **aimlessly** adverb

a
b
c
d
e
f
g
h
i
j
k
l
m
n
o
p
q
r
s
t
u
v
w
x
y
z

A
B
C
D
E
F
G
H
I
J
K
L
M
N
O
P
Q
R
S
T
U
V
W
X
Y
Z

air noun airs
1 air is the mixture of gases which surrounds the earth and which everyone breathes 2 an air is a tune 3 an air of mystery or secrecy is a feeling that things are mysterious or secret **to be in the air** is to be just an idea, and not something certain *Our plans are still in the air.* **to be on the air** is to be on the radio or television **to put on airs** is to behave grandly, as if you are important

air verb airs, airing, aired
1 to air clothes or washing is to put them in a warm place to finish drying 2 to air a room is to let fresh air into it 3 to air views or opinions is to say them so that people know them

air-conditioning noun
a system for controlling the temperature and freshness of the air in a building, so that it is kept cool in hot weather and warm in cold weather

aircraft noun aircraft
an aeroplane or a helicopter *The two aircraft passed each other over the Atlantic.*

aircraft carrier noun aircraft carriers
a large ship with a flat deck on which aircraft can take off and land

airfield noun airfields
a place where aircraft can take off and land

air force noun air forces
the part of a country's fighting force that uses aircraft

airgun noun airguns
a gun that works with compressed air

airline noun airlines
a company that takes people to places by aircraft.

airmail noun
airmail is mail that is sent by air

airport noun airports
a place where aircraft land and take off, with passenger terminals and other buildings

air raid noun air raids
an attack by bombs dropped from aircraft

airship noun airships
a large balloon with engines, designed to carry passengers or cargo

airstrip noun airstrips
a strip of land prepared for aircraft to take off and land

airtight adjective
not letting air get in or out

airy adjective airier, airiest
1 with plenty of fresh air 2 vague and insincere *They were just airy promises.*

aisle (rhymes with **mile**) noun aisles
1 a part at the side of a church 2 a passage between or beside rows of seats or pews

ajar adverb, adjective
slightly open *Please leave the door ajar.*

akimbo adverb
arms akimbo with your hands on your hips and your elbows out

alarm verb alarms, alarming, alarmed
to alarm someone is to make them frightened or anxious

alarm noun alarms
1 a warning sound or signal 2 a feeling of fear or anxiety *He cried out in alarm.*

alarm clock noun alarm clocks
a clock with a loud ring or bleep, which can be set to wake someone who is asleep

alas interjection (old use)
something you say when you are sad

albatross noun albatrosses
a large sea bird with long wings

album noun albums
1 a book in which you keep things like photographs or stamps or autographs 2 a collection of songs on a CD, record, or tape

alcohol noun
1 a colourless liquid made by fermenting sugar or starch 2 drinks containing this liquid (for example beer, wine, gin), which

affects people's behaviour and can make them drunk if they have too much **alcoholic** adjective containing alcohol

alcove noun alcoves
a part of a room where the wall is set back from the main part

alert adjective
watching for something; ready to act
alert verb alerts, alerting, alerted
to alert someone to a danger or problem is to warn them about it
alert noun alerts
an alarm **on the alert** on the lookout for danger or attack

A level noun A levels
a higher standard of examination that is taken after the GCSE, especially by pupils who want to go to university

algebra (say al-ji-bra) noun
mathematics in which letters and symbols are used to represent numbers

alias (say ay-li-as) noun aliases
a false or different name that someone uses instead of their real name
alias adverb
also named *Clark Kent, alias Superman*

alibi (say al-i-by) noun alibis
evidence that someone accused of a crime was not there when the crime was committed

alien (say ay-li-en) noun aliens
1 someone who is not a citizen of the country where they are living **2** in science fiction, a being from another world
alien adjective
1 foreign **2** not in keeping, quite unlike *Lying was alien to his nature.*

alienate verb alienates, alienating, alienated
to alienate someone is to make them unfriendly to you **alienation** noun

alight adjective
on fire, burning

alike adjective
similar, like each other
alike adverb
in the same way *He treats everybody alike.*

alive adjective
living, existing *Is he alive?*

alkali (say al-ka-ly) noun alkalis
a substance that neutralizes acids or that combines with acids to form salts

all determiner, adverb, pronoun
meaning 'everything' or 'everyone' *That is all I know. She was dressed all in white. All my books are in the desk.* **to do something all out** (informal) is to use all your ability to do it *Go all out to win.* **all the same** nevertheless; making no difference *It was raining but I went out all the same.*

Allah
the Muslim name of God

all–clear noun
a signal that a danger has passed

allegation (say a-li-gay-shun) noun allegations
you make an allegation when you accuse someone of doing something wrong

allege (say a-lej) verb alleges, alleging, alleged
to allege that someone has done something is to accuse them of it, usually without proof *He alleged that I stole his watch.*

allegiance (say a-lee-jans) noun allegiances
loyalty shown to a person or organization

allegory noun allegories
a story or poem with made-up people and places that are meant to stand for real people and places **allegorical** adjective

allergy noun
a condition that some people have that makes their body react badly to things they eat or drink or touch or breathe in, for example dust, milk, or some kinds of food **allergic** adjective someone is allergic to something if they become ill or

A

uncomfortable when they eat it or touch it *She must be allergic to goat's milk.*

alley noun alleys
1 a narrow street or passage 2 a place where you can play at skittles or tenpin bowling

alliance noun alliances
an agreement between countries to support each other and have the same enemies

alligator noun alligators
a large reptile like a crocodile

alliteration noun
alliteration is when the same letter or sound occurs several times in a group of words, for special effect, e.g. *sing a song of sixpence*

allot verb allots, allotting, allotted
to allot shares or jobs is to give them to various people

allotment noun allotments
a small rented piece of ground used for growing vegetables

allow verb allows, allowing, allowed
1 to allow someone to do something is to let them do it *Will you allow me to take a photograph? Skateboarding is not allowed.*
2 to allow an amount of money is to provide it for some reason *She was allowed £10 for books.*

allowance noun allowances
a sum of money given regularly to someone
to make allowances is to be considerate *We must make allowances for his age.*

alloy noun alloys
a metal formed from a mixture of other metals

all right adjective
1 satisfactory; reasonably good *The book was all right, but the film was better.*
2 acceptable; allowed *Is it all right to play music in here?* 3 safe and well; not harmed *Are you sure you're all right?*

all right interjection
you can also say all right when you agree to something *'Would you like to come with us?' 'All right.'*

all-round adjective
having many skills *She's a good all-round athlete.*

ally (say al-I) noun allies
1 a country in alliance with another country 2 a person who helps or cooperates with you

ally verb allies, allying, allied
to ally oneself with someone else is to form an alliance with them

almond (say ah-mond) noun almonds
an oval nut that you can eat

almost adverb
very close to but not quite *I am almost ready.*

aloft adverb
high up *The sailors climbed aloft.*

alone adjective, adverb
without any other people or other things *She lived alone on the island for a whole year. The drinks alone cost £10.*

along preposition, adverb
1 from one end of something to the other 2 on; onwards *Move along, please!*
3 accompanying someone *I have brought my brother along.*

alongside preposition, adverb
next to something

aloud adverb
in a voice that can be heard

alphabet noun alphabets
the letters used in a language, usually arranged in a set order
alphabetical adjective

already adverb
by or before now *I've already told you once.*

Alsatian (say al-say-shan) noun Alsatians
a large strong dog, also sometimes called a German shepherd

also adverb
as an extra, besides *We also need some bread.*

altar noun altars
a table or raised surface used in religious ceremonies

alter verb alters, altering, altered
to alter something is to change it
alteration noun

alternate (say ol-**ter**-nat) adjective
1 happening on every other one *In the Doldrums, laughter is frowned upon and smiling is permitted only on alternate Thursdays.* – Norton Juster, *The Phantom Tollbooth* **2** coming in turns, one after the other *alternate laughter and tears*
alternately adverb

alternate (say **ol**-ter-nayt) verb
alternates, alternating, alternated
to alternate is to happen in turns

alternative (say ol-**ter**-na-tiv) noun
alternatives
something you can choose instead of something else *If you don't like this book there is an alternative.*

alternative adjective
for you to choose instead of something else *The cafe has an alternative menu for vegetarians.*

although conjunction
in spite of the fact that *Although it was morning, the sky was still dark.*

altitude noun altitudes
the height of something, especially above sea level

alto noun altos
1 a female singer with a low voice **2** a male singer with a voice higher than a tenor's

altogether adverb
1 completely *He is altogether wrong.*
2 on the whole *Altogether, it wasn't a bad holiday.*

aluminium noun
a silver-coloured metal that is light in weight

always adverb
1 all the time, at all times **2** often,

constantly *You are always crying.* **3** whatever happens *You can always sleep on the floor.*

am
1st person singular present tense of be

a.m.
short for Latin *ante meridiem* which means 'before midday'

amalgamate verb amalgamates, amalgamating, amalgamated
1 to amalgamate things is to mix them or join them together **2** to amalgamate is to join together to form one thing

amalgamation noun
amalgamations
1 amalgamation is mixing or joining things together **2** an amalgamation is a mixture of things put together

amateur (say **am**-a-ter) noun amateurs
someone who does something because they like it, without being paid for it

amaze verb amazes, amazing, amazed
to amaze someone is to surprise them greatly **amazement** noun

ambassador noun ambassadors
someone sent to a foreign country to represent their own government

amber noun
1 a hard, clear, yellow substance used for making ornaments **2** a yellowish colour, the one used in traffic lights as a signal for caution

ambiguity noun ambiguities
1 ambiguity is uncertainty about what something means **2** an ambiguity is something that has more than one possible meaning

ambiguous adjective
having more than one possible meaning, uncertain *His reply was ambiguous.*

ambition noun ambitions
1 ambition is a strong desire to be successful in life **2** an ambition is something you want to do very much *His ambition is to play for his country.*

a
b
c
d
e
f
g
h
i
j
k
l
m
n
o
p
q
r
s
t
u
v
w
x
y
z

A
B
C
D
E
F
G
H
I
J
K
L
M
N
O
P
Q
R
S
T
U
V
W
X
Y
Z

ambitious adjective
1 an ambitious person wants very much to be successful in life 2 an ambitious idea or plan is difficult or challenging

amble verb ambles, ambling, ambled
to amble along is to walk slowly

ambulance noun ambulances
a vehicle for carrying sick or injured people

ambush noun ambushes
a surprise attack from a hidden place
ambush verb ambushes, ambushing, ambushed
to ambush someone is to attack them suddenly from a hidden place

amend verb amends, amending, amended
to amend something like a piece of writing is to change or improve it **amendment** noun

American adjective
coming from America, or to do with America
American noun Americans
a person from America

amiable adjective
friendly, good-tempered **amiably** adverb

amicable adjective
friendly **amicably** adverb

amid or **amidst** preposition
in the middle of, among

ammonia noun
a gas or liquid with a strong smell

ammunition noun
bullets, bombs, and other explosive objects used in fighting

amoeba (say a-**mee**-ba) noun amoebas
an amoeba is a tiny creature made of one cell, it can change shape and split itself in two

amok adverb
to run amok is to run about wildly

among or **amongst** preposition
1 surrounded by, in the middle of She was hiding among the bushes. 2 between Let's divide the money amongst ourselves.

amount noun amounts
a quantity or total
amount verb amounts, amounting, amounted
to amount to something is to reach it as a total The bill amounted to £55.

ampere (say **am**-pair) noun amperes
a unit for measuring the rate of flow of an electric current

ampersand noun ampersands
the sign &, which means 'and'

amphibian noun
1 an animal that can live on land and in water 2 a vehicle that can travel on land and in water **amphibious** adjective an amphibious animal or vehicle is able to live or travel on land and in water

amphitheatre noun amphitheatres
a circular or oval building without a roof, which has rows of seats arranged round a central area

ample adjective ampler, amplest
1 large, having plenty of space This car has an ample boot. 2 more than enough We had ample provisions. **amply** adverb generously

amplifier noun amplifiers
an electronic device for making music or other sounds louder

amplify verb amplifies, amplifying, amplified
1 to amplify sounds is to make them louder or stronger 2 to amplify something you say is to give more details about it

amputate verb amputates, amputating, amputated
to amputate an arm or a leg is to cut it off when it is diseased **amputation** noun

amuse verb amuses, amusing, amused
1 to amuse someone is to make them laugh or smile 2 to amuse yourself is to find pleasant things to do

amusement noun amusements
1 an amusement is something that amuses you **2** amusement is being amused; laughing, or smiling

amusing adjective
making you laugh or smile *It was an amusing story.*

an determiner (called the indefinite article)
a word used instead of **a** when the next word begins with a vowel sound or a silent **h** *Take an apple. You can hire boats for £5 an hour.*

anaemia (say a-**nee**-mi-a) noun
a poor condition of the blood that makes someone look pale
anaemic adjective

anaesthetic (say an-iss-**thet**-ik) noun
anaesthetics
a drug or gas that makes you unable to feel pain

anaesthetize (say an-**ees**-thit-ize) verb anaesthetizes, anaesthetizing, anaesthetized
to anaesthetize a person or an animal is to give them an anaesthetic

anagram noun anagrams
a word or phrase made by rearranging the letters of another word or phrase, for example *carthorse* is an anagram of *orchestra*

analogue adjective
an analogue clock or watch has hands and a dial to indicate numbers (the opposite of **digital**)

analogy noun analogies
a comparison or similarity between two things that are fairly like each other *There is an analogy between the human heart and a pump.*

analyse verb analyses, analysing, analysed
1 to analyse something is to examine it carefully **2** to analyse a substance is to divide it into its parts

analysis noun analyses
a detailed study or examination of something

anarchy noun
1 anarchy is having no government or controls, leading to a breakdown in law and order **2** complete disorder or confusion

anatomy noun
the study of the parts of the body
anatomical adjective

ancestor noun ancestors
a person who lived in the past and was in the same family as someone alive now
ancestry noun a person's ancestry is the list of all their ancestors

anchor noun anchors
a heavy object joined to a ship by a chain or rope and dropped to the bottom of the sea to stop the ship from moving

ancient adjective
1 belonging to times that were long ago **2** very old *They came from an ancient family.*

and conjunction
you use **and** to link words and phrases together *We had cakes and lemonade. Touch that and you'll get burnt. Go and buy a pen.*

anecdote noun anecdotes
a short amusing or interesting story about a real person or thing

anemone (say a-**nem**-on-i) noun anemones
1 a small flower with the shape of a cup **2** a sea anemone

angel noun angels
1 a being that some people believe in, who is a messenger or attendant of God **2** a very kind or beautiful person

angelic adjective
kind and beautiful, like an angel

anger noun
a strong feeling that you do not like what someone has said or done, making you want to quarrel or fight with them

a
b
c
d
e
f
g
h
i
j
k
l
m
n
o
p
q
r
s
t
u
v
w
x
y
z

23

A
B
C
D
E
F
G
H
I
J
K
L
M
N
O
P
Q
R
S
T
U
V
W
X
Y
Z

angle noun angles
1 the space between two lines or surfaces that meet 2 a point of view *What is your angle on this?*

angle verb angles, angling, angled
1 to angle something is to put it in a slanting position 2 to angle news or a story is to tell it in a special way *The report was angled so that the robbers looked like heroes.*

angler noun anglers
someone who fishes with a fishing rod

Anglican adjective
belonging to the Church of England

Anglican noun Anglicans
a member of the Church of England

Anglo–Saxon noun Anglo-Saxons
1 an English person, especially of the time before the Norman Conquest in 1066 2 the old form of English spoken before 1066

angry adjective angrier, angriest
feeling or showing anger **angrily** adverb

anguish noun
great suffering or unhappiness

angular adjective
1 having sharp corners 2 bony *She has a thin, angular face.*

animal noun animals
a living thing that can move and feel. The word **animal** is normally used to mean creatures that are not humans.

animated adjective
1 lively and excited 2 an animated film is one made by photographing a series of still pictures and showing them rapidly one after another, so they appear to move

animation noun
1 being lively or excited 2 a way of making films from still pictures so they appear to move

animosity noun animosities
a feeling of being an enemy towards someone *There was a lot of animosity in his voice.*

aniseed noun
a seed with a strong sweet taste like liquorice

ankle noun ankles
the part of your leg where it is joined to your foot

annex (say a-**neks**) verb annexes, annexing, annexed
to annex something, like a piece of land, is to add it to something larger

annexe (say **an**-eks) noun annexes
a building added to a larger building

annihilate (say a-**ny**-il-ayt) verb annihilates, annihilating, annihilated
to annihilate something is to destroy it completely **annihilation** noun

anniversary noun anniversaries
a day when you remember something special that happened on the same date in an earlier year

announce verb announces, announcing, announced
to announce something is to say it publicly **announcer** noun

announcement noun announcements
something that is made known publicly, especially in a newspaper or on radio or television

annoy verb annoys, annoying, annoyed
to annoy someone is to give them a feeling of not being pleased

annoyance noun annoyances
1 annoyance is the feeling of being annoyed 2 an annoyance is something that annoys you *Wasps are a great annoyance at a picnic.*

annual adjective
happening or coming every year **annually** adverb

annual noun annuals
1 a children's book of stories or comic strips that comes out once a year 2 a plant that dies when winter comes

anon.
short for **anonymous**

anonymous adjective
an anonymous book or letter is written by someone who does not give their name **anonymity** noun anonymity is keeping your name secret **anonymously** adverb

anorak noun anoraks
a thick warm jacket with a hood

anorexia (say an-er-**eks**-ee-a) noun
an illness that makes someone not want to eat **anorexic** adjective

another determiner, pronoun
a different person or thing *Have another look. May I have another?*

answer noun answers
1 an answer is what you say when someone asks you a question **2** the answer to a problem is something that solves it
answer verb answers, answering, answered
1 to answer someone is to give them an answer **2** to answer a telephone is to pick it up when it rings **to answer back** is to say something rude or cheeky as an answer

ant noun ants
a tiny insect that lives with others in a colony

antagonism noun
antagonism is a feeling of being someone's enemy

antagonize verb antagonizes, antagonizing, antagonized
to antagonize someone is to make them feel you are their enemy

Antarctic or Antarctica noun
the area round the South Pole

anteater noun anteaters
an animal with a long tongue that lives by eating ants

antelope noun antelope or antelopes
an animal like a deer, that lives in Africa and parts of Asia

antenna noun
1 antennae a long thin feeler on the head of an insect or shellfish
2 antennas an aerial

anthem noun anthems
a religious or patriotic song, usually sung by a choir or group of people

anther noun anthers
the part of a flower's stamen that contains pollen

anthill noun anthills
a mound of earth over an ants' nest

anthology noun anthologies
a collection of poems, stories, or songs in one book

anthropology noun
the study of human beings and the way they live **anthropologist** noun

anti- prefix
against something or someone, as in *antibiotic* and *anti-school*

antibiotic noun antibiotics
a drug that kills bacteria, for example penicillin

anticipate verb anticipates, anticipating, anticipated
1 to anticipate something is to expect it and be ready for it *The police were anticipating trouble.* **2** to anticipate someone is to act before they do *They anticipated us in getting the early train.*

anticipation noun
looking forward to doing something

anticlimax noun anticlimaxes
a disappointing ending or result after something exciting

anticlockwise adverb, adjective
moving in the opposite direction to the hands of a clock

antidote noun antidotes
something which takes away the bad effects of a poison or disease

a b c d e f g h i j k l m n o p q r s t u v w x y z

A

antiquated adjective
old-fashioned

antique (say an-**teek**) noun antiques
something that is valuable because it is
very old

antiseptic noun antiseptics
a chemical that kills germs

antler noun antlers
the horn of a deer, which divides into
several branches

antonym (say **ant**-o-nim) noun
antonyms
a word that is opposite in meaning to
another *'Soft' is an antonym of 'hard'.*

anvil noun anvils
a large block of iron on which a blacksmith
hammers metal into shape

anxiety noun anxieties
1 anxiety is a feeling of being worried **2** an
anxiety is something that worries you

anxious adjective
1 worried and nervous **2** eager to do
something *They were anxious to help us.*

any determiner
1 one or some *Have you any spare paper?*
2 no matter which *Come any day you like.*
3 every *Any fool knows that!*

any pronoun
one or some *I don't have any left.*

any adverb
at all; in some degree *Is the cake any good?*

anybody pronoun
anyone

anyhow adverb
1 anyway **2** (informal) carelessly, without
much thought *He does his work anyhow.*

anyone pronoun
any person

anything pronoun
any thing

anyway adverb
whatever happens; whatever the situation
may be *If it rains, we'll go anyway.*

anywhere adverb
in any place or to any place

apart adverb
1 away from each other; separately *The
male lion and cubs are kept apart.* **2** into
pieces *The book was beginning to fall apart.*
3 excluded *Joking apart, what do you think?*

apartment noun apartments
1 a set of rooms **2** (in America) a flat

apathy noun
not having much interest in something
apathetic adjective

ape noun apes
a monkey without a tail, such as a gorilla or
a chimpanzee

aphid or **aphis** noun aphids
a tiny insect that sucks juices from plants

apologetic adjective
saying you are sorry for something
apologetically adverb

apologize verb apologizes,
apologizing, apologized
to apologize to someone is to tell them you
are sorry

apology noun apologies
a statement that you are sorry for doing
something wrong

apostle noun apostles
in Christianity, one of the twelve men sent
out by Christ to tell people about God

apostrophe (say a-**pos**-tro-fi) noun
apostrophes
an apostrophe is a punctuation mark (')
used to show that letters have been left
out, as in *can't* and *we'll*. It is also used with
s to show who owns something, as in *the
cat's paws* (one cat), *the cats' paws* (more
than one cat).

appal verb appals, appalling, appalled
to appal someone is to shock them a lot *The
violence appalled everyone.*

appalling adjective
dreadful, shocking *The room was in an
appalling mess.*

apparatus noun apparatuses
an apparatus is a set of equipment for a special use

apparent adjective
1 clear, obvious *He burst out laughing for no apparent reason.* 2 appearing to be true *Police are investigating an apparent theft.*

apparently adverb
as it seems, so it appears *The door had apparently been locked.*

appeal verb appeals, appealing, appealed
1 to appeal for something is to ask for it when you need it badly *They are appealing for money to build a playpark.* 2 to appeal to someone is to interest or attract them *Rock-climbing has never appealed to me.* 3 to appeal against a decision is to ask for it to be changed

appeal noun appeals
1 an appeal is asking for something you need 2 appeal is what makes something interesting *The book has a lot of appeal for both kids and adults.* 3 an appeal is asking for a decision to be changed

appear verb appears, appearing, appeared
1 to appear is to become visible 2 to appear is also to seem *They appeared very anxious.* 3 to appear in a film or play is to take part in it

appearance noun appearances
1 coming into sight 2 taking part in a play, film, show, etc. 3 what someone looks like 4 what something seems to be

appease verb appeases, appeasing, appeased
to appease someone is to make them peaceful or calm, often by giving them what they want

appendicitis noun
an inflammation or disease of the appendix

appendix noun
1 appendixes a small tube leading off from the intestines in the body 2 appendices an extra section at the end of a book

appetite noun appetites
a desire for something, especially for food

appetizer noun appetizers
something you eat or drink before a meal, to give you an appetite

appetizing adjective
looking or smelling good to eat

applaud verb applauds, applauding, applauded
to applaud someone or something is to show that you like them, especially by clapping

applause noun
clapping or cheering after someone has given a speech or given a performance

apple noun apples
a round fruit with skin that is red, green, or yellow

appliance noun appliances
a device or gadget

applicable adjective
1 that applies to someone *This rule is now applicable to everyone.* 2 relevant *Ignore any questions which are not applicable.*

applicant noun applicants
someone who applies for something, for example a job

application noun applications
1 an application is a letter or form you use to ask for something important, such as a job 2 an application is a program for a computer or mobile phone that allows you to perform a particular activity on it 3 application is when you make a lot of effort to do something

apply verb applies, applying, applied
1 to apply something is to put it on something else *Apply a generous amount of suncream.* 2 to apply for a job is to write formally and ask for it 3 to apply to someone is to concern them *These rules apply to everybody.* 4 to apply yourself to something is to give it all your attention

A
B
C
D
E
F
G
H
I
J
K
L
M
N
O
P
Q
R
S
T
U
V
W
X
Y
Z

appoint verb appoints, appointing, appointed
1 to appoint someone is to choose them for a job 2 to appoint a time and place for a meeting is to decide when and where to have it

appointment noun appointments
1 an arrangement to meet or visit someone *an appointment with the dentist* 2 choosing someone for a job *the appointment of a new teacher*

appreciate verb appreciates, appreciating, appreciated
1 to appreciate something is to enjoy or value it 2 to appreciate a fact is to understand it *We didn't appreciate how much danger we were in.* **appreciation** noun

appreciative adjective
an appreciative person or group shows how much they enjoy or value something *I enjoy playing to an appreciative audience.*

apprehension noun apprehensions
nervous fear or worry
apprehensive adjective

apprentice noun apprentices
someone who is learning a trade or craft
apprenticeship noun

approach verb approaches, approaching, approached
1 to approach a place is to come near to it 2 to approach someone is to go to them with a request or offer 3 to approach a problem or difficulty is to start solving it

approach noun approaches
1 coming near to a place 2 a way of tackling a problem *Let's try a different approach.* 3 a way or road leading up to a building *The approach to the house had trees on each side.*

approachable adjective
friendly and easy to talk to

appropriate adjective
suitable

approval noun
thinking well of someone or something

approve verb approves, approving, approved
to approve of someone or something is to think they are good or suitable

approximate adjective
roughly correct but not exact *What is your approximate height?* **approximately** adverb

approximation noun approximations
something that is a rough estimate and not exact

apricot noun apricots
a juicy, orange-coloured fruit like a small peach, with a stone in it

April noun
the fourth month of the year

April fool noun
someone who is fooled on April Fool's Day (1 April)

apron noun aprons
a piece of clothing worn over the front of your body to protect your clothes

apt adjective
1 likely to do something *He is apt to be careless.* 2 suitable *I need to find an apt quotation.* 3 quick at learning *She is an apt pupil.*

aptitude noun aptitudes
a talent in something *You have a real aptitude for music.*

aquarium noun aquariums
a tank or building for keeping live fish

aquatic adjective
to do with water and swimming *water polo and other aquatic sports*

aqueduct noun aqueducts
a bridge that carries water across a valley

Arab noun Arabs
a member of a people inhabiting Arabia and other parts of the Middle East and North Africa **Arabian** adjective

Arabic noun
the language of the Arabs

Arabic figures or Arabic numerals plural noun
the figures 1, 2, 3, 4, and so on (compare *Roman numerals*)

arable adjective
to do with the growing of crops

arbitrary (say **ar**-bi-trer-i) adjective
done or chosen at random or without a proper reason *It was an arbitrary decision.*

arc noun arcs
part of the circumference of a circle, a curve

arcade noun arcades
a covered place to walk, with shops down each side

arch noun arches
a curved structure that helps to support a bridge or building

arch verb arches, arching, arched
to curve *The wind itself had ceased and a brilliant, deep blue sky arched high over the moorland.* – Frances Hodgson Burnett, *The Secret Garden*

archaeology (say ar-ki-**ol**-o-ji) noun
the study of ancient people from the remains of their buildings
archaeologist noun

archbishop noun archbishops
the chief bishop of a region

archer noun archers
someone who shoots with a bow and arrows

archery noun
the sport of shooting with a bow and arrows

architect (say **ar**-ki-tekt) noun architects
someone whose work is to design buildings

architecture noun
1 the work of designing buildings 2 a style of building *Victorian architecture*

Arctic noun
the area round the North Pole

are
plural and 2nd person singular present tense of be

area noun areas
1 part of a country, place, etc. 2 the space occupied by something *The area of this room is 20 square metres.*

arena (say a-**ree**-na) noun arenas
1 the level space in the middle of a stadium or sports ground 2 the place where a sports event takes place

aren't
short for *am not* or *are not*

argue verb argues, arguing, argued
1 to argue with someone is to quarrel with them 2 to argue is also to give reasons for something *She argued that the housework should be shared.*

argument noun arguments
1 a quarrel 2 a reason someone gives to try to convince someone about something

arid adjective
dry and barren

arise verb arises, arising, arose, arisen
1 to arise is to appear or to come into existence 2 (old meaning) to rise; to stand up *'Arise, Sir Lancelot.'*

aristocrat (say **a**-ris-to-krat) noun aristocrats
a nobleman or noblewoman
aristocratic adjective

arithmetic noun
the study of using numbers and working things out with them

ark noun arks
in the Bible, the ship in which Noah and his family escaped the Flood

arm noun arms
1 the part of your body between your shoulder and your hand 2 the sleeve of a coat or dress 3 the side part of a chair, on which you can rest your arm

a
b
c
d
e
f
g
h
i
j
k
l
m
n
o
p
q
r
s
t
u
v
w
x
y
z

29

arm verb arms, arming, armed
1 to arm people is to give them weapons
2 to arm is to prepare for war

armada (say ar-**mah**-da) noun armadas
a fleet of warships, especially the Spanish Armada which attacked England in 1588

armadillo noun armadillos
a South American animal whose body is covered with a shell of bony plates

armchair noun armchairs
a chair with parts on either side to rest your arms on

armed forces plural noun
the army, navy, and air force of a country

armful noun armfuls
as much of something as you can hold in your arms *Jack was carrying an armful of books.*

armistice noun armistices
an agreement to stop fighting in a war or battle

armour noun
armour is a metal covering to protect people or things in battle
armoured adjective

armpit noun armpits
the hollow part under your arm at your shoulder

arms plural noun
1 weapons *Lay down your arms.* 2 a coat of arms

army noun armies
1 a large number of soldiers ready to fight 2 a large group *They had an army of supporters.*

aroma (say a-**roh**-ma) noun aromas
a pleasant smell, for example of food
aromatic adjective

arose
past tense of arise

around adverb, preposition
1 round *A group of people stood around* the platform. 2 about *Please stop running around.*

arouse verb arouses, arousing, aroused
1 to arouse someone is to make them wake up 2 to arouse feelings in someone is to cause them to have those feelings

arrange verb arranges, arranging, arranged
1 to arrange things is to put them all in the position you want 2 to arrange a meeting or event is to organize it 3 to arrange to do something is to make sure that it happens

arrangement noun arrangements
1 arrangement is how you arrange or display something, for example flowers or a table setting 2 an arrangement is something you agree with someone else *We made an arrangement to meet outside the cinema.*

array noun arrays
a display of things for people to see *There was a huge array of pots and pans.*

arrears plural noun
in arrears owing money *He's in arrears with his rent.*

arrest verb arrests, arresting, arrested
1 to arrest someone is to take hold of them by the power of the law 2 to arrest something is to stop it *The doctors were trying to arrest the spread of disease.*
arrest noun arrests
taking hold of someone by the power of the law **under arrest** taken in and held by the police

arrival noun arrivals
1 an arrival is when someone or something arrives at a place 2 an arrival is also someone who is new or has just arrived *Have you met the new arrivals?*

arrive verb arrives, arriving, arrived
1 to arrive at a place is to get there at the end of a journey 2 to arrive is also to happen *The great day finally arrived.*

arrogance noun
arrogance is a feeling someone has that they are more important than anyone else

arrogant adjective
an arrogant person is unpleasantly proud and thinks they are more important than anyone else

arrow noun arrows
1 a pointed stick shot from a bow **2** a sign used to show direction or position

arsenal noun arsenals
a place where bullets, shells, and weapons are made or stored

arsenic noun
a strong poison made from a metallic element and used in insecticides

arson noun
the crime of deliberately setting fire to a building

art noun arts
1 art is producing something by drawing or painting or sculpture **2** the arts are subjects such as history and languages, as distinct from the sciences **3** an art is also a skill in something *the art of public speaking*

artefact noun artefacts
an object made by humans, especially one from the past that is studied by archaeologists

artery noun arteries
a tube that carries blood from your heart to other parts of your body

artful adjective
clever at getting what you want by fooling people **artfully** adverb

arthritis (say arth-**ry**-tiss) noun
a disease that makes joints in the body painful and stiff

article noun articles
1 an object or thing that you can touch or pick up **2** a piece of writing published in a newspaper or magazine **3** (in grammar) the word 'a' or 'an' (called the *indefinite article*) or the word 'the' (called the *definite article*)

articulate (say ar-**tik**-yoo-lat) adjective
an articulate person is able to speak clearly and fluently

articulate (say ar-**tik**-yoo-layt) verb
articulates, articulating, articulated
to articulate a word or phrase is to pronounce it clearly **articulation** noun

artificial adjective
made by human beings and not by nature **artificially** adverb

artillery noun artilleries
1 artillery is a collection of large guns **2** the artillery is the part of the army that uses large guns

artist noun artists
1 someone who produces art, especially a painter **2** an entertainer

artistic adjective
1 to do with art and artists **2** showing skill and beauty *an artistic flower arrangement*

artistry noun
the skill of an artist *The carving showed great artistry.*

as conjunction, adverb, preposition
1 you use **as** to link words and phrases together *As it was late, everyone had gone home.*, *She slipped as she got off the bus. It is not as easy as you think. Peter was dressed as a pirate.* **2** you can also use **as** to make similes *as flat as a pancake, as cold as ice*

asbestos noun
a fireproof material that is made up of fine soft fibres

ascend verb ascends, ascending, ascended
to ascend something like a hill or staircase is to go up it

ascent noun ascents
an ascent is a climb, usually a hard or long one

ash[1] noun ashes
ash is the powder that is left after something has been burned

a
b
c
d
e
f
g
h
i
j
k
l
m
n
o
p
q
r
s
t
u
v
w
x
y
z

ash² noun ashes
an ash or ash tree is a tree with silvery bark and winged seeds

ashamed adjective
feeling shame

ashen adjective
grey and pale *Her face was ashen.*

ashore adverb
on the shore

Asian adjective
to do with Asia

Asian noun Asians
a person from Asia

aside adverb
to or at one side; away *Step aside and let them pass.*

aside noun asides
something said so that only some people will hear

ask verb asks, asking, asked
1 to ask someone something is to speak to them so as to find out or get something **2** to ask someone to a party or event is to invite them to it **to ask for it** or **to ask for trouble** (informal) is to do something that will bring trouble

asleep adverb, adjective
sleeping

aspect noun aspects
1 one way of looking at a problem or situation *Perhaps the worst aspect of winter is the dark mornings.* **2** the direction a building faces *This room has a southern aspect.*

asphalt (say **ass**-falt) noun
a sticky black substance which is mixed with gravel to make a surface for roads and playgrounds

aspirin noun aspirins
a drug used to relieve pain or reduce fever

ass noun asses
1 a donkey **2** (informal) a fool *You are an ass!*

assassinate verb assassinates, assassinating, assassinated
to assassinate a ruler or leader is to murder them to stop them having power
assassination noun

assault noun assaults
a violent attack on someone

assault verb assaults, assaulting, assaulted
to assault someone is to attack them violently

assemble verb assembles, assembling, assembled
1 to assemble people or things is to bring them together in one place **2** to assemble is to come together in one place *Please assemble in the playground.*

assembly noun assemblies
1 an assembly is when people come together and someone speaks to them, for example in a school **2** an assembly is also a group of people who meet together, such as a parliament **3** assembly of a machine or piece of furniture is putting the parts together to make it

assent noun
assent is agreement or permission to do something *Have your parents given their assent?*

assert verb asserts, asserting, asserted
to assert something is to say it strongly and clearly **assertion** noun

assertive adjective
speaking or behaving strongly and firmly

assess verb assesses, assessing, assessed
to assess someone or something is to decide how good or useful they are

assessment noun assessments
an opinion about something after thinking about it carefully

asset noun assets
something useful or valuable to someone *Katie is a real asset to the team.*

A B C D E F G H I J K L M N O P Q R S T U V W X Y Z

assets plural noun
the property of a person or company that they could sell to raise money if they wanted to

assign verb assigns, assigning, assigned
to assign a job or task to someone is to give it to them to do *A guard was assigned to watch the prisoner.*

assignment noun assignments
a piece of work that someone is given to do

assist verb assists, assisting, assisted
to assist someone is to help them, usually in a practical way

assistance noun
help someone gets when they need information or support

assistant noun assistants
1 someone whose job is to help another person in their work **2** someone who serves in a shop

associate (say a-**soh**-shi-ayt) verb associates, associating, associated
1 to associate one thing with another is to connect them in your mind *I associate Christmas with ice and snow.* **2** to associate with someone is to spend time with them *He likes to associate with famous people.*

association noun associations
1 an organization for people sharing an interest or doing the same work *the local athletics association* **2** a connection between things

assonance (say **ass**-on-ans) noun
assonance is when the same vowel sound is repeated, for special effect, e.g. *the bright kite flies high in the sky*

assorted adjective
of various kinds; mixed and different *A large wooden trunk stood open at the foot of his bed, revealing a cauldron, broomstick, black robes and assorted spellbooks.* — J. K. Rowling, *Harry Potter and the Goblet of Fire*

assortment noun assortments
a mixture of different things or people

assume verb assumes, assuming, assumed
to assume something is to think it is true or likely without being sure of it *I assume you will be coming tomorrow.* **assumed** adjective an assumed name is one that is not the person's real name

assumption noun assumptions
something you assume or take for granted

assurance noun assurances
1 assurance is a feeling of certainty about something **2** an assurance is a promise or guarantee

assure verb assures, assuring, assured
to assure someone is to tell someone something definite *I assure you that you will be quite safe.*

asterisk noun asterisks
a star-shaped sign (*) used in printing and writing to draw attention to something

asteroid noun asteroids
one of the small planets found mainly between the orbits of Mars and Jupiter

asthma (say **ass**-ma) noun
a disease which makes breathing difficult

asthmatic adjective
suffering from asthma
asthmatic noun asthmatics
someone who is suffering from asthma

astonish verb astonishes, astonishing, astonished
to astonish someone is to surprise them very much **astonishment** noun

astound verb astounds, astounding, astounded
to astound someone is to amaze or shock them very much

astrology noun
astrology is studying how the planets and stars may affect people's lives **astrologer** noun

astronaut noun astronauts
someone who travels in a spacecraft

a b c d e f g h i j k l m n o p q r s t u v w x y z

A

B

C

D

E

F

G

H

I

J

K

L

M

N

O

P

Q

R

S

T

U

V

W

X

Y

Z

astronomical adjective
1 to do with astronomy 2 (informal) extremely large *The cost of the party was astronomical.*

astronomy noun
astronomy is studying the sun, moon, planets, and stars **astronomer** noun

at preposition
showing where someone or something is, or when something happens *I was at the hospital all morning. The postbox is at the end of the road. The match starts at 3 o'clock.*

ate
past tense of eat

atheist noun atheists
someone who does not believe in a God **atheism** noun

athlete noun athletes
someone who is good at athletics or other sports

athletic adjective
1 to do with athletics *an athletic competition* 2 good at sports; strong

athletics plural noun
physical exercises and sports such as running and jumping

atlas noun atlases
a book of maps

atmosphere noun atmospheres
1 the earth's atmosphere is the air around it 2 an atmosphere is a feeling you get in a room or at a place *There was a happy atmosphere at the fairground.*

atmospheric adjective
1 to do with the earth's atmosphere 2 having a strong atmosphere

atoll noun atolls
a ring-shaped island of coral in the sea

atom noun atoms
the smallest possible part of a chemical element **atomic** adjective

at once adverb
immediately *Come here at once!*

atrocious (say a-**troh**-shus) adjective
awful, terrible

atrocity noun atrocities
a terrible and cruel act, such as the killing of a large number of people

attach verb attaches, attaching, attached
to attach one thing to another is to fix or fasten it

attached adjective
to be attached to someone is to be fond of them

attachment noun attachments
1 an extra part you fix to a device so that it can do a special kind of work *The garden hose has an attachment for washing cars.* 2 a fondness or friendship *The boys felt a real attachment to their pet hamster.* 3 (in computing) a document that you send to someone with an email message

attack noun attacks
1 an attempt to hurt someone with violence 2 an attempt to harm someone or something by using unfriendly words 3 a sudden illness or pain

attack verb attacks, attacking, attacked
to attack someone is to try to hurt them with violence, or to harm them with unfriendly words

attain verb attains, attaining, attained
to attain something is to reach or achieve it *I have attained Grade 3 on the violin.* **attainment** noun

attempt verb attempts, attempting, attempted
to attempt to do something is to make an effort to do it

attempt noun attempts
an attempt at something is making an effort to do it

attend verb attends, attending, attended
1 to attend something like a meeting or a wedding is to be there 2 to attend school or college is to be a pupil or student there

3 to attend to someone is to look after them, especially when they are ill **4** to attend to something is to spend time dealing with it *She had some business to attend to.*

attendance noun attendances
1 attendance is being somewhere where you are supposed to be **2** the attendance at an event is the number of people who are there to see it

attendant noun attendants
someone who helps or goes with another person

attention noun
giving care or thought to someone or something **to stand to attention** is to stand with your feet together and your arms straight down, like soldiers on parade

attentive adjective
listening closely **attentively** adverb

attic noun attics
a room or space under the roof of a house

attitude noun attitudes
your attitude is the way you think or feel about something, and the way you behave

attract verb attracts, attracting, attracted
1 to attract someone is to seem pleasant to them and get their attention or interest **2** to attract something unwelcome is to make it come *Empty bottles of drink attract wasps.* **3** to attract something is also to pull it by a physical force like magnetism *Magnets attract metal pins.*

attraction noun attractions
1 attraction is the power to attract someone **2** an attraction is something pleasant that people like to see, such as a fair or a rock concert

attractive adjective
1 interesting or welcome *They made us an attractive offer of a free holiday.* **2** pleasant, good-looking

auburn adjective
auburn hair is a reddish-brown colour

auction noun auctions
a sale at which things are sold to the person who offers the most money for them **auctioneer** noun an official in charge of an auction

audible adjective
loud enough to be heard

audience noun audiences
1 the people who have come to see or hear an event like a concert or film **2** a formal interview with an important person *an audience with the Queen*

audition noun auditions
a test to see if an actor or musician is suitable for a part

auditorium (say aw-dit-**or**-i-um) noun auditoriums
the part of a building where the audience sits

August noun
the eighth month of the year

aunt noun aunts
1 the sister of your mother or father **2** your uncle's wife

auntie or **aunty** noun
aunties (informal)
an aunt

aural adjective
using the sense of hearing *an aural comprehension test*

austere adjective
1 not having much comfort or luxury **2** an austere person is severe and strict

Australian adjective
to do with Australia
Australian noun Australians
a person from Australia

authentic adjective
real, genuine **authenticity** noun

author noun authors
the writer of a book or other work such as a poem or magazine article

A

B

C

D

E

F

G

H

I

J

K

L

M

N

O

P

Q

R

S

T

U

V

W

X

Y

Z

authority noun **authorities**
1 authority is the power to give orders to other people **2** an authority on a subject is an expert on it or a book that gives you reliable information about it

authorize verb **authorizes, authorizing, authorized**
1 to authorize something is to give official permission for it **2** to authorize someone to do something is to give them permission to do it

autistic adjective
having a disability that means someone has difficulty communicating with other people

autobiography noun **autobiographies**
the story of someone's life that they have written themselves
autobiographical adjective

autograph noun **autographs**
the signature of a famous person

automatic adjective
1 an automatic process is one that works on its own, without needing attention or control by humans **2** an automatic action is one that you do without specially thinking about it **automatically** adverb

automation (say aw-tom-**ay**-shun) noun
making processes automatic, and using machines instead of people to do work

automobile noun **automobiles**
(in America)
a motor car

autumn (say **aw**-tum) noun **autumns**
the season when leaves fall off the trees, between summer and winter

 TOP TIPS
Keep it quiet! There is a silent **n** in **autumn**.

autumnal (say aw-**tum**-nal) adjective
in autumn; to do with autumn

available adjective
able to be found or used *Fresh strawberries are available in June.* **availability** noun

avalanche (say **av**-a-lahnsh) noun **avalanches**
a sudden heavy fall of rocks or snow down the side of a mountain

avenue noun **avenues**
a wide street, usually with trees along each side

average noun **averages**
1 an average is the number you get by adding several amounts together and dividing the total by the number of amounts *The average of 2, 4, 6, and 8 is 5.* **2** the average is the usual or ordinary standard *Their work is well above the average.*

average adjective
of the usual or ordinary standard

avert verb **averts, averting, averted**
1 to avert something is to turn it away *People averted their eyes from the accident.* **2** to avert something is also to stop it happening *The train driver's quick reaction had averted a disaster.*

aviary noun **aviaries**
a place where birds are kept

aviation noun
aviation is flying in aircraft

avid adjective
keen, eager *She is an avid reader.*

avoid verb **avoids, avoiding, avoided**
1 to avoid something or someone is to keep yourself away from them *They try to avoid their relations at Christmas.* **2** to avoid something is also to find a way of not doing it *We wanted to avoid extra homework.*

await verb **awaits, awaiting, awaited**
to await someone or something is to wait for them

awake adjective
not sleeping

awake verb **awakes, awaking, awoke, awoken**
1 to awake is to wake up **2** to awake someone is to wake them up

awaken verb awakens, awakening, awakened
1 to awaken is to wake up 2 to awaken someone is to wake them up

award noun awards
something such as a prize given to a person who has done something successful

award verb awards, awarding, awarded
to award something to someone is to give it to them as an award

aware adjective
to be aware of something is to know about it or realize it is there *They soon became aware of the danger.* **awareness** noun

away adverb
1 at a distance or somewhere else *I wish those people would go away. The ice cream melted so I threw it away.* 2 you can also use **away** with special meanings *They are working away at their exams. The noise gradually died away.*

away adjective
an away match is one that is played at the opponents' ground

awe noun
fear and wonder *The mountains filled him with awe.*

awful adjective
1 (informal) very bad; very great *I've been an awful fool.* 2 causing fear or horror *The dungeon was an awful sight.*

awfully adverb (informal)
very, extremely *It's awfully hot in June.*

awkward adjective
1 difficult to use or cope with *The box was an awkward shape.* 2 embarrassed and uncomfortable *He always felt awkward among strangers.*

awoke
past tense of awake verb

awoken
past participle of awake verb

axe noun axes
a tool for chopping

axe verb axes, axing, axed (informal)
to axe something is to cancel or abolish it

axis noun axes
1 a line through the centre of a spinning object 2 a line dividing something in half

axle noun axles
the rod through the centre of a wheel, on which it turns

azalea (say a-**zay**-li-a) noun azaleas
a flowering shrub like a rhododendron

azure adjective
sky-blue

Bb

babble verb babbles, babbling, babbled
1 to babble is to talk quickly, without making much sense 2 to babble is also to make a murmuring or bubbling sound *They came across a babbling brook.*

baboon noun baboons
a large kind of monkey with a long muzzle

baby noun babies
1 a very young child 2 a baby animal is a very young animal *a baby elephant*

babyish adjective
silly and childish

babysit verb babysits, babysitting, babysat
to babysit is to look after a child while its parents are out

babysitter noun babysitters
someone who babysits

bachelor noun bachelors
a man who has not married

back noun backs
1 the part of your body between your shoulders and your bottom 2 the upper part of a four-legged animal's body 3 the part of

a
b
c
d
e
f
g
h
i
j
k
l
m
n
o
p
q
r
s
t
u
v
w
x
y
z

A
B
C
D
E
F
G
H
I
J
K
L
M
N
O
P
Q
R
S
T
U
V
W
X
Y
Z

a thing that is furthest away from the front *The back of the house faces a river.*

back adjective
placed at or near the back *Let's sit in the back row.*

back adverb
1 backwards or towards the back *Go back!*
2 to where someone or something was before *When will you be coming back?* 3 to an earlier time *Think back to when you were little.*

back verb backs, backing, backed
1 to back a vehicle is to move it backwards
2 to back a horse is to bet on it winning a race 3 to back someone is to support them or give them help **to back down** is to admit you were wrong about something **to back out** is to decide not to get involved in something **to back someone up** is to give them support or help

backache noun backaches
a pain in your back, usually lasting for a long time

backbone noun backbones
your backbone is your spine

background noun backgrounds
1 the background of a picture or view is the part that is farthest away from you, behind the main subject 2 the background to an event or situation is all the things that help to explain why it happened 3 a person's background is their family, education, and what they have done in their life **in the background** not noticeable or obvious

backing noun
1 backing is support or help 2 backing is also the material that forms a support or back for something 3 the backing on a pop song is the music that is played or sung to support the main singer or tune

backlash noun backlashes
a strong and often angry reaction to something

backlog noun backlogs
a backlog is work that should have been finished but still has to be done

backstroke noun
a stroke you use when swimming on your back

backward adjective
1 facing or aimed towards the back *She walked past him without a backward glance.*
2 slow in learning or developing

backward adverb
backwards

backwards adverb
1 towards the back 2 with the back end going first 3 in the opposite order to the usual one *Can you say the alphabet backwards?*

backyard noun backyards
an open area at the back of a building

bacon noun
smoked or salted meat from the back or sides of a pig

bacteria plural noun
tiny organisms that can cause diseases

bad adjective worse, worst
1 not good or well done *We were watching a very bad film on television.* 2 someone who is bad is wicked or naughty 3 someone is bad at something when they can't do it very well *Tracy is bad at maths.* 4 serious or unpleasant *That was a bad mistake.*
5 harmful to your health *Eating fatty foods is bad for you.* **not bad** fairly good, all right

baddy noun baddies (informal)
a bad person, especially in a story or a film

badge noun badges
a small piece of metal, plastic, or cloth that you pin or sew on your clothes to tell people something about you, such as what club or school you belong to or what kind of thing you like

badger noun badgers
a grey animal with a black and white head, which lives underground and comes out at night to feed

badger verb badgers, badgering, badgered
to badger someone is to keep asking them

to do something *He kept badgering his mother for his pocket money.*

badly adverb
1 not well *They did the work badly.*
2 seriously *He was badly wounded.* 3 very much *They needed sleep badly.* **badly off** poor or unfortunate

badminton noun
a game in which players use rackets to hit a light object called a *shuttlecock* backwards and forwards across a high net

bad-tempered adjective
a bad-tempered person is one who often becomes angry

baffle verb baffles, baffling, baffled
to baffle someone is to puzzle or confuse them completely

bag noun bags
a container made of soft material, for holding or carrying things **bags of something** (informal) plenty *There's bags of room.*
bag verb bags, bagging, bagged
to bag something is to get hold of it or take it *I bagged the best seat.*

bagel noun bagels
a hard ring-shaped bread roll

baggage noun
baggage is the suitcases and bags you take on a journey

baggy adjective baggier, baggiest
baggy clothes hang loosely from your body

bagpipes plural noun
bagpipes are a musical instrument you play by squeezing air out of a bag into a set of pipes

bail[1] noun
bail is money that has to be paid or promised so that a person accused of a crime will not be kept in prison before their trial

bail[2] noun bails
bails are the two small pieces of wood placed on top of the stumps in cricket

bail verb bails, bailing, bailed
to bail water out of a boat is to scoop it over the side

Bairam (say by-**ram**) noun Bairams
either of two Muslim festivals, one in the tenth month and one in the twelfth month of the Islamic year

Baisakhi (say by-sa-ki) noun
a Sikh festival held in April

bait noun
bait is a small amount of food put on a hook or in a trap to catch fish or animals
bait verb baits, baiting, baited
to bait a hook or trap is to put the bait on it or in it, to catch fish or animals

bake verb bakes, baking, baked
1 to bake food is to cook it in an oven, especially bread or cakes 2 to bake something like clay is to make it hard by heating it in an oven 3 to bake is to become very hot, especially in the sun

baker noun bakers
someone who makes or sells bread and cakes

bakery noun bakeries
a place where bread is made or sold

balance noun balances
1 a person's balance is their feeling of being steady *He lost his balance and fell over.* 2 a balance is a device for weighing things, with two trays hanging from the ends of a horizontal bar 3 the balance of a bank account is the difference between the money paid into it and the money taken out of it 4 a balance is also an amount of money that someone owes *I will pay you the balance on Saturday.*
balance verb balances, balancing, balanced
1 to balance something is to keep it steady *He was balancing a tray on one hand.*
2 a balanced diet is one that has all the right kinds of food for being healthy

balcony noun balconies
1 a platform built out from the wall of

a
b
c
d
e
f
g
h
i
j
k
l
m
n
o
p
q
r
s
t
u
v
w
x
y
z

A
B
C
D
E
F
G
H
I
J
K
L
M
N
O
P
Q
R
S
T
U
V
W
X
Y
Z

a building, with railings round it **2** the upstairs part of a cinema or theatre

bald adjective balder, baldest
a bald person does not have much hair or any hair on their head

bale[1] noun bales
a large bundle of something like hay or straw, usually tied up tightly

bale[2] verb bales, baling, baled
to bale out is to jump out of an aircraft with a parachute

ball noun balls
1 a round object used in many games **2** anything that is made into a round shape *a ball of string* **3** a grand or formal party where people dance

ballad noun ballads
a simple song or poem that tells a story

ballerina (say bal-e-**ree**-na) noun ballerinas
a female ballet dancer

ballet (say **bal**-ay) noun ballets
a form of dancing in which a group of dancers perform special steps and movements to tell a story to music

balloon noun balloons
1 a small rubber pouch that you fill up with air or gas and use as a toy or for decoration **2** a large round or pear-shaped bag filled with a light gas or hot air, so that it can carry people into the air **3** an outline in a strip cartoon containing the words the characters are saying

TOP TIPS
Double up! There is double **l** and double **o** in **balloon**.

ballot (say **bal**-ot) noun ballots
a method of voting in secret by making a mark on a piece of paper and putting it into a box

ballpoint noun ballpoints
a pen with a tiny ball at the tip, round which the ink flows

ballroom noun ballrooms
a large room where dances are held

bamboo noun bamboos
a tall tropical plant with hard hollow stems, used for making furniture

ban verb bans, banning, banned
to ban something is to forbid people to do it

banana noun bananas
a long curved fruit with a yellow skin

band noun bands
1 a group of people playing music together **2** an organized group of people doing something together **3** a circular strip of something

band verb bands, banding, banded
to band together is to join together to form an organized group

bandage (say **ban**-dij) noun bandages
a strip of material that you wrap round a wound to protect it

bandit noun bandits
a member of a gang of robbers who attack travellers

bandstand noun bandstands
a platform for a band playing music outdoors, usually in a park

bandwagon noun bandwagons
to jump or **climb on the bandwagon** (informal) is to join in something that looks like being successful

bandy adjective bandier, bandiest
bandy legs curve outwards at the knees

bang noun bangs
1 a sudden loud noise **2** a heavy blow or knock

bang verb bangs, banging, banged
1 to bang something is to hit or shut it noisily *Don't bang the door when you go out.* **2** to bang something is to knock it hard against something else *She banged her knee on the desk.*

banger noun bangers (informal)
1 a firework that explodes noisily **2** a sausage **3** a noisy old car

banish verb banishes, banishing, banished
to banish someone is to punish them by sending them away and ordering them not to return *The wicked witch Duchess shall be banished for seven years to the tiny Isle of Stones where nothing grows and the sea-current is strong.* — Alan Temperley, *The Brave Whale* **banishment** noun

banisters plural noun
banisters are a rail with upright supports at the side of a staircase

banjo noun banjos
a musical instrument like a small guitar with a round body

bank noun banks
1 a business which looks after people's money 2 the ground beside a river or lake 3 a piece of raised or sloping ground 4 a place where something is stored and collected *a blood bank* 5 a bank of clouds is a mass of them 6 a bank of lights or switches is a row of them

bank verb banks, banking, banked
1 to bank money is to put it in a bank 2 to bank is to lean over while changing direction *The plane banked as it turned to land.* **to bank on something** is to rely on it *We're banking on the weather being good.*

bank holiday noun bank holidays
a public holiday, when the banks are closed

banknote noun banknotes
a piece of paper money

bankrupt adjective
not able to pay all the money you owe **bankruptcy** noun

banner noun banners
a large strip of cloth with writing on it, carried on a pole or between two poles in a procession or demonstration

banquet (say **bank**-wit) noun banquets
a large formal dinner, often with speeches

baptism noun baptisms
baptism is the ceremony of baptizing someone

Baptist noun Baptists
a Christian who believes that a person should not be baptized as a baby but only when he or she is old enough to understand what baptism means

baptize verb baptizes, baptizing, baptized
to baptize someone is to sprinkle them with water, or dip them in water, in a ceremony welcoming them into the Christian Church

bar noun bars
1 a long piece of something hard 2 a counter or room where drinks and refreshments are served 3 one of the small equal sections into which music is divided *A waltz has three beats in a bar.*

bar verb bars, barring, barred
1 to bar something is to fasten it with a bar 2 to bar someone from something is to prevent them from taking part in it 3 to bar someone's way is to stop them getting past

barb noun barbs
a backward-curving point on a fish hook or spear, which makes it stick in more firmly

barbarian noun barbarians
an uncivilized or savage person

barbaric or **barbarous** adjective
savage and cruel

barbecue noun barbecues
1 a metal frame used for grilling food over a charcoal fire outdoors 2 a party at which food is cooked outdoors on a barbecue

barbed wire noun
wire with sharp twisted spikes on it, used to make fences

barber noun barbers
someone whose job is to cut men's hair

bar chart noun bar charts
a diagram showing amounts as bars of equal width but different heights

bar code noun bar codes
a set of black lines that are printed on goods, library books, etc. so that they can be identified by a computer

a
b
c
d
e
f
g
h
i
j
k
l
m
n
o
p
q
r
s
t
u
v
w
x
y
z

A

B

C

D

E

F

G

H

I

J

K

L

M

N

O

P

Q

R

S

T

U

V

W

X

Y

Z

bard noun bards (old use)
a poet or minstrel

bare adjective barer, barest
1 not covered with anything *The trees were bare.* **2** empty or almost empty *The cupboard was bare.* **3** only just enough *They just had the bare necessities of life.*

bareback adjective, adverb
riding on a horse without a saddle

barely adverb
only just; with difficulty *They were barely able to see in the fog.*

bargain noun bargains
1 something that you buy cheaply
2 an agreement between two people to do something for each other *I expect you to keep your side of the bargain.* **into the bargain** as well *He lost all his money and got lost into the bargain.*

bargain verb bargains, bargaining, bargained
to bargain over something is to argue over its price **to get more than you bargained for** is to get an unwelcome surprise

barge noun barges
a long flat-bottomed boat used especially on canals

barge verb barges, barging, barged
to barge into someone is to bump clumsily into them or push them out of the way

baritone noun baritones
a male singer with a voice between a tenor and a bass

bark noun barks
1 a bark is the sound made by a dog or a fox **2** bark is the outer covering of a tree's branches or trunk

bark verb barks, barking, barked
1 a dog or fox barks when it makes its special sound **2** you can say a person barks when they speak loudly or sharply

barley noun
a kind of grain which is used for food and to make beer

barman noun barmen
a man who serves drinks in a bar

bar mitzvah noun bar mitzvahs
a religious ceremony for Jewish boys who have reached the age of 13, when they accept some of the responsibilities of an adult

barn noun barns
a building on a farm used to store things such as grain or hay

barnacle noun barnacles
a shellfish that attaches itself to rocks and the bottoms of ships

barometer (say ba-**rom**-it-er) noun barometers
an instrument that measures air pressure, used in forecasting the weather

baron noun barons
a member of the lowest rank of noblemen

baroness noun baronesses
a female baron or a baron's wife

barrack verb barracks, barracking, barracked
to barrack someone is to jeer at them in public

barracks noun barracks
the buildings where soldiers live

barrage (say ba-rahzh) noun barrages
1 heavy gunfire **2** a large amount of something *We received a barrage of complaints.* **3** a dam or barrier built across a river to make the water deeper

barrel noun barrels
1 a large container for liquids, with curved sides and flat ends **2** the metal tube of a gun, through which the shot is fired

barren adjective
barren land or plants cannot produce any crops or fruit

barricade noun barricades
a barrier, especially one put up quickly to block a street

barricade verb barricades, barricading, barricaded
to barricade a place is to block or defend it with a barrier

barrier noun barriers
1 a fence or wall put up to stop people getting past **2** something that stops you doing something *Lack of confidence can be a barrier to success.*

barrister noun barristers
a lawyer who presents legal cases in the higher courts

barrow noun barrows
1 a small cart **2** an ancient mound of earth over a grave

barter verb barters, bartering, bartered
to barter is to exchange goods for other goods, without using money

base noun bases
1 the lowest part of something, or the part on which something stands **2** a place from which an organization like an army or business is controlled

base verb bases, basing, based
to base one thing on another thing is to use the second thing as the starting point for the first *She based the story on an event in her own childhood.*

baseball noun baseballs
1 baseball is an American game like rounders, in which the players hit a ball and run round a series of four 'bases' to score points **2** a baseball is the ball used in this game

basement noun basements
a room or part of a building below ground level

bash verb bashes, bashing, bashed (informal)
to bash someone or something is to hit them hard

bash noun bashes (informal)
a hard hit **to have a bash at something** (informal) is to try it even though it is

difficult and you think you might not succeed

bashful adjective
shy

basic adjective
forming the first or most important part *He has a basic knowledge of French. Food is a basic human need.*

basically adverb
in the most important ways; essentially *She is basically lazy.*

basin noun basins
1 a deep bowl for mixing food in **2** a large container to hold water for washing your face and hands in **3** a river basin is the area of land where the river's water comes from **4** an area of water enclosed by land, where ships can stay safely

basis noun bases
1 the basis of something is what you start from or add to *These players will be the basis of a new team.* **2** a basis is the way in which something is arranged or organized *The competition is organized on a knockout basis.*

bask verb basks, basking, basked
to bask is to lie or sit comfortably warming yourself in the sun

basket noun baskets
a container made of strips of wood, cane, or wire woven together

basketball noun basketballs
1 basketball is a team game in which players try to throw a large ball through a high net hanging from a hoop **2** a basketball is the ball used in this game

bass (say bayss) adjective
forming the lowest sounds in music

bass (say bayss) noun basses
a bass singer or instrument

bassoon noun bassoons
a woodwind instrument that plays low notes

bat[1] noun bats
a shaped piece of wood used to hit the ball in cricket, baseball, and other games **to do**

a
b
c
d
e
f
g
h
i
j
k
l
m
n
o
p
q
r
s
t
u
v
w
x
y
z

A
B
C
D
E
F
G
H
I
J
K
L
M
N
O
P
Q
R
S
T
U
V
W
X
Y
Z

something off your own bat (informal) is to do it without any help from other people

bat verb bats, batting, batted
to bat is to take a turn at using a bat in cricket, baseball, and other games

bat² noun bats
a flying mammal that looks like a mouse with wings. Bats come out at night to feed.

batch noun batches
a set of things made at one time or dealt with together

bated adjective
with bated breath waiting nervously

bath noun baths
1 a bath is a large container you fill with water and get into to wash yourself 2 a bath sometimes means the water in a bath *Your bath is getting cold.* 3 the baths are also a public swimming pool

bath verb baths, bathing, bathed
1 to bath someone is to give them a bath 2 to bath is to have a bath

bathe verb bathes, bathing, bathed
1 to bathe is to go swimming in the sea or a river 2 to bathe a sore part of your body is to wash it gently

bathe noun bathes
a bathe is a swim

bathroom noun bathrooms
a room for having a bath or wash in

bat mitzvah noun bat mitzvahs
a religious ceremony for Jewish girls who have reached the age of 12, when they accept some of the responsibilities of an adult

baton noun batons
a short stick, especially one you use to conduct an orchestra or in a relay race

batsman noun batsmen
a player who uses a bat in cricket

battalion noun battalions
an army unit consisting of two or more companies

batten noun battens
a flat strip of wood used to hold something in place

batten verb
to batten something down is to fix it securely

batter verb batters, battering, battered
to batter someone or something is to hit them hard and often *The huge waves battered the rocks.*

batter noun
batter is a mixture of flour, eggs, and milk beaten together and used to make pancakes or to coat food before you fry it

battering ram noun battering rams (historical)
a heavy pole used to break through the walls and gates of a city or fort

battery noun batteries
1 a portable device for storing and supplying electricity 2 a series of cages in which animals are kept close together on a farm *Free-range hens are not kept in batteries.* 3 a set of devices that are used together, especially a group of large guns

battle noun battles
1 a fight between two armies 2 a struggle

battlefield noun battlefields
a place where a battle is or was fought

battlements plural noun
the top of a castle wall, usually with gaps through which people defending the castle could fire arrows at the enemy

battleship noun battleships
a large warship armed with powerful guns

bawl verb bawls, bawling, bawled
to bawl is to shout or cry loudly

bay noun bays
1 a place by the sea or a lake where the shore curves inwards 2 an area that is marked out to be used for parking vehicles, storing things, etc. **to keep someone at bay** is to prevent them from coming near you

bayonet noun bayonets
a steel blade that can be fixed to the end of a rifle and used for stabbing

bay window noun bay windows
a window that sticks out from the wall of a house

bazaar noun bazaars
1 a sale held to raise money for charity **2** a covered market in an Eastern country

BBC
short for *British Broadcasting Corporation*

BC
short for *before Christ*, used with dates that come before the birth of Jesus Christ *Julius Caesar came to Britain in 55 BC.*

be verb I am; you are; he, she, or it is; they are; I, he, she, or it was, you were, they were; I, you, or they have been; he, she, or it has been
1 to be is to live or exist *Three boys were in the classroom. There is a bus stop at the corner.* **2** to be someone or something is to have that position or quality *She is my teacher. You are very tall.* **3** the verb **be** can also be used to help make other verbs *They are having a good time. A man was killed on the motorway.* **4** the verb **be** can also be used instead of **go** in questions and in statements with **not** *Have you been to Paris? No, I've never been there.*

beach noun beaches
the strip of pebbles or sand close to the sea

beacon noun beacons
a light or fire used as a warning signal

bead noun beads
1 a small piece of glass, wood, or plastic with a hole through it, threaded on a string or wire to make a necklace or bracelet **2** a small drop of liquid *She had beads of sweat on her face.*

beady adjective beadier, beadiest
beady eyes are small and bright

beagle noun beagles
a type of dog with long ears, used for hunting hares

beak noun beaks
the hard pointed part of a bird's mouth

beaker noun beakers
1 a tall drinking mug, usually without a handle **2** (in science) a glass container used for pouring liquids in a laboratory

beam noun beams
1 a long thick bar of wood or metal **2** a ray of light

beak

hummingbird

puffin

sparrow

duck

hawk

pelican

A
B
C
D
E
F
G
H
I
J
K
L
M
N
O
P
Q
R
S
T
U
V
W
X
Y
Z

beam verb beams, beaming, beamed
1 to beam is to send out a beam of light or radio waves **2** you can say a person beams when they smile very happily

bean noun beans
1 a kind of plant with seeds growing in pods **2** the seed or pod of this kind of plant, eaten as food

bear[1] verb bears, bearing, bore, born or borne
1 to bear something is to carry or support it **2** to bear something such as a signature or mark is to have or show it *The letter bore her signature.* **3** to bear something is to put up with it or suffer it *I can't bear all this noise.* **4** a woman bears children when she gives birth to them *She was born in 1950. She has borne three sons.*

bear[2] noun bears
a large heavy animal with thick fur and sharp hooked claws

bearable adjective
something that is bearable is something you are able to put up with *His toothache was hardly bearable.*

beard noun beards
hair on the lower part of a man's face

bearing noun bearings
1 your bearing is the way you stand and walk **2** the direction or position of something in relation to something else **to get your bearings** is to work out where you are in relation to other things **to lose your bearings** is to forget where you are in relation to other things

beast noun beasts
1 any large four-footed animal **2** (informal) a person you think is cruel or unkind

beastly adjective (informal)
cruel or unkind *Don't be so beastly to your sister.*

beat verb beats, beating, beat, beaten
1 to beat someone or something is to hit them repeatedly, especially with a stick **2** to beat someone in a game or match is to do

better than them and win it **3** to beat a cooking mixture is to stir it quickly so that it becomes thicker **4** to beat something is to shape or flatten it by hitting it many times **5** to beat is also to make regular movements like your heart does **to beat someone up** is to attack them very violently

beat noun beats
1 a regular rhythm or stroke, like your heart makes **2** a strong rhythm in pop music **3** the regular route of a police officer

beautiful adjective
very pleasing to look at or listen to
beautifully adverb

TOP TIPS
There is a tricky bit in **beautiful**—it has three vowels in a row, **eau**.

beauty noun beauties
1 beauty is a quality that gives delight or pleasure, especially to your senses *They enjoyed the beauty of the sunset.* **2** a beauty is a particularly beautiful person or thing

beaver noun beavers
1 a brown furry animal with strong teeth and a long flat tail, which builds dams in rivers **2** a member of the most junior section of the Scout Association

became
past tense of become *The dark passageway became completely black.*

because conjunction
for the reason that *We were happy because it was a holiday.* **because of someone** or **something** for that reason; on account of them *He limped because of his bad leg.*

beckon verb beckons, beckoning, beckoned
to beckon to someone is to make a sign asking them to come to you

become verb becomes, becoming, became, become
1 to become is to start being something described *It gradually became darker.* **2** to become someone is to make them look attractive *That dress becomes you.*

bed noun beds
1 a bed is a piece of furniture for sleeping on 2 bed is the place where you sleep *I'm going to bed now.* 3 a bed is also a part of a garden where plants are grown 4 the bed of the sea or of a river is the bottom of it

bedclothes plural noun
sheets, blankets, and duvets for using on a bed

bedding noun
things for making a bed, such as sheets, blankets, and duvets

bedlam noun
a loud noise or disturbance *There was bedlam at the playgroup.*

bedraggled (say bi-**drag**-uld) adjective
wet and dirty

bedridden (say **bed**-rid-en) adjective
too ill or injured to get out of bed

bedroom noun bedrooms
a room where you sleep

bedside noun
the space beside a bed, especially the bed of someone who is ill *He sat by his son's bedside all night.*

bedspread noun bedspreads
a covering put over the top of a bed

bedstead noun bedsteads
the framework of a bed

bedtime noun
the time when you are supposed to go to bed

bee noun bees
a stinging insect that makes honey

beech noun beeches
a tree with smooth bark and glossy leaves

beef noun
the meat of an ox, bull, or cow

beefburger noun beefburgers
a hamburger

beefy adjective beefier, beefiest (informal)
a beefy person is big, with strong muscles

beehive noun beehives
a container that bees are kept in so that their honey can be collected

beeline noun
to make a beeline for something is to go quickly and directly towards it

been
past participle of be *I have been feeling poorly for a while.*

beer noun beers
beer is an alcoholic drink made from malt and hops

beet noun beet or beets
beet is a plant used as a vegetable or for making sugar

beetle noun beetles
an insect with hard shiny covers over its wings

beetroot noun beetroot
the dark red root of beet used as a vegetable

before adverb, preposition
1 earlier, or earlier than *Have you been here before? They came the day before yesterday.* 2 in front of *He stood up before the whole school.*

beforehand adverb
earlier, or before something else happens *She had tried to phone me beforehand. Let me know beforehand if you want to come on the picnic.*

beg verb begs, begging, begged
1 to beg is to ask people to give you money or food 2 to beg someone is to ask them seriously or desperately *He begged me not to tell the teacher.* **I beg your pardon** I didn't hear or understand what you said; I apologize

began
past tense of begin *The ground beneath them began to shake.*

a
b
c
d
e
f
g
h
i
j
k
l
m
n
o
p
q
r
s
t
u
v
w
x
y
z

A
B
C
D
E
F
G
H
I
J
K
L
M
N
O
P
Q
R
S
T
U
V
W
X
Y
Z

beggar noun beggars
someone who lives by begging in the street

begin verb begins, beginning, began, begun
to begin something is to start doing it

beginner noun beginners
someone who is just starting to learn or is still learning a subject

beginning noun beginnings
the start of something

begun
past participle of begin *Tears had begun to run down Emily's face.*

behalf noun
on behalf of something to help a cause *They were collecting money on behalf of cancer research.* **on someone's behalf** for them or in their name *Will you accept the prize on my behalf?*

behave verb behaves, behaving, behaved
1 to behave well or badly is to act in a good or bad way *They behaved very badly at the party.* 2 to show good manners *Why can't you behave?*

behaviour noun
1 your behaviour is the way you behave 2 animal behaviour is the way animals normally behave and treat one another

behead verb beheads, beheading, beheaded
to behead someone is to cut off their head, as a form of execution

behind adverb, preposition
1 at or to the back *The others are a long way behind. She hid behind a tree.* 2 not making good progress *He's behind the rest of the class in maths.* 3 supporting or encouraging *We're all behind you.* **behind someone's back** without them knowing about it

behind noun behinds
your behind is your bottom *He kicked me on the behind.*

beige (say bayzh) noun, adjective
a light yellow-brown colour

being noun beings
a being is a person or creature of any kind

belch verb belches, belching, belched
1 to belch is to make a noise by letting air come up from your stomach through your mouth 2 a chimney or factory belches smoke or fumes when it sends out thick smoke or fumes into the air

belch noun belches
the act or sound of belching

belfry noun belfries
the top part of a tower or steeple, in which bells hang

belief noun beliefs
1 a belief is something you believe *They have very few beliefs.* 2 belief is when you believe something

believe verb believes, believing, believed
1 to believe something is to think that it is true 2 to believe someone is to think that they are telling the truth 3 to believe in something is to think it is real or important *Do you believe in ghosts?* **believable** adjective if something is believable, you are able to believe it could happen

bell noun bells
a device that makes a ringing sound, especially a cup-shaped metal object with a clapper

bellow verb bellows, bellowing, bellowed
to bellow is to roar or shout loudly and deeply

bellows plural noun
bellows are a device for blowing out air, especially into a fire to make it burn more strongly

belly noun bellies
1 the abdomen or the stomach of a human 2 the under part of a four-legged animal

belong verb belongs, belonging, belonged
1 to belong to someone is to be their

property *The pencil belongs to me.*
2 to belong to a club or group is to be a member of it *We both belong to the tennis club.* **3** to belong somewhere is to have a special place where it goes *The butter belongs in the fridge.*

belongings plural noun
your belongings are the things that you own

beloved (say bi-**luvd** or bi-**luv**-id) adjective
greatly loved

below preposition
lower than, under *We have nice neighbours in the flat below us.*

below adverb
at a lower point, or to a lower point *I'll have the top bunk, and you can sleep below.*

belt noun belts
1 a strip of material, often leather or cloth, that you wear round your waist **2** a long narrow area *As we went further north we met a belt of rain.*

belt verb belts, belting, belted (informal)
1 to belt someone is to hit them hard **2** to belt along is to move very fast

bench noun benches
1 a long seat **2** a long table for working at

bend verb bends, bending, bent
1 to bend something is to make it curved or crooked **2** to bend is to become curved or crooked *The trees were bending in the wind.* **3** to bend is also to move the top of your body downwards *She bent down to pick up the cat.*

bend noun bends
a part where something curves or turns

beneath preposition, adverb
under *Beneath the soil there is clay.*

benefactor noun benefactors
someone who gives money or other help to a person or organization that needs it

beneficial adjective
something is beneficial when it is useful or helpful

benefit noun benefits
1 a benefit is something that is useful or helpful *A big benefit of exercise is that it makes you feel good.* **2** benefit is money that the government pays to help people who are poor, sick, or out of work **3** a benefit concert or match is one organized to raise money for a good cause

benefit verb benefits, benefiting, benefited
you benefit from something, or it benefits you, when it helps you

benevolent adjective
kind and helpful **benevolence** noun

bent adjective
curved or crooked **to be bent on something** is to be determined to do it

bequeath (rhymes with **breathe**) verb bequeaths, bequeathing, bequeathed
to bequeath something to someone is to leave it to them in a will

bereaved adjective
a bereaved person is someone with a close relative who has recently died **bereavement** noun

bereft adjective
to be bereft of something is to be deprived of it *He was bereft of hope.*

beret (say **bair**-ay) noun berets
a soft, round, flat cap

berry noun berries
a small juicy fruit

berserk adjective
to go berserk is to become extremely angry or lose control *The man went berserk and started flinging things around.*

berth noun berths
1 a sleeping place on a ship or train **2** a place where a ship is tied up

beside preposition
next to; close to *A house beside the sea.* **to be beside yourself** is to be very excited or upset *He was beside himself with anger.*

a
b
c
d
e
f
g
h
i
j
k
l
m
n
o
p
q
r
s
t
u
v
w
x
y
z

besides preposition
in addition to *Who came besides you?*

besides adverb
also; in addition to this *The coat cost too much. Besides, it's the wrong colour.*

besiege (say bi-**seej**) verb besieges, besieging, besieged
1 to besiege a place is to surround it until the people inside surrender **2** to besiege someone famous is to crowd round them *The rock group was besieged by hundreds of fans.*

best adjective
1 superlative of good and well[2] **2** most excellent; most able to do something *She's the best swimmer in the class.*

best adverb
1 in the best way; most *We'll do what suits you best.* **2** most usefully; most wisely *He is best ignored.*

best noun
the best person or thing, or the best people or things *She was the best at tennis. These apples are the best you can buy.* **to make the best of something** is to accept it and enjoy it as much as you can, even though it is not very good

best man noun
someone who helps the bridegroom at his wedding

best-seller noun best-sellers
a book or other product that has sold in very large numbers

bet noun bets
1 an agreement that you will receive money if you are correct in choosing the winner of a race or in saying something will happen, and will lose money if you are not correct **2** the money you risk losing in a bet

bet verb bets, betting, bet or betted
1 to bet, or to bet money, is to make a bet **2** (informal) to bet something is to say you are sure about it *I bet I'm right.*

betray verb betrays, betraying, betrayed
1 to betray someone is to do them harm when they are expecting your support **2** to betray something like a secret is to give it away **betrayal** noun

better adjective
comparative of good and well[2]
1 more excellent *I need a better bike.* **2** to be better is to feel well again after an illness *Are you better?*

better noun betters
a better person or thing **to get the better of someone** is to defeat or outwit them

better adverb
in a better way *Try to do it better next time.* **I had better do something** it would be better for me to do it (you can use **we, you,** and so on, instead of **I**) **to be better off** is to be more fortunate in some way, for example by having more money

better verb betters, bettering, bettered
to better something is to improve on it *She hopes to better her own record time.*

between preposition, adverb
within two or more points; among *Call me between Tuesday and Friday. The train runs between London and Glasgow. What is the difference between butter and margarine? Divide the sweets between the children. The two houses are side by side with a fence between.*

beware verb only used in the form beware
a warning to be careful *Beware of pickpockets.*

bewilder verb bewilders, bewildering, bewildered
to bewilder someone is to puzzle them completely **bewilderment** noun

bewitch verb bewitches, bewitching, bewitched
1 to bewitch someone is to put a spell on them **2** to bewitch someone is also to delight them very much *He was completely bewitched by her beauty.*

beyond preposition, adverb
farther on *Don't go beyond the end of the street. You can see the next valley and the mountains beyond.*

bias noun biases
1 bias is a strong feeling in favour of one person or side and against another *The referee was accused of bias.* **2** bias is also a tendency for a ball to swerve, especially in a game of bowls **biased** adjective someone is biased when they show that they prefer one person or side over another

bib noun bibs
a piece of cloth or plastic you put under a baby's chin during meals to protect its clothes from stains

Bible noun Bibles
the holy book of Christianity and Judaism **biblical** adjective

bibliography (say bib-lee-**og**-ra-fee) noun bibliographies
a list of books about a subject or by a particular author

bicycle noun bicycles
a two-wheeled vehicle that you ride by pushing down on pedals with your feet

bid noun bids
1 offering an amount you will pay for something, especially at an auction **2** an attempt *He will make a bid for the world record tomorrow.*

bid verb bids, bidding, bid
to bid an amount of money is to offer it for something at an auction

bide verb bides, biding, bided
to bide your time is to wait, expecting something to happen that will help you

big adjective bigger, biggest
1 more than the normal size; large **2** important *This is a big decision.* **3** elder *Have you met my big sister?*

bike noun bikes (informal)
a bicycle or motor cycle

bikini noun bikinis
a girl's or woman's two-piece swimsuit

bilingual adjective
speaking two languages well

bill[1] noun bills
1 a piece of paper that tells you how much money you owe for something **2** a plan for a new law in parliament **3** a poster giving information about something **4** a programme of entertainment *There's a magician on the bill.*

bill[2] noun bills
a bird's beak

a
b
c
d
e
f
g
h
i
j
k
l
m
n
o
p
q
r
s
t
u
v
w
x
y
z

bicycle

saddle
gears
handlebars
brake
crossbar
valve
brake block
fork
tyre
spoke
chain
pedal

A
B
C
D
E
F
G
H
I
J
K
L
M
N
O
P
Q
R
S
T
U
V
W
X
Y
Z

billiards noun
a game played with long sticks (called *cues*) and three balls on a cloth-covered table

billion noun billions
a thousand million (1,000,000,000)
billionth adjective, noun

billow verb billows, billowing, billowed
to billow is to rise up or move like waves on the sea *As she floated gently down, Mrs Twit's petticoat billowed out like a parachute, showing her long knickers.* – Roald Dahl, *The Twits*

billy goat noun billy goats
a male goat

bin noun bins
a large or deep container, especially one that you put rubbish or litter in

binary number noun binary numbers
a number that uses only the digits 0 and 1. Binary numbers are used in computer programming.

bind verb binds, binding, bound
1 to bind things is to tie them up or tie them together **2** to bind something is to wrap a piece of material round it **3** to bind a book is to fasten the pages inside a cover **4** to bind someone is to make them do something or promise something

bingo noun
a game played with cards with numbered squares. These are covered or crossed out as the numbers are called out, and the first person to complete the card wins the game.

binoculars plural noun
a device with lenses for both eyes, for making distant objects seem nearer

biography noun biographies
the story of a person's life
biographical adjective

biology noun
the science or study of living things
biological adjective **biologist** noun

birch noun birches
a thin tree with shiny bark and slender branches

bird noun birds
a feathered animal with two wings, two legs, and a beak

bird of prey noun birds of prey
a bird that feeds on animal flesh, such as an eagle or hawk

birdseed noun
seeds for caged birds to eat

bird's-eye view noun
a general view of something, seen from above

Biro noun Biros (trademark)
a kind of ballpoint pen

birth noun births
birth is the beginning of a person's or animal's life, when they come out of their mother's body

birthday noun birthdays
the anniversary of the day on which you were born

birthmark noun birthmarks
a coloured mark which has been on someone's skin since they were born

birthplace noun birthplaces
the place where someone was born

biscuit noun biscuits
a small flat kind of cake that has been baked until it is hard

bishop noun bishops
1 a senior priest in the Christian Church who is in charge of all the churches in a city or district **2** a chess piece shaped like a bishop's mitre

bison noun bison
a wild ox with shaggy hair

bit noun bits
1 a small piece or amount of something **2** the part of a horse's bridle that is put into its mouth **3** the part of a tool that cuts or grips **4** (in computing) the smallest unit

of data or memory **bits and pieces** small things of various kinds

bit
past tense of bite verb *I bit my lip, thinking hard.*

bitch noun bitches
a female dog, fox, or wolf

bite verb bites, biting, bit, bitten
1 to bite something is to cut it or hold it with your teeth **2** to bite into something is to penetrate it *The tyres bit into the mud.* **3** to accept bait *The fish are biting.* **4** to sting or hurt *a biting wind*

bite noun bites
1 to give a person or animal a bite is to bite them **2** a mark or spot made by biting *You've had an insect bite.* **3** a snack *Would you like a bite?*

bitter adjective
1 tasting sour and unpleasant **2** feeling angry and resentful because you are disappointed about something *She is very bitter about losing her place in the team.* **3** extremely cold *There was a bitter wind.*

black adjective blacker, blackest
1 of the darkest colour, the opposite of white **2** also **Black**, having dark skin **3** dismal; not hopeful *The outlook is black.* **4** very dirty

black noun blacks
1 a black colour **2** a person with dark skin

blackberry noun blackberries
a sweet black berry

blackbird noun blackbirds
a dark European songbird

blackboard noun blackboards
a dark board for writing on with chalk

blacken verb blackens, blackening, blackened
1 to blacken something is to make it black **2** to blacken someone's name is to say bad things about them

black eye noun black eyes
an eye with heavy bruises round it

black hole noun black holes
(in astronomy)
a region in space with such strong gravity that no light escapes

black ice noun
thin transparent ice on roads

blackmail verb blackmails, blackmailing, blackmailed
to blackmail someone is to get money from them by threatening to tell people something that they want to keep secret

black market noun
a black market in goods is illegal trading in them

blackout noun blackouts
1 when a person becomes unconscious for a short time **2** a time when lights are kept hidden or turned off

blacksmith noun blacksmiths
someone who makes and repairs things made of iron, and fits shoes on horses

bladder noun bladders
1 the bladder is the bag-like part of your body where urine collects **2** a bladder is also an inflatable bag inside a football

blade noun blades
1 the sharp part of a device for cutting, such as a knife or sword **2** the flat, wide part of an oar or propeller **3** a long narrow leaf of grass

blame verb blames, blaming, blamed
to blame someone is to say that they have done something wrong *My brother broke the window but they blamed me.*

blame noun
to get the blame for something is to be blamed for it **to be to blame** is to be the person who has done something wrong

blank adjective
1 not written, drawn, or printed on *The piece of paper was blank.* **2** showing no expression or interest *His face looked blank.*

blank noun blanks
1 an empty space **2** a cartridge for a gun

a
b
c
d
e
f
g
h
i
j
k
l
m
n
o
p
q
r
s
t
u
v
w
x
y
z

A
B
C
D
E
F
G
H
I
J
K
L
M
N
O
P
Q
R
S
T
U
V
W
X
Y
Z

which makes a noise but does not fire a bullet

blanket noun blankets
a large piece of thick cloth, used as a warm covering for a bed

blare verb blares, blaring, blared
to blare is to make a harsh loud sound

blast noun blasts
1 a strong rush of wind or air 2 a sharp or loud noise *The referee gave a long blast of his whistle.*

blast verb blasts, blasting, blasted
to blast something is to blow it up with explosives

blast-off noun
the launch of a spacecraft

blaze noun blazes
1 a very bright fire 2 a very bright colour or light

blaze verb blazes, blazing, blazed
1 to blaze is to burn or shine brightly
2 to blaze with a feeling is to feel it very strongly *He was blazing with anger.*
to blaze a trail is to show the way for others to follow

blazer noun blazers
a kind of jacket, often with a badge on the front

bleach noun bleaches
a substance used to clean things or make clothes white

bleach verb bleaches, bleaching, bleached
to bleach something is to make it white

bleak adjective bleaker, bleakest
1 bare and cold *The village school for younger children was a bleak brick building called Crunchem Hall Primary School.* – Roald Dahl, *Matilda* 2 dreary and miserable *The future looks bleak.*

bleary adjective blearier, bleariest
bleary eyes are tired and do not see clearly

bleat noun bleats
the cry of a sheep or goat

bleat verb bleats, bleating, bleated
a sheep or goat bleats when it makes a bleat

bleed verb bleeds, bleeding, bled
1 to bleed is to lose blood from your body, for example if you are injured 2 to bleed a person or animal is to take blood from them

bleep noun bleeps
a small high sound made by an electronic device

blemish noun blemishes
1 a mark or stain on something 2 a fault or weakness

blend verb blends, blending, blended
to blend things is to mix them together smoothly or easily

blend noun blends
a smooth mixture

bless verb blesses, blessing, blessed
1 to bless someone is to wish or bring them happiness 2 to bless someone is also to ask God to look after them

blessing noun blessings
1 a prayer or act of blessing someone
2 something you are glad of or happy about *It's a blessing that they are safe.*

blew
past tense of **blow** verb *A gusty wind blew rain into his face.*

blight noun blights
1 blight is a plant disease 2 a blight is a thing that spoils or damages something

blind adjective blinder, blindest
1 not able to see 2 without thought or understanding

blind verb blinds, blinding, blinded
1 to blind someone is to make them blind
2 a bright light blinds you when it makes you unable to see for a time

blind noun blinds
a screen for a window

blindfold noun blindfolds
a piece of cloth used to cover someone's eyes so that they cannot see where they are or what is happening

blindfold verb blindfolds, blindfolding, blindfolded
to blindfold someone is to cover their eyes with a blindfold

blindfold adjective
with a blindfold over the eyes

blink verb blinks, blinking, blinked
to blink is to shut and open your eyes quickly

bliss noun
bliss is great happiness

blister noun blisters
a swelling like a bubble on your skin

blitz noun blitzes
a sudden violent attack, especially from aircraft

blizzard noun blizzards
a severe snowstorm

bloated adjective
swollen or puffed out

blob noun blobs
a small round lump of something like paint or ice cream

block noun blocks
1 a solid piece of something hard such as wood 2 a large building or group of buildings with streets all around it 3 something that stops people getting through *They came to a road block and had to turn back.*

block verb blocks, blocking, blocked
1 to block something is to get in the way of it *Tall buildings blocked our view.* 2 to block something like a pipe or drain is to prevent water flowing through it

blockade noun blockades
when a city or port is surrounded to stop people or goods from getting in or out

blockage noun blockages
1 something that stops up a pipe or drain 2 a blocked state *Roadworks are causing blockages in the traffic.*

block capitals or **block letters** plural noun
large capital letters

blog noun blogs
a website on which someone writes regularly about their own life or opinions

blond or **blonde** adjective blonder, blondest
fair-haired

blonde noun blondes
a girl or woman with fair hair

blood noun
1 blood is the red liquid that flows through your veins and arteries 2 someone who is of noble or royal blood has ancestors who were noble or royal *He is of royal blood.*
to do something in cold blood is to do it deliberately and cruelly

bloodhound noun bloodhounds
a large breed of dog which can track people over long distances by following their scent

bloodshed noun
bloodshed is the killing and injuring of people

bloodshot adjective
eyes are bloodshot when they are streaked with red from being strained or tired

bloodstream noun
the bloodstream is the blood flowing round your body

bloodthirsty adjective bloodthirstier, bloodthirstiest
enjoying killing and violence

bloody adjective bloodier, bloodiest
1 bleeding 2 covered in blood 3 a bloody fight or battle is one in which a lot of people are killed or badly hurt

bloom verb blooms, blooming, bloomed
to bloom is to produce flowers *Look! The roses have bloomed!*

bloom noun blooms
a bloom is a flower **in bloom** trees

A

B

C

D

E

F

G

H

I

J

K

L

M

N

O

P

Q

R

S

T

U

V

W

X

Y

Z

and plants are in bloom when they are producing flowers

blossom noun blossoms
1 a blossom is a flower, especially on a fruit tree 2 blossom is a mass of flowers on a tree
blossom verb blossoms, blossoming, blossomed
1 a tree or bush blossoms when it produces flowers 2 to blossom is also to develop into something very fine or good *She has blossomed into a lovely singer.*

blot noun blots
1 a spot or blob of ink 2 a flaw or fault
blot verb blots, blotting, blotted
1 to blot something is to make a blot on it 2 to blot paper is to dry it with blotting paper **to blot something out** is to remove it or make it invisible

blotch noun blotches
an untidy patch of colour **blotchy** adjective

blouse noun blouses
a loose piece of clothing like a shirt that girls and women wear

blow noun blows
1 a hard knock or hit 2 a shock or disappointment *Losing the cup final was a terrible blow.* 3 the action of blowing
blow verb blows, blowing, blew, blown
1 to blow is to force out air from your mouth or nose *He blew on his cold hands to warm them up.* 2 to move in the wind *Her hat blew off.* 3 to blow something is to form it by blowing *Let's blow bubbles.* 4 to blow something such as a whistle is to make a sound with it 5 a fuse or light bulb blows when it melts or breaks **to blow something up** is to destroy it with an explosion **to blow up** is to be destroyed in an explosion

blowlamp or **blowtorch** noun blowlamps, blowtorches
a device for aiming a strong flame at a surface, especially to remove old paint

blue adjective bluer, bluest
1 of the colour of a bright cloudless sky 2 sad and miserable *I'm feeling blue.* 3 rude or obscene *They were telling blue jokes.*

blue noun blues
a blue colour **out of the blue** with no warning *My friend turned up out of the blue.*

bluebell noun bluebells
a blue wild flower

bluebottle noun bluebottles
a large blue fly that makes a loud buzz

blueprint noun blueprints
a detailed plan of something that is going to be built

blues plural noun
blues is a type of music that is often sad **to get the blues** is to feel sad and miserable

bluff verb bluffs, bluffing, bluffed
to bluff someone is to make them think that you will do something that you don't intend to do or that you know something that you don't really know

bluff noun bluffs
a bluff is something that someone says or does to bluff someone else, for example an empty promise or threat *He said he'd report us, but that was just a bluff.*

blunder noun blunders
a careless mistake

blunt adjective blunter, bluntest
1 having an edge that is not good for cutting 2 saying what you mean without trying to be polite or tactful

blur verb blurs, blurring, blurred
to blur something is to make it unclear or smeared
blur noun blurs
an unclear shape with no definite outline *Without her glasses on, everything was a blur.*

blurb noun blurbs
a short description of a book that is printed on the back and meant to attract your attention and make you want to buy it

blurt verb blurt, blurting, blurted
to blurt something out is to say it suddenly, without thinking

blush verb blushes, blushing, blushed
to blush is to have a strong pink colour in

your face because you are embarrassed or ashamed

bluster verb blusters, blustering, blustered
to bluster is to boast or make threats that don't mean very much

blustery adjective
blustery weather is when the wind is blowing in gusts

boar noun boars
1 a wild pig 2 a male pig

board noun boards
1 a board is a flat piece of wood, used in building 2 a board is also a flat piece of wood or cardboard used to play games with, for example a dartboard or a chess board 3 a board is also a group of people who run a company or organization 4 board is daily meals supplied in return for money or work *The price of the holiday includes full board.*
on board aboard a ship

board verb boards, boarding, boarded
1 to board a ship or train or aircraft is to get on it for a journey 2 to board is to get meals and accommodation **to board something up** is to cover it with boards

boarder noun boarders
1 a child who lives at a boarding school during the term 2 a lodger

board game noun board games
a game played on a board, such as chess or draughts

boarding school noun
boarding schools
a school in which the pupils live during the term

boast verb boasts, boasting, boasted
to boast about something that you own or that you have done is to talk proudly about it, often in order to impress people

boastful adjective
a boastful person likes to talk a lot about the things they own or the things they have done **boastfully** adverb

boat noun boats
a vehicle designed to float and travel on water **to be in the same boat** is to share the same problems or difficulties

bob verb bobs, bobbing, bobbed
to bob is to move gently up and down, like something floating on water

bobble noun bobbles
a small round ball of something soft such as wool, used as a decoration on a hat or clothing

bobsleigh or **bobsled** noun
bobsleighs, bobsleds
a large sledge with two sets of runners

bodily adjective
to do with your body

bodily adverb
by taking hold of someone's body *He was picked up bodily and bundled into the car.*

body noun bodies
1 the body is the flesh and bones and other parts of a person or animal 2 the body is also the main part of a person or animal, not including the head, arms, or legs 3 a body is a dead person or corpse 4 the body of something is the main part of it *They entered the huge body of the castle.* 5 a body of people is a group of them in one place 6 a body is a distinct object or piece of matter *Stars and planets are heavenly bodies.*

bodyguard noun bodyguards
a guard who protects someone from being attacked

bog noun bogs
bog or a bog is an area of wet spongy ground

bogus adjective
false; not real or genuine *He gave a name that turned out to be bogus.*

boil[1] verb boils, boiling, boiled
1 to boil a liquid is to heat it until it starts to bubble and give off vapour 2 to boil is to start bubbling, like water 3 to boil food is to cook it in boiling water **to be**

boiling (informal) is to be very hot *It's boiling outside.*

boil² noun boils
a painful red swelling on the skin

boiler noun boilers
a container for heating water or making steam

boisterous adjective
noisy and lively

bold adjective bolder, boldest
1 brave and adventurous 2 clear and easy to see *bold colours* 3 printed in thick black type

bollard noun bollards
1 a short thick post put up on a road, used to keep out traffic 2 a short thick post on a ship or quay, that ropes are tied to

bolster verb bolsters, bolstering, bolstered
to bolster something such as a feeling is to increase it *Her win last week has really bolstered her confidence.* **to bolster something up** is to support it when it is weak

bolt noun bolts
1 a sliding bar for fastening a door or window 2 a thick metal pin for fastening things together 3 a flash of lightning **a bolt from the blue** an unwelcome surprise

bolt verb bolts, bolting, bolted
1 to bolt a door or window is to fasten it with a bolt 2 to bolt is to run away in panic, as a horse does 3 to bolt food is to swallow it too quickly

bomb noun bombs
a container with explosives, which blows up when it is detonated

bomb verb bombs, bombing, bombed
to bomb a place is to attack it with bombs

bombard verb bombards, bombarding, bombarded
1 to bombard a place is to attack it with heavy gunfire 2 to bombard someone with questions or complaints is to direct a large number of questions or complaints at them **bombardment** noun

bomber noun bombers
1 an aircraft built to drop bombs 2 a person who plants or sets off a bomb

bond noun bonds
1 a shared experience or feeling that brings people close together 2 bonds are ropes or chains used to tie people up

bondage noun
bondage is being a slave

bone noun bones
a bone is one of the hard pieces of a skeleton **to have a bone to pick with someone** is to have a reason to argue with them about something

bonfire noun bonfires
a large fire lit out of doors

bonnet noun bonnets
1 the hinged cover over the front part of a car 2 a baby's or woman's hat with strings that tie under the chin

bonus noun bonuses
1 an extra payment that someone gets for their work 2 an extra advantage or reward

bony adjective bonier, boniest
1 bony people or animals have bones without much flesh on them 2 full of bones 3 thin and hard, like a bone

boo verb boos, booing, booed
to boo is to shout out that you don't like what someone has said or done, like an angry audience in a theatre

booby prize noun booby prizes
a prize given as a joke to someone who comes last in a contest

booby trap noun booby traps
something designed to hit or injure someone when they do not expect it

book noun books
a set of sheets of paper, usually with printing or writing on, fastened together inside a cover

book verb books, booking, booked
1 to book something such as a seat in a theatre or on a train, or a room in a hotel, is to arrange for it to be kept for you
2 to book someone is to record their name in a book or list

bookcase noun bookcases
a piece of furniture with shelves for holding books

bookkeeping noun
bookkeeping is recording details of all the money that a business receives and spends

booklet noun booklets
a small book with paper covers

bookmaker noun bookmakers
a person whose business is taking bets, especially bets made on horse races

bookmark noun bookmarks
1 something you use to mark a place in a book **2** a link you have made on a computer to one of your favourite websites

boom noun booms
1 a deep hollow sound **2** a time when people are well off **3** a long pole at the bottom of a sail to keep it stretched **4** a long pole carrying a microphone
boom verb booms, booming, boomed
1 to boom is to make a deep hollow sound, like a heavy gun **2** to boom is also to speak in a loud deep voice **3** to boom is also to grow quickly or be prosperous *Business is booming.*

boomerang noun boomerangs
a curved stick which moves in a curve and comes back to you when you throw it.

boost verb boosts, boosting, boosted
to boost something is to increase its size or value or power *Being in the drama group has really boosted his confidence.*

booster noun boosters
1 something that increases the power of a system, especially a radio or television transmitter **2** an additional engine or rocket for a spacecraft **3** an additional dose of a vaccine

boot noun boots
1 a heavy shoe that covers the ankle and sometimes part of your leg **2** the space for luggage at the back of a car
boot verb boots, booting, booted
1 to boot someone is to kick them hard
2 to boot up a computer is to switch it on and start it

booth noun booths
a small compartment for a special purpose, such as making a telephone call or having your photo taken

booty noun
booty is the valuable things that invading soldiers or pirates take from others by force

border noun borders
1 the border between two countries is the line where they meet *We're about to cross the Scottish border.* **2** an edge *There is a black border around the poster.* **3** a flower bed

borderline adjective
only just acceptable or valid

bore[1] verb bores, boring, bored
1 to bore someone is to make them feel tired and uninterested **2** to bore a hole is to drill it through something
bore noun bores
a dull or uninteresting person or thing

bore[2]
past tense of **bear**[1] *His fellow soldiers bore him off the field.*

boredom noun
a feeling of tiredness and lack of interest

boring adjective
dull and uninteresting *The book was really boring.*

born or **borne**
past participle of **bear**[1] *Their son was born on the 17th of December. She has borne three children.*

borough (say **bu**-ro) noun boroughs
an important town or district with its own local council

a
b
c
d
e
f
g
h
i
j
k
l
m
n
o
p
q
r
s
t
u
v
w
x
y
z

A
B
C
D
E
F
G
H
I
J
K
L
M
N
O
P
Q
R
S
T
U
V
W
X
Y
Z

borrow verb borrows, borrowing, borrowed
to borrow something is to have it for a time and then return it to its owner

bosom noun bosoms
a woman's breasts

boss noun bosses (informal)
a person who is in charge of a business or group of workers
boss verb bosses, bossing, bossed (informal)
to boss someone is to order them around

bossy adjective bossier, bossiest (informal)
a bossy person is fond of ordering people about

botany noun
botany is the study of plants
botanical adjective a botanical garden is one that has a lot of interesting plants that the public can go and see
botanist noun

both determiner, pronoun
the two of them, not just one *I want them both in the team.*
both adverb
you use **both** with **and** to say two things about something or someone *He is both friendly and helpful.*

bother verb bothers, bothering, bothered
1 to bother someone is to cause them trouble or worry **2** to be bothered to do something is to take trouble over it
bother noun
bother is trouble or worry

bottle noun bottles
a glass or plastic container with a narrow neck for holding liquids
bottle verb bottles, bottling, bottled
to bottle something is to put it in a bottle **to bottle something up** is to keep something you are worried about to yourself

bottle bank noun bottle banks
a large tank or drum for putting glass bottles and jars in for recycling

bottleneck noun bottlenecks
a place where traffic is slowed down or stuck by a blockage or hazard

bottom noun bottoms
1 the bottom of something is its lowest point **2** the bottom of a garden is the farther end of it, away from the house **3** your bottom is the part of you that you sit on, also called your buttocks

bottomless adjective
1 very deep **2** not seeming to have any limit *I don't have a bottomless purse.*

bough (rhymes with **cow**) noun boughs
a large branch of a tree that reaches out from the trunk

bought
past tense and past participle of **buy** verb
I bought the baby some lovely toys to play with. She looked at the map she had bought.

boulder noun boulders
a very large smooth stone

bounce verb bounces, bouncing, bounced
1 to bounce is to spring back when thrown against something, like a rubber ball **2** to bounce something like a ball is to throw it so that it bounces
bounce noun bounces
1 a bounce is the action of bouncing **2** bounce is liveliness, such as a young child or puppy has **bouncy** adjective a bouncy person is lively and full of energy

bound[1]
past tense and past participle of **bind** *She bound his arm firmly with the bandage. The prisoners had been bound and gagged.*

bound[2] adjective
to be bound for a place is to be travelling towards it *This train is bound for London.* **to be bound to do something** is to have to do it or be likely to do it *He is bound to come.*

bound³ verb bounds, bounding, bounded
to bound is to leap or to run with leaping steps
bound noun bounds
a leaping movement

boundary noun boundaries
a line that marks a limit *the boundary between north and south*

bounds plural noun
a place that is **out of bounds** is somewhere you are not allowed to go *The teachers' common room is out of bounds to pupils.*

bouquet (say boo-**kay** or boh-**kay**) noun bouquets
a bunch of flowers

bout (say bowt) noun bouts
1 a period of illness *I've just had a bout of flu.* **2** a boxing or wrestling fight

boutique (say boo-**teek**) noun boutiques
a small shop, especially one that sells fashionable clothes

bow¹ (rhymes with **go**) noun bows
1 a knot made with loops **2** the stick used for playing a stringed musical instrument such as a violin or cello **3** a long curved piece of wood with a tight string joining its ends, used for shooting arrows

bow² (rhymes with **cow**) noun bows
the front part of a ship

bow³ (rhymes with **cow**) verb bows, bowing, bowed
to bow is to bend your body forwards to show respect or as a greeting
bow (rhymes with **cow**) noun bows
a movement of bowing your body *The pianist stood up to take a bow.*

bowels plural noun
the bowels are the intestines

bowl¹ noun bowls
1 a deep round dish for eating from **2** the rounded part of a spoon

bowl² verb bowls, bowling, bowled (in cricket)
1 to bowl is to send the ball towards the batsman **2** to bowl someone is to get them out by hitting the wicket with the ball
bowl noun bowls
a heavy ball used in the game of bowls or tenpin bowling

bow-legged adjective
a bow-legged person has legs that curve outwards at the knees

bowler noun bowlers
1 someone who bowls in cricket **2** a hat with a rounded top and a narrow brim

bowling noun
1 bowling is the game of bowls **2** bowling is also another game, in which you have to knock down skittles with a ball you roll down an alley **3** the action of throwing a cricket ball

bowls plural noun
a game played on a smooth piece of grass, in which you roll heavy balls towards a small target ball called the 'jack'

bow tie noun bow ties
a tie in the form of a bow, worn by men as part of formal dress

box noun boxes
1 a container made of wood or cardboard, often with a lid **2** a small rectangle that you fill in on a form or computer screen **3** a special compartment or booth, such as a phone box or a witness box in a law court
box verb boxes, boxing, boxed
1 to box is to fight with the fists **2** to box something is to put it into a box

boxer noun boxers
1 someone who boxes **2** a breed of dog that looks like a bulldog

Boxing Day noun Boxing Days
the first weekday after Christmas Day

box office noun box offices
a place where you can buy seats for the theatre or cinema

a
b
c
d
e
f
g
h
i
j
k
l
m
n
o
p
q
r
s
t
u
v
w
x
y
z

A
B
C
D
E
F
G
H
I
J
K
L
M
N
O
P
Q
R
S
T
U
V
W
X
Y
Z

boy noun boys
a male child **boyish** adjective

boycott verb boycotts, boycotting, boycotted
to boycott something is to refuse to buy it or have anything to do with it *They boycotted the buses when the fares went up.*

boyfriend noun boyfriends
someone's boyfriend is the male friend they have a romantic relationship with

bra noun bras (informal)
a piece of underwear women wear to support their breasts

brace noun braces
1 a device for holding something in place 2 a wire device for straightening the teeth

bracelet noun bracelets
a small band or chain you wear round your wrist

braces plural noun
braces are a pair of stretching straps worn over the shoulders to hold trousers up

bracken noun
bracken is a kind of large fern that grows in open country

bracket noun brackets
1 a kind of punctuation mark used in pairs round words or figures to separate them from what comes before and after. Brackets are round ( ) or square [ ]. 2 a support attached to a wall to hold up a shelf or light fitting

brag verb brags, bragging, bragged
to brag is to boast

braid noun braids
1 a plait 2 a decorative ribbon or band

Braille noun
Braille is a system of writing or printing using raised dots, which blind people can read by touch

brain noun brains
1 your brain is the part inside the top of your head that controls your body 2 brain
also means a person's mind or intelligence *He's got a good brain.*

brainy adjective brainier, brainiest (informal)
clever, intelligent *She's the brainiest child in the school.*

brake noun brakes
a device for making a vehicle stop or slow down

brake block noun
a block that can be made to press against a wheel, used as a brake on a bicycle

bramble noun brambles
a bramble is a blackberry bush or a prickly bush like it

bran noun
the outer parts of the seeds of grain which is usually left when the grain is made into flour

branch noun branches
1 a part that sticks out from the trunk of a tree 2 a part of a railway or river or road that leads off from the main part 3 a part of a large organization

branch verb branches, branching, branched
to branch is to form a branch **to branch out** is to start doing something new

brand noun brands
a particular make or kind of goods *Just get a cheap brand of tea.*

brand verb brands, branding, branded
to brand sheep or cattle is to mark them with a hot iron to identify them as yours

brandish verb brandishes, brandishing, brandished
to brandish something is to wave it about *Before Eddie knew what was happening, Mad Uncle Jack had leapt to his feet and was brandishing a small ceremonial sword.* – Philip Ardagh, *Terrible Times*

brand–new adjective
completely new

brandy noun brandies
brandy is a kind of strong alcoholic drink

brass noun
1 brass is an alloy made from copper and zinc 2 brass also means the wind instruments made of brass, such as trumpets and trombones

brass band noun brass bands
a musical band made up of brass instruments

brassy adjective brassier, brassiest
1 having the colour of brass 2 loud and harsh *We heard a brassy laugh.* 3 cheeky and showy

brave adjective braver, bravest
ready to face danger or suffering

brave noun braves
a Native American warrior **bravely** adverb **bravery** noun

brawl noun brawls
a noisy fight or quarrel

brawny adjective brawnier, brawniest
a brawny person has a strong body and muscles

bray verb brays, braying, brayed
to bray is to make a noise like a donkey

brazen adjective
1 shameless or cheeky 2 made of brass

brazier (say bray-zi-er) noun braziers
a metal container holding hot coal

breach noun breaches
1 the breaking of an agreement or rule 2 a gap or broken place in something like a wall

bread noun
bread is food made by baking flour and water, usually with yeast

breadth noun breadths
a thing's breadth is its width from side to side

breadwinner noun breadwinners
the member of a family who earns most of the money

break verb breaks, breaking, broke, broken
1 to break something is to make it go into several pieces by hitting it or dropping it 2 to break is to stop working properly *I think my watch must have broken.* 3 to break a law or rule or promise is to fail to keep it or observe it 4 the weather breaks when it changes after being hot 5 waves break over rocks when they fall and froth over them 6 a boy's voice breaks when it starts to go deeper at about the age of 14 7 to break a record is to do better than the previous holder, for example in athletics **to break down** a machine or vehicle breaks down when it stops working properly **to break off** is to stop doing something for a time *We broke off for lunch.* **to break out** is to start and spread rapidly, like a disease or fighting **to break the news** is to make it known **to break up 1** people break up when they leave one another after a long time together 2 school breaks up when it closes at the end of term

break noun breaks
1 a broken place; a gap 2 a sudden dash or attempt to escape 3 a short rest from work 4 (informal) a piece of luck; a fair chance *Give me a break.*

breakable adjective
easy to break *Be careful with that box—there are breakable things in it.*

breakage noun breakages
something that is broken *All breakages must be paid for.*

breakdown noun breakdowns
1 a sudden failure to work, especially by a car *We had a breakdown on the motorway.* 2 a failure or collapse of an organization or arrangement *There has been a breakdown of communications.* 3 a period of mental illness caused by anxiety or depression 4 a detailed look at the parts of something to make it easier to understand *Here's a breakdown of last season's football results.*

breaker noun breakers
a wave breaking on the shore

a
b
c
d
e
f
g
h
i
j
k
l
m
n
o
p
q
r
s
t
u
v
w
x
y
z

A
B
C
D
E
F
G
H
I
J
K
L
M
N
O
P
Q
R
S
T
U
V
W
X
Y
Z

breakfast noun breakfasts
breakfast is the first meal of the day

breakneck adjective
dangerously fast *He drove at breakneck speed.*

breakthrough noun breakthroughs
an important piece of progress, for example in medical research

breakwater noun breakwaters
a wall built out into the sea to protect a harbour or coast against heavy waves

breast noun breasts
1 one of the two parts on the front of a woman's body where milk is produced after she has had a baby 2 a person's or animal's chest

breaststroke noun
a stroke you use when swimming on your front, by pushing your arms forward and bringing them round and back

breath (say breth) noun breaths
the air that you take into your lungs and send out again **to be out of breath** is to gasp for air after exercise

breathe (say breeth) verb breathes, breathing, breathed
to breathe is to take air into your lungs through your nose or mouth and send it out again

breather noun breathers (informal)
a pause for a rest *We all need a breather.*

breathless adjective
short of breath

breathtaking adjective
extremely beautiful or delightful

bred verb
past tense and past participle of breed verb *My uncle bred pigeons for racing. Humans have bred dogs for all sorts of jobs.*

breech noun breeches
the part of a gun barrel where the bullets are put in

breeches (say brich-iz) plural noun
short trousers that fit tightly at the knee

breed verb breeds, breeding, bred
1 to breed is to produce offspring
2 to breed animals is to keep them in order to get young ones from them 3 to breed something like illness or poverty is to cause it

breed noun breeds
a variety of similar animals

breeder noun breeders
someone who breeds animals

breeze noun breezes
a gentle wind

breezy adjective breezier, breeziest
1 slightly windy 2 bright and cheerful

brew verb brews, brewing, brewed
1 to brew beer or tea is to make it
2 to be brewing is to start or develop *Trouble is brewing.*

brewer noun brewers
someone whose work is to make beer

brewery noun breweries
a place where beer is made

briar noun briars
another spelling of brier

bribe noun bribes
a bribe is money or a gift offered to someone to make them do something
bribe verb bribes, bribing, bribed
to bribe someone is to give them a bribe
bribery noun

brick noun bricks
1 a small hard block of baked clay used in building 2 a rectangular block of something

bricklayer noun bricklayers
a worker who builds with bricks

bridal adjective
to do with brides

bride noun brides
a woman on her wedding day

bridegroom noun bridegrooms
a man on his wedding day

bridesmaid noun bridesmaids
a girl or unmarried woman who helps the bride at her wedding

bridge noun bridges
1 a bridge is a structure built over a river, railway, or road, to allow people to cross it **2** the bridge of a ship is the high platform above the deck, from where the ship is controlled **3** the bridge of your nose is the bony upper part of your nose **4** bridge is a card game rather like whist

bridle noun bridles
the part of a horse's harness that fits over its head

brief adjective briefer, briefest
lasting a short time or using only a few words **in brief** in a few words

brief noun briefs
a brief is a set of instructions about a job to be done, especially one given to a lawyer about a case

brief verb briefs, briefing, briefed
to brief someone is to give them instructions about a job to be done
briefly adverb

briefcase noun briefcases
a flat case for keeping documents and papers in

briefs plural noun
short underpants

brier noun briers
a thorny bush, especially a wild rose bush

brigade noun brigades
1 an army unit usually consisting of three battalions **2** a group of people in uniform, for example the fire brigade

brigadier noun brigadiers
an army officer who commands a brigade and is higher in rank than a colonel

brigand noun brigands
an old word for a robber or outlaw *The chief brigand was a ferocious-looking man, with*

two belts full of bullets criss-cross over his shoulders. — Philip Pullman, *The Scarecrow and his Servant*

bright adjective brighter, brightest
1 giving out a strong light; shining **2** a bright colour is strong and vivid **3** clever *He's a bright lad.* **4** cheerful
brightly adverb **brightness** noun

brighten verb brightens, brightening, brightened
1 to brighten something is to make it brighter **2** to brighten is to become brighter, like the sky when the weather improves

brilliance noun
1 brilliance is bright light *the brilliance of the summer sky* **2** brilliance is also being very intelligent or clever

brilliant adjective
1 a brilliant person is very intelligent or clever **2** (informal) really good or enjoyable *That was a brilliant film!* **3** very bright and sparkling

brim noun brims
1 the edge round the top of a container **2** the bottom edge of a hat that sticks out

brimming adjective
completely full

brine noun
brine is salty water

bring verb brings, bringing, brought
to bring someone or something is to make them come with you to a place **to bring someone round** is to make them conscious again after they have fainted **to bring someone up** is to look after them and educate them as a child **to bring something about** is to make it happen **to bring something off** is to achieve something difficult or unexpected **to bring something up** is to mention it in a conversation

brink noun
the edge of a steep or dangerous place

brisk adjective brisker, briskest
quick and lively **briskly** adverb

a
b
c
d
e
f
g
h
i
j
k
l
m
n
o
p
q
r
s
t
u
v
w
x
y
z

65

A
B
C
D
E
F
G
H
I
J
K
L
M
N
O
P
Q
R
S
T
U
V
W
X
Y
Z

bristle noun bristles
a short, stiff hair

British adjective
to do with Great Britain

Briton noun Britons
someone born in Great Britain

brittle adjective brittler, brittlest
hard but likely to break or snap

broad adjective broader, broadest
1 wide and open *They walked down a broad avenue.* 2 broad daylight is clear and full daylight 3 general, not detailed *a broad outline*

broadband noun
a system for connecting computers to the Internet and sending information very quickly

broad bean noun broad beans
a type of large flat bean

broadcast noun broadcasts
a radio or television programme

broadcast verb broadcasts, broadcasting, broadcast
to broadcast a radio or television programme is to transmit it or take part in it

broaden verb broadens, broadening, broadened
to broaden something is to make it broader

broadly adverb
in general terms *They were broadly right.*

broccoli noun
a vegetable with green or purple heads on green stalks

TOP TIPS
Double up the **c** in **broccoli** (but the **l** stays single)!

brochure noun brochures
a booklet containing information, especially about a place

brogue noun brogues
1 a strong kind of shoe 2 a strong accent *He spoke with an Irish brogue.*

broke[1]
past tense of **break** verb *He never broke a promise.*

broke[2] adjective (informal)
not having any money

broken
past participle of **break** verb *He was sure he had broken his leg.*

broken adjective
1 broken English is English spoken with a strong foreign accent and lots of mistakes 2 a broken home is a home in which the parents have separated

bronchitis (say brong-ky-tiss) noun
bronchitis is a disease of the lungs

bronze noun
1 bronze is an alloy of copper and tin 2 bronze is also a yellow-brown colour

bronze medal noun bronze medals
a medal made of bronze, usually awarded as the third prize

brooch (rhymes with **coach**) noun brooches
a piece of jewellery that can be pinned on to clothes

brood noun broods
a brood is a number of young birds hatched together

brood verb broods, brooding, brooded
1 birds such as chickens brood when they sit on eggs to hatch them 2 to brood over something is to keep on thinking and worrying about it

broody adjective broodier, broodiest
1 a broody hen is one that wants to hatch its eggs 2 a broody person is one who keeps on thinking and worrying about things

brook noun brooks
a small stream

broom noun brooms
1 a broom is a brush with a long handle, for sweeping 2 broom is a shrub with yellow, white, or pink flowers

broomstick noun broomsticks
the handle of a broom

broth noun broths
broth is a thin kind of soup

brother noun brothers
your brother is a man or boy who has the same parents as you

brother-in-law noun brothers-in-law
a person's brother-in-law is the brother of their husband or wife, or the husband of their sister

brought
past tense and past participle of bring
She brought out a bowl of trifle. Have you brought presents?

brow noun brows
1 your brow is your forehead **2** your brows are your eyebrows **3** the brow of a hill is the top of it

brown adjective browner, brownest
1 of the colour of earth, wood, or toast **2** suntanned
brown noun
a brown colour

Brownie noun Brownies
a junior member of the Guides

brownie noun brownies
a small chocolate cake with nuts

browse verb browses, browsing, browsed
1 to browse is to read or look at something casually **2** animals browse when they feed on grass or leaves

bruise noun bruises
a dark mark that appears on your skin when it is hit or hurt
bruise verb bruises, bruising, bruised
to bruise your skin or a part of your body is to get a bruise on it

brunette noun brunettes
a woman with dark brown or black hair

brush noun brushes
1 a device with hairs or bristles for sweeping, painting, or arranging the hair **2** a fox's bushy tail
brush verb brushes, brushing, brushed
1 to brush something is to use a brush on it *Have you brushed your hair yet?* **2** to brush against someone is to touch them gently as you pass them **to brush something aside** is to ignore it **to brush something up** is to improve your knowledge of it *You need to brush up on your maths.*

Brussels sprout noun Brussels sprouts
a green vegetable like a tiny cabbage

brutal adjective
savage and cruel **brutality** noun
brutally adverb

brute noun brutes
1 a cruel person **2** an animal

bubble noun bubbles
1 a thin transparent ball of liquid filled with air or gas **2** a small ball of air in a liquid or a solid
bubble verb bubbles, bubbling, bubbled
a liquid bubbles when it produces bubbles, as it does when it boils

bubble gum noun
bubble gum is a kind of chewing gum that you can blow into a bubble out of the front of your mouth

bubbly adjective bubblier, bubbliest
1 full of bubbles, like fizzy water **2** a bubbly person is cheerful and lively

buccaneer noun buccaneers
an old word for a pirate

buck noun bucks
a male deer, rabbit, or hare
buck verb bucks, bucking, bucked
a horse bucks when it jumps with its back arched

bucket noun buckets
a container with a handle, for carrying liquids or something such as sand

a
b
c
d
e
f
g
h
i
j
k
l
m
n
o
p
q
r
s
t
u
v
w
x
y
z

A

B

C

D

E

F

G

H

I

J

K

L

M

N

O

P

Q

R

S

T

U

V

W

X

Y

Z

buckle noun buckles
a clip at the end of a belt or strap for fastening it
buckle verb buckles, buckling, buckled
1 to buckle something is to fasten it with a buckle **2** to buckle is to bend or give way under a strain *The arm of the crane was beginning to buckle.*

bud noun buds
a flower or leaf before it has opened

Buddhism (say **buud**-izm) noun
Buddhism is a religion that started in Asia and follows the teachings of Buddha
Buddhist noun

budding adjective
showing great promise *The new class had several budding musicians.*

budge verb budges, budging, budged
to budge is to move slightly *The door was stuck and wouldn't budge.*

budgerigar (say **bud**-jer-i-gar) noun
budgerigars
a small brightly coloured Australian bird often kept as a pet in a cage

budget noun budgets
1 the money someone plans to spend on something **2** a plan for earning and spending money
budget verb budgets, budgeting, budgeted
to budget is to plan how much you are going to spend

budgie noun budgies (informal)
a budgerigar

buff adjective
of a dull yellow colour

buffalo noun buffalo or buffaloes
a wild ox with long curved horns

buffer noun buffers
1 something that softens a blow or collision, especially a device on a railway engine or wagon or at the end of a railway line **2** (in computing) a memory in which data can be stored for a time, especially while being sent from one device to another

buffet (say **buu**-fay) noun buffets
1 a cafe or place for buying drinks and snacks **2** a meal where guests serve themselves

bug noun bugs
1 a tiny insect **2** (informal) a germ that causes illness *I may have a tummy bug.*
3 a hidden microphone **4** a fault or problem in a computer program that stops it working properly
bug verb bugs, bugging, bugged
1 to bug a place is to put a hidden microphone into it **2** (informal) to bug someone is to annoy them *This loud music is really beginning to bug me.*

bugle (say **byoo**-gul) noun bugles
a brass instrument like a small trumpet

build verb builds, building, built
to build something is to make it by putting the parts together **to build something up** is to make it larger or stronger *Regular exercise will build up your health.* **to build up** is to become larger or stronger *The work was starting to build up.*
build noun builds
your build is the shape of your body

builder noun builders
someone who puts up buildings

building noun buildings
1 a building is a structure that someone has built, such as a house or a block of flats **2** building is the business of making houses and other structures

building society noun building societies
an organization like a bank that lends money to people for them to buy houses

build-up noun
1 a gradual increase in the amount of something **2** the part of a story or series of events which is before the most important part and leads up to it

built-in adjective
made into a permanent part of something
The house had built-in kitchen units.

built-up adjective
a built-up area is one with lots of houses and other buildings

bulb noun bulbs
1 the glass part of an electric light, with a wire inside that glows when you switch it on 2 an onion-shaped root which grows into a plant or flower when it is put in the ground

bulge noun bulges
a part that sticks out; a swelling

bulge verb bulges, bulging, bulged
to bulge is to stick out or swell

bulk noun
1 a thing's bulk is its size, especially when it is large 2 the bulk of something is most of it *He spends the bulk of his time on the computer.* **in bulk** in large quantities

bulky adjective bulkier, bulkiest
taking up a lot of space

bull noun bulls
1 the male of the cattle family 2 a male seal, whale, or elephant

bulldog noun bulldogs
a breed of dog with a short thick neck

bulldozer noun bulldozers
a heavy vehicle with a wide metal blade in front, used to clear or flatten land **bulldoze** verb

bullet noun bullets
a piece of shaped metal shot from a rifle or pistol

bulletin noun bulletins
a short announcement of news on radio or television

bulletproof adjective
able to stop bullets getting through

bullfight noun bullfights
in Spain, a public entertainment in which people challenge bulls, and sometimes kill them **bullfighter** noun

bullion noun
gold or silver in the form of bars

bullock noun bullocks
a young bull

bull's-eye noun bull's-eyes
the centre of a target

bully verb bullies, bullying, bullied
to bully someone is to hurt or frighten them when they are weaker

bully noun bullies
someone who bullies people

bulrush noun bulrushes
a tall reed which grows in water or on boggy land

bulwarks plural noun
a ship's side above the level of the deck

bumblebee noun bumblebees
a large kind of bee with a loud buzz

bump verb bumps, bumping, bumped
1 to bump something is to knock against it accidentally 2 to bump along is to move along unsteadily, like an old car **to bump into someone** (informal) is to meet them unexpectedly

bump noun bumps
1 an accidental knock 2 a swelling or lump

bumper[1] noun bumpers
a bar along the front or back of a motor vehicle to protect it in collisions

bumper[2] adjective
unusually large or fine *We had a bumper crop of apples this year.*

bumpy adjective bumpier, bumpiest
having lots of bumps

bun noun buns
1 a small, round, sweet cake 2 a round bunch of hair that some women make at the back of their head

bunch noun bunches
a number of things joined or tied together, such as fruit or flowers or keys *He was eating a bunch of grapes.*

a
b
c
d
e
f
g
h
i
j
k
l
m
n
o
p
q
r
s
t
u
v
w
x
y
z

A
B
C
D
E
F
G
H
I
J
K
L
M
N
O
P
Q
R
S
T
U
V
W
X
Y
Z

bundle noun bundles
a number of things tied or wrapped loosely together, such as clothes or papers
bundle verb bundles, bundling, bundled
1 to bundle things together is to tie or wrap them loosely **2** to bundle someone into a room or car is to push them there hurriedly *They bundled him into the back of a taxi.*

bung verb bungs, bunging, bunged
to bung something up (informal) is to block it

bungalow noun bungalows
a house with all the rooms on one floor

bungle verb bungles, bungling, bungled
to bungle something is to do it badly and clumsily

bunk noun bunks
a narrow bed fixed to a wall, as on a ship

bunk bed noun bunk beds
a single bed with another bed above it or below it

bunker noun bunkers
1 a container for storing fuel such as coal **2** a hollow filled with sand, made as an obstacle on a golf course **3** an underground shelter

bunny noun bunnies (informal)
a rabbit

buoy (say boi) noun buoys
a floating object fixed to the bottom of the sea and used to mark a channel or a stretch of shallow water

buoyant adjective
1 able to float **2** lively and cheerful *He was in a buoyant mood.* **buoyancy** noun

burden noun burdens
1 a heavy load **2** something troublesome that you have to put up with

bureau (say **bewr**-oh) noun bureaux
1 a writing desk with drawers **2** an office or department *They will tell you at the Information Bureau.*

burger noun burgers
a hamburger

burglar noun burglars
someone who breaks into a building to steal things **burglary** noun burglary is the crime of stealing things from a building

burgle verb burgles, burgling, burgled
to burgle someone is to steal from their house

burial noun burials
putting a dead body in a grave

burly adjective burlier, burliest
a burly person is big and strong

burn verb burns, burning, burnt or burned
1 to burn something is to damage or destroy it by fire or strong heat **2** to burn is to be damaged or destroyed by fire or heat **3** to be burning is to be on fire **4** to be burning is also to feel very hot

burn noun burns
1 an injury or mark caused by fire or strong heat **2** the firing of a spacecraft's rocket

burner noun burners
the part of a lamp or cooker that forms the flame

burning adjective
a burning wish or desire is one that is very strong

burp verb burps, burping, burped
to burp is to make a noise through your mouth by letting air come up from your stomach

burp noun burps
the act or sound of burping

burr noun burrs
part of a plant that clings to your clothes or hair

burrow noun burrows
a hole dug by an animal such as a rabbit or fox

burrow verb burrows, burrowing, burrowed
1 an animal burrows when it digs a

burrow **2** to burrow is also to dig or search deeply *He burrowed in his pockets to find a pound coin.*

burst verb **bursts, bursting, burst**
1 to burst is to break apart suddenly **2** to burst something is to make it break apart **3** to be bursting with energy or excitement is to have a lot of energy or to be very excited **to burst in** is to rush in noisily or clumsily **to burst into tears** is to suddenly start crying **to burst out laughing** is to start laughing noisily

burst noun **bursts**
1 a split caused by something bursting *There's a burst in one of the pipes.* **2** something short and quick *a burst of gunfire*

bury verb **buries, burying, buried**
1 to bury something is to put it under the ground **2** to bury someone is to put them in a grave when they are dead **to bury the hatchet** is to agree to stop quarrelling or fighting

bus noun **buses**
a large road vehicle for carrying passengers

bush noun **bushes**
1 a bush is a plant like a small tree with a lot of stems or branches **2** the bush is wild land, especially in Australia or Africa

bushy adjective **bushier, bushiest**
thick and hairy *His dad has bushy eyebrows.*

busily adverb
in a busy way

business (say **biz**-niss) noun **businesses**
1 a business is an organization that makes money by selling goods or services *His uncle worked in a garage business.* **2** business is what an organization does to make money *She has made a career in the banking business.* **3** a person's business is what concerns them and no one else *Mind your own business.* **4** a business is also an affair or subject *I am tired of the whole business.* **to go out of business** is to stop trading because you are not making enough money

businesslike adjective
efficient and practical

busker noun **buskers**
someone who plays music in the street, hoping for money from people passing by

bus stop noun **bus stops**
a place where a bus regularly stops

bust[1] noun **busts**
1 a sculpture of a person's head and shoulders **2** a woman's breasts

bust[2] adjective (informal)
1 broken *My watch is bust.* **2** bankrupt

bustle verb **bustles, bustling, bustled**
to bustle is to be in a hurry or rushing about busily *Mum bustled into the kitchen, stuffing papers into her briefcase.* — Catherine MacPhail, *Granny Nothing*

busy adjective **busier, busiest**
1 a busy person is one with a lot to do **2** a busy place is one with a lot going on **3** a busy telephone line is one that someone is already using

busybody noun **busybodies**
someone who interferes in other's affairs

but conjunction
you use **but** to join two words or statements that say different or opposite things *I wanted to go but I couldn't.*

but preposition
except *There's no one here but me.*

butcher noun **butchers**
1 someone who runs a shop that cuts and sells meat **2** a person who kills people cruelly

butchery noun
butchery is the cruel killing of many people

butler noun **butlers**
a male servant in charge of other servants in a large private house

butt[1] noun **butts**
the thicker end of a weapon or tool

butt[2] noun **butts**
a large barrel

butt[3] noun butts
someone people often make fun of *James always seems to be the butt of your jokes.*

butt[4] verb butts, butting, butted
to butt someone is to hit them hard with your head **to butt in** is to interrupt suddenly or rudely

butter noun
butter is a fatty yellow food made from cream

buttercup noun buttercups
a yellow wild flower

butter-fingers noun
butter-fingers (informal)
someone who is clumsy and keeps dropping things

butterfly noun butterflies
1 an insect with a thin body and large white or brightly coloured wings **2** a stroke you use when swimming on your front, by raising both arms together over your head

butterscotch noun butterscotches
butterscotch is a kind of hard toffee

buttocks plural noun
your buttocks are the part of the body on which you sit, your bottom

button noun buttons
1 a flat plastic or metal disc sewn on clothes and passed through a buttonhole to fasten them **2** a small knob you press to work an electric device

button verb buttons, buttoning, buttoned
to button clothes or to button up clothes is to fasten them with buttons

buttonhole noun buttonholes
1 a slit for a button to pass through **2** a flower worn on a lapel

buttress noun buttresses
a support built against a wall

buy verb buys, buying, bought
to buy something is to get it by paying for it *I bought a CD yesterday.* **buyer** noun

buy noun buys
something you buy *That was a good buy.*

buzz noun buzzes
a sharp humming sound, like bees make

buzz verb buzzes, buzzing, buzzed
to buzz is to make a buzzing sound

buzzard noun buzzards
a bird of prey like a large hawk

buzzer noun buzzers
an alarm or signalling device that makes a buzzing noise

by preposition, adverb
1 near, close *Sit by me.* **2** using; by means of *I fixed the tyre by sticking on a patch.* **3** before *Do your homework by tomorrow.* **4** past *She went by the window. I can't get by.* **by and large** mostly, on the whole **by the way** a phrase you use to add something else to what you have said *I'll see you later. Where is Dad, by the way?*

bye-bye interjection (informal)
goodbye

by-election noun by-elections
an election in one district only, when a Member of Parliament has died or resigned

by-law noun by-laws
a law which only applies to a particular town, district, etc.

bypass noun bypasses
a road that takes traffic round the edge of a town or city rather than going through the centre

by-product noun by-products
something useful that is made while something else is being made

bystander noun bystanders
someone who sees something happening but takes no part in it

byte noun bytes (in computing)
a unit that measures data or memory

Cc

c
1 short for **Celsius** 2 100 in Roman numerals

cab noun **cabs**
1 a taxi 2 the place for the driver in a lorry, bus, train, or crane

cabaret (say **kab**-a-ray) noun **cabarets**
a show in a nightclub or restaurant, with singers and dancers

cabbage noun **cabbages**
a large, round, green vegetable with layers of closely packed leaves

cabin noun **cabins**
1 a hut or shelter 2 one of the small rooms on a ship for sleeping in 3 the part of an aircraft where the passengers sit

cabinet noun **cabinets**
1 a cupboard with shelves and doors, used for storing things 2 the group of chief ministers who run the government

cable noun **cables**
1 a thick rope, wire, or chain used for lifting heavy loads or tying up ships 2 a bundle of wires inside a tube, used for transmitting electricity or electrical signals 3 a telegram sent overseas

cable car noun
a small cabin that hangs from a moving cable, used for carrying people up and down the side of a mountain.

cable television noun
a television system in which programmes are transmitted along underground cables into people's houses

cackle noun **cackles**
1 a cackle is the clucking of a hen
2 a cackle is also a loud silly laugh
3 cackle is stupid chattering

cactus noun **cacti**
a fleshy plant that grows in hot dry places

caddie noun **caddies**
someone whose job is to help a golfer by carrying the clubs and giving advice

cadet noun **cadets**
a young person who is being trained for the armed forces or the police

cadge verb **cadges, cadging, cadged**
to cadge something is to get it by asking for it in a blunt or direct way

cafe (say **kaf**-ay) noun **cafes**
a place that sells hot and cold drinks and light meals

cafeteria (say kaf-e-**teer**-i-a) noun **cafeterias**
a cafe where customers serve themselves from a counter

caffeine noun
caffeine is a substance in tea and coffee and some other drinks, which keeps you awake and makes you feel active

cage noun **cages**
an enclosure made of bars or wires, for keeping birds or animals so that they can't get away

cagoule noun **cagoules**
a lightweight waterproof jacket

cake noun **cakes**
1 a sweet food made from a baked mixture of flour, eggs, fat, and sugar 2 something made into a lump rather like a cake, such as soap **a piece of cake** (informal) something very easy to do

caked adjective
covered with something that has dried hard, like mud

calamine noun
a pink powder used to make a soothing liquid to put on your skin

calamity noun **calamities**
a disaster **calamitous** adjective

a
b
c
d
e
f
g
h
i
j
k
l
m
n
o
p
q
r
s
t
u
v
w
x
y
z

73

A
B
C
D
E
F
G
H
I
J
K
L
M
N
O
P
Q
R
S
T
U
V
W
X
Y
Z

calcium noun
a grey-white element contained in teeth, bones, and lime

calculate verb calculates, calculating, calculated
1 to calculate something is to work it out by arithmetic or with a calculator **2** to calculate on something is to plan round it *They were calculating on a fine day for the picnic.*

calculation noun calculations
something you work out by using numbers or other information

calculator noun calculators
a machine for adding up figures and doing other calculations with numbers

calendar noun calendars
a chart or display that shows the days of the year

 TOP TIPS There is a tricky bit in **calendar**—it ends in **ar**.

calf¹ noun calves
1 a young cow or ox **2** a young seal, whale, or elephant

calf² noun calves
the back part of your leg below your knee

call noun calls
1 a shout or cry *They heard a call for help.* **2** a short visit *She decided to pay her father a call.* **3** a telephone conversation with someone
call verb calls, calling, called
1 to call is to shout out **2** to call someone is to telephone them *I'll call you at the weekend.* **3** to call someone near you is to ask them to come to you **4** to call on someone is to visit them **5** to be called something is to have it as your name *His friend was called Damon.* **6** to call something a certain thing is to describe it that way *I call that a swindle.* **to call someone names** is to be rude to them or insult them **to call something off** is to cancel it

call centre noun call centres
a large office where people deal with telephone calls made to a company by customers

callous adjective
a callous person is very unkind and doesn't care about other people's feelings

calm adjective calmer, calmest
1 quiet and still, like the sea or the weather **2** someone is calm when they are not excited or agitated *Please keep calm.*
calmly adverb **calmness** noun

calorie noun calories
a unit for measuring the amount of heat or the energy produced by food

calves
plural of calf

calypso noun calypsos
a West Indian folk song which is made up as the singer goes along

camcorder noun camcorders
a video camera that can record pictures and sound

came
past tense of come *The truck came to a stop.*

camel noun camels
a large animal with a long neck and one or two humps on its back *Arabian camels have one hump, and Bactrian camels have two.*

camera noun cameras
a device for taking photographs, films, or television pictures

camouflage (say **kam**-o-flahzh) noun
a way of hiding things by making them look like part of their surroundings

camp noun camps
a place where people live in tents or huts or caravans for a short time
camp verb camps, camping, camped
1 to camp or go camping is to have a holiday in a tent **2** to camp is also to put up a tent or tents *Let's camp here for the night.*
camper noun **camping** noun

campaign noun campaigns
1 a planned series of actions, especially

to get people to support you or become interested in something *a campaign for human rights* **2** a series of battles in one area or with one aim

campaign verb campaigns, campaigning, campaigned
to campaign is to carry out a plan of action to raise people's interest in something such as a good cause *They are campaigning to stop the destruction of the rainforests.*

campsite noun campsites
a place for camping

can[1] verb present tense can; past tense could
1 to be able to do something or to know how to do it *Can you lift this stone? They can speak French.* **2** (informal) to be allowed to do something *Can I go home?*

can[2] noun cans
a sealed metal container holding food or drink

canal noun canals
1 a long channel specially dug and filled with water for boats to travel along **2** a tube in the body of a human being or animal *The canals in your ears help you balance.*

canary noun canaries
a small yellow bird that sings, often kept in a cage as a pet

cancel verb cancels, cancelling, cancelled
1 to cancel something planned is to say that it will not be done or not take place after all **2** to cancel an order or instruction is to stop it **3** to cancel a stamp or ticket is to mark it so that it cannot be used again
cancellation noun

cancer noun cancers
a serious disease in which a harmful growth forms in the body

candidate noun candidates
1 someone who has applied for a job or position **2** someone who is taking an exam

candle noun candles
a stick of wax with a wick through it, giving light when it is burning

candlelight noun
candlelight is the light given out by a candle

candlestick noun candlesticks
a holder for a candle or candles

candy noun candies
1 candy is crystallized sugar **2** a candy is a sweet

candyfloss noun
candyfloss is a fluffy mass of sugar that has been spun into fine threads

cane noun canes
a cane is the hollow stem of a reed or tall grass
cane verb canes, caning, caned
to cane someone is to beat them with a cane

canine adjective
to do with dogs

canine tooth noun canine teeth
a canine tooth is a pointed tooth at the front of the mouth. Human beings have four of these.

cannibal noun cannibals
1 a person who eats human flesh **2** an animal that eats animals of its own kind
cannibalism noun

cannon noun cannon or cannons
a large gun that fires heavy balls made of metal or stone

cannonball noun cannonballs
a heavy metal or stone ball fired from a cannon

cannot
can not *I cannot believe it.*

canoe noun canoes
a light narrow boat driven with paddles
canoe verb canoes, canoeing, canoed
to canoe is to travel in a canoe
canoeist noun

canopy noun canopies
a covering that hangs over something

can't
short for **cannot** *We can't see them.*

canteen noun canteens
a restaurant in a factory or office or school, where the people working there can get a meal or snack

canter verb canters, cantering, cantered
to canter is to go at a gentle gallop

canvas noun canvases
1 canvas is strong coarse cloth 2 a canvas is a piece of this kind of cloth used for painting on

canvass verb canvasses, canvassing, canvassed
to canvass people is to visit them to ask them for their support, especially in an election

canyon noun canyons
a deep valley with a river running through it

cap noun caps
1 a soft hat without a brim but often with a peak 2 a cover or top

cap verb caps, capping, capped
1 to cap something is to cover it 2 to cap a story or joke is to tell one that is better

capable adjective
able to do something **capability** noun **capably** adverb

capacity noun capacities
1 ability to do something *He has a great capacity for work.* 2 the amount that something can hold 3 the position someone occupies *He was there in his capacity as our leader.*

cape¹ noun capes
a piece of high land sticking out into the sea

cape² noun capes
a cloak

caper verb capers, capering, capered
to caper is to jump about playfully

caper noun capers
1 a leap or jump 2 (informal) an activity or adventure

capital noun capitals
1 the capital of a country is the most important city in it 2 capital is money or property that can be used to make more money

capitalism (say **kap**-i-ta-lizm) noun
capitalism is a system in which the wealth of a country is owned by private individuals and not by the state **capitalist** noun

capital letter noun capital letters
a large letter of the kind used at the start of a name or a sentence, such as A, B, C

capital punishment noun
capital punishment is when someone is killed as a punishment for a crime, such as murder or treason

capsize verb capsizes, capsizing, capsized
to capsize is to overturn in a boat in the water

capsule noun capsules
1 a hollow pill containing medicine 2 a small spacecraft or pressurized cabin

captain noun captains
1 an officer in charge of a ship or aircraft 2 an officer in the army or navy 3 the leader in a sports team

caption noun captions
1 the words printed beside a picture to describe it 2 a heading in a newspaper or magazine

captivate verb
to captivate someone is to charm them or make them interested **captivating** adjective

captive noun captives
a prisoner

captive adjective
imprisoned; unable to escape

captivity noun
1 captivity is being held prisoner
2 an animal in captivity is one kept in a zoo or wildlife park rather than living in the wild

captor noun captors
someone who has captured a person or animal

capture verb captures, capturing, captured
1 to capture an animal or person is to catch or imprison them 2 (in computing) to capture data is to put it into a form that a computer can accept

capture noun
catching or imprisoning an animal or person

car noun cars
1 a private motor vehicle 2 a railway carriage *The train has a dining car.*

caramel noun caramels
1 caramel is burnt sugar used to give a sweet taste to food 2 a caramel is a sweet made from butter, milk, and sugar

carat noun carats
1 a measure of weight for precious stones 2 a measure of the purity of gold

caravan noun caravans
1 a vehicle towed by a car and used for living in, especially by people on holiday 2 a large number of people travelling together, especially across a desert

carbohydrate noun carbohydrates
a compound of carbon, oxygen, and hydrogen *Sugar and starch are carbohydrates.*

carbon noun
carbon is an element found in charcoal, graphite, diamonds, and other substances

carbon dioxide noun
a colourless gas made by humans and animals breathing

carbon monoxide noun
a colourless poisonous gas found especially in the exhaust fumes of motor vehicles

car-boot sale noun car-boot sales
an outdoor sale where people sell things which they have brought by car

carcass noun carcasses
the dead body of an animal or bird

card noun cards
1 card is thick stiff paper 2 a card is a piece of thick paper that you use to put information on or to send greetings to someone, for example a business card or a birthday card 3 a card is also a playing card 4 a card is also a small piece of plastic that a bank or building society issues to a customer, with an electronic strip recording details of their account **cards** is a game with playing cards **something is on the cards** when it is likely to happen

cardboard noun
cardboard is thick stiff paper

cardigan noun cardigans
a knitted jumper fastened with buttons down the front

cardinal noun cardinals
one of the most senior priests in the Roman Catholic Church

cardinal number noun cardinal numbers
a number for counting things, for example 1, 2, 3 (compare *ordinal number*)

care noun cares
1 care is worry or trouble *She was free from care.* 2 care is also serious thought or attention *Take more care with your homework.* 3 care is also protection or supervision *You can leave your dog in my care.* **to take care of someone** or **something** is to look after them *Please could you take care of the cat while I'm away?*

care verb cares, caring, cared
to care about something or someone is to feel interested or concerned about them **to care for someone** is to look after them *He cared for his wife when she was ill.* **to care for something** is to like it or want it *I don't much care for fried food.*

a
b
c
d
e
f
g
h
i
j
k
l
m
n
o
p
q
r
s
t
u
v
w
x
y
z

A
B
C
D
E
F
G
H
I
J
K
L
M
N
O
P
Q
R
S
T
U
V
W
X
Y
Z

career noun careers
a person's career is what they have been trained to do to earn a living and make progress during their lives

career verb careers, careering, careered
to career along or down somewhere is to rush along wildly *The beast was careering through the tunnels, crashing, bellowing, thundering through the maze.* – Alan Gibbons, *Shadow of Minotaur*

carefree adjective
not having any worries or responsibilities

careful adjective
making sure that you do something well without any mistakes and without causing any danger *She is a careful driver. He was always careful to give the correct answer in class.* **carefully** adverb

careless adjective
not taking care; clumsy **carelessly** adverb **carelessness** noun

caress (say ka-**ress**) noun caresses
a gentle and loving touch

caress verb caresses, caressing, caressed
to caress someone is to touch them gently and fondly

caretaker noun caretakers
someone who looks after a large building

cargo noun cargoes
cargo or a cargo is the goods carried in a ship or aircraft

Caribbean (say ka-ri-**bee**-an) adjective
to do with the West Indies

caricature noun caricatures
a drawing or description of someone that exaggerates their features and makes them look funny or absurd

carnation noun carnations
a garden flower with a sweet smell

carnival noun carnivals
a festival or celebration with a procession of people in fancy dress

carnivore noun carnivores
an animal that eats meat **carnivorous** adjective

carol noun carols
a hymn or song that you sing at Christmas time **carolling** noun carolling is singing carols, usually in the street or going from house to house

carp noun carp
a freshwater fish

carpenter noun carpenters
someone who makes things, especially parts of buildings, out of wood **carpentry** noun

carpet noun carpets
a thick soft covering for a floor

carriage noun carriages
1 a carriage is one of the separate sections of a train where passengers sit **2** a carriage is also a passenger vehicle pulled by horses **3** carriage is taking goods from one place to another *You will have to pay extra for carriage.*

carriageway noun carriageways
the part of a road that vehicles travel on

carrier bag noun carrier bags
a large bag for holding shopping

carrot noun carrots
a long, thin, orange-coloured vegetable

carry verb carries, carrying, carried
1 to carry something is to lift it and take it somewhere **2** to carry something is also to have it with you *I always carry my mobile in my pocket.* **3** a sound carries when it can be heard a long way away **to be carried away** is to become very excited **to carry on** is to continue doing something *They carried on chatting.* **to carry something out** is to put it into practice *Will you please carry out my orders?*

cart noun carts
a small vehicle for carrying loads **to put the cart before the horse** is to do things in the wrong order

cart verb carts, carting, carted (informal)
to cart something somewhere is to carry or transport it, especially when it is heavy or tiring *I've been carting these books around the school all afternoon.*

carthorse noun carthorses
a large heavy horse

cartilage (say **kar**-ti-lij) noun
cartilage is tough and flexible tissue attached to a bone

carton noun cartons
a lightweight cardboard box

cartoon noun cartoons
1 a drawing that is funny or tells a joke
2 a series of drawings that tell a story
3 an animated film **cartoonist** noun

cartridge noun cartridges
1 a container holding film to be put into a camera or ink to be put into a pen 2 the case containing the explosive for a bullet or shell

cartwheel noun cartwheels
a somersault done sideways, with your arms and legs spread wide

carve verb carves, carving, carved
1 to carve wood or stone is to make something artistic by cutting it carefully
2 to carve meat is to cut it into slices

cascade noun cascades
a waterfall or a series of waterfalls

cascade verb cascades, cascading, cascaded
to cascade is to tumble down like the water in a waterfall

case¹ noun cases
1 a container 2 a suitcase

case² noun cases
1 an example of something existing or happening *We've had four cases of chickenpox. It's just a case of being patient.*
2 a crime or incident that the police or a law court are investigating *The next case was a murder.* **in case** because something may happen *Take an umbrella in case it rains.*

cash noun
cash is coins and banknotes that you use to pay for something

cash verb cashes, cashing, cashed
to cash a cheque is to exchange it for coins and banknotes **to cash in on something** (informal) is to take advantage of it

cashier noun cashiers
someone in charge of the money in a bank, office, or shop

cash register noun cash registers
a machine that records and stores money received in a shop

cask noun casks
a barrel

casket noun caskets
a small box for jewellery or other small objects

casserole noun casseroles
1 a covered dish in which food is cooked
2 the food cooked in a dish of this kind

cassette noun cassettes
a small sealed case containing recording tape or film on spools that turn when it is put in a tape recorder or camera

cast verb casts, casting, cast
1 to cast something is to throw it 2 to cast a vote is to make your vote in an election
3 to cast something made of metal or plaster is to make it in a mould 4 to cast a play or film is to choose the performers for it **to cast off** is to untie a boat and start sailing in it

cast noun casts
1 a shape you make by pouring liquid metal or plaster into a mould 2 the performers in a play or film

castanets plural noun
two pieces of wood or ivory held in one hand and clapped together to make a clicking sound, as in Spanish dancing

castaway noun castaways
someone who has been left in a deserted place, especially after a shipwreck

a
b
c
d
e
f
g
h
i
j
k
l
m
n
o
p
q
r
s
t
u
v
w
x
y
z

castle

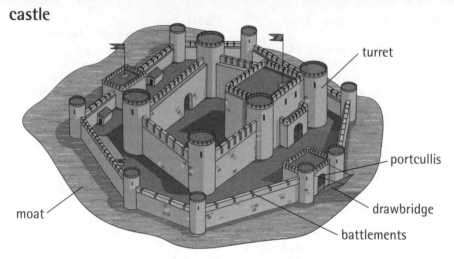

turret

portcullis

drawbridge

battlements

moat

castle noun **castles**
1 a large old building with heavy stone walls and battlements, made to protect people in it from attack 2 a piece in chess, also called a *rook*

castor (say **kah**-ster) noun **castors**
a small wheel on the leg of a piece of furniture

castor oil noun
a yellow oil made from the seeds of a tropical plant, used as medicine

castor sugar noun
finely ground white sugar

casual adjective
1 not deliberate or planned *It was just a casual remark.* 2 casual clothes are informal clothes that you wear for leisure time 3 not regular or permanent *His dad was doing casual work.* **casually** adverb

casualty noun **casualties**
someone killed or injured in war or in an accident

cat noun **cats**
1 a small furry animal, usually kept as a pet and known for catching mice 2 a larger member of the same family, for example a lion, tiger, or leopard **to let the cat out of the bag** is to give away a secret

catalogue noun **catalogues**
a list of goods for sale or of books in a library

catalyst (say **kat**-a-list) noun **catalysts**
1 something that starts or speeds up a chemical reaction 2 something important that results in a change

catamaran noun **catamarans**
a sailing boat with two hulls fixed side by side

catapult noun **catapults**
a small weapon made from a forked stick with elastic attached to each fork, used for shooting pellets or small stones

catastrophe (say ka-**tas**-tro-fi) noun **catastrophes**
a great or sudden disaster
catastrophic adjective

catch verb **catches, catching, caught**
1 to catch something is to get hold of it, for example a ball that is coming towards you 2 to catch an animal is to capture it and not let it escape 3 to catch someone is to discover them doing something wrong *He was caught going home early.* 4 to catch an illness is to get it from someone else 5 to catch a bus or train is to get on it before it leaves 6 to catch something someone says

is to manage to hear it *I'm afraid I didn't catch your question.* **7** to catch your clothes is to get them entangled in something *I've caught my sleeve on a bramble.* **to catch fire** is to start burning **to catch on** (informal) is to become popular, as a craze or fashion does **to catch someone out** is to show that they are wrong or mistaken **to catch up with someone** is to reach them when they have been ahead of you

catch noun **catches**
1 something caught or worth catching *They had a large catch of fish.* **2** a hidden difficulty or snag *The car was so cheap there had to be a catch.* **3** a device for fastening a door or window

catching adjective
a disease is catching when people catch it easily, so that it spreads quickly

catchphrase noun **catchphrases**
a phrase that someone famous has used and a lot of people now use

catchy adjective **catchier, catchiest**
pleasant and easy to remember, like a tune

category noun **categories**
a group or division of similar people or things *I'm going to enter the competition in the under-twelves category.*

cater verb **caters, catering, catered**
to cater for someone or something is to give them what they need

caterer noun **caterers**
someone whose job is to provide food for people, especially at an important function

caterpillar noun **caterpillars**
a long creeping creature that turns into a butterfly or moth

cathedral noun **cathedrals**
a large and important church in a major city, with a bishop in charge of it

Catherine wheel noun
Catherine wheels
a round flat firework that spins round and throws out sparks as it burns

Catholic adjective
belonging to the Roman Catholic Church
Catholic noun **Catholics**
a member of the Roman Catholic Church

catkin noun **catkins**
a tiny flower hanging down from a willow or hazel

Catseye noun **Catseyes** (trademark)
a stud containing small pieces of glass or plastic that reflect the lights of vehicles, set in a row in the road to help drivers see their way at night

cattle plural noun
cattle are cows and bulls and other large grass-eating animals

caught
past tense and past participle of **catch** verb *I caught Hannah looking at me. I think you've caught a cold.*

cauldron noun **cauldrons**
a large round iron cooking pot used especially by witches in stories

cauliflower noun **cauliflowers**
a kind of cabbage with a large head of white flowers

cause noun **causes**
1 what makes something happen, a reason *You have no cause for complaint.* **2** the aim or purpose that a group of people are working for *They were raising money for a good cause.*
cause verb **causes, causing, caused**
to cause something is to make it happen

caution noun **cautions**
1 caution is being careful to avoid danger or mistakes **2** a caution is a warning
cautionary adjective a cautionary story is one that gives a warning about a danger or difficulty

a
b
c
d
e
f
g
h
i
j
k
l
m
n
o
p
q
r
s
t
u
v
w
x
y
z

A
B
C
D
E
F
G
H
I
J
K
L
M
N
O
P
Q
R
S
T
U
V
W
X
Y
Z

cautious adjective
careful to avoid a risk or difficulty
cautiously adverb

cavalry noun
soldiers who fight on horseback or in
armoured vehicles

cave noun caves
a large hole in the side of a hill or cliff, or
under the ground
cave verb caves, caving, caved
to cave or go caving is to explore caves **to
cave in** is to collapse

caveman or **cavewoman** noun
cavemen, cavewomen
a person who lived in a cave in
prehistoric times

cavern noun caverns
a cave, especially a deep or dark cave

cavity noun cavities
a hollow or hole

CD CDs
short for **compact disc**

CD player noun CD players
a machine for playing compact discs

CD–ROM noun CD-ROMs
short for *compact disc read-only memory*, a
system for storing information that can be
viewed on the screen of a computer

cease verb ceases, ceasing, ceased
to cease doing something is to stop doing it

ceasefire noun ceasefires
an agreement to stop using weapons, made
by people who are fighting a war

ceaseless adjective
going on all the time, not stopping

cedar noun cedars
an evergreen tree with hard
sweet-smelling wood

ceiling (say **see**-ling) noun ceilings
1 the flat surface along the top of a room
2 the highest limit that something can

reach *They agreed to put a ceiling on pay.*

TOP TIPS In **ceiling**, e before i is the right way
round.

celebrate verb celebrates,
celebrating, celebrated
to celebrate a day or event is to do
something special to show that it
is important

celebrated adjective
famous, well known *He won a prize to meet a
celebrated film star.*

celebration noun celebrations
a celebration is a party or other special
event to celebrate something

celebrity noun celebrities
a famous person, especially in show
business or on television

celery noun
a vegetable with crisp white or green stems

cell noun cells
1 a small room, especially in a prison
2 a tiny part of a living creature or plant
3 a device for producing electric current
using chemicals

cellar noun cellars
an underground room for storing things

cello (say **chel**-oh) noun cellos
a large stringed musical instrument, which
you play by placing it upright between the
knees and using a bow **cellist** noun

cellular adjective
1 made of cells, or having cells *the cellular
structure of living things* 2 a cellular
telephone is one that uses a network of
radio stations to cover a wide area

Celsius adjective
using a scale for measuring temperature in
which water freezes at 0 degrees and boils
at 100 degrees

cement noun
1 cement is a mixture of lime and clay used
in building to make floors and join bricks
together 2 cement is also a strong glue

cemetery (say **sem**-e-tri) noun
cemeteries
a place where dead people are buried

censor verb **censors, censoring, censored**
to censor films, plays, or books is to look at them to make sure that they are suitable for people to see, and to take out any parts that do not seem suitable
censor noun **censors**
someone whose job is to censor films, plays, and books **censorship** noun

census noun **censuses**
an official count or survey of the number of people or the volume of traffic in a place

cent noun **cents**
a coin worth one-hundredth of a dollar or euro, used in the USA and some other countries

centenary noun **centenaries**
the hundredth anniversary of something special or important

centigrade adjective
a non-technical word for **Celsius**

centimetre noun **centimetres**
one-hundredth of a metre, about four-tenths of an inch

centipede noun **centipedes**
a small long creature with many pairs of legs

central adjective
1 at or near the centre of something 2 most important *She will have the central role in the play.* **centrally** adverb in a central position

central heating noun
central heating is a system of heating a building by sending hot water, hot air, or steam round it in pipes

centre noun **centres**
1 the middle of something 2 an important place *Vienna is one of the great music centres of Europe.* 3 a building or place for a special purpose, such as a sports centre or a shopping centre

centre verb **centres, centring, centred**
when you centre a word or picture on a computer you move it to the middle of the screen

centre forward noun **centre forwards**
the middle player in the front line of a team in football or hockey

centurion noun **centurions**
an officer in the ancient Roman army, originally commanding a hundred men

century noun **centuries**
1 a period of a hundred years 2 a hundred runs scored by one batsman in an innings at cricket

centurion

helmet

sword

shield

a
b
c
d
e
f
g
h
i
j
k
l
m
n
o
p
q
r
s
t
u
v
w
x
y
z

A
B
C
D
E
F
G
H
I
J
K
L
M
N
O
P
Q
R
S
T
U
V
W
X
Y
Z

ceramics plural noun
ceramics is the art of making pottery

cereal noun cereals
1 a grass that produces seeds which are used as food 2 a breakfast food made from seeds of this kind

ceremonial adjective
to do with a ceremony, or used in a ceremony ceremonial robes

ceremonious adjective
ceremonious behaviour is formal and dignified He made a ceremonious bow. **ceremoniously** adverb

ceremony (say se-ri-mo-ni) noun ceremonies
1 ceremony is the formal actions carried out at a wedding, funeral, or other important occasion 2 a ceremony is a formal event such as a wedding or funeral

certain adjective
1 something is certain when it is definitely true or is going to happen 2 you are certain about something when you know it is definitely true **to make certain** is to make sure

certainly adverb
as a fact, without any doubt They were certainly here last night.

certainty noun certainties
1 a certainty is something that is sure to happen 2 certainty is being sure

certificate noun certificates
an official document that records an important event or achievement, such as someone's birth or passing an exam

certify verb certifies, certifying, certified
to certify something is to say in writing that it is true

chaffinch noun chaffinches
a small bird

chain noun chains
1 a row of metal rings fastened together 2 a line of people 3 a connected series

of things The story told of a strange chain of events.

chain letter noun chain letters
a letter someone sends you asking you to copy it and send it to several other people, who are supposed to do the same

chain reaction noun chain reactions
a series of happenings, each causing the next

chain saw noun chain saws
a saw with teeth on a chain that is moved round very fast by a motor

chair noun chairs
1 a seat with a back for one person 2 the person who is in charge of a meeting

chairlift noun chairlifts
a set of seats hanging from a moving cable, carrying people up the side of a mountain

chairman or **chairperson** noun chairmen, chairpersons
the person who is in charge of a meeting

chalet (say shal-ay) noun chalets
a small house, usually built of wood

chalk noun chalks
1 a kind of soft white rock 2 a soft white or coloured stick of a similar rock, used for writing on blackboards **chalky** adjective

challenge verb challenges, challenging, challenged
to challenge someone is to demand that they perform some feat or take part in a fight **challenger** noun

challenge noun challenges
something difficult that someone has to do

chamber noun chambers
1 (old use) a room 2 a hall used for meetings of a parliament or council

chameleon (say ka-mee-li-on) noun chameleons
a small lizard that can change the colour of its skin to match its surroundings and appear almost invisible

champagne (say sham-**payn**) noun
a bubbly white French wine

champion noun champions
1 the best person in a sport or competition
2 someone who supports a cause by fighting or speaking for it *Martin Luther King was a champion of human rights.*

championship noun championships
a contest to decide who is the best player or competitor in a game or sport

chance noun chances
1 a chance is a possibility or opportunity *This is your only chance to see them.*
2 chance is the way things happen accidentally *It was pure chance that we met.* **by chance** accidentally, without any planning *We found the place by chance.* **to take a chance** is to take a risk

chancellor noun chancellors
1 an important government or legal official
2 the chief minister of the government in some European countries

chandelier (say shan-de-**leer**) noun chandeliers
a light fitting that hangs from the ceiling and has a lot of bright bulbs

change verb changes, changing, changed
1 to change something or someone is to make them different 2 to change is to become different *My gran said I'd changed since she'd last seen me.* 3 to change one thing for another is to exchange them *I'm going to change my bike for a new one.* 4 to change money is to give coins or notes of small values in exchange for higher value money *Can you change a £5 note?* 5 to change trains or buses is to get off one and get on another *Change at York for the train to Durham.*

change noun changes
1 change is the process of changing 2 your change is the money you get back when you give more money than the price of something you are buying, for example if you don't have the right money 3 a change of clothes is a set of fresh clothes **to do**

something for a change is to do it because it is different or unusual *Let's walk home for a change.*

changeable adjective
likely to change, often changing *The weather has been very changeable.*

channel noun channels
1 a stretch of water joining two seas, like the English Channel between Britain and France 2 a television or radio station that transmits on a particular frequency 3 a way for water to flow along 4 the part of a river or sea that is deep enough for ships to sail on

chant noun chants
a tune, especially one that is often repeated

chant verb chants, chanting, chanted
to chant words is to say them or call them out in a special rhythm

chaos (say kay-oss) noun
chaos is complete disorder or confusion *The room was in chaos.*

chaotic (say kay-**ot**-ik) adjective
completely confused or in a mess

chap noun chaps (informal)
a man or boy *What a funny chap he is.*

chapatti noun chapattis
a flat thin cake of Indian bread made without yeast

chapel noun chapels
1 a small church or part of a large church
2 a room in a large house, used for worship

chapped adjective
having rough cracked skin

chapter noun chapters
a section of a book

char verb chars, charring, charred
to char something is to scorch it or blacken it with fire

character noun characters
1 the special nature and qualities of a person or thing 2 a person in a story or play

a b c d e f g h i j k l m n o p q r s t u v w x y z

85

characteristic noun characteristics
something that makes a person or thing noticeable or different from others

characteristic adjective
typical, what you would expect of someone

characterize verb characterizes, characterizing, characterized
1 to characterize something is to provide it with its special character or qualities *Stony beaches and grey seas characterize the south coast of England.* 2 to characterize someone is to describe their character in a certain way *His friends characterized him as boastful.*

charades (say sha-**rahdz**) noun
charades is a game in which people have to guess a word or the title of a book or film when other people act it out

charcoal noun
charcoal is a black substance made by burning wood slowly

charge noun charges
1 the price asked for something 2 an accusation that someone committed a crime *He is facing three charges of burglary.* 3 an attack in a battle 4 the amount of explosive needed to fire a weapon 5 the amount of an electric current **to be in charge of something** or **someone** is to be the one who decides what will happen to them

charge verb charges, charging, charged
1 to charge a price for something is to ask people to pay it 2 to charge someone is to accuse them of committing a crime 3 to charge in a battle is to rush to attack the enemy

chariot noun chariots
a horse-drawn vehicle with two wheels, used in ancient times for fighting and racing

charitable adjective
1 a charitable person or act is one that is kind and generous 2 a charitable organization is one that gives money or other kinds of help to those who need it

charity noun charities
1 charity is giving money and help to other people 2 a charity is an organization that helps those in need

charm noun charms
1 charm is being pleasant and attractive 2 a charm is a magic spell 3 a charm is also something small worn or carried to bring good luck

charm verb charms, charming, charmed
1 to charm someone is to give them pleasure or delight 2 to charm someone is also to put a spell on them

charming adjective
pleasant and attractive

chart noun charts
1 a large plan or map 2 a diagram or list with information set out in columns or rows 3 a list of the most popular CDs and recordings that are sold

charter noun charters
1 an official document explaining people's rights or privileges 2 the hire of an aircraft or vehicle for a special purpose

charter verb charters, chartering, chartered
to charter an aircraft or vehicle is to hire it for a special journey

chase verb chases, chasing, chased
to chase someone is to go quickly after them to try to catch them up

chase noun chases
a chase is when you chase someone

chasm (say ka-zum) noun chasms
a deep opening in the ground

chassis (say **shass**-i) noun chassis
the frame and wheels of a vehicle, which support the body

chat noun chats
a friendly or informal talk with someone

chat verb chats, chatting, chatted
to chat to someone is to talk to them in a friendly or informal way **chatty** adjective

chat room noun chat rooms
a place on the Internet where people can have a conversation by sending messages to each other

chatter verb chatters, chattering, chattered
1 to talk quickly or stupidly; to talk too much 2 to make a rattling noise

chauffeur (say shoh-fer) noun chauffeurs
someone who is paid to drive a large smart car for someone important

cheap adjective cheaper, cheapest
1 something cheap does not cost much 2 you call something cheap when it is shoddy or inferior **cheaply** adverb

cheat verb cheats, cheating, cheated
1 to cheat someone is to trick them so they lose something 2 to cheat is to try to do well in an exam or game by breaking the rules

cheat noun cheats
someone who cheats

check verb checks, checking, checked
1 to check something is to make sure that it is correct or all right 2 to check someone or something is to make them stop or slow down **to check in** is to sign your name to show you have arrived at a hotel or to show your ticket at an airport **to check out** is to pay your bill and leave a hotel

check noun checks
1 a check is when you check something 2 check in chess is when the king is threatened by another piece 3 a check is a pattern of squares

checkmate noun checkmates
checkmate in chess is when one side wins by trapping the other side's king

checkout noun checkouts
the place where you pay for your shopping in a supermarket or a large shop

check-up noun check-ups
a careful check or examination

cheek noun cheeks
1 your cheek is the side of your face below your eye 2 cheek, or a cheek, is being rude or impolite

cheek verb cheeks, cheeking, cheeked
to cheek someone is to be rude to them

cheeky adjective cheekier, cheekiest
rude or impolite, without being unpleasant or nasty **cheekily** adverb

cheer noun cheers
a shout praising or supporting someone

cheer verb cheers, cheering, cheered
1 to cheer someone is to support them by cheering 2 to cheer someone is to comfort or encourage them **to cheer someone up** is to make them more cheerful **to cheer up** is to become more cheerful

cheerful adjective
happy and bright

cheerio interjection (informal)
goodbye

cheese noun cheeses
cheese is a white or yellow food made from milk. Cheese can be hard like Cheddar or soft like some French cheeses.

cheetah noun cheetahs
a large spotted animal of the cat family, which can run very fast

chef (say shef) noun chefs
the chief cook in a hotel or restaurant

chemical noun chemicals
a substance used in or made by chemistry

chemical adjective
to do with chemistry or made by chemistry

chemist noun chemists
1 someone who makes or sells medicines 2 an expert in chemistry

chemistry noun
chemistry is the study of the way substances combine and react with one another

cheque noun cheques
a written form instructing a bank to pay money out of an account

chequered adjective
marked with a pattern of squares

cherish verb cherishes, cherishing, cherished
to cherish something is to look after it lovingly

cherry noun cherries
a small, bright red fruit with a large stone

chess noun
a game for two players played with sixteen pieces (called *chessmen*) each on a board (called a *chessboard*) of 64 squares

chest noun chests
1 a chest is a large strong box 2 your chest is the front part of your body between your neck and your waist **to get something off your chest** (informal) is to admit something you are worried about or feel bad about

chestnut noun chestnuts
1 a hard brown nut 2 the tree that produces this kind of nut

chest of drawers noun chests of drawers
a piece of furniture with drawers for holding clothes

chew verb chews, chewing, chewed
to chew food is to grind it into pieces between your teeth **chewy** adjective chewy food is tough and needs a lot of chewing

chewing gum noun
a sticky flavoured gum for chewing

chick noun chicks
a young bird

chicken noun chickens
1 a chicken is a young hen 2 chicken is the meat of a hen used as food

chicken adjective (informal)
cowardly

chicken verb chickens, chickening, chickened
to chicken out of something (informal) is to avoid it because you are afraid

chickenpox noun
a disease that produces red itchy spots on your skin

chief noun chiefs
1 a leader or ruler 2 the most important person, the boss

chief adjective
1 having the highest rank or power 2 most important

chiefly adverb
mainly, mostly *Peter is the one who is chiefly to blame.*

chieftain noun chieftains
the chief of a tribe or clan

child noun children
1 a young person, a boy or girl 2 someone's son or daughter *Whose child is that?*

childhood noun childhoods
the time when you are a child

childish adjective
silly and immature *Don't be childish!*

childminder noun childminders
a person who is paid to look after children while their parents are out at work

childproof adjective
not able to be opened or operated by small children *The car has childproof door locks.*

chill noun chills
1 chill is an unpleasant feeling of being cold 2 a chill is a cold that makes you shiver

chill verb chills, chilling, chilled
to chill something is to make it cold

chilli noun chillies
the hot-tasting pod of a red pepper

chilly adjective chillier, chilliest
1 slightly cold 2 unfriendly *They went to see the head and got a chilly reception.*

chime noun chimes
a ringing sound made by a bell

chime verb chimes, chiming, chimed
to chime is to ring *The clock chimes every quarter-hour.*

chimney noun chimneys
a tall pipe or passage that carries away smoke from a fire

chimney sweep noun chimney sweeps
someone who cleans the soot out of chimneys

chimpanzee noun chimpanzees
an small African ape with black fur and large eyes

chin noun chins
your chin is the part of your face under your mouth

china noun
china is thin and delicate pottery

chink noun chinks
1 a narrow opening *He looked through a chink in the curtains.* 2 a clinking sound *They heard the chink of coins.*

chip noun chips
1 a small piece of something 2 a place where a small piece has been knocked off something 3 a small piece of fried potato 4 a small counter used in gambling games 5 a silicon chip

chip verb chips, chipping, chipped
to chip something is to knock a small piece off it by accident **to chip in** is to make a suggestion or comment during a conversation that other people are having

chirp verb chirps, chirping, chirped
to chirp is to make short sharp sounds like a small bird

chirpy adjective chirpier, chirpiest
(informal)
lively and cheerful

chisel noun chisels
a tool with a sharp end for shaping wood or stone

chisel verb chisels, chiselling, chiselled
to chisel wood or stone is to shape or cut it with a chisel

chivalry noun
being ready to help people who are less strong than you are **chivalrous** adjective

chlorine noun
a chemical used to disinfect water

chlorophyll noun
the substance that makes plants green

chock-a-block or **chock-full** adjective, adverb
a place that is chock-a-block is completely full so there is hardly any room to move

chocolate noun chocolates
1 chocolate is a sweet brown food 2 a chocolate is a sweet made of or covered with chocolate 3 chocolate is also a sweet powder used for making drinks

 TOP TIPS There is a tricky bit in **chocolate**—it has an **o** in the middle.

choice noun choices
1 choice is the process of choosing or the power to choose *I'm afraid we have no choice.* 2 a choice is what someone chooses *Let me know your choice of book.*

choir noun choirs
a group of singers, especially in a church

choke verb chokes, choking, choked
1 to choke on something is to be unable to breathe properly because it is stuck in your throat 2 to choke someone is to stop them breathing properly 3 to choke something is to block it up

choke noun chokes
a valve in a motor vehicle that controls the mixture of air and petrol

cholera (say **kol**-er-a) noun
cholera is a severe infectious disease that affects the intestines

cholesterol (say ko-**less**-te-rol) noun
cholesterol is a substance found in the cells of your body which helps to carry fat in the bloodstream

chomp verb chomps, chomping, chomped
if you chomp on something you chew it

a b **c** d e f g h i j k l m n o p q r s t u v w x y z

89

A
B
C
D
E
F
G
H
I
J
K
L
M
N
O
P
Q
R
S
T
U
V
W
X
Y
Z

choose verb chooses, choosing, chose, chosen
to choose something or someone is to decide that you want them rather than any of the others

choosy adjective choosier, choosiest (informal)
a choosy person is fussy and difficult to please

chop verb chops, chopping, chopped
1 to chop something up is to cut it into small pieces 2 to chop something is to cut or hit it with a heavy blow
chop noun chops
1 a chopping blow 2 a small thick slice of meat

chopper noun choppers
1 a small axe 2 (informal) a helicopter

choppy adjective choppier, choppiest
a choppy sea is fairly rough with lots of small waves

chopsticks plural noun
a pair of thin sticks used for eating Chinese or Japanese food

choral (say **kor**-al) adjective
for a choir or chorus

chord (say kord) noun chords
a number of musical notes sounded together

chore (say chor) noun chores
a tedious or difficult task

chorus (say **kor**-us) noun choruses
1 a group of people singing or speaking together 2 a piece of music sung by a group of people 3 the words repeated after every verse of a song or poem

chose
past tense of choose He chose carefully from the library.

chosen
past participle of choose I have chosen a name for my dog.

christen verb christens, christening, christened
to christen a child is to baptize it and give it a name **christening** noun the ceremony at which a child is baptized

Christian noun Christians
someone who believes in Christ
Christian adjective
to do with Christ or Christians

Christianity noun
the religion of Christians

Christian name noun Christian names
a first name, for example John and Mary

Christmas noun Christmases
the time of celebrating the birth of Christ on 25 December

chrome or **chromium** noun
a shiny silvery metal

chronic adjective
a chronic illness or problem is one that lasts for a long time

chronicle noun chronicles
a list of events with their dates

chronology noun
the arrangement of events in the order in which they happened, especially in history or geology **chronological** adjective

chrysalis (say **kris**-a-lis) noun chrysalises
the hard cover a caterpillar makes round itself before it turns into a butterfly or moth

chrysanthemum noun chrysanthemums
a garden flower that blooms in autumn

chubby adjective chubbier, chubbiest
plump and healthy

chuck verb chucks, chucking, chucked (informal)
to chuck something is to throw it roughly He chucked a brick through the window.

chuckle verb chuckles, chuckling, chuckled
to chuckle is to laugh quietly

chuckle noun chuckles
a quiet laugh

chug verb chugs, chugging, chugged
to chug is to move with the sound of a slow-running engine

chum noun chums (informal)
a friend

chunk noun chunks
a thick lump of something **chunky** adjective big and thick

church noun churches
1 a church is a building where Christians worship 2 a church is also a particular Christian religion, for example the Church of England

churchyard noun churchyards
the ground round a church, used as a graveyard

churn noun churns
1 a large container for milk 2 a machine for making butter

churn verb churns, churning, churned
1 to churn butter is to make it in a churn
2 to churn something is to stir it vigorously **to churn something out** (informal) is to produce lots of it very quickly

chute (say shoot) noun chutes
a steep channel for people or things to slide down

chutney noun
chutney is a spicy mixture of fruit and peppers in a sauce, eaten with meat or cheese

cider noun ciders
cider is an alcoholic drink made from apples

cigar noun cigars
a roll of compressed tobacco leaves for smoking

cigarette noun cigarettes
a small thin roll of shredded tobacco in thin paper for smoking

cinder noun cinders
a small piece of coal or wood that is partly burned

cinema noun cinemas
1 a cinema is a place where people go to see films 2 cinema is the art or business of making films *recent trends in British cinema*

cinnamon noun
a yellow-brown spice

circle noun circles
1 a round flat shape, the shape of a coin or wheel 2 a balcony in a cinema or theatre
3 a number of people who have the same interests *She belongs to a writers' circle.*

circle verb circles, circling, circled
1 to circle is to move in a circle *Vultures circled overhead.* 2 to circle a place is go round it *The space probe circled Mars.*

circuit (say **ser**-kit) noun circuits
1 a circular line or journey 2 a racecourse
3 the path of an electric current

circular adjective
round like a circle

circular noun circulars
a letter or advertisement sent to a lot of people

circulate verb circulates, circulating, circulated
1 to circulate is to move around and come back to the beginning *Blood circulates in the body.* 2 to circulate something like a letter or notice is to send it to a lot of people

circulation noun circulations
1 the movement of blood around your body
2 the number of copies of each issue of a newspaper or magazine that are sold

circumference noun circumferences
the line or distance round something, especially round a circle

circumstance noun circumstances
1 a circumstance is a fact or event that makes a difference to something *He won under difficult circumstances.* 2 a person's circumstances are how much money they

a
b
c
d
e
f
g
h
i
j
k
l
m
n
o
p
q
r
s
t
u
v
w
x
y
z

A

B

C

D

E

F

G

H

I

J

K

L

M

N

O

P

Q

R

S

T

U

V

W

X

Y

Z

have, where they live, and the sort of life they lead

circus noun circuses
an entertainment with clowns, acrobats, and animals, usually performed in a large tent

cistern noun cisterns
a water tank

citizen noun citizens
a citizen of a place is someone who was born there or who lives there

citizenship noun
1 the citizenship of a country is the right to live there and be a citizen of it *She has applied for American citizenship.* 2 citizenship is also the duties a person has when they are the citizen of a country *The school has lessons in citizenship.*

citrus fruit noun
citrus fruits are juicy fruits with a tough skin, such as oranges, lemons, limes, and grapefruit

city noun cities
a large and important town, often having a cathedral

civic adjective
to do with a city or its citizens *the civic authorities*

civil adjective
1 to do with the citizens of a place 2 to do with the ordinary people and not those who are in the armed forces 3 a civil person is polite and courteous to other people

civilian noun civilians
someone who is an ordinary citizen and not in the armed forces

civilization noun civilizations
1 a civilization is a society or culture at a particular time in history *They were learning about the Bronze Age civilization.* 2 civilization is a developed or organized way of life *We are studying a primitive society with little civilization.*

civilize verb civilizes, civilizing, civilized
to civilize someone is to improve their education and manners

civil war noun civil wars
a war fought between people of the same country, such as the English Civil War (1642–51) or the American Civil War (1861–65)

clad adjective
clothed or covered *The story was about a knight clad in shining armour.*

claim verb claims, claiming, claimed
1 to claim something is to ask for it when you think it belongs to you *I'd like to claim the three weeks' money you owe me.* 2 to claim something is to state or assert it *They claimed they had been at home all evening.*

claim noun claims
1 an act of claiming 2 something claimed

claimant noun claimants
someone who makes a claim, especially for a right or benefit

clam noun clams
a shellfish

clamber verb clambers, clambering, clambered
to clamber is to climb up or over something difficult using your hands and feet *We clambered over the slippery rocks.*

clammy adjective clammier, clammiest
damp and slimy

clamp noun clamps
a device for holding things together

clamp verb clamps, clamping, clamped
to clamp something is to fit a clamp on it **to clamp down on something** is to be strict about it *The teachers decided to clamp down on homework.*

clan noun clans
a number of families with the same ancestor *The Scottish clans include the Campbells and the MacDonalds.*

clang verb **clangs, clanging, clanged**
to make a loud ringing sound

clank verb **clanks, clanking, clanked**
to make a loud sound like heavy pieces of metal banging together

clap verb **claps, clapping, clapped**
to clap is to make a noise by hitting the palms of your hands together, especially to show you like something

clap noun **claps**
1 a round of clapping, especially to show you like something *They gave the winners a loud clap.* 2 a clap of thunder is a sudden sound of loud thunder

clarify verb **clarifies, clarifying, clarified**
to clarify something is to explain it and make it easier to understand
clarification noun

clarinet noun **clarinets**
a woodwind instrument with a low tone
clarinettist noun

clarity noun
clarity is a clear quality *They spoke with clarity.*

clash verb **clashes, clashing, clashed**
1 to clash is to make a loud sound like cymbals banging together 2 two events clash when they happen at the same time *My favourite TV programmes clash at 8 o'clock tonight.* 3 two or more people clash when they have a fight or argument *Gangs of rival supporters clashed outside the ground.*

clash noun **clashes**
1 a clashing sound 2 a fight or argument

clasp verb **clasps, clasping, clasped**
to clasp someone or something is to hold them tightly

clasp noun **clasps**
1 a device for fastening things 2 a tight grasp

class noun **classes**
1 a class is a group of similar people, animals, or things 2 a class is also a division according to how good or important something is *Send the letter by first class post.* 3 a class is also a group of children or students who are taught together 4 class is a system of different ranks in society **to have class** (informal) is to look smart or behave elegantly

class verb **classes, classing, classed**
to class things is to put them in classes or groups

classic noun **classics**
a book, film, or story that is well known and thought to be very good and important

classic adjective
1 a classic story is one that most people think is very good and important 2 very typical or common *They made the classic mistake of leaving things to the last moment.* **classics** the study of the ancient Greek and Latin languages and writers

classical adjective
1 to do with Greek and Latin literature 2 classical music is serious music, often written in the past and still played

classified adjective
1 classified advertisements in newspapers are organized into types or subjects 2 classified information is officially secret and not told to the public

classify verb **classifies, classifying, classified**
to classify things is to put them in classes or groups **classification** noun

classmate noun **classmates**
your classmates are the people in the same class as you at school

classroom noun **classrooms**
a room where lessons are given at a school

clatter noun
a loud noise of things being rattled or banged

clatter verb **clatters, clattering, clattered**
to clatter is to make a clatter

clause noun **clauses**
1 (in grammar) a part of a sentence that has

a
b
c
d
e
f
g
h
i
j
k
l
m
n
o
p
q
r
s
t
u
v
w
x
y
z

its own verb **2** a part of a contract, treaty, or law

claw noun **claws**
one of the hard sharp nails that some birds and animals have on their feet

claw verb **claws, clawing, clawed**
to claw something is to grasp or scratch it with a claw or hand

clay noun
clay is a sticky kind of earth, and is used for making bricks and pottery

clean adjective **cleaner, cleanest**
1 something is clean when it does not have any dirt or stains on it **2** fresh, not yet used *Start on a clean page.* **3** not rude or offensive *I hope your jokes are clean ones.* **4** fair and honest *They wanted a clean fight.*

clean verb **cleans, cleaning, cleaned**
to clean something is to make it clean

cleaner noun **cleaners**
1 someone who cleans rooms or offices **2** something used for cleaning **the cleaners** a firm which cleans clothes

cleanliness (say **klen**-li-nes) noun
the practice of keeping things clean

cleanly adverb
neatly, exactly *He cut the brick cleanly in two.*

cleanse (say klenz) verb **cleanses, cleansing, cleansed**
to cleanse something is to clean it and make it pure **cleanser** noun

clear adjective **clearer, clearest**
1 easy to see or hear or understand *He spoke with a clear voice.* **2** free from things that get in the way or are not wanted *Make sure the table's clear for dinner.*

clear adverb
1 clearly *Speak loud and clear.* **2** completely *He got clear away.* **3** at a distance from something *You'd better stand clear of the gates.*

clear verb **clears, clearing, cleared**
1 to clear something is to make it free of

unwanted things *Will you clear the table for dinner?* **2** to clear is to become clearer *After the storm, the sky slowly cleared.* **3** to clear someone is to find out that they are not to blame for something people thought they had done **4** to clear something is to jump over it without touching it **to clear off** or **clear out** (informal) is to go away **to clear something out** is to empty or tidy it **to clear up** is to make things tidy

clearance noun **clearances**
1 clearance between two things is how close together they are when one passes the other or comes near it *There was not much clearance between the bridge and the top of the bus.* **2** clearance to do something is official permission for it to happen *The pilot wanted clearance for take-off.* **3** clearance is moving away things that are in the way or not wanted

clearing noun **clearings**
an open space in a wood or forest

clearly adverb
1 in a clear way *We could see the house clearly.* **2** obviously *They were clearly going to win.*

clef noun **clefs**
a sign that shows the pitch of a stave in music

clench verb **clenches, clenching, clenched**
to clench your teeth or fingers is to close them tightly

clergy plural noun
the clergy are the priests and other officials of a Christian Church

clergyman noun **clergymen**
a man who is one of the clergy

clergywoman noun **clergywomen**
a woman who is one of the clergy

clerical adjective
1 to do with the routine work in an office, such as filing and writing letters **2** to do with the clergy

A
B
C
D
E
F
G
H
I
J
K
L
M
N
O
P
Q
R
S
T
U
V
W
X
Y
Z

clerk (say klark) noun **clerks**
someone who works in an office to keep records and accounts and file papers

clever adjective **cleverer, cleverest**
quick to learn and understand things; skilful
cleverly adverb

cliché (say **klee**-shay) noun **clichés**
a phrase that people use a lot, so that it does not mean very much, for example *in this day and age* and *have a nice day*

click noun **clicks**
a short sharp sound *She heard a click as someone turned on the light.*

click verb **clicks, clicking, clicked**
1 to make a short sharp sound **2** to press a button on a mouse to select something on a computer screen *Click here to move to the next section.*

client noun **clients**
someone who gets help or advice from a professional person such as a lawyer or architect; a customer

cliff noun **cliffs**
a steep rock face, especially on the coast

cliffhanger noun **cliffhangers**
a story or situation that is exciting because you do not know what will happen next

climate noun **climates**
the usual sort of weather in a particular area

climax noun **climaxes**
the most important or exciting part of a story or series of events

climb verb **climbs, climbing, climbed**
1 to climb or climb up something is go up it **2** to climb down something is to go down it **3** to climb is to grow or rise upwards, like a tall plant or a building **to climb down** is to admit that you have been wrong about something or have had to change your mind

climb noun **climbs**
an act of climbing *It's a long climb to the top of the hill.*

climber noun **climbers**
someone who climbs hills and mountains for sport

cling verb **clings, clinging, clung**
to cling to someone or something is to hold on tightly *The child was clinging to its mother.*

clingfilm noun
clingfilm is a thin clear sheet of plastic that sticks to itself easily and is used for wrapping food

clinic noun **clinics**
a place where people see doctors for treatment or advice

clink verb **clinks, clinking, clinked**
to make a short ringing sound, like a coin being dropped

clip noun **clips**
a fastener for keeping things together

clip verb **clips, clipping, clipped**
1 to clip things together is to fasten them with a clip **2** to clip something is to cut it with shears or scissors

clip art noun
pictures that you can copy from a CD-ROM or the Internet and use on your computer

clipboard noun **clipboards**
a board that you can carry around, with a clip at the top to hold papers

clipper noun **clippers**
an old type of fast sailing ship

clippers plural noun
clippers are large scissors for clipping

clipping noun **clippings**
a piece cut from a newspaper or magazine

cloak noun **cloaks**
a piece of outdoor clothing, usually without sleeves, that hangs loosely from your shoulders

cloakroom noun **cloakrooms**
1 a place where you can leave coats and bags while you are visiting a building **2** a lavatory

a
b
c
d
e
f
g
h
i
j
k
l
m
n
o
p
q
r
s
t
u
v
w
x
y
z

A
B

clobber verb clobbers, clobbering, clobbered (informal)
to clobber someone is to hit them very hard

C

clock noun clocks
an instrument that shows what the time is

D
E

clockwise adverb, adjective
moving round a circle in the same direction as the hands of a clock

F

clockwork adjective
worked by a spring which you wind up

G
H

clog verb clogs, clogging, clogged
to clog something is to block it up accidentally

I

clog noun clogs
a shoe with a wooden sole

J
K

cloister noun cloisters
a covered path that is open on one side and goes round a courtyard or along the side of a cathedral or monastery

L
M

clone noun clones
an animal or plant made from the cells of another animal or plant

N

clone verb clones, cloning, cloned
to clone something is copy it

O

close[1] (say klohss) adjective
closer, closest
1 near, either in time or place *They were close to finding the answer. The shops were quite close to their new house.* **2** careful and detailed *Please pay close attention.* **3** tight; with little empty space *They got the wardrobe in but it was a close fit.* **4** a close race or finish is one in which competitors are nearly equal at the end **5** stuffy; without fresh air *It's very close in this room.*

P
Q
R
S
T
U

close (say klohss) adverb closer, closest
at a close distance *The children were following close behind.*

V
W

close (say klohss) noun closes
1 a street that is closed at one end **2** an enclosed area, especially round a cathedral

X
Y

close[2] (say klohz) verb closes, closing, closed
1 to close something is to shut it **2** to close an event or meeting is to finish it **to close**

Z

down is to stop doing business *Several shops in the High Street have closed down recently.*
to close in is to get nearer *The police closed in around the house.*

closely (say **klohss**-li) adverb
1 carefully, with attention *His friends were watching closely.* **2** tightly *The box was closely packed with toys.*

close-up (say **klohss**-up) noun
close-ups
a photograph or film taken at short range

clot noun clots
1 a mass of thick liquid like blood or cream that has become nearly solid **2** (informal) a stupid person

clot verb clots, clotting, clotted
to clot is to form into clots, like blood or cream

cloth noun cloths
1 cloth is material woven from wool, cotton, or some other fabric **2** a cloth is a piece of this material

clothe verb clothes, clothing, clothed
to clothe someone is to put clothes on them

clothes plural noun
clothes are the things you wear to cover your body

clothing noun
clothing is the clothes you wear

cloud noun clouds
1 a mass of water vapour floating in the air **2** a mass of smoke or something else dense in the air

cloud verb clouds, clouding, clouded
to cloud or cloud over is to become full of clouds *In the afternoon the sky clouded over.*
cloudless adjective a cloudless sky does not have any clouds

cloudburst noun cloudbursts
a sudden heavy downpour of rain

cloudy adjective cloudier, cloudiest
1 full of clouds **2** hard to see through *The glass contained a cloudy liquid.*

clout verb clouts, clouting, clouted
to clout someone is to give them a hard blow

clove noun cloves
the dried bud of a tropical tree used as a spice

clover noun
a small wild plant, usually with leaves in three parts

clown noun clowns
1 a circus performer who dresses up and wears bright face paint and does silly things to make people laugh 2 an amusing or silly person
clown verb clowns, clowning, clowned
to clown is to behave like a clown

club noun clubs
1 a heavy stick 2 a stick for playing golf 3 a group of people who meet together because they are interested in the same thing 4 a playing card with a black clover leaf printed on it
club verb clubs, clubbing, clubbed
to club someone is to hit them hard with a heavy stick **to club together** is to join with other people in doing something, especially raising money

cluck verb clucks, clucking, clucked
to make a noise like a hen

clue noun clues
something that helps you to solve a puzzle or a mystery

clueless adjective (informal)
stupid, having no idea how to do something

clump noun clumps
a cluster of trees or plants

clumsy adjective clumsier, clumsiest
a clumsy person is careless and awkward, and likely to knock things over or drop things **clumsily** adverb **clumsiness** noun

clung
past tense and past participle of cling She clung to the side of the boat. The child had clung to her hand.

cluster noun clusters
a group of people or things close together

clutch¹ verb clutches, clutching, clutched
to clutch something or clutch at something is to grab hold of it
clutch noun clutches
1 a tight grasp 2 a device for disconnecting the engine of a motor vehicle from its gears and wheels

clutch² noun clutches
a set of eggs in a nest

clutter verb clutters, cluttering, cluttered
to clutter a place up is to make it untidy or messy
clutter noun
clutter is a lot of things left around untidily

cm
short for centimetre or centimetres

Co.
short for company

coach noun coaches
1 a comfortable single-deck bus used for long journeys 2 a carriage of a railway train 3 a carriage pulled by horses 4 a person who trains or instructs people in a sport or skill
coach verb coaches, coaching, coached
to coach someone is to instruct or train them in a sport or skill

coal noun
coal is a hard black mineral used as fuel

coarse adjective coarser, coarsest
1 rough, not delicate or smooth 2 rude or offensive You have a very coarse sense of humour.

coast noun coasts
the seashore and the land close to it **the coast is clear** there is no one about to catch you or stop you doing something
coast verb coasts, coasting, coasted
to coast is to ride downhill without using power They stopped pedalling and coasted down the slope.

a
b
c
d
e
f
g
h
i
j
k
l
m
n
o
p
q
r
s
t
u
v
w
x
y
z

coastal adjective
by the coast or near the coast

coastguard noun **coastguards**
someone whose job is to keep watch on coasts to prevent smuggling

coastline noun
the edge of the land by the sea

coat noun **coats**
1 a piece of clothing with sleeves that covers most of the body and is worn outdoors over other clothes **2** a layer of paint

coat verb **coats, coating, coated**
to coat something is to cover it with a coating

coating noun **coatings**
a covering or layer, especially of paint

coat of arms noun **coats of arms**
a design on a shield or building, representing a historic family or town

coax verb **coaxes, coaxing, coaxed**
to coax someone is to persuade them gently or patiently

cobbler noun **cobblers**
someone whose job is to mend shoes

cobbles plural noun
cobbles are a surface of cobblestones on a road **cobbled** adjective

cobblestone noun **cobblestones**
a small smooth and rounded stone sometimes used in large numbers to pave roads in towns

cobra (say **koh**-bra) noun **cobras**
a poisonous snake

cobweb noun **cobwebs**
a net of thin sticky threads that spiders spin to catch insects

cock noun **cocks**
a male bird, especially a male fowl

cock verb **cocks, cocking, cocked**
1 to cock your eye or ear is to turn it in a particular direction **2** to cock a gun is to make it ready to fire

cockerel noun **cockerels**
a young male fowl

cocker spaniel noun **cocker spaniels**
a kind of small spaniel with a golden brown coat and long hanging ears

cockle noun **cockles**
an edible shellfish

coat of arms

helmet

shield

banner

motto

cockney noun cockneys
1 a cockney is someone born in the East End of London **2** cockney is a kind of English spoken by people from this part of London

cockpit noun cockpits
the place in an aircraft where the pilot sits

cockroach noun cockroaches
a dark brown insect

cocky adjective cockier, cockiest (informal)
conceited and cheeky

cocoa noun cocoas
1 a hot drink that tastes of chocolate **2** the powder from which you make this drink

coconut noun coconuts
a large round nut containing a milky juice, that grows on palm trees

cocoon noun cocoons
the covering round a pupa

cod noun cod
a large edible sea fish

code noun codes
1 a set of signs and letters for sending messages secretly **2** a set of rules *the Highway Code, a code of behaviour*
code verb codes, coding, coded
1 to code a message is to use special signs and letters, so that other people cannot understand it **2** to code data is to put it into a form that can be accepted by a computer

co-education noun
the teaching of boys and girls together
co-educational adjective

coffee noun coffees
1 a hot drink made from the roasted and crushed beans of a tropical plant **2** the powder from which you make this drink

coffin noun coffins
a long box in which a dead body is buried or cremated

cog noun cogs
one of a number of pieces sticking out from the edge of a wheel and allowing it to drive another wheel

coil noun coils
a circle or spiral of rope or wire
coil verb coils, coiling, coiled
to coil something is to wind it into circles or spirals

coin noun coins
a piece of metal money
coin verb coins, coining, coined
1 to coin money is to manufacture it **2** to coin a new word is to invent it

coinage noun coinages
1 a country's coinage is the system of money that it uses **2** a coinage is also a new word or phrase that someone has invented

coincide verb coincides, coinciding, coincided
to coincide is to happen at the same time as something else *The end of term coincides with my birthday.*

coincidence noun coincidences
coincidence, or a coincidence, is when two things can happen by chance at the same time

coke noun
coke is a solid fuel made out of coal

cola noun colas
cola is a sweet, brown, fizzy drink

colander (say **kul**-an-der) noun colanders
a bowl with holes, for draining water from vegetables

cold adjective colder, coldest
1 low in temperature, not hot or warm **2** a cold person is unfriendly and distant
coldly adverb **coldness** noun
cold noun colds
1 cold weather or temperature **2** a cold is an illness that makes your nose run and gives you a sore throat

cold-blooded adjective
1 a cold-blooded animal has blood that changes temperature according to the

a
b
c
d
e
f
g
h
i
j
k
l
m
n
o
p
q
r
s
t
u
v
w
x
y
z

surroundings *Lizards are cold-blooded animals.* **2** cruel, ruthless

coleslaw noun
a salad made of chopped cabbage covered in mayonnaise

collaborate verb collaborates, collaborating, collaborated
1 people collaborate when they work together or share their information **2** to collaborate with an enemy is to work secretly on their side **collaboration** noun

collaborator noun
1 someone who works with someone else or shares ideas with them **2** someone who betrays their country during a war by sharing information with the enemy

collage (say kol-ahzh or kol-**ah**zh) noun collages
a picture made by arranging scraps of paper and other things on a card

collapse verb collapses, collapsing, collapsed
1 to collapse is to fall or break into pieces because of too much weight **2** someone collapses when they fall from being very weak or ill

collapse noun collapses
an act of collapsing

collapsible adjective
a collapsible piece of furniture or equipment can be folded up into a smaller space

collar noun collars
1 the part of a piece of clothing that goes round your neck **2** a band that goes round an animal's neck

collate verb collates, collating, collated
to collate pieces of information is to collect and arrange them in an organized way *They had to collate the results in the form of a graph.*

colleague noun colleagues
someone's colleague is a person they work with

collect verb collects, collecting, collected
1 to collect things is to get them together from various places, especially as a hobby *She collects stamps, and I collect coins.* **2** to collect someone or something is to go and get them **collector** noun

collection noun collections
1 things you have collected as a hobby **2** money given by people at a meeting or concert or church service

collective adjective
involving several people or things *It was a collective decision.*

collective noun noun collective nouns
a singular noun that is a name for a group of things or people, for example *choir, flock, government*

college noun colleges
a place where people continue to study after they have left school

collide verb collides, colliding, collided
to collide with something is to hit it while moving *The bicycle collided with the car.*

collie noun collies
a breed of dog with a long pointed muzzle and long hair

collision noun collisions
a crash between moving vehicles *There has been a collision on the motorway.*

colloquial adjective
colloquial language is used for conversation but not for formal speech or writing *'Chuck' is a colloquial word for 'throw'.*

colon noun colons
a punctuation mark (:) used to separate parts of a sentence or before items in a list *There are two things I love about my room: the walls are bright yellow and you can see the sea out of the window.*

colonel (say ker-nel) noun colonels
a senior army officer

A
B
C
D
E
F
G
H
I
J
K
L
M
N
O
P
Q
R
S
T
U
V
W
X
Y
Z

colonial adjective
from or to do with a country's
colonies abroad

colonist noun colonists
a person who goes to live in a
colony abroad

colony noun colonies
1 a country that another another country
governs and sends people out to live
there 2 a group of people or animals
living together

colossal adjective
huge, enormous *The monster did not laugh.
He set off, up from the earth, beating his
colossal wings. – Ted Hughes, The Iron Man*

colour noun colours
1 the quality of being red, green, blue,
and so on, produced by rays of light of
different wavelengths 2 the use of all
colours, not just black and white *Is this film
in colour?* 3 the colour of someone's skin
4 a substance used to give colour to things
5 the special flag of a ship or regiment

colour verb colours, colouring,
coloured
to colour something is to give it a colour or
colours with paints or crayons

colour–blind adjective
not able to see or distinguish between some
colours, usually red and green

coloured adjective
having a particular colour

colourful adjective
1 having a lot of bright colours 2 lively *The
film was a colourful story of life on board a
pirate ship.*

colouring noun
1 colouring is a substance you add to
something to give it a special colour
2 a person's colouring is the colour and
appearance of their skin and hair

colourless adjective
not having any colour *Many gases
are colourless.*

colt noun colts
a young male horse

column noun columns
1 a pillar 2 something long and narrow *They
could see a column of smoke in the distance.*
3 a strip of printing in a book or newspaper
4 a regular feature in a newspaper *He
always read the sports column.*

 TOP TIPS Keep it quiet! There is a silent **n** in
column.

coma (say **koh**-ma) noun comas
someone is in a coma when they are
unconscious for a long time

comb noun combs
1 a tool with teeth for making the hair tidy
2 the red fleshy crest on the head of some
birds, such as cockerels

comb verb combs, combing, combed
1 to comb the hair is to tidy it with a comb
2 to comb an area is to search it carefully
for something lost *We combed the woods all
day but couldn't find our dog.*

combat noun combats
a fight or contest

combat verb combats, combating,
combated
to combat something bad or unpleasant is
to fight it and try to get rid of it *The police
force combats crime.*

combination noun combinations
1 combination is joining or mixing things
2 a combination is a group of things that
have been joined or mixed together

combine (say kom-**byn**) verb combines,
combining, combined
to combine things is to join them or mix
them together

combustion noun
combustion is what happens when
something burns

come verb comes, coming, came, come
1 to come is to move towards the person or
place that is here, and is the opposite of **go**
*Do you want to come to my house? Has that
letter come yet?* 2 to come is also to occur

a
b
c
d
e
f
g
h
i
j
k
l
m
n
o
p
q
r
s
t
u
v
w
x
y
z

A
B
C
D
E
F
G
H
I
J
K
L
M
N
O
P
Q
R
S
T
U
V
W
X
Y
Z

or be present *The pictures come at the end of the book.* **to come about** is to happen **to come across someone** is to meet them by chance **to come by something** is to get it *How did you come by that watch?* **to come round** or **come to** is to revive after being unconscious **to come true** is to actually happen *Their holiday was a dream come true.*

comeback noun **comebacks**
someone makes a comeback when they start doing something again that they have been famous for in the past

comedian noun **comedians**
someone who entertains people with humour and jokes

comedy noun **comedies**
1 a comedy is a play or film that makes people laugh 2 comedy is using humour to make people laugh

comet noun **comets**
an object moving across the sky with a bright tail of light

comfort noun
1 comfort is a feeling of relief from worry or pain 2 your comforts are the things you have around you that you enjoy and that make life pleasant

comfort verb **comforts, comforting, comforted**
to comfort someone is to make them feel happier when they are feeling sad or worried

comfortable adjective
1 pleasant to use or wear *a comfortable chair* 2 free from worry or pain *The nurse made the patient comfortable.*
comfortably adverb

comic noun **comics**
1 a children's magazine that has stories with pictures 2 a comedian

comic or **comical** adjective
funny, making people laugh
comically adverb

comic strip noun **comic strips**
a series of drawings that tell a story

comma noun **commas**
a punctuation mark (,) used to mark a pause in a sentence or between items in a list

command noun **commands**
1 a command is an instruction telling someone to do something 2 command is authority or control *Who has command of these soldiers?* 3 a command of a subject is the skill or ability to understand it *She has a good command of Spanish.*

command verb **commands, commanding, commanded**
1 to command someone is to tell them to do something 2 to command a group of people is to be in charge of them *A centurion commanded a hundred soldiers.*

commander noun **commanders**
someone who commands, especially a senior naval officer

commandment noun **commandments**
a sacred command, especially one of the Ten Commandments of Moses

commando noun **commandos**
a soldier trained for making dangerous raids

commemorate verb **commemorates, commemorating, commemorated**
to commemorate a past event is to do something special so that people remember it **commemoration** noun

commence verb **commences, commencing, commenced**
to commence something is to begin it **commencement** noun

commend verb **commends, commending, commended**
to commend someone is to praise them *He was commended for bravery.* **commendable** adjective **commendation** noun

comment noun **comments**
a remark or opinion

commentary noun commentaries
a description of an event by someone who is watching it, especially for radio or television

commentator noun commentators
a person who gives a commentary, especially of a sports event
commentate verb

commerce noun
commerce is trade, or buying and selling goods

commercial adjective
1 connected with trade and making money
2 paid for by advertising *a commercial radio station*

commercial noun commercials
an advertisement, especially on television or radio

commit verb commits, committing, committed
to commit a crime is to do something against the law **to commit yourself to something** is to decide to do it or to promise that you will do it

commitment noun commitments
1 commitment is being determined to do something 2 a commitment is something you have promised to do

committee noun committees
a group of people who meet to organize or discuss something

commodity noun commodities
something that can be bought and sold *commodities like coffee, cocoa, and sugar*

common adjective commoner, commonest
1 ordinary or usual *The dandelion is a common plant.* 2 happening or used often *Traffic jams are common where we live.* 3 shared by many people *The story was common knowledge. Music was their common interest.*

common noun commons
a piece of open land that anyone can use

commonplace adjective
ordinary, familiar

common room noun common rooms
a room for teachers or pupils to relax in at a school or college

commonwealth noun commonwealths
a group of countries cooperating together **the Commonwealth** an association of Britain and various other countries, such as Canada, Australia, and New Zealand

commotion noun commotions
an uproar *The cocker spaniel heard the commotion and he ran out from the barn to join in the chase.* – E. B. White, *Charlotte's Web*

communal adjective
shared by several people

commune noun communes
a group of people who live in the same house and share the money and work

communicate verb communicates, communicating, communicated
to communicate news or information is to pass it on to other people
communicative adjective a communicative person is willing to talk to people and give them information

communication noun communications
1 communication is giving people useful information and telling them about things that have happened 2 a communication is a message or piece of information that someone gives you 3 communication is also a form of technology for passing on information, for example television and text messages

Communion noun
Communion is the Christian ceremony in which holy bread and wine are given to worshippers.

community noun communities
the people living in one area

a
b
c
d
e
f
g
h
i
j
k
l
m
n
o
p
q
r
s
t
u
v
w
x
y
z

commute noun commutes, commuting, commuted
to travel from home to work every morning and back again in the evening **commuter** noun

compact adjective
small and neat

compact disc noun compact discs
a small plastic and metal disc on which music or information is stored as digital signals and is read by a laser beam. Usually called CD.

companion noun companions
a companion is someone who spends a lot of time with you **companionship** noun
companionship is being with someone and enjoying their friendship

company noun companies
1 a company is a group of people, especially a business firm 2 company is having people with you *Jill was lonely and longed for some company.* 3 a company is an army unit consisting of two or more platoons

comparable (say kom-per-a-bul) adjective
able to be compared, similar

comparative adjective
compared with something else *After the noise of her own house she enjoyed the comparative peace of her friend's place.*

comparative noun comparatives
the form of an adjective or adverb that expresses 'more' *The comparative of 'big' is 'bigger', and the comparative of 'bad' is 'worse'.*

comparatively adverb
in comparison, relatively *They all went to bed comparatively late.*

compare verb compares, comparing, compared
1 to compare things is to see how they are similar *Compare your answers.* 2 to compare with something is to be as good as it *Our football pitch cannot compare with Wembley Stadium.*

comparison noun comparisons
comparison, or a comparison, is thinking about several things and seeing how they are similar or different

compartment noun compartments
a special place or section where you can put something *The coach had a luggage compartment under the floor.*

compass noun compasses
an instrument with a magnetized needle that shows which direction you are facing

compasses noun
compasses, or a pair of compasses, are a device for drawing circles

compassion noun
compassion is pity or mercy you show to people who are suffering **compassionate** adjective

compatible adjective
1 people are compatible when they are able to live or exist together without trouble 2 machines and devices are compatible when they can be used together

compel verb compels, compelling, compelled
to compel someone to do something is to force them to do it

compensate verb compensates, compensating, compensated
to compensate someone is to give them something to make up for something they have lost or suffered **compensation** noun

compère (say kom-pair) noun compères
someone who introduces the performers in a show or broadcast

compete verb competes, competing, competed
to compete in a competition is to try to win it by being better than other people

competent adjective
having the skill or knowledge to do something well *He is a competent football player.* **competence** noun

competition noun competitions
a game or race in which you try to do better than other people

competitive adjective
a competitive person enjoys competing with other people and likes to win

competitor noun competitors
1 someone who competes in a game or race
2 if two companies are competitors, they sell the same type of product or service

compile verb compiles, compiling, compiled
to compile information is to collect and arrange it, especially in a book *She compiled a collection of children's poems.* **compilation** noun a collection of information, stories, or poems, that someone has put together

complacent adjective
smugly satisfied with the way things are, without wanting to improve them

complain verb complains, complaining, complained
to complain about something is to say that you are not pleased about it

complaint noun complaints
1 you make a complaint when you are not pleased about something 2 you suffer from a complaint when you are slightly ill

complement noun complements
the amount needed to fill or complete something *This ship has a full complement of sailors.*

complementary adjective
1 complementary colours and designs go well together 2 complementary parts together make up a whole

complete adjective
1 having all its parts, with nothing missing *I hope the tool kit is complete.* 2 finished, achieved *By evening the jigsaw puzzle was complete.* 3 utter, total *It came as a complete surprise.*

complete verb completes, completing, completed
to complete something is to finish it or make it complete **completion** noun

completely adverb
totally, utterly *You are completely wrong.*

complex adjective
difficult and complicated **complexity** noun

complex noun complexes
1 a group of buildings, such as a sports centre 2 something that someone has a strange attitude or obsession about *He has a complex about winning.*

complexion noun complexions
the colour or appearance of your skin

complicate verb complicates, complicating, complicated
to complicate something is to make it difficult or awkward

complicated adjective
difficult to understand or cope with because it has so many parts or details

complication noun complications
1 a difficult or awkward situation 2 a difficulty that makes something worse

compliment noun compliments
words or actions that show you approve of a person or thing

complimentary adjective
1 praising someone or saying good things about them *She liked Neil and was very complimentary about him.* 2 given to someone free of charge *We were given complimentary tickets for the match.*

component noun components
one of the parts that a machine is made of

compose verb composes, composing, composed
1 to compose music or poetry is to write it 2 to be composed of several people or things is to be made up of them *The class is composed of children up to the age of 8.* **composer** noun

a
b
c
d
e
f
g
h
i
j
k
l
m
n
o
p
q
r
s
t
u
v
w
x
y
z

A
B
C
D
E
F
G
H
I
J
K
L
M
N
O
P
Q
R
S
T
U
V
W
X
Y
Z

composition noun **compositions**
1 composition is composing or writing something 2 a composition is a piece of music or an essay

compost noun
compost is a mixture of decayed leaves, grass, and other natural refuse, and is used as manure

compound[1] noun **compounds**
1 a substance that is made of two or more parts or ingredients 2 (in grammar) a word that is made from two or more other words, such as *bathroom* and *newspaper*

compound[2] noun **compounds**
a fenced area containing buildings

comprehend verb **comprehends, comprehending, comprehended**
to comprehend something is to understand it

comprehension noun **comprehensions**
1 comprehension is understanding 2 a comprehension is an exercise that tests or helps your understanding of a language

comprehensive adjective
including everything or everyone *a comprehensive list*

comprehensive school noun **comprehensive schools**
a secondary school for children of all abilities

compress verb **compresses, compressing, compressed**
1 to compress something is to press it or squeeze it together 2 to be compressed is to be forced into a small space **compression** noun

compromise (say **kom**-pro-myz) verb **compromises, compromising, compromised**
to compromise is to accept less than you really wanted, especially so as to settle a disagreement *We both wanted to sit beside Mum, so we compromised by swapping seats every half-hour.*

compromise (say **kom**-pro-myz) noun **compromises**
accepting less than you really wanted

compulsory adjective
something is compulsory when you have to do it *Wearing seat belts is compulsory.*

compute verb **computes, computing, computed**
to compute something is to calculate it

computer noun **computers**
an electronic machine that does word processing, sorts data, and does rapid calculations

comrade noun **comrades**
a friend or companion

con verb **cons, conning, conned** (informal)
to con someone is to swindle them

concave adjective
a concave surface is curved like the inside of a circle or ball (the opposite of *convex*)

conceal verb **conceals, concealing, concealed**
to conceal something is to hide it carefully or cleverly **concealment** noun

conceit noun
conceit is thinking a lot about how clever or attractive you are **conceited** adjective

conceive verb **conceives, conceiving, conceived**
1 to conceive an idea or plan is to form it in your mind 2 a woman conceives when she becomes pregnant

concentrate verb **concentrates, concentrating, concentrated**
1 to concentrate on something is to think hard about it 2 to concentrate people or things is to bring them together in one place

concentrated adjective
a liquid is concentrated when it is made stronger by having water removed from it

concentration noun
concentration is thinking hard
about something

concentric adjective
circles that are concentric are placed
one inside another and have the
same centre

concept noun concepts
an idea *the concept of right and wrong*

conception noun conceptions
1 conception is forming an idea in your
mind 2 conception is also when a woman
becomes pregnant

concern verb concerns, concerning,
concerned
1 to concern someone is to be important
or interesting to them 2 to concern
something is to be about a particular
subject *This story concerns a shipwreck.*
3 to worry someone

concern noun concerns
1 something that matters to someone *I
think that is my concern.* 2 a business

concerning preposition
on the subject of; in connection with *The
head teacher wrote to all parents concerning
the school report.*

concert noun concerts
a performance of music

concertina noun concertinas
a portable musical instrument that you
squeeze to push air past reeds

concerto (say kon-**cher**-toh) noun
concertos
a piece of music for a solo instrument and
an orchestra *a violin concerto*

concession noun concessions
something that someone allows you to
have or do, to be helpful or to reach an
agreement *As a special concession, parents
may park in the teachers' car park on
Sports Day.*

concise adjective
giving a lot of information in a few words

conclude verb concludes, concluding,
concluded
1 to conclude something is to end it 2 to
conclude something is also to decide about
it *The jury concluded that he was not guilty.*

conclusion noun conclusions
1 the ending of something 2 a decision that
you reach after a lot of thought

concrete noun
cement mixed with water and gravel or sand
and used in building

concrete adjective
real, definite *We need concrete evidence.*

concussion noun
a temporary injury to the brain that is
caused by a hard knock and leaves you
feeling dizzy or unconscious

condemn verb condemns,
condemning, condemned
1 to condemn someone or something is to
say that you strongly disapprove of them
2 to condemn criminals is to sentence
them to a punishment *He was condemned
to death.* 3 to condemn a building is
to declare that it is not fit to be used
condemnation noun

condensation noun
drops of liquid formed from vapour that
has condensed

condense verb condenses,
condensing, condensed
1 to condense a piece of writing is to make
it shorter 2 to condense is to change into
water or other liquid *Steam condenses on
cold windows.*

condensed adjective
a condensed liquid, such as milk, is one that
is made stronger or thicker

condition noun conditions
1 the state in which a person or thing is *This
bike is in good condition.* 2 something that
must happen if something else is to happen
*Learning to swim is a condition of going
sailing. You can come on condition that you
bring your sister too.*

a
b
c
d
e
f
g
h
i
j
k
l
m
n
o
p
q
r
s
t
u
v
w
x
y
z

conduct (say kon-**dukt**) verb conducts, conducting, conducted
1 to conduct someone is to lead or guide them 2 to conduct something is to organize or manage it 3 to conduct an orchestra or band is to direct it in a piece of music 4 to conduct electricity or heat is to allow it to pass along *Copper conducts electricity well.*

conduct (say **kon**-dukt) noun
a person's conduct is their behaviour

conductor noun conductors
1 someone who conducts an orchestra or band 2 something that conducts electricity or heat 3 someone who collects the fares on a bus or coach

cone noun cones
1 an object which is circular at one end and pointed at the other end 2 an ice cream cornet 3 the fruit of a pine, fir, or cedar

confectioner noun confectioners
someone who makes or sells sweets
confectionery noun confectionery is sweets and cakes that a shop sells

confer verb confers, conferring, conferred
1 to confer a title or honour on someone is to give it to them 2 to confer is to have a discussion

conference noun conferences
a meeting for discussion

confess verb confesses, confessing, confessed
to confess to something wrong is to admit that you have done it

confession noun confessions
an act of admitting that you have committed a crime or done wrong *The burglar made a full confession.*

confetti plural noun
tiny bits of coloured paper thrown at the bride and bridegroom after a wedding

confide verb confides, confiding, confided
to confide in someone is to tell them a secret

confidence noun
1 you have confidence when you are sure that you are right or can do something 2 confidence in someone is trusting or believing them **in confidence** as a secret *He told me all this in confidence.*

confidence trick noun confidence tricks
a trick to get money out of someone by deceiving them into giving their trust

confident adjective
1 being sure that you are right or can do something 2 certain that something will happen *We are confident it will be an enjoyable day.*

confidential adjective
information is confidential when it has to be kept secret **confidentially** adverb

confine verb confines, confining, confined
1 to confine something is to restrict or limit it *Please confine your comments to points of fact.* 2 to confine someone is to lock them up or shut them in a place **confinement** noun

confirm verb confirms, confirming, confirmed
1 to confirm something is to say that it is true or to show that it is true 2 to confirm an arrangement is to make it definite *Please write to confirm your order.* 3 to confirm someone is to make them a full member of a Christian Church

confirmation noun
a fact or piece of information that shows something is true or has happened *You will receive confirmation of your booking by email.* **Confirmation** a Christian ceremony that makes someone a full member of a Christian Church

confiscate verb confiscates, confiscating, confiscated
to confiscate something is to take it away from someone as a punishment **confiscation** noun

conflict (say **kon**-flikt) noun **conflicts**
a fight or disagreement *the conflict in the Middle East, Jack was trying to resolve a conflict between his parents.*

conflict (say kon-**flikt**) verb **conflicts, conflicting, conflicted**
two things conflict when they contradict or disagree with one another *The two reports of the incident conflict.*

conform verb **conforms, conforming, conformed**
to conform is to follow other people's rules or ideas about something

confront verb **confronts, confronting, confronted**
1 to confront someone is to challenge them face to face for a fight or argument *The police decided to confront the criminals there and then.* **2** to confront a problem or difficulty is to deal with it firmly and positively **confrontation** noun

confuse verb **confuses, confusing, confused**
1 to confuse someone is to make them puzzled or muddled **2** to confuse things is to mistake one thing for another **confusing** adjective **confusion** noun

congested adjective
crowded, especially with people or traffic **congestion** noun

congratulate verb **congratulates, congratulating, congratulated**
to congratulate someone is to tell them how pleased you are about something they have done **congratulations** plural noun

congregation noun **congregations**
the people who take part in a church service

congress noun **congresses**
a large meeting or conference **Congress** the parliament or government of the USA

conical adjective
shaped like a cone

conifer (say **kon**-i-fer) noun **conifers**
an evergreen tree with cones **coniferous** adjective

conjunction noun **conjunctions**
a word that joins other words and parts of a sentence, e.g. *and, but,* and *whether*

conjure verb **conjures, conjuring, conjured**
to conjure is to perform tricks that look like magic **conjurer** noun

conker noun **conkers**
a hard and shiny brown nut that grows on a horse chestnut tree **conkers** a game played with conkers threaded on pieces of string

connect verb **connects, connecting, connected**
to connect things is to join them together

connection noun **connections**
1 a link between things **2** joining together

connective noun **connectives** (in grammar)
a word or phrase that links clauses or sentences, for example *because, however,* or *on the other hand*

conquer verb **conquers, conquering, conquered**
to conquer a people or country is to defeat them and take them over *William I conquered England. He managed to conquer all his fears.* **conqueror** noun

conquest noun **conquests**
a victory over another country or people

conscience (say **kon**-shens) noun
a feeling people have about what is right or wrong

conscientious (say kon-shee-**en**-shus) adjective
careful and hard-working **conscientiously** adverb

conscious (say **kon**-shus) adjective
1 awake and knowing what is happening **2** aware of something *Are you conscious of the danger you are in?* **3** deliberate *She has made a conscious effort to improve.* **consciously** adverb **consciousness** noun

a
b
c
d
e
f
g
h
i
j
k
l
m
n
o
p
q
r
s
t
u
v
w
x
y
z

A
B
C
D
E
F
G
H
I
J
K
L
M
N
O
P
Q
R
S
T
U
V
W
X
Y
Z

consecutive adjective
things are consecutive when they come one after another in a list or sequence

consensus noun
an agreement between most people about something *There was a consensus that the law should be changed.*

consent noun
consent is agreement or permission
consent verb **consents, consenting, consented**
to consent to something is to agree to it or permit it

consequence noun **consequences**
1 a consequence is something which happens because of an event or action *His injury was the consequence of an accident.*
2 consequence is the importance that something has *It is of no consequence.*
consequently adverb as a result

conservation noun
conservation is keeping buildings and natural surroundings in a good state
conservationist noun

Conservative noun **Conservatives**
someone who supports the Conservative Party, a British political party

conservative adjective
1 a conservative person doesn't like change and wants things to stay the same 2 a conservative estimate or guess is a careful or cautious one

conservatory noun **conservatories**
a room built on the back or side of a house, with glass walls and a glass roof

conserve verb **conserves, conserving, conserved**
to conserve something is to keep it from being changed or spoilt

consider verb **considers, considering, considered**
1 to consider something is to think carefully about it 2 to consider something is also to believe it *We consider that people should be allowed to follow their own religion.*

considerable adjective
large or important *The journey takes a considerable time.* **considerably** adverb very much *Her new house is considerably larger.*

considerate adjective
kind and thoughtful towards other people

consideration noun **considerations**
1 consideration is careful thought or attention 2 a consideration is a serious thought or reason *Money is a major consideration in this plan.*

considering preposition
in view of *The car goes well, considering its age.*

consist verb **consists, consisting, consisted**
to consist of something is to be made from it *The meal consisted of pasta and cheese.*

consistency noun **consistencies**
1 consistency is being the same 2 the consistency of a liquid is how thick it is

consistent adjective
1 always the same, regular 2 always acting in the same way **consistently** adverb

consolation noun **consolations**
consolation is comfort or sympathy given to someone

consolation prize noun **consolation prizes**
a prize given to someone who does not win a main prize

console (say kon-**sohl**) verb **consoles, consoling, consoled**
to console someone is to give them comfort or sympathy

consonant noun **consonants**
a letter that is not a vowel

conspicuous adjective
something conspicuous stands out and is easy to see or notice

conspiracy noun **conspiracies**
a plot to do something bad or illegal
conspirator noun

conspire verb conspires, conspiring, conspired
if people conspire, they plot together

constable noun constables
an ordinary member of the police

constant adjective
1 not changing; continual 2 a constant person is loyal and faithful **constancy** noun constancy is being loyal and faithful **constantly** adverb continually, all the time *They are constantly complaining.*

constellation noun constellations
a group of stars that you can see in the sky at night

constipated adjective
someone is constipated when they cannot empty their bowels easily to get rid of the waste in their body **constipation** noun

constituency noun constituencies
a district of the country that chooses its own Member of Parliament

constituent noun constituents
1 a part of something 2 someone who lives in the district of a particular Member of Parliament

constitute verb constitutes, constituting, constituted
to constitute something is to form it or make it up *50 states constitute the USA.*

constitution noun constitutions
1 the set of principles or laws by which a country is governed 2 a person's condition or state of health **constitutional** adjective

construct verb constructs, constructing, constructed
to construct something is to build it

construction noun constructions
1 construction is the process of building 2 a construction is something that someone has built

constructive adjective
helpful and positive *Their criticism was very constructive.*

consul noun consuls
an official representative of one country, living in another country

consult verb consults, consulting, consulted
to consult a person or book is to look for information or advice **consultation** noun

consultant noun consultants
1 a person who provides professional advice 2 a senior hospital doctor

consume verb consumes, consuming, consumed
1 to consume food or drink is to eat or drink it 2 to consume something is to use it up or destroy it *The building was consumed by fire.*

consumer noun consumers
someone who buys goods or services

consumption noun
the using up of food or fuel *The consumption of oil has increased.*

contact noun contacts
1 contact is touching someone or something 2 contact is also communication *I've lost contact with my uncle.* 3 a contact is a person you communicate with

contact verb contacts, contacting, contacted
to contact someone is to get in touch with them

contact lens noun contact lenses
a small plastic lens worn against the eyeball instead of glasses

contagious (say kon-**tay**-jus) adjective
you catch a contagious disease by having contact with people or things that are already infected with it

contain verb contains, containing, contained
to contain something is to have it inside *This book contains a great deal of information.*

container noun containers
1 something that is designed to contain things 2 a large box-shaped container for taking goods abroad by sea

a b c d e f g h i j k l m n o p q r s t u v w x y z

111

A
B
C
D
E
F
G
H
I
J
K
L
M
N
O
P
Q
R
S
T
U
V
W
X
Y
Z

contaminate verb contaminates, contaminating, contaminated
to contaminate something is to make it dirty or impure **contamination** noun

contemplate verb contemplates, contemplating, contemplated
1 to contemplate something is to look hard at it or think about it **2** to contemplate doing something is to plan or intend to do it **contemplation** noun

contemporary adjective
1 people or things are contemporary when they belong to the same time *Florence Nightingale was contemporary with Queen Victoria.* **2** modern or up to date *We like contemporary music.*

contempt noun
a feeling of strong disapproval when you despise someone or something **contemptible** adjective someone or something is contemptible when people strongly disapprove of them or despise them

contemptuous adjective
to be contemptuous of someone or something is to strongly disapprove of them **contemptuously** adverb

contend verb contends, contending, contended
1 to contend is to struggle or compete **2** to contend something is to state or claim it *I contend that we've been treated unfairly.* **contender** noun someone who takes part in a competition

content[1] (say **kon**-tent) noun
1 the amount of a substance that there is in something *Drink milk with a low fat content.* **2** the content of a book, magazine, or piece of writing is what you read in it

content[2] (say kon-**tent**) adjective
happy and willing *Are you content to stay behind?* **contentment** noun

contented (say kon-**tent**-id) adjective
happy and satisfied *After his big dinner he looked very contented.*

contents (say kon-tents) plural noun
1 the contents of a box or other container are what is inside it **2** the contents of a book or magazine are the things you read in it

contest (say kon-test) noun contests
a competition

contest (say kon-**test**) verb contests, contesting, contested
to contest something is to argue about it *After her death, relatives contested her will.*

contestant (say kon-**test**-ant) noun contestants
someone who takes part in a contest or competition

context noun contexts
the context of a word or phrase is the words that come before or after it and help to tell you what it means

continent noun continents
one of the main masses of land in the world, which are Africa, Antarctica, Asia, Oceania, Europe, North America, and South America **the Continent** the mainland of Europe from the point of view of people living in Britain *Please see illustration on following page.*

continental adjective
on a continent, especially Europe from the point of view of people living in Britain *We thought we'd have a continental holiday this year.*

continual adjective
happening repeatedly *I get fed up with his continual shouting.* **continually** adverb

continue verb continues, continuing, continued
to continue something, or to continue to do something, is to go on doing it **continuation** noun

continuity noun
the process of going on without any breaks or changes

continuous adjective
going on all the time; without a break *We*

continent

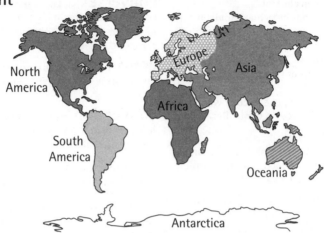

North America

Europe

Asia

Africa

South America

Oceania

Antarctica

could hear a *continuous hum from the fridge*.
continuously adverb

contour noun **contours**
1 the contour of something is its shape or outline **2** a line on a map joining points that are the same height above sea level

contract (say **kon**-trakt) noun
contracts
a legal agreement
contract (say kon-**trakt**) verb
contracts, contracting, contracted
1 to contract is to become smaller *Heated metal contracts as it cools.* **2** to contract to do something is to make a contract about it **3** to contract an illness is to catch it *She contracted pneumonia.* **contraction** noun

contradict verb **contradicts, contradicting, contradicted**
to contradict someone or something is to say they are wrong or untrue
contradiction noun

contraption noun **contraptions**
a clumsy or strange-looking device or machine

contrary adjective
1 (say **kon**-tra-ri) one thing is contrary to another when they are opposites or contradict one another *The two sisters had*
contrary views about computer games.
2 (say kon-**trair**-i) someone who is contrary is obstinate and difficult to deal with *Mary, Mary, quite contrary*. **on the contrary** the opposite is true *'Are you pleased?' 'On the contrary, I'm very annoyed.'*

contrast (say kon-**trahst**) verb
contrasts, contrasting, contrasted
1 to contrast two things is to show they are different **2** one thing contrasts with another when it is clearly different
contrast (say **kon**-trahst) noun
contrasts
1 the action of contrasting **2** a clear difference **3** the amount of difference between colours or tones

contribute verb **contributes, contributing, contributed**
1 to contribute to something is to give money to help it **2** to contribute to a result is to help cause it *His tiredness contributed to the accident*. **contribution** noun
contributor noun

contrive verb **contrives, contriving, contrived**
1 to contrive something is to plan or invent it in a clever way **2** to contrive to do something is to manage to do it though it is probably foolish or dangerous *He contrived to get stuck in the lift near the fifth floor.*

a
b
c
d
e
f
g
h
i
j
k
l
m
n
o
p
q
r
s
t
u
v
w
x
y
z

113

A
B
C
D
E
F
G
H
I
J
K
L
M
N
O
P
Q
R
S
T
U
V
W
X
Y
Z

control noun controls
1 control is the power to make someone or something do what you want **2** the controls of a machine are the switches and levers that make it work
control verb controls, controlling, controlled
to control something or someone is to have power over what they do **controller** noun

controversial adjective
a controversial action or statement is one that is likely to cause people to have strong opinions and disagree about it

controversy (say **kon**-tro-ver-si or kon-**trov**-er-si) noun controversies
a long argument or disagreement

convalescent adjective
recovering from an illness **convalescence** noun

convenience noun conveniences
1 convenience is usefulness and comfort **2** a convenience is something that is useful, such as central heating **3** a convenience is also a public lavatory

convenient adjective
easy to use or reach **conveniently** adverb

convent noun convents
a group of buildings where nuns live and work

convention noun conventions
an accepted way of doing things

conventional adjective
done in the accepted way; usual, traditional **conventionally** adverb

converge verb converges, converging, converged
to converge is to come together *The two roads converge at the pub. Thousands of fans converged on the football ground.*

conversation noun conversations
conversation, or a conversation, is when you talk to someone for a while **conversational** adjective

converse[1] (say kon-**verss**) verb
converses, conversing, conversed
to converse is to talk together *They conversed in low voices.*

converse[2] (say **kon**-verss) noun
the converse of something is the opposite of it

conversion noun conversions
conversion, or a conversion, is changing or converting something

convert (say kon-**vert**) verb converts, converting, converted
1 to convert something is to change it for a new purpose **2** to convert someone is to persuade them to change their religion or beliefs **3** (in rugby football) to convert a try is to kick a goal after scoring

convert (say **kon**-vert) noun converts
someone who has changed their beliefs **convertible** adjective something is convertible when it can be changed from one form or shape to another

convex adjective
a convex surface is curved like the outside of a circle or ball (the opposite of *concave*)

convey verb conveys, conveying, conveyed
1 to convey someone or something is to take them somewhere **2** to convey a message or idea is to get someone to understand it

conveyor belt noun conveyor belts
a long belt or chain for carrying goods in a factory

convict (say kon-**vikt**) noun convicts
a criminal in a prison
convict (say kon-**vikt**) verb convicts, convicting, convicted
to convict someone of a crime is to decide at their trial that they are guilty of it and punish them

conviction noun convictions
1 being convicted of a crime **2** being convinced of something; a strong opinion

convince verb convinces, convincing, convinced
to convince someone is to persuade them about something

convoy noun convoys
a group of ships or vehicles travelling together

cook verb cooks, cooking, cooked
to cook food is to make it ready to eat by heating it
cook noun cooks
someone who cooks, especially as their job

cooker noun cookers
a device with an oven and hot surfaces for cooking food

cookery noun
the art or skill of cooking food

cool adjective cooler, coolest
1 not very warm; fairly cold 2 a cool person is calm and not easily excited 3 (informal) good or fashionable *He looks cool in those glasses.* **coolly** adverb calmly **coolness** noun
cool verb cools, cooling, cooled
1 to cool something is to make it cool 2 to cool is to become cool

coop noun coops
a cage for poultry

cooperate verb cooperates, cooperating, cooperated
to cooperate with people is to work helpfully with them **cooperative** adjective

cooperation noun
1 cooperation is working together to achieve something 2 you give someone your cooperation when you do what they ask and help them

coordinate (say koh-**or**-din-ayt) verb coordinates, coordinating, coordinated
to coordinate people or things is to get them to work well together
coordinate (say koh-**or**-din-at) noun coordinates
two numbers or letters used to show the position of something on a graph or map *The coordinates of point P are (4,2).*

coordination noun
1 coordination is organizing people or things so that they work well together 2 the coordination of parts of your body, for example your hands and your eyes, is making them help each other and work well together

coot noun coots
a water bird with a hard white plate on its forehead

cop noun cops (informal)
a police officer

cope verb copes, coping, coped
to cope with something awkward or difficult is to deal with it successfully

copper noun coppers
1 copper is a reddish-brown metal used for making wire and pipes 2 copper is also a reddish-brown colour 3 a copper is a coin made of copper or bronze 4 (informal) a copper is a police officer

copy noun copies
1 something made to look exactly like something else 2 something written out a second time 3 one newspaper, magazine, or book *We each have a copy of 'Alice in Wonderland'.*
copy verb copies, copying, copied
1 to copy something is to make a copy of it 2 to copy someone is to do the same as them 3 to copy a computer file or program or piece of text is to make another one that is exactly the same, usually one that you store somewhere else **copier** noun a machine for copying pages

coral noun
coral is a hard substance made of the skeletons of tiny sea creatures

cord noun cords
a cord is a piece of thin rope

cordial adjective
warm and friendly *We got a cordial welcome.* **cordially** adverb
cordial noun cordials
a sweet drink

a
b
c
d
e
f
g
h
i
j
k
l
m
n
o
p
q
r
s
t
u
v
w
x
y
z

115

corduroy (say **kor**-der-oi) noun
thick cotton cloth with ridges along it

core noun cores
the part in the middle of something

corgi noun corgis
a small breed of dog with short legs and large upright ears

cork noun corks
1 cork is the lightweight bark of a kind of oak tree 2 a cork is a piece of this bark used to close a bottle

corkscrew noun corkscrews
1 a device for removing corks from bottles 2 a spiral

cormorant noun cormorants
a large black sea bird

corn[1] noun
grain *a field of corn*

corn[2] noun corns
a small hard lump on your toe or foot

corned beef noun
tinned beef preserved with salt

corner noun corners
1 the point where two lines, roads, or walls meet 2 a kick from the corner of a football field; a hit from the corner of a hockey field

corner verb corners, cornering, cornered
1 to corner someone is to trap them *The police cornered the escaped prisoner.* 2 to corner is to go round a corner *The car cornered slowly and accelerated up the road.*

cornet noun cornets
1 a long cone-shaped biscuit open at the top for ice cream 2 a musical instrument like a trumpet

cornfield noun cornfields
a field where corn grows

cornflakes plural noun
toasted maize flakes eaten for breakfast

cornflour noun
fine flour used for making puddings

cornflower noun cornflowers
a blue wild flower

corny adjective cornier, corniest (informal)
a corny joke is one that is feeble and often repeated

coronation noun coronations
the ceremony of crowning a king or queen

coroner noun coroners
an official who holds an inquiry into the cause of an unnatural death

corporal noun corporals
a soldier just below sergeant in rank

corporal adjective
to do with the human body

corporal punishment noun
punishment by hitting or beating someone

corporation noun corporations
a group of people elected to govern a town

corps (say kor) noun corps
1 a large unit of soldiers 2 a special army unit *He is in the Medical Corps.*

corpse noun corpses
a dead body

corral (say ko-**rahl**) noun corrals
an enclosure for horses or cattle

correct adjective
1 true or accurate; without any mistakes *Your answers are all correct.* 2 proper, suitable *Is that the correct way to talk to your parents?* **correctly** adverb

correct verb corrects, correcting, corrected
to correct a piece of work is to mark the mistakes in it, or to put them right

correction noun corrections
1 correction is correcting something 2 a correction is a change made to something in order to correct it

correspond verb corresponds, corresponding, corresponded
1 to correspond with something is to agree with it or match it *Your story corresponds*

A B C D E F G H I J K L M N O P Q R S T U V W X Y Z

with what I heard. **2** to correspond with someone is to exchange letters with them

correspondence noun
1 similarity or agreement **2** letters or writing letters

correspondent noun
correspondents
1 someone who writes letters **2** someone employed to send news or articles to a newspaper or television channel

corridor noun corridors
1 a long narrow passage from which doors open into rooms or compartments **2** a route an aircraft follows

corrode verb corrodes, corroding, corroded
to corrode is to wear away by rust or be eaten away by a chemical **corrosion** noun

corrugated adjective
shaped into folds or ridges *The roof was made of corrugated iron.*

corrupt adjective
a corrupt person is dishonest in carrying out their responsibilities or duties, for example by taking bribes

corrupt verb
1 to corrupt someone is to make them dishonest, especially when they have important responsibilities **2** in a computer, a bug or other problem corrupts a file when it makes it impossible to read or use

corruption noun
corruption is dishonest behaviour by people who are in authority or have important responsibilities

corset noun corsets
a tight piece of underwear worn round the hips and waist

cosmetics plural noun
substances like lipstick and face powder, for making the skin or hair look beautiful or different

cosmic (say **koz**-mik) adjective
to do with the universe

cosmonaut noun cosmonauts
a Russian astronaut

cost verb costs, costing, cost
to cost a certain amount is to have that amount as its price *The book only cost £5 last year.*

cost noun costs
what you have to spend to do or get something *the cost of admission to the zoo* **at all costs** or **at any cost** no matter what the cost or difficulty may be

costly adjective costlier, costliest
expensive

costume noun costumes
clothes, especially for a particular purpose or of a particular period

cosy adjective cosier, cosiest
warm and comfortable

cot noun cots
a baby's bed with high sides

cottage noun cottages
a small house, especially in the country

cotton noun
1 a soft white substance covering the seeds of a tropical plant **2** thread made from this substance **3** cloth made from cotton thread

couch noun couches
a long soft seat or sofa

couch potato noun couch potatoes
(informal)
a person who spends a lot of time watching television

cough (say kof) verb coughs, coughing, coughed
to cough is to push air suddenly out of your lungs with a harsh noise

cough noun coughs
1 the action or sound of coughing **2** an illness which makes you cough a lot

could
past tense of **can**[1] *Jamie could feel his heart thumping.*

couldn't
short for *could not*

council noun councils
a group of people chosen to organize or discuss something, especially to plan the affairs of a town

councillor noun councillors
a member of a council

counsel noun counsels
1 advice 2 the barrister or barristers involved in a case in a law court

counsel verb counsels, counselling, counselled
to counsel someone is to give them advice

counsellor noun counsellors
someone who gives advice, especially as their job

count[1] verb counts, counting, counted
1 to count is to use numbers to find out how many people or things there are in a place 2 to count or count out is to say numbers in their proper order 3 to count someone or something is to include them in a total *There are 30 in the class, counting the teacher.* 4 to count is to have a particular value or importance *Playing well counts a lot even if you lose.* **to count on someone** or **something** is to rely on them

count noun counts
1 the total reached by counting 2 one of the things that someone is accused of *He was found guilty on all counts.*

count[2] noun counts
a foreign nobleman

countable adjective
able to be counted

countdown noun countdowns
a counting down to 0, especially before launching a rocket

countenance noun countenances
someone's face or the expression on their face

counter noun counters
1 a long table where customers are served in a shop or cafe 2 a small plastic disc used in board games

counterfeit (say **kown**-ter-fit) adjective
faked to deceive or swindle people *They were using counterfeit money.*

countess noun countesses
the wife or widow of a count or earl; a female earl

countless adjective
too many to count; very many

country noun countries
1 a country is a part of the world where a particular nation of people lives 2 the country is the countryside

countryman or **countrywoman**
noun countrymen, countrywomen
1 a man or woman who lives in the countryside 2 a fellow countryman is someone who lives in the same country

countryside noun
an area with fields, woods, and villages, away from towns

county noun counties
one of the areas that a country is divided into, for example Kent in England, Fife in Scotland, and Powys in Wales

couple noun couples
a couple is two people or things

couple verb couples, coupling, coupled
to couple things is to join them together

coupon noun coupons
a piece of paper that gives you the right to receive or do something

courage noun
being courageous

courageous adjective
ready to face danger or pain

courgette noun courgettes
a kind of vegetable like a small marrow

courier (say **koor**-i-er) noun couriers
1 someone who carries a message

2 someone employed to guide and help people on holiday, especially abroad

course noun **courses**
1 the direction in which something moves along *The ship's course was to the west.* **2** a series of lessons or exercises in learning something *My Mum's starting a cookery course at last.* **3** a part of a meal, such as the meat course or the pudding course **4** a racecourse or golf course **in due course** eventually; at the right time **in the course of something** while it is happening **of course** naturally; certainly *Of course they will help us. 'Will you help us?' 'Of course!'*

court noun **courts**
1 a law court **2** an enclosed place for games like tennis or netball **3** a courtyard **4** the place where a king or queen lives **5** the people who are usually at a king's or queen's court
court verb **courts, courting, courted**
to court someone is to try to win their love or support

courteous (say **ker**-ti-us) adjective
friendly and polite towards other people
courteously adverb **courtesy** noun

court martial noun **courts martial**
1 a court for trying offenders against military law **2** a trial in this court

courtship noun
courting someone, especially a boyfriend or girlfriend

courtyard noun **courtyards**
a paved area surrounded by walls or buildings

cousin noun **cousins**
your cousin is a child of your uncle or aunt

cove noun **coves**
a small bay

cover verb **covers, covering, covered**
1 to cover something is to put something else over it to hide or protect it **2** to cover a distance is to travel over it *We managed to cover ten miles a day.* **3** to cover a subject is to deal with or include it *This book covers* everything you need to know about football. **4** to cover something is to be enough money for it *I expect £2 will cover my fare.* **5** to cover someone is to aim a gun at or near them *I've got you covered.* **to cover something up** is to make sure no one knows about something wrong or illegal

cover noun **covers**
1 a cover is something used for covering something else; a lid or wrapper **2** cover is a place where someone can hide or take shelter

coverage noun
the amount of time or space given to reporting an event on radio, on television, or in a newspaper

cover-up noun **cover-ups**
a cover-up is when people in power prevent other people knowing about something wrong or illegal *The government were accused of a cover-up of their mistakes.*

cow noun **cows**
a large female animal kept by farmers for its milk and beef

coward noun **cowards**
someone who has no courage and runs away from danger and difficulties
cowardice noun **cowardly** adjective

cowboy noun **cowboys**
1 a man who rides round looking after the cattle on a large farm in America **2** (informal) a person who uses dishonest methods in business, especially in building

cowslip noun **cowslips**
a wild plant that has yellow flowers in spring

cox noun **coxes**
someone who steers a racing boat

coy adjective
shy; pretending to be shy or modest
coyly adverb

crab noun **crabs**
a shellfish with ten legs

crab apple noun **crab apples**
a small sour apple

A
B
C
D
E
F
G
H
I
J
K
L
M
N
O
P
Q
R
S
T
U
V
W
X
Y
Z

crack noun **cracks**
1 a line on the surface of something where it has broken but not come completely apart; a narrow gap *There's a crack in this cup.* **2** a sudden sharp noise *They heard the crack of a pistol shot.* **3** a sudden sharp blow *He got a crack on the head.*

crack verb **cracks, cracking, cracked**
1 to crack something is to make a crack in it **2** something cracks when it splits without breaking *The plate has cracked.* **3** to crack is to make a sudden sharp noise **4** to crack a joke is to tell it

cracker noun **crackers**
1 a pretty paper tube with a small gift inside it, which bangs when two people pull it apart **2** a thin biscuit

crackle verb **crackles, crackling, crackled**
to make small cracking sounds, like a fire

crackling noun
the hard skin of roast pork

cradle noun **cradles**
1 a cot for a baby **2** a supporting frame for something

craft noun **crafts**
1 a craft is an activity which needs skill with the hands **2** a boat **3** craft is cunning or trickery

craftsman or **craftswoman**
noun **craftsmen, craftswomen**
someone who is skilled at making things with the hands **craftsmanship** noun the skill of a craftsman or craftswoman

crafty adjective **craftier, craftiest**
cunning and clever **craftily** adverb **craftiness** noun

crag noun **crags**
a steep piece of rough rock **craggy** adjective

cram verb **crams, cramming, crammed**
1 to cram things is to force them into a small space **2** to cram is to study very hard for an examination

cramp noun **cramps**
pain caused by a muscle tightening suddenly

cramp verb **cramps, cramping, cramped**
to cramp someone is to restrict their freedom or growth

cramped adjective
in a space that is too small or tight *We felt very cramped sleeping three in the same room.*

crane noun **cranes**
1 a large machine for lifting and moving heavy objects **2** a large bird with long legs and neck

crane verb **cranes, craning, craned**
to crane your neck is to stretch it so that you can see something

crane–fly noun **crane-flies**
an insect with long thin legs

crank noun **cranks**
1 an L-shaped rod used to turn or control something **2** a person with weird or unusual ideas

cranky adjective **crankier, crankiest**
weird or unusual

cranny noun **crannies**
a crevice; a narrow hole or space

crash noun **crashes**
1 the loud noise of something falling or breaking **2** a collision between road vehicles, causing damage

crash verb **crashes, crashing, crashed**
1 to crash is to collide or fall violently **2** to crash a vehicle is to have a crash while driving it **3** to crash along or through something is to move violently and loudly

crash helmet noun **crash helmets**
a padded helmet worn by cyclists and motorcyclists

crate noun **crates**
a container in which goods are transported

crater noun craters
1 the mouth of a volcano 2 a hole in the ground made by a bomb

crave verb craves, craving, craved
to crave something is to want it very badly

crawl verb crawls, crawling, crawled
1 to crawl is to move along on your hands and knees 2 to crawl is also to move slowly in a vehicle 3 to be crawling with something unpleasant is to be full of it or covered in it *This room's crawling with cockroaches.*

crawl noun
1 a crawling movement 2 a powerful swimming stroke with the arms hitting the water alternately

crayon noun crayons
a coloured pencil for drawing or writing

craze noun crazes
a brief enthusiasm for something

crazy adjective crazier, craziest
mad or weird **crazily** adverb **craziness** noun

creak noun creaks
a sound like the noise made by a stiff door opening

creak verb creaks, creaking, creaked
to make a creak **creaky** adjective

cream noun creams
1 the rich fatty part of milk 2 a yellow-white colour 3 a food containing or looking like cream 4 something that looks like cream, for example face cream
creamy adjective

crease noun creases
1 a line made in something by folding or pressing it 2 a line on a cricket pitch showing where the batsman should stand

crease verb creases, creasing, creased
to crease something is to make a crease in it

create verb creates, creating, created
to create something is to make it exist
creation noun

creative adjective
showing imagination and thought as well

as skill *The older children have started some creative writing.* **creativity** noun

creator noun creators
someone who creates something

creature noun creatures
a living animal or person

crèche (say kresh) noun crèches
a place where babies or small children are looked after while their parents are busy

credit noun
1 honour or approval *Give her credit for her honesty.* 2 a system of allowing someone to pay for something later on *Do you want cash now or can I have it on credit?* 3 an amount of money in an account at a bank or building society **credits** the list of people who have helped to produce a film, television programme, etc.

credit verb credits, crediting, credited
1 to credit something is to believe it *Can you credit that?* 2 to credit someone with something is to enter it as a credit in their bank account *We will credit you with a £50 refund.*

creditable adjective
deserving praise

credit card noun credit cards
a card allowing someone to buy goods on credit

creed noun creeds
a set or statement of beliefs

creek noun creeks
1 a narrow inlet 2 (in Australia, New Zealand, or America) a small stream

creep verb creeps, creeping, crept
1 to creep is to move along with the body close to the ground 2 to creep about is to move quietly or secretly **to creep up on someone** is to go up to them quietly from behind

creep noun creeps
1 a creeping movement 2 (informal) a nasty or unpleasant person **the creeps** (informal) a feeling of fear or disgust

121

A
B
C
D
E
F
G
H
I
J
K
L
M
N
O
P
Q
R
S
T
U
V
W
X
Y
Z

creeper noun creepers
a plant that grows close to the ground or up walls

creepy adjective creepier, creepiest (informal)
weird and slightly frightening

cremate verb cremates, cremating, cremated
to cremate a dead body is to burn it into fine ashes instead of burying it
cremation noun

crematorium (say krem-a-**tor**-i-um) noun crematoria
a place where dead bodies are cremated

crêpe (say krayp) noun crêpes
1 cloth or paper with a wrinkled surface 2 a kind of thin French pancake

crept
past tense and past participle of creep verb
He got up and crept down the stairs. An angry look had crept into his face.

crescent noun crescents
1 a narrow curved shape, pointed at both ends, like a new moon 2 a curved street

cress noun
a green plant used in salads and sandwiches

crest noun crests
1 a tuft of hair, feathers, or skin on an animal's head 2 the top of a hill or wave

crevice noun crevices
a crack in rock or in a wall

crew noun crews
the people who work on a ship or aircraft

crib noun cribs
1 a baby's cot 2 a framework containing fodder for animals

crib verb cribs, cribbing, cribbed
to crib someone else's work is to copy it

cricket[1] noun
a game played outdoors by two teams with a ball, two bats, and two wickets
cricketer noun

cricket[2] noun crickets
an insect like a grasshopper

cried
past tense and past participle of cry verb
'Look out!' cried Tom. After he had cried a long time, he wiped his eyes.

crime noun crimes
an act that breaks the law

criminal noun criminals
someone who has committed one or more crimes

criminal adjective
to do with crime or criminals

crimson noun, adjective
a dark red colour

crinkle verb crinkles, crinkling, crinkled
to crinkle something is to crease or wrinkle it **crinkly** adjective

cripple verb cripples, crippling, crippled
1 to cripple someone is to make them unable to walk properly 2 to cripple something is to damage it so it will not work properly

crisis (say **kry**-sis) noun crises
an important or difficult time or situation

crisp adjective crisper, crispest
1 very dry so that it breaks easily 2 firm and fresh *I'd like a nice crisp apple.* 3 cold and frosty *We woke up to a crisp winter morning.*

crisp noun crisps
a thin fried slice of potato, sold in packets

criss-cross adjective, adverb
with crossing lines

critic noun critics
1 a person who criticizes someone or something 2 someone who gives opinions on books, plays, films, music, or other performances

critical adjective
1 criticizing 2 to do with critics or criticism 3 serious, amounting to a crisis **critically** adverb in a critical way; seriously

criticism (say krit-i-si-zum) noun
criticisms
an opinion or judgement about something,
usually pointing out its faults

criticize (say krit-i-syz) verb criticizes,
criticizing, criticized
to criticize something or someone is to give
an opinion pointing out their faults

croak noun croaks
a deep sound, like a frog makes

croak verb croaks, croaking, croaked
to make a croak

crochet (say kroh-shay) noun
a kind of needlework done with a
hooked needle

crock noun crocks
1 a large pot made out of clay 2 (informal)
an old or worn-out person or thing

crockery noun
dishes, plates, and cups and saucers used
for eating

crocodile noun crocodiles
a large reptile living in hot countries, with a
thick skin, long tail, and huge jaws

crocodile tears plural noun
sorrow that is not genuine

crocus noun crocuses
a small spring flower that is yellow, purple,
or white

croft noun crofts
a small farm in Scotland **crofter** noun

croissant (say krwa-sahn) noun
croissants
a crescent-shaped roll of rich pastry,
first made in France and usually eaten
for breakfast

crook noun crooks
1 (informal) someone who cheats or robs
people; a criminal 2 a shepherd's or bishop's
stick with a curved end

crooked (say kruuk-id) adjective
1 bent or twisted 2 (informal) dishonest
or criminal

croon verb croons, crooning, crooned
to croon is to sing softly or sentimentally

crop noun crops
1 something grown for food, especially in a
field *They had a good crop of wheat last year.*
2 a riding whip with a loop instead of a lash

crop verb crops, cropping, cropped
to crop something is to cut or bite the top
off it *They could see sheep in a field, cropping
the grass.* **to crop up** is to happen or appear
unexpectedly

cross noun crosses
1 a mark or shape like + or x 2 an upright
post with another post across it 3 an animal
produced by mixing one breed with another
*A mule is a cross between a donkey and
a horse.*

cross verb crosses, crossing, crossed
1 to cross something is to go across it *She
crossed the room to meet him.* 2 to cross
your fingers or legs is to put one over
the other **to cross something out** is to
draw a line across something because it is
unwanted or wrong

cross adjective
1 angry or bad-tempered 2 going from one
side to another *There were cross winds on the
bridge.* **crossly** adverb **crossness** noun

crossbar noun crossbars
a horizontal bar between two upright bars

crossbow noun crossbows
a kind of bow used for shooting arrows,
held like a gun and fired by pulling a trigger

cross-country noun
a running race through fields and country

cross-examine verb
cross-examines, cross-examining,
cross-examined
to cross-examine someone is to
question them about information
they have given, usually in a law court
cross-examination noun

cross-eyed adjective
having eyes that appear to look in
different directions

a
b
c
d
e
f
g
h
i
j
k
l
m
n
o
p
q
r
s
t
u
v
w
x
y
z

crossing noun crossings
a place where people can cross a road or railway

cross-legged adverb, adjective
having crossed legs

crossroads noun crossroads
a place where two or more roads cross one another

cross-section noun cross-sections
1 a drawing of something as if it has been cut through 2 a sample that includes all the different types of something *A cross-section of parents said they wanted an after-school club.*

crosswise adverb, adjective
with one thing crossing another

crossword noun crosswords
a puzzle with blank squares in which you put the letters of words worked out from clues

crotchet (say **kroch**-it) noun crotchets
a musical note equal to half a minim, written ♩

crouch verb crouches, crouching, crouched
to crouch is to lower your body, with your arms and legs bent

crow noun crows
a large black bird **as the crow flies** in a straight line

crow verb crows, crowing, crowed
1 to make a noise like a cock 2 to boast; to be proudly triumphant

crowbar noun crowbars
an iron bar used as a lever

crowd noun crowds
a large number of people in one place

crowd verb crowds, crowding, crowded
1 to crowd or crowd round is to form a crowd 2 to crowd a place is to make it uncomfortably full of people *The town is crowded with tourists in summer.*

crown noun crowns
1 a crown is an ornamental headdress worn by a king or queen 2 the crown is the king or queen of a country *This land belongs to the crown.* 3 the top of the head 4 the middle part of a road, which is higher than the sides

crown verb crowns, crowning, crowned
1 to crown someone is to make them king or queen 2 to crown something is to form the top of it 3 to crown an achievement is to finish it happily *Their efforts were crowned with success.*

crow's-nest noun crow's-nests
a lookout position at the top of a ship's mast

crucial (say kroo-shal) adjective
extremely important

crucifix noun crucifixes
a model of the Cross or of Christ on the Cross

crucify verb crucifies, crucifying, crucified
to crucify someone is to execute them by fixing their hands and feet to a cross and leaving them to die. The Romans used this method of executing criminals. **crucifixion** noun

crude adjective cruder, crudest
1 natural; not purified *The country exported crude oil.* 2 rough and simple *They stayed in a crude hut in the mountains.* 3 rude or dirty *The boys were telling each other crude jokes.*

cruel adjective crueller, cruellest
causing pain and suffering to others *They were ruled by a cruel tyrant. War is cruel.* **cruelly** adverb **cruelty** noun

cruise noun cruises
a holiday on a ship, usually visiting different places

cruise verb cruises, cruising, cruised
1 to cruise is to sail or travel at a gentle speed 2 to cruise is also to have a cruise on a ship

cruiser noun cruisers
1 a fast warship 2 a large motor boat

A B **C** D E F G H I J K L M N O P Q R S T U V W X Y Z

crumb noun crumbs
a tiny piece of bread or cake

crumble verb crumbles, crumbling, crumbled
1 to crumble something is to break it into small pieces 2 to crumble is to be broken into small pieces **crumbly** adjective

crumpet noun crumpets
a soft flat cake made with yeast, toasted and eaten with butter

crumple verb crumples, crumpling, crumpled
1 to crumple something is to make it creased 2 to crumple is to become creased

crunch noun crunches
the noise made by chewing hard food or walking on gravel

crunch verb crunches, crunching, crunched
to crunch something is to chew or crush it with a crunch **crunchy** adjective

crusade noun crusades
1 a military expedition to Palestine made by Christians in the Middle Ages 2 a campaign against something that you think is bad **crusader** noun

crush verb crushes, crushing, crushed
1 to crush something is to press it so that it gets broken or damaged 2 to crush an enemy is to defeat them

crush noun crushes
1 a crowd; a crowded place
2 a fruit-flavoured drink 3 (informal) a sudden liking you have for someone

crust noun crusts
1 the hard outside part of something, especially of a loaf 2 the rocky outer part of a planet

crustacean (say krus-**tay**-shan) noun crustaceans
a shellfish

crutch noun crutches
a stick that fits under the arm, used as a support in walking

cry verb cries, crying, cried
1 to cry is to shout 2 to cry is also to let tears fall from your eyes

cry noun cries
1 a loud shout 2 a period of weeping

crypt noun crypts
a large room underneath a church

crystal noun crystals
1 a clear mineral rather like glass
2 a small solid piece of a substance with a symmetrical shape, such as snow and ice **crystalline** adjective

crystallize verb crystallizes, crystallizing, crystallized
to form into crystals

cub noun cubs
a young animal, especially a lion, tiger, fox, or bear **Cub** a junior Scout

cube noun cubes
1 an object that has six square sides, like a box or dice 2 the result of multiplying something by itself twice *The cube of 3 is 3 x 3 x 3 = 27.*

cube verb cubes, cubing, cubed
1 to cube a number is to multiply it by itself twice *4 cubed is 4 x 4 x 4 = 64.* 2 to cube something is to cut it into small cubes

cube root noun cube roots
a number that gives another number if it is multiplied by itself twice *2 is the cube root of 8.*

cubic adjective
1 shaped like a cube 2 a cubic metre or foot is the volume of a cube with sides that are one metre or foot long

cubicle noun cubicles
a small division of a room

cuboid noun cuboids
an object with six rectangular sides

cuckoo noun cuckoos
a bird that makes a sound like 'cuck-oo', and lays its eggs in other birds' nests

cucumber noun cucumbers
a long green vegetable, eaten raw

a
b
c
d
e
f
g
h
i
j
k
l
m
n
o
p
q
r
s
t
u
v
w
x
y
z

A B **C** D E F G H I J K L M N O P Q R S T U V W X Y Z

cud noun
half-digested food that a cow brings back from its first stomach to chew again

cuddle verb cuddles, cuddling, cuddled
to cuddle someone is to put your arms closely round them and squeeze them in a loving way **cuddly** adjective a cuddly person or thing is nice to cuddle

cue¹ noun cues
something that tells an actor when to start speaking or come on the stage

cue² noun cues
a long stick used to strike the ball in billiards or snooker

cuff noun cuffs
1 the end of a sleeve that fits round your wrist 2 a blow given to someone with your hand

cuff verb cuffs, cuffing, cuffed
to cuff someone is to hit them with the hand

cul-de-sac noun cul-de-sacs
a street that is closed at one end

culminate verb culminates, culminating, culminated
to reach the end or the most important part *Their long struggle for freedom culminated in victory.* **culmination** noun

culprit noun culprits
someone who is to blame for something

cult noun cults
1 a religion 2 being extremely keen on someone or something *The TV series is a bit of a cult now.*

cultivate verb cultivates, cultivating, cultivated
1 to cultivate land is to grow crops on it 2 to cultivate something is to try to make it grow or develop **cultivation** noun

cultivated adjective
having good manners and education

cultural adjective
a cultural activity is one to do with education and learning

culture noun cultures
1 culture is the development of the mind by education and learning 2 a culture is the customs and traditions of a people *They were studying Greek culture.*

cunning adjective
clever at deceiving people *Said the cunning Spider to the Fly, 'Dear Friend, what can I do, / To prove the warm affection I've always felt for you?'* – Mary Howitt, The Spider and the Fly

cup noun cups
1 a small container with a handle, from which you drink liquid 2 a prize in the form of a silver cup, usually with two handles

cup verb cups, cupping, cupped
to cup your hands is to form them into the shape of a cup *John lifted up one of the eggs, cupping it carefully in his hands.* – Alexander McCall Smith, Akimbo and the Crocodile Man

cupboard (say **kub**-erd) noun cupboards
a compartment or piece of furniture with a door, for storing things

cupful noun cupfuls
as much as a cup will hold

curate (say **kewr**-at) noun curates
a member of the clergy who helps a vicar

curator (say kewr-**ay**-ter) noun curators
someone in charge of a museum or art gallery

curb verb curbs, curbing, curbed
to curb a feeling is to hold it back or hide it *You must curb your anger.*

curd noun curds
a thick substance formed when milk turns sour

curdle verb curdles, curdling, curdled
to curdle is to form into curds

cure verb cures, curing, cured
1 to cure someone who is ill is to make them better 2 to cure something bad is to stop it 3 to cure food is to treat it so as to preserve it *Fish can be cured in smoke.*

cure noun **cures**
something that cures a person or thing *They are still trying to find a cure for cancer.*

curfew noun **curfews**
a time or signal after which people must stay indoors until the next day

curiosity noun **curiosities**
1 curiosity is being curious **2** a curiosity is something strange or interesting

curious adjective
1 wanting to find out about things **2** strange or unusual *a curious kind of handwriting* **curiously** adverb

curl noun **curls**
a curve or coil, especially of hair

curl verb **curls, curling, curled**
to curl is to form into curls **to curl up** is to sit or lie with your knees drawn up

curly adjective **curlier, curliest**
full of curls

currant noun **currants**
1 a small black fruit made from dried grapes **2** a small juicy berry, or the bush that produces it

currency noun **currencies**
money that is in use in a place *You can pay with Russian currency.*

current noun **currents**
a flow of water, air, or electricity

current adjective
happening or used now **currently** adverb
now, at the moment *The admission charge is currently £10.*

curriculum noun **curriculums** or **curricula**
a course of study

curry noun **curries**
food cooked with spices that make it taste hot

curse noun **curses**
1 a call or prayer for someone to be harmed or killed **2** something very unpleasant **3** an angry word or words

curse verb **curses, cursing, cursed**
to curse someone is to use a curse against them

cursor noun **cursors**
a movable flashing signal on a computer screen, showing where new data will go

curtain noun **curtains**
a piece of material hung at a window or door, or at the front of a stage

curtsy noun **curtsies**
a bow made by bending the knees, done by women as a mark of respect

curtsy verb **curtsies, curtsying, curtsied**
to curtsy is to make a curtsy

curvature noun **curvatures**
a curving or bending, especially of the earth's horizon

curve noun **curves**
a line that bends smoothly

curve verb **curves, curving, curved**
to curve is to bend smoothly

cushion noun **cushions**
a fabric cover filled with soft material so that it is comfortable to sit on or rest against

cushion verb **cushions, cushioning, cushioned**
to cushion someone is to protect them from harm *When he fell down the stairs, the rug at the bottom cushioned his fall.*

custard noun
a sweet yellow sauce eaten with puddings

custom noun **customs**
1 the usual way of doing things *It is the custom to go on holiday in the summer.* **2** regular business from customers *That rude man at the corner shop won't get my custom any more.* **customs** are the group of officials at a port or airport to whom people coming into a country declare what goods they have with them

customary adjective
something that is customary is usually done or done according to a custom

a
b
c
d
e
f
g
h
i
j
k
l
m
n
o
p
q
r
s
t
u
v
w
x
y
z

customer noun customers
someone who uses a shop, bank, or business

customize noun customizes, customizing, customized
to customize something is to alter it for a special use

cut verb cuts, cutting, cut
1 to cut something is to divide it or make a slit in it with a knife or scissors 2 to cut something like prices or taxes is to reduce them 3 to cut a pack of playing cards is to divide it 4 to cut a corner is to go across it rather than round it 5 to cut a meeting or lesson is to stay away from it 6 a baby cuts a tooth when it has a new tooth coming **to cut and paste** is to remove text on a computer screen from one place and put it in another place **to cut someone off** is to interrupt them *She cut me off before I could finish my sentence.* **to cut something out** (informal) is to stop doing it *Cut out the talking!*

cut noun cuts
1 an act of cutting; the result of cutting *Your hair could do with a cut.* 2 a small wound caused by something sharp 3 (informal) a share *I want a cut of the profits.*

cute adjective cuter, cutest (informal)
attractive in a quaint or simple way

cutlass noun cutlasses
a short sword with a wide curved blade

cutlery noun
knives, forks, and spoons used for eating

cutlet noun cutlets
a thick slice of meat still on the bone

cut-out noun cut-outs
something cut out of paper or cardboard

cut-price adjective
sold at a reduced price

cutting noun cuttings
1 something cut from a newspaper or magazine 2 a piece cut off a plant to grow as a new plant 3 a deep passage cut through high ground for a railway or road

cycle noun cycles
1 a bicycle 2 a series of events that are regularly repeated *Rainfall is part of the water cycle.*

cycle verb cycles, cycling, cycled
to cycle is to ride a bicycle **cyclist** noun

cyclone noun cyclones
a strong wind rotating round a calm central area

cygnet (say **sig**-nit) noun cygnets
a young swan

cylinder noun cylinders
1 an object with straight sides and circular ends 2 part of an engine in which a piston moves

cylindrical adjective
shaped like a cylinder

cymbal noun cymbals
a cymbal is a round, slightly hollowed metal plate that you hit to make a ringing sound in music

cynic (say **sin**-ik) noun cynics
someone who doubts that anything is good or worthwhile **cynical** adjective

cypress noun cypresses
an evergreen tree with dark leaves

Dd

dab noun dabs
a gentle touch with something soft
dab verb dabs, dabbing, dabbed
to dab something is to touch it gently with something soft *I dabbed my eyes with a handkerchief.*

dabble verb dabbles, dabbling, dabbled
1 to dabble something is to splash it about in water 2 to dabble in something is to do it as a hobby or not very seriously *She likes to dabble in photography.*

dachshund (say **daks**-huund or **daks**-huunt) noun **dachshunds**
a small dog with a long body and short legs

dad noun **dads** (informal)
father

daddy noun **daddies** (informal)
father

daddy-long-legs noun **daddy-long-legs**
a crane-fly

daffodil noun **daffodils**
a yellow flower that grows from a bulb

daft adjective **dafter, daftest**
silly or stupid

dagger noun **daggers**
a short pointed knife, used as a weapon
daintily adverb **daintiness** noun

dahlia (say **day**-li-a) noun **dahlias**
a garden plant with
brightly-coloured flowers

daily adjective, adverb
something that happens daily happens
every day

dainty adjective **daintier, daintiest**
small and delicate **daintily** adverb
daintiness noun

dairy noun **dairies**
a place where milk, butter, cream, and
cheese are made or sold

daisy noun **daisies**
a small flower with white petals and a
yellow centre

dale noun **dales**
a valley

Dalmatian noun **Dalmatians**
a large dog that is white with black or
brown spots

dam noun **dams**
a wall built across a river to hold the
water back
dam verb **dams, damming, dammed**
to dam a river is to build a dam across it

damage verb **damages, damaging, damaged**
to damage something is to injure or harm it
damage noun
damage is injury or harm *The storm caused a lot of damage.*

damages plural noun
damages are money paid to someone to
make up for an injury or loss

Dame noun **Dames**
the title of a lady who has been given the
equivalent of a knighthood

dame noun **dames**
a comic middle-aged woman in a
pantomime, usually played by a man

damn verb **damns, damning, damned**
to damn something is to say it is bad
or wrong

damp adjective **damper, dampest**
slightly wet; not quite dry
damp noun
damp or the damp is wetness in the air or
on something **dampness** noun

dampen verb **dampens, dampening, dampened**
1 to dampen something is to make it damp
2 to dampen sound or noise is to make
it softer

damson noun **damsons**
a small purple plum

dance verb **dances, dancing, danced**
to dance is to move about in time to music
dance noun **dances**
1 a piece of music or set of movements
for dancing 2 a party or gathering where
people dance

dancer noun **dancers**
someone who dances

dandelion noun **dandelions**
a yellow wild flower with jagged leaves

dandruff noun
dandruff is small white flakes of dead skin
in a person's hair

a
b
c
d
e
f
g
h
i
j
k
l
m
n
o
p
q
r
s
t
u
v
w
x
y
z

A

B

C

D

E

F

G

H

I

J

K

L

M

N

O

P

Q

R

S

T

U

V

W

X

Y

Z

danger noun dangers
something that is dangerous

dangerous adjective
likely to harm you **dangerously** adverb

dangle verb dangles, dangling, dangled
to swing or hang down loosely

dappled adjective
marked with patches of different colours
She was a strong, well-made animal, of a bright dun colour, beautifully dappled, and with a dark-brown mane and tail. – Anna Sewell, *Black Beauty*

dare verb dares, daring, dared
1 to dare to do something is to be brave or bold enough to do it 2 to dare someone to do something is to challenge them to do it *I dare you to climb that tree.*

dare noun dares (informal)
a challenge to do something risky

daredevil noun daredevils
a person who enjoys doing dangerous things

daring adjective
bold or brave

dark adjective darker, darkest
1 with little or no light 2 deep and rich in colour *She wore a dark green coat.*

dark noun
1 dark or the dark is when there is no light *Cats can see in the dark.* 2 dark is also the time when it becomes dark just after sunset *Be home before dark.* **darkness** noun

darken verb darkens, darkening, darkened
1 to darken something is to make it dark 2 to darken is to become dark *The sky suddenly darkened.*

darkroom noun darkrooms
a room kept dark for developing and printing photographs

darling noun darlings
someone who is loved very much

darn verb darns, darning, darned
to darn a hole is to mend it by sewing across it

dart noun darts
an object with a sharp point that you throw at a dartboard in the game of **darts**

dartboard noun dartboards
a round target at which you throw darts

dash noun dashes
1 a quick rush or a hurry *They made a dash for the door.* 2 a dash of something is a small amount of it 3 a short line (–) used in writing or printing

dash verb dashes, dashing, dashed
1 to dash somewhere is to rush there 2 to dash something is to hurl it and smash it *In her anger she dashed the cup against the wall.*

dashboard noun dashboards
a panel with dials and controls in front of the driver of a car

data (say **day**-ta) plural noun
data is pieces of information

database noun databases
a store of information held in a computer

date[1] noun dates
1 the day of the month, or the year, when something happens or happened 2 an appointment to go out with someone

date verb dates, dating, dated
1 to date something is to work out how old it is *Trees can be dated by the number of rings in their wood.* 2 to date something such as a letter is to put the date on it *a letter dated 1950* 3 to date from a time is to have existed from then *The church dates from the 15th century.* 4 to date is also to seem old-fashioned *Some fashions date very quickly.*

date[2] noun dates
a sweet brown fruit that grows on a palm tree

daughter noun daughters
a girl or woman who is someone's child

dawdle verb dawdles, dawdling, dawdled
to walk or do something too slowly

dawn noun dawns
the time of the day when the sun rises

dawn verb dawns, dawning, dawned
1 to dawn is to begin to become light in the morning 2 something dawns on you when you begin to realize it

day noun days
1 the 24 hours between midnight and the next midnight 2 the light part of the day 3 a period in time *Write about what it was like in Queen Victoria's day.*

daybreak noun
the first light of day; dawn

daydream verb daydreams, daydreaming, daydreamed
to have pleasant thoughts about things you would like to happen

daylight noun
1 the light of day 2 dawn *They left before daylight.*

daze noun
to be in a daze is to be unable to think or see clearly

dazed adjective
someone is dazed when they can't think or see clearly

dazzle verb dazzles, dazzling, dazzled
a light dazzles you when it shines so brightly in your eyes that you are blinded for a moment

dead adjective
1 no longer alive 2 no longer working or active *The phone went dead.* 3 a dead place is not at all lively *This town is dead at the weekend.* 4 complete, sure *It was a dead loss.*

deaden verb deadens, deadening, deadened
to deaden pain or noise is to make it weaker

dead end noun dead ends
a road or passage that is closed at one end

dead heat noun dead heats
a race in which two or more winners finish exactly together

deadline noun deadlines
the time by which you must finish doing something

deadlock noun
a situation in which people cannot agree or settle an argument

deadly adjective deadlier, deadliest
likely to kill *The liquid in the glass was a deadly poison.*

deaf adjective deafer, deafest
unable to hear **deafness** noun

deafen verb deafens, deafening, deafened
a noise deafens you when it is very loud *The noise from the party upstairs was deafening me.*

deal verb deals, dealing, dealt
1 to deal something is to hand it out 2 to deal in something is to buy and sell it *He deals in scrap metal.* 3 to deal playing cards is to give them to players in a card game **to deal with someone** or **something** is to spend time sorting them out *I'll deal with you later.* **to deal with something** is to be concerned with it *This book deals with cacti.*

deal noun deals
1 an agreement or bargain 2 someone's turn to give out playing cards *Whose deal is it?* **a good deal** or **a great deal** a large amount

dealer noun dealers
1 someone who buys and sells things 2 the person dealing at cards

dean noun deans
1 an important member of the clergy in a cathedral or large church 2 the head of part of a college or university

dear adjective dearer, dearest
1 loved very much 2 you use dear as the usual way of beginning a letter *Dear Mary* 3 expensive

death noun deaths
dying; the end of life

deathly adjective
like death; very quiet or spooky

debate noun debates
a formal discussion about a subject

debate verb debates, debating, debated
to debate is to discuss or argue about something

debris (say deb-ree) noun
debris is scattered pieces that are left after something has been destroyed

debt (say det) noun debts
something that someone owes **to be in debt** is to owe money

debut (say day-bew or day-boo) noun debuts
someone's first public appearance as a performer

decade noun decades
a period of ten years

decathlon (say dek-ath-lon) noun decathlons
an athletics competition in which you take part in ten different events

decay verb decays, decaying, decayed
to rot or go bad

decay noun
decay is going bad or rotting

deceased (say di-seest) adjective
a formal word for dead

deceit (say di-seet) noun
deceit is telling lies or doing something dishonest

deceitful adjective
someone who is deceitful tells lies or does something dishonest **deceitfully** adverb

deceive (say di-seev) verb deceives, deceiving, deceived
to deceive someone is to make them believe something that is not true

December noun
the last month of the year

decency noun
decency is respectable and honest behaviour

decent adjective
1 respectable and honest 2 of good enough quality *Was it a decent film?* **decently** adverb

deception noun deceptions
1 deception is making someone believe something that is not true 2 a deception is a trick or a lie

deceptive adjective
not what it seems to be *The sunshine was deceptive and the wind made it very cold.*

decibel noun decibels
a unit for measuring how loud a sound is

decide verb decides, deciding, decided
1 to decide something is to make up your mind about it or make a choice 2 to decide a contest or argument is to settle it

decided adjective
very definite and clear *She spoke in a decided voice. He walked with a decided limp.*

decidedly adverb
very much *She was looking decidedly worried.*

deciduous adjective
a deciduous tree loses its leaves in autumn

decimal adjective
a decimal system uses tens or tenths to count things

decimal noun decimals
a decimal fraction

decimal fraction noun decimal fractions
a fraction with tenths shown as numbers after a dot (⅓ is 0.3; 1½ is 1.5)

decimal point noun decimal points
the dot in a decimal fraction

decipher to dedication

decipher (say di-**sy**-fer) verb **deciphers, deciphering, deciphered**
to decipher writing is to work out what it means when it is in code or difficult to read

decision noun **decisions**
a decision is what someone has decided

decisive adjective
1 ending or deciding something important *The decisive battle of the war was fought here.* **2** a decisive person decides things quickly and firmly **decisively** adjective

deck noun **decks**
1 a floor on a ship or bus **2** the part of a record player where the record is put for playing

deckchair noun **deckchairs**
a folding chair with a seat of canvas or plastic material

declaration noun **declarations**
an official or public statement

declare verb **declares, declaring, declared**
to declare something is to say it clearly and openly

decline verb **declines, declining, declined**
1 to decline is to become weaker or smaller **2** to decline an offer is to refuse it politely

decode verb **decodes, decoding, decoded**
to decode something written in code is to work out its meaning

decompose verb **decomposes, decomposing, decomposed**
to decay or rot **decomposition** noun

decorate verb **decorates, decorating, decorated**
1 to decorate something is to make it look more beautiful or colourful **2** to decorate a room or building is to put fresh paint or paper on the walls **3** to decorate someone is to give them a medal for bravery

decoration noun **decorations**
1 decorations are the paint, wallpaper, and ornaments that make a place look more attractive **2** decoration is making something look more attractive or colourful **3** a decoration is a medal

decorative adjective
used to made to look something look colourful and pretty *decorative ribbons*

decorator noun **decorators**
a person whose job is to paint rooms and buildings and to put up wallpaper

decoy (say **dee**-koi or di-**koi**) noun **decoys**
something used to tempt a person or animal into a trap

decrease (say di-**kreess**) verb **decreases, decreasing, decreased**
1 to decrease something is to make it smaller or less **2** to decrease is to become smaller or less

decrease (say **dee**-kreess) noun **decreases**
the amount by which something decreases

decree noun **decrees**
an official order or decision

decree verb **decrees, decreeing, decreed**
to decree something is to give an official order that it must happen

decrepit (say dik-**rep**-it) adjective
old and weak

dedicate verb **dedicates, dedicating, dedicated**
1 to dedicate yourself or your life to something is to spend all your time doing it *She dedicated her working life to nursing.* **2** to dedicate a book to someone is to name them at the beginning, as a sign of friendship or thanks

dedication noun **dedications**
1 dedication is hard work and effort **2** a dedication is a message at the beginning of a book in which you name someone as a sign of friendship or thanks

A
B
C
D
E
F
G
H
I
J
K
L
M
N
O
P
Q
R
S
T
U
V
W
X
Y
Z

deduce verb **deduces, deducing, deduced**
to deduce a fact or answer is to work it out from what you already know is true *She deduced from my smile that I had won the prize.*

deduct verb **deducts, deducting, deducted**
to deduct an amount is to subtract it from a total *His Dad deducted 50 pence from his pocket money for breaking a window.*

deduction noun **deductions**
1 something that you work out by reasoning **2** an amount taken away from a bigger amount

deed noun **deeds**
1 something that someone has done **2** a legal document that shows who owns something

deep adjective **deeper, deepest**
1 going down or back a long way from the top or front **2** measured from top to bottom or from front to back *The hole was two metres deep.* **3** intense or strong *The room was painted a deep blue.* **4** a deep voice is very low in pitch **deeply** adverb very, extremely *She was deeply upset.*

deepen verb **deepens, deepening, deepened**
to deepen is to become deeper *The pool deepened to 2 metres half way along.*

deep-freeze noun **deep-freezes**
a freezer for food

deer noun **deer**
a fast-running, graceful animal. The male has antlers.

deface verb **defaces, defacing, defaced**
to deface something is to spoil its appearance by writing or drawing on it

defeat verb **defeats, defeating, defeated**
to defeat someone is to beat them in a game or battle

defeat noun **defeats**
1 defeat is losing a game or battle **2** a defeat is a lost game or battle

defect (say **dee**-fekt) noun **defects**
a flaw or weakness

defect (say di-**fekt**) verb **defects, defecting, defected**
to defect is to desert a country or cause and join the other side

defective adjective
something is defective when it has flaws or faults or doesn't work properly

defence noun **defences**
1 something that protects you *High walls were built around the city as a defence against enemy attacks.* **2** protecting yourself or a place from an attack or from criticism *In her defence, she thought she was acting for the best.* **3** the players whose job is to stop the other team scoring in football and other games **defenceless** adjective someone who is defenceless cannot protect themselves

defend verb **defends, defending, defended**
1 to defend someone or something is to protect them from an attack **2** to defend an idea, belief, or person is to argue in support of them **3** to defend an accused person is to try to prove that they are innocent **defender** noun

defendant noun **defendants**
a person accused of something in a law court

defensive adjective
1 used to defend something *We need to take defensive measures.* **2** a defensive person is anxious about being criticized

defer verb **defers, deferring, deferred**
to defer something is to put it off until later *She deferred her departure until Saturday.*

defiant adjective
openly showing that you refuse to obey someone **defiance** noun **defiantly** adverb

deficiency noun **deficiencies**
a lack or shortage **deficient** adjective

defile verb defiles, defiling, defiled
to defile something is to make it dirty
or impure

define verb defines, defining, defined
1 to define a word is to explain what it
means 2 to define an idea or problem is to
show exactly what it is

definite adjective
fixed or certain *Is it definite that we are
going to move?*

 TOP TIPS There is a tricky bit in **definite**—it
ends in **ite**.

definite article noun definite
articles
the word **the**

definitely adverb, interjection
certainly, without doubt *We are definitely
going to the party.*

definition noun definitions
an explanation of what a word means

deflate verb deflates, deflating,
deflated
1 to deflate a tyre or balloon is to let air out
of it 2 to deflate someone is to make them
feel less confident or proud

deflect verb deflects, deflecting,
deflected
to deflect something that is moving is
to make it go in a different direction
deflection noun

deforestation noun
the cutting down of a large number of trees
in an area

deformed adjective
not properly shaped **deformity** noun

defrost verb defrosts, defrosting,
defrosted
1 to defrost a refrigerator or freezer is to
remove the ice from it 2 to defrost frozen
food is to thaw it out

deft adjective defter, deftest
skilful and quick *a few deft strokes with a
paintbrush* **deftly** adverb

defuse verb defuses, defusing, defused
1 to defuse a bomb is to remove its fuse
so that it will not blow up 2 to defuse
a situation is to make it less dangerous
or tense

defy verb defies, defying, defied
1 to defy someone is to refuse to obey
them 2 to defy something is to prevent it
happening *The door defied all attempts to
open it.* 3 to defy someone to do something
is to challenge them *I defy you to find
anything cheaper.*

degenerate verb degenerates,
degenerating, degenerated
to degenerate is to become worse *The game
degenerated into a succession of fouls.*

degrade verb degrades, degrading,
degraded
to degrade someone is to humiliate them

degree noun degrees
1 a unit for measuring temperature *Water
boils at 100 degrees centigrade, or 100°C.*
2 a unit for measuring angles *There are 90
degrees (90°) in a right angle.* 3 the level or
amount of something *I agree with you to a
large degree.* 4 an award to someone at a
university or college who has successfully
finished a course *She has a degree in English.*

dehydrated adjective
dried up, with all the water removed
dehydration noun someone suffers from
dehydration when they lose too much water
from their body

deity (say **dee**-i-ti or **day**-i-ti) noun
deities
a god or goddess

dejected adjective
sad or depressed **dejection** noun

delay verb delays, delaying, delayed
1 to delay someone is to make them
late 2 to delay something is to put it off
until later 3 to delay is to wait before
doing something

delay noun delays
1 delaying or waiting *Do it without delay.*
2 the period you have to wait when

a
b
c
d
e
f
g
h
i
j
k
l
m
n
o
p
q
r
s
t
u
v
w
x
y
z

A

something happens late *There will be a delay of 20 minutes.*

B

delegate (say **del**-i-gayt) verb
delegates, delegating, delegated
to delegate someone is to choose them to do a job that you are responsible for

C

D

delegate (say **del**-i-gat) noun delegates
a person who represents other people at a meeting or conference **delegation** noun a delegation is a group of delegates

E

F

delete verb deletes, deleting, deleted
to delete something is to cross it out or remove it **deletion** noun

G

H

deliberate (say di-**lib**-er-at) adjective
1 done on purpose *It was a deliberate lie.*
2 slow and careful *He has a deliberate way of talking.* **deliberately** adverb

I

J

deliberate (say di-**lib**-er-ayt) verb
deliberates, deliberating, deliberated
to deliberate is to think carefully about something **deliberation** noun

K

L

delicacy noun delicacies
1 delicacy is being delicate **2** a delicacy is something small and tasty to eat

M

N

delicate adjective
1 fine and graceful *The cloth had delicate embroidery.* **2** fragile and easily damaged
3 becoming ill easily **4** a delicate situation needs great care **delicately** adverb

O

P

Q

delicatessen noun delicatessens
a shop that sells cooked meats, cheeses, salads, etc.

R

S

delicious adjective
tasting or smelling very pleasant

T

delight verb delights, delighting, delighted
to delight someone is to please them a lot

U

V

delight noun delights
great pleasure

W

delightful adjective
giving great pleasure *It's the most delightful surprise ever.* **delightfully** adverb

X

Y

delirious adjective
1 in a confused state of mind because you

Z

are ill or have a high fever **2** extremely excited or enthusiastic **deliriously** adverb

delirium noun deliriums
1 the confused state of mind of people who are ill or have a high fever
2 wild excitement

deliver verb delivers, delivering, delivered
1 to deliver letters, milk, or newspapers is to take them to a house or office **2** to deliver a speech or lecture is to give it to an audience
3 to deliver a baby is to help with its birth

delivery noun deliveries
1 delivery is when letters or goods are taken to a house or office **2** a person's delivery is the way they give a speech or lecture
3 giving birth to a baby

delta noun deltas
a triangular area at the mouth of a river where it spreads into branches

delude verb deludes, deluding, deluded
to be deluded is to believe something that is not true

deluge noun deluges
1 a large flood **2** a heavy fall of rain
3 something coming in great numbers *After the speech there was a deluge of questions.*

deluge verb deluges, deluging, deluged
to be deluged with something is to get a huge amount of it *We have been deluged with replies.*

delusion noun delusions
a false belief

demand verb demands, demanding, demanded
to demand something is to ask for it forcefully

demand noun demands
1 a demand is a very firm request for something **2** demand is a desire to have something *There's not much demand for ice cream at this time of year.*

demanding adjective
1 asking for many things *Toddlers can be*

very demanding. **2** needing a lot of time or effort *She has a demanding job.*

demo noun **demos** (informal)
a demonstration

democracy noun **democracies**
1 democracy is government by leaders elected by the people **2** a democracy is a country governed in this way

democrat noun **democrats**
a person who believes in or supports democracy

democratic adjective
a democratic idea or process is one that involves ordinary people and takes account of their views

demolish verb **demolishes, demolishing, demolished**
to demolish a building is to knock it down and break it up **demolition** noun

demon noun **demons**
1 a devil or evil spirit **2** a fierce or forceful person

demonstrate verb **demonstrates, demonstrating, demonstrated**
1 to demonstrate something is to show or prove it **2** to demonstrate is to take part in a demonstration

demonstration noun **demonstrations**
1 showing how to do or work something **2** a march or meeting to show everyone what you think about something *There will be a demonstration against the new motorway.*

demonstrator noun **demonstrators**
1 someone who takes part in a demonstration or meeting **2** someone who demonstrates something

demoralize verb **demoralizes, demoralizing, demoralized**
to demoralize someone is to make them lose confidence or courage

den noun **dens**
1 the home of a wild animal *a lion's den* **2** a hiding place, especially for children

denial noun **denials**
saying that something is not true

denim noun
strong cotton cloth, used to make jeans

denominator noun **denominators**
the number below the line in a fraction. In ¼ the 4 is the denominator.

denote verb **denotes, denoting, denoted**
to denote something is to indicate or mean it *In road signs, P denotes a car park.*

denounce verb **denounces, denouncing, denounced**
to denounce someone or something is to speak strongly against them, or accuse them of something *They denounced him as a spy.*

dense adjective **denser, densest**
1 thick *The fog was getting very dense.*
2 packed close together *They walked through a dense forest.* **densely** adverb thickly, close together *a densely populated area*

density noun **densities**
how thick or tightly packed something is

dent noun **dents**
a hollow made in a surface by hitting it or pressing it

dent verb **dents, denting, dented**
to dent something is to make a dent in it

dental adjective
to do with the teeth or dentistry

dentist noun **dentists**
a person who is trained to treat teeth, fill them or take them out, and fit false ones

denture noun **dentures**
a set of false teeth

deny verb **denies, denying, denied**
1 to deny something is to say that it is not true **2** to deny a request is to refuse it

deodorant noun **deodorants**
a powder or liquid that removes unpleasant smells

a
b
c
d
e
f
g
h
i
j
k
l
m
n
o
p
q
r
s
t
u
v
w
x
y
z

A
B
C

D

E
F
G
H
I
J
K
L
M
N
O
P
Q
R
S
T
U
V
W
X
Y
Z

depart verb departs, departing, departed
to depart is to go away or leave
departure noun

department noun departments
one part of a large organization or shop

department store noun
department stores
a large shop that sells many different kinds of goods

depend verb depends, depending, depended
to depend on someone or **something** is to rely on them *We depend on you for help.*
to depend on something is to be decided or controlled by it *Whether we can have a picnic depends on the weather.*

dependable adjective
if someone or something is dependable, they are reliable and you can depend on them

dependant noun dependants
a person who depends on someone else, especially for money *She has two dependants, a son and a daughter.*

dependent adjective
depending or relying on someone *He was dependent on his father. She has two dependent children.* **dependence** noun

depict verb depicts, depicting, depicted
1 to depict something is to show it in a painting or drawing **2** to depict a scene is to describe it *The story depicted a small village in Austria.*

deplore verb deplores, deploring, deplored
to deplore something is to dislike it very much because it upsets or annoys you

deport verb deports, deporting, deported
to deport someone is to send them out of a country **deportation** noun

deposit noun deposits
1 an amount of money you pay into a bank or building society **2** a sum of money paid as the first instalment of a bigger sum **3** a layer of matter in or on the earth *deposits of oil and gas under the ground*

deposit verb deposits, depositing, deposited
1 to deposit something is to put it down somewhere **2** to deposit money is to pay it into a bank or building society

depot (say dep-oh) noun depots
1 a place where things are stored **2** a place where buses or trains are kept and repaired

depress verb depresses, depressing, depressed
to depress someone is to make them very sad

depressed adjective
someone who is depressed feels very sad and without hope

depression noun depressions
1 a feeling of great sadness and lack of hope **2** a long period when there is less trade and business than usual and many people have no work **3** a shallow hollow or dip in the ground

deprive verb deprives, depriving, deprived
to deprive someone of something is to take it away from them *Prisoners are deprived of their freedom.*

deprived adjective
without all the things you need to live a happy and comfortable life, like enough food and good housing

depth noun depths
how deep something is *What is the depth of the river here?* **in depth** thoroughly **out of your depth 1** in water that is too deep to stand in **2** trying to do something that is too difficult for you

deputize verb deputizes, deputizing, deputized
to deputize for someone is to act as their deputy

deputy noun deputies
a person who acts as a substitute or chief assistant for someone and does that person's job when they are away

derail verb derails, derailing, derailed
a train is derailed when something causes it to leave the track

derby (say **dar**-bi) noun derbies
a sports match between two teams from the same city or area

derelict (say **de**-re-likt) adjective
abandoned and left to fall into ruin *The factory is now completely derelict.*

deride verb derides, deriding, derided
to deride someone or something is to treat them with scorn *He was derided for his beliefs.*

derision noun
scorn or ridicule *They treated him with derision.*

derivation noun derivations
where a word comes from

derive verb derives, deriving, derived
to get something from another person or thing *She derived a lot of pleasure from music. Many English words are derived from Latin.*

derrick noun derricks
1 a kind of large crane for lifting things
2 a tall framework that holds the machinery used for drilling an oil well

descant noun descants
a tune sung or played above another tune

descend verb descends, descending, descended
to descend something like a hill or staircase is to go down it **to be descended from someone** is to be in the same family as them but living at a later time

descendant noun descendants
a person's descendants are the people who are descended from them

descent noun descents
a descent is a climb down, usually a hard or long one

describe verb describes, describing, described
to describe something or someone is to say what they are like

description noun descriptions
1 description is saying what someone or something is like *She's a writer who's very good at description.* 2 a description is something you write or say that describes what someone or something is like *He gave the police a description of the robbers.* **descriptive** adjective a descriptive word or piece of writing describes someone or something *a descriptive poem*

desert (say **dez**-ert) noun deserts
a large area of very dry, often sandy, land

desert (say di-**zert**) verb deserts, deserting, deserted
to desert someone or something is to leave them without intending to return **desertion** noun

deserted adjective
a place is deserted when there is nobody there

deserter noun deserters
a soldier who runs away from the army

desert island noun desert islands
a tropical island where nobody lives

deserts (say di-**zerts**) plural noun
someone's deserts are what they deserve *He got his deserts.*

deserve verb deserves, deserving, deserved
to deserve something is to be worthy of it or to have a right to it **deservedly** adverb rightly, because it is deserved *She is friendly and deservedly popular.*

design noun designs
1 the way that something is made or arranged 2 a drawing that shows how something is to be made 3 lines and shapes forming a pattern

a
b
c
d
e
f
g
h
i
j
k
l
m
n
o
p
q
r
s
t
u
v
w
x
y
z

139

A

B

D

C

E

F

G

H

I

J

K

L

M

N

O

P

Q

R

S

T

U

V

W

X

Y

Z

design verb designs, designing, designed
to design something is to make a design or plan for it **designer** noun

designate verb designates, designating, designated
to designate something is to choose it for a special purpose *The meadow was designated a picnic area.*

desirable adjective
worth having or doing *It is desirable for you to come with us.*

desire verb desires, desiring, desired
to desire something is to want it very much
desire noun desires
a feeling of wanting something very much

desk noun desks
1 a piece of furniture with a flat top and drawers, used for writing, reading, or working at **2** a counter at which a cashier or receptionist sits

desktop adjective
small enough to use on a desk *I've bought a desktop computer.*

desolate adjective
1 lonely and sad **2** a desolate place is empty, with no people living there *They had come to the edge of a clearing in the wood, a desolate place like a quarry strewn with boulders, with stagnant pools of water between the rocks.* – Elizabeth Goudge, *The Little White Horse* **desolation** noun

despair noun
despair is a complete loss of hope
despair verb despairs, despairing, despaired
to despair is to lose hope completely

despatch noun despatches and verb despatches, despatching, despatched
a different spelling of *dispatch*

desperate adjective
1 extremely serious or hopeless *We were in a desperate situation.* **2** ready to do anything to get out of a difficulty *There are three*

desperate criminals at large. **3** needing or wanting something very much *She was desperate to go home.* **desperation** noun

 TOP TIPS
There is a tricky bit in **desperate**—it has an **e** in the middle.

desperately adverb
1 extremely; seriously *She was desperately worried about what she had seen.* **2** if you do something desperately, you do it in a despairing or reckless way *'Please don't call the police,' she said desperately.*

despicable adjective
very unpleasant or evil

despise verb despises, despising, despised
to despise someone is to hate them and have no respect at all for them

despite preposition
in spite of *They went out despite the rain.*

dessert (say di-**zert**) noun desserts
fruit or a sweet food eaten at the end of a meal

dessertspoon noun dessertspoons
a medium-sized spoon used for eating puddings

destination noun destinations
the place you are travelling to

destined adjective
intended by fate; meant to happen *They felt they were destined to win.*

destiny noun destinies
your destiny is what is intended for you in the future; your fate *His destiny was to travel the world.*

destroy verb destroys, destroying, destroyed
to destroy something is to ruin it or put an end to it

destroyer noun destroyers
a fast warship

destruction noun
destruction is completely destroying something *the destruction of the rainforests*

destructive adjective
something that is destructive causes a lot of damage

detach verb detaches, detaching, detached
to detach something is to remove it or separate it *Detach the coupon from the bottom of the page.* **detachable** adjective

detached adjective
1 able to stand back from a situation and not get emotionally involved in it *She was watching with a detached expression, as though the argument had nothing to do with her.* 2 a detached house is one that is not joined to another house

detachment noun detachments
a detachment is a special group of people, especially soldiers

detail noun details
1 a small piece of information 2 a small part of a design or picture or piece of decoration **detailed** adjective **in detail** describing or dealing with everything fully

detain verb detains, detaining, detained
1 to detain someone is to keep them in a place 2 to detain someone is also to keep them waiting *I'll try not to detain you for long.*

detect verb detects, detecting, detected
to detect something is to discover or notice it **detection** noun **detector** noun

detective noun detectives
a person, especially a police officer, who investigates crimes

detention noun detentions
detention is when someone is made to stay in a place, especially made to stay late in school as a punishment

deter verb deters, deterring, deterred
to deter someone is to put them off doing something

detergent noun detergents
a kind of washing powder or liquid

deteriorate verb deteriorates, deteriorating, deteriorated
to deteriorate is to become worse *The weather was starting to deteriorate.* **deterioration** noun

determination noun
a strong intention to achieve something, even though it is difficult

determine verb determines, determining, determined
to determine something is to decide it or work it out *The task was to determine the height of the mountain.*

determined adjective
having your mind firmly made up

determiner noun determiners
(in grammar)
a word (such as *a*, *the*, and *many*) that introduces a noun

deterrent noun deterrents
something that is meant to put people off doing something, such as a powerful weapon

detest verb detests, detesting, detested
to detest something or someone is to dislike them very much *I truly detested that Jamie. He was just the most annoying person in the whole world to have to sit next to.* — Jacqueline Wilson, *The Lottie Project*
detestable adjective horrid

detonate verb detonates, detonating, detonated
to detonate a bomb is to make it explode
detonation noun **detonator** noun

detour noun detours
a roundabout route you use instead of the normal route

deuce noun
a tennis score when each player has 40 points and needs two more points in a row to win the game

devastate verb devastates, devastating, devastated
to devastate a place is to ruin or destroy

a
b
c
d
e
f
g
h
i
j
k
l
m
n
o
p
q
r
s
t
u
v
w
x
y
z

it, making it impossible to live in **devastation** noun

devastated adjective
someone is devastated when they are extremely shocked and upset

develop verb develops, developing, developed
1 to develop something is to make it bigger or better 2 to develop is to become bigger or better 3 to develop land is to put up new buildings on it 4 to develop photographic film is to treat it with chemicals so that pictures appear on it

development noun developments
1 a development is something interesting that has happened *Have there been any developments since I last saw you?* 2 development is putting up new buildings

device noun devices
a piece of equipment used for a particular purpose *We need a device for opening tins.* **to leave someone to their own devices** is to leave them alone to do as they wish and not tell them what to do

devil noun devils
an evil spirit or person **devilish** adjective

devious adjective
1 using unfair and dishonest methods *He got rich by devious means.* 2 not straight or direct *The coach took us by a devious route to avoid the traffic jams.*

devise verb devises, devising, devised
to devise a plan or idea is to think it up

devote verb devotes, devoting, devoted
to devote yourself or your time to something is to spend all your time doing it *They devote all their free time to sport.*

devoted adjective
loving and loyal *They are devoted parents.*

devotion noun
great love or loyalty

devour verb devours, devouring, devoured
to devour something is to eat or swallow it greedily *Latch and the beasts sat round the kitchen table drinking tea and devouring an overlooked packet of digestive biscuits.* – Debi Gliori, *Pure Dead Wicked*

devout adjective
deeply religious

dew noun
tiny drops of water that form during the night on the ground and other surfaces out of doors **dewy** adjective

dhoti (say doh-ti) noun dhotis
a long piece of cloth worn by some Hindu men around the lower part of their bodies

diabetes (say dy-a-bee-teez) noun
a disease in which there is too much sugar in a person's blood

diabetic (say dy-a-bet-ik) noun diabetics
a person suffering from diabetes
diabetic adjective
suffering from diabetes

diabolical adjective
like a devil; very wicked

diagnose verb diagnoses, diagnosing, diagnosed
to diagnose a disease is to find out what it is and what treatment is needed

diagnosis noun diagnoses
a doctor makes a diagnosis when they decide what disease someone has

diagonal noun diagonals
a straight line joining opposite corners **diagonally** adverb

diagram noun diagrams
a drawing or picture that shows the parts of something or how it works

dial noun dials
a circular piece of plastic or card with numbers or letters round it

dial verb dials, dialling, dialled
to dial a telephone number is to choose it by pressing numbered buttons

dialect noun dialects
the form of a language used by people in one area of the country but not in the rest of the country

dialogue noun dialogues
talk between people, especially in a play, film, or book

diameter noun diameters
1 a line drawn from one side of a circle to the other, passing through the centre 2 the length of this line

diamond noun diamonds
1 a very hard jewel that looks like clear glass 2 a shape which has four equal sides but which is not a square 3 a playing card with red diamond shapes on it

diaphragm (say dy-a-fram) noun diaphragms
the muscular layer inside your body between your chest and your abdomen, used when you breathe

diarrhoea (say dy-a-ree-a) noun
an illness that makes you have to keep going to the toilet and the waste matter you empty from your bowels is very watery

diary noun diaries
a book with a separate space to write in for each day of the year, in which you write down what happens each day or to plan what you need to do in the future

dice noun dice
a small cube marked with one to six dots on each side, thrown to give a number in some games

dictate verb dictates, dictating, dictated
1 to dictate something is to speak or read it aloud for someone else to write down 2 to dictate to someone is to give them orders in a bossy way **dictation** noun dictation, or a dictation, is an exercise in writing down what someone reads out

dictator noun dictators
a ruler who has complete power over the people of a country

dictionary noun dictionaries
a book with words listed in alphabetical order, so that you can find out what a word means and how to spell it

did
past tense of **do** Where did you go to school before?

didn't
short for did not

die verb dies, dying, died
to die is to stop living **to die down** is to gradually become less strong The wind died down at last. **to die out** is to gradually disappear The tiger is beginning to die out.

diesel noun diesels
1 a diesel is an engine that works by burning oil in compressed air 2 diesel is fuel for this kind of engine

diet noun diets
1 a diet is special meals that someone eats to be healthy or to lose weight Mum's on a diet. 2 someone's diet is the food they normally eat

diet verb diets, dieting, dieted
to diet is to keep to a special diet, especially in order to lose weight

differ verb differs, differing, differed
1 to differ from something is to be not the same as it 2 to differ is to disagree The two writers differ on this point.

difference noun differences
1 the way in which something is different from something else 2 the amount between two numbers The difference between 8 and 3 is 5.

different adjective
one person or thing is different from another when they are not the same **differently** adverb

difficult adjective
needing a lot of effort or skill; not easy

difficulty noun difficulties
1 difficulty is not being easy; trouble *I had difficulty answering most of the questions.*
2 a difficulty is something that causes a problem

diffuse verb diffuses, diffusing, diffused
to diffuse something is to spread it widely or thinly *A rosy light seemed to diffuse itself through the room.* **diffusion** noun

dig verb digs, digging, dug
1 to dig soil or the ground is to break it up and move it **2** to dig a hole is to make it
3 to dig someone is to poke them *He dug me in the ribs.* **digger** noun

dig noun digs
1 a place where archaeologists dig to look for ancient remains **2** a sharp thrust or poke *She gave me a dig in the ribs with her elbow.*
3 an unpleasant remark *What he said was clearly a dig at me.*

digest verb digests, digesting, digested
to digest food is to soften and change it in the stomach and intestine so that the body can absorb it **digestion** noun

digestive adjective
to do with digesting food

digit (say **dij**-it) noun digits
1 any of the numbers from 0 to 9 **2** a finger or toe

digital adjective
1 to do with or using digits **2** a digital computer or recording stores the data or sound as a series of binary digits
3 a digital clock or watch has a row of digits to indicate numbers (the opposite of *analogue*)

dignified adjective
having dignity

dignity noun
a calm and serious manner

dike noun dikes
1 a long wall or embankment to hold back water and prevent flooding **2** a ditch for draining water from land

dilemma noun dilemmas
an awkward choice between two possible actions, either of which would cause difficulties

dilute verb dilutes, diluting, diluted
to dilute a liquid is to make it weaker by mixing it with water

dim adjective dimmer, dimmest
only faintly lit and difficult to see
dimly adverb to see something dimly is to find it hard to see clearly

dim verb dims, dimming, dimmed
a light dims when it becomes less bright *As the curtain rose, the lights dimmed.*

dimension noun dimensions
1 a measurement such as length, width, area, or volume *What are the dimensions of the box?* **2** a feature of something *The day trips added another dimension to our holiday.*

diminish verb diminishes, diminishing, diminished
1 to diminish something is to make it smaller **2** to diminish is to become smaller

diminutive (say dim-**in**-yoo-tiv) adjective
very small

diminutive noun diminutives
a word, name, or ending of a word that shows that something is small, e.g. the name *Tiny Tim* or the word *piglet*

dimple noun dimples
a small hollow on a person's cheek or chin

din noun
a loud noise

dine verb dines, dining, dined
to dine is to have dinner **diner** noun

dinghy (say **ding**-i) noun dinghies
a kind of small boat

dingy (say **din**-ji) adjective dingier, dingiest
shabby and dirty-looking

dinner noun dinners
the main meal of the day, eaten either in the middle of the day or in the evening

A B C **D** E F G H I J K L M N O P Q R S T U V W X Y Z

dinosaur noun dinosaurs
a prehistoric reptile, often of enormous size

dip verb dips, dipping, dipped
1 to dip something is to put it into a liquid and then take it out again *Dip the brush in the paint.* 2 to dip is to go or slope downwards *The road dips steeply after the hill.* 3 to dip a vehicle's headlights is to lower the beam so that they do not dazzle other drivers

dip noun dips
1 dipping 2 a downward slope 3 a quick swim 4 a mixture into which things are dipped

diploma noun diplomas
a certificate awarded for skill in a particular subject

diplomacy noun
1 the business of keeping friendly with other nations 2 dealing with other people without upsetting or offending them

diplomatic adjective
1 to do with diplomacy 2 tactful and courteous **diplomat** noun someone who works in diplomacy

dire adjective direr, direst
dreadful or serious *The refugees are in dire need of food and shelter.*

direct adjective
1 as straight or quick as possible 2 frank and honest **directness** noun

direct verb directs, directing, directed
1 to direct someone is to show them the way 2 to direct a film or play is to decide how it should be made or performed

direction noun directions
1 a direction is the way you go to get somewhere 2 direction is directing something **directions** information on how to use or do something or how to get somewhere

directly adverb
1 by a direct route *Go directly to the shop.* 2 immediately *I want you to come directly.*

director noun directors
1 a person who is in charge of something, especially one of a group of people managing a company 2 a person who decides how a film or play should be made or performed

directory noun directories
a book containing a list of people with their telephone numbers and addresses

direct speech noun
someone's words written down exactly in the way they were said, for example, *'I want to go home,' said Josh.*

dirt noun
earth or soil; anything that is not clean

dirty adjective dirtier, dirtiest
1 covered with dirt; not clean 2 rude or offensive *Someone has written dirty words on the wall.* 3 unfair or mean *That was a dirty trick.* **dirtily** adverb **dirtiness** noun

dis– prefix
1 showing the opposite of something, as in *dishonest* 2 showing that something has been taken away or apart, as in *disarm* or *dismantle*

disability noun disabilities
something that prevents someone from using their body in the usual way

disabled adjective
having a disease or injury that makes it difficult for someone to use their body properly

disadvantage noun disadvantages
something that hinders you or makes things difficult

disagree verb disagrees, disagreeing, disagreed
1 to disagree with someone is to have or express a different opinion from them 2 to disagree with someone is also to have a bad effect on them *Rich food disagrees with me.* **disagreement** noun

disagreeable adjective
unpleasant

a
b
c
d
e
f
g
h
i
j
k
l
m
n
o
p
q
r
s
t
u
v
w
x
y
z

A
B
C
D
E
F
G
H
I
J
K
L
M
N
O
P
Q
R
S
T
U
V
W
X
Y
Z

disappear verb disappears, disappearing, disappeared
1 to disappear is to become impossible to see; to vanish **2** to disappear is also to stop happening or existing *Her nervousness soon disappeared.* **disappearance** noun

TOP TIPS
Double up the **p** in **disappear** and **disappoint** (but the **s** stays single)!

disappoint verb disappoints, disappointing, disappointed
to disappoint someone is to fail to do what they want **disappointing** adjective **disappointment** noun

disapprove verb disapproves, disapproving, disapproved
to disapprove of someone or something is to have a bad opinion of them **disapproval** noun

disarm verb disarms, disarming, disarmed
1 to disarm is to reduce the size of armed forces **2** to disarm someone is to take away their weapons **disarmament** noun

disaster noun disasters
1 a very bad accident or misfortune, often one where many people are killed or injured **2** a complete failure *The first performance of our play was a disaster.* **disastrous** adjective causing great misfortune; going completely wrong **disastrously** adverb

disc noun discs
1 a round flat object **2** a round, flat piece of plastic on which sound, pictures, or other data is recorded

discard verb discards, discarding, discarded
to discard something is to throw it away

discharge verb discharges, discharging, discharged
1 to release someone *She was discharged from hospital yesterday.* **2** to send something out *Vehicles must not discharge smoke.*

disciple noun disciples
a follower of a political or religious leader, especially one of Christ's first followers

discipline noun
1 training people to obey rules and punishing them if they don't **2** the control you have over how you behave *You need lots of discipline to learn the piano.*

disc jockey noun disc jockeys
someone who introduces and plays records on the radio or at a club

disclose verb discloses, disclosing, disclosed
to disclose information or a secret is to tell someone about it

disco noun discos
a place or party where records are played for dancing

discolour verb discolours, discolouring, discoloured
to discolour something is to spoil its colour

discomfort noun
being uncomfortable

disconnect verb disconnects, disconnecting, disconnected
to disconnect something is to break its connection or detach it **disconnection** noun

discontented adjective
unhappy and not satisfied **discontent** noun

discount noun discounts
an amount by which a price is reduced

discourage verb discourages, discouraging, discouraged
1 to discourage someone is to take away their enthusiasm or confidence **2** to discourage someone from doing something is to try to persuade them not to do it **discouragement** noun

discover verb discovers, discovering, discovered
to discover something is to find it or learn about it, especially by chance or for the first time

discovery noun discoveries
1 finding or learning about something, especially by chance or for the first time

Columbus is famous for the discovery of America. **2** something that is found or learned about for the first time *This drug was an important discovery in the history of medicine.*

discreet adjective
being careful in what you say and do, especially when you have a secret to keep **discreetly** adverb

discriminate verb discriminates, discriminating, discriminated
1 to discriminate between things is to notice the differences between them, or to prefer one thing to another **2** to discriminate between people is to treat them differently or unfairly because of their race, sex, or religion

discrimination noun
1 discrimination is treating people differently or unfairly because of their race, sex, or religion **2** discrimination is also the ability to notice the differences between things

discus (say dis-kuss) noun discuses
a thick heavy disc thrown in an athletic contest

discuss (say dis-kuss) verb discusses, discussing, discussed
to discuss a subject is to talk with other people about it or to write about it in detail

discussion noun discussions
1 a conversation about a subject **2** a piece of writing in which you look at a subject from different points of view

disease noun diseases
a disease is an illness or sickness **diseased** adjective

disembark verb disembarks, disembarking, disembarked
to disembark is to get out of a boat or aircraft

disgrace noun
1 disgrace is shame *You have brought disgrace to your family.* **2** a disgrace is a person or thing that is so bad that people

should feel ashamed *This room is an absolute disgrace.* **disgraceful** adjective **disgracefully** adverb

disgrace verb disgraces, disgracing, disgraced
to disgrace someone or something is to bring them shame

disguise verb disguises, disguising, disguised
to disguise someone or something is to make them look different so that other people won't recognize them

disguise noun disguises
clothes or make-up you put on to change the way you look so that people won't recognize you

disgust noun
a strong feeling of dislike or contempt

disgust verb disgusts, disgusting, disgusted
to disgust someone is to make them feel disgust **disgusted** adjective **disgusting** adjective

dish noun dishes
1 a plate or bowl for food **2** food that has been prepared for eating

dish verb dishes, dishing, dished
to dish something out (informal) is to give it to people

dishcloth noun dishcloths
a cloth you use for washing or drying dishes

dishevelled adjective
untidy in appearance

dishonest adjective
not honest or truthful **dishonesty** noun **dishonestly** adverb

dishwasher noun dishwashers
a machine for washing dishes automatically

disinfect verb disinfects, disinfecting, disinfected
to disinfect something is to treat it to kill all the germs in it

disinfectant noun disinfectants
a liquid used to disinfect things

a
b
c
d
e
f
g
h
i
j
k
l
m
n
o
p
q
r
s
t
u
v
w
x
y
z

A

disintegrate verb disintegrates, disintegrating, disintegrated
to disintegrate is to break up into small pieces **disintegration** noun

disinterested adjective
not favouring one side more than the other; impartial

disk noun disks
a disc, especially one used to store computer data

dislike verb dislikes, disliking, disliked
to dislike someone or something is not to like them

dislike noun dislikes
a feeling of not liking someone or something

dislocate verb dislocates, dislocating, dislocated
to dislocate a bone or joint in your body is to make it come out of its proper place by accident **dislocation** noun

dislodge verb dislodges, dislodging, dislodged
to dislodge something is to move it from its place

disloyal adjective
not loyal

dismal adjective
gloomy and sad **dismally** adverb

dismantle verb dismantles, dismantling, dismantled
to dismantle something is to take it to pieces

dismay noun
a feeling of strong disappointment and surprise **dismayed** adjective

dismiss verb dismisses, dismissing, dismissed
1 to dismiss someone is to tell them that they have to leave, especially to leave their job 2 to dismiss an idea or suggestion is to reject it **dismissal** noun

B
C
D
E
F
G
H
I
J
K
L
M
N
O
P
Q
R
S
T
U
V
W
X
Y
Z

dismount verb dismounts, dismounting, dismounted
to dismount is to get off a horse or bicycle

disobedience noun
refusing to obey someone **disobedient** adjective

disobey verb disobeys, disobeying, disobeyed
to disobey someone is to refuse to do what they tell you to do

disorder noun disorders
1 disorder is confusion or disturbance 2 a disorder is an illness **disorderly** adjective
behaving in a wild and noisy way

dispatch noun dispatches
a report or message

dispatch verb dispatches, dispatching, dispatched
to dispatch something or someone is to send them somewhere

dispense verb dispenses, dispensing, dispensed
1 to dispense something is to give it out to people *The machine dispenses drinks and snacks.* 2 to dispense medicine is to prepare it for patients **to dispense with something** is to do without it

dispenser noun dispensers
a device that gives you things, especially in special amounts *There is a soap dispenser above each washbasin.*

disperse verb disperses, dispersing, dispersed
1 to disperse people is to send them away in various directions *The police dispersed the crowd.* 2 to disperse is to go off in various directions **dispersal** noun

displace verb displaces, displacing, displaced
1 to displace something is to move it from its place *Some roof tiles had been displaced by the wind.* 2 to displace someone is to take their place *Last year she displaced him as captain.*

display verb displays, displaying, displayed
to display something is to arrange it so that it can be clearly seen

display noun displays
1 a show or exhibition 2 the showing of information on a computer screen

displease verb displeases, displeasing, displeased
to displease someone is to annoy them

disposable adjective
something that is disposable is made to be thrown away after it has been used

disposal noun
getting rid of something **at your disposal** ready for you to use

dispose verb disposes, disposing, disposed
to be disposed to do something is to be ready and willing to do it *They were not disposed to help us.* **to dispose of something** is to get rid of it

disposition noun dispositions
a person's nature or qualities *He has a cheerful disposition.*

disprove verb disproves, disproving, disproved
to disprove something is to prove that it is not true

dispute noun disputes
a quarrel or disagreement

disqualify verb disqualifies, disqualifying, disqualified
to disqualify someone is to remove them from a race or competition because they have broken the rules **disqualification** noun

disregard verb disregards, disregarding, disregarded
to disregard someone or something is to take no notice of them

disrespect noun
lack of respect; rudeness **disrespectful** adjective **disrespectfully** adverb

disrupt verb disrupts, disrupting, disrupted
to disrupt something is to stop it running smoothly or throw it into confusion *Floods have disrupted local traffic.* **disruption** noun **disruptive** adjective

dissatisfied adjective
not satisfied or pleased **dissatisfaction** noun

dissect verb dissects, dissecting, dissected
to dissect something is to cut it up so that you can examine it **dissection** noun

dissolve verb dissolves, dissolving, dissolved
1 to dissolve something is to mix it with a liquid so that it becomes part of the liquid 2 to dissolve is to melt or become liquid *As the book sank into the green sea the ink dissolved from its pages. And as each page washed blank, the spell written upon it was broken.* – Alan Temperley, *The Brave Whale*

dissuade verb dissuades, dissuading, dissuaded
to dissuade someone is to persuade them not to do something

distance noun distances
the amount of space between two places or things **in the distance** a long way off but able to be seen

distant adjective
1 far away 2 a person who is distant is not friendly or sociable

distil verb distils, distilling, distilled
to distil a liquid is to purify it by boiling it and condensing the vapour

distillery noun distilleries
a place where spirits such as whisky are produced

distinct adjective
1 easily heard or seen; clear or definite *You have made a distinct improvement.* 2 clearly separate or different *A rabbit is quite distinct from a hare.* **distinctly** adverb

a
b
c
d
e
f
g
h
i
j
k
l
m
n
o
p
q
r
s
t
u
v
w
x
y
z

distinction noun distinctions
1 a distinction is a clear difference between two things 2 distinction is excellence or honour *She is a writer of distinction.* 3 a distinction is also a high mark in an examination

distinctive adjective
clearly different from all the others and easy to recognize or notice *The school has a distinctive blue football strip.*

distinguish verb distinguishes, distinguishing, distinguished
1 to distinguish things is to notice the differences between them 2 to distinguish something is to see or hear it clearly

distinguished adjective
famous, successful, and much admired by other people *There was a distinguished scientist visiting the school.*

distort verb distorts, distorting, distorted
1 to distort something is to change it into a strange shape *His face was distorted with anger.* 2 to distort facts is to change them so that they are untrue or misleading **distortion** noun

distract verb distracts, distracting, distracted
to distract someone is to take their attention away from what they are doing *Don't distract the bus driver.* **distraction** noun

distress noun
great sorrow, suffering, or trouble **in distress** a ship or plane is in distress when it is in difficulty and needs help

distress verb distresses, distressing, distressed
to distress someone is to make them feel very upset or worried

distribute verb distributes, distributing, distributed
1 to distribute things is to give them out or deliver them *The teacher distributed textbooks to the class.* 2 to distribute something is to share it among a number of people *The money was distributed among all the local schools.* 3 to distribute something is also to spread or scatter it around *Make sure your weight is evenly distributed.* **distribution** noun

district noun districts
part of a town or country

distrust noun
lack of trust; suspicion **distrustful** adjective not trusting people

distrust verb distrusts, distrusting, distrusted
to think that someone or something cannot be trusted

disturb verb disturbs, disturbing, disturbed
1 to disturb someone is to interrupt them or spoil their peace 2 to disturb someone is also to worry or upset them 3 to disturb something is to move it from its right position **disturbance** noun

disused adjective
no longer used *The house was next to a disused warehouse.*

ditch noun ditches
a narrow trench to hold or carry away water

dither verb dithers, dithering, dithered
to dither is to hesitate nervously

ditto noun
the same again

divan noun divans
a bed or couch without a raised back or sides

dive verb dives, diving, dived
1 to dive is to go into water head first 2 to dive is also to move downwards quickly *The aeroplane then dived.*

diver noun divers
1 a swimmer who dives 2 someone who works under water using special breathing equipment 3 a bird that dives for its food
Please see illustration on following page.

diverse adjective
very different from each other and of

diver

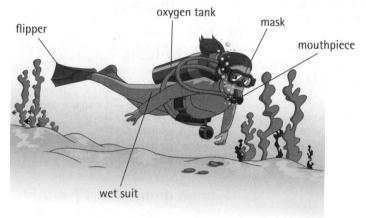

flipper

oxygen tank

mask

mouthpiece

wet suit

several different kinds *He has a diverse collection of comics.* **diversity** noun

diversion noun **diversions**
1 a different way for traffic to go when the usual road is closed **2** something amusing or entertaining

divert verb **diverts, diverting, diverted**
1 to divert something is to change the direction it is moving in **2** to divert someone is to amuse or entertain them

divide verb **divides, dividing, divided**
1 to divide something is to separate it into smaller parts or shares **2** (in mathematics) to divide a number by another number is to find out how many times the second number is contained in the first *Divide six by two and you get three (6÷2 = 3).*

dividend noun **dividends**
a share in the profit a business makes

divine adjective
1 belonging to God or coming from God **2** like a god **3** (informal) excellent; extremely beautiful **divinity** noun

divine verb **divines, divining, divined**
to divine is to find hidden water or metal by holding a Y-shaped stick called a **divining rod**

division noun **divisions**
1 the process of dividing numbers or things

2 a dividing line or partition **3** one of the parts into which something is divided

divorce noun **divorces**
the legal ending of a marriage

divorce verb **divorces, divorcing, divorced**
a husband and wife divorce when they end their marriage by law

Diwali (say di-**wah**-li) noun
a Hindu festival held in October or November

DIY
short for **do-it-yourself**

dizzy adjective **dizzier, dizziest**
giddy and feeling confused **dizzily** adverb **dizziness** noun

DJ
short for **disc jockey**

do verb **does, doing, did, done**
1 to do something is to perform it or deal with it *Are you doing your work? I can't do this sum.* **2** to do well is to manage; to do badly is not to manage very well **3** you say that something will do when it is all right or suitable *I'd really like some football boots but trainers will do.* **4** you also use **do** with other verbs in special ways *Do you want this? He does not want it. I do like crisps. We work as hard as they do.* **to do away with**

something (informal) is to get rid of it
to do something up is to fasten it *Do up your coat.* **to do without something** is to manage without having it

docile adjective
gentle and obedient

dock[1] noun **docks**
a part of a harbour where ships are loaded, unloaded, or repaired

dock verb **docks, docking, docked**
1 a ship docks when it comes into a dock
2 spacecraft dock when they join together in orbit

dock[2] noun **docks**
a place for the prisoner on trial in a law court

dock[3] verb **docks, docking, docked**
1 to dock an animal's tail is to cut it short 2 to dock someone's pay is to take something off it as a penalty

dock[4] noun
a weed with broad leaves

docker noun **dockers**
a person whose job is loading and unloading ships

dockyard noun **dockyards**
an open area with docks and equipment for building or repairing ships

doctor noun **doctors**
a person trained to heal sick or injured people

doctrine (say **dok**-trin) noun **doctrines**
a religious or political belief

document noun **documents**
1 an important written or printed piece of paper 2 (in computing) something stored in a computer or on a disk, such as a piece of text or a picture **documentation** noun a collection of documents

documentary noun **documentaries**
a film or a television programme that tells you about real events or situations

doddery adjective
someone who is doddery is shaking or unsteady because they are old

doddle noun (informal)
you say that something is a doddle when it is very easy to do

dodge verb **dodges, dodging, dodged**
to dodge something is to move quickly to avoid it

dodge noun **dodges**
1 a dodging movement 2 a trick; a clever way of doing something

dodgem noun **dodgems**
a small electrically driven car at a fair, in which you drive round an enclosure, dodging and bumping other cars

dodgy adjective **dodgier, dodgiest** (informal)
1 awkward or tricky 2 dishonest or not reliable

doe noun **does**
a female deer, rabbit, or hare

does
3rd singular present tense of **do** *She does what she likes.*

doesn't
short for *does not He doesn't understand.*

dog noun **dogs**
a four-legged animal that barks, often kept as a pet

dog–eared adjective
a dog-eared book has the corners of its pages bent or worn because it has been read so much

dogged (say **dog**-id) adjective
not giving up in spite of difficulties; obstinate **doggedly** adverb

do–it–yourself adjective
suitable for anyone to make or use at home, rather than paying for someone else to do it

doldrums plural noun
the ocean regions near the equator, where

there is little or no wind **in the doldrums**
bored and unhappy

dole noun (informal)
the dole is money paid by the government
to unemployed people

doll noun dolls
a toy model of a person, especially a baby
or child

dollar noun dollars
a unit of money in the United States and
some other countries

dolly noun dollies (informal)
a doll

dolphin noun dolphins
a sea mammal like a small whale with a
snout like a beak

domain noun domains
an area that is ruled or controlled
by someone

dome noun domes
a roof shaped like the top half of a ball

domestic adjective
1 to do with the home 2 a domestic animal
is tame and kept at home

domesticated adjective
1 a domesticated animal is trained to live
with people 2 a domesticated person enjoys
household work and home life

dominant adjective
most powerful or important
dominance noun

dominate verb dominates,
dominating, dominated
to dominate people is to control them by
being the most powerful **domination** noun

dominion noun dominions
1 rule or authority 2 an area ruled by
one ruler

domino noun dominoes
a small, flat, oblong piece of wood or plastic
with dots (1 to 6) or a blank space at each
end, used in the game of **dominoes**

donate verb donates, donating,
donated
to donate something, especially money,
is to give it to a charity or organization
donation noun

done
past participle of do *I have done
nothing wrong.*

donkey noun donkeys
an animal that looks like a small horse with
long ears

donor noun donors
someone who gives something *New blood
donors are needed.*

don't
short for *do not Don't cycle on the pavement.*

doodle noun doodles
a quick drawing or scribble

doodle verb doodles, doodling,
doodled
to doodle is to draw a doodle *I get my felt
tips and doodle all around my name, drawing
a little sun on one side and a cloud with
raindrops on the other.* — Jacqueline Wilson,
Little Darlings

doom noun
a grim fate like ruin or death

doom verb dooms, dooming, doomed
to be doomed to something is to have a
grim fate you cannot avoid

door noun doors
a movable panel that opens and closes the
entrance to a room, building, or cupboard

doorstep noun doorsteps
the step or piece of ground outside a door

doorway noun doorways
the opening into which a door fits

dopey adjective dopier, dopiest
(informal)
1 half asleep 2 stupid

dormitory noun dormitories
a room for several people to sleep in,
especially in a school

a
b
c
d
e
f
g
h
i
j
k
l
m
n
o
p
q
r
s
t
u
v
w
x
y
z

A
B
C
D
E
F
G
H
I
J
K
L
M
N
O
P
Q
R
S
T
U
V
W
X
Y
Z

dose noun doses
the amount of a medicine that you are meant to take at one time

dossier (say **doss**-i-er or **doss**-i-ay) noun dossiers
a set of documents with information about a person or event

dot noun dots
a tiny spot

dot verb dots, dotting, dotted
to dot something is to mark it with dots

dotty adjective dottier, dottiest
(informal)
crazy or silly

double adjective
1 twice as much or twice as many 2 having two of something *double doors* 3 suitable for two people *a double bed*

double noun doubles
1 double is twice the amount or cost 2 a double is someone who looks like someone else 3 you play doubles in tennis when you play with someone else against another pair of players

double verb doubles, doubling, doubled
1 to double something is to make it twice as big 2 to double is to become twice as big **to double up** is to bend over because you are in pain or laughing so much

double bass noun double basses
a musical instrument with strings, like a large cello

double-cross verb double-crosses, double-crossing, double-crossed
to double-cross someone is to cheat or betray them when you are supposed to be supporting them

double-decker noun double-deckers
a bus with two floors, one above the other

doubly adverb
twice as much *It's doubly important that you should go.*

doubt noun doubts
not feeling sure about something

doubt verb doubts, doubting, doubted
to doubt something is to feel unsure about it *I doubt whether he is telling the truth.*

doubtful adjective
1 having doubts *She looked doubtful.*
2 making you feel doubt *Their story was very doubtful.* **doubtfully** adverb

doubtless adverb
certainly; without any doubt

dough noun
a thick mixture of flour and water used for making bread or pastry

doughnut noun doughnuts
a round or ring-shaped bun that has been fried and covered with sugar

dove noun doves
a kind of pigeon, often used as a symbol of peace

dowel noun dowels
a wooden or metal pin for holding together two pieces of wood or stone

down[1] adverb, preposition
1 to or in a lower place *It fell down. Run down the hill.* 2 along *Go down to the shops.*

down[2] noun
very soft feathers or hair *Ducks are covered with down.*

downcast adjective
1 looking downward *Her eyes were downcast.* 2 sad or dejected

downfall noun downfalls
1 a person's downfall is their ruin or fall from power 2 a heavy fall of rain or snow

downhill adverb
down a slope

download verb downloads, downloading, downloaded (in computing)
to download data is to transfer it from a larger system to a smaller one

download noun downloads
data that has been downloaded

downpour noun **downpours**
a heavy fall of rain

downright adjective
complete, total *a downright lie*

downright adverb
thoroughly, extremely *I felt downright angry about it.*

downs plural noun
grass-covered hills *Let's have a picnic on the downs.*

downstairs adverb, adjective
to or on a lower floor

downstream adverb
in the direction that a river or stream flows

downward or **downwards** adjective, adverb
going towards what is lower

doze verb **dozes, dozing, dozed**
to doze is to sleep lightly **dozy** adjective
someone is dozy when they are feeling sleepy

dozen noun **dozens**
a set of twelve

Dr
short for **Doctor**

drab adjective **drabber, drabbest**
1 dull and without colour *His clothes were drab.* **2** dreary and uninteresting

draft noun **drafts**
a rough plan for something you are going to write

draft verb **drafts, drafting, drafted**
to draft something you are going to write is to make a rough plan of it

drag verb **drags, dragging, dragged**
1 to drag something heavy is to pull it along **2** to drag a river or lake is to search it with nets and hooks

drag noun (informal)
something annoying or tedious

dragon noun **dragons** (in stories)
a winged lizard-like monster that breathes fire

dragonfly noun **dragonflies**
an insect with a long body and two pairs of transparent wings

drain noun **drains**
1 a pipe or ditch for taking away water or sewage **2** something that uses up your strength or money

drain verb **drains, draining, drained**
1 to drain water is to take it away with drains **2** to drain is to flow or trickle away **3** to drain a glass or bottle is to empty liquid out of it **4** to drain someone is to exhaust them
drainage noun

drake noun **drakes**
a male duck

drama noun **dramas**
1 drama is writing or performing plays **2** a drama is a play **3** a drama is also a series of exciting events

dramatic adjective
1 to do with drama **2** exciting and impressive *A dramatic change has taken place.* **dramatically** adverb

dramatics plural noun
performing plays

dramatist noun **dramatists**
someone who writes plays

dramatize verb **dramatizes, dramatizing, dramatized**
1 to dramatize a story is to make it into a play **2** to dramatize an event is to exaggerate it *Why do you always dramatize everything?* **dramatization** noun

drank
past tense of **drink** verb *Grandad drank his tea.*

drape verb **drapes, draping, draped**
to drape something like cloth is to hang it loosely over something

drastic adjective
having a strong or violent effect
drastically adverb

a
b
c
d
e
f
g
h
i
j
k
l
m
n
o
p
q
r
s
t
u
v
w
x
y
z

draught (rhymes with **craft**) noun
draughts
a current of cold air indoors
draughty adjective

draughts noun
a game played with 24 round pieces on a chessboard

draughtsman noun draughtsmen
1 someone who draws plans **2** a piece used in the game of draughts

draw verb draws, drawing, drew, drawn
1 to draw a picture or outline is to form it with a pencil or pen **2** to draw something is to pull it *She drew her chair up to the table.* **3** to draw people is to attract them *The fair drew large crowds.* **4** to draw is to end a game or contest with the same score on both sides *They drew 2-2 last Saturday.* **5** to draw the curtains is to open or close them **6** to draw near is to come nearer *The ship was drawing nearer.*

draw noun draws
1 a raffle or similar competition in which the winner is chosen by picking tickets or numbers at random **2** a game that ends with the same score on both sides **3** an attraction

drawback noun drawbacks
a disadvantage

drawbridge noun drawbridges
a bridge over a moat, hinged at one end so that it can be raised or lowered

drawer noun drawers
a sliding box-like container in a piece of furniture

drawing noun drawings
something drawn with a pencil or pen

drawing pin noun drawing pins
a short pin with a large flat top that you use for fixing paper to a surface

drawl verb drawls, drawling, drawled
to speak very slowly or lazily

dread verb dreads, dreading, dreaded
to dread something is to fear it very much

dread noun
great fear

dreadful adjective
very bad *We've had dreadful weather.*
dreadfully adverb

dreadlocks plural noun
hair in long tightly-curled ringlets, worn especially by Rastafarians

dream noun dreams
1 things you seem to see while you are sleeping **2** something you imagine; an ambition or ideal *His dream is to be famous.*
dreamy adjective like a dream; not real

dream verb dreams, dreaming, dreamt or dreamed
1 to dream is to have a dream **2** to dream is also to want something badly *She dreams of being a ballet dancer.* **3** to dream something is to think it may happen *I never dreamt she would leave.*

dreary adjective drearier, dreariest
1 dull or boring **2** gloomy **dreariness** noun

dredge verb dredges, dredging, dredged
to dredge something is to drag it up, especially mud from the bottom of water
dredger noun

drench verb drenches, drenching, drenched
to drench someone or something is to soak them *They got drenched in the rain.*

dress noun dresses
1 a dress is a woman's or girl's piece of clothing, having a top and skirt in one **2** dress is clothes or costume *We have to wear fancy dress.*

dress verb dresses, dressing, dressed
1 to dress is to put clothes on **2** to dress a wound is to put a bandage or plaster it **3** to dress food is to prepare it for cooking or eating

dresser noun dressers
a sideboard with shelves at the top

dressing noun dressings
1 a sauce of oil, vinegar, and spices for a

salad **2** a bandage or plaster used to cover a wound

dressing gown noun dressing gowns
a loose light indoor coat you wear over pyjamas or a nightdress

dressmaker noun dressmakers
a person whose job is to make clothes for women

drew
past tense of **draw** verb *Toby drew in a deep breath.*

dribble verb dribbles, dribbling, dribbled
1 to dribble is to let saliva trickle out of your mouth **2** to dribble is also to kick a ball gently in front of you as you run forward

dried
past tense and past participle of **dry** verb *He dried himself with a towel. The mud had dried on his shoes.*

drier noun driers
a device for drying hair or washing

drift verb drifts, drifting, drifted
1 to drift is to be carried gently along by water or air **2** to drift is also to live casually or wander about without any real plan or purpose

drift noun drifts
1 a drifting movement **2** a mass of snow or sand piled up by the wind **3** the general meaning of what someone says *Do you get my drift?*

driftwood noun
wood floating on the sea or washed ashore

drill noun drills
1 a tool for making holes **2** repeated exercises in military training, gymnastics, or sport **3** a set way of doing something *Do you know the drill?*

drill verb drills, drilling, drilled
1 to drill a hole is to make a hole with a drill **2** to drill is to do repeated exercises

drink verb drinks, drinking, drank, drunk
1 to drink is to swallow liquid **2** to drink can also mean to have a lot of alcohol *Don't drink and drive.*

drink noun drinks
1 a liquid for drinking **2** an alcoholic drink

drip verb drips, dripping, dripped
1 to drip is to fall in drops **2** to drip is also to let liquid fall in drops *The tap was dripping.*

drip noun drips
a falling drop of liquid

dripping noun
fat that melts from roasted meat and is allowed to set

drive verb drives, driving, drove, driven
1 to drive a vehicle is to operate it **2** to drive someone or something is to make them move **3** to drive someone into a state or feeling is to force them into it *That music is driving me mad!* **driver** noun

drive noun drives
1 a drive is a journey in a vehicle **2** drive is energy and enthusiasm **3** a drive is a road leading to a house **4** a drive is a powerful stroke of the ball in cricket, golf, and other games

drizzle noun
gentle rain

drizzle verb drizzles, drizzling, drizzled
to rain gently

drone verb drones, droning, droned
1 to drone is to make a low humming sound **2** you can also say that someone drones when they talk in a boring voice

drone noun drones
1 a droning sound **2** a male bee

drool verb drools, drooling, drooled
to drool is to dribble continuously

droop verb droops, drooping, drooped
to hang down weakly

drop noun drops
1 a tiny amount of liquid **2** a fall or

a b c **d** e f g h i j k l m n o p q r s t u v w x y z

decrease *There has been a sharp drop in attendance.* **droplet** noun a small drop

drop verb drops, dropping, dropped
1 to drop is to fall 2 to drop something is to let it fall 3 to drop is also to become less or lower *The temperature suddenly dropped.* **to drop in** is to visit someone casually **to drop out** is to stop taking part in something

drought (rhymes with out) noun droughts
a long period of dry weather

drove
past tense of **drive** verb *Uncle Gareth drove them all the way home.*

drown verb drowns, drowning, drowned
1 to drown is to die from being under water and unable to breathe 2 to drown a person or animal is to kill them by forcing them to stay under water 3 to drown sounds is to make so much noise that they cannot be heard

drowsy adjective drowsier, drowsiest
sleepy **drowsily** adverb **drowsiness** noun

drug noun drugs
1 a substance that kills pain or cures a disease 2 a substance that people take because it affects their senses or their mind. Some drugs cause addiction or are illegal.

drug verb drugs, drugging, drugged
to drug someone is to make them unconscious with drugs

Druid noun Druids
a priest of an ancient religion in Britain and France

drum noun drums
1 a musical instrument made of a cylinder with a thin skin stretched over one end or both ends 2 a cylindrical container *There was a row of oil drums along the side of the road.*

drum verb drums, drumming, drummed
1 to drum is to play a drum or drums 2 to drum on something is to tap it repeatedly *He drummed his fingers on the table.* **drummer** noun

drumstick noun drumsticks
1 a stick used for hitting a drum 2 the lower part of a cooked bird's leg

drunk[1] adjective
not able to control your behaviour through drinking too much alcohol

drunk noun drunks
someone who is drunk **drunkard** noun a person who is often drunk

drunk[2]
past participle of **drink** verb *Have you drunk all the juice?*

dry adjective drier, driest
1 not wet or damp 2 boring and dull *The book I'm reading is rather dry.* 3 funny in a clever and sarcastic way *He has a very dry sense of humour.* **drily** adverb **dryness** noun

dry verb dries, drying, dried
1 to dry is to become dry 2 to dry something is to make it dry

dry-cleaning noun
a method of cleaning clothes using chemicals rather than water

dual adjective
having two parts or aspects; double *This building has a dual purpose.*

dual carriageway noun dual carriageways
a road with several lanes in each direction

dub verb dubs, dubbing, dubbed
1 to change or add new sound to the sound on a film *It's a Japanese film but has been dubbed into English.* 2 to give someone a name or title

dubious adjective
1 feeling doubtful or uncertain *I'm dubious about our chances of winning.* 2 probably not honest or not good

duchess noun duchesses
a duke's wife or widow

duck noun ducks
1 a web-footed water bird with a flat beak 2 a batsman's score of nought at cricket

A B C **D** E F G H I J K L M N O P Q R S T U V W X Y Z

duck verb ducks, ducking, ducked
1 to duck is to bend down quickly to avoid something 2 to duck someone is to push them under water quickly

duckling noun ducklings
a young duck

duct noun ducts
a tube or pipe

due adjective
1 expected to arrive *The train is due in five minutes.* 2 needing to be paid *Payment for the trip is due next week.* **due to something** or **someone** because of something or someone *The traffic jam was due to an accident.* **in due course** eventually; at the expected time

due adverb
directly *The camp is due north.*

duel noun duels
a fight between two people, especially with pistols or swords

duet noun duets
a piece of music for two players or two singers

duffel coat noun duffel coats
a thick overcoat with a hood

dug
past tense and past participle of **dig** verb *He dug in his pocket for some change. The dog has dug a hole in the lawn.*

dugout noun dugouts
1 an underground shelter 2 a canoe made by hollowing out a tree trunk

duke noun dukes
a member of the highest rank of noblemen

dull adjective duller, dullest
1 not bright or clear; gloomy *It was a dull day.* 2 boring *What a dull programme.* 3 not sharp *I had a dull pain.* 4 stupid *You are a dull boy.* **dully** adverb **dullness** noun

duly adverb
rightly; as expected *They promised to come, and later they duly arrived.*

dumb adjective dumber, dumbest
1 unable to speak; silent 2 (informal) stupid

dumbfounded adjective
unable to say anything because you are so astonished

dummy noun dummies
1 something made to look like a person or thing; an imitation 2 an imitation teat for a baby to suck

dump noun dumps
1 a place where something, especially rubbish, is left or stored 2 (informal) if you call a place a dump, you do not like it

dump verb dumps, dumping, dumped
1 to dump something is to get rid of it when you do not want it 2 to dump something somewhere is to put it down carelessly

dumpling noun dumplings
a lump of boiled or baked dough

dumpy adjective dumpier, dumpiest
short and fat

dune noun dunes
a hill of loose sand formed by the wind

dung noun
solid waste matter from an animal

dungarees plural noun
trousers with a piece in front covering your chest, held up by straps over your shoulders

dungeon (say **dun**-jon) noun dungeons
an underground prison cell

dunk verb dunks, dunking, dunked
to dunk something is to dip it into a liquid

duo noun duos
a pair of people, especially playing music

duplicate (say **dew**-pli-kat) noun duplicates
something that is exactly the same as something else; an exact copy

duplicate (say **dew**-pli-kayt) verb duplicates, duplicating, duplicated
to duplicate something is to make an exact copy of it **duplication** noun

159

durable adjective
lasting and strong

duration noun
the time something lasts

during preposition
while something else is going on *Let's meet in the playground during the interval.*

dusk noun
the time of the day just after sunset when it is starting to get dark

dust noun
a fine powder made up of tiny pieces of dry earth or other material

dust verb dusts, dusting, dusted
1 to dust things is to clear the dust off them **2** to dust something is to sprinkle it with dust or powder *You can dust the cake with sugar.*

dustbin noun dustbins
a bin for household rubbish

duster noun dusters
a cloth for dusting things

dustman noun dustmen
a person whose job is to empty dustbins

dustpan noun dustpans
a pan into which you brush dust

dusty adjective dustier, dustiest
covered with or full of dust

dutiful adjective
doing your duty; obedient
dutifully adverb

duty noun duties
1 your duty is what you have to do, perhaps as part of your job **2** a duty is a kind of tax

duvet (say **doo**-vay) noun duvets
a kind of quilt used instead of other bedclothes

DVD noun DVDs
short for *digital versatile disc*, a disc on which large amounts of sound and pictures can be stored, especially films

dwarf noun dwarfs or dwarves
a very small person or thing

dwarf verb dwarfs, dwarfing, dwarfed
to dwarf something is to make it seem very small *The skyscraper dwarfs all the buildings round it.*

dwell verb dwells, dwelling, dwelt
to dwell in a place is to live there **to dwell on something** is to think or talk about it constantly

dwelling noun dwellings
a house or other place to live in

dwindle verb dwindles, dwindling, dwindled
to get smaller gradually *A trickle of woodsmoke from the Schloss chimneys slowly dwindled to a thin line, etching a message of embers and ash across the night sky.*
— Debi Gliori, *Pure Dead Magic*

dye verb dyes, dyeing, dyed
to dye something is to change its colour by putting it in a special liquid

dye noun dyes
a liquid used to dye things

dying
present participle of **die** *The wind is dying down.* **to be dying to do something** is to be very eager to do it *I'm dying to see the film.*

dyke noun dykes
another spelling of **dike**

dynamic adjective
energetic and active

dynamite noun
a powerful explosive

dynamo noun dynamos
a machine that makes electricity

dynasty (say **din**-a-sti) noun dynasties
a series of kings and queens from the same family

dyslexia (say dis-**lek**-si-a) noun
special difficulty in being able to read and spell words **dyslexic** adjective

Ee

each determiner, pronoun
each person or thing in a group is every one of them when you think of them separately *Each film lasts an hour. You get ten marks for each of these questions. We all knew each other.*

eager adjective
badly wanting to do something or to have something; enthusiastic **eagerly** adverb **eagerness** noun

eagle noun eagles
a large bird of prey with strong eyesight

ear¹ noun ears
1 the part of your body that you hear with **2** an ear, or a good ear, for something is the ability to hear something clearly and understand it well *She has an unusually good ear for music.*

ear² noun ears
the spike of seeds at the top of a stalk of corn

earache noun
a pain inside your ear

eardrum noun eardrums
a membrane in the ear that vibrates when sound reaches it

earl noun earls
a British nobleman

earlobe noun earlobes
the rounded part that hangs down at the bottom of your ear

early adverb, adjective earlier, earliest
1 arriving or happening before the usual or expected time *Jane caught a bus and got home early.* **2** happening near the beginning *The team was helped by an early goal. They became friends early in their lives.*

earmark verb earmarks, earmarking, earmarked
to earmark something, especially money, is to put it aside for a special purpose

earn verb earns, earning, earned
1 to earn money is to get it by working for it **2** to earn a reward or praise is to do something good so that you deserve it

earnest adjective
serious about something you want to do or about something important **earnestly** adverb

earnings plural noun
earnings are money that someone earns

earphones plural noun
earphones are a set of two small flat speakers joined by a band that fits over your ears so that you can listen to music without other people hearing it

earplugs plural noun
earplugs are a pair of small plugs that fit into your ears to cut out loud sounds

earring noun earrings
an ornament worn on the ear

earshot noun
a sound is in earshot when it is close enough for you to be able to hear it

earth noun earths
1 the earth is the planet that we live on **2** earth is soil or the ground **3** an earth is a hole or burrow where a fox or badger lives **4** an earth is also a connection to the ground to complete an electric circuit you use **on earth** with words like *what, who,* and *where* to make the point stronger *What on earth are you doing?*

earthly adjective
to do with life on earth

earthquake noun earthquakes
a violent movement of part of the earth's surface caused by pressure that has built up underneath

earthworm noun earthworms
a common worm that is found in the soil

a
b
c
d
e
f
g
h
i
j
k
l
m
n
o
p
q
r
s
t
u
v
w
x
y
z

A
B
C
D

E

F
G
H
I
J
K
L
M
N
O
P
Q
R
S
T
U
V
W
X
Y
Z

earthy adjective **earthier, earthiest**
like earth or soil

earwig noun **earwigs**
a crawling garden insect with pincers at the end of its body

ease noun
to do something with ease is to do it without any difficulty or trouble **to be at ease** is to be comfortable and relaxed *She liked Tony and felt at ease with him.*

ease verb **eases, easing, eased**
1 to ease something unpleasant is to make it easier or less troublesome **2** a pain or problem eases when it becomes less severe or troublesome **3** to ease something is to move it gently into position

easel noun **easels**
a stand or frame for holding a painting so an artist can work on it

easily adverb
1 without difficulty; with ease *Pencil marks can be easily rubbed out afterwards.* **2** by far *This was easily the best victory of his career.* **3** very likely *They could easily be wrong.*

east noun
1 the direction in which the sun rises **2** the part of a country or city that is in this direction

east adjective, adverb
1 towards the east or in the east **2** coming from the east *An east wind made the day very cold.*

Easter noun
a Christian festival in spring, commemorating Christ's rising from the dead

easterly adjective
an easterly wind is one that blows from the east

eastern adjective
coming from or to do with the east

eastward or **eastwards**
adjective, adverb
towards the east

easy adjective **easier, easiest**
something easy can be done or understood without trouble *He started with easy questions. The machine is easy to use.* **to take it easy** is to relax or go carefully

eat verb **eats, eating, ate, eaten**
to eat food is to chew it and swallow it

eaves plural noun
eaves are the overhanging edges of a roof

ebb noun
the movement of the tide when it is going out

ebb verb **ebbs, ebbing, ebbed**
1 the tide ebbs when it goes away from the land **2** a good feeling ebbs or ebbs away when it becomes much weaker *When he saw his opponent his courage ebbed away.*

ebony noun
ebony is a hard black wood

eccentric (say ik-**sen**-trik) adjective
behaving strangely **eccentricity** noun

echo noun **echoes**
a second sound that you hear when the original sound is reflected off a hard surface such as walls or high rocks

echo verb **echoes, echoing, echoed**
1 to echo is to make an echo **2** to echo something said is to repeat it

eclair (say ay-**klair**) noun **eclairs**
a finger-shaped cake of pastry with a cream filling

eclipse noun **eclipses**
An eclipse is the blocking of light from the sun or moon, causing a short period of darkness. An eclipse of the sun happens when the moon comes between the sun and the earth and blocks out the light from the sun. An eclipse of the moon happens when the earth comes between the moon and the sun and casts a dark shadow on the surface of the moon.
Please see illustration on following page.

ecology (say ee-**kol**-o-ji) noun
ecology is the study of living creatures and plants in their surroundings

eclipse

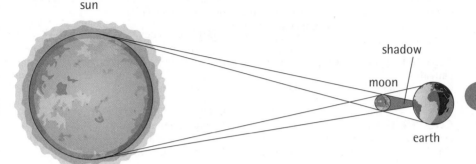

sun

shadow

moon

earth

economic (say eek-o-**nom**-ik or ek-o-**nom**-ik) adjective
to do with economics or the economy

economical (say eek-o-**nom**-ik-al) adjective
using money and resources carefully
economically adverb

economics (say eek-o-**nom**-iks or ek-o-**nom**-iks) noun
economics is the study of how money is used and how goods and services are provided and used

economist (say i-**kon**-o-mist) noun economists
someone who studies economics

economize (say i-**kon**-o-myz) verb economizes, economizing, economized
to economize is to use money more carefully

economy (say i-**kon**-o-mi) noun economies
1 an economy is a country's or family's income and the way it is spent
2 economy is being careful with money **3** economies are ways of saving money

ecstasy noun ecstasies
ecstasy is a feeling of great delight or joy
ecstatic adjective

eczema (say **ek**-si-ma) noun
eczema is a skin disease that causes rough itching patches

edge noun edges
1 the part along the side or end of something **2** the sharp part of a knife or other cutting device **to be on edge** is to feel nervous and irritable

edge verb edges, edging, edged
1 to edge is to move gradually and carefully *He edged carefully round the puddles in the garden.* **2** to edge something is to form a border to it

edgeways adverb
with the edge outwards or forwards

edgy adjective edgier, edgiest
nervous and irritable

edible adjective
an edible substance is one that you can eat, and is not poisonous

edit verb edits, editing, edited
1 to edit a book, newspaper, or magazine is to get it ready for publishing **2** to edit a film or tape recording is to choose parts of it and put them in the right order

edition noun editions
1 the form in which something is published *There is a special illustrated edition of the book.* **2** all the copies of a newspaper, magazine, or book issued at the same time

A B C D E F G H I J K L M N O P Q R S T U V W X Y Z

editor noun editors
1 someone who prepares a book, newspaper, or magazine for publishing 2 the person who manages a newspaper and is in charge of everything that is published in it

educate verb educates, educating, educated
to educate someone is to teach them and give them knowledge and skills

education noun
education, or an education, is the process of teaching people and giving them knowledge and skills **educational** adjective

eel noun eels
a long thin fish that looks like a snake

eerie adjective eerier, eeriest
weird and frightening *It was dark outside and there was an eerie silence.* **eerily** adverb **eeriness** noun

effect noun effects
1 something that happens because of something else *The drink had a strange effect on Alice.* 2 a general impression *The lights made a cheerful effect.*

effective adjective
producing what you want; successful *The program is much more effective if it is linked to the Internet.* **effectively** adverb **effectiveness** noun

effervescent (say ef-er-**vess**-ent) adjective
an effervescent liquid is fizzy and gives off bubbles **effervescence** noun

efficient adjective
doing work well; effective **efficiency** noun **efficiently** adverb

effort noun efforts
1 effort is using energy or hard work 2 an effort is an attempt

effortless adjective
something that is effortless doesn't need much work or effort *The team won another effortless victory.*

e.g.
for example *There are lots of ways of finding out, e.g. ask a teacher.*

egg¹ noun eggs
1 an oval or round object with a thin shell that birds, fish, reptiles, and insects lay, and in which their offspring develop 2 a hen's or duck's egg used as food

egg² verb eggs, egging, egged
to egg someone on is to encourage them with taunts or dares *He didn't want to dance but his friends egged him on.*

Eid (say eed) noun
a Muslim festival that marks the end of the fast of Ramadan

eiderdown (say I-der-down) noun eiderdowns
a quilt stuffed with soft material

eight noun eights
the number 8

eighteen noun eighteens
the number 18 **eighteenth** adjective, noun

eighth adjective, noun
the next after the seventh **eighthly** adverb in the eighth place; as the eighth one

eighty noun eighties
the number 80 **eightieth** adjective, noun

either determiner
1 one or the other of two people or things *Either road will take us there.* 2 both of two things *The houses on either side were all boarded up.*

either pronoun
one or the other of two people or things *Either of them might have stolen the bag.*

either adverb
also; similarly *I didn't rush, but I didn't hang about either.*

either conjunction
either ... or ... one thing or another, but not both *You can choose either a CD or a DVD. The soldiers were all either killed or badly injured.*

eject verb ejects, ejecting, ejected
1 to eject something is to send it out with force **2** to eject someone is to make them leave

elaborate (say i-**lab**-er-at) adjective
complicated or detailed

elastic noun
cord or material with strands of rubber in it so that it can stretch

elastic adjective
able to stretch and then return to its original shape or length **elasticity** noun

elated adjective
very pleased and excited

elbow noun elbows
the joint in the middle of your arm, where it bends

elbow verb elbows, elbowing, elbowed
to elbow someone is to push or prod them with your elbow

elder adjective
older *Apparently Arthur has an elder brother.*

elderberry noun
a small black berry from a tree with white flowers called an *elder*

elderly adjective
rather old

eldest adjective
oldest *Their eldest son George was born in 1660.*

elect verb elects, electing, elected
to elect someone is to choose them by voting

election noun elections
the process of voting for people, especially for Members of Parliament

electorate noun
a country's electorate is all the people who can vote in an election

electric or **electrical** adjective
to do with electricity, or worked by electricity **electrically** adverb

electrician noun electricians
someone whose job is to fit and repair electrical equipment

electricity noun
electricity is a kind of energy used to produce light and heat, and to make machines work

electrify verb electrifies, electrifying, electrified
1 to electrify something is to make it work by electricity, or to give it an electric charge **2** to electrify someone is to excite or startle them *Her singing electrified the audience.* **electrification** noun

electrocute verb electrocutes, electrocuting, electrocuted
to electrocute someone is to kill them when a large charge of electricity passes through them **electrocution** noun

electronic adjective
electronic equipment uses transistors and silicon chips **electronically** adverb

electronics plural noun
electronics is the use or study of electronic devices

elegant adjective
graceful and smart **elegance** noun **elegantly** adverb

element noun elements
1 (in science) a substance that cannot be split up into simpler substances, for example copper and oxygen **2** a part of something **3** the elements of a subject are the basic facts to do with it *Next term you will learn the elements of algebra.* **4** the elements are forces that make the weather, such as rain and wind **5** a wire or coil that gives out heat in an electric heater or cooker **to be in your element** is to be doing something you enjoy

elementary adjective
dealing with the simplest stages of something; easy

elephant noun elephants
a very large animal found in Africa and

a
b
c
d
e
f
g
h
i
j
k
l
m
n
o
p
q
r
s
t
u
v
w
x
y
z

India, with a thick grey skin, large ears, a trunk, and tusks

elevate verb elevates, elevating, elevated
to elevate something is to lift it or raise it to a higher position

elevator noun elevators (in America)
a lift for carrying people from one floor to another in a large building

eleven noun elevens
1 the number 11 2 a team of eleven people in cricket, football, and other sports
eleventh adjective, noun

elf noun elves
a tiny mischievous fairy in stories

eligible adjective
a person is eligible for something when they are qualified or suitable for it

eliminate verb eliminates, eliminating, eliminated
to eliminate someone or something is to get rid of them **elimination** noun

elite noun elites
a group of people with special privileges

elk noun elk or elks
a large kind of deer

ellipse noun ellipses
an oval shape **elliptical** noun

elm noun elms
a tall tree with large rough leaves

elocution noun
elocution is the art of speaking clearly and correctly

elongated adjective
made longer; lengthened

eloquent adjective
speaking well and expressing ideas clearly
eloquence noun

else adverb
besides; instead Nobody else knows. **or else**
otherwise Run or else you'll be late.

elsewhere adverb
somewhere else

elude verb eludes, eluding, eluded
1 to elude someone is to escape from them or avoid being caught by them 2 something eludes you when you cannot find it or remember it

elusive adjective
difficult to find or catch Deer are elusive animals.

elves
plural of elf

email noun emails
1 a system of sending messages from one computer to another by means of a network. Email is short for electronic mail.
2 a message sent by email
email verb emails, emailing, emailed
you email someone when you send them a message by email

embankment noun embankments
a long wall or bank of earth that holds back water or supports a road or railway

embark verb embarks, embarking, embarked
to embark is to go on board a ship
to embark on something is to begin something important

embarrass verb embarrasses, embarrassing, embarrassed
to embarrass someone is to make them feel shy or awkward **embarrassment** noun

TOP TIPS
Double up! There is double **r** and double **s** in **embarrass**.

embassy noun embassies
a building where an ambassador from another country lives and has an office

embers plural noun
the embers of a fire are small pieces of coal or wood that keep glowing when the fire is going out

emblem noun emblems
a symbol that stands for something The dove is an emblem of peace.

embrace verb embraces, embracing, embraced
1 to embrace someone is to hold them closely in your arms 2 to embrace a cause or belief is to accept it or adopt it 3 to embrace several things is to include them *The treaty embraces seventeen countries.*

embroider verb embroiders, embroidering, embroidered
to embroider cloth is to decorate it by stitching in designs or pictures **embroidery** noun

embryo noun embryos
a baby or young animal that is growing in the womb

emerald noun emeralds
1 a green jewel 2 a bright green colour

emerge verb emerges, emerging, emerged
to emerge is to come out or appear **emergence** noun

emergency noun emergencies
a sudden dangerous event that needs to be dealt with very quickly

emigrant noun emigrants
someone who leaves their own country and goes to live in another country

emigrate verb emigrates, emigrating, emigrated
to emigrate is to leave your own country and go and live in another country **emigration** noun

eminent adjective
famous and respected *Britain's most eminent mountaineer died ten years ago.* **eminence** noun

emission noun emissions
1 the action of sending something out 2 something that is emitted, for example fumes or radiation

emit verb emits, emitting, emitted
to emit something such as smoke or fumes is to send it out

emotion noun emotions
1 an emotion is a strong feeling in your mind, such as love or fear 2 emotion is being excited or upset *Tears of emotion flooded his eyes.*

emotional adjective
1 an emotional person expresses their feelings openly 2 an emotional event or experience is one that excites strong feelings in people

emperor noun emperors
the ruler of an empire

emphasis noun emphases
special importance given to something or extra attention drawn to something

emphasize verb emphasizes, emphasizing, emphasized
to emphasize something is to give it special importance or draw special attention to it

emphatic adjective
an emphatic statement or expression is one that you make very firmly or strongly *He agreed, with an emphatic nod of the head.* **emphatically** adverb

empire noun empires
1 a group of countries ruled by one person or group of people 2 a large group of businesses or shops under the control of one person or group of people

employ verb employs, employing, employed
1 to employ someone is to pay them to work for you 2 to employ something is to use it

employee (say im-**ploi**-ee) noun employees
someone who works for another person or group of people

employer noun employers
a person or organization that has people working for them

employment noun
1 employment is having paid work 2 employment is a paid job

A
B
C
D
E
F
G
H
I
J
K
L
M
N
O
P
Q
R
S
T
U
V
W
X
Y
Z

empress noun empresses
a female emperor, or the wife of an emperor

empty adjective emptier, emptiest
an empty place or container has nothing or no one in it *The shop had an empty flat above it. Diana waved her empty glass, hoping for more.* **emptiness** noun

empty verb empties, emptying, emptied
1 to empty something is to make it empty 2 to empty is to become empty *After the show the hall quickly emptied.*

emu (say ee-mew) noun emus
a large Australian bird that cannot fly, like an ostrich but smaller

emulate verb emulates, emulating, emulated
to emulate someone is to do what they do because you respect or admire them

emulsion noun emulsions
1 emulsion is a creamy or slightly oily liquid 2 emulsion, or emulsion paint, is a kind of water paint used for decorating buildings

enable verb enables, enabling, enabled
to enable someone to do something is to make it possible for them *A calculator will enable you to multiply and divide quickly.*

enamel noun enamels
1 enamel is a shiny glassy substance that is baked on to metal or pottery to form a hard bright surface 2 enamel is also the hard shiny surface of teeth 3 an enamel paint is a hard glossy paint

encampment noun encampments
a military camp

enchant verb enchants, enchanting, enchanted
1 to enchant someone is to delight or please them 2 to enchant someone is also to put a magic spell on them in stories **enchanted** adjective **enchanting** adjective beautiful or delightful **enchantment** noun

encircle verb encircles, encircling, encircled
to encircle something or someone is to surround them *The lake was completely encircled by a road.*

enclose verb encloses, enclosing, enclosed
1 to enclose an area is to put a fence or wall round it 2 to enclose something is to put it in an envelope or packet with a letter

enclosure noun enclosures
1 a piece of ground with a fence or wall round it 2 something you put in an envelope or packet together with a letter

encore (say on-kor) noun encores
an extra item performed at a concert or show when the audience has clapped or cheered the main items

encounter verb encounters, encountering, encountered
1 to encounter someone is to meet them unexpectedly 2 to encounter something is to experience it *We have encountered difficulties.*

encourage verb encourages, encouraging, encouraged
1 to encourage someone is to give them confidence or hope *We were encouraged by your support.* 2 to encourage someone to do something is to urge and help them to do it *They try to encourage schools to take part in these road safety schemes. This behaviour should not be encouraged.* **encouragement** noun

encyclopedia noun encyclopedias
a book or set of books containing a lot of information on a particular subject, or on all subjects, often with headings arranged in alphabetical order like a dictionary **encyclopedic** adjective

end noun ends
1 the end of something is the last part of it or the point where it stops *Holly stood at the end of the pier. Kenny thought he would never reach the end of his work.* 2 each end of a sports pitch is the part defended by one team or player 3 an end is an aim or purpose *They used the money for their own ends.* **on end 1** upright *His hair stood on end.*

2 continuously *She spoke for two hours on end.*

end verb ends, ending, ended
1 to end something is to finish it **2** to end is to finish

endanger verb endangers, endangering, endangered
to endanger someone or something is to cause them danger, especially of being injured

endeavour verb endeavours, endeavouring, endeavoured
to endeavour to do something is to try hard to do it *He endeavoured to get the job finished that day.*

ending noun endings
the last part of something *They all wanted a story with a happy ending.*

endless adjective
never stopping *Top athletes need endless training.* **endlessly** adverb

endure verb endures, enduring, endured
1 to endure pain or suffering is to put up with it **2** to endure is to continue or last **endurance** noun

enemy noun enemies
1 someone who is opposed to someone else and wants to harm them **2** a nation or army that is at war with another country

energetic adjective
1 an energetic person has a lot of energy **2** an energetic activity needs a lot of energy *They then performed an energetic dance.* **energetically** adverb

energy noun energies
1 energy is the ability to do work or provide power, for example electrical energy **2** a person's energy is the strength they have to do things

enforce verb enforces, enforcing, enforced
to enforce a law or order is to make people obey it **enforcement** noun

engage verb engages, engaging, engaged
1 to engage someone is to give them a job **2** to engage someone in conversation is to talk to them **3** to engage the enemy is to start a battle

engaged adjective
1 someone is engaged when they have promised to marry someone **2** a telephone line or lavatory is engaged when someone is already using it

engagement noun engagements
1 a promise to marry someone **2** an appointment to meet someone or do something **3** a battle

engine noun engines
1 a machine that turns energy into motion **2** a vehicle that pulls a railway train

engineer noun engineers
a person who designs and builds machines, roads, and bridges

engineering noun
engineering is the designing and building of machines, roads, bridges, and other large buildings

engrave verb engraves, engraving, engraved
to engrave a surface is to carve figures or words on it

engrossed adjective
to be engrossed in something is to concentrate on it and ignore other things around you *He was so engrossed in his work that he didn't hear her come in.*

engulf verb engulfs, engulfing, engulfed
to engulf something is to flow over it and swamp it *The town was engulfed by smoke from a huge forest fire.*

enhance verb enhances, enhancing, enhanced
to enhance something is to make it more valuable or attractive *The colour pictures enhance the book.* **enhancement** noun

A
B
C
D
E
F
G
H
I
J
K
L
M
N
O
P
Q
R
S
T
U
V
W
X
Y
Z

enjoy verb enjoys, enjoying, enjoyed
1 to enjoy something is to get pleasure from it **2** to enjoy yourself is to have a good time **enjoyable** adjective **enjoyment** noun

enlarge verb enlarges, enlarging, enlarged
to enlarge something is to make it larger **enlargement** noun

enlist verb enlists, enlisting, enlisted
1 to enlist is to join the army, navy, or air force **2** to enlist someone's help is to ask them to help you **enlistment** noun

enormity noun
something very wicked or harmful *People don't realize the enormity of the disaster created by this war.*

enormous adjective
very large; huge **enormously** adverb hugely; a lot *I enjoyed the party enormously.* **enormousness** noun

enough determiner, noun, adverb
as much or as many as you need or can cope with

enquire verb enquires, enquiring, enquired
to enquire about something is to ask for information about it *He enquired if I was well.*

enquiry noun enquiries
a question you ask when you want information *Her enquiry was about the time of the next train.*

enrage verb enrages, enraging, enraged
to enrage a person or animal is to make them very angry

enrich verb enriches, enriching, enriched
to enrich something is to make it richer

enrol verb enrols, enrolling, enrolled
1 to enrol in a society or class is to become a member of it **2** to enrol someone is to make them a member **enrolment** noun

ensue verb ensues, ensuing, ensued
to ensue is to happen or come after something else, often as a result of it

ensure verb ensures, ensuring, ensured
to ensure that something happens or has happened is to make sure of it *Please ensure that you leave the room tidy when you go.*

entangle verb entangles, entangling, entangled
to entangle something is to get it tangled or caught up **entanglement** noun

enter verb enters, entering, entered
1 to enter a place is to come into it or go into it **2** to enter something in a list or book is to write or record it there **3** to enter data in a computer is to key it in **4** to enter for a competition or examination is to take part in it

enterprise noun enterprises
1 enterprise is being bold and adventurous **2** an enterprise is a difficult or important task or project

enterprising adjective
an enterprising person or activity is one that is exciting or adventurous

entertain verb entertains, entertaining, entertained
1 to entertain someone is to amuse them or give them pleasure, as a singer or comedian does **2** to entertain people is to have them as guests and give them food and drink **entertainer** noun **entertainment** noun

enthusiasm noun enthusiasms
1 enthusiasm is a feeling of excitement and interest you show for something **2** an enthusiasm is a strong liking or interest

enthusiast noun enthusiasts
a person who has a strong interest in something *Her brother is a hockey enthusiast.*

enthusiastic adjective
full of enthusiasm *She is very enthusiastic about breeding mice.* **enthusiastically** adverb

entire adjective
whole or complete *The entire school gathered*

in the field for a photograph. **entirely** adverb completely; in every way *The brothers look entirely different.* **entirety** noun the entirety of something is all of it

entitle verb entitles, entitling, entitled to entitle someone to something is to give them a right to it *The voucher entitles you to a free drink with your pizza.* **entitlement** noun

entrance¹ (say **en**-transs) noun entrances
1 the way into a place 2 coming into a room or on to a stage or arena *Everyone clapped when the clowns made their entrance.*

entrance² (say in-**trahnss**) verb entrances, entrancing, entranced to entrance someone is to delight or enchant them

entrant noun entrants someone who goes in for a competition or examination

entreat verb entreats, entreating, entreated to entreat someone is to ask them seriously or earnestly **entreaty** noun

entrust verb entrusts, entrusting, entrusted to entrust someone with something, or to entrust something to someone, is to give it to them to look after

entry noun entries
1 an entrance 2 something written in a list or diary

envelop (say in-**vel**-op) verb envelops, enveloping, enveloped to envelop something is to cover or wrap it completely *The mountain was enveloped in mist.*

envelope (say **en**-ve-lohp or **on**-ve-lohp) noun envelopes a wrapper or covering, especially for a letter

envious adjective you are envious of someone when they have something you would like to have too **enviously** adverb

environment noun environments
1 surroundings, especially as they affect people and other living things *Some animals and plants can die out if their environment is damaged.* 2 the environment is the natural world of the land and sea and air **environmental** adjective

TOP TIPS There is a tricky bit in **environment** —it has an **n** in the middle.

envy noun an unhappy feeling you have when you want something that someone else has got
envy verb envies, envying, envied to envy someone is to feel envy about them

enzyme noun enzymes a chemical substance that humans, animals, and plants produce and that sets off processes such as the digestion of food

epic noun epics
1 a story or poem about heroes 2 an exciting or spectacular film

epidemic noun epidemics a disease that spreads quickly among the people of an area

epilepsy noun epilepsy is a disease of the nervous system, which causes periods of unconsciousness and uncontrolled body movements

epileptic adjective to do with epilepsy *an epileptic fit*
epileptic noun epileptics someone who suffers from epilepsy

episode noun episodes
1 one event that is part of a series of happenings or forms part of a story 2 one programme in a radio or television serial

epitaph noun epitaphs words written on a tomb or describing a person who has died

epoch (say **ee**-pok) noun epochs a long period of time in the past, during which important events happened

a b c d e f g h i j k l m n o p q r s t u v w x y z

171

A
B
C
D
E
F
G
H
I
J
K
L
M
N
O
P
Q
R
S
T
U
V
W
X
Y
Z

equal adjective
things are equal when they are the same in amount, size, or value **to be equal to something** is to have the strength or ability to do it *She was equal to the task.*

equal noun **equals**
a person or thing that is equal to another *He thought he was his sister's equal at maths.*

equal verb **equals, equalling, equalled**
to equal something is to be the same in amount, size, or value

equality noun
equality is being equal

equalize verb **equalizes, equalizing, equalized**
to equalize things is to make them equal

equalizer noun **equalizers**
a goal or point that makes the scores in a game equal

equally adverb
in the same way or to the same extent *You are all equally to blame.*

equation (say i-**kway**-zhon) noun **equations** (in mathematics)
a statement that two amounts are equal, for example 3 + 4 = 2 + 5

equator (say i-**kway**-ter) noun
an imaginary line round the earth at an equal distance from the North and South Poles **equatorial** adjective

equestrian adjective
to do with horse-riding

equilateral (say ee-kwi-**lat**-er-al) adjective
an equilateral triangle has all its sides equal

equinox noun **equinoxes**
the time of year when day and night are equal in length (about 20 March in spring and about 22 September in autumn)

equip verb **equips, equipping, equipped**
to equip someone or something is to supply them with what is needed *Are you equipped for mountaineering?*

equipment noun
equipment is a set of things needed for a special purpose

equivalent adjective
things are equivalent when they are equal in value, importance, or meaning **equivalence** noun

era (say **eer**-a) noun **eras**
a long period of history

erase verb **erases, erasing, erased**
1 to erase something written is to rub it out
2 to erase a recording on magnetic tape is to wipe it out **eraser** noun a piece of rubber or plastic for rubbing out writing

erect adjective
standing straight up

erect verb **erects, erecting, erected**
to erect something is to set it up or build it **erection** noun

erode verb **erodes, eroding, eroded**
to erode something is to wear it away *Water has eroded the rocks.*

erosion noun
erosion is the wearing away of the earth's surface by the action of water and wind

errand noun **errands**
a short journey to take a message or fetch something

erratic (say i-**rat**-ik) adjective
not reliable or regular **erratically** adverb

error noun **errors**
a mistake

erupt verb **erupts, erupting, erupted**
1 a volcano erupts when it shoots out lava
2 something powerful or violent erupts when it suddenly happens *An argument erupted over a disputed goal.* **eruption** noun

escalate verb **escalates, escalating, escalated**
to escalate is to become gradually greater or more serious *The riots escalated into a war.*

escalator noun escalators
a staircase with a revolving band of steps moving up or down

escape verb escapes, escaping, escaped
1 to escape is to get free or get away
2 to escape something is to avoid it *He escaped the washing-up.*

escape noun escapes
1 an act of escaping *an escape of prisoners*
2 a way to escape *He suddenly saw his escape, and ran for it.*

escort (say ess-kort) noun escorts
1 a person or group who accompanies someone, especially to give protection
2 a group of vehicles, ships, or aircraft accompanying someone or something

escort (say i-skort) verb escorts, escorting, escorted
to escort someone or something is to act as an escort to them

Eskimo noun Eskimos or Eskimo
one of the people who live in very cold parts of North America, Greenland, and Siberia

especially adverb
chiefly; more than anything else *I like cheese, especially strong cheese.*

espionage (say ess-pi-on-ahzh) noun
espionage is spying on other countries or people

esplanade noun esplanades
a flat open area for walking, especially by the sea

–ess suffix
used to make feminine forms of words, for example *lioness* and *actress*

essay noun essays
a short piece of writing on one subject

essence noun essences
1 the most important quality or ingredient of something 2 a concentrated liquid

essential adjective
something is essential when it is very important and you must have it or do it *A car is essential in the country.*
essentially adverb basically; in many ways *The two stories are essentially the same.*

essential noun essentials
something you must have or do

establish verb establishes, establishing, established
1 to establish a business, government, or relationship is to start it on a firm basis 2 to establish a fact is to show that it is true *He managed to establish his innocence.*

establishment noun establishments
1 a place where people do business
2 establishing something

estate noun estates
1 an area of land with a set of houses or factories on it 2 a large area of land belonging to one person 3 everything that a person owns when they die

estate agent noun estate agents
someone whose business is selling or letting buildings and land

esteem verb esteems, esteeming, esteemed
to esteem someone or something is to think they are excellent

estimate (say ess-ti-mat) noun estimates
a rough calculation or guess about an amount or value

estimate (say ess-ti-mayt) verb estimates, estimating, estimated
to estimate is to make an estimate

estimation noun
1 estimation is making a rough estimate
2 a person's estimation is their opinion *It is very good in my estimation.*

estuary (say ess-tew-er-i) noun estuaries
the mouth of a large river where it flows into the sea

etc.
short for et cetera, a Latin phrase used after a list to mean 'and other similar things'

a
b
c
d
e
f
g
h
i
j
k
l
m
n
o
p
q
r
s
t
u
v
w
x
y
z

or 'and so on' *We study maths, English, science, etc.*

etch verb etches, etching, etched
to etch a picture is to make it by engraving on a metal plate with an acid **etching** noun

eternal adjective
lasting for ever; not ending or changing **eternally** adverb **eternity** noun time that goes on for ever

ether (say **ee**-ther) noun
1 ether is a colourless liquid that evaporates easily, and is used as an anaesthetic or a solvent 2 the ether is the upper air

ethnic adjective
belonging to a particular national or racial group

EU
short for **European Union**

eucalyptus (say yoo-ka-**lip**-tus) noun eucalyptuses
an evergreen tree from which an oil is obtained

euphemism noun euphemisms
a word or phrase which is used instead of an impolite or less tactful one; 'pass away' is a euphemism for 'die'

euro noun euros or euro
the currency used in many countries in the European Union

European adjective
coming from Europe or to do with Europe
European noun Europeans
a European person

euthanasia (say yooth-an-**ay**-zi-a) noun
euthanasia is causing someone to die gently and without pain when they are suffering from a disease that cannot be cured

evacuate verb evacuates, evacuating, evacuated
to evacuate people is to move them away from a dangerous place **evacuation** noun **evacuee** noun someone who is evacuated, especially during a war

evade verb evades, evading, evaded
to evade someone or something is to make an effort to avoid them

evaluate verb evaluates, evaluating, evaluated
to evaluate something is to estimate its value **evaluation** noun

evaporate verb evaporates, evaporating, evaporated
to evaporate is to change from liquid into steam or vapour **evaporation** noun

evasion noun evasions
1 evasion is evading something 2 an evasion is an answer that tries to avoid the question being asked

evasive adjective
trying to avoid answering something; not honest or straightforward

eve noun eves
the day or evening before an important day, for example Christmas Eve

even adjective
1 level and smooth 2 calm and stable *He has a very even temper.* 3 equal *Our scores were even.* 4 (in mathematics) able to be divided exactly by two *6 and 14 are even numbers.* **to get even with someone** is to take revenge on them **evenly** adverb **evenness** noun

even verb evens, evening, evened
1 to even something is to make it even 2 to even or even out is to become even

even adverb
used to emphasize another word *You haven't even started your work! I ran fast, but she ran even faster. She even ignored her mother.* **even so** although that is correct

evening noun evenings
the time at the end of the day before night time

event noun events
1 something that happens, especially something important 2 an item in an athletics contest *The next event will be the long jump.*

eventful adjective
full of happenings, especially remarkable or exciting ones *They had an eventful train journey across the USA.*

eventual adjective
happening at last or as a result *He had many failures before his eventual success.*

eventually adverb
finally, in the end *We eventually managed to get the door open.*

ever adverb
1 at any time *It's the best present I've ever had.* **2** always *ever hopeful* **3** (informal) used for emphasis *Why ever didn't you tell me?* **ever so** or **ever such** (informal) very much *I'm ever so pleased. She's ever such a nice girl.*

evergreen adjective
having green leaves all through the year

evergreen noun evergreens
an evergreen tree

everlasting adjective
lasting for ever or for a long time

every determiner
all the people or things of a particular kind; each *Every child should learn to swim.* **every other** each alternate one; every second one *Every other house had a garage.*

everybody pronoun
everyone

everyday adjective
happening or used every day; ordinary *Just wear your everyday clothes.*

everyone pronoun
every person; all people *Everyone likes her.*

everything pronoun
1 all things; all *Everything you need is here.* **2** the only or most important thing *Beauty is not everything.*

everywhere adverb
in all places

evict verb evicts, evicting, evicted
to evict someone is to make them move out of their house **eviction** noun

evidence noun
evidence is facts and information that give people reason to believe something

evident adjective
obvious; clearly seen *It is evident that he is lying.* **evidently** adverb

evil adjective
an evil person or action is one that is wicked and harmful

evil noun evils
evil, or an evil, is something wicked or harmful

evolution (say ee-vo-**loo**-shon) noun
1 gradual change into something different **2** the development of animals and plants from earlier or simpler forms of life

evolve verb evolves, evolving, evolved
to develop gradually or naturally

ewe (say yoo) noun ewes
a female sheep

ex- prefix
meaning something or someone that used to be, as in *ex-boyfriend*

exact adjective
1 completely correct **2** giving all the details *He gave an exact description of the people he saw running away.* **exactly** adverb **exactness** noun

exaggerate verb exaggerates, exaggerating, exaggerated
to exaggerate something is to make it seem bigger or better or worse than it really is **exaggeration** noun

exalt verb exalts, exalting, exalted
1 to exalt someone is to make them higher in rank **2** to exalt someone is also to praise them highly

exam noun exams (informal)
an examination

examination noun examinations
1 a test of someone's knowledge or skill **2** a close inspection of something

a b c d e f g h i j k l m n o p q r s t u v w x y z

A
B
C
D
E
F
G
H
I
J
K
L
M
N
O
P
Q
R
S
T
U
V
W
X
Y
Z

examine verb examines, examining, examined
to examine something is to look at it closely or in detail

examiner noun examiners
a person who sets and marks an examination to test students' knowledge

example noun examples
1 a single thing or event that shows what others of the same kind are like 2 a person or thing that you should copy or learn from **for example** as an example

exasperate verb exasperates, exasperating, exasperated
to exasperate someone is to make them very annoyed **exasperation** noun

excavate verb excavates, excavating, excavated
to excavate a piece of land is to dig in it, especially in building or archaeology **excavation** noun

exceed verb exceeds, exceeding, exceeded
1 to exceed an amount or achievement is to be more than it or do better than it 2 to exceed a rule or limit is to go beyond it when you are not supposed to *The driver was exceeding the speed limit.*

excel verb excels, excelling, excelled
to excel at something is to be very good at it, and better than everyone else

excellent adjective
extremely good; of the best kind **excellence** noun

except preposition
not including; apart from *Everyone got a prize except me.*

exception noun exceptions
1 something or someone that does not follow the normal rule 2 something that is left out

exceptional adjective
unusual *She has exceptional skill.* **exceptionally** adverb *exceptionally heavy rain*

excerpt noun excerpts
a piece taken from a book or story or film

excess noun excesses
excess, or an excess, is too much of something *We have an excess of food.*

excessive adjective
too much or too great **excessively** adverb

exchange verb exchanges, exchanging, exchanged
to exchange something is to give it and receive something else for it

exchange noun exchanges
1 a place where telephone lines are connected to each other when a call is made 2 a place where company shares are bought and sold 3 a process of exchanging things

excite verb excites, exciting, excited
to excite someone is to make them eager and enthusiastic about something *The thought of the outing excited them.* **excitable** adjective an excitable person is easily excited **excitedly** adverb

excitement noun excitements
1 excitement is being excited 2 an excitement is something that excites you

exclaim verb exclaims, exclaiming, exclaimed
to exclaim is to shout or cry out

exclamation noun exclamations
1 exclamation is shouting or crying out 2 an exclamation is a word or phrase you say out loud that expresses a strong feeling such as surprise or pain

exclamation mark noun exclamation marks
the punctuation mark (!) placed after an exclamation

exclude verb excludes, excluding, excluded
1 to exclude someone or something is to keep them out 2 to exclude something is to leave it out *Do not exclude the possibility of rain.* **exclusion** noun

exclusive adjective
1 not shared with others *Today's newspaper has an exclusive report about the match.*
2 allowing only a few people to be involved *They joined an exclusive club.*
exclusively adverb

excursion noun **excursions**
a short journey or outing made for pleasure

excuse (say iks-**kewss**) noun **excuses**
a reason given to explain why something wrong has been done
excuse (say iks-**kewz**) verb **excuses, excusing, excused**
1 to excuse someone is to forgive them
2 to excuse someone something is to allow them not to do it *Please may I be excused swimming?* **excuse me** a polite apology for interrupting or disagreeing
excusable adjective

execute verb **executes, executing, executed**
1 to execute someone is to put them to death as a punishment **2** to execute something is to perform or produce it *She executed the somersault perfectly.*
execution noun **executioner** noun

executive noun **executives**
a senior person with authority in a business or government organization

exempt adjective
not having to do something that others have to do *Old people are sometimes exempt from paying bus fares.*

exercise noun **exercises**
1 exercise is using your body to make it strong and healthy **2** an exercise is a piece of work done for practice
exercise verb **exercises, exercising, exercised**
1 to exercise is to do exercises **2** to exercise an animal is to give it exercise **3** to exercise something is to use it *You will have to exercise patience.*

exercise book noun **exercise books**
a book for writing in

exert verb **exerts, exerting, exerted**
to exert oneself or one's ability is to make an effort to get something done *He exerted all his strength to bend the bar.*
exertion noun

exhale verb **exhales, exhaling, exhaled**
to exhale is to breathe out **exhalation** noun

exhaust noun **exhausts**
1 the waste gases from an engine **2** the pipe these gases are sent out through
exhaust verb **exhausts, exhausting, exhausted**
1 to exhaust someone is to make them very tired **2** to exhaust something is to use it up completely **exhaustion** noun

exhibit verb **exhibits, exhibiting, exhibited**
to exhibit something is to show it in public, especially in a gallery or museum
exhibitor noun
exhibit noun **exhibits**
something displayed in a gallery or museum

exhibition noun **exhibitions**
a collection of things put on display for people to look at

exile verb **exiles, exiling, exiled**
to exile someone is to send them away from their country
exile noun **exiles**
1 exile is having to live away from your own country *He was in exile for ten years.* **2** an exile is a person who is exiled

exist verb **exists, existing, existed**
1 to exist is to have life or be real *Do ghosts exist?* **2** to exist is also to stay alive *They existed on biscuits and water.*

existence noun **existences**
1 existing or being **2** staying alive *It was a real struggle for existence.*

exit noun **exits**
1 the way out of a place **2** going out of a room or going off a stage or arena *The clowns then made their exit.*
exit verb **exits, exiting, exited**
to exit is to leave a stage or arena

a
b
c
d
e
f
g
h
i
j
k
l
m
n
o
p
q
r
s
t
u
v
w
x
y
z

A

exotic adjective
unusual and colourful, especially because it comes from another part of the world

B

expand verb expands, expanding, expanded
1 to expand something is to make it larger **2** to expand is to become larger **expansion** noun

C

D

E

expanse noun expanses
a wide area

F

expect verb expects, expecting, expected
1 to expect something is to think that it will probably happen *We expected it would rain.* **2** to be expecting someone is to be waiting for them to arrive **3** to expect something is to think that it ought to happen *She expects us to be quiet.*

G

H

I

J

expectant adjective
1 full of expectation or hope **2** an expectant mother is a woman who is pregnant

K

L

expectation noun expectations
1 expectation is expecting something or being hopeful **2** an expectation is something you hope to get

M

N

expecting adjective
a woman is expecting when she is pregnant

O

expedition noun expeditions
a journey made in order to do something *They are going on a climbing expedition.*

P

Q

expel verb expels, expelling, expelled
1 to expel something is to send or force it out *The fan expels stale air and fumes.* **2** to expel someone is to make them leave a school or country *He was expelled for bullying.*

R

S

T

U

V

expenditure noun
expenditure is when you spend money or use effort *We must reduce our expenditure.*

W

X

expense noun expenses
expense, or an expense, is the cost of doing something

Y

Z

expensive adjective
costing a lot of money

experience noun experiences
1 experience is what you learn from doing and seeing things **2** an experience is something that has happened to you

experience verb experiences, experiencing, experienced
to experience something is to have it happen to you

experienced adjective
having gained skill or knowledge from much experience

experiment noun experiments
a test made in order to study what happens

experiment verb experiments, experimenting, experimented
to experiment is to carry out experiments **experimentation** noun

experimental adjective
1 used in or to do with experiments *experimental work* **2** something is experimental when it is being tried out to see how good or successful it is *experimental robots*

expert noun experts
someone who has skill or special knowledge in something

expert adjective
having great knowledge or skill

expertise (say eks-per-teez) noun
expertise is expert ability or knowledge

expire verb expires, expiring, expired
to expire is to come to an end or to stop being usable *Your TV licence has expired.* **expiry** noun

explain verb explains, explaining, explained
1 to explain something is to make it clear to someone else **2** to explain a fact or event is to show why it happens *His accident explains his absence.*

explanation noun explanations
something you say that explains something or gives reasons for it *He gave*

an explanation for what had happened.
explanatory adjective an explanatory statement is one that explains something

explode verb explodes, exploding, exploded
1 to explode is to burst or suddenly release energy with a loud bang **2** to explode a bomb is to set it off **3** to explode is to increase suddenly or quickly *The city's population exploded to 3 million in a year.*

exploit (say **eks**-ploit) noun exploits
a brave or exciting deed

exploit (say iks-**ploit**) verb exploits, exploiting, exploited
1 to exploit resources is to use or develop them **2** to exploit someone is to use them selfishly **exploitation** noun

explore verb explores, exploring, explored
1 to explore a place is to travel through it to find out more about it **2** to explore a subject is to examine it carefully *We need to explore all the possibilities.* **exploration** noun **explorer** noun

explosion noun explosions
1 the exploding of a bomb or other weapon **2** a sudden or quick increase *There was a population explosion after the war.*

explosive noun explosives
explosive, or an explosive, is a substance that can explode

explosive adjective
likely to explode; able to cause an explosion

export (say iks-**port**) verb exports, exporting, exported
1 when a company exports things, it sends them to another country to sell **2** (in computing) when you export information on a computer, you move it from one file to another, or from one computer to another

export (say **eks**-port) noun exports
something that is sent abroad to be sold

expose verb exposes, exposing, exposed
1 to expose something is to reveal or uncover it **2** to expose someone is to show that they are to blame for something **3** to expose a photographic film is to let light reach it in a camera, so as to take a picture

exposure noun exposures
1 exposure is being harmed by the weather when in the open without enough protection **2** an exposure is a single photograph or frame on a film

express adjective
going or sent quickly

express noun expresses
a fast train stopping at only a few stations

express verb expresses, expressing, expressed
to express an idea or feeling is to put it into words

expression noun expressions
1 the look on a person's face that shows what they are thinking or feeling **2** a word or phrase **3** a way of speaking or performing music that expresses feelings **expressive** adjective an expressive look or statement is one that shows your feelings

expulsion noun expulsions
expulsion, or an expulsion, is when someone is driven away or made to leave

exquisite adjective
very delicate or beautiful *Next came a tall, beautiful woman clothed in a splendid trailing gown, trimmed with exquisite lace as fine as cobweb.* — L. Frank Baum, *The Road to Oz*

extend verb extends, extending, extended
1 to extend is to stretch out **2** to extend something is to make it longer or larger **3** to extend a greeting or welcome is to offer it

extension noun extensions
1 extension is extending or being extended **2** an extension is something added on, especially to a building **3** an extension is also an extra telephone in an office or house

extensive adjective
covering a large area *The bomb caused extensive damage.* **extensively** adverb over a

A

large area *She travelled extensively with her children.*

extent noun extents
1 the area or length of something 2 an amount or level *The extent of the damage was enormous.*

exterior noun exteriors
the outside of something

exterminate verb exterminates, exterminating, exterminated
to exterminate a people or breed of animal is to kill all the members of it
extermination noun

external adjective
outside **externally** adverb

extinct adjective
1 an animal or bird is extinct when there are no more examples of it alive 2 a volcano is extinct when it is not burning or active any more **extinction** noun

extinguish verb extinguishes, extinguishing, extinguished
to extinguish a fire or light is to put it out
extinguisher noun

extra adjective
more than usual; added *There is an extra charge for taking a bicycle on the train.*

extra noun extras
1 an extra person or thing 2 someone acting as part of the crowd in a film or play

extra– prefix
1 more than usual, as in *extra-special*
2 outside or beyond something, as in *extraterrestrial*

extract (say **eks**-trakt) noun extracts
1 a piece taken from a book, play, or film
2 something obtained from something else *a plant extract*

extract (say iks-**trakt**) verb extracts, extracting, extracted
to extract something is to remove it or take it out of something else

extraction noun
1 a person's extraction is the place or people they come from *She is of*

Indian extraction. 2 extraction is taking something out

extraordinary adjective
unusual or very strange
extraordinarily adverb

extraterrestrial adjective
existing in or coming from another planet
extraterrestrial noun extraterrestrials
a living thing from another planet, especially in science fiction

extravagant adjective
spending or using too much of something
extravagance noun **extravagantly** adverb

extreme adjective
1 very great or strong *They were suffering from extreme cold.* 2 farthest away *She lives in the extreme north of the country.*

extreme noun extremes
1 something very great, strong, or far away
2 either end of something

extremely adverb
as much or as far as possible; very much *They are extremely pleased.*

extremity (say iks-**trem**-it-ee) noun extremities
an extreme point; the very end of something

exuberant adjective
very cheerful or lively **exuberance** noun

exult verb exults, exulting, exulted
to rejoice or be very pleased
exultant adjective **exultation** noun

eye noun eyes
1 the organ of your body used for seeing *Please see illustration on following page.* 2 the small hole in a needle 3 the centre of a storm

eye verb eyes, eyeing, eyed
to eye someone or something is to look at them closely

eyeball noun eyeballs
the ball-shaped part of your eye, inside your eyelids

eye

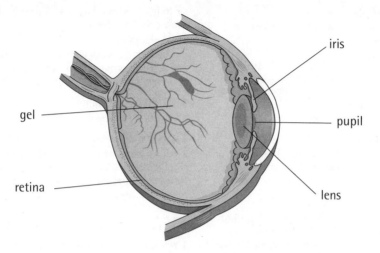

iris

gel

pupil

retina

lens

eyebrow noun **eyebrows**
the curved fringe of hair growing above
each eye

eyelash noun **eyelashes**
one of the short hairs that grow on
your eyelids

eyelid noun **eyelids**
the upper or lower fold of skin that can
close over your eyeball

eyesight noun
a person's eyesight is their ability to see

eyesore noun **eyesores**
something that is ugly to look at

eyewitness noun **eyewitnesses**
someone who actually saw something
happen, especially an accident or crime

Ff

F
short for **Fahrenheit**

fable noun **fables**
a short story which teaches a lesson about

how people should behave, often with
animals as characters

fabric noun **fabrics**
cloth

fabulous adjective
1 very great *The prince had fabulous
wealth.* **2** (informal) wonderful; marvellous
3 described in stories and fables,
not existing in real life *Dragons are
fabulous creatures.*

face noun **faces**
1 the front part of your head, where your
eyes, nose, and mouth are **2** the look on a
person's face *She had a friendly face.* **3** the
front or upper side of something *Put the
cards face down.* **4** one of the surfaces of a
shape *A cube has six faces.* **5** the side of a
mountain or cliff *They reached the face of
the rock.*

face verb **faces, facing, faced**
1 to face in a certain direction is to look
there or have the front in that direction
*Please face the front. The church faces the
school.* **2** to face a problem or danger is to
accept that you have to deal with it

facet (say **fass**-it) noun **facets**
one small surface of an object such as a
diamond, which reflects light and makes
it sparkle

facial adjective
on or to do with your face *Smiling is a facial expression.*

facility (say fa-**sil**-i-ti) noun facilities
a place where you can take part in an activity, or a piece of equipment that helps you to do things *The school has facilities for computing and sport.*

fact noun facts
fact, or a fact, is something that is true or certain **as a matter of fact** or **in fact** really *I'm leaving this morning. Now, in fact.*

factor noun factors
1 one of the reasons for something *Hard work has been a factor in her fame.* **2** a number by which a larger number can be divided exactly, without leaving a remainder *2 and 3 are factors of 6.*

factory noun factories
a large building where machines are used to make things in large amounts

factual adjective
containing facts, not stories *a factual book that tells you lots of interesting things about the Harry Potter series* **factually** adverb

fad noun fads
something that is popular for only a short time *There used to be a fad for Pokemon.*

fade verb fades, fading, faded
1 to lose colour, freshness, or strength **2** to fade or fade away is to disappear gradually

faggot noun faggots
1 a bundle of sticks tied together, used for building or as fuel for a fire **2** a meat ball made of baked chopped liver

Fahrenheit (say **fa**-ren-hyt) adjective
using a scale for measuring temperature that gives 32 degrees for freezing water and 212 degrees for boiling water

fail verb fails, failing, failed
1 to fail is to try to do something but not be able to do it **2** to fail an exam or test is not to pass it **3** to fail is also to become weak or useless or to come to an end *The batteries are failing.* **4** to fail to do something is not

to do it when you should *My friend failed to show up at the cinema.*

fail noun fails
not being successful in an examination *She has five passes and one fail.* **without fail** definitely or always *I'll be there without fail.*

failing noun failings
a fault or weakness

failure noun failures
1 failure is not being successful **2** a failure is someone or something that has failed *He was unhappy and felt a failure. It got really dark when there was a power failure.*

faint adjective fainter, faintest
1 weak; not clear or distinct **2** nearly unconscious, often because you are exhausted or very hungry

faint verb faints, fainting, fainted
to faint is to become unconscious for a short time **faintly** adverb **faintness** noun

faint-hearted adjective
not having much courage or confidence

fair¹ adjective fairer, fairest
1 right or just; honest *It's not fair to cheat in games.* **2** light in colour *The sisters both had fair hair.* **3** quite good *We've got a fair chance of winning.* **4** weather is fair when it is fine and not raining **fairness** noun

fair² noun fairs
1 an outdoor entertainment with rides, amusements, and stalls. Fairs move from town to town. **2** an exhibition or market *a craft fair*

fairground noun fairgrounds
a place where a fair is held

fairly adverb
1 quite or rather *It is fairly hard.* **2** honestly; justly *He promised to treat everyone fairly.*

fairy noun fairies
an imaginary small creature with wings and magic powers

fairyland noun
a place where fairies live; an imaginary place

fairy story or fairy tale noun
fairy stories, fairy tales
a story about fairies or magic

faith noun faiths
1 faith is strong belief or trust *We have a lot of faith in her.* 2 a faith is a religion

faithful adjective
loyal and trustworthy **faithfully** adverb **faithfulness** noun

fake noun fakes
a copy of something made to deceive people into thinking it is real

fake adjective
not real or genuine *fake diamonds*

fake verb fakes, faking, faked
1 to fake something is to make it look real in order to deceive people 2 to fake something is also to pretend to have it *He was always faking illness so he could miss PE.*

falcon noun falcons
a small kind of hawk

fall verb falls, falling, fell, fallen
1 to come down quickly towards the ground 2 numbers or prices fall when they get lower or smaller 3 a city or castle falls when it is captured 4 soldiers fall when they die in battle 5 when silence falls it becomes quiet 6 to fall sick or ill is to become ill 7 a look or glance falls on someone when it is directed at them **to fall back on something** or **someone** is to rely on them in a difficulty **to fall for someone** is to start loving them **to fall for something** is to be tricked into believing it **to fall out** is to quarrel and stop being friends **to fall through** is to fail to happen *Our plans have fallen through.*

fall noun falls
1 a time when a person or thing falls *My grandma had a bad fall.*
2 (in America) autumn

fallow adjective
land that is fallow has been ploughed but not planted with crops *The field was left fallow every three years.*

falls plural noun
a waterfall *Niagara Falls*

false adjective falser, falsest
1 untrue or incorrect 2 faked; not genuine *false tears* **falsely** adverb **falseness** noun

falsehood noun falsehoods
1 falsehood is telling lies 2 a falsehood is a lie

falter verb falters, faltering, faltered
1 to falter is to keep stopping when you move or speak 2 to falter is also to become weaker *His courage began to falter.*

fame noun
fame is being famous **famed** adjective

familiar adjective
1 well-known; often seen or experienced *It was a familiar sight.* 2 knowing something well *Are you familiar with this story?* 3 very friendly **familiarity** noun

family noun families
1 parents and their children, sometimes including grandchildren and other relations 2 a group of animals, plants, or things that are alike in some way *The tiger is a member of the cat family.*

family tree noun family trees
a diagram showing how people in a family are related and who their ancestors are

famine noun famines
famine, or a famine, is a severe shortage of food that causes many people to die

famished adjective
extremely hungry

famous adjective
known to a lot of people *Her uncle is a famous scientist.*

fan¹ noun fans
a device for making the air move about, in order to cool people or things

fan verb fans, fanning, fanned
to fan something is to send a draught of air at it *She fanned her face with her hand.* **to fan out** is to spread out in the shape of a fan *Lloyd could see the men in brown overalls fanning out across the Dome, like hounds searching for a scent.* — Gillian Cross, *The Revenge of the Demon Headmaster*

183

fan² noun fans
an enthusiastic follower or supporter of someone or something

fanatic (say fa-**nat**-ik) noun fanatics
someone who is too enthusiastic about something **fanatical** adjective

fanciful adjective
imagined rather than based on the way things really are *fanciful pictures of castles*

fancy noun fancies
1 fancy is imagination 2 a fancy is a liking or desire for something

fancy adjective fancier, fanciest
decorated; not plain

fancy verb fancies, fancying, fancied
1 to fancy something is to want it *Does anyone fancy an ice cream?* 2 to fancy something unusual is to imagine or think of it *Just fancy him riding a horse!*

fancy dress noun
unusual costume that you wear to a party or dance, often to make you look like someone else

fanfare noun fanfares
a short burst of music, often with trumpets and to announce something

fang noun fangs
a long sharp tooth

fantastic adjective
1 strange or unusual *Some of my companions pass the time by carving sea monsters' teeth into fantastic shapes, or by engraving pictures on them.* – Richard Platt, *Pirate Diary* 2 (informal) excellent **fantastically** adverb

fantasy noun fantasies
1 something pleasant that you imagine but is not likely to happen *His fantasy is to play football for England.* 2 a very imaginative story

far adverb farther, farthest
1 a long way *We didn't go far.* 2 much; by a great amount *She's a far better singer than I am.* **so far** up to now

far adjective farther, farthest
distant; opposite *She swam to the far side of the river.*

far-away adjective
distant *I'd love to go to far-away places.*

farce noun farces
1 a farce is a far-fetched or absurd kind of comedy 2 farce, or a farce, is a series of ridiculous events *The match ended up in farce.*

fare noun fares
the money you pay to travel on a bus, train, ship, or aircraft

fare verb fares, faring, fared
to fare is to get on or make progress *How did you fare in your exam?*

farewell interjection
goodbye

far-fetched adjective
unlikely to be true; difficult to believe

farm noun farms
1 an area of land where someone grows crops and keeps animals for food 2 the buildings on land of this kind 3 a farmhouse

farm verb farms, farming, farmed
1 to farm is to grow crops and raise animals for food 2 to farm land is to use it for growing crops

farmer noun farmers
someone who owns or looks after a farm

farmhouse noun farmhouses
the house where a farmer lives

farmyard noun farmyards
the open area surrounded by farm buildings

farther adverb, adjective
at or to a greater distance; more distant *She lives farther from the school than I do.*

farthest adverb, adjective
at or to the greatest distance; most distant

farthing noun farthings
an old British coin that was worth a quarter of an old penny

fascinate verb fascinates, fascinating, fascinated
to fascinate someone is to attract or interest them very much **fascination** noun

 TOP TIPS There is a tricky bit in **fascinate** —the s sound is spelt **sc**.

fashion noun fashions
1 fashion, or a fashion, is the style of clothes or other things that most people like at a particular time 2 a way of doing something *The man spoke in a friendly fashion.*

fashion verb fashions, fashioning, fashioned
to fashion something is to make it in a particular shape or style

fashionable adjective
something is fashionable when it follows a style that is popular at a particular time

fast¹ adjective faster, fastest
1 moving or done quickly *He's a fast runner.*
2 allowing fast movement *This is a fast road.*
3 a watch or clock is fast when it shows a time later than the correct time 4 secure; firmly held in place *Make sure the rope is fast.* 5 a fast colour is one that is not likely to fade

fast adverb
1 quickly 2 firmly **fast asleep** deeply asleep

fast² verb fasts, fasting, fasted
to fast is to go without food

fasten verb fastens, fastening, fastened
to fasten something is to join it firmly to something else **fastener** or **fastening** noun

fat noun fats
1 the white greasy part of meat 2 an oily or greasy substance used in cooking

fat adjective fatter, fattest
1 having a very thick round body 2 thick *What a fat book!* 3 fat meat is meat with a lot of fat

fatal adjective
1 causing someone's death *There has been a fatal accident on the motorway.* 2 likely to have bad results *He then made a fatal mistake.* **fatally** adverb

fatality noun fatalities
a death caused by war or an accident

fate noun fates
1 a power that is thought to make things happen 2 someone's fate is what has happened or will happen to them

father noun fathers
a male parent

father–in–law noun fathers–in–law
the father of your husband or wife

fathom verb fathoms, fathoming, fathomed
to fathom something difficult or tricky is to work it out *I can't fathom how you did it.*

fathom noun fathoms
a unit used in measuring the depth of water, equal to 1.83 metres or 6 feet

fatigue (say fa-**teeg**) noun
1 extreme tiredness 2 weakness in metals, caused by stress

fatten verb fattens, fattening, fattened
1 to fatten something is to make it fat 2 to fatten is to become fat

fattening adjective
fattening food is food that is likely to make you fat

fatty adjective fattier, fattiest
fatty food contains a lot of fat

fault noun faults
1 something wrong that spoils a person or thing; a flaw or mistake 2 the responsibility or blame for something *It's my fault we are late.*

fault verb faults, faulting, faulted
to fault something is to find faults in it

faultless adjective
something is faultless when it is perfect and has nothing wrong with it

a
b
c
d
e
f
g
h
i
j
k
l
m
n
o
p
q
r
s
t
u
v
w
x
y
z

A
B
C
D
E
F
G
H
I
J
K
L
M
N
O
P
Q
R
S
T
U
V
W
X
Y
Z

faulty adjective **faultier, faultiest**
having a fault or faults; not
working properly

fauna (say **faw**-na) noun
the animals that live in an area or during a
period of time

favour noun **favours**
1 a favour is something kind that you do for
someone *Will you do me a favour?* **2** favour
is approval or goodwill *The idea found
favour with most people.* **to be in favour of
someone** or **something** is to like or support
them

favour verb **favours, favouring,
favoured**
to favour someone or something is to like or
support them, or prefer them to others

favourable adjective
1 helpful or suitable *favourable
weather for sailing* **2** showing approval
favourably adverb

favourite adjective
liked more than others *This is my
favourite book.*

favourite noun **favourites**
the person or thing that you like best *This
book is my favourite.*

favouritism noun
favouritism is when someone is unfairly
kinder to one person than to others

fawn noun **fawns**
1 a young deer **2** a light brown colour

fax noun **faxes**
1 a machine that sends copies of documents
electronically through a telephone line
2 a copy made this way

fax verb **faxes, faxing, faxed**
to fax a document is to send a copy of it
using a fax machine

fear noun **fears**
fear, or a fear, is a feeling that something
unpleasant may happen

fear verb **fears, fearing, feared**
1 to fear someone or something is to be
afraid of them **2** to fear something is also to

be anxious or sad about it *I feared we would
be too late.*

fearful adjective
1 frightened *Within a dozen paces I came
upon what I perceived to be a wolf pup. I was
not fearful for I could see that he was too
weak to do me harm.* – Michael Morpurgo,
The Last Wolf **2** (informal) awful or horrid
They had a fearful quarrel. **fearfully** adverb

fearless adjective
having no fear *The great knights were
fearless when it came to anything you could
stick your sword into.* – Martyn Beardsley, *Sir
Gadabout and the Ghost* **fearlessly** adverb

fearsome adjective
frightening *'As I was saying,' the Scarecrow
went on, 'the brigands were a fearsome crew.
Armed to the teeth, every single one.'
– Philip Pullman, *The Scarecrow and his
Servant*

feasible adjective
able to be done; possible or likely

feast noun **feasts**
a large and splendid meal for a lot of people

feast verb **feasts, feasting, feasted**
to feast is to have a feast

feat noun **feats**
a brave or clever deed

feather noun **feathers**
a bird's feathers are the very light pieces
that grow from its skin and cover its body

feature noun **features**
1 your features are the different parts
of your face *He has handsome features.*
2 an important or noticeable part of
something; a characteristic **3** a newspaper
article or television programme on a
particular subject

feature verb **features, featuring,
featured**
1 to feature something is to make it an
important part of something *Ancient
Egyptian stories often featured magic.*
2 to feature in something is to be an
important part of it

February noun
the second month of the year

TOP TIPS
February can be difficult to spell —the letter **r** appears twice!

fed
past tense and past participle of **feed** verb
He fed us hearty meals of soup. Have you fed the dog?

federal adjective
to do with a system in which different states of a country are ruled by a central government, but each state still makes some of its own laws

federation noun
a group of different states that have joined together under a central government

fed up adjective (informal)
bored or unhappy

fee noun fees
a payment or charge

feeble adjective feebler, feeblest
weak; not having much strength or force
Years went over, and the Giant grew very old and feeble. — Oscar Wilde, The Selfish Giant
feebly adverb

feed verb feeds, feeding, fed
1 to feed a person or animal is to give them food 2 to feed on something is to eat it *Sheep feed on grass.* 3 to feed a machine is to put paper, coins, or other things into it

feed noun feeds
1 a feed is a meal 2 feed is food for animals

feedback noun
someone gives you feedback when they speak to you about something you have done for them *Your teacher will give you feedback on your homework.*

feel verb feels, feeling, felt
1 to feel something is to touch it to find out what it is like 2 to feel a feeling or emotion is to experience it *I feel very angry about being left out.* **to feel like something** is to want it

feel noun
what something is like when you touch it
Her dress has a funny feel about it.

feeler noun feelers
an insect's feelers are the two long thin parts that extend from the front of its body and are used for feeling

feeling noun feelings
1 feeling is the ability to feel or touch things *She lost the feeling in her right hand.* 2 feeling is also what a person feels in the mind, such as love or fear *I have hurt her feelings.* 3 a feeling is what you think about something *My feeling is that he's right.*

feet
plural of **foot**

feline adjective
to do with cats; like a cat

fell[1]
past tense of **fall** verb *He was so tired he fell asleep instantly.*

fell[2] verb fells, felling, felled
1 to fell a tree is to cut it down 2 to fell someone is to knock them down

fell[3] noun fells
a piece of wild hilly country

fellow noun fellows
1 a friend or companion; someone who belongs to the same group 2 (informal) a man or boy *He's a clever fellow.*

fellow adjective
of the same group or kind *She arranged a meeting with her fellow teachers.*

fellowship noun fellowships
1 fellowship is friendship 2 a fellowship is a group of friends; a society

felt[1]
past tense and past participle of **feel** verb
I felt sorry for her, He had felt a sharp pain in his leg.

felt[2] noun
thick woollen material

a
b
c
d
e
f
g
h
i
j
k
l
m
n
o
p
q
r
s
t
u
v
w
x
y
z

A

felt-tip pen or
felt-tipped pen noun
felt-tip pens, felt-tipped pens
a pen with a tip made of felt or fibre

B

C

female adjective
belonging to the sex that produces young
by giving birth or laying eggs
female noun females
a female person or animal

D

E

feminine adjective
to do with women or like women; suitable
for women **femininity** noun

F

G

fen noun fens
an area of low-lying marshy or flooded land

H

fence noun fences
a wooden or metal barrier round an area
of land
fence verb fences, fencing, fenced
1 to fence something or to fence it in is to
put a fence round it **2** to fence is to fight
with long narrow swords called *foils*, as
a sport

I

J

K

L

M

fencing noun
a sport that involves fighting with swords

N

O

fend verb fends, fending, fended
to fend for yourself is to take care of
yourself **to fend someone** or **something
off** is to keep them away from yourself
when they are attacking you

P

Q

R

fender noun fenders
1 a low guard placed round a fireplace to
stop coal from falling into the room
2 (in America) a bumper on a car

S

T

fern noun ferns
a plant with feathery leaves and no flowers

U

V

ferocious adjective
fierce or savage *Stig looked up, and for a
moment Barney felt quite frightened at the
ferocious scowl on his face, and was glad to
be high up out of his reach.* – Clive King,
Stig of the Dump **ferociously** adverb

W

X

Y

ferocity noun
fierceness

Z

ferret noun ferrets
a small fierce animal with a long thin body,
used for catching rabbits and rats
ferret verb ferrets, ferreting, ferreted
to ferret, or ferret about, is to search busily
for something

ferry noun ferries
a boat that takes people or things across a
river or other stretch of water
ferry verb ferries, ferrying, ferried
to ferry people or things is to take them
from one place to another, especially by
boat or car

fertile adjective
1 land that is fertile is good for growing
crops and plants **2** people or animals that
are fertile can produce babies or young
animals **fertility** noun

fertilize verb fertilizes, fertilizing,
fertilized
1 to fertilize the soil is to add chemicals or
manure to it so that crops and plants grow
better **2** to fertilize an egg or plant is to
put male cells into it so that it develops its
young or seeds **fertilization** noun

fertilizer noun fertilizers
chemicals or manure added to the soil to
make crops and plants grow better

fervent adjective
very enthusiastic about something
He is a fervent supporter of the team.
fervently adverb

fervour noun
strong feeling or great enthusiasm

festival noun festivals
1 a time of celebration, especially for
religious reasons **2** an organized set of
concerts, shows, or other events, especially
one that is arranged every year

festive adjective
to do with joyful celebrating

festivities plural noun
parties and other events that are held to
celebrate something

fetch verb fetches, fetching, fetched
1 to fetch something or someone is to go and get them **2** something fetches a particular price when it is sold for that price *My old bike fetched £10.*

fete (say fayt) noun fetes
an outdoor event with stalls, games, and things for sale, often held to raise money

fetters plural noun
fetters are chains put round a prisoner's ankles

feud (say fewd) noun feuds
a bitter quarrel between two people or families that lasts a long time
feud verb feuds, feuding, feuded
people feud when they keep up a quarrel for a long time

fever noun fevers
1 a person has a fever when their body temperature is higher than usual because they are ill **2** fever is excitement or agitation

feverish adjective
1 someone is feverish when they have a slight fever **2** excited or frantic *There was feverish activity getting the hall ready for the show.* **feverishly** adverb

few determiner fewer, fewest
not many
few pronoun
a small number of people or things **a good few** or **quite a few** a fairly large number

fiancé (say fee-**ahn**-say) noun fiancés
a woman's fiancé is the man who she is engaged to be married to

fiancée (say fee-**ahn**-say) noun fiancées
a man's fiancée is the woman who he is engaged to be married to

fiasco (say fi-**ass**-koh) noun fiascos
a complete failure *The party turned into a fiasco.*

fib noun fibs
a lie about something unimportant

fib verb fibs, fibbing, fibbed
to fib is to tell a lie about something unimportant **fibber** noun

fibre (say **fy**-ber) noun fibres
1 a fibre is a very thin thread **2** fibre is a substance made up of thin threads **3** fibre is also a substance in food that your body cannot digest but that moves the rest of the food quickly through your body and helps you to digest it

fickle adjective
someone is fickle when they often change their mind or do not stay loyal to one person or group

fiction noun fictions
1 fiction is writing, such as stories and novels, about events that have not really happened **2** a fiction is something untrue or made up

fictional adjective
a fictional character or event exists only in a story, not in real life

fictitious adjective
made up by someone and untrue

fiddle noun fiddles (informal)
a violin
fiddle verb fiddles, fiddling, fiddled
1 to fiddle is to play the violin **2** to fiddle with something is to keep touching or playing with it with your fingers *Stop fiddling with the CD player.* **fiddler** noun

fiddly adjective (informal)
awkward to use or do because it involves handling small objects *Making the model of the ship was quite a fiddly job.*

fidelity (say fi-**del**-i-ti) noun
fidelity is being faithful or loyal

fidget verb fidgets, fidgeting, fidgeted
to make small restless movements because you are bored or nervous **fidgety** adjective

field noun fields
1 a piece of land with crops or grass growing on it **2** an area of interest or study *She wants to work in the field of science.*

a
b
c
d
e
f
g
h
i
j
k
l
m
n
o
p
q
r
s
t
u
v
w
x
y
z

field verb fields, fielding, fielded
to field a ball in cricket or other games is to stop it or catch it **fielder** noun

field trip noun field trips
a visit to a place with your school to study something in its natural environment

fiend (say feend) noun fiends
1 a devil or evil spirit 2 a wicked or cruel person

fiendish adjective
1 wicked or cruel 2 very difficult or complicated *That was a fiendish puzzle.* **fiendishly** adverb

fierce adjective fiercer, fiercest
1 angry and violent and likely to attack you 2 strong or intense *The heat from the fire was fierce.* **fiercely** adverb **fierceness** noun

fiery adjective fierier, fieriest
1 full of flames or heat *The building looked like a fiery ghost, with great bursts of flame coming from the windows. — Lemony Snicket, A Series of Unfortunate Events* 2 easily made angry *He had a fiery temper.*

fifteen noun fifteens
the number 15 **fifteenth** adjective, noun

fifth adjective, noun
the next after the fourth **fifthly** adverb in the fifth place; as the fifth one

fifty noun fifties
the number 50 **fiftieth** adjective, noun

fig noun figs
a soft fruit full of small seeds

fight noun fights
1 a struggle against someone, using hands or weapons 2 an attempt to achieve or overcome something *We can all help in the fight against crime.*

fight verb fights, fighting, fought
1 to fight someone is to have a fight with them 2 to fight something is to try to stop it *They fought the fire all night.*

fighter noun fighters
1 someone who fights 2 a fast military plane that attacks other aircraft

figurative adjective
figurative language uses words for special effect and not in their usual way, often in order to describe what something is like. For example *flood* in *a flood of letters* is a figurative meaning of the word.

figure noun figures
1 one of the symbols that stand for numbers, such as 1, 2, and 3 2 the shape of someone's body 3 a diagram or illustration in a book or magazine 4 a pattern or shape *He drew a figure of eight.*

figure verb figures, figuring, figured
1 to appear or take part in something *His name does not figure in the list of entrants.* 2 to think that something is probably true *I figure the best thing to do is to wait.* **to figure something out** is to work it out *Can you figure out the answer?*

figure of speech noun figures of speech
a special way of using words that makes what you say or write interesting, such as a metaphor or a simile

filament noun filaments
a thread or thin wire

file¹ noun files
a metal tool with a rough surface that you rub on things to make them smooth or shape them
file verb files, filing, filed
to file something is to make it smooth or shape it with a file

file² noun files
1 a box or folder for keeping papers in 2 a set of information that has been stored under one name in a computer **to walk in single file** is to walk one behind the other
file verb files, filing, filed
1 to file a paper or document is to put it in a box or folder 2 to file is to walk one behind the other

filings plural noun
tiny pieces of metal that have been rubbed from a larger piece

fill verb fills, filling, filled
1 to fill something is to make it full **2** to fill is to become full *The room was filling quickly.* **3** to fill a tooth is to put a filling in it **to fill in a form** is to write answers to all the questions on it **to fill something up** is to fill it completely
fill noun fills
enough to make you full *Eat your fill.*

fillet noun fillets
a piece of fish or meat without bones

filling noun fillings
1 a piece of metal put in your tooth by a dentist to replace a decayed part **2** food you put inside a pie, sandwich, or cake

filly noun fillies
a young female horse

film noun films
1 a series of moving pictures that tells a story, such as those shown in a cinema or on television **2** a roll or piece of thin plastic that you put in some types of camera to take photographs **3** a very thin layer of something *The table was covered in a film of grease.*
film verb films, filming, filmed
to film something is to make a film of it

filter noun filters
1 a device for removing dirt or other unwanted things from a liquid or gas that passes through it **2** a system allowing a line of traffic to move in one direction while other lines are held up
filter verb filters, filtering, filtered
1 to filter a liquid or gas is to pass it through a filter **2** to move gradually *People started to filter into the hall.*

filth noun
disgusting dirt

filthy filthier, filthiest adjective
very dirty

fin noun fins
1 a thin flat part that sticks out from a fish's body and helps it to swim **2** a small part that sticks out from an aircraft or rocket and helps it to balance

final adjective
1 coming at the end; last **2** a decision is final when it puts an end to argument or doubt *You must not go, and that's final!*
final noun finals
the last of a series of contests, that decides the overall winner

finale (say fin-ah-li) noun finales
the last part of a show or piece of music

finalist noun finalists
a person or team taking part in a final

finally adverb
1 after a long time, at last *We finally got there around midnight.* **2** as the last thing *Finally, I would like to thank my parents.*

finance noun
1 finance is the use and control of money **2** someone's finances are the amount of money or funds they have
finance verb finances, financing, financed
to finance something is to provide money for it

financial adjective
to do with money

finch noun finches
a small bird with a short thick beak

find verb finds, finding, found
1 to find something is to see or get it by chance or by looking for it **2** to find something is also to learn it by experience *He found that digging is hard work.* **to find someone out** is to discover that they have done something wrong **to find something out** is to get information about it

findings plural noun
things someone has found out

fine[1] adjective finer, finest
1 of high quality; excellent *They cooked a fine meal.* **2** the weather is fine when it is sunny and not raining **3** very thin or delicate *The curtains were made of a fine material.* **4** made of small particles *The sand*

on the beach was very fine. **finely** adverb into fine or small parts *Slice the tomato finely.*

fine² noun fines
money that someone must pay as a punishment

fine verb fines, fining, fined
to fine someone is to make them pay money as a punishment

finger noun fingers
1 one of the long thin parts that stick out on your hand 2 something that is shaped like a finger

finger verb fingers, fingering, fingered
to finger something is to touch it with your fingers

fingernail noun fingernails
the hard covering at the end of your finger

fingerprint noun fingerprints
a mark made by the pattern of curved lines on the tip of your finger

finicky adjective
fussy or hard to please

finish verb finishes, finishing, finished
1 to finish something is to bring it to an end 2 to finish is to come to an end

finish noun finishes
the end of something

fiord (say fi-**ord**) noun fiords
in Norway, a narrow strip of water coming in from the sea between high cliffs

fir noun firs
an evergreen tree with leaves like needles

fire noun fires
1 fire, or a fire, is the flames, heat, and light that come from burning things 2 coal or wood burning in a grate or furnace to give heat 3 a device using electricity or gas to heat a room 4 the shooting of guns *Hold your fire!* **to set fire to something** is to start it burning

fire verb fires, firing, fired
1 to fire a gun is to shoot it 2 (informal) to fire someone is to dismiss them from their job 3 to fire pottery or bricks is to bake them in an oven to make them hard

firearm noun firearms
a gun or rifle

fire brigade noun fire brigades
a team of people whose job is to put out fires and rescue people from fires

fire engine noun fire engines
a large vehicle that carries firefighters and equipment to fight fires

fire extinguisher noun fire extinguishers
a metal cylinder containing water or foam for spraying over a fire to put it out

firefighter noun firefighters
a member of a fire brigade

fireman noun firemen
a man who is a member of a fire brigade

fireplace noun fireplaces
an open space for a fire in the wall of a room

fireproof adjective
something is fireproof when it can stand great heat without burning

fireside noun firesides
the part of a room near the fire

fire station noun fire stations
the headquarters of a fire brigade

firewood noun
wood suitable for burning as fuel

firework noun fireworks
a cardboard tube containing chemicals that give off pretty sparks and lights and sometimes make loud noises

firm noun firms
a business organization *She works for a clothing firm.*

firm adjective firmer, firmest
1 fixed or solid so that it will not move 2 definite and not likely to change *She has made a firm decision to go.* **firmly** adverb **firmness** noun

fish

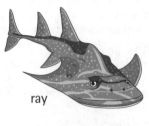

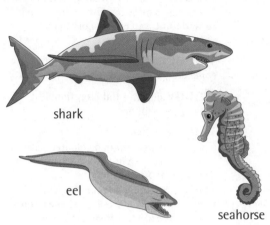

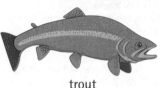

shark

ray

eel

seahorse

trout

first adjective
1 coming before all others **2** the most important *He plays football in the first team at school.*

first adverb
before everything else *Finish your work first.*

first noun
a person or thing that is first **at first** at the beginning; to start with

first aid noun
simple medical treatment that is given to an injured person before a doctor comes

first–class adjective
1 belonging to the best part of a service *Send the letter by first-class post.*
2 excellent

first floor noun **first floors**
the next floor above the ground floor

first–hand adjective, adverb
you get first-hand information directly, rather than from other people or from books

firstly adverb
as the first thing *Firstly, let me tell you about our holiday.*

first–rate adjective
excellent

fish noun **fish** or **fishes**
an animal that lives and breathes in water

fish verb **fishes, fishing, fished**
to fish is to try to catch fish

fisherman noun **fishermen**
someone who tries to catch fish, either as a job or as a sport

fishmonger noun **fishmongers**
a shopkeeper who sells fish

fishy adjective **fishier, fishiest**
1 smelling or tasting of fish **2** (informal) suspicious or a bit strange *His excuse was rather fishy.*

fist noun **fists**
your hand when it is tightly closed with your fingers bent into your palm

fit[1] adjective **fitter, fittest**
1 healthy and strong because you get a lot of exercise **2** suitable or good enough *It was a meal fit for a king.* **3** ready or likely *They worked till they were fit to collapse.* **to see fit** or **think fit to do something** is to decide or choose to do it

fit verb **fits, fitting, fitted**
1 to fit someone or something is to be the right size and shape for them *Her shoes did not fit her.* **2** to fit something is to put it into place *We need to fit a new lock on the door.*

a
b
c
d
e
f
g
h
i
j
k
l
m
n
o
p
q
r
s
t
u
v
w
x
y
z

fit to flamingo

A
B
C
D
E
F
G
H
I
J
K
L
M
N
O
P
Q
R
S
T
U
V
W
X
Y
Z

3 to fit something is to be suitable for it *The music fitted the party perfectly.*

fit noun
the way something fits *The coat is a good fit.*

fit² noun fits
1 a sudden illness, especially one that makes you move violently or become unconscious
2 (informal) a sudden outburst *He rushed off in a fit of rage.*

fitness noun
being healthy and strong because of doing a lot of exercise

fitted adjective
made to fit something exactly *The room has a fitted carpet.*

fitter noun fitters
someone who fits clothes or machinery

fitting adjective
suitable or proper
fitting noun fittings
fittings are pieces of furniture or equipment in a room or building

five noun fives
the number 5

fiver noun fivers (informal)
a five-pound note; £5

fix verb fixes, fixing, fixed
1 to fix something is to join it firmly to something else or to put it where it will not move **2** to fix something is also to decide or settle it *We have fixed a date for the party.*
3 to fix something that is broken is to mend it *He's fixing my bike.* **to fix something up** is to arrange or organize something
fix noun fixes (informal)
an awkward situation *I'm in a fix.*

fixture noun fixtures
1 a sports event planned for a particular day **2** something fixed in its place, like a cupboard or a washbasin

fizz verb fizzes, fizzing, fizzed
1 to fizz is to make a hissing or spluttering sound **2** liquid fizzes when it produces a lot of small bubbles **fizzy** adjective

fizzle verb fizzles, fizzling, fizzled
to fizzle is to make a slight hissing sound
to fizzle out is to end in a disappointing or unsuccessful way

flabbergasted adjective (informal)
completely astonished

flabby adjective flabbier, flabbiest
fat and soft; not firm

flag¹ noun flags
a piece of material with a coloured pattern or shape on it, often used as the symbol of a country or organization
flag verb flags, flagging, flagged
to become weak or droop **to flag a vehicle down** is to make the driver stop by waving your hand

flag² noun flags
a flat slab of paving stone

flagpole noun flagpoles
a pole that a flag is attached to

flagship noun flagships
the main ship in a navy's fleet, which has the commander of the fleet on board

flagstone noun flagstones
a flat slab of paving stone

flake noun flakes
1 a very light thin piece of something *Flakes of old paint came off the wall.* **2** a piece of falling snow
flake verb flakes, flaking, flaked
to flake is to come off in light thin pieces

flaky adjective flakier, flakiest
something that is flaky is likely to break into light thin pieces *flaky pastry*

flame noun flames
a bright strip of fire that flickers and leaps
flame verb flames, flaming, flamed
to flame is to produce flames or become bright red

flamingo noun flamingos
a large wading bird with long legs, a long neck, and pale pink feathers

flammable adjective
something that is flammable can be set alight easily

flan noun flans
a pie without any pastry on top

flank noun flanks
the side of something, especially an animal's body or an army

flannel noun flannels
1 a flannel is a piece of soft cloth you use to wash yourself 2 flannel is a soft woollen material

flap noun flaps
1 a part that hangs down from one edge of something, usually to cover an opening 2 the action or sound of flapping 3 (informal) a panic or fuss *Don't get in a flap.*

flap verb flaps, flapping, flapped
1 to flap something is to move it up and down or from side to side *The bird flapped its wings.* 2 to flap is to wave about *The sails were flapping in the breeze.*

flapjack noun flapjacks
a cake made from oats and syrup

flare verb flares, flaring, flared
1 to flare is to burn with a sudden bright flame 2 to flare is also to become suddenly angry 3 things flare or flare out when they get gradually wider

flare noun flares
1 a bright light fired into the sky as a signal 2 a gradual widening, especially in skirts or trousers

flash noun flashes
1 a sudden bright burst of light 2 a device for making a brief bright light when you take a photograph 3 a sudden display of anger or humour **to happen in a flash** is to happen immediately or very quickly

flash verb flashes, flashing, flashed
1 to make a sudden bright burst of light 2 to flash past or across is to approach and go past very fast *The train flashed past into the distance.*

flashback noun flashbacks
going back in a film or story to something that happened earlier *The hero's childhood was shown in flashbacks.*

flashy adjective flashier, flashiest
showy and expensive *flashy clothes*

flask noun flasks
1 a bottle with a narrow neck
2 a vacuum flask

flat adjective flatter, flattest
1 having no curves or bumps; smooth and level 2 spread out; lying at full length *Lie flat on the ground.* 3 dull or uninteresting *He spoke in a flat voice.* 4 complete; not changing *We got a flat refusal.* 5 a liquid is flat when it is no longer fizzy 6 a tyre is flat when it is punctured and has lost its air 7 feet are flat when they do not have the normal shape underneath 8 below the proper musical pitch *The clarinet was flat.* **flatness** noun

flat adverb
exactly and no more *He won the race in ten seconds flat.* **flat out** as fast as possible *They worked flat out to get their homework finished in time.*

flat noun flats
1 a set of rooms for living in, usually on one floor of a building 2 (in music) the note that is a semitone lower than the natural note; the sign ♭ indicates this

flatly adverb
in a definite way, leaving no room for doubt *They flatly refused to go.*

flatten verb flattens, flattening, flattened
1 to flatten something is to make it flat
2 to flatten is to become flat

flatter verb flatters, flattering, flattered
to flatter someone is to praise them more than they deserve, often because you want to please them **flattery** noun

flaunt verb flaunts, flaunting, flaunted
to flaunt something is to show it off

A

too proudly *He is always flaunting his expensive clothes.*

B

flavour noun flavours
flavour, or a flavour, is the taste and smell of a food or drink

C

flavour verb flavours, flavouring, flavoured
to flavour food or drink is to give it a particular taste and smell

D

E

F

flavouring noun flavourings
something added to food or drink to give it a particular flavour

G

flaw noun flaws
a fault that stops a person or thing from being perfect *Toby saw the flaw in his plan.*

H

I

flawless adjective
perfect, with no faults

J

K

flax noun
a plant that produces fibres that are used to make cloth and seeds that are used to make oil

L

M

flea noun fleas
a small jumping insect that sucks blood

N

fleck noun flecks
a small piece or speck *There were flecks of dirt on the table.*

O

P

fled
past tense and past participle of **flee** *People fled in panic as the fire started. He had fled from England, never to return.*

Q

R

S

flee verb flees, fleeing, fled
to flee is to run away from something

T

fleece noun fleeces
1 a sheep's fleece is the wool that covers its body 2 a type of jacket or top made from a soft warm material

U

V

fleece verb fleeces, fleecing, fleeced
to fleece a sheep is to shear it

W

X

fleet noun fleets
a number of ships, aircraft, or vehicles owned by one country or company

Y

Z

fleeting adjective
very brief; passing quickly *I caught a fleeting glimpse of him.*

flesh noun
the soft substance of the bodies of people and animals, made of muscle and fat

flew
past tense of **fly** verb *The door flew open.*

flex noun flexes
flexible wire for carrying an electric current

flex verb flexes, flexing, flexed
to flex something is to move or bend it *Try flexing your muscles.*

flexible adjective
1 easy to bend or stretch 2 able to be changed *Our plans are flexible.*
flexibility noun

flick noun flicks
a quick light hit or movement

flick verb flicks, flicking, flicked
to flick something is to hit or move it with a flick *Harry flicked his wand at the oil lamps as he entered and they illuminated the shabby but cosy room.* — J. K. Rowling, *Harry Potter and the Deathly Hallows*

flicker verb flickers, flickering, flickered
to burn or shine unsteadily

flight[1] noun flights
1 flight is the action of flying *She looked up to see a flock of birds in flight.* 2 a flight is a journey in an aircraft or rocket 3 a flight is also a group of flying birds or aircraft 4 a flight of stairs is one set of stairs

flight[2] noun flights
running away; escape

flimsy adjective flimsier, flimsiest
light and thin; fragile *flimsy tissue paper, a flimsy wooden hut*

flinch verb flinches, flinching, flinched
to make a sudden movement because you are frightened or in pain

fling verb flings, flinging, flung
to fling something is to throw it violently or carelessly *He flung his shoes under the bed.*

flint noun flints
1 flint is a very hard kind of stone 2 a flint is a piece of this stone or hard metal used to produce sparks

flip verb flips, flipping, flipped
to flip something is to turn it over quickly *We were flipping pancakes in the kitchen.*

flippant adjective
not being serious when you should be *Don't be flippant about his illness.*

flipper noun flippers
1 one of the limbs that water animals such as seals and turtles have to help them swim 2 a flat rubber shoe shaped like a duck's foot, that you wear on your feet to help you swim

flirt verb flirts, flirting, flirted
to flirt with someone is to talk to them as if you wanted to get them to love you, not seriously but just for fun

flit verb flits, flitting, flitted
to flit is to fly or move lightly and quickly *A moth flitted across the room.*

float verb floats, floating, floated
1 to float is to stay or move on the surface of a liquid or in the air 2 to float something is to make it stay on the surface of a liquid

float noun floats
1 a device designed to float *She learned to swim with the help of floats.* 2 a vehicle with a platform used for delivering milk or for carrying a display in a parade

flock noun flocks
a group of sheep, goats, or birds

flock verb flocks, flocking, flocked
to flock is to gather or move in a crowd *People flocked to see the fireworks.*

flog verb flogs, flogging, flogged
1 to flog someone is to beat them severely with a whip or stick 2 (informal) to flog something is to sell it

flood noun floods
1 a large amount of water spreading over a place that is usually dry 2 a great amount of something *The TV station received a flood of complaints.*

flood verb floods, flooding, flooded
1 to flood something is to cover it with a large amount of water 2 a river floods when it flows over its banks 3 to arrive in large amounts *Offers of help came flooding in from all over the country.*

floodlight noun floodlights
a lamp that gives a broad bright beam, used to light up a public building or a sports ground at night **floodlit** adjective

floor noun floors
1 the part of a room that people walk on 2 all the rooms on the same level in a building *The sports department is on the top floor.*

floor verb floors, flooring, floored
to floor someone is to knock them down

floorboard noun floorboards
one of the long flat boards in a wooden floor

flop verb flops, flopping, flopped
1 to flop, or flop down, is to fall or sit down heavily 2 to flop is also to fall or hang loosely or heavily *Her hair flopped over her eyes.* 3 (informal) to flop is to be a failure

flop noun flops
1 the movement or sound of sudden falling or sitting down 2 (informal) a failure or disappointment *The play was a complete flop.*

floppy adjective floppier, floppiest
hanging loosely or heavily *Our dog has huge floppy ears.*

flora (say flor-a) noun
the plants that live in an area or during a period of time

floral adjective
made of flowers or to do with flowers

florist noun florists
a shopkeeper who sells flowers

197

A
B
C
D
E
F
G
H
I
J
K
L
M
N
O
P
Q
R
S
T
U
V
W
X
Y
Z

flower

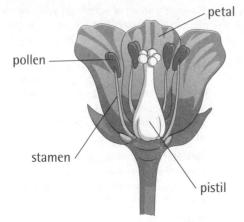

petal

pollen

stamen

pistil

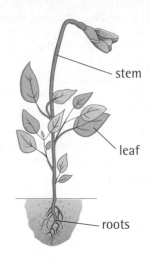

stem

leaf

roots

floss noun
a mass of silky thread or fibres

flounder verb flounders, floundering, floundered
to move or struggle clumsily because you are in difficulties *The animals floundered in the shallows at the river's edge, trampling the banks to mud, treading on each other.* – Ted Hughes, *How the Whale Became and Other Stories*

flour noun
a fine powder made from corn or wheat and used for making bread, cakes, and pastry

flourish verb flourishes, flourishing, flourished
1 to flourish is to grow or develop strongly; to be successful **2** to flourish something is to wave it about *Mrs Brown flourished a big spoon.*

flourish noun flourishes
if you do something with a flourish, you do in a dramatic way that people will notice *He signed his name with a flourish.*

flow verb flows, flowing, flowed
1 to flow is to move along smoothly, like a river does **2** to flow is also to hang loosely *She had golden flowing hair.*

flow noun flows
a continuous steady movement of something

flower noun flowers
1 the part of a plant from which the seed or fruit develops **2** a plant with a flower *The daffodil is my favourite flower.* **to be in flower** is to be producing flowers

flower verb flowers, flowering, flowered
a plant flowers when it produces flowers

flowerpot noun flowerpots
a pot in which plants are grown

flowery adjective
1 decorated with flowers or pictures of them *The room had flowery wallpaper.* **2** using fancy words *He had a flowery style of writing.*

flown
past participle of **fly** verb *A gorgeous butterfly had flown into the room.*

flu noun
an infectious disease that causes pain in your muscles and fever

fluctuate verb fluctuates, fluctuating, fluctuated
to keep changing **fluctuation** noun

flue noun flues
a pipe that takes smoke and fumes away from a stove or boiler

fluent adjective
skilful at speaking, especially a foreign language

fluff noun
fluff is the small soft bits that come off wool and cloth **fluffy** adjective soft like fluff

fluid noun fluids
a substance that flows easily, like liquids and gases

fluke noun flukes
a success that you achieve by unexpected good luck

flung
past tense and past participle of **fling** He flung his arms up to protect himself. He was flung backwards by the blast.

fluorescent adjective
a fluorescent light or lamp is one that produces a bright light by means of radiation

fluoride noun
a chemical that is thought to help prevent tooth decay

flurry noun flurries
a sudden gust of wind or rain or snow

flush verb flushes, flushing, flushed
1 to flush is to go slightly red in the face **2** to flush something is to clean or remove it with a fast flow of liquid
flush noun flushes
1 a slight blush **2** a fast flow of water

flustered adjective
nervous and confused Aunty Rose looked around her like a flustered hen. 'What are you all talking about?' she asked. — Michael Morpurgo, Tom's Sausage Lion

flute noun flutes
a musical instrument consisting of a long pipe with holes that are covered by fingers or keys. You play it by holding it to one side of your mouth and blowing over a hole at one end.

flutter verb flutters, fluttering, fluttered
1 to move with a quick flapping of wings A butterfly fluttered in through the window. **2** to move or flap quickly and lightly The flags fluttered in the breeze.
flutter noun flutters
a fluttering movement **to be in a flutter** is to be nervous and excited

fly verb flies, flying, flew, flown
1 to fly is to move through the air with wings or in an aircraft **2** to fly is also to wave in the air Flags were flying. **3** to fly something is to make it move through the air They were flying model aircraft. **4** to fly is to move or pass quickly The door flew open. The weeks just flew by.
fly noun flies
1 a small flying insect with two wings **2** the front opening of a pair of trousers

flying saucer noun flying saucers
a saucer-shaped flying object believed to come from outer space, especially in science fiction stories

flyover noun flyovers
a bridge that carries one road over another

foal noun foals
a young horse

foam noun
1 a mass of tiny bubbles on top of a liquid **2** a spongy kind of rubber or plastic, used inside cushions and mattresses
foam verb foams, foaming, foamed
to foam is to form a mass of tiny bubbles

focus noun focuses or foci
1 the point at which something appears most clearly to your eye or in a lens **2** the part of something that people pay most attention to **to be in focus** is to appear clearly and not blurred **to be out of focus** is to appear blurred
focus verb focuses, focusing, focused
1 to focus your eye or a camera lens is to adjust it so that objects appear clearly **2** to

A

focus your attention on something is to concentrate on it

B

fodder noun
fodder is food for horses and farm animals

C

foe noun foes (old use)
an enemy

D

E

foetus (say fee-tus) noun foetuses
a developing embryo, especially an unborn human baby

F

fog noun fogs
thick mist which makes it difficult to see
foggy adjective

G

H

foghorn noun foghorns
a loud horn for warning ships in fog of danger

I

J

foil¹ noun foils
very thin sheets of metal, sometimes used to wrap food

K

L

foil² noun foils
a long narrow sword you use in fencing

M

foil³ verb foils, foiling, foiled
to foil someone or something is to stop them from succeeding *Police foiled the kidnapping plan.*

N

O

fold¹ verb folds, folding, folded
1 to fold something is to bend it so that one part lies over another part 2 to fold is to bend or move in this way *The table folds up when we are not using it.* 3 to fold your arms is to put one of your arms over the other one and hold them against your chest

P

Q

R

S

fold noun folds
a line where something has been folded

T

fold² noun folds
an enclosure for sheep

U

V

folder noun folders
1 a folding cardboard or plastic cover you use to keep loose papers in 2 a place where a set of files are grouped together in a computer

W

X

Y

foliage noun
the leaves of a tree or plant

Z

folk plural noun
people

folk dance noun folk dances
a dance in the traditional style of a country

folklore noun
old beliefs and legends

folk song noun folk songs
a song in the traditional style of a country

follow verb follows, following, followed
1 to follow someone or something is to go or come after them, or to do something after they have 2 to follow someone's instructions or advice is to obey them 3 to follow a road or path is to go along it 4 to follow a sport or team is to take an interest in them or support them *Which football team do you follow?* 5 to follow something is to understand it *I couldn't follow the film's plot.*

follower noun followers
a person who follows or supports someone or something

following preposition
after or as a result of *Following the break-in, my parents had new locks fitted.*

fond adjective fonder, fondest
kind and loving *She wished me a fond farewell.* **to be fond of someone** or **something** is to like them very much
fondly adverb **fondness** noun

font noun fonts
a stone or wooden basin in a church, to hold water for baptism

food noun foods
anything that a plant or animal can take into its body to make it grow or give it energy

food chain noun food chains
a series of plants and animals, each of which is eaten as food by the one above in the series
Please see illustration on following page.

food chain

hawk

↑

snake

↑

grasshopper

↑

grass

fool noun fools
1 a silly or stupid person 2 a jester or clown *Stop playing the fool.* 3 a pudding made of fruit mixed with custard or cream
fool verb fools, fooling, fooled
to fool someone is to trick or deceive them
to fool about or **fool around** is to behave in a silly or stupid way

foolhardy adjective foolhardier, foolhardiest
bold but foolish; reckless
foolhardiness noun

foolish adjective
stupid **foolishly** adverb **foolishness** noun

foolproof adjective
a plan or method is foolproof when it is easy to follow and cannot easily go wrong

foot noun feet
1 the lower part of your leg below your ankle 2 the lowest part of something *They met up at the foot of the hill.* 3 a measure of length, 12 inches or about 30 centimetres
on foot walking

football noun footballs
1 a game played by two teams which try to kick an inflated ball into their opponents' goal 2 the ball used in this game

footballer noun footballers
someone who plays football

foothill noun foothills
a low hill near the bottom of a mountain or range of mountains

foothold noun footholds
a place where you can put your foot when you are climbing

footing noun
your footing is the position of your feet when you are standing firmly on something *He lost his footing and slipped.*

footpath noun footpaths
a path for people to walk along, especially one in the countryside

footprint noun footprints
a mark made by a foot or shoe

a b c d e f g h i j k l m n o p q r s t u v w x y z

A
B
C
D
E
F
G
H
I
J
K
L
M
N
O
P
Q
R
S
T
U
V
W
X
Y
Z

footstep noun footsteps
the sound made each time your foot touches the ground when you are walking or running

for preposition
used to show
1 purpose or direction *This letter is for you. We set out for home. Let's go for a walk.* **2** length of time or distance *We've been waiting for hours. They walked for three miles.* **3** price or cost *She bought it for £2.* **4** a replacement *I swapped my broken pencil for a new one.* **5** cause or reason *He was rewarded for bravery. I only did it for fun.* **6** a particular person or thing *I feel sorry for you. She has a good ear for music.* **7** support *Are you for us or against us?* **for ever** always

for conjunction
because *They paused, for they heard a noise.*

forbid verb forbids, forbidding, forbade, forbidden
1 to forbid someone to do something is to tell them that they must not do it **2** to forbid something is not to allow it *Running is forbidden in the school corridor.*

forbidding adjective
looking stern or threatening *The sky was dark and forbidding.*

force noun forces
1 strength or power **2** an organized team of soldiers or police **in force** a law or rule is in force if it exists and has to be obeyed *Is the rule still in force?*

force verb forces, forcing, forced
1 to force someone to do something is to use your power or strength to make them do it **2** to force something is to break it open using your strength

forceful adjective
strong and effective **forcefully** adverb

forceps (say for-seps) plural noun
a pair of pincers or tongs that a dentist or surgeon uses

forcibly adverb
if you do something forcibly, you use a lot of force

ford noun fords
a shallow place where you can wade or drive across a river

fore adjective
at or towards the front

forecast noun forecasts
a statement about what is likely to happen, especially what the weather is likely to be

forecast verb forecasts, forecasting, forecast or forecasted
to forecast something is to say what is likely to happen *The weather report forecasts snow for tomorrow.*

forecourt noun forecourts
an area in front of a petrol station or large building

forefathers plural noun
your forefathers are your ancestors

forefinger noun forefingers
the finger next to your thumb

foreground noun foregrounds
the part of a scene or view that is nearest to you

forehead (say **for**-hed or **fo**-rid) noun foreheads
the part of your face above your eyes

foreign adjective
1 belonging to or coming from another country **2** strange or unnatural *Lying is foreign to her nature.*

foreigner noun foreigners
a person from another country

foreman noun foremen
a worker who is in charge of other workers in a group

foremost adjective
most important *Holly became the LEP's foremost expert in the Artemis Fowl cases, and was invaluable in the fight against the People's most feared enemy. — Eoin Colfer, Artemis Fowl*

forename noun forenames
a person's first name

foresee verb foresees, foreseeing, foresaw, foreseen
to foresee something is to realize that it is likely to happen

foresight noun
the ability to realize that something is likely to happen in the future and prepare for it

forest noun forests
a large area of trees growing close together

forester noun foresters
someone whose job is to look after a forest

forestry noun
forestry is planting forests and looking after them

foretell verb foretells, foretelling, foretold
to foretell something is to say it will happen *Among other things the witch told her that she understood all magic arts, and that she could foretell the future, and knew the healing powers of herbs and plants. — Andrew Lang, The Red Fairy Book*

forever adverb
continually or always *He is forever complaining.*

forfeit noun forfeits
something that is taken away from you as a penalty for doing something wrong

forfeit verb forfeits, forfeiting, forfeited
to forfeit something is to lose it as a penalty

forgave
past tense of forgive *He had done his best, so she forgave him.*

forge[1] noun forges
a place where metal is heated and shaped; a blacksmith's workshop

forge verb forges, forging, forged
1 to forge metal is to shape it by heating and hammering **2** to forge money or a signature is to copy it in order to deceive people

forge[2] verb forges, forging, forged
to forge ahead is to make progress with a strong effort

forgery noun forgeries
1 forgery is copying something in order to deceive people **2** a forgery is a copy of something made to deceive people

forget verb forgets, forgetting, forgot, forgotten
1 to forget something is to fail to remember it **2** to forget something is also to stop thinking about it *Try to forget your worries.*

forgetful adjective
tending to forget things **forgetfulness** noun

forget–me–not noun forget-me-nots
a plant with small blue flowers

forgive verb forgives, forgiving, forgave, forgiven
to forgive someone is to stop being angry with them for something they have done **forgiveness** noun

fork noun forks
1 a small device with prongs for lifting food to your mouth **2** a large device with prongs used for digging or lifting things **3** a place where a road or river divides into two or more parts

fork verb forks, forking, forked
1 to fork something is to dig or lift it with a fork **2** to fork is to divide into two or more branches *The tunnel suddenly forked into two. One passage was nice and wide, the other narrow. — Enid Blyton, Five On a Secret Trail*

fork–lift truck noun fork-lift trucks
a truck with two metal bars at the front for lifting and moving heavy loads

forlorn adjective
looking sad and lonely

form noun forms
1 a form is a kind or type of thing *planes and other forms of transport* **2** the form of something is its shape and general

a
b
c
d
e
f
g
h
i
j
k
l
m
n
o
p
q
r
s
t
u
v
w
x
y
z

203

appearance *They could see a shadowy form in front of them.* **3** a form is also a class in a school **4** a form is also a piece of paper with printed questions and spaces for the answers

form verb forms, forming, formed
1 to form something is to shape or make it **2** to form is to come into being or develop *Icicles formed on the window.*

formal adjective
1 something that is formal strictly follows certain rules or customs *She is very formal and never calls me by my first name.* **2** a formal event is official or has a ceremony *The formal opening of the bridge takes place tomorrow.* **3** formal language strictly follows the rules of grammar, has longer words, and does not have friendly or slang words **formally** adverb

formality noun
formality is behaviour that follows certain rules and customs

format noun formats
1 the way something is arranged or organized *What will the format of the lesson be?* **2** the way the information is arranged in a computer file or disk *The files are in MP3 format.* **3** the shape and size of a book or magazine

formation noun formations
1 the action of forming something *This chapter is about the formation of ice crystals.* **2** something that is formed *We were studying formations of rock.* **3** a special pattern or arrangement *The aircraft were flying in formation.*

former adjective
earlier; in the past *In former times the house had been an inn. He is a former President of the US.* **the former** the first of two people or things just mentioned *If it's a choice between a picnic or a swim I prefer the former.*

 TOP TIPS
Some words are used in pairs, such as **former** and **latter**.

formerly adverb
once; previously

formidable (say for-mid-a-bul) adjective
1 deserving respect because of being so powerful or impressive *The Sheepdog was a formidable Twilight Barker. Tonight, with the most important news in Dogdom to send out, he surpassed himself.* – Dodie Smith, *The Hundred and One Dalmatians* **2** very difficult to deal with or do *This is a formidable task.*

formula noun formulas or formulae
1 a set of chemical symbols showing what a substance consists of H_2O is the formula for water. **2** a rule or problem in maths shown as a sequence symbols and numbers $2a + 4b = 4c$. **3** a list of what you need to make something **4** one of the groups into which racing cars are placed according to their engine size, for example Formula 1

formulate verb formulates, formulating, formulated
to formulate an idea or plan is to work it out and express it clearly and exactly

forsake verb forsakes, forsaking, forsook, forsaken
to forsake someone is to abandon them

fort noun forts
a building that has been strongly built against attack

forth adverb
forwards or onwards

fortification noun fortifications
a tower or wall that is built to help defend a place against attack

fortify verb fortifies, fortifying, fortified
1 to fortify a place is to make it strong against attack **2** to fortify someone is to make them feel stronger *A bowl of hot soup will fortify you.*

fortnight noun fortnights
a period of two weeks **fortnightly** adverb something that happens fortnightly happens every two weeks

A B C D E **F** G H I J K L M N O P Q R S T U V W X Y Z

fortress noun **fortresses**
a castle or town that has been strongly built
against attack

fortunate adjective
lucky **fortunately** adverb

fortune noun **fortunes**
1 fortune is luck or chance **2** a fortune is a
large amount of money

fortune-teller noun
fortune-tellers
someone who tells you what will happen to
you in the future **fortune-telling** verb

forty noun **forties**
the number 40 **fortieth** adjective, noun

forward adjective
1 going towards the front **2** placed in the
front **3** too eager or bold

forward adverb
forwards

forward noun **forwards**
a player in an attacking position in a team
at football, hockey, and other games

forwards adverb
to or towards the front; in the direction you
are facing

fossil noun **fossils**
the remains of a prehistoric animal or plant
that has been in the ground for a very
long time and become hardened in rock
fossilized adjective a fossilized animal or
plant has been formed into a fossil

foster verb **fosters, fostering, fostered**
to foster someone is to look after someone
else's child as if they were your own, but
without adopting them

foster child noun **foster children**
a child brought up by foster parents

foster parent noun **foster parents**
a parent who is fostering a child

fought
past tense and past participle of **fight** verb
*I fought my way towards the front. He had
just fought with his best friend.*

foul adjective **fouler, foulest**
1 disgusting; tasting or smelling unpleasant
2 breaking the rules of a game *That was a
foul shot.* **foulness** noun

foul noun **fouls**
an action that breaks the rules of
a game

foul verb **fouls, fouling, fouled**
to foul a player in a game is to commit a
foul against them

found¹ verb **founds, founding, founded**
to found an organization or society
is to start it or set it up *When was the
hospital founded?*

found²
past tense and past participle of **find** *They
suddenly found themselves surrounded by
tigers. I have found the book I had lost.*

foundation noun **foundations**
1 a building's foundations are the solid
base under the ground on which it is built
2 the basis for something *His story had
no foundation in truth.* **3** the founding
of something

founder¹ noun **founders**
someone who founds something *Guru
Nanak was the founder of the Sikh religion.*

founder² verb **founders, foundering,
foundered**
1 to founder is to fill with water and sink
The ship foundered on the rocks.
2 to founder is to fail completely *Their plans
have foundered.*

foundry noun **foundries**
a factory or workshop where metal or
glass is made

fountain noun **fountains**
a structure in which jets of water shoot up
into the air, used to decorate a park or other
place outdoors

fountain pen noun **fountain pens**
a pen that can be filled with a cartridge
or a supply of ink that flows through its
sharp nib

a
b
c
d
e
f
g
h
i
j
k
l
m
n
o
p
q
r
s
t
u
v
w
x
y
z

A
B
C
D
E

F

G
H
I
J
K
L
M
N
O
P
Q
R
S
T
U
V
W
X
Y
Z

four noun fours
the number 4 **to be on all fours** is to be on your hands and knees

fourteen noun fourteens
the number 14 **fourteenth** adjective, noun

fourth adjective, noun
the next after the third **fourthly** adverb in the fourth place; as the fourth one

fowl noun fowl or fowls
a bird, such as a chicken or duck, that is kept for its eggs or meat

fox noun foxes
a wild animal that looks like a dog with a long furry tail

fox verb foxes, foxing, foxed
to fox someone is to puzzle them

foxglove noun foxgloves
a tall plant with flowers like the fingers of gloves

foyer (say **foi**-ay) noun foyers
the entrance hall of a cinema, theatre, or hotel

fraction noun fractions
1 a number that is not a whole number, for example ½ or 0.5 2 a tiny part or amount of something

fractionally adverb
by a small amount; very slightly *The ball was fractionally over the line.*

fracture verb fractures, fracturing, fractured
to fracture something, especially a bone, is to break it

fracture noun fractures
the breaking of something, especially a bone

fragile (say **fra**-jyl) adjective
easy to break or damage
fragility noun

fragment noun fragments
1 a small piece broken off something 2 a small part *She overheard fragments of conversation.*

fragrance (say **fray**-granss) noun fragrances
a thing's fragrance is the sweet or pleasant smell it has

fragrant (say **fray**-grant) adjective
having a sweet or pleasant smell

frail adjective frailer, frailest
weak or fragile **frailty** noun

frame noun frames
1 a set of wooden or metal strips that fit round the outside of a picture or mirror to hold it 2 a rigid structure that supports something *I've broken the frame of my glasses.* 3 a human body *He has a small frame.*

frame verb frames, framing, framed
1 to frame a picture is to put a frame round it 2 to frame laws or questions is to put them together 3 (informal) to frame someone is to make them seem guilty of a crime by giving false evidence against them

framework noun frameworks
1 a structure that supports something 2 a basic plan or system

franchise noun franchises
1 the franchise is the right to vote in elections 2 a franchise is a licence to sell a firm's goods or services in a certain area

frank adjective franker, frankest
honest and saying exactly what you think *I'll be frank with you.*

frank verb franks, franking, franked
to frank a letter or parcel is to mark it with a postmark **frankly** adverb

frantic adjective
wildly anxious or excited **frantically** adverb

fraud noun frauds
1 fraud is the crime of getting money by tricking people; a fraud is a swindle 2 a fraud is also someone who is not what they pretend to be

fraught adjective
1 someone is fraught when they are tense and upset 2 a situation is fraught when it is full of problems and makes you worried

frayed adjective
1 frayed material is worn and ragged at the edge *Your shirt collar is frayed.* 2 tempers or nerves are frayed when people feel strained or upset *Tempers were becoming frayed.*

freak noun freaks
1 a very strange or abnormal person, animal, or thing 2 (informal) someone who is a keen fan of something *She is a fitness freak.*

freckle noun freckles
a small brown spot on someone's skin
freckled adjective

free adjective freer, freest
1 able to do what you want to do or go where you want to go 2 not costing any money *Entrance to the museum is free.*
3 available; not being used or occupied *Is this seat free?* 4 not busy doing something *Are you free tomorrow morning?* 5 generous *She is very free with her money.* **to be free of something** is not to have it or be affected by it *The roads are free of ice.*

free verb frees, freeing, freed
to free someone or something is to make them free **freely** adverb to do something freely is to do it as you want, without anyone or anything stopping you

freedom noun
the right to go where you like or do what you like

freehand adjective, adverb
to draw something freehand is to do it without using a ruler or compasses

free-range adjective
1 free-range hens are allowed to move about freely in the open instead of being caged 2 free-range eggs are those laid by free-range hens

freewheel verb freewheels, freewheeling, freewheeled
to freewheel is to ride a bicycle without pedalling

freeze verb freezes, freezing, froze, frozen
1 to freeze is to turn into ice, or to become covered with ice *The pond froze last night.*
2 to be freezing or to be frozen is to be very cold *My hands are frozen.* 3 to freeze food is to store it at a low temperature to preserve it 4 a person or animal freezes when they suddenly stand still with fright 5 to freeze pay or prices is to keep them at a fixed level and not change them

freezer noun freezers
a large refrigerator for keeping food frozen

freight (say frayt) noun
goods carried by road or in a ship or aircraft

freighter noun freighters
a ship or aircraft for carrying goods

frenzy noun frenzies
to be in a frenzy is to be wildly excited or angry about something **frenzied** adjective

frequency noun frequencies
1 how often something happens 2 being frequent 3 the number of vibrations made each second by a wave of sound or light

frequent (say **free**-kwent) adjective
happening often
frequent (say fri-**kwent**) verb
frequents, frequenting, frequented
to frequent a place is to visit it often
frequently adverb

fresh adjective fresher, freshest
1 newly made or produced; not old or used *We need fresh bread.* 2 not tinned or preserved *Would you like some fresh fruit?* 3 cool and clean *It's nice to be in the fresh air.* 4 fresh water is water that is not salty **freshly** adverb newly or recently done *Here are some freshly made biscuits.*
freshness noun

freshen verb freshens, freshening, freshened
1 to freshen something is to make it fresh
2 to freshen is to become fresh

freshwater adjective
freshwater fish live in rivers or lakes and not the sea

a
b
c
d
e
f
g
h
i
j
k
l
m
n
o
p
q
r
s
t
u
v
w
x
y
z

A
B
C
D
E
F
G
H
I
J
K
L
M
N
O
P
Q
R
S
T
U
V
W
X
Y
Z

fret verb frets, fretting, fretted
to fret is to worry or be upset about something
fret noun
frets are the bars on the neck of a guitar where you press the strings

fretful adjective
worried and upset

friar noun friars
a man who is a member of a Roman Catholic order and has vowed to live a life of poverty

friction noun
1 the rubbing of one thing against another
2 disagreement and quarrelling

Friday noun Fridays
the sixth day of the week

fridge noun fridges (informal)
a refrigerator

friend noun friends
your friend is someone you like and who likes you

friendless adjective
someone who is friendless has no friends *A friendless, bitter old man, Roxanne's grandfather was interested in nothing unless there was some money in it.* – Michael Morpurgo, *The Dancing Bear*

friendly adjective friendlier, friendliest
kind and pleasant **friendliness** noun

friendship noun friendships
friendship, or a friendship, is being friends with someone

frieze (say freez) noun friezes
a strip of designs or pictures along the top of a wall

frigate noun frigates
a small fast warship

fright noun frights
a sudden feeling of fear

frighten verb frightens, frightening, frightened
to frighten someone is to make them afraid

frightful adjective
awful; very great or bad *It's a frightful shame.* **frightfully** adverb awfully *I'm frightfully sorry.*

frill noun frills
1 a strip of pleated material used to decorate the edge of a dress or curtain
2 an unnecessary extra *We lead a simple life with no frills.* **frilly** adjective

fringe noun fringes
1 a straight line of short hair that hangs down over your forehead 2 a decorative edge of hanging threads on something like a piece of clothing or a curtain 3 the edge of something *We walked around on the fringe of the crowd.*

frisk verb frisks, frisking, frisked
1 to frisk is to skip or leap playfully
2 (informal) to frisk someone is to search them by moving your hands over their body

frisky adjective friskier, friskiest
playful or lively

fritter[1] noun fritters
a slice of meat, potato, or fruit that is covered in batter and fried

fritter[2] verb fritters, frittering, frittered
to fritter something or fritter it away is to waste it gradually *He frittered all his money on comics.*

frivolity noun
playfulness

frivolous adjective
light-hearted and playful; not serious

frizzy adjective frizzier, frizziest
frizzy hair has tight short curls

fro adverb
to and fro backwards and forwards

frock noun frocks
a girl's or woman's dress

frog noun frogs
a small jumping animal that can live both in water and on land

frogman noun **frogmen**
a swimmer equipped with a rubber suit and flippers and breathing apparatus for swimming under water

frolic verb **frolics, frolicking, frolicked**
to frolic is to spend time playing in a lively and cheerful way

frolic noun **frolics**
a lively cheerful game or entertainment

from preposition
used to show:
1 a beginning or starting point *She comes from London. Buses run from 8 o'clock.* **2** distance *We are a mile from home.* **3** separation *Get the sweets from him.* **4** origin or source *Get water from the tap.* **5** cause *I was shivering from cold.* **6** difference *Can you tell one twin from the other?*

front noun **fronts**
1 the part of a person or thing that faces forwards *The front of the house is blue.* **2** the part of a thing or place that is furthest forward *Go to the front of the class.* **3** a road or promenade that runs alongside the seashore **4** the place where fighting is happening in a war *More troops were moved to the front.* **5** in weather systems, the forward edge of an approaching mass of air *There is a warm front out in the Atlantic.*
in front at or near the front

front adjective
placed at or near the front *We sat in the front row.*

frontier noun **frontiers**
the boundary between two countries or regions

frost noun **frosts**
1 powdery ice that forms on things in freezing weather **2** weather with a temperature below freezing point

frostbite noun
harm done to a person's body by very cold weather **frostbitten** adjective

frosting noun
sugar icing you put on cakes

frosty adjective
1 so cold that there is frost *It was a frosty morning.* **2** unfriendly *She gave us a frosty look.*

froth noun
a white mass of tiny bubbles on or in a liquid

froth verb **froths, frothing, frothed**
to froth is to form a froth **frothy** adjective

frown verb **frowns, frowning, frowned**
to frown is to wrinkle your forehead because you are angry or worried

frown noun **frowns**
the wrinkling of your forehead when you frown

froze
past tense of **freeze** *The girl froze on the spot.*

frozen
past participle of **freeze** *The entire river had frozen solid.*

frugal (say **froo**-gal) adjective
1 spending very little money *The girls tried to be frugal with their pocket money.* **2** costing little money *They ate a frugal meal.*

fruit noun **fruit** or **fruits**
1 the seed container that grows on a tree or plant and is often used as food, such as apples, oranges, and bananas **2** the result of doing something *He lived to see the fruits of his efforts.*

fruitful adjective
something is fruitful when it is successful or has good results *Their work was fruitful.*

fruitless adjective
something is fruitless when it is unsuccessful or has no results *It was a fruitless search.*

fruity adjective **fruitier, fruitiest**
tasting like fruit

frustrate verb **frustrates, frustrating, frustrated**
to frustrate someone is to prevent them

a
b
c
d
e
f
g
h
i
j
k
l
m
n
o
p
q
r
s
t
u
v
w
x
y
z

A

B

C

D

E

F

G

H

I

J

K

L

M

N

O

P

Q

R

S

T

U

V

W

X

Y

Z

from doing something or from succeeding in something, in a way that annoys them

frustration noun
the feeling of annoyance you have when you cannot do what you want to do

fry verb fries, frying, fried
to fry food is to cook it in hot fat

frying pan noun frying pans
a shallow pan in which things are fried

fudge noun
a soft sweet made with milk, sugar, and butter

fuel noun fuels
something that is burnt to make heat or power, such as coal and oil

fuel verb fuels, fuelling, fuelled
to fuel something is to provide it with material to burn to make heat or power

fugitive (say **few**-ji-tiv) noun fugitives
a person who is running away from something, especially from the police

fulfil verb fulfils, fulfilling, fulfilled
1 to fulfil something is to achieve it or carry it out *She fulfilled her dream of appearing on television.* **2** to fulfil a prophecy is to make it come true

fulfilment noun
the feeling that you have achieved something important

full adjective
1 if a building or container is full, it contains as much or as many as it possibly can *The cinema was full.* **2** having many people or things *You are full of ideas.* **3** complete *Tell me the full story.* **4** the greatest possible *They drove at full speed.* **5** fitting loosely; having many folds *She's wearing a full skirt.* **fullness** noun **in full** not leaving anything out

full adverb
completely; very *You knew full well what I wanted.* **fully** adverb completely

full moon noun full moons
the moon when you can see the whole of it as a bright disc

full stop noun full stops
the dot used as a punctuation mark at the end of a sentence or an abbreviation

TOP TIPS

A full stop brings a stop to the sentence! After the full stop, use a capital letter.

full-time adjective, adverb
you do something full-time when you do it for all the normal working hours of the day *She has a full-time job. She works full-time.*

fumble verb fumbles, fumbling, fumbled
to fumble is to handle or feel for something clumsily *He fumbled in the dark for the light switch.*

fume verb fumes, fuming, fumed
1 to fume is to give off strong-smelling smoke or gas **2** to be fuming is to be very angry

fumes plural noun
strong-smelling smoke or gas

fun noun
amusement or enjoyment **to make fun of someone** or **something** is to make them look silly or make people laugh at them

function noun functions
1 what someone or something does or ought to do *The function of a doctor is to cure sick people.* **2** an important event or party **3** a basic operation of a computer or calculator

function verb functions, functioning, functioned
to function is to work properly or perform a function *The chair also functions as a small table.*

functional adjective
practical and useful *functional objects such as knives, forks, and spoons*

fund noun funds
a fund is an amount of money collected or kept for a special purpose *They started a fund for refugees.*

fundamental adjective
basic and necessary *Let me explain the fundamental rules of the game.*
fundamentally adverb basically

funeral noun funerals
the ceremony where a person who has died is buried or cremated

fungus noun fungi
a plant without leaves or flowers that grows on other plants or on decayed material, such as mushrooms and toadstools

funnel noun funnels
1 a tube that is wide at the top and narrow at the bottom, to help you pour things into bottles or other containers 2 a chimney on a ship or steam engine

funny adjective funnier, funniest
1 something that is funny makes you laugh or smile *We heard a funny joke.* 2 strange or odd *There's a funny smell in here.*
funnily adverb

funny bone noun funny bones
part of your elbow which gives you a strange tingling feeling if you knock it

fur noun furs
1 the soft hair that covers some animals 2 animal skin with the hair on it, used for clothing; fabric that looks like animal skin with hair on it *She was wearing a fur hat.*

furious adjective
1 very angry 2 violent or extreme *They were travelling at a furious speed.*

furiously adverb
1 to say something furiously is to say it very angrily 2 to do something furiously is to put a lot of effort into doing it *We worked furiously to get the poster finished in time.*

furl verb furls, furling, furled
to furl a sail or flag or umbrella is to roll it up and fasten it *Pegasus snorted, then calmly furled his wings as he chomped.*
– Francesca Simon, *Helping Hercules*

furlong noun furlongs
one-eighth of a mile, 220 yards or about 201 metres

furnace noun furnaces
an oven in which great heat can be produced for making glass or heating metals

furnish verb furnishes, furnishing, furnished
to furnish a room or building is to put furniture in it

furniture noun
tables, chairs, beds, cupboards, and other movable things that you need inside a building

furrow noun furrows
1 a long cut in the ground made by a plough 2 a deep wrinkle on the skin

furry adjective furrier, furriest
1 soft and hairy like fur 2 covered with fur

further adverb, adjective
1 at or to a greater distance; more distant *I can't walk any further.* 2 more *We need further information.*

further verb furthers, furthering, furthered
to further something is to help it make progress *We want to further the cause of peace.*

furthermore adverb
also; moreover

furthest adverb, adjective
at or to the greatest distance; most distant

furtive adjective
cautious, trying not to be seen *He gave a furtive glance and helped himself to the biscuits.*

fury noun furies
violent or extreme anger

fuse[1] noun fuses
a safety device containing a short piece of wire that melts if too much electricity passes through it

a
b
c
d
e
f
g
h
i
j
k
l
m
n
o
p
q
r
s
t
u
v
w
x
y
z

fuse verb fuses, fusing, fused
1 a piece of electrical equipment fuses when it stops working because a fuse has melted *The lights have fused.* **2** to fuse things is to blend them together, especially through melting

fuse² noun fuses
a device for setting off an explosive

fuselage (say **few**-ze-lahzh) noun fuselages
the main body of an aircraft

fusion (say **few**-zhon) noun
the action of blending or joining together

fuss noun fusses
fuss, or a fuss, is unnecessary excitement or worry about something that is not important **to make a fuss of someone** is to pay a lot of attention to them in a kind way
fuss verb fusses, fussing, fussed
to fuss is to be excited or worried about something that is not important

fussy adjective fussier, fussiest
1 worrying too much about something that is not important **2** full of unnecessary details or decorations **fussily** adverb **fussiness** noun

futile (say **few**-tyl) adjective
useless or having no purpose
futility noun

future noun
1 the time that will come **2** what is going to happen in the time that will come **in future** from now onwards

future tense noun
The future tense is the form of a verb that shows that something is going to happen in the time that will come. In English, the future tense uses 'will' and 'shall' in front of the verb, for example *I shall come tomorrow.*

fuzzy adjective fuzzier, fuzziest
1 blurred or not clear **2** soft and fluffy

Gg

g
short for **gram** or **grams**

gabble verb gabbles, gabbling, gabbled
to gabble is to talk so quickly that it is difficult to hear the words

gable noun gables
the three-sided part of a wall between two sloping roofs

gadget (say **gaj**-it) noun gadgets
a small device or tool that helps you with a particular task

Gaelic (say **gay**-lik (in Ireland) or **gal**-ik (in Scotland)) noun
a language that is spoken in Ireland and (in a different form) in the Highlands of Scotland

gag noun gags
1 something put over someone's mouth to stop them from speaking **2** (informal) a joke
gag verb gags, gagging, gagged
to gag someone is to put a gag over their mouth

gain verb gains, gaining, gained
1 to gain something is to get it when you did not have it before **2** a clock or watch gains when it goes ahead of the correct time **to gain on someone** is to come closer to them when you are following them
gain noun gains
something you have got that you did not have before; profit

gala (say **gah**-la) noun galas
1 a festival **2** a series of sports contests, especially in swimming

galaxy (say **gal**-ak-si) noun galaxies
a very large group of stars
galactic adjective

gale noun gales
a very strong wind

galleon

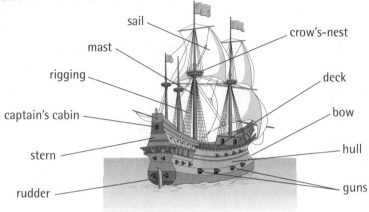

sail
crow's-nest
mast
rigging
deck
captain's cabin
bow
stern
hull
rudder
guns

a
b
c
d
e
f
g
h
i
j
k
l
m
n
o
p
q
r
s
t
u
v
w
x
y
z

gallant adjective
brave or courteous **gallantly** adverb
gallantry noun

galleon noun **galleons**
a large Spanish sailing ship used in the 16th and 17th centuries

gallery noun **galleries**
1 a platform sticking out from the inside wall of a building **2** the highest set of seats in a cinema or theatre **3** a long room or passage **4** a building or room for showing works of art

galley noun **galleys**
the kitchen in a ship

gallon noun **gallons**
a measure of liquid, 8 pints or about 4.5 litres

gallop noun **gallops**
1 the fastest pace that a horse can go
2 a fast ride on a horse

gallop verb **gallops, galloping, galloped**
1 a horse gallops when it runs very fast
2 to gallop is to ride fast on a horse

gallows plural noun
gallows are a framework with a noose for hanging criminals

galore adjective
in large amounts *The players were scoring runs galore.*

gamble verb **gambles, gambling, gambled**
1 to gamble is to play a betting game for money **2** to gamble with something is to take great risks with it **gambler** noun

gamble noun **gambles**
1 a bet or chance *His idea of a gamble was a pound on the lottery.* **2** a risk *We were taking a bit of a gamble on the weather being good.*

game noun **games**
1 something that you can play, usually with rules *a game of draughts, Children zap human figures on their electronic games.*
2 a trick or scheme *It was difficult to know what their game might be.* **3** wild animals or birds hunted for sport or food **to give the game away** is to reveal a secret

game adjective
1 able and willing to do something *Are you game for a swim?* **2** brave *She's a game lass.*

gamekeeper noun **gamekeepers**
someone whose job is to protect game birds and animals, especially from poachers

gander noun **ganders**
a male goose

A
B
C
D
E
F

G

H
I
J
K
L
M
N
O
P
Q
R
S
T
U
V
W
X
Y
Z

gang noun gangs
1 a group of people who do things together
2 a group of criminals

gang verb gangs, ganging, ganged
to gang up on someone is to form a group
to oppose them or frighten them

gangplank noun gangplanks
a plank for walking on to or off a ship

gangster noun gangsters
a member of a gang of violent criminals

gangway noun gangways
1 a gap left for people to move along
between rows of seats or through a crowd
2 a movable bridge for getting on or off
a ship

gaol noun, verb
a different spelling of jail

gaoler noun
a different spelling of jailer

gap noun gaps
1 an opening or break in something
2 an interval

gape verb gapes, gaping, gaped
1 to gape is to open your mouth wide
2 to gape is also to stare in amazement

garage (say **ga**-rahzh or **ga**-rij) noun
garages
1 a building for keeping motor vehicles in
2 a place where motor vehicles are serviced
and repaired and where petrol is sold

garbage noun
garbage is household refuse or rubbish

garden noun gardens
a piece of ground where flowers, fruit, or
vegetables are grown *He jumped over the
fence into the next-door garden.*

gardener noun gardeners
someone who looks after gardens, especially
as a job

gardening noun
gardening is looking after a garden

gargle verb gargles, gargling, gargled
to wash your throat by holding liquid at the
back of your mouth and washing it out

gargoyle noun gargoyles
an ugly or comical carving of a face on a
building, especially one that sticks out from
a gutter and sends out rainwater through
its mouth

garland noun garlands
a wreath of flowers worn as a decoration

garlic noun
a plant with a bulb divided into sections
(called *cloves*), which have a strong smell
and taste and are used in cooking

garment noun garments
a piece of clothing

garnish verb garnishes, garnishing,
garnished
to garnish a dish of food is to decorate it
with extra items such as salad

garrison noun garrisons
troops who stay in a town or fort to
defend it

garter noun garters
a band of elastic to hold up a sock
or stocking

gas noun gases
1 gas, or a gas, is a substance, such as
oxygen, that can move freely and is not
liquid or solid 2 a gas that burns and is used
for heating or cooking **gaseous** adjective in
the form of a gas

gas verb gasses, gassing, gassed
to gas someone is to kill or injure them with
a poisonous gas

gash noun gashes
a long deep cut or wound

gasoline noun (in America)
petrol

gasometer (say gas-**om**-it-er) noun
gasometers
a large round tank in which gas is stored

gasp verb **gasps, gasping, gasped**
1 to gasp is to breathe in suddenly when you are shocked or surprised **2** to gasp is also to struggle to breathe when you are ill or tired **3** to gasp something is to say it in a breathless way

gastric adjective
to do with the stomach

gate noun **gates**
1 a movable barrier, usually on hinges, used as a door in a wall or fence **2** a barrier used to control the flow of water in a dam or lock **3** a place where you wait before you board an aircraft **4** the number of people attending a football match

gateau (say **gat**-oh) noun **gateaux**
a rich cream cake

gateway noun **gateways**
an opening containing a gate

gather verb **gathers, gathering, gathered**
1 to gather is to come together **2** to gather people or things is to bring them together **3** to gather flowers or fruit is to pick them **4** to gather a piece of information is to hear or read about it *I gather you went to the same school as me?*

gathering noun **gatherings**
an assembly or meeting of people; a party

gaudy adjective **gaudier, gaudiest**
very showy and bright

gauge (say gayj) noun **gauges**
1 a measuring instrument, such as a fuel gauge **2** one of the standard sizes of something **3** the distance between a pair of railway lines

gauge verb **gauges, gauging, gauged**
to gauge something is to measure it or estimate it *We can gauge the size of the cave from the time it takes for an echo to reach us.*

gaunt adjective
a gaunt person is thin and tired-looking

gauntlet noun **gauntlets**
a glove with a wide covering for the wrist **to run the gauntlet** is to face a lot of criticism or risks **to throw down the gauntlet** is to offer a challenge

gauze noun
gauze is thin transparent material

gave
past tense of **give** *He gave me a sympathetic look.*

gaze verb **gazes, gazing, gazed**
to gaze at something or someone is to look at them hard for a long time

gaze noun **gazes**
a long steady look

GCSE
short for **General Certificate of Secondary Education**

gear noun **gears**
1 a gear is a set of toothed wheels working together in a machine, especially those connecting the engine to the wheels of a vehicle **2** gear is equipment or clothes *He had left all his fishing gear behind by the river.*

gee interjection
1 a command to a horse to go on or go faster *Gee up!* **2** an exclamation of surprise or disappointment

geese
plural of **goose**

gel noun **gels**
gel is a substance like jelly, especially one used to give a style to hair

gelatine noun
gelatine is a clear tasteless substance used to make jellies

gem noun **gems**
1 a precious stone or jewel **2** an excellent person or thing *Her auntie's a real gem.*

gender (say **jen**-der) noun **genders**
your gender is whether you are male or female

gene (say jeen) noun **genes**
the part of a living cell that controls which characteristics (such as the colour of your hair or eyes) you inherit from your parents

a
b
c
d
e
f
g
h
i
j
k
l
m
n
o
p
q
r
s
t
u
v
w
x
y
z

genealogy (say jeen-ee-**al**-o-jee) noun
genealogies
1 genealogy is the study of the history of families 2 a genealogy is a list or diagram of the members of a family

general adjective
1 to do with most people or things *The general opinion is that there needs to be a new school building.* 2 not detailed or specialized *That is the general idea.* **in general** usually; to do with most people
general noun **generals**
an army officer of high rank

generalize verb **generalizes, generalizing, generalized**
to generalize is to say things about people or things generally **generalization** noun

generally adverb
usually; to do with most people

general practitioner noun
general practitioners
a doctor who treats all kinds of diseases and sends people to specialists if necessary

generate verb **generates, generating, generated**
to generate something is to produce or create it

generation noun **generations**
1 a single stage in a family *Three generations were included: children, parents, and grandparents.* 2 all the people born about the same time *His generation grew up during the war.*

generator noun **generators**
a machine for producing electricity

generosity noun
being generous and ready to give a lot *Thanks to the public's generosity, the appeal has raised a lot of money.*

generous adjective
ready to give or share what you have **generously** adverb

genetic (say ji-**net**-ik) adjective
to do with genes or with characteristics inherited from parents **genetically** adverb

genetics plural noun
genetics is the study of genes and genetic behaviour

genial adjective
kind and pleasant

genie noun **genies**
a magical being in stories who can grant wishes

genius noun **geniuses**
1 an unusually clever person 2 an unusually great ability

genre noun **genres**
A genre is one type of writing. Poetry, adventure stories, and fairy tales are examples of different genres.

gent noun **gents** (informal)
a gentleman; a man

gentle adjective **gentler, gentlest**
kind and quiet; not rough or severe **gentleness** noun **gently** adverb

gentleman noun **gentlemen**
1 a man 2 a well-mannered or honest man *He's a real gentleman.* **gentlemanly** adjective polite and courteous

genuine adjective
1 something is genuine when it is real and not fake 2 a person is genuine when they are honest and sincere **genuinely** adverb

geography noun
geography is the science or study of the world and its climate, peoples, and products **geographical** adjective a geographical area is a region of the earth that you can see on a map

geology (say ji-**ol**-o-ji) noun
geology is the study of the earth's crust and its layers **geologist** noun **geological** adjective

geometry noun
geometry is the study of lines, angles, surfaces, and solids in mathematics

geranium (say je-**ray**-ni-um) noun
geraniums
a plant with red, pink, or white flowers

gerbil (say **jer**-bil) noun **gerbils**
a small brown animal with long back legs

germ noun **germs**
a tiny living thing, especially one that causes a disease

germinate verb **germinates, germinating, germinated**
a seed germinates when it starts growing and developing **germination** noun

gesticulate verb **gesticulates, gesticulating, gesticulated**
to make movements with your hands and arms while you are talking

gesture (say **jes**-cher) noun **gestures**
a movement or action which expresses what you feel

get verb **gets, getting, got**
This word has many meanings, depending on the words that go with it.
1 to get something is to obtain or receive it *I got a new bike yesterday.* **2** to get (for example) angry or upset is to become angry or upset **3** to get to a place is to reach it *We had to borrow money to get home.* **4** to get something (for example) on or off is take it on or off *I can't get my shoe on.* **5** to get (for example) a meal is to prepare it **6** to get an illness is to catch it *I think she's got measles.* **7** to get someone to do something is to persuade or order them to do it *Lara might get him to say yes.* **8** (informal) to get something is to understand it *Do you get what I mean?* **to get by** is to manage with what you have **to get on** is to make progress, or to be friendly with someone **to get out of something** is to avoid having to do it **to get over something** is to recover from an illness or shock **to get your own back** is to have your revenge **to have got to do something** is to have no choice about it

getaway noun **getaways**
an escape

geyser (say **gee**-zer or **gy**-zer) noun **geysers**
a natural spring that shoots up columns of hot water

ghastly adjective **ghastlier, ghastliest**
horrible; awful

ghetto (say **get**-oh) noun **ghettos**
an area of a city, often a slum area, where a group of people live who are treated unfairly compared with other people

ghost noun **ghosts**
the spirit of a dead person seen by a living person **ghostly** adjective unreal or frightening *The moon gave a ghostly light to the scene.*

ghoulish (say **gool**-ish) adjective
enjoying looking at things to do with death and suffering

giant noun **giants**
1 a creature in stories, like a huge man **2** something that is much larger than the usual size

giant adjective
huge

giddy adjective **giddier, giddiest**
feeling unsteady or dizzy **giddily** adverb **giddiness** noun

gift noun **gifts**
1 a present **2** a talent *She has a special gift for drawing.*

gifted adjective
a gifted person has a special talent or ability

gigantic adjective
huge; enormous *Suddenly the boy let out a gigantic belch which rolled around the Assembly Hall like thunder.* – Roald Dahl, *Matilda*

giggle verb **giggles, giggling, giggled**
to giggle is to laugh in a silly way

giggle noun **giggles**
1 a silly laugh **2** (informal) something amusing; a joke *We did it for a giggle.*

gild verb **gilds, gilding, gilded**
to gild something is to cover it with a thin layer of gold paint or gold

gills plural noun
the gills are the part of a fish's body that it breathes through

a b c d e f g h i j k l m n o p q r s t u v w x y z

gimmick noun **gimmicks**
something unusual done or used to attract people's attention

gin noun
gin is a strong alcoholic drink

ginger noun
1 ginger is a hot-tasting tropical root, used as a flavouring for food 2 ginger is also a reddish-yellow colour

gingerbread noun
a cake or biscuit flavoured with ginger

gingerly adverb
you do something gingerly when you do it carefully and cautiously because you are not sure about it

gipsy noun **gipsies**
a different spelling of **gypsy**

giraffe noun **giraffes**
a tall African animal with a very long neck

girder noun **girders**
a metal beam supporting part of a building or bridge

girdle noun **girdles**
a belt or cord worn around your waist

girl noun **girls**
1 a female child 2 a young woman
girlish adjective

girlfriend noun **girlfriends**
1 someone's girlfriend is the female friend they have a romantic relationship with 2 a female friend

giro noun **giros**
a system of sending money directly from one bank account or Post Office account to another

girth noun **girths**
1 the measurement round something 2 a band fastened round a horse's belly to keep its saddle in place

gist (say jist) noun
the main points or general meaning of a speech or conversation

give verb **gives, giving, gave, given**
1 to give someone something is to let them have it *She gave me a sweet.* 2 to give (for example) a laugh or shout is to laugh or shout out 3 to give a performance is to present or perform something *They gave a concert to raise money.* 4 something gives if it bends or goes down under a strain *Will this branch give if I sit on it?* **to give in** is to surrender **to give up** is to stop doing or trying something **to give way** is to break or collapse **giver** noun

given adjective
stated or agreed in advance *Work out how much you can do in a given time.*

glacial (say **glay**-shal) adjective
made of ice or formed by glaciers

glacier (say **glas**-i-er) noun **glaciers**
a mass of ice moving slowly along a valley

glad adjective **gladder, gladdest**
happy and pleased **gladly** adverb **gladness** noun

gladden verb **gladdens, gladdening, gladdened**
to gladden someone is to make them glad

gladiator noun **gladiators**
a man who fought with a sword or other weapons at public shows in ancient Rome

glamorize verb **glamorizes, glamorizing, glamorized**
to glamorize something is to make it attractive and exciting

glamorous adjective
attractive and exciting

glamour noun
1 the glamour of something is what makes it attractive or exciting *Just think of the glamour of competing in the Olympics.* 2 a person's glamour is their beauty or attractiveness *The Basic Brown was the most common type of dragon, a serviceable beast but without much glamour.* – Cressida Cowell, *How to Train Your Dragon*

glance verb **glances, glancing, glanced**
1 to glance at something is to look at it

quickly **2** to glance off something is to hit it and slide off *The ball glanced off his bat.*

glance noun glances
a quick look

gland noun glands
an organ of the body that separates substances from the blood, so that they can be used or passed out of the body
glandular adjective glandular fever is a disease that affects glands in the body

glare verb glares, glaring, glared
1 to glare is to shine with a bright or dazzling light **2** to glare at someone is to look angrily at them *The bald man glared down at the children and spoke to them in a frightening whisper.* – Lemony Snicket, *A Series of Unfortunate Events*

glare noun glares
1 a strong light **2** an angry stare

glaring adjective
1 very bright **2** very obvious and embarrassing *Fortunately there were no glaring mistakes in their work.*

glass noun glasses
1 glass is a hard brittle substance that lets light through **2** a glass is a container made of glass, for drinking out of **3** a glass is also a mirror or a lens

glasses plural noun
spectacles or binoculars

glassful noun glassfuls
as much as a glass will hold

glassy adjective glassier, glassiest
1 like glass **2** dull; without liveliness or expression *He gave a glassy stare.*

glaze verb glazes, glazing, glazed
1 to glaze something is to cover or fit it with glass **2** to glaze pottery is to give it a shiny surface **3** to glaze is to become glassy *Her eyes glazed and she fainted.*

glaze noun glazes
a shiny surface

glazier noun glaziers
someone whose job is to fit glass into windows and doors

gleam noun gleams
1 a beam of soft light, especially one that comes and goes **2** a clear sign of something *She could see the gleam of excitement in his eyes.*

gleam verb gleams, gleaming, gleamed
to gleam is to shine with beams of soft light

glee noun
glee is when you feel happy and excited about something

glen noun glens
a narrow valley, especially in Scotland

glide verb glides, gliding, glided
1 to glide is to fly or move smoothly **2** to glide is also to fly without using an engine

glider noun gliders
an aircraft that does not use an engine and floats on air currents

glimmer noun glimmers
a faint light

glimmer verb glimmers, glimmering, glimmered
to glimmer is to shine with a faint light

glimpse verb glimpses, glimpsing, glimpsed
to glimpse something is to see it briefly

glimpse noun glimpses
a brief view of something

glint verb glints, glinting, glinted
to glint is to shine with a flash of light *High upon the slope to our right, in among the trees, a little frozen waterfall glinted brilliantly.* – Philip Pullman, *Count Karlstein*

glint noun glints
a brief flash of light

glisten verb glistens, glistening, glistened
to shine like something wet or oily

glitter verb glitters, glittering, glittered
to shine with tiny flashes of light *There was the dragon she had longed for and dreamed of. Its green scales glittered, his eyes were bright and black.* – Helen Cresswell, *Dragon Ride*

a
b
c
d
e
f
g
h
i
j
k
l
m
n
o
p
q
r
s
t
u
v
w
x
y
z

gloat verb gloats, gloating, gloated
to be pleased in an unkind way that you have succeeded or that someone else has been hurt or upset

global adjective
to do with the whole world **globally** adverb

global warming noun
global warming is the gradual increase in the average temperature of the earth's climate, caused by the greenhouse effect

globe noun globes
1 a globe is something shaped like a ball, especially one with a map of the world on it 2 the globe is the world

gloom noun
gloom is a depressed condition or feeling

gloomy adjective gloomier, gloomiest
1 almost dark; not well lit 2 sad or depressed **gloomily** adverb **gloominess** noun

glorify verb glorifies, glorifying, glorified
1 to glorify someone is to praise them highly 2 to glorify something is to make it seem splendid **glorification** noun

glorious adjective
splendid or magnificent **gloriously** adverb

glory noun glories
1 glory is fame and honour 2 a thing's glory is its splendour or beauty

gloss noun glosses
the shine on a smooth surface

glossary noun glossaries
a list of words with their meanings explained *Your Science book has a glossary of technical terms.*

glossy adjective glossier, glossiest
smooth and shiny

glove noun gloves
a covering for the hand, with a separate division for each finger

glow noun
1 a brightness and warmth without flames

They sat and finished their drinks in the glow from the fire. 2 a warm or cheerful feeling *Sarah felt a deep glow of satisfaction at her win.*

glow verb glows, glowing, glowed
to glow is to shine with a soft light

glower (rhymes with **flower**) verb glowers, glowering, glowered
to glower is to stare with an angry look

glow-worm noun glow-worms
an insect with a tail that gives out a green light

glucose noun
glucose is a type of sugar found in fruits and honey

glue noun glues
glue is a thick liquid for sticking things together

glue verb glues, gluing, glued
to glue something is to stick it with glue

glum adjective glummer, glummest
sad or depressed **glumly** adverb

glutton noun gluttons
someone who is greedy and enjoys eating too much **gluttony** noun

gnarled (say narld) adjective
twisted and knobbly, like an old tree

gnash (say nash) verb gnashes, gnashing, gnashed
to gnash your teeth is to grind them together

TOP TIPS Keep it quiet! There is a silent **g** in **gnash**, **gnat**, **gnaw**, and **gnome**.

gnat (say nat) noun gnats
a tiny fly that bites

gnaw (say naw) verb gnaws, gnawing, gnawed
to gnaw something hard is to keep biting it

gnome (say nohm) noun gnomes
a kind of dwarf in fairy tales that usually lives underground

go verb goes, going, went, gone
1 to go is to move or lead from one place to

another *Let's go in and see Mrs Cooper. We'll have to go soon. This road goes to Bristol.* **2** a machine or device goes when it is working *My watch isn't going. A car that doesn't go is not much use.* **3** you say that someone or something has gone when they are no longer there and you can't find them *All her money had gone.* **4 Go** also has many special uses shown in these examples *The milk went sour. The plates go on that shelf. The party went well. The gun went bang.* **to be going to do something** is to be ready to do it **to go in for something** is to take part in it **to go off** is to explode **to go off someone** or **something** is to stop liking them **to go on** is to happen or continue *What's going on?*

go noun **goes**
1 a go is a turn or try *May I have a go?*
2 (informal) a go is also a successful try *They made a go of it.* **on the go** always working or moving

go-ahead noun
permission to do something *The Council has given the go-ahead for a recycling scheme in the area.*

go-ahead adjective
adventurous and keen to try out new methods

goal noun **goals**
1 the two posts that the ball must go between to score a point in football, hockey, and other games **2** a point scored in football, hockey, netball, and other games **3** something that you try to do or to achieve *Her goal is to become a pilot.*

goalie noun **goalies** (informal)
a goalkeeper

goalkeeper noun **goalkeepers**
the player who guards the goal in football and hockey

goalpost noun **goalposts**
each of the upright posts of a goal in sports

goat noun **goats**
an animal with horns, belonging to the same family as sheep

gobble verb **gobbles, gobbling, gobbled**
to gobble something is to eat it quickly and greedily

gobbledegook or **gobbledygook** noun
the pompous technical language used by officials that is difficult to understand

goblet noun **goblets**
a drinking glass with a long stem and a base

goblin noun **goblins**
an evil or mischievous fairy in stories

God noun
the creator of the Universe in Christian, Jewish, and Muslim belief

god noun **gods**
a male being that is worshipped

godchild noun **godchildren**
a child that a godparent promises to see brought up as a Christian. A boy is a **godson** and a girl is a **god-daughter**.

goddess noun **goddesses**
a female being that is worshipped

godparent noun **godparents**
a person at a child's christening who promises to see that it is brought up as a Christian. A man is a **godfather** and a woman is a **godmother**.

goggles plural noun
goggles are large glasses that you wear to protect your eyes from wind, water, or dust

gold noun
1 gold is a precious yellow metal **2** gold is also a bright yellow colour

golden adjective
1 made of gold **2** coloured like gold **3** precious or excellent *It was a golden opportunity.*

golden wedding noun **golden weddings**
the 50th anniversary of a wedding

A
B
C
D
E
F
G
H
I
J
K
L
M
N
O
P
Q
R
S
T
U
V
W
X
Y
Z

goldfinch noun goldfinches
a small, brightly-coloured bird with yellow feathers in its wings

goldfish noun goldfish
a small red or orange fish, often kept as a pet

golf noun
golf is an outdoor game played on a prepared course by hitting a small ball into a series of small holes, using a club
golfer noun **golfing** noun

gone
past participle of go verb *I don't know where Jack has gone.*

gong noun gongs
a large metal disc that makes a deep hollow sound when it is hit

good adjective better, best
1 of the kind that people like, want, or praise *They wanted to have a good time.* **2** kind *It was good of you to come.* **3** well-behaved *Be a good boy.* **4** healthy; giving benefit *Exercise is good for you.* **5** thorough; large enough *Let's give it a good clean.* **6** quite large or long *It's a good walk to the station.*

good noun
1 something good or right *Do good to others.* **2** benefit or advantage *I'm telling you for your own good.* **for good** for ever **no good** useless

goodbye interjection
a word you use when you leave someone or at the end of a telephone call

Good Friday noun
the Friday before Easter, when Christians remember Christ's death on the Cross

good-looking adjective
attractive or handsome

good-natured adjective
kind

goodness noun
1 goodness is being good **2** a thing's goodness is the good it does

goods plural noun
goods are things that people buy and sell

goodwill noun
goodwill is a kindly and helpful feeling towards people

gooey adjective
sticky or slimy

goose noun geese
a water bird with webbed feet, larger than a duck

gooseberry noun gooseberries
a small green fruit that grows on a prickly bush

goose pimples plural noun
goose pimples are lots of tiny bumps you get on the skin when you are cold or afraid

gore verb gores, goring, gored
to gore a person or animal is to wound them savagely with a horn or tusk *Several dogs had been gored by a wild boar.*

gorge noun gorges
a narrow valley with steep sides

gorgeous adjective
magnificent; beautiful

gorilla noun gorillas
a large strong African ape

gorse noun
gorse is a prickly bush with small yellow flowers

gory adjective gorier, goriest
1 covered in blood **2** involving a lot of killing

gosh interjection (informal)
an exclamation of surprise

gosling noun goslings
a young goose

gospel noun gospels
1 the gospel is the teachings of Jesus Christ **2** gospel is something you can safely believe *You can take what she says as gospel.* **the Gospels** the first four books of the New Testament

gossip verb gossips, gossiping, gossiped
to gossip is to talk a lot about other people
gossip noun gossips
1 gossip is talk or rumours about other people 2 a gossip is someone who likes talking about other people

got
past tense and past participle of get *I got a bike for my birthday. I've got homework to do.*

gouge (say gowj) verb gouges, gouging, gouged
to gouge something is to press or scoop it out

govern verb governs, governing, governed
to govern a country or organization is to be in charge of it

government noun governments
the group of people who are in charge of a country

governor noun governors
someone who governs or runs a place

gown noun gowns
a loose flowing piece of clothing

GP
short for general practitioner

grab verb grabs, grabbing, grabbed
to grab something is to take hold of it firmly or suddenly

grace noun graces
1 grace is beauty, especially in movement 2 someone behaves with grace when they are kind and friendly to people

graceful adjective
beautiful and elegant in movement or shape
gracefully adverb

gracious adjective
1 kind and pleasant to other people 2 merciful **graciously** adverb

grade noun grades
a step in a scale of quality, value, or rank

grade verb grades, grading, graded
to grade things is to sort or divide them into grades

gradient (say gray-di-ent) noun gradients
1 a slope 2 the amount that a road or railway slopes

gradual adjective
happening slowly but steadily
gradually adverb

graduate (say grad-yoo-at) noun graduates
someone who has a degree from a university or college

graduate (say grad-yoo-ayt) verb graduates, graduating, graduated
1 to graduate is to get a university degree 2 to graduate something is to divide it into graded sections, or to mark it so that it can be used for measuring *The ruler was graduated in millimetres.* **graduation** noun

graffiti (say gra-fee-tee) plural noun
graffiti is words or drawings scribbled on a wall

grain noun grains
1 grain is cereals when they are growing or after they have been harvested 2 a grain is the hard seed of a cereal 3 a grain of something is a small amount of it *The story had a grain of truth in it.* 4 the grain on a piece of wood is the pattern of lines going through it

gram noun grams
a unit of weight in the metric system, a thousandth of a kilogram

grammar noun grammars
1 grammar is the rules for using words 2 a grammar is a book that gives the rules for using words

TOP TIPS
There is a tricky bit in **grammar**—it ends in **ar.**

grammar school noun grammar schools
a kind of secondary school

223

A
B
C
D
E
F
G
H
I
J
K
L
M
N
O
P
Q
R
S
T
U
V
W
X
Y
Z

granny knot

granny knot, crossings are opposite

reef knot, crossings are the same

grammatical adjective
something you say or write is grammatical when it follows the rules of grammar

grand adjective **grander, grandest**
1 great or splendid **2** a grand total is one that includes everything **grandly** adverb

grandad noun **grandads** (informal)
grandfather

grandchild noun **grandchildren**
a child of a person's son or daughter. A girl is a **grand-daughter** and a boy is a **grandson**.

grandeur noun
grandeur is greatness and splendour

grandfather noun **grandfathers**
the father of a person's mother or father

grandfather clock noun
grandfather clocks
a clock in a tall wooden case

grandma noun **grandmas** (informal)
grandmother

grandmother noun **grandmothers**
the mother of a person's mother or father

grandpa noun **grandpas** (informal)
grandfather

grandparent noun **grandparents**
a grandmother or grandfather

grandstand noun **grandstands**
a building at a racecourse or sports ground, that is open at the front with rows of seats for spectators

granite noun
granite is a very hard kind of rock

granny noun **grannies** (informal)
grandmother

granny knot noun **granny knots**
a reef knot with the strings crossed the wrong way

grant verb **grants, granting, granted**
to grant someone something is to give or allow them what they have asked for **to take something for granted** is to assume that it is true or will happen

grant noun **grants**
something given, especially a sum of money

grape noun **grapes**
a small green or purple fruit that grows in bunches on a vine

grapefruit noun **grapefruit**
a large, round, yellow citrus fruit with soft juicy flesh

grapevine noun grapevines
1 a climbing plant on which grapes grow
2 to hear something on the grapevine is to be told it by friends and people you know *We heard the rumour on the grapevine.*

graph noun graphs
a diagram that shows how two amounts are related

graphic adjective
1 short and lively *He gave a graphic account of the journey.* **2** to do with drawing or painting *She is a graphic artist.*
graphically adverb

graphics plural noun
graphics are diagrams, lettering, and drawings, especially pictures that are produced by a computer

graphite noun
graphite is a soft kind of carbon used for the lead in pencils

grapple verb grapples, grappling, grappled
1 to grapple someone or grapple with someone is to fight them **2** to grapple something is to hold it tightly **3** to grapple with a problem is to try to deal with it

grasp verb grasps, grasping, grasped
1 to grasp someone or something is to hold them tightly **2** to grasp something is to understand it

grasp noun
1 a firm hold **2** a person's grasp of something is how well they understand it *His grasp of English was limited.*

grasping adjective
greedy for money or possessions

grass noun grasses
1 grass is a green plant with thin stalks **2** a piece of grass is an area of ground covered with grass **grassy** adjective

grasshopper noun grasshoppers
a jumping insect that makes a shrill noise

grate[1] noun grates
1 a metal framework that keeps fuel in the fireplace **2** a fireplace

grate[2] verb grates, grating, grated
1 to grate something is to shred it into small pieces **2** to grate is to make an unpleasant noise by rubbing something *The chalk grated on the blackboard.*

grateful adjective
feeling glad that someone has done something for you *I was grateful for their kindness in giving me food and drink.*
gratefully adverb

grating noun gratings
a framework of metal bars placed across an opening

gratitude noun
you show gratitude when you are grateful or thankful for something

grave[1] noun graves
the place where a dead body is buried

grave[2] adjective graver, gravest
serious or solemn *We've had grave news.*
gravely adverb

gravel noun
gravel is small stones mixed with coarse sand, used to make paths

gravestone noun gravestones
a stone monument over a grave

graveyard noun graveyards
a place where dead bodies are buried

gravity noun
1 gravity is the force that pulls all objects in the universe towards each other **2** the earth's gravity is the force that pulls everything towards itself **3** the importance or seriousness of a situation

gravy noun
a hot brown sauce made from meat juices

graze verb grazes, grazing, grazed
1 to graze is to feed on growing grass **2** to graze your skin is to scrape it slightly against something rough

graze noun grazes
a sore place where skin has been scraped

a
b
c
d
e
f
g
h
i
j
k
l
m
n
o
p
q
r
s
t
u
v
w
x
y
z

A

B

C

D

E

F

G

H

I

J

K

L

M

N

O

P

Q

R

S

T

U

V

W

X

Y

Z

grease noun
grease is thick fat or oil **greasy** adjective

great adjective greater, greatest
1 very large 2 very important or
distinguished *She was a great writer.*
3 (informal) very good or enjoyable *It's
great to see you again.* 4 older or younger
by one generation, as in *great-grandmother*
and *great-grandson* **greatly** adjective
greatness noun

greed noun
greed is being greedy and wanting
too much

greedy adjective greedier, greediest
wanting more food or money than you need
greedily adverb

green adjective greener, greenest
1 of the colour of grass and leaves
2 concerned with protecting the
natural environment
green noun greens
1 green is a green colour 2 a green is an
area of grass

greenery noun
green leaves or plants

greengage noun greengages
a kind of green plum

greengrocer noun greengrocers
someone who keeps a shop that sells fruit
and vegetables **greengrocery** noun a
greengrocer's shop

greenhouse noun greenhouses
a glass building that is kept warm inside for
growing plants

greenhouse effect noun
the warming of the earth's surface by gases
(called **greenhouse gases**) such as methane
and carbon dioxide, which trap heat in the
earth's atmosphere

greens plural noun
greens are green vegetables, such as
cabbage and spinach

greet verb greets, greeting, greeted
1 to greet someone is to welcome them

when they arrive *His cat Moxie greeted him
with a soft miaow.* 2 to greet something is to
respond to it in a certain way *They greeted
the news with loud cheering.*

greeting noun greetings
a greeting is the words or actions used
to greet someone **greetings** are good
wishes when you meet someone or talk to
them

grenade noun grenades
a small bomb, usually thrown by hand

grew
past tense of **grow** *The road grew busier as
we neared the town.*

grey adjective greyer, greyest
of the colour between black and white, like
ashes or dark clouds
grey noun
a grey colour

greyhound noun greyhounds
a slim dog with smooth hair, used in racing

grid noun grids
a framework or pattern of bars or lines
crossing each other

grief noun
grief is deep sadness or sorrow people feel
when someone has died **to come to grief** is
to have an accident or misfortune

grievance noun grievances
something that people are unhappy or
angry about

grieve verb grieves, grieving, grieved
1 to grieve is to feel sad or sorrowful 2 to
grieve someone is to make them feel very
sad *It grieves me to have to tell you this.*

grievous adjective
1 causing great sadness 2 serious *We have
suffered a grievous loss.* **grievously** adverb

grill noun grills
1 an element or burner on a cooker, that
sends heat downwards 2 grilled food
3 a grating
grill verb grills, grilling, grilled
1 to grill food is to cook it under a grill 2 to

grill someone is to question them closely and severely *The police grilled him for hours.*

grim adjective **grimmer, grimmest**
1 stern or severe 2 frightening or unpleasant *They had a grim experience.*
grimly adverb

grimace noun **grimaces**
a strange or twisted expression on your face

grime noun
grime is a layer of dirt on a surface
grimy adjective

grin noun **grins**
a smile showing your teeth

grin verb **grins, grinning, grinned**
to grin is to smile showing your teeth

grind verb **grinds, grinding, ground**
1 to grind something is to crush it into a powder 2 to grind something hard is to sharpen or polish it by rubbing it on a rough surface **grinder** noun

grindstone noun **grindstones**
a rough round revolving stone used for grinding things **to keep your nose to the grindstone** is to keep working hard

grip verb **grips, gripping, gripped**
1 to grip something is to hold it tightly
2 a story, film, game, or other activity grips you when you find it very interesting or exciting

grip noun **grips**
1 a firm hold on something 2 a handle

grisly adjective **grislier, grisliest**
disgusting or horrible *He met a grisly end by being eaten by a bear.*

gristle noun
gristle is the tough rubbery part of meat
gristly adjective

grit noun
1 grit is tiny pieces of stone or sand
2 a person's grit is their courage and determination to do something difficult
gritty adjective

grit verb **grits, gritting, gritted**
1 to grit your teeth is to clench them tightly

when in pain or trouble 2 to grit a road or path is to put grit on it

grizzly bear noun **grizzly bears**
a large bear of North America

groan verb **groans, groaning, groaned**
to groan is to make a long deep sound when in pain or distress

groan noun **groans**
a long deep sound of pain or distress

grocer noun **grocers**
someone who keeps a shop that sells food, drink, and other goods for the house

grocery noun **groceries**
a grocer's shop **groceries** goods sold by a grocer

groggy adjective **groggier, groggiest**
dizzy or unsteady, especially from illness or injury

groin noun **groins**
the flat part between your thighs and your trunk

groom noun **grooms**
1 someone whose job is to look after horses
2 a bridegroom

groom verb **grooms, grooming, groomed**
1 to groom a horse or other animal is to clean and brush it 2 to groom the hair or a beard is to make it neat and trim

groove noun **grooves**
a long narrow channel cut in the surface of something

grope verb **gropes, groping, groped**
to grope for something is to feel about for it when you cannot see it

gross adjective **grosser, grossest**
1 fat and ugly 2 having bad manners; crude or vulgar 3 very bad or shocking *They showed gross stupidity.* 4 a person's gross income or the gross profits of a business are the total amount before taxes and other amounts have been taken off
grossly adverb someone grossly exaggerates something when they exaggerate a lot

a
b
c
d
e
f
g
h
i
j
k
l
m
n
o
p
q
r
s
t
u
v
w
x
y
z

A

gross noun gross
a gross is twelve dozen or 144

B

grotesque (say groh-**tesk**) adjective
strange and ugly **grotesquely** adverb

C

D

grotty adjective **grottier, grottiest**
(informal)
unpleasant or dirty

E

F

ground¹ noun **grounds**
1 the ground is the surface of the earth 2 a ground is a sports field

G

ground²
past tense and past participle of **grind**
Sarah scowled and ground her teeth. The ship had ground to a halt.

H

I

grounded adjective
1 aircraft are grounded when they are prevented from flying, for example because of the weather 2 (informal) someone is grounded when they are not allowed to go out

J

K

L

M

ground floor noun **ground floors**
in a building, the floor that is level with the ground

N

grounds plural noun
1 the grounds for something are the reasons that explain it or justify it *There are grounds for suspecting that a crime has been committed.* 2 the gardens of a large house 3 bits of coffee at the bottom of a cup

O

P

Q

R

groundsheet noun **groundsheets**
a piece of waterproof material for spreading on the ground, especially in a tent

S

groundsman noun **groundsmen**
someone whose job is to look after a sports ground

T

U

group noun **groups**
a number of people, animals, or things that belong together in some way

V

group verb **groups, grouping, grouped**
to group people or things is to make them into a group

W

X

grouse¹ verb **grouses, grousing, groused**
to grumble or complain

Y

Z

grouse² noun grouse
a large bird hunted as game

grove noun **groves**
a group of trees; a small wood

grovel verb **grovels, grovelling, grovelled**
1 to grovel is to crawl on the ground 2 to grovel is to be extremely humble and obedient towards someone, usually because you want something from them

grow verb **grows, growing, grew, grown**
1 a person grows when they become bigger with age 2 a plant or seed grows when it develops in the ground 3 to grow something is to plant it in the ground and look after it *She grows lovely roses.* 4 to grow is also to become *By now it was growing dark on the moor. He grew richer and richer.* **to grow on someone** is to become more attractive to them *This music grows on you.* **to grow out of something** is to become too big or too old for it **to grow up** is to become an adult **grower** noun

growl verb **growls, growling, growled**
to growl is to make a deep rough sound, like an angry dog

growl noun **growls**
a deep rough sound

grown-up noun **grown-ups**
an adult

growth noun **growths**
1 growth is growing or development 2 a growth is something that has grown, especially something unwanted in the body such as a tumour

grub noun **grubs**
1 a grub is a tiny creature that will become an insect; a larva 2 (informal) grub is food

grubby adjective **grubbier, grubbiest**
rather dirty

grudge noun **grudges**
a dislike of someone because you think they have harmed you, or because you are jealous

grudge verb **grudges, grudging, grudged**
to grudge someone something is to feel unwilling to let them have it
grudgingly adverb you do something grudgingly when you don't really want to do it, and only do it because you have to

gruelling adjective
a gruelling test or journey or other experience is one that is very hard and tiring

gruesome adjective
horrible or disgusting to look at

gruff adjective **gruffer, gruffest**
having a rough unfriendly voice or manner
gruffly adverb

grumble verb **grumbles, grumbling, grumbled**
to complain in a bad-tempered way

grumpy adjective **grumpier, grumpiest**
bad-tempered **grumpily** adverb
grumpiness noun

grunt verb **grunts, grunting, grunted**
to grunt is to make a snorting sound like a pig
grunt noun **grunts**
a snort like that of a pig

guarantee noun **guarantees**
a formal promise to do something, especially to repair something you have sold someone if it goes wrong
guarantee verb **guarantees, guaranteeing, guaranteed**
to guarantee something is to make a promise to do it

guard verb **guards, guarding, guarded**
1 to guard something or someone is to keep them safe 2 to guard a prisoner is to prevent them from escaping **to guard against something** is to be careful to prevent it happening
guard noun **guards**
1 guard is protecting or guarding people or things *He was kept on constant guard after his attempts to escape.* 2 a guard is

someone who protects a person or place, or a group of people guarding a prisoner 3 a guard is also an official in charge of a railway train 4 a guard is a shield or device protecting people from the dangers of a fire or machinery

guardian noun **guardians**
1 someone who protects something
2 someone who is legally in charge of a child instead of the child's parents

guerrilla (say ge-**ril**-a) noun **guerrillas**
a member of a small army or band that fights by means of surprise attacks

guess noun **guesses**
an opinion or answer that you give without working it out in detail or being sure of it
guess verb **guesses, guessing, guessed**
to guess is to make a guess

guest (say gest) noun **guests**
1 a person who is invited to visit or stay at someone's house 2 someone staying at a hotel 3 a performer in a show in which someone else is the main performer

guest house noun **guest houses**
a kind of small hotel

guidance noun
guidance is giving help or information to someone, or telling them how to do something

guide noun **guides**
1 someone who shows people the way, helps them, or points out interesting sights 2 a book that tells you about a place **Guide** a member of the Girl Guides Association, an organization for girls
guide verb **guides, guiding, guided**
to guide someone is to show them the way or help them do something *He guided her into the sitting room where the piano was.*

guide dog noun **guide dogs**
a dog specially trained to lead a blind person

guidelines plural noun
guidelines are rules and information about how to do something

a
b
c
d
e
f
g
h
i
j
k
l
m
n
o
p
q
r
s
t
u
v
w
x
y
z

A B C D E F **G** H I J K L M N O P Q R S T U V W X Y Z

guild (say gild) noun **guilds**
a society of people with similar skills or interests

guillotine (say gil-o-teen) noun **guillotines**
1 a machine once used in France for beheading people 2 a device with a sharp blade for cutting paper

guilt noun
1 guilt is an unpleasant feeling you have when you have done something wrong 2 a person's guilt is the fact that they have done something wrong *Everyone was convinced of their guilt.*

guilty adjective **guiltier, guiltiest**
1 someone is guilty when they have done wrong 2 someone feels guilty when they know they have done wrong

guinea noun **guineas**
a British gold coin worth 21 shillings or £1.05, no longer in use

guinea pig noun **guinea pigs**
1 a small furry animal without a tail, kept as a pet 2 a person who is used in an experiment

guitar noun **guitars**
a musical instrument played by plucking its strings **guitarist** noun

gulf noun **gulfs**
a large area of sea partly surrounded by land

gull noun **gulls**
a seagull

gullet noun **gullets**
the tube from the throat to the stomach

gullible adjective
someone is gullible when they can be easily fooled about something

gully noun **gullies**
a narrow channel that carries water

gulp verb **gulps, gulping, gulped**
1 to gulp something is to swallow it quickly or greedily 2 to gulp is to make a loud swallowing noise, especially out of fear

gulp noun **gulps**
a loud swallowing noise

gum[1] noun **gums**
the firm fleshy part of the mouth that holds the teeth

gum[2] noun **gums**
1 a sticky substance used as glue 2 chewing gum

gun noun **guns**
1 a weapon that fires shells or bullets from a metal tube 2 a pistol fired to signal the start of a race 3 a device that forces a substance such as grease out of a tube

gunboat noun **gunboats**
a small warship

gunfire noun
gunfire is the firing of guns, or the noise they make

gunman noun **gunmen**
a man armed with a gun

gunner noun **gunners**
someone who works with guns, especially in the army

gunpowder noun
gunpowder is a type of explosive

gunshot noun **gunshots**
gunshot is the shot that some guns fire

gurdwara noun **gurdwaras**
a building where Sikhs worship

gurgle verb **gurgles, gurgling, gurgled**
to make a bubbling sound *Water gurgled down the waste pipe. Anna's clear voice gurgled with laughter.*

guru noun **gurus**
1 a Hindu religious teacher 2 a wise and respected teacher

Guru Granth Sahib noun
the holy book of the Sikh religion

gush verb **gushes, gushing, gushed**
1 to gush is to flow quickly 2 to gush is also to talk quickly and with excitement

gust noun gusts
a sudden rush of wind or rain
gusty adjective

gut noun guts
the lower part of the digestive system;
the intestine
gut verb guts, gutting, gutted
1 to gut a dead fish or animal is to remove
its insides before cooking it **2** to gut a place
is to remove or destroy the inside of it
Flames gutted the bedroom of the flat.

guts plural noun
1 your guts are your insides, especially
your stomach and intestines **2** (informal) a
person has guts when they show courage
and determination to do something
difficult

gutter noun gutters
a long narrow channel at the side of a
street or along the edge of a roof, to carry
away rainwater

guy[1] noun guys
1 a figure in the form of Guy Fawkes, burnt
on or near 5 November in memory of the
Gunpowder Plot to blow up Parliament in
1605 **2** (informal) a man

guy[2] or **guy-rope** noun
guys, guy-ropes
a rope used to hold something in place,
especially a tent

guzzle verb guzzles, guzzling, guzzled
to guzzle food or drink is to eat or drink
it greedily

gym (say jim) noun gyms (informal)
1 a gym is a gymnasium **2** gym is the
exercises and games you do in PE

gymkhana (say jim-**kah**-na) noun
gymkhanas
a show of horse-riding contests and
other events

gymnasium noun gymnasiums
a large room equipped for gymnastics and
other exercises

gymnast noun gymnasts
an expert in gymnastics

gymnastics plural noun
gymnastics are exercises and movements
that show the body's agility and strength

gypsy noun gypsies
a member of a community of people, also
called **travellers**, who live in caravans
or similar vehicles and travel from place
to place

Hh

habit noun habits
something that you do often and almost
without thinking

habitat noun habitats
an animal's or plant's habitat is the place
where it naturally lives or grows

habitual adjective
something is habitual when you do
it regularly *her brother's face with its
habitual smile*

hack verb hacks, hacking, hacked
to hack something is to chop or cut
it roughly

hacker noun hackers
someone who uses a computer to get access
to a company's or government's computer
system without permission

hacksaw noun hacksaws
a saw with a thin blade for cutting metal

had
past tense and past participle of have *I had
to bite my tongue to stop myself answering
back. He had had a brilliant day.*

haddock noun haddock
a sea fish used for food

hadn't
short for *had not He hadn't seen her come in.*

hag noun hags
an ugly old woman

A
B
C
D
E
F
G
H
I
J
K
L
M
N
O
P
Q
R
S
T
U
V
W
X
Y
Z

haggard adjective
looking ill or very tired

haggis noun haggises
a Scottish food made from some of the
inner parts of a sheep mixed with oatmeal

haggle verb haggles, haggling,
haggled
to argue about a price or agreement

haiku (say **hy**-koo) noun haiku
a Japanese short poem, with three lines and
17 syllables in the pattern 5, 7, 5

hail[1] noun
frozen drops of rain
hail verb hails, hailing, hailed
it hails or it is hailing when hail falls

hail[2] verb hails, hailing, hailed
to hail someone is to call out or wave to
them to get their attention

hailstone noun hailstones
a piece of hail

hair noun hairs
1 hair is the soft covering that grows on the
heads and bodies of people and animals
2 a hair is one of the fine threads that
makes up this soft covering

hairbrush noun hairbrushes
a brush for tidying your hair

haircut noun haircuts
cutting a person's hair when it gets too
long; the style into which it is cut

hairdresser noun hairdressers
someone whose job is to cut and arrange
people's hair

hairpin noun hairpins
a pin for keeping your hair in place

hair-raising adjective
terrifying or dangerous

hairstyle noun hairstyles
a way or style of arranging your hair

hairy adjective hairier, hairiest
1 having a lot of hair **2** (informal)
dangerous or risky

Hajj noun
the Hajj is the journey to Mecca that
all Muslims try to make at least once in
their lives

hake noun hake
a sea fish used for food

halal adjective
halal meat is prepared according to
Muslim law

half noun halves
each of the two equal parts that something
is or can be divided into
half adverb
partly; not completely *This meat is only
half cooked.*

half-baked adjective (informal)
a half-baked plan or idea has not been
properly worked out

half-hearted adjective
not very enthusiastic **half-heartedly** adverb

half-mast noun
a flag is at half-mast when it is lowered to
halfway down its flagpole, as a sign that
someone important has died

halfpenny (say **hayp**-ni) noun
halfpennies or halfpence
an old British coin that was worth half
a penny

half-term noun half-terms
a short holiday from school in the middle of
a school term

half-time noun half-times
a short break in the middle of a game

halfway adverb, adjective
at a point half the distance or amount
between two places or times

halibut noun halibut
a large flat sea fish used for food

hall noun halls
1 a space or passage inside the front
door of a house **2** a very large room
for meetings, concerts, or other large

gatherings of people **3** a large important building or house, such as a town hall

hallo interjection
a word used to greet someone or to attract their attention

Hallowe'en noun
the night of 31 October, when people used to think that ghosts and witches might appear

hallucination noun **hallucinations**
something you think you can see or hear when it is not really there

halo noun **haloes**
a circle of light, especially one shown round the head of a saint or angel in a painting

halt verb **halts, halting, halted**
to halt is to stop
halt noun
to call a halt is to stop something **to come to a halt** is to stop

halter noun **halters**
a rope or strap put round a horse's head so that it can be controlled

halting adjective
slow and uncertain *He has a halting walk.*

halve verb **halves, halving, halved**
1 to halve something is to divide it into halves **2** to halve something is to reduce to half its size or amount *If the shop had another checkout it would halve the queues.*

halves
plural of **half** noun

ham noun **hams**
1 ham is meat from a pig's leg **2** (informal) a ham is an actor who is not very good and acts in a very exaggerated way

hamburger noun **hamburgers**
a round flat cake of minced beef that is fried and usually eaten in a bread roll

hammer noun **hammers**
a tool with a heavy metal head at the end of a handle, used for hitting nails in or beating out things

hammer verb **hammers, hammering, hammered**
1 to hammer something is to hit it with a hammer **2** to hammer is to knock loudly *We heard someone hammering on the door.* **3** (informal) to hammer someone in a game or contest is to defeat them completely

hammock noun **hammocks**
a bed made of a strong net or piece of cloth hung up above the ground or floor

hamper[1] noun **hampers**
a large box-shaped basket with a lid

hamper[2] verb **hampers, hampering, hampered**
to hamper someone or something is to get in their way or make it difficult for them to work

hamster noun **hamsters**
a small furry animal with cheek pouches, often kept as a pet

hand noun **hands**
1 the part of your body at the end of your arm **2** a pointer on a clock or watch **3** the cards held by one player in a card game **4** a worker, especially a member of a ship's crew **5** side or direction *the right-hand side, on the other hand* **at hand** near or close by **to do or make something by hand** is to do or make it using your hands **to give someone a hand** is to help them **hands down** winning easily or completely **on hand** ready and available **to get out of hand** is to get out of control

hand verb **hands, handing, handed**
to hand something to someone is to give or pass it to them

handbag noun **handbags**
a small bag for holding money, keys, and other personal items

handbook noun **handbooks**
a book that gives useful facts about something

handcuffs plural noun
a pair of metal rings joined by a chain, used for locking a person's wrists together

a
b
c
d
e
f
g
h
i
j
k
l
m
n
o
p
q
r
s
t
u
v
w
x
y
z

A B C D E F G **H** I J K L M N O P Q R S T U V W X Y Z

handful noun handfuls
1 as much as you can carry in one hand
2 a small number of people or things *There were only a handful of people in the audience.*
3 (informal) a troublesome person

handheld adjective
a handheld electronic device is one that you can hold in your hand and carry around with you

handicap noun handicaps
1 a disadvantage 2 a disability affecting a person

handicapped adjective
1 suffering from a disadvantage 2 suffering from a disability

handicraft noun handicrafts
artistic work done with your hands, such as woodwork and pottery

handiwork noun
something you have done or made using your artistic skill

handkerchief (say **hang**-ker-cheef) noun handkerchiefs
a square piece of material for wiping your nose

handle noun handles
the part of a thing by which you can hold or control it or pick it up

handle verb handles, handling, handled
1 to handle something is to touch or feel it with your hands 2 to handle a task or problem is to deal with it *I thought you handled the situation very well.*

handlebars plural noun
a bar with a handle at each end, used to steer a bicycle or motor cycle

handrail noun handrails
a rail for holding on to for support

handsome adjective handsomer, handsomest
1 attractive or good-looking *I have no children of my own, and as you are the cleverest and handsomest young man I've ever met, I think I would like to make you the Prince of Narnia. — C. S. Lewis, The Lion, The Witch and the Wardrobe* 2 large or generous *They have made a handsome offer.*

handstand noun handstands
an exercise in which you balance on your hands with your feet in the air

handwriting noun
writing done by hand; a person's style of writing **handwritten** adjective written by hand, not typed or printed

handy adjective handier, handiest
useful or convenient

handyman noun handymen
someone who does small jobs or repairs in the house

hang verb hangs, hanging, hung
1 to hang something is to fix the top part of it to a hook or nail *Hang your coat on one of the pegs.* 2 something hangs when it is supported from the top and does not touch the ground *The bat was hanging by its feet.* 3 to hang wallpaper is to paste it in strips on to a wall 4 to hang is to float in the air 5 (in this meaning, the past tense and past participle are **hanged**) to hang someone is to execute them by hanging them from a rope that tightens around their neck *He was hanged in 1950.* **to hang about** or **hang around** is to wait around doing nothing **to hang on** (informal) is to wait *Hang on! I'm not ready yet.* **to hang on to something** is to hold it tightly **to hang up** is to end a telephone conversation by putting back the receiver or by pressing a button

hangar noun hangars
a large shed where aircraft are kept

hanger noun hangers
a curved piece of wood, plastic, or wire with a hook at the top, that you use to hang clothes up on

hang-glider noun hang-gliders
a frame like a large kite on which a person can glide through the air **hang-gliding** noun

hank noun hanks
a coil or piece of wool or thread

hanker verb hankers, hankering, hankered
to hanker after something is to want it badly *The penguin, who had always hankered after the good life, recognized that this was as near to it as any penguin could decently hope for.* – Alan Rusbridger, *The Coldest Day in the Zoo*

hanky noun hankies (informal)
a handkerchief

Hanukkah noun
a Jewish festival held in December

haphazard (say hap-**haz**-erd) adjective
done or chosen at random, with no particular order or plan *The books were arranged on the shelf in a haphazard way.*

happen verb happens, happening, happened
to happen is to take place or occur **to happen to do something** is to do it by chance without planning it *I happened to see him in the street.*

happening noun happenings
something that happens; an unusual event

happily adverb
1 to do something happily is to do it in a happy way *She was singing happily.*
2 in a contended or willing way *Since my sister was doing the dusting, I happily did the washing-up.*

happiness noun
being happy *Her eyes were shining with happiness.*

happy adjective happier, happiest
1 pleased or contented 2 satisfied that something is good *My teacher is happy with my work this term.* 3 lucky or fortunate *By a happy coincidence, we met Jenny in town.*

happy-go-lucky adjective
being cheerful and not worrying about the future

harass (say **ha**-ras) verb harasses, harassing, harassed
to harass someone is to annoy or trouble them a lot **harassed** adjective **harassment** noun

harbour noun harbours
a place where ships can shelter or unload

harbour verb harbours, harbouring, harboured
to harbour a criminal is to give them shelter

hard adjective harder, hardest
1 firm or solid; not soft *The ground was hard.* 2 difficult *These sums are quite hard.* 3 severe or harsh *There has been a hard frost.* 4 energetic; using great effort *She is a hard worker.* **hard up** short of money **hardness** noun

hard adverb harder, hardest
1 with great effort *We must work hard.* 2 with a lot of force *It was raining hard.*

hardboard noun
stiff board made of compressed wood pulp

hard-boiled adjective
a hard-boiled egg is one that has been boiled until it is hard

hard disk noun hard disks
a disk fitted inside a computer, able to store large amounts of data

harden verb hardens, hardening, hardened
1 to harden is to become hard *Wait for the varnish to harden.* 2 to harden something is to make it hard *What's the best way to harden a conker?*

hardly adverb
only just; only with difficulty *She was hardly able to walk.*

hardship noun hardships
1 hardship is suffering or difficulty 2 a hardship is something that causes suffering

hardware noun
1 tools and other pieces of equipment you use in the house and garden 2 the machinery and electronic parts of a computer, not the software

hard-wearing adjective
able to stand a lot of wear

hardy adjective **hardier, hardiest**
able to endure cold or difficult conditions

hare noun **hares**
a fast-running animal like a large rabbit

hark verb **harks, harking, harked** (old-fashioned use)
to hark is to listen **to hark back** is to return to an earlier subject

harm verb **harms, harming, harmed**
to harm someone or something is to hurt or damage them

harm noun
injury or damage **harmful** adjective causing injury or damage **harmless** adjective not at all dangerous

harmonica noun **harmonicas**
a mouth organ

harmonious adjective
1 music is harmonious when it is pleasant to listen to 2 peaceful and friendly **harmoniously** adverb

harmonize verb **harmonizes, harmonizing, harmonized**
1 musicians or singers harmonize when they play or sing together with notes that combine in a pleasant way with the main tune 2 to harmonize is to combine together in an effective or pleasant way **harmonization** noun

harmony noun **harmonies**
1 a pleasant combination of musical notes played or sung at the same time 2 agreement or friendship *They live in perfect harmony.* **harmonic** adjective to do with musical harmony

harness noun **harnesses**
the straps put over a horse's head and round its neck to control it

harness verb **harnesses, harnessing, harnessed**
1 to harness a horse is to put a harness on it 2 to harness something is to control it and make use of it *They tried to harness the power of the wind to make electricity.*

harp noun **harps**
a musical instrument made of a frame with strings stretched across it that you pluck with your fingers **harpist** noun

harp verb **harps, harping, harped**
to harp on about something is to keep on talking about it in an annoying way *He keeps harping on about all the work he has to do.*

harpoon noun **harpoons**
a spear attached to a rope, fired from a gun to catch whales and large fish

harpsichord noun **harpsichords**
a musical instrument like a piano but with the strings plucked and not struck

harrow noun **harrows**
a heavy device pulled over the ground to break up the soil

harsh adjective **harsher, harshest**
1 rough and unpleasant 2 cruel or severe **harshly** adverb **harshness** noun

harvest noun **harvests**
1 the time when farmers gather in the corn, fruit, or vegetables they have grown 2 the crop that is gathered in

harvest verb **harvests, harvesting, harvested**
to harvest crops is to gather them in

has
3rd person singular of **have** *He has a very nice nature.*

hash noun **hashes**
a mixture of small pieces of meat and vegetables, usually fried

hasn't
short for *has not*

hassle noun **hassles** (informal)
hassle or a hassle is something that is difficult or causes problems

hassle verb **hassles, hassling, hassled**
to hassle someone is to annoy them or cause them problems

haste noun
hurry or speed **to make haste** is to hurry

hasten verb hastens, hastening, hastened
1 to hasten is to hurry 2 to hasten something is to speed it up

hasty adjective hastier, hastiest
hurried; done too quickly *a hasty decision* **hastily** adverb **hastiness** noun

hat noun hats
a covering for the head

hatch¹ noun hatches
an opening in a floor, wall, or door, usually with a covering

hatch² verb hatches, hatching, hatched
1 to hatch is to break out of an egg *The chicks hatched this morning.* 2 to hatch an egg is to keep it warm until a young bird hatches from it 3 to hatch a plan is to form it

hatchet noun hatchets
a small axe

hate verb hates, hating, hated
to hate someone or something is to dislike them very much

hate noun hates
1 hate is a feeling of great dislike
2 (informal) a hate is someone or something that you dislike very much *Sweetcorn is one of my hates.*

hateful adjective
hated; very nasty **hatefully** adverb

hatred (say **hay**-trid) noun
a strong feeling of great dislike

hat trick noun hat tricks
getting three goals, wickets, or victories one after another

haughty (say **haw**-ti) adjective
haughtier, haughtiest
proud of yourself and looking down on other people **haughtily** adverb **haughtiness** noun

haul verb hauls, hauling, hauled
to haul something is to pull it using a lot of power or strength *The topmen hurried aloft*
while on the deck the rest of us hauled the thick anchor cable from its locker. — Richard Platt, *Pirate Diary*

haul noun hauls
an amount that someone has gained; a catch or booty *The thieves made a haul of over £6 million. The trawler brought home a large haul of fish.*

haunt verb haunts, haunting, haunted
1 a ghost haunts a place or person when it appears often 2 to haunt a place is to visit it often 3 an idea or memory haunts someone when they are always thinking of it **haunted** adjective a haunted place is one that people think is visited by ghosts

have verb has, having, had
This word has many meanings, depending on the words that go with it.1 to have something is to own or possess it *We haven't any money.* 2 to contain something *I thought this tin had biscuits in it.* 3 to have (for example) a party is to organize it 4 to have (for example) a shock or accident is to experience it *I'm afraid she has had an accident.* 5 to have to do something is to be obliged or forced to do it *We really have to go now.* 6 to have something (for example) mended or built is to get someone to mend or build it *I'm having my watch mended.* 7 to have (for example) a letter is to receive it *I had an email from my cousin.* 8 the verb **have** can also be used to help make other verbs *They have gone. Has he seen my book? We had eaten them.* **to have someone on** (informal) is to fool them

haven (say **hay**-ven) noun havens
1 a safe place 2 a harbour

haven't
short for *have not*

haversack noun haversacks
a strong bag you carry on your back

hawk¹ noun hawks
a bird of prey with very strong eyesight and a hooked beak

hawk² verb hawks, hawking, hawked
to hawk things is to go from place to place selling them **hawker** noun

a
b
c
d
e
f
g
h
i
j
k
l
m
n
o
p
q
r
s
t
u
v
w
x
y
z

A

B

C

D

E

F

G

H

I

J

K

L

M

N

O

P

Q

R

S

T

U

V

W

X

Y

Z

hawthorn noun **hawthorns**
a thorny tree with small red berries

hay noun
cut grass that is dried and used to feed animals

hay fever noun
an allergy to pollen that makes you sneeze and makes your eyes water or itch

haystack noun **haystacks**
a large neat pile of stored hay

hazard noun **hazards**
a risk or danger

hazardous adjective
something is hazardous when it is dangerous or risky *Cold and hunger drove me to ever more desperate and hazardous escapades.* – Michael Morpurgo, *The Last Wolf*

haze noun **hazes**
thin mist

hazel noun **hazels**
1 a type of small nut tree 2 a nut from this tree 3 a light brown colour

hazy adjective **hazier, haziest**
1 misty *hazy sunshine* 2 vague and unclear *I have a hazy memory of that day.*
hazily adverb **haziness** noun

he pronoun, noun
a male person or animal: used as the subject of a verb

head noun **heads**
1 the part of your body containing your brains, eyes, and mouth 2 brains or intelligence *Use your head!* 3 a talent or ability *He has a good head for sums.* 4 the side of a coin on which someone's head is shown 5 a person *It costs £3 per head.* 6 the top or front of something, such as a pin or nail 7 the person in charge *She's the head of this school.* **to keep your head** is to stay calm **off the top of your head** (informal) without preparation or thinking carefully *He gave an answer off the top of his head.*

head verb **heads, heading, headed**
1 to head a group or organization is to lead it or be the person in charge 2 to head a ball is to hit it with your head 3 to head in a particular direction is to start going there *They headed for home.* **to head someone off** is to get in front of them in order to turn them aside

headache noun **headaches**
1 a pain in your head that goes on hurting 2 (informal) a problem or difficulty

headdress noun **headdresses**
a decorative covering for the head

header noun **headers**
the act of hitting the ball with your head in football

head first adverb
with your head at the front *I dived in head first.*

heading noun **headings**
a word or words at the top of a piece of printing or writing

headland noun **headlands**
a piece of high land sticking out into the sea

headlight noun **headlights**
a strong light at the front of a vehicle

headline noun **headlines**
a heading in a newspaper, printed in large type

headlong adverb, adjective
1 falling head first 2 in a hasty or thoughtless way *He's always rushing headlong into trouble.*

headmaster noun **headmasters**
a male headteacher

headmistress noun **headmistresses**
a female headteacher

head-on adverb, adjective
with the front parts hitting each other *They had a head-on collision.*

headphones plural noun
a listening device that fits over the top of your head

headquarters noun **headquarters**
the place from which an organization is controlled

headteacher noun **headteachers**
the person in charge of a school

heal verb **heals, healing, healed**
1 to heal someone is to make them healthy **2** a wound or injury heals when it gets better *The cut soon healed.* **3** to heal a disease is to cure it **healer** noun

health noun
1 the condition of a person's body or mind *His health is bad.* **2** being healthy *We wished the couple health and happiness.*

healthy adjective **healthier, healthiest**
1 free from illness; having good health **2** good for you *Fresh air is healthy.* **healthily** adverb **healthiness** noun

heap noun **heaps**
a pile, especially an untidy pile **heaps** (informal) a large amount *We've got heaps of time.*

heap verb **heaps, heaping, heaped**
1 to heap things is to pile them up **2** to

heap something is to put large amounts on it *She heaped his plate with food.*

hear verb **hears, hearing, heard**
1 to hear is to take in sounds through the ears **2** to hear a sound is to take it in through the ear **3** to hear news or information is to receive it **4** you hear from someone when they write to you or phone you

hearing noun **hearings**
1 the ability to hear **2** a chance to be heard *Please give me a fair hearing.* **3** a trial in court

hearing aid noun **hearing aids**
a device to help a deaf person to hear

hearse (say herss) noun **hearses**
a vehicle for taking a coffin to a funeral

heart noun **hearts**
1 the part of the body inside your chest that pumps blood around your body **2** a person's feelings or emotions *She has a kind heart.* **3** courage or enthusiasm *We must take heart.* **4** the middle or most important part of something **5** a curved shape representing a heart, or a playing card with this shape on it **to break someone's heart** is to make them very unhappy **by heart** by using your memory

heart

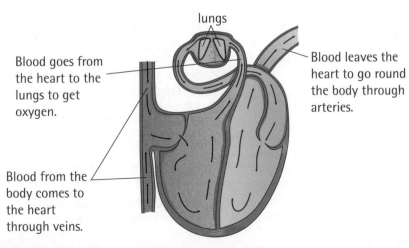

lungs

Blood goes from the heart to the lungs to get oxygen.

Blood leaves the heart to go round the body through arteries.

Blood from the body comes to the heart through veins.

A
B
C
D
E
F
G
H
I
J
K
L
M
N
O
P
Q
R
S
T
U
V
W
X
Y
Z

heart attack noun heart attacks
a sudden failure of the heart to work properly, causing pain and sometimes death

hearth (say harth) noun hearths
the floor of a fireplace or the area near it

heartless adjective
cruel or without pity

hearty adjective heartier, heartiest
1 strong and healthy **2** enthusiastic or sincere *Hearty congratulations!* **3** a hearty meal is large and filling **heartily** adverb **heartiness** noun

heat noun heats
1 being hot; great warmth **2** a race or contest to decide who will take part in the final

heat verb heats, heating, heated
1 to heat something, or heat something up, is to make it hot **2** to heat, or heat up, is to become hot

heater noun heaters
a device for heating a place, especially a room or a car

heath noun heaths
wild flat land, often covered with heather or bushes

heathen noun heathens
someone who does not believe in any of the world's chief religions

heather noun
a low bush with small purple, pink, or white flowers

heatwave noun heatwaves
a long period of hot weather

heave verb heaves, heaving, heaved
1 to heave something is to lift or move it with great effort **2** (informal) to heave something is to throw it **to heave a sigh** is to sigh deeply

heaven noun
1 the place where, in some religions, good people are thought to go when they die and where God and the angels are thought to live **2** a very pleasant place or condition **the heavens** the sky

heavenly adjective
1 to do with the sky or in the sky **2** (informal) pleasing or delicious *Pauline sipped her drink. It was very hot, but simply heavenly—the sort of drink certain to make a cold feel better.* — Noel Streatfeild, *Ballet Shoes*

heavy adjective heavier, heaviest
1 weighing a lot; hard to lift or carry **2** you talk about how heavy something is when you are talking about how much it weighs **3** strong or severe *Heavy rain was falling. He brought his fist down upon the table with a heavy blow.* **4** hard or difficult *The climb up the hill was heavy going.* **heavily** adverb with a lot of weight or force **heaviness** noun

heavyweight noun heavyweights
1 a heavy person **2** a boxer or wrestler of the heaviest weight

Hebrew noun
the language of the ancient Jews, or a modern form of the language used in Israel

hectare (say hek-tar) noun hectares
a unit of area equal to 10,000 square metres or just over 2 acres

hectic adjective
very active or busy *It's been a hectic morning.*

he'd
short for *he had, he should,* or *he would*

hedge noun hedges
a row of bushes forming a barrier or boundary

hedge verb hedges, hedging, hedged
1 to hedge a field or other area is to surround it with a hedge **2** to hedge is also to avoid giving a definite answer *He wasn't sure, so he tried to hedge.*

hedgehog noun hedgehogs
a small animal covered with prickles

hedgerow noun hedgerows
a row of bushes forming a hedge

heed verb heeds, heeding, heeded
to heed something is to pay attention to it
heed noun
attention given to something
heedless adjective to be heedless of
something is to take no notice of it

heel noun heels
1 the back part of your foot **2** the part of a
sock or shoe round or under the back part
of your foot **to take to your heels** is to run
away
heel verb heels, heeling, heeled
to heel a shoe is to mend its heel

hefty adjective heftier, heftiest
big and strong

heifer (say hef-er) noun heifers
a young female cow

height noun heights
1 how high someone or something is
2 a high place *She's afraid of heights.*
3 the highest or most important part of
something *We shall be going at the height of
the holiday season.*

TOP TIPS
There is a tricky bit in **height**—it
begins with **hei**.

heighten verb heightens,
heightening, heightened
1 to heighten something is to make it higher
or more intense **2** to heighten is to become
higher or more intense *Their excitement
heightened as the kick-off approached.*

heir (say air) noun heirs
someone who inherits money or a title
heiress noun a female heir

held
past tense and past participle of **hold** verb
*He held out his hand. She should have held
her tongue.*

helicopter noun helicopters
a kind of aircraft without wings, lifted by a
large horizontal propeller on top

helium (say hee-li-um) noun
a colourless gas that is lighter than air and
is sometimes used in balloons

helix noun helices
a three-dimensional spiral, shaped like
a screw

hell noun
1 a place where, in some religions, wicked
people are thought to be punished after
they die and where the Devil is thought
to live **2** a very unpleasant place
or situation

he'll
short for *he will*

hellish adjective
very unpleasant or difficult

hello interjection
a word used to greet someone or to attract
their attention

helm noun helms
the handle or wheel used to steer a ship

helmet noun helmets
a strong covering that you wear to protect
your head

help verb helps, helping, helped
1 to help someone is to do something
useful for them or make things easier
for them **2** when you cannot help doing
something, you cannot avoid doing it *I can't
help coughing.* **3** to help yourself to food is
to take some
help noun helps
1 doing something useful for someone
2 someone who does something, especially
housework, for someone

helper noun helpers
someone who helps another person

helpful adjective
giving help; useful **helpfully** adverb

helping noun helpings
a portion of food at a meal

helpless adjective
not able to do things or look after yourself
helplessly adverb

helter-skelter noun helter-skelters
a spiral slide at a fair

a
b
c
d
e
f
g
h
i
j
k
l
m
n
o
p
q
r
s
t
u
v
w
x
y
z

hem noun hems
the edge of a piece of cloth that has been folded over and sewn down

hem verb hems, hemming, hemmed
to hem material is to fold it over and sew down its edge **to hem someone in** is to surround them or restrict their movements

hemisphere noun hemispheres
1 half a sphere 2 half the earth *Australia is in the southern hemisphere.*

hemp noun
a plant that produces coarse fibres from which cloth and ropes are made

hen noun hens
a female bird, especially a chicken

hence adverb
1 from this time on 2 therefore

heptagon noun heptagons
a shape with seven straight sides **heptagonal** adjective

her pronoun
a word used for *she* when it is the object of a verb, or when it comes after a preposition *I can see her. He took the books from her.*

her determiner
belonging to her *That is her book.*

herald noun heralds
1 an official who in the past used to make announcements or carry messages for a king or queen 2 someone or something that is a sign of things to come

herald verb heralds, heralding, heralded
to herald something or someone is to say or show that they are coming

heraldry noun
the study of coats of arms

herb noun herbs
a plant used for flavouring or for making medicines **herbal** adjective

herbivore noun herbivores
an animal that only eats plants

herd noun herds
a large group of animals, especially cattle

herd verb herds, herding, herded
to herd animals or people is to gather them together or move them in a large group

here adverb
in or to this place **here and there** in various places or directions

hereditary adjective
passed down to a child from a parent

heredity (say hir-**ed**-it-ee) noun
the passing down of characteristics from parents to children through their genes

heritage noun heritages
things that have been passed from one generation to another; a country's history and traditions *Music is part of our cultural heritage.*

hermit noun hermits
someone who lives alone and keeps away from people, often for religious reasons

hero noun heroes
1 a man or boy who has done something very brave 2 the most important man or boy in a story, film, or play

heroic (say hi-**roh**-ik) adjective
like a hero; very brave *a heroic soldier, heroic deeds* **heroically** adverb

heroine noun heroines
1 a woman or girl who has done something very brave 2 the most important woman or girl in a story, film, or play

heroism (say **her**-oh-izm) noun
being a hero; great bravery

heron noun herons
a wading bird with long legs and a long neck

herring noun herring or herrings
a sea fish that swims in large groups and is used for food

hers pronoun
belonging to her *Those books are hers.*

herself pronoun
she or her and nobody else, used to refer back to the subject of a verb *She has hurt*

A B C D E F G **H** I J K L M N O P Q R S T U V W X Y Z

herself. **by herself** on her own; alone *She did the work all by herself.*

he's
short for *he is* and (before a verb in the past tense) *he has*

hesitant adjective
being slow or uncertain when you speak or move **hesitantly** adverb

hesitate verb hesitates, hesitating, hesitated
to hesitate is to be slow or uncertain when you speak or move

hesitation noun
1 hesitation is when you hesitate *Without hesitation, they ran from the scene.*
2 a hesitation is a pause

hexagon noun hexagons
a flat shape with six sides
hexagonal adjective

hey interjection
an exclamation used to express surprise or to call someone's attention

hi interjection
an exclamation used to greet someone or to call their attention

hibernate (say **hy**-ber-nayt) verb hibernates, hibernating, hibernated
animals hibernate when they sleep for a long time during cold weather
hibernation noun

hiccup noun hiccups
a high gulping sound made when your breath is briefly interrupted

hiccup verb hiccups, hiccupping, hiccupped
to make a high gulping sound

hide verb hides, hiding, hid, hidden
1 to hide is to get into a place where you cannot be seen or found *I hid behind a tree.* 2 to hide someone or something is to keep them from being seen *The gold was hidden in a cave.* 3 to hide information is to keep it secret *Are you hiding the truth from me?*

hide-and-seek noun
a game in which one person looks for others who are hiding

hideous adjective
very ugly or unpleasant *Aunt Sponge had a long-handled mirror on her lap and she kept picking it up and gazing at her own hideous face.* – Roald Dahl, *James and the Giant Peach* **hideously** adverb

hideout noun hideouts
a place where someone hides

hiding¹ noun
to go into hiding is to hide yourself so that people cannot find you

hiding² noun hidings
a thrashing or beating

hieroglyphics (say hyr-o-**glif**-iks) plural noun
pictures or symbols used in ancient Egypt to represent words

higgledy-piggledy adverb, adjective
in disorder; completely mixed up

high adjective higher, highest
1 reaching a long way up *They could see a high building.* 2 far above the ground or sea *The clouds were high in the sky.* 3 measuring from top to bottom *The post is two metres high.* 4 above average in amount or importance *They are people of a high rank. Prices are high.* 5 lively; happy *They are in high spirits.* 6 a high note is one at the top end of a musical scale

high jump noun
an athletic contest in which competitors jump over a high bar

highland adjective
in the highlands; to do with the highlands

highlands plural noun
mountainous country, especially in Scotland

highlight noun highlights
the most interesting part of something *We watched the highlights of the match on the TV.*

highlight verb highlights, highlighting, highlighted
to highlight something is to draw attention to it

highlighter noun highlighters
a pen with bright coloured ink that you spread over words on paper to draw attention to them

highly adverb
extremely *He is highly amusing.* **to think highly of someone** is to admire them very much

highly-strung adjective
very sensitive or nervous

Highness noun Highnesses
a title of a prince or princess *His Royal Highness, the Prince of Wales*

high-pitched adjective
high in sound

high-rise adjective
a high-rise building is a tall one with many storeys

high school noun high schools
a secondary school

hijack verb hijacks, hijacking, hijacked
to hijack an aircraft or vehicle is to take control of it by force during a journey **hijacker** noun

hike noun hikes
a long walk in the countryside
hike verb hikes, hiking, hiked
to hike is to go for a long walk in the countryside **hiker** noun

hilarious adjective
very funny **hilariously** adverb **hilarity** noun
loud laughter

hill noun hills
a piece of ground that is higher than the ground around it **hilly** adjective

hillside noun hillsides
the side of a hill

hilt noun hilts
the handle of a sword or dagger

him pronoun
a word used for *he* when it is the object of a verb, or when it comes after a preposition
I like him. I gave it to him.

himself pronoun
he or him and nobody else, used to refer back to the subject of a verb *He has hurt himself.* **by himself** on his own; alone *He did the work all by himself.*

hind[1] (say hynd) adjective
at the back *The donkey had hurt one of its hind legs.*

hind[2] (say hynd) noun hinds
a female deer

hinder (say **hin**-der) verb hinders, hindering, hindered
to hinder someone is to get in their way, or to make it difficult for them to do something **hindrance** noun

Hindi noun
a language spoken in northern India

Hindu noun Hindus
someone who believes in **Hinduism**, one of the religions of India

hinge noun hinges
a joining device on which a door, gate, or lid swings when it opens
hinge verb hinges, hinging, hinged
to hinge on something is to depend on it *It all hinges on the weather.*

hinged adjective
a hinged door, window, or lid is fixed on a hinge

hint noun hints
1 a slight indication or suggestion *Give me a hint of what you want for your birthday.*
2 a useful piece of advice *He was always giving us hints on model-making.*
hint verb hints, hinting, hinted
to hint is to suggest something without actually saying it *She hinted that she'd like to have a puppy.*

hip[1] noun hips
your hips are the bony parts at the side

of your body between your waist and your thighs

hip² interjection
a word that you say when you give a cheer *Hip, hip, hooray!*

hippo noun hippos (informal)
a hippopotamus

hippopotamus noun hippopotamuses
a very large African animal that lives near water

hire verb hires, hiring, hired
to hire something is to pay to use it for a time
hire noun
something is for hire when you can hire it

his determiner, pronoun
belonging to him *Those books are his.*

hiss verb hisses, hissing, hissed
to make a sound like a continuous *s*, as some snakes do

historian noun historians
someone who writes or studies history

historic adjective
famous or important in history

historical adjective
1 to do with history 2 that really happened in the past *The story is based on historical events.*

history noun histories
1 what happened in the past 2 the study of past events 3 a description of important events

hit verb hits, hitting, hit
1 to hit someone or something is to come up against them with force, or to give them a blow 2 something hits you when you suddenly realize or feel it *The answer suddenly hit me.* 3 to hit a place or people is to have a bad effect on them *Famine hit the poorer countries.* 4 to hit a note is to reach it when you are singing **to hit it off with someone** is to get on well with them when

you meet them **to hit on something** is to think of an idea suddenly

hit noun hits
1 a knock or stroke 2 a shot that hits the target 3 a successful song or show

hitch verb hitches, hitching, hitched
1 to hitch something is to tie it up with a loop 2 (informal) to hitch a lift is to hitch-hike **to hitch something up** is to pull it up quickly or with a jerk *He hitched up his trousers.*
hitch noun hitches
1 a slight difficulty or delay 2 a knot

hitch-hike verb hitch-hikes, hitch-hiking, hitch-hiked
to hitch-hike is to travel by getting lifts in other people's vehicles
hitch-hiker noun

hither adverb (old use)
to or towards this place

hive noun hives
1 a beehive 2 a very busy place *The classroom was a hive of activity.*

HMS
short for *His* or *Her Majesty's Ship*

ho interjection
an exclamation of triumph or surprise, etc.

hoard noun hoards
a hidden store of something valuable
hoard verb hoards, hoarding, hoarded
to hoard things is to collect them and store them away **hoarder** noun

hoarding noun hoardings
a tall fence covered with advertisements

hoar frost noun
white frost

hoarse adjective hoarser, hoarsest
having a rough or croaking voice *He was hoarse from shouting.*

hoax noun hoaxes
a trick played on someone in which they are told about something but it is not true *The bomb scare was a hoax.*

A
B
C
D
E
F
G
H
I
J
K
L
M
N
O
P
Q
R
S
T
U
V
W
X
Y
Z

hoax verb hoaxes, hoaxing, hoaxed
to hoax someone is to trick them by telling them about something that is not true

hobble verb hobbles, hobbling, hobbled
to walk with unsteady steps, especially because your feet are sore

hobby noun hobbies
something that you enjoy doing in your spare time

hockey noun
an outdoor game played by two teams with long curved sticks and a small hard ball

hoe noun hoes
a gardening tool with a long handle and a metal blade, used for scraping up weeds and making soil loose

hoe verb hoes, hoeing, hoed
to hoe ground is to scrape it or dig it with a hoe

hog noun hogs
a male pig **to go the whole hog** (informal) is to do something completely or thoroughly

hog verb hogs, hogging, hogged (informal)
to hog something is to take more than your fair share of it

Hogmanay noun
New Year's Eve in Scotland

hoist verb hoists, hoisting, hoisted
to hoist something is to lift it up using ropes or pulleys

hold verb holds, holding, held
1 to hold something is to have it in your hands **2** to hold something is to possess it or be the owner of it *She holds the world high jump record.* **3** to hold a party, meeting, or event is to organize it *The 2008 Olympic Games were held in China.* **4** a container holds an amount when that is what you can put in it *This jug holds a litre.* **5** to hold someone or something is to support them *This plank won't hold my weight.* **6** to hold someone is to keep them and stop them getting away *They held the thief until help arrived.* **7** something like the weather holds when it stays the same *Will this good weather hold?* **8** to hold an opinion is to believe it **hold it** (informal) stop; wait a minute **to hold on** (informal) is to wait *Hold on! I'm not ready yet.* **to hold on to something** is to keep holding it **to hold out** is to last or continue **to hold someone up** is to rob them with threats of force **to hold someone** or **something up** is to hinder or delay them *We were held up by the traffic.*

hold noun holds
1 holding something *Don't lose hold of the rope.* **2** the part of a ship or aeroplane where cargo is stored **to get hold of someone** is to make contact with them *I want to invite Jane to the party but I can't get hold of her.*

holdall noun holdalls
a large portable bag or case

holder noun holders
a person or thing that holds something

hold–up noun hold-ups
1 a delay **2** a robbery with threats or force

hole noun holes
1 a gap or opening made in something **2** an animal's burrow *a rabbit hole*
holey adjective full of holes

Holi noun
a Hindu festival held in the spring

holiday noun holidays
a day or time when you do not go to work or school; a time when you go away to enjoy yourself

hollow adjective
having an empty space inside; not solid
hollow verb hollows, hollowing, hollowed
to hollow something is to make it hollow *We always hollow out a pumpkin at Hallowe'en.*
hollow noun hollows
1 a hollow place **2** a small valley

holly noun
an evergreen bush with shiny prickly leaves and red berries

246

holocaust (say **hol**-o-kawst) noun
holocausts
great destruction, especially because of
a fire

hologram noun holograms
a type of photograph made by laser beams,
that appears to have depth as well as height
and width

holster noun holsters
a leather case for a pistol, usually attached
to a belt

holy adjective holier, holiest
1 to do with God and treated with religious
respect 2 a holy person is devoted to God or
a religion **holiness** noun

home noun homes
1 the place where you live 2 the place
where you were born or where you feel you
belong 3 a place where people are looked
after *She went to a home for the elderly.*
4 the place that you try to reach in a game
The far end of the gym is home. **to feel at
home** is to feel comfortable and happy

home adverb
1 to or at the place where you live *Go home!
Is she home yet?* 2 to the place aimed at
Push the bolt home.

home verb homes, homing, homed
to home in on something is to aim for it

homeless adjective
not having a place to live

homely adjective
simple or ordinary **homeliness** noun

home-made adjective
made at home and not bought from a shop

homesick adjective
sad or upset because you are away from
home **homesickness** noun

homestead noun homesteads
a farmhouse and the land around it

homeward or **homewards**
adverb, adjective
towards home; going or leading towards
home

homework noun
school work that you have to do at home

homing adjective
trained to fly home *He kept homing pigeons.*

homograph noun homographs
a word spelt the same as another word but
with a different meaning, such as *lead* (the
metal) and *lead* (for a dog)

homonym noun homonyms
a **homograph** or **homophone**

homophone noun homophones
a word with the same sound as another
word but with a different spelling and
meaning, such as *son* and *sun*

honest adjective
truthful and able to be trusted; not stealing,
cheating, or telling lies **honesty** noun

honestly adverb
1 to say something honestly is to say it
truthfully 2 to do something honestly is to
do it without stealing or cheating 3 you say
honestly when you want to show you are
really telling the truth *It was an accident,
honestly.* 4 you can also say honestly when
you are annoyed by something *Honestly, I'm
tired of being told what to do!*

honey noun
a sweet sticky food made by bees

honeycomb noun honeycombs
a wax framework made by bees to hold
their honey and eggs

honeymoon noun honeymoons
a holiday that a newly-married couple
spend together

honeysuckle noun
a climbing plant with sweet-smelling yellow
or pink flowers

honk noun honks
a loud sound like the one made by a car
horn or a wild goose

honk verb honks, honking, honked
to make a honking sound

a
b
c
d
e
f
g
h
i
j
k
l
m
n
o
p
q
r
s
t
u
v
w
x
y
z

A
B
C
D
E
F
G
H
I
J
K
L
M
N
O
P
Q
R
S
T
U
V
W
X
Y
Z

honour noun honours
1 honour is great respect or reputation
2 an honour is something given to a person who deserves it because of the good work they have done 3 an honour is also something a person is proud to do *It is an honour to meet you.*

honour verb honours, honouring, honoured
1 to honour someone is to show them respect or to give them an honour
2 to honour a promise or agreement is to keep it

honourable adjective
someone is honourable when they can be trusted and always try to do the right thing **honourably** adverb

hood noun hoods
1 a covering of soft material for the head and neck, usually part of a coat or sweatshirt 2 a folding roof or cover **hooded** adjective a hooded person is wearing a hood

hoody or hoodie noun
hoodies (informal)
a sweatshirt with a hood

hoof noun hoofs or hooves
the hard, bony part of the foot of horses, cattle, or deer

hook noun hooks
a piece of bent or curved metal or plastic for hanging things on or catching hold of something **hooked** adjective a hooked nose or beak has a curved shape like a hook
hook verb hooks, hooking, hooked
1 to hook something is to fasten it with or on a hook 2 to hook a fish is to catch it with a hook

hooligan noun hooligans
a rough or noisy person

hoop noun hoops
a large ring made of metal, wood, or plastic

hoopla noun
a game in which you try to throw hoops round an object, which you then win

hooray interjection
a shout of joy or approval; a cheer

hoot noun hoots
1 a sound like the one made by an owl or a car horn 2 a jeer
hoot verb hoots, hooting, hooted
to hoot is to make a sound like an owl or a car horn

hooter noun hooters
a horn or other device that makes a hoot

hop^1 verb hops, hopping, hopped
1 to hop is to jump on one foot 2 animals hop when they move in jumps 3 (informal) to hop is also to move quickly *Hop in and I'll give you lift.* **hop it** (informal) go away
hop noun hops
a jump you make on one foot

hop^2 noun hops
a climbing plant used to give beer its flavour

hope noun hopes
1 the feeling of wanting something to happen, and thinking that it will happen
2 a person or thing that makes you feel like this *She is our big hope for a gold medal.*
hope verb hopes, hoping, hoped
to hope for something is to want it and expect it to happen

hopeful adjective
1 having hope 2 likely to be good or successful *The future did not seem very hopeful.*

hopefully adverb
1 in a hopeful way 2 I hope that... *Hopefully we can all go to the sea tomorrow.*

hopeless adjective
1 without hope 2 very bad at something *I'm hopeless at cricket.* **hopelessly** adverb

hopscotch noun
a game in which you hop into squares drawn on the ground

horde noun hordes
a large group or crowd

horizon (say ho-**ry**-zon) noun horizons
the line where the sky appears to meet the
land or sea

horizontal (say ho-ri-**zon**-tal)
adjective
level or flat; going across from left to right
horizontally adverb

hormone noun hormones
a substance made in your body that
controls things like how you develop
and grow

horn noun horns
1 a kind of pointed bone that grows on
the head of a bull, cow, ram, and other
animals 2 a brass musical instrument
that you blow 3 a device for making a
warning sound

hornet noun hornets
a large kind of wasp

horoscope noun horoscopes
your horoscope is an astrologer's forecast
about what will happen to you, based on
your zodiac sign

horrible adjective
very unpleasant or nasty **horribly** adverb

horrid adjective
nasty or unkind

horrific adjective
shocking or terrifying **horrifically** adverb

horrify verb horrifies, horrifying,
horrified
to horrify someone is to make them feel
shocked and disgusted

horror noun horrors
1 horror is great fear or disgust 2 a horror
is a person or thing you really dislike

horse noun horses
1 a four-legged animal used for riding on
or pulling carts 2 a tall box that you
jump over when you are doing
gymnastics

horseback noun
to be on horseback is to be riding a horse

horse chestnut noun horse
chestnuts
a large tree that produces dark brown nuts
called conkers

horseman noun horsemen
a man who rides a horse, especially a
skilful rider

horsepower noun horsepower
a unit for measuring the power of an
engine, equal to 746 watts

horseshoe noun horseshoes
a U-shaped piece of metal nailed as a shoe
to a horse's hoof

horsewoman noun horsewomen
a woman who rides a horse, especially a
skilful rider

horticulture noun
the art of planning and looking
after gardens

hose noun hoses
a long flexible tube through which liquids
or gases can travel

hospitable adjective
welcoming to people; liking to give
hospitality **hospitably** adverb

hospital noun hospitals
a place where sick or injured people are
given medical treatment

hospitality noun
welcoming people and giving them food
and entertainment

host¹ noun hosts
someone who has guests and looks
after them

host² noun hosts
a large number of people or things

hostage noun hostages
someone who is held prisoner until the
people who are holding them get what
they want

hostel noun hostels
a building with rooms where students or
other people can stay cheaply

A

hostess noun hostesses
a woman who has guests and looks after them

B

hostile adjective
1 unfriendly and angry *In the bedroom, the children were grouped in two corners of the room, regarding each other in hostile silence. – Emma Thompson, Nanny McPhee and the Big Bang* 2 opposed to someone or something **hostility** noun

C

D

E

F

hot adjective hotter, hottest
1 having a high temperature; very warm 2 having a burning taste like pepper or mustard 3 excited or angry *He has a hot temper.* **to be in hot water** (informal) is to be in trouble or difficulty

G

H

I

hot cross bun noun hot cross buns
a spicy bun with a cross marked on it, eaten at Easter

J

K

hot dog noun hot dogs
a hot sausage in a bread roll

L

hotel noun hotels
a building where people pay to stay for the night and have meals

M

N

hothouse noun hothouses
a heated greenhouse

O

hotly adverb
strongly or forcefully *He hotly denied that he'd done it.*

P

Q

hotpot noun hotpots
a kind of stew

R

hot–water bottle noun hot-water bottles
a container that you fill with hot water to make a bed warm

S

T

U

hound noun hounds
a dog used for hunting or racing

V

hound verb hounds, hounding, hounded
to hound someone is to keep on chasing and bothering them *We were hounded by newspaper reporters.*

W

X

Y

hour noun hours
1 one of the twenty-four parts into which

Z

a day is divided 2 a particular time *Why are you up at this hour?*

hourglass noun hourglasses
an old-fashioned device for telling the time, with sand running from one half of a glass container into the other through a narrow middle part

hourly adjective, adverb
every hour; done once an hour

house (say howss) noun houses
1 a building where people live, usually designed for one family 2 a building used for a special purpose *They passed the opera house.* 3 a building for a government assembly, or the assembly itself, for example the Houses of Parliament or the House of Commons 4 one of the divisions in some schools for sports competitions and other events

house (say howz) verb houses, housing, housed
to house someone or something is to provide a house or room for them

houseboat noun houseboats
a boat for living in

household noun households
all the people who live together in the same house

householder noun householders
someone who owns or rents a house

housekeeper noun housekeepers
a person employed to look after a household

house–proud adjective
very careful to keep a house clean and tidy

house–trained adjective
an animal that is house-trained is trained to be clean in the house

house–warming noun house-warmings
a party you have to celebrate moving into a new home

housewife noun housewives
a woman who stays at home to look after

her children and do the housework rather than doing a paid job

housework noun
the work of cooking and cleaning that has to be done in a house

housing noun **housings**
1 housing is accommodation or houses
2 a housing is a cover or guard for a piece of machinery

hover verb **hovers, hovering, hovered**
1 to hover is to stay in one place in the air
2 to hover round someone is to wait near them to watch what they do

hovercraft noun **hovercraft**
a vehicle that travels just above the surface of water or land, supported by a strong current of air sent downwards by its engines

how adverb
1 in what way *How did you do it?* 2 to what extent *How much do you want?* 3 in what condition *How are you?* **how do you do?** a more formal greeting when you meet someone

however adverb
1 no matter how; in whatever way *You will never catch him, however hard you try.* 2 nevertheless *It was snowing; however, he went out.*

however conjunction
in any way *You can do it however you like.*

howl noun **howls**
a long loud cry like an animal in pain

howl verb **howls, howling, howled**
to howl is to make a long loud cry like an animal in pain, or to weep loudly

HQ
short for **headquarters**

hub noun **hubs**
the centre of a wheel

huddle verb **huddles, huddling, huddled**
to crowd together with other people for warmth or comfort *Behind the village was a stony field where a flock of thin sheep huddled together under the shadow of a few*

spindly apple trees. — Vivian French, *Under the Moon*

hue noun **hues**
a colour or tint

huff noun
to be in a huff is to be annoyed or offended

hug verb **hugs, hugging, hugged**
1 to hug someone is to clasp them tightly in your arms 2 to hug something is to keep close to it *The ship hugged the shore.*

hug noun **hugs**
clasping someone tightly in your arms

huge adjective **huger, hugest**
extremely large **hugely** adverb greatly; very

hulk noun **hulks**
1 the remains of an old decaying ship
2 a large clumsy person or thing

hull noun **hulls**
the main part or framework of a ship

hullabaloo noun **hullabaloos**
an uproar *Quite a hullabaloo was breaking out upstairs, and most of the sounds were by no means pleasant.* — Alan Garner, *The Weirdstone of Brisingamen*

hullo interjection
a word used to greet someone or to attract their attention

hum verb **hums, humming, hummed**
1 to hum is to sing a tune with your lips closed 2 to hum is also to make a low continuous sound like a bee

hum noun **hums**
a humming sound

human noun **humans**
a man, woman, or child; a human being

human adjective
to do with humans

human being noun **human beings**
a man, woman, or child; a human

humane (say hew-**mayn**) adjective
showing kindness and a wish to cause

A

as little suffering or pain as possible
humanely adverb

B

humanitarian (say hew-man-i-**tair**-i-an) adjective
concerned with helping humanity and relieving suffering

C

D

humanity noun
1 all the people in the world **2** being human **3** kindness and sympathy to other people

E

F

humble adjective humbler, humblest
modest and not proud **humbly** adverb

G

H

humid (say **hew**-mid) adjective
damp and warm in the air
humidity noun

I

humiliate verb humiliates, humiliating, humiliated
to humiliate someone is to make them feel ashamed or foolish in front of other people
humiliation noun

J

K

L

humility noun
being humble

M

hummingbird noun hummingbirds
a small tropical bird that makes a humming sound by beating its wings rapidly

N

O

humorous adjective
amusing or funny

P

humour noun
1 being amusing; what makes people laugh **2** being able to enjoy things that are funny *He has a good sense of humour.* **3** a person's mood *Keep him in a good humour.*

Q

R

S

humour verb humours, humouring, humoured
to humour someone is to keep them happy by doing what they want

T

U

V

hump noun humps
1 a rounded lump or mound **2** a lump on a person's back

W

hump verb humps, humping, humped
to hump something heavy is to carry it with difficulty on your back

X

Y

Z

humus (say hew-mus) noun
rich earth made by decayed plants

hunch[1] noun hunches
a feeling that you can guess what will happen *I have a hunch that she won't come.*

hunch[2] verb hunches, hunching, hunched
to hunch your shoulders is to bring them up and forward so that your back is rounded

hunchback noun hunchbacks
someone with a hump on their back

hundred noun hundreds
the number 100 **hundredth** adjective, noun

hung
past tense and past participle of **hang** *Her hair hung round her shoulders. Lanterns were hung around the hall.*

hunger noun
the feeling you get when you want or need to eat

hungry adjective hungrier, hungriest
you are hungry when you want or need to eat **hungrily** adverb

hunk noun hunks
a large piece or chunk of something

hunt verb hunts, hunting, hunted
1 to hunt animals is to chase and kill them for food or sport **2** to hunt for something is to look hard for it

hunt noun hunts
1 a time when a group of people chase and kill animals for food or sport **2** a group of people who go hunting

hunter or huntsman noun
hunters, huntsmen
someone who hunts for sport

hurdle noun hurdles
1 an upright frame that runners jump over in hurdling **2** a problem or difficulty

hurdling noun
racing in which the runners run and jump over hurdles **hurdler** noun

hurl verb hurls, hurling, hurled
to hurl something is to throw it as far as you can

hurrah or **hurray** interjection
a shout of joy or approval; a cheer

hurricane noun hurricanes
a severe storm with a strong wind

hurry verb hurries, hurrying, hurried
1 to hurry is to move or act quickly
2 to hurry someone is to try to make them be quick **hurriedly** adverb
hurry noun
moving quickly; doing something quickly **in a hurry** hurrying or impatient *They were in a hurry to catch their train.*

hurt verb hurts, hurting, hurt
1 to hurt a person or animal is to harm them or cause them pain 2 part of your body hurts when you feel pain there 3 to hurt someone is also to upset them by doing or saying something unkind
hurt noun
pain or injury **hurtful** adjective a hurtful remark upsets someone because it is unkind

hurtle verb hurtles, hurtling, hurtled
to move quickly or dangerously *The front three rows of students drew backwards as the carriage hurtled ever lower, coming in to land at a tremendous speed.*
— J. K. Rowling, *Harry Potter and the Goblet of Fire*

husband noun husbands
the man that a woman is married to

hush verb hushes, hushing, hushed
to hush someone is to make them be quiet
to hush something up is to prevent people knowing about it
hush noun
silence or quiet *Let's have a bit of hush.*

husk noun husks
the dry outer covering of a seed

husky[1] adjective huskier, huskiest
you say a voice is husky when it is deep and rough *She has a husky voice.* **huskily** adverb

husky[2] noun huskies
a large strong dog used in the Arctic for pulling sledges

hustle verb hustles, hustling, hustled
1 to hustle is to hurry 2 to hustle someone is to push them rudely

hut noun huts
a small roughly made house or shelter

hutch noun hutches
a box or cage for a rabbit or other pet animal

hyacinth noun hyacinths
a sweet-smelling flower that grows from a bulb

hybrid noun hybrids
1 an animal or plant that combines two different species *A mule is a hybrid of a donkey and a mare.* 2 something that is a mixture of two things

hydrangea (say hy-**drayn**-ja) noun hydrangeas
a shrub with large pink, blue, or white flowers

hydrant noun hydrants
an outdoor water tap connected to the main water supply, for fixing a hose to

hydraulic adjective
worked by the movement of water or other liquid

hydroelectric adjective
using water power to make electricity

hydrogen noun
a very light gas which with oxygen makes water

hyena (say hy-**ee**-na) noun hyenas
a wild animal that looks like a wolf and makes a shrieking howl

hygiene (say **hy**-jeen) noun
keeping clean and healthy and free of germs

hygienic adjective
clean and healthy and free of germs

a
b
c
d
e
f
g
h
i
j
k
l
m
n
o
p
q
r
s
t
u
v
w
x
y
z

A
B
C
D
E
F
G
H
I
J
K
L
M
N
O
P
Q
R
S
T
U
V
W
X
Y
Z

hymn noun hymns
a Christian religious song, especially one
that praises God

hyperactive adjective
unable to relax and always moving about or
doing things

hyphen noun hyphens
a short dash used to join words or parts
of words together, for example in
house-proud **hyphenated** adjective
a word is hyphenated when it is spelt with
a hyphen

hypnosis (say hip-**noh**-sis) noun
to be under hypnosis is to be in a
condition like a deep sleep in which
a person follows the instructions of
another person

hypnotism (say **hip**-no-tizm) noun
hypnotizing people **hypnotist** noun

hypnotize verb hypnotizes,
hypnotizing, hypnotized
to hypnotize someone is to put them to
sleep by hypnosis

hypocrite (say **hip**-o-krit) noun
hypocrites
someone who pretends to be a better
person than they really are **hypocrisy** noun
hypocritical adjective

hypothermia noun
a person suffers from hypothermia
when they become so cold that their
body temperature falls well below
normal

hysteria noun
wild uncontrollable excitement or
emotion

hysterical adjective
1 suffering from hysteria **2** very excited
3 (informal) very funny
hysterically adverb

hysterics plural noun
a fit of hysteria **to be in hysterics**
(informal) is to be laughing a lot

Ii

I pronoun
a word used by someone to speak about
himself or herself

ice noun ices
1 ice is frozen water **2** an ice is an ice cream

ice verb ices, icing, iced
1 to ice or ice up is to become covered in
ice **2** to ice a cake is to put icing on it

ice age noun
a time in the past when ice covered large
areas of the earth's surface

iceberg noun icebergs
a large mass of ice floating in the sea, with
most of it under water

ice cream noun ice creams
1 ice cream is a sweet creamy frozen food
2 an ice cream is a portion of this

ice hockey noun
ice hockey is a game like hockey played
on ice

iceberg

ice lolly noun ice lollies
a piece of flavoured ice on a stick

ice-skating noun
ice-skating is moving on ice wearing special boots with blades on the bottom

icicle noun icicles
a thin pointed piece of hanging ice formed from dripping water

icing noun
icing is a sugary substance for decorating cakes

icon noun icons
1 a small picture or symbol standing for a program on a computer screen 2 a painting of a holy person

ICT
short for *information and communication technology*

icy adjective icier, iciest
1 an icy road has ice on it 2 an icy wind is very cold 3 very unfriendly; hostile *He gave them an icy stare.*

I'd
short for *I had, I should,* or *I would*

idea noun ideas
something that you have thought of; a plan

ideal adjective
exactly what you want; perfect
ideally adverb if things were perfect *Ideally, I'd like to live by the sea.*

ideal noun ideals
something that is perfect or the best thing to have; a very high standard

identical adjective
exactly the same *Daniel and Sammy are identical twins.* **identically** adverb

identification noun
1 identification is any document, such as a passport, that proves who you are 2 identification is the process of discovering who someone is or what something is

identify verb identifies, identifying, identified
to identify someone or something is to discover who or what they are *The police have identified the car used in the robbery.* **to identify with someone** is to understand or share their feelings or opinions

identity noun identities
who someone is or what something is *Can you discover the identity of our mystery guest?*

idiom (say id-i-om) noun idioms
a phrase or group of words that together have a special meaning that is not obvious from the words themselves, for example *to be in hot water* means to be in trouble or difficulty

idiomatic adjective
a person's language is idiomatic when it is natural and uses a lot of idioms

idiot noun idiots (informal)
a stupid or foolish person

idiotic adjective (informal)
stupid or foolish *That was an idiotic thing to do.*

idle adjective idler, idlest
1 a person is idle when they are lazy or doing nothing 2 a machine is idle when it is not being used 3 idle talk or gossip is talk that is silly or pointless **idly** adverb

idle verb idles, idling, idled
a machine or engine idles when it is working slowly

idol noun idols
1 a famous person who is admired by a lot of people 2 a statue or image that people worship as a god

idolize verb idolizes, idolizing, idolized
to idolize someone is to admire them very much

i.e.
short for the Latin *id est*, which means 'that is', used to explain something *The world's highest mountain (i.e. Mount Everest) is in the Himalayas.*

a
b
c
d
e
f
g
h
i
j
k
l
m
n
o
p
q
r
s
t
u
v
w
x
y
z

A
B
C
D
E
F
G
H
I
J
K
L
M
N
O
P
Q
R
S
T
U
V
W
X
Y
Z

if conjunction
1 on condition that *I'll tell you what happened if you promise to keep it secret.* **2** although; even though *I'll finish this job if it kills me!* **3** whether *Do you know if lunch is ready?* **if only...** I wish... *If only I could go with you!*

igloo noun **igloos**
an Inuit round house made of blocks of hard snow

igneous (say **ig**-ni-us) adjective
igneous rocks are formed by the action of a volcano

ignite verb **ignites, igniting, ignited**
1 to ignite something is to set fire to it **2** to ignite is to catch fire

ignition noun
1 igniting **2** ignition is the system in a motor engine that starts the fuel burning

ignorance noun
not knowing about something or knowing very little

ignorant adjective
not knowing about something; knowing very little

ignore verb **ignores, ignoring, ignored**
to ignore someone or something is to take no notice of them

ill adjective
1 not well; in bad health **2** bad or harmful *There were no ill effects.*
ill adverb
badly *She was ill-treated.*

I'll
short for *I shall* or *I will*

illegal adjective
something is illegal when it is against the law **illegally** adverb

illegible (say i-**lej**-i-bul) adjective
illegible writing is not clear enough to read

illiterate (say i-**lit**-er-at) adjective
unable to read or write

illness noun **illnesses**
1 illness is being ill **2** an illness is something that makes people ill; a disease

illogical adjective
not logical or having any good reason

illuminate verb **illuminates, illuminating, illuminated**
1 to illuminate a place or street is to light it up or decorate it with lights **2** to illuminate something difficult is to make it clearer **illuminations** plural noun lights put up to decorate a place or street

illusion noun **illusions**
1 something that you think is real or happening but is not **2** an idea or belief you have that is not true

illustrate verb **illustrates, illustrating, illustrated**
1 to illustrate something is to show it with pictures or examples **2** to illustrate a book is to put pictures in it

illustration noun **illustrations**
1 an illustration is a picture in a book **2** an illustration is also an example that helps to explain something

illustrator noun **illustrators**
a person who produces the illustrations in a book

illustrious (say i-**lus**-tri-us) adjective
famous

I'm
short for *I am*

image noun **images**
1 a picture or statue of a person or thing **2** what you see in a mirror or through a lens **3** a person who looks very much like another *She is the image of her mother.* **4** the way that people think of a person or thing

imagery noun
imagery is the use of words to produce pictures in the mind of the reader

imaginary adjective
not real; existing only in your mind

imagination noun imaginations
your ability to form pictures and ideas in your mind

imaginative adjective
showing that you are good at thinking of new and exciting ideas *Her stories are always very imaginative.*

imagine verb imagines, imagining, imagined
to imagine something or someone is to form a picture of them in your mind **imaginable** adjective

imam noun imams
a Muslim religious leader

imbecile (say im-bi-seel) noun imbeciles (informal)
a very stupid person

imitate verb imitates, imitating, imitated
to imitate someone or something is to do the same as them **imitation** noun **imitator** noun

immature adjective
1 not fully grown or developed **2** behaving in a silly or childish way **immaturity** noun

immediate adjective
1 happening or done without any delay **2** nearest; with nothing or no one between *The Smiths are our immediate neighbours.*

immediately adverb
without any delay; at once *You must come immediately.*

immense adjective
huge **immensely** adverb extremely

immerse verb immerses, immersing, immersed
1 to immerse something is to put it completely into a liquid **2** to be immersed in something is to be very interested or involved in it **immersion** noun

immigrant noun immigrants
someone who has come into a country to live there

immigrate verb immigrates, immigrating, immigrated
to immigrate is to come into a country to live there **immigration** noun

immobile adjective
not moving *After a few minutes, the crocodiles became quite immobile, their giant heads resting in the warm sand, their tails stretched out behind them.*
— Alexander McCall Smith, *Akimbo and the Crocodile Man*

immobilize verb immobilizes, immobilizing, immobilized
to immobilize something is to stop it moving or working

immoral adjective
not following the usual standards of right and wrong **immorality** noun

immortal adjective
someone who is immortal lives for ever and never dies **immortality** noun

immune adjective
someone is immune to a disease if they cannot catch it **immunity** noun

immunize verb immunizes, immunizing, immunized
to immunize someone is to make them safe from a disease, usually by giving them an injection **immunization** noun

imp noun imps
1 a small devil **2** a naughty child **impish** adjective

impact noun impacts
1 the force of one thing hitting another **2** a strong influence or effect *The Internet has a big impact on our lives.*

impair verb impairs, impairing, impaired
to impair something is to harm or weaken it *The accident has impaired his health.*

impale verb impales, impaling, impaled
to impale something is to push a sharp pointed object through it

a
b
c
d
e
f
g
h
i
j
k
l
m
n
o
p
q
r
s
t
u
v
w
x
y
z

A
B
C
D
E
F
G
H
I
J
K
L
M
N
O
P
Q
R
S
T
U
V
W
X
Y
Z

impartial adjective
fair and not supporting one side more than the other *A referee must be impartial.*

impatient adjective
annoyed because you cannot wait for something to happen **impatience** noun **impatiently** adverb

impede verb impedes, impeding, impeded
to impede someone or something is to hinder them or get in their way

imperative adjective
1 essential *Speed is imperative.*
2 in grammar, an imperative word expresses a command, like *come* in *Come here!*

imperceptible adjective
too small or gradual to be noticed *The change in the weather was imperceptible.*

imperfect adjective
not perfect or complete **imperfection** noun **imperfectly** adverb

imperial adjective
1 belonging to an empire or its rulers
2 an imperial unit or measure is a non-metric one such as gallon, ounce, or yard

impersonal adjective
1 not showing friendly human feelings *The letter was a bit impersonal.* 2 not referring to a particular person

impersonate verb impersonates, impersonating, impersonated
to impersonate someone is to pretend to be them **impersonation** noun **impersonator** noun

impertinent adjective
rude to someone and not showing them respect **impertinence** noun

implement (say **im**-pli-ment) noun implements
a tool or device you use to do something

implement (say **im**-pli-ment) verb implements, implementing, implemented
to implement a plan or idea is to put it into action

implication noun implications
1 an implication is something that someone suggests without actually saying it
2 an implication is also a possible effect or result *She began to realize the implications of her actions.*

implore verb implores, imploring, implored
to implore someone to do something is to beg them to do it

imply verb implies, implying, implied
to imply something is to suggest it without actually saying it *Are you implying that I'm lazy?*

impolite adjective
not having good manners; not respectful and thoughtful towards other people

import (say im-**port**) verb imports, importing, imported
to import goods is to bring them in from another country to sell them

import (say **im**-port) noun imports
something brought in from another country to be sold

important adjective
1 needing to be taken seriously; having a great effect *This is an important decision.* 2 an important person is powerful or influential **importance** noun **importantly** adverb seriously *Try to win the match but, more importantly, don't lose.*

impose verb imposes, imposing, imposed
1 to impose something on someone is to make them have to put up with it *The new school rules were imposed against all our wishes.* 2 to impose a charge or tax is to make people pay it

imposing adjective
looking important and impressive

imposition noun impositions
something that someone is made to suffer, especially as a punishment

impossible adjective
1 not possible 2 (informal) very annoying

He is impossible! **impossibility** noun
impossibly adverb

impostor noun **impostors**
someone who is not what he or she
pretends to be

impractical adjective
1 impractical people are not good at
making or doing things **2** not likely to work
or be useful *Their ideas are impractical.*

impress verb **impresses, impressing,
impressed**
1 to impress someone is to make them
admire you **2** to impress something
on someone is to make them realize or
remember it

impression noun **impressions**
1 a vague idea that you have about
something **2** the effect that something has
on your mind or feelings **3** an imitation of a
person or a sound

impressive adjective
something is impressive when it makes you
admire it **impressively** adverb

imprison verb **imprisons, imprisoning,
imprisoned**
to imprison someone is to put them in
prison **imprisonment** noun

improbable adjective
unlikely **improbability** noun

impromptu (say im-**promp**-tew)
adjective, adverb
done without any rehearsal or preparation

improper adjective
1 not proper; wrong **2** rude or indecent

improve verb **improves, improving,
improved**
to make something better, or to become
better **improvement** noun

improvise verb **improvises,
improvising, improvised**
1 to improvise is to do something without
any rehearsal or preparation, especially
to play music without rehearsing **2** to

improvise something is to make it quickly
with what is to hand **improvisation** noun

impudent adjective
not respectful; rude **impudence** noun

impulse noun **impulses**
1 a sudden desire to do something **2** a push;
a driving force

impulsive adjective
doing things suddenly without much
thought **impulsively** adverb

impure adjective
not pure **impurity** noun

in preposition, adverb
1 showing position at or inside something
*They live in London. Please come in. She fell
in the water. Then the others fell in.* **2 In**
also has some special uses, shown by the
following examples: *We came in April. I
paid in cash. They are watching a serial in
four parts. He is in the army. We knocked
on the door but no one was in.* **to be in for
something** is to be likely to get it *You're in
for a shock.* **to be in on something** is to
take part in something *I want to be in on
this game.*

in– prefix
meaning 'not', as in *inefficient*

inability noun
inability is being unable to do something

inaccessible adjective
an inaccessible place is impossible to reach

inaccurate adjective
not accurate **inaccuracy** noun
inaccurately adverb

inaction noun
inaction is lack of action

inactive adjective
not working or doing anything
inactivity noun

inadequate adjective
not enough **inadequacy** noun
inadequately adverb

a
b
c
d
e
f
g
h
i
j
k
l
m
n
o
p
q
r
s
t
u
v
w
x
y
z

A

inanimate (say in-**an**-im-at) adjective
not living or moving

B

inappropriate adjective
not appropriate or suitable
inappropriately adverb

C

D

inattentive adjective
not listening or paying attention

E

inaudible adjective
not able to be heard

F

G

incapable adjective
unable to do something *They are incapable of understanding the problem.*

H

incapacity noun
incapacity is inability or disability

I

J

incendiary adjective
an incendiary bomb or device is one that starts a fire

K

L

incense (say in-senss) noun
incense is a substance that makes a spicy smell when it is burnt

M

incense (say in-**senss**) verb incenses, incensing, incensed
to incense someone is to make them very angry

N

O

incentive noun incentives
something that encourages a person to do something or to work harder

P

Q

incessant adjective
going on without stopping, usually in an annoying way *They were bothered by the incessant noise.* **incessantly** adverb

R

S

T

inch noun inches
a measure of length, one twelfth of a foot or about 2½ centimetres

U

incident noun incidents
an event, usually a strange or unusual one

V

W

incidental adjective
happening along with something else; not so important **incidentally** adverb

X

Y

incinerator noun incinerators
a device for burning rubbish

Z

inclination noun inclinations
a feeling that makes you want to do something *He suddenly had an inclination to look through the keyhole.*

incline (say in-**klyn**) verb inclines, inclining, inclined
to incline is to lean or bend **to be inclined to do something** is to feel like doing it *I'm inclined to wait until later.*

incline (say **in**-klyn) noun inclines
a slope

include verb includes, including, included
to include something or someone is to make or consider them as part of a group of things *Did you include Peter in the party?*
inclusion noun

inclusive adjective
including everything; including all the things mentioned *We want to stay from Monday to Thursday inclusive.*

income noun incomes
the money that a person earns regularly

incompatible adjective
1 not able to live or exist together without trouble **2** machines and devices are incompatible when they cannot be used together

incompetent adjective
unable to do something properly
incompetence noun

incomplete adjective
not complete **incompletely** adverb

incomprehensible adjective
not able to be understood

incongruous (say in-**kong**-roo-us) adjective
not suitable and out of place

inconsiderate adjective
not thinking of other people

inconsistent adjective
not consistent **inconsistency** noun
inconsistently adverb

inconspicuous adjective
not noticeable or remarkable

inconvenient adjective
not convenient; awkward
inconvenience noun

incorporate verb incorporates, incorporating, incorporated
to incorporate something is to include it as a part of something else
incorporation noun

incorrect adjective
not correct; wrong **incorrectly** adverb

increase (say in-**kreess**) verb increases, increasing, increased
1 to increase something is to make it bigger **2** to increase is to become bigger **increasingly** adverb more and more *They were becoming increasingly angry.*

increase (say **in**-kreess) noun increases
1 increasing **2** the amount by which something increases

incredible adjective
unbelievable **incredibly** adverb

incredulous adjective
finding it difficult to believe someone
incredulity noun

incubate verb incubates, incubating, incubated
to incubate eggs is to hatch them by keeping them warm **incubation** noun

incubator noun incubators
a specially heated container for keeping newly born babies warm and well supplied with oxygen

indebted adjective
owing something to someone

indecent adjective
not decent; improper **indecency** noun
indecently adverb

indeed adverb
used for emphasis *The dog was very wet indeed.*

indefinite adjective
not definite; vague and unclear

indefinite article noun indefinite articles
the word *a* or *an*

indefinitely adverb
for an indefinite or unlimited time

indent verb indents, indenting, indented
to indent a line of print or writing is to begin it further to the right than usual

indentation noun indentations
a dent or hollow made in something

independent adjective
1 free from the control of another person or country **2** not needing help from other people **independence** noun
independently noun

index noun indexes
a list of names or topics, usually in alphabetical order at the end of a book

index finger noun index fingers
the finger next to the thumb

indicate verb indicates, indicating, indicated
to indicate something is to point it out or show that it is there **indication** noun a sign of something

indicative adjective
being a sign of something

indicator noun indicators
1 something that tells you what is happening **2** a flashing light on a vehicle, to show that it is turning left or right

indifferent adjective
1 you are indifferent to something when you have no interest in it at all **2** not very good; ordinary *He is an indifferent cricketer.*
indifference noun

indigestion noun
indigestion is pain caused by difficulty in digesting food

a
b
c
d
e
f
g
h
i
j
k
l
m
n
o
p
q
r
s
t
u
v
w
x
y
z

indignant adjective
angry at something that seems wrong or unjust *'Stupid things!' Alice began in a loud, indignant voice.* – Lewis Carroll, *Alice's Adventures in Wonderland* **indignantly** adverb **indignation** noun

indigo noun
a deep blue colour

indirect adjective
not direct or straight **indirectly** adverb

indirect speech noun
indirect speech is when someone's words are given in a changed form reported by someone else, as in *He said that he would come* (reporting the words 'I will come')

indispensable adjective
essential

indistinct adjective
not clear **indistinctly** adverb

indistinguishable adjective
impossible to see or hear, or to tell apart from something else

individual adjective
1 of or for one person **2** single or separate **individually** adverb separately; one by one

individual noun individuals
an individual is one person

individuality noun
individuality is the things that make one person or thing different from another

indoor adjective
placed or done inside a building *We like indoor sports.*

indoors adverb
inside a building

induce verb induces, inducing, induced
1 to induce someone to do something is to persuade them to do it **2** to induce a pregnant woman is to start the birth of her baby artificially

indulge verb indulges, indulging, indulged
to indulge someone is to let them have

or do what they want **to indulge in something** is to have or do something that you really like

indulgent adjective
kind and allowing people to do what they want **indulgence** noun

industrial adjective
to do with industry

industrialize verb industrializes, industrializing, industrialized
to industrialize a country is to increase or develop its industry **industrialization** noun

industrious adjective
hard-working **industriously** adverb

industry noun industries
1 industry is making or producing goods to sell, especially in factories **2** an industry is a branch of this, such as the motor industry **3** industry is also working hard

ineffective adjective
not effective; not working well **ineffectively** adverb

ineffectual adjective
not achieving anything **ineffectually** adverb

inefficient adjective
not working well and wasting time or energy **inefficiency** noun **inefficiently** adverb

inequality noun inequalities
inequality is not being equal

inert adjective
not moving or reacting

inertia (say in-er-sha) noun
inertia is being inert or slow to take action

inevitable adjective
something is inevitable when it cannot be avoided **inevitability** noun **inevitably** adverb

inexhaustible adjective
that you cannot use up completely; never-ending

inexpensive adjective
not expensive; cheap

inexperience noun
inexperience is lack of experience
inexperienced adjective

inexplicable adjective
impossible to explain **inexplicably** adverb

infamous (say in-fa-mus) adjective
well-known for being bad or wicked

infant noun infants
a baby or young child **infancy** noun the
time when someone is a baby or young child

infantile adjective
1 childish and silly 2 to do with babies or
young children

infantry noun
infantry are soldiers trained to fight on foot

infect verb infects, infecting, infected
to infect someone is to pass on a disease
to them

infection noun infections
1 infection is infecting someone 2 an
infection is an infectious disease

infectious adjective
1 an infectious disease is one that can
spread from one person to another
2 something like laughter or fear is
infectious when it spreads to other people

infer verb infers, inferring, inferred
to infer something is to work it out from
what someone says or does *I infer from your
uniform that you are the postman.*

inferior adjective
not as good or important as something else;
lower in position or quality **inferiority** noun

inferior noun inferiors
a person who is lower in position or rank
than someone else

infernal adjective
like hell or to do with hell

inferno (say in-**fer**-noh) noun infernos
a fierce fire

infested adjective
a place is infested with (for example) insects
or rats when it is full of them

infiltrate verb infiltrates, infiltrating,
infiltrated
to infiltrate a place or organization is
to get into it without being noticed
infiltration noun

infinite (say **in**-fi-nit) adjective
endless; too large to be measured or
imagined **infinitely** adverb

infinitive (say in-**fin**-i-tiv) noun
infinitives
the form of a verb that does not change
to indicate a particular person or tense. In
English it often comes after *to*, as in *to go*
and *to hit.*

infinity (say in-**fin**-i-ti) noun
infinity is an infinite number or distance

infirm adjective
someone is infirm when they are weak
because they are ill or old **infirmity** noun

infirmary noun infirmaries
a place for sick people; a hospital

inflame verb inflames, inflaming,
inflamed
1 a part of the body is inflamed when it has
become red and sore 2 to inflame someone
is to make them angry

inflammable adjective
an inflammable material can be set alight

inflammation noun inflammations
a painful swelling or sore place on the body

inflammatory adjective
likely to make people angry

inflatable adjective
something is inflatable when it can be filled
with air to make it swell up

inflate verb inflates, inflating, inflated
1 to inflate something is to fill it with air or
gas so that it swells up 2 to inflate a claim
or statement is to exaggerate it

a
b
c
d
e
f
g
h
i
j
k
l
m
n
o
p
q
r
s
t
u
v
w
x
y
z

A

inflation noun
inflation is a general rise in prices

B

inflect verb inflects, inflecting,
inflected
to inflect your voice is to change the sound
of it when you speak

C

D

inflexible adjective
that you cannot bend or change *There are a
lot of inflexible rules.* **inflexibility** noun

E

F

inflict verb inflicts, inflicting, inflicted
to inflict something on someone is to make
them suffer it *She inflicted a severe blow
on him.*

G

H

influence noun influences
the power to affect someone or something

I

influence verb influences,
influencing, influenced
to influence someone or something is to
have an effect on what they are or do *The
tides are influenced by the moon.*

J

K

L

influential adjective
having a big influence; important

M

influenza (say in-floo-**en**-za) noun
influenza is flu

N

O

inform verb informs, informing,
informed
to inform someone of something is to tell
them about it **to inform against** or **on
someone** is to give information about them,
especially to the police

P

Q

R

informal adjective
not formal; casual and relaxed
informality noun **informally** adverb

S

T

informant noun informants
a person who gives information

U

information noun
information is facts or what someone
tells you

V

W

information technology noun
information technology is ways of storing,
arranging, and giving out information,
especially the use of computers and
telecommunications

X

Y

Z

informative (say in-**form**-a-
tiv) adjective
containing a lot of helpful information

informed adjective
you are informed about something when
you know about it

informer noun informers
a person who tells the police about
someone else

infrequent adjective
not frequent **infrequently** adverb

infuriate verb infuriates, infuriating,
infuriated
to infuriate someone is to make them
very angry

ingenious adjective
1 clever at doing things **2** cleverly made or
done **ingeniously** adverb **ingenuity** noun

ingot noun ingots
a lump of gold or silver that has been cast
in the form of a brick

ingrained adjective
deeply fixed *She was accused of
ingrained idleness.*

ingratitude noun
ingratitude is not showing that you are
grateful for something that someone has
done for you

ingredient (say in-**greed**-i-ent) noun
ingredients
1 one of the parts of a mixture **2** one of the
items used in a recipe

inhabit verb inhabits, inhabiting,
inhabited
to inhabit a place is to live in it

inhabitant noun inhabitants
an inhabitant of a place is someone who
lives there

inhale verb inhales, inhaling, inhaled
1 to inhale is to breathe in **2** to inhale
something is to breathe it in

inhaler noun inhalers
a device for taking medicine by inhaling it

inherent (say in-**heer**-ent) adjective
naturally or permanently part of something
inherently adverb

inherit verb inherits, inheriting,
inherited
1 to inherit money, property, or a title is
to receive it when its previous owner dies
2 to inherit qualities or characteristics is to
get them from your parents or ancestors
inheritance noun

inhibited adjective
not relaxed enough to show or talk about
your feelings

inhospitable (say in-hos-**pit**-a-bul or
in-**hos**-pit-a-bul) adjective
1 unfriendly to visitors 2 an inhospitable
place is difficult to live in because it gives
no shelter *They reached an inhospitable
rocky island.*

inhuman adjective
cruel; without pity or kindness
inhumanity noun

initial noun initials
the first letter of a word or name, especially
of someone's forename
initial adjective
first; of the beginning *the initial stages of
the work* **initially** adverb at the beginning

initiate (say in-**ish**-i-ayt) verb initiates,
initiating, initiated
1 to initiate something is to start it 2 to
initiate someone is to admit them as a
member of a society or group, often with
special ceremonies **initiation** noun

initiative (say in-**ish**-a-tiv) noun
initiatives
1 the action that starts something *She
took the initiative in planning the party.*
2 initiative is the ability or power to start
things or to get them done on your own

inject verb injects, injecting, injected
1 to inject someone is to put a medicine
or drug through their skin using a hollow
needle 2 to inject something is to add it
Try to inject some humour into the story.
injection noun

injure verb injures, injuring, injured
to injure someone is to harm or hurt them

injury noun injuries
injury, or an injury, is harm or damage done
to someone

injustice noun injustices
injustice, or an injustice, is unjust action
or treatment

ink noun inks
ink is a black or coloured liquid used for
writing and printing

inkling noun
a slight idea or suspicion *I had an inkling
that we'd find them in here.*

inland adverb
in or towards a place on land and away
from the coast

in-laws plural noun
a person's in-laws are the relatives of their
husband or wife *We're going to visit the
in-laws at Easter.*

inlet noun inlets
a strip of water reaching into the land from
a sea or lake

inn noun inns
a hotel or pub, especially in the country

inner adjective
inside; nearer the centre
innermost adjective furthest inside *'Ask for
the High Priest,' said the Phoenix. 'Say that
you have a secret to unfold that concerns
my worship, and he will lead you to the
innermost sanctuary.'* – Edith Nesbit, *The
Phoenix and the Carpet*

innings noun innings
the time when a cricket team or player
is batting

innocence noun
1 innocence is when someone is not guilty
of doing something wrong 2 innocence is
also lack of experience of the world and the
evil things in it

innocent adjective
1 not guilty of doing something wrong

a
b
c
d
e
f
g
h
i
j
k
l
m
n
o
p
q
r
s
t
u
v
w
x
y
z

A

2 not knowing much about the world and the evil things in it **innocently** adverb

B

innocuous adjective
harmless

C

innovation noun innovations
1 innovation is inventing or using new things 2 an innovation is something new that you have just invented or started using

D

E

inoculate verb inoculates, inoculating, inoculated
to inoculate someone is to inject them to protect them against a disease
inoculation noun

F

G

H

in-patient noun in-patients
someone who stays at a hospital for treatment

I

J

input noun inputs
what you put into something, especially data put into a computer

K

input verb inputs, inputting, input
to input data or programs is to put them into a computer

L

M

inquest noun inquests
an official investigation to decide why someone died

N

O

inquire verb inquires, inquiring, inquired
1 to inquire about something is to ask about it 2 to inquire into something is to make an official investigation of it

P

Q

R

inquiry noun inquiries
an official investigation

S

inquisitive adjective
always trying to find out things, especially about other people *Goldipig was a very inquisitive little swine, always poking her snout into other people's business.* – Dick King-Smith, *Goldipig and the Three Bears*
inquisitively adverb

T

U

V

W

X

insane adjective
not sane; mad **insanely** adverb
insanity noun

Y

Z

insanitary adjective
not clean or healthy

inscribe verb inscribes, inscribing, inscribed
to inscribe something is to write or carve it on a surface

inscription noun inscriptions
words written or carved on a monument, stone, or coin, or written in the front of a book

insect noun insects
a small animal with six legs and a body divided into three parts
Please see illustration on following page.

insecticide noun insecticides
a poisonous chemical used for killing insects

insecure adjective
1 not safe or protected properly 2 not feeling safe or confident **insecurely** adverb
insecurity noun

insensitive adjective
not sensitive or thinking about the feelings of other people **insensitively** adverb
insensitivity noun

inseparable adjective
1 unable to be separated 2 people are inseparable when they are very good friends and always together *The two girls were inseparable during the summer.*

insert verb inserts, inserting, inserted
to insert something is to put it into something else **insertion** noun

inshore adjective, adverb
on the sea near or nearer to the shore

inside noun insides
1 the inner side, surface, or part; the part nearest to the middle 2 (informal) your insides are your stomach or abdomen **inside out** with the inside turned so that it faces outwards

inside adjective
on the inside of something *Look on an inside page.*

inside adverb, preposition
in or to the inside of something *Come inside. It's inside that box.*

insect

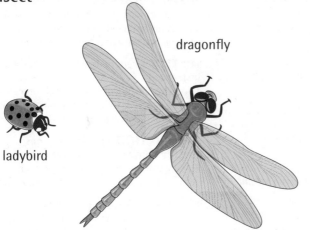

dragonfly

ladybird

fly

insight noun insights
1 insight is being able to see the truth about things 2 an insight is an understanding of something

insignificant adjective
not important or influential
insignificance noun

insincere adjective
not sincere **insincerely** adverb
insincerity noun

insist verb insists, insisting, insisted
to insist something is to be very firm in saying it *He insisted that he was innocent.*
to insist on something is to demand it *We insist on seeing the head teacher.*

insistent adjective
insisting on doing or having something
insistence noun

insolent adjective
very rude and insulting *Malfoy gave Professor Lupin an insolent stare. – J. K. Rowling, Harry Potter and the Prisoner of Azkaban* **insolence** noun

insoluble adjective
1 impossible to dissolve *Some chemicals are insoluble.* 2 impossible to solve *It is an insoluble problem.*

insomnia noun
insomnia is being unable to sleep

inspect verb inspects, inspecting, inspected
to inspect something or someone is to look carefully at them, especially to check them

inspection noun inspections
an inspection is a close or careful look at something to check it

inspector noun inspectors
1 someone employed to inspect things or people 2 a police officer next in rank above a sergeant

inspiration noun inspirations
an inspiration is a person or thing that encourages you and fills you with ideas

inspire verb inspires, inspiring, inspired
to inspire someone is to fill them with ideas or enthusiasm

install verb installs, installing, installed
1 to install something is to put it in position ready for use *We want to install central heating.* 2 to install someone is to put them into an important position with a ceremony *He was installed as pope.* **installation** noun

instalment noun instalments
one of the parts into which something

a b c d e f g h i j k l m n o p q r s t u v w x y z

267

A
B
C
D
E
F
G
H
I
J
K
L
M
N
O
P
Q
R
S
T
U
V
W
X
Y
Z

is divided so that it is spread over a period of time *He is paying for his bike in monthly instalments. The story was in three instalments.*

instance noun instances
an example **for instance** for example

instant adjective
1 happening immediately *It has been an instant success.* **2** an instant food or drink can be made very quickly *Do you like instant coffee?*

instant noun instants
a moment *I don't believe it for an instant.*

instantaneous adjective
happening or done in an instant, or without any delay *Mrs. Cobb had taken an instantaneous and illogical dislike to the Rev. Mr. Burch in the afternoon.* – Kate Douglas Wiggin, *Rebecca of Sunnybrook Farm*
instantaneously adverb

instantly adverb
to do something instantly is to do it without any delay

instead adverb
in place of something else; as a substitute *There were no potatoes, so we had rice instead.*

instep noun insteps
the top of your foot between the toes and the ankle

instinct noun instincts
a natural tendency to do or feel something without being taught *Spiders spin webs by instinct.* **instinctive** adjective instinctive behaviour follows instinct, not thought **instinctively** adverb

institute noun institutes
an organization set up to study something or for some other purpose, or the building used by it

institute verb institutes, instituting, instituted
to institute something is to establish it or start it

institution noun institutions
1 a large organization **2** something that is an established habit or custom *Going for a swim on Sunday was a family institution.*

instruct verb instructs, instructing, instructed
1 to instruct someone is to teach them a subject or skill **2** to instruct someone is also to give them information or orders

instruction noun instructions
1 instruction is teaching a subject or skill **2** an instruction is an order or piece of information *Follow the instructions carefully.*

instrument noun instruments
1 a device for making musical sounds **2** a device for delicate or scientific work

instrumental adjective
1 instrumental music uses musical instruments without any singing **2** to be instrumental in something is to be helpful in making it happen *She was instrumental in getting him a job.*

insufficient adjective
not enough

insulate verb insulates, insulating, insulated
to insulate something is to cover it to stop heat, cold, or electricity from passing in or out **insulation** noun

insulin noun
insulin is a chemical that controls how much sugar there is in the blood

insult (say in-**sult**) verb insults, insulting, insulted
to insult someone is to speak or behave in a rude way that offends them

insult (say **in**-sult) noun insults
a rude remark or action that offends someone

insurance noun
insurance is a business agreement to receive money or compensation if you suffer a loss or injury, in return for a regular payment

insure verb insures, insuring, insured
to insure yourself or your goods is to
protect them with insurance

intact adjective
complete and not damaged *Despite the
storm our tent was still intact.*

intake noun intakes
1 taking something in 2 the number of
people or things taken in *The school had a
high intake of pupils this year.*

integral (say in-ti-gral) adjective
1 that is an essential part of something
Your heart is an integral part of your body.
2 whole or complete

integrate (say in-ti-grayt) verb
integrates, integrating, integrated
1 to integrate different things or parts is
to make them into a whole 2 to integrate
people, especially of different origins,
is to bring them together into a single
community **integration** noun

integrity (say in-teg-ri-ti) noun
integrity is being honest and behaving well

intellect noun intellects
the ability to think and work things out
with your mind

intellectual adjective
1 involving the intellect 2 able to think
effectively; keen to study and learn
intellectually adverb

intellectual noun intellectuals
an intellectual person

intelligence noun
1 your intelligence is your ability to think
and learn 2 intelligence is also secret
information, especially about the military
operations of a country

intelligent adjective
good at thinking and learning
intelligently adverb

intelligible adjective
able to be understood *The message was
barely intelligible.*

intend verb intends, intending,
intended
1 to intend to do something is to have
it in mind as a plan *She was intending to
go swimming.* 2 to intend someone to do
something is to want them to do it

intense adjective
1 very strong or great *The heat was intense.*
2 having or showing strong feelings
intensely adverb

intensify verb intensifies,
intensifying, intensified
1 to intensify something is to make it
more intense 2 to intensify is to become
more intense

intensity noun intensities
the intensity of something is how strong or
great it is

intensive adjective
using a lot of effort; thorough *We have
made an intensive search.* **intensively** adverb

intent adjective
showing a lot of attention and interest **to
be intent on something** is to be eager or
determined to do it

intent noun intents
a person's intent is what they intend to do

intention noun intentions
what you intend to do; a plan

intentional adjective
done on purpose; deliberate
intentionally adverb

intently adverb
to listen or look intently is to do so with a
lot of attention and interest *For a moment
everything was quiet as Milo, Tock, and
the Humbug looked intently at the bottle,
wondering what Dr Dischord would do next.*
— Norton Juster, *The Phantom Tollbooth*

inter- prefix
meaning between two or more people
or things, as in *interchangeable*
and *inter-school*

a
b
c
d
e
f
g
h
i
j
k
l
m
n
o
p
q
r
s
t
u
v
w
x
y
z

A B C D E F G H I J K L M N O P Q R S T U V W X Y Z

interact verb interacts, interacting, interacted
two people or things interact when they have an effect on one another *It is interesting to watch how young children interact.* **interaction** noun

interactive adjective (in computing)
allowing information to be sent in either direction between a computer system and its user

intercept verb intercepts, intercepting, intercepted
to intercept someone or something is to stop them going from one place to another **interception** noun

interchange noun interchanges
a place where you can move from one main road or motorway to another

interchangeable adjective
things are interchangeable when they can be changed or swapped round

intercom noun intercoms
a device for communicating by radio or telephone

interest verb interests, interesting, interested
to interest someone is to make them want to look or listen or take part in something

interest noun interests
1 interest is being interested 2 an interest is a thing that interests you 3 interest is also extra money you have to pay back regularly for a loan

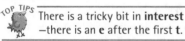
TOP TIPS There is a tricky bit in **interest** —there is an **e** after the first **t**.

interfere verb interferes, interfering, interfered
1 to interfere in something is to become involved in it when it has nothing to do with you 2 to interfere is to get in the way

interference noun
1 interference is interfering in something 2 interference is also a crackling or distorting of a radio or television signal

interior noun interiors
the inside of something

interjection noun interjections
an exclamation, such as *oh!*

interlock verb interlocks, interlocking, interlocked
to interlock is to fit into one another *The gearwheels interlocked.*

interlude noun interludes
1 an interval 2 music played during an interval

intermediate adjective
coming between two things in place, order, or time

intermission noun intermissions
an interval in a play or film

intermittent adjective
happening at intervals
intermittently adverb

intern verb interns, interning, interned
to intern someone is to imprison them in a special camp or building, usually during a war **internment** noun

internal adjective
of or in the inside of something
internally adverb

international adjective
to do with more than one country *Interpol is an international police organization.*
internationally adverb

Internet noun
the Internet is the computer network that allows people all over the world to share information and send messages

interpret verb interprets, interpreting, interpreted
1 to interpret something is to explain what it means 2 to interpret a foreign language is to translate it into another language
interpretation noun

interpreter noun interpreters
a person who translates what someone says into another language

interrogate verb interrogates, interrogating, interrogated
to interrogate someone is to question them closely in order to get information **interrogation** noun **interrogator** noun

interrupt verb interrupts, interrupting, interrupted
1 to interrupt someone is to stop them talking 2 to interrupt something is to stop it continuing **interruption** noun

intersect verb intersects, intersecting, intersected
to intersect something is to cross or divide it *The cloth had a design of intersecting lines.*

intersection noun intersections
a place where lines or roads cross each other

interval noun intervals
a time between two events or between two parts of a play or film **at intervals** with some time or distance between each one; not continuously

intervene verb intervenes, intervening, intervened
1 to intervene is to come between two events *During the intervening years they went abroad.* 2 to intervene in an argument or fight is to interrupt it in order to stop it or affect the result **intervention** noun

interview noun interviews
a meeting with someone to ask them questions or discuss something
interview verb interviews, interviewing, interviewed
to interview someone is to have an interview with them

interviewer noun interviewers
a person who interviews someone, especially on radio or television

intestine noun or
intestines plural noun
the long tube along which food passes from the stomach

intimate (say **in**-ti-mat) adjective
1 very friendly with someone 2 intimate thoughts are thoughts that are private or personal 3 detailed *They have an intimate knowledge of the town.* **intimately** noun

intimate (say **in**-ti-mayt) verb
intimates, intimating, intimated
to intimate something is to hint at it or suggest it *He has not yet intimated what his plans are.*

intimidate verb intimidates, intimidating, intimidated
to frighten a person with threats into doing something **intimidation** noun

into preposition
1 expressing movement to the inside of something *Go into the house.* 2 **Into** also has some special uses, shown by the following examples: *He got into trouble. She went into acting. 3 into 12 goes 4 times.*

intolerable adjective
unbearable *The noise outside was intolerable.* **intolerably** adverb

intolerant adjective
not tolerant; not willing to put up with people **intolerance** noun **intolerantly** adverb

intonation noun intonations
1 the pitch or tone of a voice or musical instrument 2 when you speak, your intonation is the way you use the pitch of your voice to alter the meaning of what you are saying, for example when asking a question

intrepid adjective
brave or fearless *'Perhaps most of the brave defenders were killed quite early in the siege and all the provisions eaten, and now there are only a few intrepid survivors.'* – Edith Nesbit, *Five Children and It*

intricate adjective
an intricate pattern or design is detailed and complicated **intricacy** noun **intricately** adverb

intrigue (say in-**treeg**) verb intrigues, intriguing, intrigued
to intrigue someone is to interest them

a
b
c
d
e
f
g
h
i
j
k
l
m
n
o
p
q
r
s
t
u
v
w
x
y
z

very much and make them curious
intriguing adjective

intrigue (say **in**-treeg) noun intrigues
a secret plot

introduce verb introduces,
introducing, introduced
1 to introduce someone is to make them
known to other people **2** to introduce
something is to get it into general use

introduction noun introductions
1 introducing someone or something **2** a
piece at the beginning of a book, explaining
what it is about **introductory** adjective
coming at the beginning of something

intrude verb intrudes, intruding,
intruded
to intrude is to come in or join in without
being wanted

intruder noun intruders
someone who forces their way into a place
where they are not supposed to be

intrusion noun intrusions
an intrusion is coming in where you are
not wanted

intrusive adjective
something is intrusive when it is not wanted
and gets in the way

intuition (say in-tew-**ish**-on) noun
intuition is the power to know or
understand things without having to think
hard **intuitive** adjective

Inuit noun Inuit or Inuits
one of the people who live in very cold
parts of North America

inundate verb inundates, inundating,
inundated
to inundate someone is to overwhelm them
with a large number of things *We've been
inundated with complaints.* **inundation** noun

invade verb invades, invading, invaded
to invade a country or place is to attack and
enter it

invader noun invaders
an invader is someone who invades a place

invalid[1] (say **in**-va-leed or **in**-va-lid)
noun invalids
someone who is ill or weakened by a
long illness

invalid[2] (say in-**val**-id) adjective
not valid *This passport is invalid.*

invaluable adjective
very valuable

invariable adjective
never changing; always the same

invariably adverb
always

invasion noun invasions
when an army or a large number of people
attack and enter a place

invent verb invents, inventing,
invented
1 to invent something is to be the first
person to make it or think of it **2** to
invent a story or excuse is to make it
up **invention** noun **inventive** adjective
someone is being inventive when they
cleverly think of new ideas **inventor** noun

inverse adjective
reversed or opposite **inversely** adverb
inverse noun
the opposite of something

invert verb inverts, inverting, inverted
to invert something is to turn it upside
down **inversion** noun

invertebrate (say in-**vert**-i-brat)
noun invertebrates
an animal without a backbone, such as a
worm or an amoeba

inverted commas plural noun
punctuation marks (" ") or (' ') that you put
round spoken words and quotations

invest verb invests, investing, invested
1 to invest money is to use it to earn
interest or make a profit **2** to invest
someone is to give them an honour or
medal or special title *He was invested as
Prince of Wales.*

A B C D E F G H I J K L M N O P Q R S T U V W X Y Z

investigate verb investigates, investigating, investigated
to investigate something or someone is to find out as much as you can about them *Police are investigating the robbery.*
investigation noun **investigator** noun

investment noun investments
1 money someone invests 2 something someone invests money in *Houses are a safe investment.*

invigorate verb invigorates, invigorating, invigorated
to fill someone with energy
invigorating adjective

invincible adjective
not able to be defeated

invisible adjective
not visible; not able to be seen
invisibility noun

invitation noun invitations
a request for someone to do something, such as come to a party

invite verb invites, inviting, invited
1 to invite someone is to ask them to come to a party or do something special 2 to invite something unwelcome is to make it likely to happen by your actions *You are inviting trouble by doing that.*

inviting adjective
attractive or tempting

invoice noun invoices
a list of goods sent or of work done, with the prices charged

involuntary adjective
not deliberate; done without thinking

involve verb involves, involving, involved
1 to involve something is to need it or result in it *The job involved a lot of effort.*
2 to be involved in something is to take part in it *We are involved in charity work.*
involvement noun

involved adjective
long and complicated

inward adjective
on the inside, or facing the inside
inward adverb
inwards

inwardly adverb
in your thoughts; privately *Titus shut his eyes like a clam and inwardly vowed never to grow old. – Debi Gliori, Pure Dead Magic*

inwards adverb
towards the inside

ion noun ions
an electrically charged particle

IQ noun IQs
a measure of someone's intelligence, calculated from the results of a test

iris noun irises
1 the coloured part of your eyeball 2 a flower with long pointed leaves

iron noun irons
1 iron is a strong heavy metal 2 an iron is a device that you heat up and press on clothes to make them smooth 3 an iron is also a tool made of iron

iron verb irons, ironing, ironed
to iron clothes is to smooth them with an iron **to iron something out** is to solve a difficulty gradually and carefully

ironic (say I-**ron**-ik) or
ironical (say I-**ron**-ikal) adjective
1 an ironic situation is strange because the opposite happens to what you might expect 2 you are being ironic when you say the opposite of what you mean
ironically adverb

ironmonger noun ironmongers
someone who keeps a shop that sells tools, nails, and other metal things

irony (say I-ro-ni) noun ironies
1 irony is saying the opposite of what you mean in order to emphasize it or be funny, for example *What a lovely day* when it is pouring with rain 2 an irony is an unexpected or strange event or situation *The irony is that she had sold all her jewels the day before the burglars broke in.*

a
b
c
d
e
f
g
h
i
j
k
l
m
n
o
p
q
r
s
t
u
v
w
x
y
z

273

A
B

irrational adjective
not reasonable or sensible
irrationally adverb

C

irregular adjective
1 not regular; not usual **2** against the rules
irregularity noun **irregularly** adverb

D

irrelevant (say i-**rel**-i-vant) adjective
not relevant; not having anything
to do with what is being discussed
irrelevance noun

E
F

irresistible adjective
too strong or attractive or tempting
to resist

G
H

irresponsible adjective
not thinking enough about the effects
of your actions **irresponsibility** noun
irresponsibly adverb

I
J

irrigate verb irrigates, irrigating,
irrigated
to irrigate land is to supply it with
water so that crops can grow
irrigation noun

K
L
M

irritable adjective
easily annoyed; bad-tempered
irritability noun **irritably** adverb

N
O

irritate verb irritates, irritating,
irritated
1 to irritate someone is to annoy them
2 to irritate a part of your body is to make
it itch or feel sore **irritant** noun an irritant
is something that makes you sore

P
Q
R

irritation noun irritations
1 irritation is being annoyed **2** an irritation
is something that annoys you

S
T

is
3rd person singular present tense of be
Everything is back to normal.

U
V

–ish suffix
meaning 'somewhat; rather like something',
as in *boyish* and *reddish*

W
X

Islam (say **iz**-lahm) noun
Islam is the religion of Muslims.
Islamic adjective

Y
Z

island noun islands
a piece of land surrounded by water
islander noun

isle noun isles
an island

–ism suffix
meaning a belief or a system of thought,
such as *Hinduism*

isn't
short for *is not*

isolate verb isolates, isolating, isolated
to isolate someone or something is to
keep them apart from others *Patients
with the disease need to be isolated.*
isolation noun

isosceles triangle (say I-**sos**-i-
leez) noun isosceles triangles
a triangle with two sides the same length

issue verb issues, issuing, issued
1 to issue something is to send it or give
it out to people *They issued blankets to
the refugees.* **2** to issue a book or piece of
information is to publish it **3** to issue is to
come out of something *Smoke was issuing
from the chimney.*

issue noun issues
1 an issue is a subject that people are
discussing *What are the most important
issues?* **2** an issue of a magazine or
newspaper is the edition sold on a particular
day *There's a good poster in this week's
issue of my football magazine.* **3** the issue
of documents is making them available
to people

–ist suffix
meaning someone who does a particular
job, such as an *anaesthetist*

it pronoun
1 the thing being talked about, used as the
subject or object of a verb **2** It also has
some special uses, as in: *It is raining. We
must go it alone.*

italics (say it-**al**-iks) plural noun
letters printed with a slant, *like this*

itch noun itches
1 a tickling feeling in your skin that makes you want to scratch it **2** a longing to do something *He has an itch to go to America.*

itch verb itches, itching, itched
a part of your body itches when it makes you want to scratch it

itchy adjective itchier, itchiest
part of your body is itchy when it makes you want to scratch it

item noun items
one thing in a list or group of things

itinerary (say I-**tin**-er-er-i) noun
itineraries
a list of places to be visited on a journey

–itis suffix
used in names of diseases in which part of the body is inflamed, such as *bronchitis*

it'll
short for *it will It'll be good to get home.*

its determiner, pronoun
of it; belonging to it *The cat hurt its paw.*

it's
short for *it is* and (before a verb in the past tense) *it has It's raining. It's been raining.*

itself pronoun
it and nothing else, used to refer back to the subject of a verb *I think the cat has hurt itself.* **by itself** on its own, alone *The house stands by itself in a wood.*

ITV
short for *Independent Television*

I've
short for *I have*

ivory noun
1 ivory is the hard creamy-white substance that forms elephants' tusks
2 a creamy-white colour

ivy noun
ivy is a climbing evergreen plant with shiny leaves

Jj

jab verb jabs, jabbing, jabbed
1 to jab someone or something is to poke them roughly *Eddie felt something jab him in the back. He turned to find that it was Malcolm the stuffed stoat's nose.* — Philip Ardagh, *Terrible Times* **2** to jab something is to push it roughly into something else

jab noun jabs
1 a quick hit with something pointed or a fist **2** (informal) an injection

jabber verb jabbers, jabbering, jabbered
to chatter a lot or to speak quickly and not clearly

jack noun jacks
1 a piece of equipment for lifting something heavy off the ground, especially a car **2** a playing card with a picture of a young man **3** a small white ball that you aim at in the game of bowls

jack verb jacks, jacking, jacked
to jack something is to lift it with a jack

jackal noun jackals
a wild animal rather like a dog

jackdaw noun jackdaws
a bird like a small crow

jacket noun jackets
1 a short coat covering the top half of the body **2** a paper cover for a book
3 a wrapping round a boiler to insulate it

jacket potato noun jacket potatoes
a potato that is baked without being peeled

jack–in–the–box noun
jack-in-the-boxes
a toy figure that springs out of a box when you lift the lid

jackknife verb jackknifes, jackknifing, jackknifed
an articulated lorry jackknifes when it goes

a
b
c
d
e
f
g
h
i
j
k
l
m
n
o
p
q
r
s
t
u
v
w
x
y
z

A

out of control, with the trailer skidding round towards the cab

B

jackpot noun jackpots
an amount of prize money that increases until someone wins it

C

D

jacuzzi (say ja-**koo**-zi) noun jacuzzis
a large bath with jets of water that massage the body under the water

E

jade noun
jade is a hard green stone which is carved to make ornaments

F

G

jaded adjective
tired and bored because you have had too much of something

H

I

jagged (say **jag**-id) adjective
having an uneven edge with sharp points

J

K

jaguar noun jaguars
a large fierce South American animal of the cat family, rather like a leopard

L

M

jail noun jails
a prison
jail verb jails, jailing, jailed
to jail someone is to put them in prison

N

O

jailer noun jailers
a person in charge of a jail

P

Q

Jain (rhymes with **main**) noun Jains
a believer in an Indian religion rather like Buddhism

R

S

jam noun jams
1 a sweet food made of fruit boiled with sugar until it is thick **2** a lot of people or cars or other things crowded together so that it is difficult to move **to be in a jam** (informal) is to be in a difficult situation

T

U

jam verb jams, jamming, jammed
1 to jam something is to make it stuck and difficult to move **2** to jam is to become stuck *The door has jammed.* **3** to jam something is to push or squeeze it with force *I jammed on the brakes.*

V

W

X

Y

jamboree noun jamborees
1 a large party or celebration **2** a rally of Scouts

Z

jammy adjective jammier, jammiest
1 covered with jam **2** (informal) very lucky

jangle verb jangles, jangling, jangled
to make a harsh ringing sound

January noun
the first month of the year

jar¹ noun jars
a container made of glass or pottery

jar² verb jars, jarring, jarred
1 to jar is to give you an unpleasant shock or jolt *I jarred every bone in my body.*
2 to jar is also to make a harsh sound *All that shrieking really jars on my ears.*

jargon noun
jargon is words used by people in a particular profession, that are difficult for other people to understand *The guide is full of computer jargon.*

jaundice noun
jaundice is a disease that makes the skin turn yellow

jaunt noun jaunts
a short trip for fun

jaunty adjective jauntier, jauntiest
lively and cheerful

javelin noun javelins
a light spear used for throwing in athletics competitions

jaw noun jaws
1 one of the two bones that hold the teeth **2** the lower part of the face; the mouth and teeth of a person or animal **3** the part of a tool that grips something

jay noun jays
a noisy brightly-coloured bird

jazz noun
jazz is a kind of music with a strong rhythm

jazzy adjective jazzier, jazziest
bright and colourful

jealous adjective
1 unhappy or resentful because you feel that someone is better or luckier

than you **2** upset because you think that someone you love loves someone else more **jealously** adverb

 TOP TIPS
There is a tricky bit in **jealous**—it begins with **jea**.

jeans plural noun
casual trousers made of denim

Jeep noun Jeeps (trademark)
a small sturdy motor car that can be driven over rough ground

jeer verb jeers, jeering, jeered
to laugh rudely at someone and shout insults at them

jelly noun jellies
1 a soft sweet food with a fruit flavour **2** any soft slippery substance

jellyfish noun jellyfish
a sea animal with a body like jelly and tentacles that can sting

jerk verb jerks, jerking, jerked
1 to jerk is to make a sudden sharp movement **2** to jerk something is to pull it suddenly
jerk noun jerks
a sudden sharp movement

jerky adjective jerkier, jerkiest
moving with sudden sharp movements **jerkily** adverb

jersey noun jerseys
a pullover with sleeves

jest noun jests
a joke; to say something **in jest** is to be joking
jest verb jests, jesting, jested
to jest is to make jokes

jester noun jesters
a professional entertainer at a royal court in the Middle Ages

jet¹ noun jets
1 a stream of liquid, gas, or flame forced out of a narrow opening **2** a narrow opening from which a jet comes out **3** an aircraft driven by jet engines

jet verb jets, jetting, jetted
1 to jet is to come out in a strong stream
2 (informal) to jet is to travel in jet aircraft

jet² noun
1 jet is a hard black mineral **2** a deep glossy black colour

jet engine noun jet engines
an engine that drives an aircraft forward by sending out a powerful jet of hot gas at the back

jet lag noun
jet lag is extreme tiredness that someone feels after a long plane journey because they have not got used to the different time zones

jet-propelled adjective
driven by jet engines

jetty noun jetties
a small landing stage for boats

Jew noun Jews
1 a member of the race of people descended from the ancient Hebrews **2** someone who believes in Judaism

jewel noun jewels
1 a precious stone **2** an ornament containing precious stones

jeweller noun jewellers
someone who sells or makes jewellery

jewellery noun
jewellery is jewels or ornaments that people wear

Jewish adjective
1 a Jewish person practises Judaism **2** to do with Judaism

jib noun jibs
1 a triangular sail of a ship, stretching forward from the mast **2** the arm of a crane that lifts things

jiffy noun (informal)
a moment *I won't be a jiffy.*

jig noun jigs
a lively jumping dance

A
B
C
D
E
F
G
H
I
J
K
L
M
N
O
P
Q
R
S
T
U
V
W
X
Y
Z

jig verb jigs, jigging, jigged
to jig is to move up and down with quick jerks

jigsaw noun jigsaws
1 a saw that can cut curved shapes 2 a jigsaw puzzle

jigsaw puzzle noun jigsaw puzzles
a puzzle made of differently shaped pieces that you fit together to make a picture

jingle verb jingles, jingling, jingled
to jingle is to make a tinkling or clinking sound

jingle noun jingles
1 a tinkling or clinking sound *Just as I was getting ready to go to sleep I heard a jingle of harness and a grunt, and a mule passed me shaking his wet ears.* — Rudyard Kipling, *The Jungle Book* 2 a simple tune or song that is used in an advertisement

job noun jobs
1 work that someone does regularly to earn a living *He got a job as a postman.* 2 a piece of work that needs to be done *We'll have tea when we've finished this job.*

jockey noun jockeys
someone who rides horses in races

jodhpurs (say **jod**-perz) plural noun
jodhpurs are trousers for riding a horse, fitting closely from the knee to the ankle

jog verb jogs, jogging, jogged
1 to jog is to run slowly, especially for exercise 2 to jog someone is to give them a slight knock or push **to jog someone's memory** is to help them remember something **jogger** noun

join verb joins, joining, joined
1 to join things together, or join one thing to another, is to put or fix them together 2 two or more things join when they come together 3 to join a society or group is to become a member of it **to join in** is to take part in something

join noun joins
a place where things join

joiner noun joiners
someone whose job is to make furniture and other things out of wood

joint noun joints
1 a place where things are fixed together 2 the place where two bones fit together 3 a large piece of meat

joint adjective
shared or done by two or more people or groups *The song was a joint effort.*

jointly adverb
two or more people jointly do something when they do it together

joist noun joists
a long beam supporting a floor or ceiling

joke noun jokes
something that you say or do to make people laugh

joke verb jokes, joking, joked
to joke is to make jokes, or to talk in a way that is not serious

joker noun jokers
1 someone who makes jokes 2 an extra playing card with a picture of a jester on it

jolly adjective jollier, jolliest
happy and cheerful

jolly adverb (informal)
very *That film was jolly good!*

jolly verb jollies, jollying, jollied
to jolly someone along is to make them more cheerful

jolt verb jolts, jolting, jolted
1 to jolt something or someone is to hit them or move them suddenly and sharply 2 to jolt is to make a sudden sharp movement *The bus jolted to a halt.*

jolt noun jolts
1 a sudden sharp movement *The plane landed with a jolt.* 2 a surprise or shock

jostle verb jostles, jostling, jostled
to jostle someone is to push them roughly

jot noun
a tiny amount *I don't care a jot.*

jot verb jots, jotting, jotted
to jot something down is to write it quickly

jotter noun jotters
a notebook

joule noun joules (in science)
a unit of work or energy

journal noun journals
1 a newspaper or magazine 2 a diary

journalist noun journalists
someone whose job is to write news stories for a newspaper, magazine, or in television or radio or for a news website **journalism** noun

journey noun journeys
1 going from one place to another 2 the distance or time you take to travel somewhere *The town is a day's journey away.*

journey verb journeys, journeying, journeyed
to journey is to go from one place to another

joust verb jousts, jousting, jousted
to joust is to fight on horseback with lances, as knights did in medieval times

jovial adjective
cheerful and jolly *Half a dozen jovial lads were talking about skates in another part of the room. – Louisa May Alcott, Little Women*

joy noun joys
1 joy is great happiness or pleasure 2 a joy is something that gives happiness

joyful adjective
very happy **joyfully** adverb

joyous adjective
full of joy; causing joy *The following days were some of the most joyous that Clara had spent on the mountain. – Johanna Spyri, Heidi* **joyously** adverb

joyride noun joyrides (informal)
a ride in a stolen car for amusement

joystick noun joysticks
1 (informal) the lever that controls the movement of an aircraft 2 a lever

for controlling the cursor on a screen, especially in computer games

jubilant (say joo-bi-lant) adjective
very happy because you have won or succeeded

jubilation noun
jubilation is rejoicing because you have won or succeeded

jubilee noun jubilees
a special anniversary of an important event

Judaism (say joo-day-izm) noun
Judaism is the religion of the Jewish people.

judge noun judges
1 someone who hears cases in a law court and decides what should be done 2 someone who decides who has won a contest or competition 3 someone who is good at forming opinions or making decisions about things *She's a good judge of musical ability.*

judge verb judges, judging, judged
1 to judge something is to act as judge in a law case or a competition 2 to judge an amount is to estimate or guess what it is 3 to judge something is to form an opinion about it

judgement noun judgements
1 judgement is acting as judge for a law case or a contest 2 a judgement is the decision made by a law court 3 judgement is also the ability to make decisions wisely 4 someone's judgement is their opinion *In my judgement, you're making a big mistake.*

judicial (say joo-dish-al) adjective
to do with law courts, judges, or decisions made in law courts

judicious (say joo-dish-us) adjective
showing good sense or judgement

judo (say joo-doh) noun
judo is a Japanese form of unarmed combat for sport

jug noun jugs
a container for pouring liquids, with a handle and lip

juggernaut noun juggernauts
a very large articulated lorry

juggle verb juggles, juggling, juggled
to juggle objects is to keep tossing and catching them so that you keep them moving in the air without dropping any
juggler noun

juice noun juices
1 the liquid from fruit, vegetables, or other food 2 a liquid produced by the body, such as the digestive juices **juicy** adjective

jukebox noun jukeboxes
a machine that automatically plays a record of your choice when you put a coin in

July noun
the seventh month of the year

jumble verb jumbles, jumbling, jumbled
to jumble things is to mix them up in a confused way

jumble noun
a confused mixture of things; a muddle

jumble sale noun jumble sales
a sale of second-hand goods to raise money

jumbo jet noun jumbo jets
a large jet aircraft for carrying a lot of passengers

jump verb jumps, jumping, jumped
1 to jump is to move suddenly from the ground into the air 2 to jump a fence or other obstacle is to go over it by jumping 3 to jump up or out is to move quickly or suddenly *He jumped out of his seat.* 4 to jump in or out of a vehicle is to get in or out quickly **to jump the queue** is to go in front of people before it is your turn

jump noun jumps
1 a sudden movement into the air 2 an obstacle to jump over

jumper noun jumpers
a pullover with sleeves

jump suit noun jump suits
a piece of clothing made in one piece and covering the whole body

jumpy adjective jumpier, jumpiest
nervous and anxious

junction noun junctions
a place where roads or railway lines join

June noun
the sixth month of the year

jungle noun jungles
a thick tangled forest, especially in tropical countries

junior adjective
1 younger 2 for young children *She goes to a junior school.* 3 lower in rank or importance
junior noun juniors
1 a younger person *Peter is my junior.* 2 a person of lower rank or importance

junk¹ noun
junk is old worthless things that should be thrown away *The garage is full of junk.*

junk² noun junks
a Chinese sailing boat

junk food noun
junk food is food that is not nourishing, usually containing a lot of sugar and starch

juror noun jurors
a member of a jury

jury noun juries
a group of people (usually twelve) chosen to make a decision about a case in a law court, especially whether a person accused of a crime is innocent or guilty

just adjective
1 fair and right; giving proper thought to everybody 2 deserved *He got his just reward.* **justly** adverb
just adverb
1 exactly *It's just what I wanted.* 2 only; simply *I just wanted another cake.* 3 barely; by only a short amount *The ball hit her just below the knee.* 4 a short time ago *They had just gone.*

justice noun justices
1 justice is being just or having fair treatment 2 justice is also the actions of the

A
B
C
D
E
F
G
H
I
J
K
L
M
N
O
P
Q
R
S
T
U
V
W
X
Y
Z

law *They were tried in a court of justice.*
3 a justice is a judge or magistrate

justify verb **justifies, justifying, justified**
to justify something is to show that it is reasonable or necessary *Do you think that you were justified in taking such a risk?*
justifiable adjective able to be justified
justification noun a justification for something is a good reason for doing it

jut verb **juts, jutting, jutted**
to jut, or to jut out, is to stick out

juvenile (say **joo**-vi-nyl) adjective
to do with young people
juvenile noun **juveniles**
a young person who is not yet an adult

Kk

kaleidoscope (say kal-I-dos-kohp)
noun **kaleidoscopes**
a tube that you look through to see brightly-coloured patterns which change as you turn the end of the tube

kayak

kangaroo noun **kangaroos**
an Australian animal that moves by jumping on its strong back legs

karaoke (say ka-ri-**oh**-ki) noun
karaoke is a party entertainment in which people sing songs with a recorded background played from a special machine

karate (say ka-**rah**-ti) noun
karate is a Japanese method of self-defence using the hands, arms, and feet

kayak (say **ky**-ak) noun **kayaks**
a small canoe with a covering that fits round the canoeist's waist

kebab noun **kebabs**
small pieces of meat or vegetables grilled on a skewer

keel noun **keels**
the long piece of wood or metal along the bottom of a boat **to be on an even keel** is to be steady
keel verb **keels, keeling, keeled**
to keel over is to fall sideways or overturn

keen adjective **keener, keenest**
1 enthusiastic or eager *She is keen on swimming. We are keen to go.* **2** strong or sharp *The knife had a keen edge. There was a keen wind.* **keenly** adverb a keenly

a b c d e f g h i **j k** l m n o p q r s t u v w x y z

A B C D E F G

K

L M N O P Q R S T U V W X Y Z

fought contest is one in which people are competing very hard **keenness** noun

keep verb keeps, keeping, kept
1 to keep something is to have it and not get rid of it **2** to keep something in a place is to put it there when you are not using it **3** to keep (for example) well or still is to continue to be well or still **4** to keep someone (for example) warm or happy is to cause them to continue to be warm or happy **5** something keeps when it lasts without going bad *Will the milk keep until tomorrow?* **6** to keep doing something is to continue to do it *They kept laughing at her.* **7** to keep your word or promise is to honour it and not break it **8** to keep animals or pets is to have them and look after them **to keep something up** is to continue doing it *Keep up the good work!* **to keep up with someone** is to go as fast as them

keep noun keeps
1 someone's keep is the food or money they need to live *They have to earn their keep.*
2 a keep is a strong tower in a castle **for keeps** (informal) to keep; permanently *Is this football mine for keeps?*

keeper noun keepers
1 someone who looks after the animals in a zoo **2** a goalkeeper

keeping noun
something is in your keeping when you are looking after it *The diaries are in safe keeping.* **to be in keeping with something** is to fit in with it or be suitable

keg noun kegs
a small barrel

kennel noun kennels
a shelter for a dog

kept
past tense and past participle of keep verb *Tom kept out of sight. I have kept the letter.*

kerb noun kerbs
the edge of a pavement

kerbstone noun kerbstones
a long square stone used to make a kerb

kernel noun kernels
the part inside the shell of a nut

kestrel noun kestrels
a kind of small falcon

ketchup noun
ketchup is a thick sauce made from tomatoes

kettle noun kettles
a container with a spout and handle, used for boiling water in

kettledrum noun kettledrums
a drum made of skin stretched over a large metal bowl

key noun keys
1 a piece of metal shaped so that it opens a lock **2** a small lever that you press with your finger, on a piano or keyboard **3** a device for winding up a clock or clockwork toy **4** a scale of musical notes *It is played in the key of C major.* **5** something that solves a problem or mystery *Police think they have found the key to the crime.*

keyboard noun keyboards
a set of keys on a piano, typewriter, or computer

keyhole noun keyholes
the hole through which you put a key into a lock

keynote noun keynotes
1 the note on which a key in music is based *The keynote of C major is C.* **2** the main idea in something that is said, written, or done

key word or **key phrase** noun
key words, key phrases
1 one of the most important words or phrases in a text, that helps you to understand what the text is about **2** a word or phrase that you type into a computer when you are searching for information

kg
short for kilogram or kilograms

khaki (say kah-ki) noun
a dull yellow-brown colour, often used for army uniforms

kibbutz noun **kibbutzim**
a farming commune in Israel

kick verb **kicks, kicking, kicked**
1 to kick someone or something is to hit them with your foot 2 to kick is to move your legs about vigorously 3 a gun kicks when it moves back sharply as it is fired

kick noun **kicks**
1 a kicking movement 2 the sudden backwards movement a gun makes when it is fired

kick-off noun **kick-offs**
the start of a football match

kid noun **kids**
1 a young goat 2 (informal) a child

kid verb **kids, kidding, kidded** (informal)
to kid someone is to deceive or tease them

kidnap verb **kidnaps, kidnapping, kidnapped**
to kidnap someone is to capture them by force, usually to get a ransom **kidnapper** noun

kidney noun **kidneys**
each of two organs in your body that remove waste products from your blood and send them as urine to your bladder

kill verb **kills, killing, killed**
1 to kill a person or animal is to make them die 2 to kill something like an idea or plan is to make sure it does not happen

killer noun **killers**
a person who kills someone

kiln noun **kilns**
an oven for hardening or drying pottery or bricks

kilo noun **kilos**
a kilogram

kilobyte noun **kilobytes** (in computing)
a unit that measures data or memory, equal to 1,024 bytes

kilogram noun **kilograms**
a unit of weight equal to 1,000 grams or about 2.2 pounds

kilometre (say kil-o-mee-ter or kil-**om**-i-ter) noun **kilometres**
a unit of length equal to 1,000 metres or about ⅝ of a mile

kilowatt noun **kilowatts**
a unit of electrical power equal to 1,000 watts

kilt noun **kilts**
a kind of pleated skirt worn by men as part of traditional Scottish dress

kin noun
a person's family or relatives **your next of kin** is your closest relative

kind[1] noun **kinds**
a type or sort of something *What kind of food do you like?* **kind of** (informal) in a way, to some extent *We kind of hoped we would come.*

kind[2] adjective **kinder, kindest**
helpful and friendly **kindness** adjective

kindergarten (say **kin**-der-gar-ten) noun **kindergartens**
a school or class for very young children

kind-hearted adjective
kind and generous

kindle verb **kindles, kindling, kindled**
1 to kindle something is to get it to burn 2 to kindle is to start burning

kindling noun
kindling is small pieces of wood for lighting fires

kindly adverb
1 in a kind way 2 please *Kindly close the door.*

kindly adjective **kindlier, kindliest**
kind *She gave a kindly smile.* **kindliness** noun

kinetic (say kin-**et**-ik) adjective
to do with movement, or produced by movement, as in *kinetic energy*

king noun **kings**
1 a man who has been crowned as the ruler of a country 2 a piece in chess that has to be captured to win the game 3 a

a
b
c
d
e
f
g
h
i
j
k
l
m
n
o
p
q
r
s
t
u
v
w
x
y
z

playing card with a picture of a king
kingly adjective

kingdom noun kingdoms
a country that is ruled by a king or queen

kingfisher noun kingfishers
a brightly-coloured bird that lives near water and catches fish

king–size or **king–sized** adjective
larger than the usual size

kink noun kinks
a short twist in a rope, wire, or piece of hair

kiosk (say kee-osk) noun kiosks
1 a telephone box **2** a small hut or stall where you can buy newspapers, sweets, and drinks

kipper noun kippers
a smoked herring

kiss noun kisses
touching someone with your lips as a sign of affection or greeting
kiss verb kisses, kissing, kissed
to kiss someone is to give them a kiss

kiss of life noun
blowing air from your mouth into someone else's to help them to start breathing again, especially after an accident

kit noun kits
1 equipment or clothes that you need to do a sport, a job, or some other activity **2** a set of parts sold to be fitted together to make something *a model aircraft kit*

kitchen noun kitchens
a room where food is prepared and cooked

kite noun kites
a light frame covered with cloth or paper that you fly in the wind at the end of a long piece of string

kitten noun kittens
a very young cat

kitty¹ noun kitties
1 an amount of money that you can win in a card game **2** an amount of money that you put aside for a special purpose

kitty² noun kitties (informal)
a kitten

kiwi (say kee-wee) noun kiwis
a New Zealand bird that cannot fly

kiwi fruit noun kiwi fruits
a fruit with thin hairy skin, soft green flesh, and black seeds

km
short for **kilometre** or **kilometres**

knack noun
a special skill or talent *There's a knack to putting up a deckchair.*

knave noun knaves (old use)
1 a dishonest man **2** a jack in a pack of playing cards

knead verb kneads, kneading, kneaded
to knead dough or something else soft is to press and stretch it with your hands

knee noun knees
the joint in the middle of your leg

kneecap noun kneecaps
the bony part at the front of your knee

kneel verb kneels, kneeling, knelt
to bend your legs so you are resting on your knees

knew
past tense of **know** *I knew we would be friends.*

knickers plural noun
underpants worn by women or girls

knife noun knives
a cutting instrument made of a short blade set in a handle
knife verb knifes, knifing, knifed
to knife someone is to stab them with a knife

knight noun knights
1 a man who has been given the honour that lets him put 'Sir' before his name **2** a warrior who had been given the rank of a nobleman, in the Middle Ages **3** a piece in chess, with a horse's head **knighthood** noun

a man receives a knighthood when he is made a knight

knight verb knights, knighting, knighted
to knight someone is to make them a knight

knit verb knits, knitting, knitted
to knit something is to make it by looping together threads of wool or other material, using long needles or a machine

knitting noun
1 knitting is the activity of making things by knitting 2 knitting is also something that is being made this way

knives
plural of knife noun

knob noun knobs
1 the round handle of a door or drawer 2 a control to adjust a radio or television set 3 a lump of something

knock verb knocks, knocking, knocked
1 to knock something is to hit it hard or bump into it *Oops, I knocked the vase over.* 2 to knock is to hit something with your hand or fist *Who's knocking at the door?* 3 (informal) to knock someone or something is to criticize them **to knock someone out** is to hit them so that they become unconscious

knock noun knocks
the act or sound of hitting something

knocker noun knockers
a device for knocking on a door

knockout noun knockouts
1 knocking someone out 2 a game or contest in which the loser in each round has to drop out

knot noun knots
1 a fastening made by tying or looping two ends of string, rope, or ribbon together 2 a round spot on a piece of wood where a branch once joined it 3 a unit for measuring the speed of ships and aircraft, 2,025 yards (or 1,852 metres) per hour 4 a knot of people is a small group of them standing close together

knot verb knots, knotting, knotted
to knot something is to tie or fasten it with a knot

knotty adjective knottier, knottiest
1 full of knots 2 difficult or puzzling *It's a knotty problem.*

know verb knows, knowing, knew, known
1 to have something in your mind that you have learned or discovered 2 to know a person or place is to recognize them or it or be familiar with them or it *I've known him for years.*

know-all noun know-alls
someone who behaves as if they know everything

know-how noun
know-how is the skill or knowledge you need for a particular job

knowing adjective
a knowing look is one that shows that you know something

knowingly adverb
1 in a knowing way *He winked at me knowingly.* 2 deliberately *She would never have done such a thing knowingly.*

knowledge (say nol-ij) noun
knowledge is what someone or everybody knows

 TOP TIPS
Keep it quiet! There is a silent **k** in **knowledge**.

knowledgeable (say nol-ij-a-bul) adjective
knowing a lot about something
knowledgeably adverb

knuckle noun knuckles
a joint in your finger

koala (say koh-ah-la) noun koalas
a furry Australian animal that looks like a small bear

Koran (say kor-ahn) noun
the holy book of Islam

A
B
C
D
E
F
G
H
I
J
K
L
M
N
O
P
Q
R
S
T
U
V
W
X
Y
Z

kosher (say **koh**-sher) adjective
kosher food is food prepared according to Jewish religious law

kung fu (say kuung-**foo**) noun
kung fu is a Chinese method of self-defence rather like karate

L
short for **learner**

label noun labels
a piece of paper, cloth, or metal fixed on or beside something to show what it is or to give other information about it such as its price
label verb labels, labelling, labelled
to label something is to put a label on it

laboratory (say la-**bo**-ra-ter-i) noun laboratories
a room or building equipped for scientific work

laborious adjective
needing a lot of effort; very hard

labour noun
1 labour is hard work 2 labour is also the movements of a woman's womb when a baby is born **Labour** the Labour Party, a socialist political party

labourer noun labourers
someone who does hard work with their hands, especially outdoors

Labrador noun Labradors
a large black or light-brown dog

laburnum noun laburnums
a tree with hanging yellow flowers

labyrinth noun labyrinths
a complicated set of passages or paths; a maze *McDougal's cave was but a vast*

labyrinth of crooked aisles that ran into each other and out again and led nowhere.
– Mark Twain, *The Adventures of Tom Sawyer*

lace noun laces
1 lace is thin material with decorative patterns of holes in it 2 a lace is a piece of thin cord used to tie up a shoe or boot
lacy adjective
lace verb laces, lacing, laced
1 to lace up a shoe or boot is to fasten it with a lace 2 to lace a drink is to add strong spirits to it

lack noun
there is a lack of something when there is not any of it or there is not enough of it *The trip was cancelled because of lack of interest.*
lack verb lacks, lacking, lacked
to lack something is to be without it *He lacks courage.*

lacquer noun
lacquer is a kind of varnish

lacrosse noun
lacrosse is a game using a stick with a net on it (called a *crosse*) to catch and throw a ball

lad noun lads
a boy or young man

ladder noun ladders
1 a device to help you climb up or down something, made of upright pieces of wood, metal, or rope with steps called rungs across them 2 a run of damaged stitches in tights or a stocking

laden adjective
carrying a heavy load

ladle noun ladles
a large deep spoon with a long handle, which you use for serving soup or other liquids

lady noun ladies
1 a polite name for a woman
2 a well-mannered woman, or a woman of high social standing **Lady** the title of a noblewoman

ladybird to landing

ladybird noun ladybirds
a small flying beetle, usually red with black spots

ladylike adjective
polite and quiet, as a lady is supposed to be *'No, thank you,' said Sylvia, in as ladylike a tone as she could muster. 'I never touch chocolate.'* – Joan Aiken, *The Wolves of Willoughby Chase*

ladyship noun
a title for a woman of high social standing

lag[1] verb lags, lagging, lagged
to lag is to go too slowly and not keep up with others *The little boy was lagging behind.*

lag[2] verb lags, lagging, lagged
to lag pipes or boilers is to wrap them with insulating material to keep in the heat

lager (say **lah**-ger) noun lagers
a light beer

lagoon noun lagoons
a lake separated from the sea by banks of sand or reefs

laid
past tense and past participle of lay[1] *Doug laid a hand on the boy's shoulder. My brother had laid the table.*

lain
past participle of lie[1] *She had lain awake all night.*

lair noun lairs
the place where a wild animal lives

lake noun lakes
a large area of water completely surrounded by land

lama noun lamas
a Buddhist priest or monk in Tibet and Mongolia

lamb noun lambs
1 a lamb is a young sheep **2** lamb is the meat from young sheep

lame adjective lamer, lamest
1 not able to walk normally **2** weak and not very convincing *What a lame excuse.* **lamely** adverb

lament verb laments, lamenting, lamented
to lament something is to express grief or disappointment about it **lamentation** noun

lament noun laments
a song or poem that expresses grief or regret

laminated adjective
1 made of layers joined together **2** permanently covered in a kind of plastic for protection

lamp noun lamps
a device for producing light from electricity, gas, or oil

lamp-post noun lamp-posts
a tall post in a street or public place, with a lamp at the top

lampshade noun lampshades
a cover for the bulb of an electric lamp, to soften the light

lance noun lances
a long spear

lance corporal noun lance corporals
a soldier between a private and a corporal in rank

land noun lands
1 land or the land is all the dry parts of the world's surface **2** land is an area of ground **3** a land is a country or nation

land verb lands, landing, landed
1 to land is to come down to the ground from the air *Where did the arrow land?* **2** to land is also to arrive in a ship or aircraft **3** to land someone or something is to bring them to a place by means of a ship or aircraft **4** (informal) to land someone in difficulty or trouble is to cause them difficulty or trouble **to land up** (informal) is to get to a particular place or situation *They landed up in France.*

landing noun landings
the floor at the top of a flight of stairs

a b c d e f g h i j k l m n o p q r s t u v w x y z

287

landlady noun landladies
1 a woman who lets rooms to lodgers
2 a woman who looks after a pub

landlord noun landlords
1 a person who rents a house or land to someone else, or lets rooms to lodgers
2 a person who looks after a pub

landmark noun landmarks
an object on land that you can easily see from a distance

landowner noun landowners
a person who owns a large amount of land

landscape noun landscapes
1 a view of a particular area of town or countryside 2 a picture of the countryside

landslide noun landslides
1 a landslide is when earth or rocks slide down the side of a hill 2 a landslide is also an overwhelming victory in an election

lane noun lanes
1 a narrow road, especially in the country
2 a strip of road for a single line of traffic
3 a strip of track or water for one runner or swimmer in a race

language noun languages
1 language is the use of words in speech and writing 2 a language is the words used in a particular country or by a particular group of people 3 a language is also a system of signs or symbols giving information, especially in computing

lanky adjective lankier, lankiest
tall and thin

lantern noun lanterns
a transparent case for holding a light and shielding it from the wind

lap¹ noun laps
1 the flat area from the waist to the knees, formed when a person is sitting down
2 going once round a racecourse

lap verb laps, lapping, lapped
to lap someone in a race is to be more than one lap ahead of them

lap² verb laps, lapping, lapped
1 to lap liquid is to drink it with the tongue, as a cat or dog does 2 waves lap when they make a gentle splash on rocks or the shore

lapel (say la-**pel**) noun lapels
the flap folded back at each front edge of a coat or jacket

lapse noun lapses
1 a slight mistake or fault 2 the passing of time *After a lapse of three months work began again.*

lapse verb lapses, lapsing, lapsed
1 to lapse into a state is to pass gradually into it *He lapsed into unconsciousness.* 2 a contract or document lapses when it is no longer valid *My passport has lapsed.*

laptop noun laptops
a computer small enough to be held and used on your lap

lapwing noun lapwings
a black and white bird with a crest on its head and a shrill cry

larch noun larches
a tall deciduous tree that produces small cones

lard noun
lard is white greasy fat from pigs, used in cooking

larder noun larders
a cupboard or small room for storing food

large adjective larger, largest
more than the ordinary or average size; big
to be at large is to be free and dangerous *The escaped prisoners were still at large.*
largeness noun

largely adverb
mainly; mostly *His success is largely a matter of hard work.*

lark¹ noun larks
a small sandy-brown bird; a skylark

lark² noun larks (informal)
something amusing; a bit of fun *They just did it for a lark.*

lark verb larks, larking, larked
to lark about is to have fun or play tricks

larva noun larvae
an insect in the first stage of its life, after it comes out of the egg

lasagne (say la-**zan**-ya) noun
lasagne is pasta in the form of flat sheets, cooked with minced meat or vegetables and a white sauce

laser (say **lay**-zer) noun lasers
a device that makes a very strong narrow beam of light

lash noun lashes
1 an eyelash 2 a stroke with a whip
lash verb lashes, lashing, lashed
1 to lash someone or something is to hit them with a whip or like a whip *Rain lashed the window.* 2 to lash something is to tie it tightly *During the storm they lashed the boxes to the mast.* **to lash out** is to speak or hit out angrily

lass noun lasses
a girl or young woman

lasso (say la-**soo**) noun lassos
a rope with a loop at the end which tightens when you pull the rope, used for catching cattle

last[1] adjective
1 coming after all the others; final *Try not to miss the last bus.* 2 most recent or latest *Where were you last night?* **the last straw** a final or added thing that makes a problem unbearable
last adverb
at the end; after everything or everyone else *He came last in the race.*
last noun
a person or thing that is last *I think I was the last to arrive.* **at last** finally; at the end

last[2] verb lasts, lasting, lasted
1 to continue *The journey lasts for two hours.* 2 to go on without being used up *How long will our supplies last?*

lastly adverb
in the last place; finally

latch noun latches
a small bar fastening a gate or door

late adjective, adverb later, latest
1 after the proper or expected time 2 near the end of a period of time *They came late in the afternoon.* 3 recent *Do you have the latest news?* 4 no longer alive *They saw the tomb of the late king.* **lateness** noun

lately adverb
recently *She has been very tired lately.*

latent (say **lay**-tent) adjective
existing but not yet active, developed, or visible

lateral adjective
to do with the sides of something

lathe (say layth) noun lathes
a machine for holding and turning pieces of wood or metal while you shape them

lather noun lathers
the thick foam you get when you mix soap with water

Latin noun
Latin is the language of the ancient Romans.

latitude noun latitudes
1 the distance of a place north or south of the equator, measured in degrees 2 freedom to do what you want or make decisions

latter adjective
later *We'd like a holiday in the latter part of the year.* **the latter** the second of two people or things just mentioned *If it's a choice between a picnic or a swim I prefer the latter.*

 TOP TIPS
Some words are used in pairs, such as latter and former.

latterly adverb
recently

lattice noun lattices
a framework of crossed strips with spaces between

laugh verb laughs, laughing, laughed
to laugh is to make sounds that show you

a
b
c
d
e
f
g
h
i
j
k
l
m
n
o
p
q
r
s
t
u
v
w
x
y
z

A
B
C
D
E
F
G
H
I
J
K
L
M
N
O
P
Q
R
S
T
U
V
W
X
Y
Z

are happy or that you think something is funny

laugh noun laughs
1 the sound you make when you laugh 2 (informal) something that is fun or amusing *Yesterday's party was quite a laugh.*

laughable adjective
silly and deserving to be laughed at

laughter noun
laughter is laughing or the sound of laughing

launch¹ verb launches, launching, launched
1 to launch a ship is to send it into the water for the first time 2 to launch a rocket is to send it into space 3 to launch a new idea or product is to make it available for the first time

launch noun launches
the launching of a ship or spacecraft

launch² noun launches
a large motor boat

launch pad noun launch pads
a platform from which rockets are sent into space

launder verb launders, laundering, laundered
to launder clothes is to wash and iron them

launderette noun launderettes
a shop with washing machines that people pay to use

laundry noun laundries
1 laundry is clothes to be washed 2 a laundry is a place where clothes are sent or taken to be washed and ironed

laurel noun laurels
an evergreen bush with smooth shiny leaves

lava noun
lava is molten rock that flows from a volcano, or the solid rock formed when it cools

lavatory noun lavatories
a toilet

lavender noun
1 lavender is a shrub with pale purple flowers that smell very sweet 2 a pale purple colour

lavish adjective
1 generous *They are lavish with their gifts.* 2 plentiful *What a lavish meal!*

law noun laws
1 a rule or set of rules that everyone must keep 2 something that always happens, for example the law of gravity

law court noun law courts
a room or building where a judge and jury or magistrates decide whether someone has broken the law

lawful adjective
allowed or accepted by the law
lawfully adverb

lawless adjective
a lawless place does not have any proper laws *It was a lawless country.*

lawn noun lawns
an area of mown grass in a garden

lawnmower noun lawnmowers
a machine with revolving blades for cutting grass

lawsuit noun lawsuits
a dispute or claim that is brought to a law court to be settled

lawyer noun lawyers
a person whose job is to help people with the law

lax adjective
not strict; tolerant *Discipline was very lax.*

lay¹ verb lays, laying, laid
1 to lay something somewhere is to put it down in a particular place or in a particular way 2 to lay a table is to arrange things on it for a meal 3 to lay an egg is to produce it 4 to lay plans is to form or prepare them
to lay someone off is to stop employing them **to lay something on** is to supply or provide it

lay²
past tense of lie¹ *Tom lay in his sleeping bag.*

layer noun layers
something flat that lies on or under something else *The cake had a layer of icing on top and a layer of jam inside.*

layman noun laymen
a person who does not have special knowledge of a subject

layout noun layouts
the arrangement or design of something

laze verb lazes, lazing, lazed
to laze is to spend time in a lazy way

lazy adjective lazier, laziest
not wanting to work; doing as little as possible **lazily** adverb **laziness** noun

lb.
short for **pound** or **pounds** in weight

l.b.w.
short for *leg before wicket*

lead¹ (say leed) verb leads, leading, led
1 to lead a person or animal is to guide them, especially by going in front 2 to lead an activity is to be in charge of it 3 to lead in a race or contest is to be winning it 4 a road or path leads somewhere when it goes in that direction *This road leads to the beach.* **to lead to something** is to cause it *Their carelessness led to the accident.*

lead (say leed) noun leads
1 the first or front place or position *Who's in the lead now?* 2 help or guidance *Just follow my lead.* 3 a strap or cord for leading a dog 4 an electric wire *Don't trip over that lead.*

lead² (say led) noun leads
1 lead is a soft heavy grey metal 2 a lead is the writing substance (graphite) in the middle of a pencil

leader noun leaders
1 someone who leads or is in charge 2 an article in a newspaper, giving the editor's opinion **leadership** noun

leaf noun leaves
1 a flat and usually green growth on a tree or plant, growing from its stem 2 a page of a book **to turn over a new leaf** is to make a fresh start and improve your behaviour **leafy** adjective

leaflet noun leaflets
a piece of paper printed with information

league (say leeg) noun leagues
1 a group of teams that play matches against each other 2 a group of countries that have agreed to work together for a particular reason **to be in league with someone** is to work or plot together

leak noun leaks
1 a hole or crack through which liquid or gas escapes 2 the revealing of some secret information

leak verb leaks, leaking, leaked
1 something leaks when it lets something out through a hole or crack *The sink is leaking.* 2 liquid or gas leaks out when it escapes from a container 3 to leak secret information is to reveal it **leakage** noun

lean¹ verb leans, leaning, leaned or leant
1 to lean is to bend your body towards something or over it 2 to lean something is to put it into a sloping position *Do not lean bicycles against the window.* 3 to lean against something is to rest against it

lean² adjective leaner, leanest
1 lean meat has little fat 2 a lean person is thin

leap noun leaps
1 a high or long jump 2 a sudden increase or advance

leap verb leaps, leaping, leapt or leaped
1 to leap is to jump high or a long way 2 to leap is also to increase or advance suddenly

leapfrog noun
a game in which each player jumps with

legs apart over another player who is bending down

leap year noun leap years
a year with an extra day in it, on 29 February

learn verb learns, learning, learnt or learned
1 to learn something is to find out about it and gain knowledge or skill in it *She's learning to play the guitar.* **2** to learn something is to discover some news *I was sorry to learn that he was ill.*

learned (say **ler**-nid) adjective
clever and knowledgeable

learner noun learners
someone who is learning something, for example how to drive a car

learning noun
learning is knowledge you get by studying

lease noun leases
an agreement to let someone use a building or land for a fixed period in return for a payment **a new lease of life** is a chance to go on being active or useful

leash noun leashes
a strap or cord for leading a dog

least determiner, adverb
less than all the others *I get the least pocket money. I like this one least.*

least pronoun
the smallest amount *I got the least.* **at least**
1 not less than what is mentioned *It will cost at least £50.* **2** anyway *He's at home; at least I think he is.*

leather noun leathers
leather is a strong material made from animals' skins

leave verb leaves, leaving, left
1 to leave a person, place, or group is to go away from them **2** to leave something is to let it stay where it is or remain as it is *You can leave your bags by the door.* **3** to leave something to someone is to give it to them in a will **to leave something** or **someone out** is not to include them **to be left over**

is to remain when other things have been used

leave noun
permission, especially to be away from work

leaves
plural of leaf

lectern noun lecterns
a stand to hold a Bible or other large book from which you read

lecture noun lectures
1 a talk about a subject to an audience or a class **2** a long or serious warning given to someone *We got a lecture about closing the windows.*

lecture verb lectures, lecturing, lectured
to lecture is to give a lecture **lecturer** noun

led
past tense and past participle of lead[1] verb
He led the way in to the cave. One thing had led to another.

ledge noun ledges
a narrow shelf

lee noun
the sheltered side of something, away from the wind

leek noun leeks
a long green and white vegetable like an onion with broad leaves

leer verb leers, leering, leered
to leer at someone is to look at them in an unpleasant or evil way

leeward adjective
facing away from the wind

left[1] adjective, adverb
1 on or towards the west if you think of yourself as facing north **2** in favour of political and social change

left noun
the left side

left[2]
past tense and past participle of leave verb
The train left at 2 o'clock. Mum had left the door open for us.

left-hand adjective
on the left side of something

left-handed adjective
using the left hand more than the right hand

leftovers plural noun
food that has not been eaten by the end of a meal

leg noun legs
1 one of the parts of a human's or animal's body on which they stand or move **2** one of the parts of a pair of trousers that cover your legs **3** each of the supports of a chair or other piece of furniture **4** one part of a journey **5** each of a pair of matches between the same teams in a competition

legacy noun legacies
something given to someone in a will

legal adjective
1 allowed by the law **2** to do with the law or lawyers **legally** adverb

legalize verb legalizes, legalizing, legalized
to legalize something is to make it legal

legend (say lej-end) noun legends
an old story handed down from the past

legendary adjective
1 mentioned in legends *the legendary knight Sir Galahad* **2** very famous *His football ability is legendary.*

legible adjective
clear enough to read *Make sure your writing is legible.*

legion noun legions
1 a division of the ancient Roman army **2** a group of soldiers, or men who used to be soldiers

legislate verb legislates, legislating, legislated
to legislate is to make laws **legislation** noun

legitimate (say li-**jit**-i-mat) adjective
1 allowed by a law or rule **2** (old use) born of parents who were married to each other

leisure noun
leisure is free time, when you can do what you like **to do something at leisure** is to do it without hurrying

leisurely adjective
done with plenty of time, without hurrying *They took a leisurely stroll down to the river.*

lemon noun lemons
1 a yellow citrus fruit with a sour taste **2** a pale yellow colour

lemonade noun lemonades
a drink with a lemon flavour

lend verb lends, lending, lent
1 to lend something to someone is to let them have it for a short time **2** when a bank lends someone money it gives them money which they must pay back plus an extra amount called interest **to lend a hand** is to help someone

length noun lengths
1 how long something is **2** a piece of something cut from a longer piece, for example rope, wire, or cloth **3** the distance of a swimming pool from one end to the other **at length** after a while; eventually

 TOP TIPS
Keep it quiet! There is a silent **g** in **length**.

lengthen verb lengthens, lengthening, lengthened
1 to lengthen something is to make it longer **2** to lengthen is to become longer

lengthways or **lengthwise** adverb
from end to end; along the longest part of something *Slice the carrots lengthways.*

lengthy adjective lengthier, lengthiest
going on for a long time *He gave a lengthy speech.*

lenient (say **lee**-ni-ent) adjective
not as strict as expected, especially when punishing someone

lens

light rays

object

image

lens

film

lens noun lenses
1 a curved piece of glass or plastic used to focus images of things, or to concentrate light **2** the transparent part of the eye, behind the pupil

Lent noun
Lent is a period of about six weeks before Easter when some Christians give up something they enjoy.

lent
past tense and past participle of **lend** *My sister lent me her dress for the party. Dad had lent him £5 yesterday.*

lentil noun lentils
a kind of small bean

leopard (say **lep**-erd) noun leopards
a large spotted wild animal of the cat family

leotard (say **lee**-o-tard) noun leotards
a close-fitting piece of clothing worn by acrobats and dancers

leper noun lepers
someone who has leprosy

leprosy noun
leprosy is an infectious disease that affects the skin and nerves, and causes parts of the body to waste away

less determiner, adverb
smaller; not so much *Make less noise. It hurts less now.*

less pronoun
a smaller amount *I have less than you.*

less preposition
minus; deducting *I have three pounds, less the pound I owe my brother.*

–less suffix
forming adjectives meaning 'lacking something' or 'free from something', such as *smokeless* and *useless*

lessen verb lessens, lessening, lessened
1 to lessen something is to make it smaller or not so much **2** to lessen is to become smaller or not so much

lesser adjective
smaller or less great *The high king ruled over the lesser kings.*

lesson noun lessons
1 the time when someone is teaching you **2** something that you have to learn **3** a passage from the Bible read aloud as part of a church service

lest conjunction (old use)
so that something should not happen *He ran away lest he should be seen.*

let verb lets, letting, let
1 to let someone do something is to allow them to do it 2 to let something happen is to cause it or not prevent it *Don't let your bike slide into the ditch.* 3 to let a house or room or building is to allow someone to use it in return for payment 4 to let someone in or out is to allow them to go in or out **to let on** (informal) is to reveal a secret *If I tell you, don't let on.* **to let someone down** is to disappoint them **to let someone off** is to excuse them from a punishment or duty **to let something off** is to make it explode **to let up** is to relax or do less work

lethal adjective
something that is lethal can kill you

let's verb (informal)
shall we? *Let's go to the park.*

letter noun letters
1 one of the symbols used for writing words, such as *a*, *b*, or *c* 2 a written message sent to another person

letter box noun letter boxes
a box or slot into which letters are delivered or posted

lettering noun
lettering is letters drawn or painted

lettuce noun lettuces
a green vegetable with crisp leaves used in salads

leukaemia (say lew-**kee**-mi-a) noun
leukaemia is a disease in which there are too many white cells in the blood

level adjective
1 flat or horizontal *The ground is level near the house.* 2 at the same height or position *Are these pictures level?*

level verb levels, levelling, levelled
1 to level something is to make it flat or horizontal 2 to level, or to level out, is to become horizontal 3 to level a gun at a target is to aim it

level noun levels
1 height or position *Fix the shelf at eye level.* 2 a standard or grade of achievement *She has reached level 3 in gymnastics.* 3 a device that shows if something is horizontal 4 a flat or horizontal surface

level crossing noun level crossings
a place where a road crosses a railway at the same level

lever noun levers
a bar that is pushed or pulled to lift something heavy, force something open, or make a machine work

liability noun liabilities
1 liability is being responsible for something 2 a liability is also a disadvantage or handicap

liable adjective
1 likely to do or get something *Loud noises are liable to upset her. Parking on the yellow lines makes you liable to a fine.* 2 responsible for something *The company is not liable for damage during delivery.*

liar noun liars
someone who tells lies

liberal adjective
1 tolerant of other people's point of view 2 generous *She is liberal with her money.* **Liberal** a supporter of the Liberal Party, now part of the Liberal Democrats **liberally** adverb in large amounts or generously *Pour the cream on liberally.*

liberate verb liberates, liberating, liberated
to liberate someone is to set them free **liberation** noun

liberty noun liberties
liberty is freedom **to take liberties** is to behave too casually or informally

librarian noun librarians
someone who looks after a library or works in one

library noun libraries
a place where books are kept for people to use or borrow

lice
plural of louse

a
b
c
d
e
f
g
h
i
j
k
l
m
n
o
p
q
r
s
t
u
v
w
x
y
z

licence noun licences
an official document allowing someone to do or use or own something

license verb licenses, licensing, licensed
to license someone to do something is to give them a licence to do it *The ship was not licensed to carry passengers.*

lichen (say ly-ken) noun lichens
a dry-looking plant that grows on rocks, walls, trees, and other surfaces

lick verb licks, licking, licked
1 to lick something is to move your tongue over it 2 (informal) to lick someone is to defeat them

lick noun licks
the act of moving your tongue over something

lid noun lids
1 a cover for a box or jar 2 an eyelid

lie[1] verb lies, lying, lay, lain
1 to lie is to be in or get into a flat position, especially to rest with your body flat as it is in bed *He lay on the grass. The cat has lain here all night.* 2 to lie is also to be or remain a certain way *The castle was lying in ruins. The valley lay before us.* **to lie low** is to keep yourself hidden

lie[2] verb lies, lying, lied
to lie is to say something that you know is not true

lie noun lies
something you say that you know is not true

lieutenant (say lef-ten-ant) noun lieutenants
an officer in the army or navy

life noun lives
1 a person's or animal's life is the time between their birth and death 2 life is being alive and able to grow 3 life is also all living things *Is there life on Mars?* 4 life is also liveliness *She is full of life.* 5 the life of a famous person is the story of what they have done

lifebelt noun lifebelts
a large ring that will float, used to support someone's body in water

lifeboat noun lifeboats
a boat for rescuing people at sea

life cycle noun life cycles
the series of changes in the life of a living thing *The diagram shows the life cycle of a frog.*

lifeguard noun lifeguards
someone whose job is to rescue swimmers who are in difficulty

life jacket noun life jackets
a jacket of material that will float, used to support a person in water

lifeless adjective
1 without life 2 unconscious

lifelike adjective
looking exactly like a real person or thing

lifelong adjective
lasting throughout someone's life

lifespan noun lifespans
how long a person or animal or plant lives

lifestyle noun lifestyles
the way of life of a person or a group of people

lifetime noun lifetimes
the period of time during which someone is alive

lift verb lifts, lifting, lifted
1 to lift something is to pick it up or move it to a higher position 2 to lift is to rise or go upwards

lift noun lifts
1 a movement upwards 2 a device for taking people or goods from one floor to another in a building 3 a ride in someone else's car or other vehicle

lift-off noun lift-offs
when a rocket or spacecraft takesoff

light[1] noun lights
1 light is the form of energy that makes things visible, the opposite of darkness

There was not enough light to see the garden.
2 a light is something that provides light or a flame, especially an electric lamp *Switch on the light.*

light adjective **lighter, lightest**
1 full of light; not dark **2** pale *The house was painted light blue.*

light verb **lights, lighting, lit or lighted**
1 to light something is to start it burning **2** to light is to begin to burn *The fire won't light.* **3** to light a place is to give it light *The streets were lit by gas lamps.* **to light up** is to become bright with lights **to light something up** is to make it bright with lights

light² adjective **lighter, lightest**
1 not heavy; weighing little **2** not large or strong *There is a light wind.* **3** not needing much effort *They were doing some light work in the garden.* **4** pleasant and entertaining rather than serious *We prefer light music.* **lightly** adverb gently or only a little *It began to snow lightly.*

lighten verb **lightens, lightening, lightened**
1 to lighten something is to make it lighter or brighter **2** to lighten is to become lighter

lighter noun **lighters**
a device for lighting something like a cigarette or a fire

light-hearted adjective
1 cheerful; free from worry **2** not serious **light-heartedly** adverb **light-heartedness** noun

lighthouse noun **lighthouses**
a tower with a bright light at the top to guide ships and warn them of danger

lighting noun
lighting is lamps or the light they provide

lightning noun
lightning is a flash of bright light in the sky during a thunderstorm

lightning conductor noun
lightning conductors
a metal wire or rod fixed on a building to divert lightning into the earth

lightweight adjective
less than average weight

light year noun **light years**
the distance that light travels in one year (about 9.5 million million kilometres or 6 million million miles)

like¹ verb **likes, liking, liked**
to like someone or something is to think they are pleasant or satisfactory **should like or would like** to want *I should like to see him.*

like² preposition
1 resembling; similar to; in the manner of *He cried like a baby.* **2** such as *We need things like knives and forks.* **3** typical of *It was like her to forgive him.*

likeable adjective
pleasant and easy to like

likely adjective **likelier, likeliest**
probable; expected to happen or to be true or suitable *It's likely that it will rain this afternoon.*

liken verb **likens, likening, likened**
to liken one thing to another is to compare them or show that they are similar

likeness noun **likenesses**
a resemblance

likewise adverb
similarly; in the same way

liking noun **likings**
a feeling that you like something or someone *She has a great liking for chocolate.*

lilac noun **lilacs**
1 lilac is a bush with sweet-smelling purple or white flowers **2** a pale purple colour

lily noun **lilies**
a trumpet-shaped flower grown from a bulb

limb noun **limbs**
a leg, arm, or wing

limber verb **limbers, limbering, limbered**
to limber up is to do exercises to be ready for a sport or athletic activity

lime¹ noun limes
a green fruit like a small round lemon

lime² noun limes
a tree with yellow blossom

lime³ noun
lime is a white chalky powder (calcium oxide) used in making cement or as a fertilizer

limelight noun
to be in the limelight is to get a lot of publicity and attention

limerick (say **lim**-er-ik) noun limericks
an amusing poem with five lines and a strong rhythm

limestone noun
limestone is rock from which lime (calcium oxide) is made, used in building and in making cement

limit noun limits
1 a line or point that you cannot or should not pass *You must obey the speed limit.* 2 a line or edge where something ends *The white line marks the limit of the road.*

limit verb limits, limiting, limited
to limit something or someone is to keep them within a limit *You are limited to one choice each.* **limitation** noun a thing that stops something or someone from going beyond a certain point

limited adjective
kept within limits; not great *The choice was limited.*

limp¹ verb limps, limping, limped
to limp is to walk with difficulty because something is wrong with your leg or foot
limp noun limps
a limping movement

limp² adjective limper, limpest
not stiff or firm; without much strength *He gave me a limp handshake.* **limply** adverb

limpet noun limpets
a small shellfish that attaches itself firmly to rocks

line¹ noun lines
1 a long thin mark made on a surface 2 a row or series of people or things 3 a length of something long and thin like rope, string, or wire 4 a number of words together in a play, film, poem, or song 5 a railway or a length of railway track 6 a company operating a transport service of ships, aircraft, or buses 7 a way of working or behaving; a type of business *What line are you in?* **in line** 1 forming a straight line 2 obeying or behaving well

line verb lines, lining, lined
1 to line something is to mark it with lines 2 to line a place is to form an edge or border along it *People lined the streets to watch the race.* **to line up** is to form lines or rows *The children lined up in the playground.* **to line things up** is to set them up in a line or row

line² verb lines, lining, lined
to line material or a piece of clothing is to put a lining on it

line graph noun line graphs
a simple graph, using a line to show how two amounts are related

linen noun
1 linen is cloth made from flax, used to make shirts, sheets, tablecloths, and so on 2 linen is also things made of this cloth

liner noun liners
a large ship or aircraft, usually carrying passengers

linesman noun linesmen
an official in football, tennis, and other games who decides whether the ball has crossed a line

linger verb lingers, lingering, lingered
to linger is to stay for a long time or be slow to leave *The smell of her perfume lingered in the room.*

linguist noun linguists
an expert in languages, or someone who can speak several languages well
linguistic adjective to do with languages

lining noun linings
a layer of material covering the inside of something

link noun links
1 one of the rings in a chain 2 a connection between two things
link verb links, linking, linked
to link things is to join them together

lino noun
lino is linoleum

lint noun
lint is a soft material for covering wounds

lion noun lions
a large strong flesh-eating animal found in Africa and India

lioness noun lionesses
a female lion

lip noun lips
1 each of the two fleshy edges of the mouth 2 the edge of something hollow such as a cup or a crater 3 the pointed part at the top of a jug or saucepan, for pouring from

lip-read verb lip-reads, lip-reading, lip-read
to lip-read is to understand what someone is saying by watching the movements of their lips, not by hearing their voice

lipstick noun lipsticks
a stick of a waxy substance for colouring the lips

liquid noun liquids
a substance (such as water or oil) that can flow but is not a gas
liquid adjective
in the form of a liquid; flowing freely

liquidizer noun liquidizers
a device for making food into a pulp or a liquid

liquor (say lik-er) noun liquors
liquor is alcoholic drink

liquorice (say lik-er-iss) noun
liquorice is a soft black sweet with a strong taste, which comes from the root of a plant

lisp noun lisps
a fault in speaking, in which s and z are pronounced like th
lisp verb lisps, lisping, lisped
to lisp is to speak with a lisp

list¹ noun lists
a number of names or figures or items written or printed one after another
list verb lists, listing, listed
to list things is to write or say them one after another

list² verb lists, listing, listed
a ship lists when it leans over to one side in the water

listen verb listens, listening, listened
to listen to someone or something is to pay attention so that you can hear them *Listen to me. I like listening to music.* **listener** noun

listless adjective
too tired to be active or enthusiastic
listlessly adverb

lit
past tense and past participle of light¹
verb *His face lit up. Emil had lit three large candles.*

literacy (say lit-er-a-si) noun
literacy is the ability to read and write

literal adjective
1 meaning exactly what it says 2 word for word *Write out a literal translation.*

literally adverb
really; exactly as stated *The noise made me literally jump out of my seat.*

literary (say lit-er-er-i) adjective
to do with literature; interested in literature

literate (say lit-er-at) adjective
able to read and write

literature noun
literature is books or writing, especially the best or most famous

a
b
c
d
e
f
g
h
i
j
k
l
m
n
o
p
q
r
s
t
u
v
w
x
y
z

---

litre (say **lee**-ter) noun litres
a measure of liquid, 1,000 cubic centimetres or about 1¾ pints

litter noun litters
1 litter is rubbish or untidy things left lying about 2 a litter is a number of young animals born to one mother at one time

litter verb litters, littering, littered
to litter a place is to make it untidy with litter

little adjective, determiner less, least
1 small; not great or not much *She brought a little boy. We have very little time.* 2 a small amount of something *Have a little sugar.*
little by little gradually

little noun
a small amount

little adverb
hardly or not at all

live[1] (rhymes with **give**) verb lives, living, lived
1 to live is to be alive 2 to live in a particular place is to have your home there *She is living in Glasgow.* 3 to live in a certain way is to pass your life in that way *He lived as a hermit.* **to live on something** is to have it as food or income *The islanders lived mainly on fish. No one can live on £50 a week.*

live[2] (rhymes with **hive**) adjective
1 alive 2 carrying electricity 3 broadcast while it is actually happening, not from a recording

livelihood (say **lyv**-li-huud) noun livelihoods
a person's livelihood is the way in which they earn a living

lively adjective livelier, liveliest
cheerful and full of life and energy
liveliness noun

TOP TIPS
There is no adverb *livelily*, because it would be too difficult to say!

liver noun livers
1 a large organ in the body that produces bile and helps keep the blood clean 2 an animal's liver used as food

lives
plural of life

livestock noun
livestock is farm animals

livid adjective
1 very angry 2 of a dark blue-grey colour, like bruised skin

living noun livings
1 the way that a person lives *They have a good standard of living.* 2 a means of earning money *What do you do for a living?*

living room noun living rooms
a room for sitting and relaxing in

lizard noun lizards
a reptile with a scaly skin, four legs, and a long tail

llama (say **lah**-ma) noun llamas
a South American animal with woolly fur

load noun loads
1 something that is being carried 2 an amount that can be carried 3 (informal) a large amount *It's a load of nonsense.*

load verb loads, loading, loaded
1 to load something is to put things into it so they can be carried *I'll go and load the back of the car.* 2 to load someone with something is to give them large amounts of it *They loaded him with gifts.* 3 to load a gun is to put a bullet or shell into it 4 to load a machine is to put something into it, such as dishes in a dishwasher 5 to load a computer is to enter programs or data on it 6 to load dice is to put a weight into them to make them fall in a special way

loaf[1] noun loaves
a shaped mass of bread baked in one piece

loaf[2] verb loafs, loafing, loafed
to loaf or loaf about is to loiter or waste time

loam noun
loam is rich fertile soil

loan noun loans
something that has been lent to someone,

especially money **on loan** being lent *The books are on loan from the library.*

loan verb loans, loaning, loaned
to loan something is to lend it

loath (rhymes with **both**) adjective
unwilling *I was loath to go.*

loathe (rhymes with **clothe**) verb loathes, loathing, loathed
to loathe something or someone is to dislike them very much

loathsome adjective
making you feel disgusted; horrible *'Now you've done it, you loathsome pest!' whispered the Earthworm to the Centipede.* — Roald Dahl, *James and the Giant Peach*

loaves
plural of loaf¹

lob verb lobs, lobbing, lobbed
to lob something is to throw or hit it high into the air

lobby noun lobbies
an entrance hall

lobby verb lobbies, lobbying, lobbied
to lobby politicians or officials is to try to influence them or persuade them of something

lobe noun lobes
the rounded part at the bottom of the ear

lobster noun lobsters
a large shellfish with eight legs and two claws

local adjective
1 belonging to a particular place or area *Where is your local library?* 2 affecting a certain part of the body *You'll need a local anaesthetic.* **locally** adverb to live or shop locally is to do so nearby, in the area where you are

local noun locals (informal)
1 a local is someone who lives in a particular district 2 someone's local is the pub nearest their home

locality noun localities
a place and the area that surrounds it

locate verb locates, locating, located
1 to locate something is to discover where it is *I have located the fault.* 2 to be located in a place is to be situated there *The cinema is located in the High Street.*

location noun locations
the place where something is *What is the exact location of the submarine?* when a film is filmed **on location** it is filmed in natural surroundings, not in a studio

loch noun lochs
a lake in Scotland

lock¹ noun locks
1 a fastening that is opened with a key or other device 2 a section of a canal or river with gates at each end, so that the level of water can be raised or lowered to allow boats to pass from one level to another 3 the distance that a vehicle's front wheels can turn **lock, stock, and barrel** completely

lock verb locks, locking, locked
1 to lock a door or window or lid is to fasten or secure it with a lock 2 to lock something somewhere is to put it in a safe place that can be fastened with a lock 3 to lock is to become fixed in one place, or to jam

lock² noun locks
a few strands of hair formed into a loop

locker noun lockers
a small cupboard for keeping things safe, often in a changing room

locket noun lockets
a small case holding a photograph or lock of hair, worn on a chain round the neck

locomotive noun locomotives
a railway engine

locust noun locusts
an insect like a large grasshopper, which flies in swarms that eat all the plants in an area

lodge noun lodges
1 a small house 2 a room or small house at the entrance to a large house or building

a
b
c
d
e
f
g
h
i
j
k
l
m
n
o
p
q
r
s
t
u
v
w
x
y
z

A
B
C
D
E
F
G
H
I
J
K
L
M
N
O
P
Q
R
S
T
U
V
W
X
Y
Z

lodge verb lodges, lodging, lodged
1 to lodge is to become fixed or get stuck somewhere *The ball lodged in the branches.* 2 to lodge somewhere is to stay there as a lodger 3 to lodge someone is to give them a place to sleep **to lodge a complaint** is to make an official complaint

lodger noun lodgers
someone who pays to live in someone else's house

lodgings plural noun
a room or set of rooms that a person rents in someone else's house

loft noun lofts
the room or space under the roof of a house

lofty adjective loftier, loftiest
1 high or tall 2 noble and proud *They have lofty ideas.* **loftily** adverb in a proud, haughty way

log noun logs
1 a large piece of a tree that has fallen or been cut down 2 a detailed record of what happens each day, especially on a journey or voyage

log verb logs, logging, logged
to log information is to put it in a log **to log in** is to gain access to a computer **to log out** is to finish using a computer

logbook noun logbooks
a book in which a log of a voyage is kept

logic noun
logic is a system of thinking and working out ideas

logical adjective
using logic or worked out by logic **logically** adverb

logo noun logos
a printed symbol used by a business or other organization as its emblem

loiter verb loiters, loitering, loitered
to stand about not doing anything

loll verb lolls, lolling, lolled
to sit or lie in an untidy and lazy way

lollipop noun lollipops
a hard sticky sweet on the end of a stick

lollipop woman or lollipop man noun
lollipop women, lollipop men
an official who uses a circular sign on a stick to signal traffic to stop so that children can cross the road

lolly noun lollies (informal)
a lolly is a lollipop or an ice lolly

lone adjective
on its own; solitary *a lone rider*

lonely adjective lonelier, loneliest
1 unhappy because you are on your own 2 far from other inhabited places; not often used or visited *They passed through a lonely village.* **loneliness** noun

long¹ adjective longer, longest
1 big when measured from one end to the other *They walked up a long path.* 2 taking a lot of time *I'd like a long holiday.* 3 measuring from one end to the other *A cricket pitch is 22 yards long.*

long adverb longer, longest
1 for a long time *Have you been waiting long?* 2 a long time before or after *They left long ago.* **as long as** or **so long as** provided that; on condition that *I'll come as long as I can bring my dog.*

long² verb longs, longing, longed
to long for something is to want it very much *Matilda longed for her parents to be good and loving and understanding and honourable and intelligent.* — Roald Dahl, *Matilda*

long division noun
long division is dividing one number by another and writing down all the calculations

longitude (say long-i-tewd or lon-ji-tewd) noun longitudes
longitude is the distance of a place east or west, measured in degrees from an imaginary line that passes through Greenwich in London

long jump noun
an athletics contest of jumping as far as possible along the ground with one leap

long-range adjective
covering a long distance or period of time

long-sighted adjective
able to see things clearly when they are at a distance but not when they are close

long-term adjective
to do with a long period of time

loo noun loos (informal)
a toilet

look verb looks, looking, looked
1 to look is to use your eyes to see something, or to turn your eyes towards something 2 to look in a particular direction is to face it *Look right and left before you cross.* 3 to look (for example) happy or sad is to appear that way **to look after something** or **someone** is to protect them or take care of them **to look down on someone** is to despise them **to look for something** or **someone** is to try to find them **to look forward to something** is to be waiting eagerly for it to happen **to look out** is to be careful **to look up to someone** is to admire or respect them

look noun looks
1 a look is the act of looking *Take a look at this.* 2 the expression on someone's face *She gave me a surprised look.* 3 the look of someone or something is their appearance *I don't like the look of that dog.*

look-alike noun look-alikes
someone who looks very like a famous person

looking-glass noun looking-glasses (old use)
a glass mirror

lookout noun lookouts
1 a place from which you watch for something 2 someone whose job is to keep watch 3 watching or being watchful *Keep a lookout for snakes.* 4 (informal) something that is your lookout is your concern or problem *It's your lookout if you get hurt.*

loom[1] noun looms
a machine for weaving cloth

loom[2] verb looms, looming, loomed
to loom or loom up is to appear large and threatening *Then a monstrous three-headed hell-hound loomed up, lashing its snake tail, with serpent heads writhing all over its back.* – Francesca Simon, *Helping Hercules*

loop noun loops
the shape made by a curve crossing itself; a piece of string, ribbon, or wire made into this shape

loop verb loops, looping, looped
to loop something is to make it into a loop

loophole noun loopholes
1 a narrow opening 2 a way of getting round a law or rule without quite breaking it

loose adjective looser, loosest
1 not tight or firmly fixed *a loose tooth* 2 not tied up or shut in *The dog got loose.* **to be on the loose** is to be free after escaping **loosely** adverb **looseness** noun

loosen verb loosens, loosening, loosened
1 to loosen something is to make it loose 2 to loosen is to become loose

loot noun
loot is stolen things

loot verb loots, looting, looted
to loot a place is to rob it violently, especially during a war or riot **looter** noun

lopsided adjective
uneven, with one side lower than the other *She had a lopsided smile.*

lord noun lords
1 a nobleman, especially one who is allowed to use the title 'Lord' in front of his name 2 (old use) a master or ruler **Our Lord** a name used by Christians for Jesus Christ **the Lord** a name for God

lordly adjective
1 relating to a lord 2 proud; haughty

a b c d e f g h i j k l m n o p q r s t u v w x y z

303

Lord Mayor noun
the mayor of a large city

lordship noun
a title for a lord or a man of high social standing

lorry noun lorries
a large motor vehicle for carrying goods

lose verb loses, losing, lost
1 to lose something is to no longer have it, especially because you cannot find it *I've lost my hat.* 2 to lose a contest or game is to be beaten in it *We lost last Friday's match.* 3 a clock or watch loses when it gives a time that is earlier than the correct time **to lose your way** is not to know where you are
loser noun

loss noun losses
1 losing something 2 something you have lost **to be at a loss** is to be puzzled or unable to do something

lost
past tense and past participle of lose *She lost her balance and fell backwards. She realised she had lost her purse.*

lost adjective
1 not knowing where you are or not able to find your way *I think we're lost.* 2 missing or strayed *a lost dog*

lot noun lots
1 **a lot** is a large number of people or things 2 **a lot** can also mean very much *Thanks a lot.* 3 a lot is a piece of land 4 at an auction, a lot is one item or group of items for sale **to draw lots** is to choose one person or thing from a group by a method that depends on chance **the lot** or **the whole lot** everything

lotion noun lotions
a liquid that you put on your skin

lottery noun lotteries
a way of raising money by selling numbered tickets and giving prizes to people who have the winning tickets

lotto noun
lotto is a game like bingo

loud adjective louder, loudest
1 noisy; easily heard 2 bright or gaudy *The room was painted in loud colours.*
loudly adverb **loudness** noun

loudspeaker noun loudspeakers
a device that changes electrical impulses into sound, for reproducing music or voices

lounge noun lounges
a room in a house, hotel, or airport for sitting in and relaxing

lounge verb lounges, lounging, lounged
to lounge is to sit or stand in a relaxed or lazy way *Sirius was lounging in his chair at his ease, tilting it back on two legs.*
— J. K. Rowling, *Harry Potter and the Order of the Phoenix*

louse noun lice
a small insect that sucks the blood of animals or the juices of plants

lousy adjective lousier, lousiest
1 full of lice 2 (informal) very bad or unpleasant

lout noun louts
a bad-mannered man

lovable adjective
someone is lovable when they are easy to love

love noun loves
1 love is a feeling of liking someone or something very much; great affection or kindness 2 someone's love is a person or thing that they love 3 in a game such as tennis, love is a score of nothing **to be in love** is to love another person very deeply

love verb loves, loving, loved
to love someone or something is to like them very much

lovely adjective lovelier, loveliest
1 beautiful 2 (informal) very pleasant or enjoyable **loveliness** noun

lover noun lovers
someone who loves something *a music lover*

A
B
C
D
E
F
G
H
I
J
K
L
M
N
O
P
Q
R
S
T
U
V
W
X
Y
Z

loving adjective
feeling or showing love *a loving son, a loving look* **lovingly** adverb

low[1] adjective **lower, lowest**
1 only reaching a short way up; not high
2 below average in amount or importance *They are people of a low rank. Prices are low.*
3 unhappy *I'm feeling low.* 4 a low note is one at the bottom end of a musical scale **lowness** noun

low[2] verb **lows, lowing, lowed**
to low is to make a sound like a cow

lower verb **lowers, lowering, lowered**
to lower something is move it down

lower case noun
lower case is small letters, not capitals

lowland adjective
to do with the lowlands

lowlands plural noun
low-lying country, especially in the south of Scotland

lowly adjective **lowlier, lowliest**
humble **lowliness** noun

loyal adjective
always true to your friends; faithful **loyally** adverb **loyalty** noun

lozenge noun **lozenges**
1 a small sweet tablet, especially one that contains medicine
2 a diamond-shaped design

Ltd.
in names of companies, short for limited

lubricant noun **lubricants**
oil or grease for lubricating machinery

lubricate verb **lubricates, lubricating, lubricated**
to lubricate something like machinery is to put oil or grease on it so that it moves smoothly **lubrication** noun

lucid (say **loo**-sid) adjective
1 something is lucid when it is clear and easy to understand 2 someone is lucid when they are able to think clearly again after being ill

luck noun
1 luck is the way things happen by chance, without being planned 2 luck is also good fortune

luckily adverb
by a lucky chance; fortunately *Luckily it stayed warm all day.*

lucky adjective **luckier, luckiest**
having or bringing good luck

ludicrous (say loo-di-krus) adjective
extremely silly or absurd **ludicrously** adverb

ludo noun
ludo is a game played with dice and counters on a board

lug verb **lugs, lugging, lugged**
to lug something heavy is to carry it or drag it with difficulty

luggage noun
luggage is the suitcases and bags you take on a journey

lukewarm adjective
1 slightly warm 2 not very keen or enthusiastic *They got a lukewarm response.*

lull verb **lulls, lulling, lulled**
to lull someone is to soothe or calm them
lull noun **lulls**
a short period of quiet or rest *There was a lull in the fighting.*

lullaby noun **lullabies**
a song that you sing to send a baby to sleep

lumber noun
lumber is unwanted furniture or other things
lumber verb **lumbers, lumbering, lumbered**
1 to lumber is to move along clumsily and heavily *A shadow under the trees moved and came lumbering out into the sunlight towards us. A monkey, a giant monkey.* — Michael Morpurgo, *Kensuke's Kingdom* 2 (informal) to lumber someone is to leave them with something unpleasant or difficult to do

a
b
c
d
e
f
g
h
i
j
k
l
m
n
o
p
q
r
s
t
u
v
w
x
y
z

lumberjack noun lumberjacks
someone whose job is to cut down trees or transport them

luminous (say loo-mi-nus) adjective
shining or glowing in the dark *Eerie green light was provided by luminous fish that hung from the rocky walls and floated overhead.* — Alan Temperley, *The Brave Whale*
luminosity noun

lump¹ noun lumps
1 a solid piece of something **2** a swelling
lumpy adjective

lump verb lumps, lumping, lumped
to lump different things together is to put them together in the same group

lump² verb lumps, lumping, lumped
to lump it (informal) is to put up with something you don't like *You'll have to like it or lump it.*

lunacy (say loo-na-si) noun lunacies
lunacy is madness

lunar adjective
to do with the moon

lunatic (say loo-na-tik) noun lunatics
a mad person

lunch noun lunches
a meal eaten in the middle of the day

lung noun lungs
each of the two organs in your chest, used for breathing

lunge verb lunges, lunging, lunged
to make a sudden movement forwards *Just as the creature lunged forwards to kill him, Hiccup was grabbed around the ankle by one of Stoick's hairy hands, and pulled back through the hole he had climbed in.* — Cressida Cowell, *How to Be a Pirate*

lupin noun lupins
a garden plant with tall spikes of flowers

lurch¹ verb lurches, lurching, lurched
to lurch is to stagger or lean suddenly
lurch noun lurches
a sudden staggering or leaning movement

lurch² noun
to leave someone in the lurch is to desert them when they are in difficulty

lure verb lures, luring, lured
to lure a person or animal is to tempt them into a trap or difficulty

lurk verb lurks, lurking, lurked
to wait quietly where you cannot be seen

luscious (say lush-us) adjective
tasting or smelling delicious *He would buy one luscious bar of chocolate and eat it all up, every bit of it, right then and there.* — Roald Dahl, *Charlie and the Chocolate Factory*

lush adjective lusher, lushest
growing thickly and healthily *Below the garden a green field lush with clover sloped down to the hollow where the brook ran and where scores of white birches grew.* — L. M. Montgomery, *Anne of Green Gables*

lustre (say lus-ter) noun lustres
a thing's lustre is its brightness or brilliance

lustrous adjective
shiny or bright

lute noun lutes
a musical instrument rather like a guitar but with a deeper and rounder body. It was used a lot in the Middle Ages.

luxurious adjective
something, like a hotel, that is luxurious is very comfortable and expensive

luxury noun luxuries
1 a luxury is something expensive that you enjoy but do not really need **2** luxury is having a very comfortable and expensive lifestyle *They led a life of luxury.*

Lycra noun (trademark)
Lycra is a thin stretchy material used especially for sports clothing.

lying
present participle of **lie¹** *Her clothes were lying in a heap. I know you're lying to me.*

A B C D E F G H I J K **L** M N O P Q R S T U V W X Y Z

lynch verb **lynches, lynching, lynched**
to lynch someone is to execute them without a proper trial

lyre noun **lyres**
an ancient musical instrument like a small harp

lyrical adjective
sounding like a song or a poem

lyrics plural noun
the words of a popular song

Mm

m
short for **metre, metres, miles,** or **millions**

ma noun **mas** (informal)
mother

mac noun **macs** (informal)
a raincoat

macabre (say mak-**ah**br) adjective
strange and horrible

macaroni noun
macaroni is pasta in the form of short tubes

machine noun **machines**
a piece of equipment made of moving parts that work together to do a job

machine–gun noun **machine–guns**
a gun that can keep firing bullets quickly one after another

machinery noun
1 machinery is machines generally *farm machinery* 2 machinery is a mechanism *The lift's machinery is faulty.*

mackerel noun **mackerel**
a sea fish used as food

mad adjective **madder, maddest**
1 having something wrong with your mind; not sane 2 very foolish 3 very keen *She's mad about rock music.* **like mad** (informal)

with great speed, energy, or enthusiasm
madness noun

madam noun
a word sometimes used when speaking or writing politely to a woman, instead of her name *Can I help you, madam?*

madden verb **maddens, maddening, maddened**
to madden someone is to make them mad or angry

made
past tense and past participle of **make** *I made a cake for your birthday. I have made a mistake.*

madly adverb
extremely; very much *They are madly in love.*

magazine noun **magazines**
1 a paper-covered publication with articles or stories, which comes out regularly 2 the part of a gun that holds the cartridges 3 a store for weapons and ammunition or for explosives 4 a device that holds film for a camera or slides for a projector

maggot noun **maggots**
the larva of some kinds of fly

magic noun
1 magic is the power to make impossible things happen 2 magic is also performing clever tricks

magical adjective
1 done by magic or as if by magic
2 wonderful; marvellous **magically** adverb

magician noun **magicians**
1 someone who does magic tricks 2 a man with magic powers; a wizard

magistrate noun **magistrates**
a judge in a local court who deals with some less serious cases

magma noun
magma is the molten substance beneath the earth's crust
Please see illustration on following page.

magnet noun **magnets**
a piece of metal that can attract iron or

a
b
c
d
e
f
g
h
i
j
k
l
m
n
o
p
q
r
s
t
u
v
w
x
y
z

magma

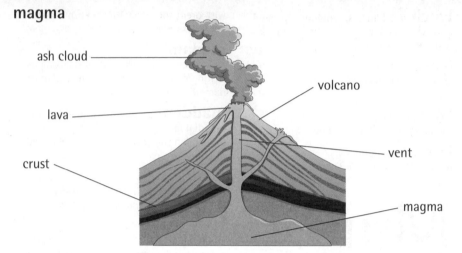

ash cloud

volcano

lava

vent

crust

magma

A B C D E F G H I J K L **M** N O P Q R S T U V W X Y Z

steel and that points north and south when it is hung in the air **magnetism** noun the attraction of a magnet

magnetic adjective
having or using the powers of a magnet

magnetize verb magnetizes, magnetizing, magnetized
to magnetize something is to make it into a magnet

magnificent adjective
1 looking splendid or impressive *There was a whirr and flutter of wings and down from the dawn sky flew a magnificent white horse.* — Francesca Simon, *Helping Hercules* **2** excellent *We had a magnificent meal.* **magnificence** noun **magnificently** adverb

magnify verb magnifies, magnifying, magnified
to magnify something is to make it look bigger than it really is **magnification** noun

magnifying glass noun
magnifying glasses
a lens that magnifies things

magnitude noun magnitudes
magnitude is how large or important something is

magnolia noun magnolias
a tree with large white or pale pink flowers

magpie noun magpies
a black and white bird, related to the crow

mahogany (say ma-**hog**-a-ni) noun
mahogany is a hard brown wood used for making furniture

maid noun maids
1 a female servant **2** (old use) a girl

maiden noun maidens (old use)
a girl

maiden name noun maiden names
a woman's family name before she gets married

mail¹ noun
1 mail is letters and parcels sent by post **2** mail is also electronic mail

mail verb mails, mailing, mailed
to mail something is to send it by post or by electronic mail

mail² noun
armour made of metal rings joined together

maim verb maims, maiming, maimed
to maim someone is to injure them so badly that part of their body is damaged for life

main adjective
largest or most important

main or **mains** noun
the main pipe or cable in a system carrying water, gas, or electricity to a building

mainland noun
the mainland is the main part of a country or continent, not the islands around it

mainly adverb
chiefly or usually; almost completely

maintain verb maintains, maintaining, maintained
1 to maintain something is to keep it in good condition 2 to maintain a belief is to have it or state it *I maintain that animals should not be hunted.* 3 to maintain someone is to provide money for them

maintenance noun
1 maintenance is keeping something in good condition 2 maintenance is also money for food and clothing

maisonette noun maisonettes
a small flat or house

maize noun
maize is a tall kind of corn with large seeds

majestic adjective
stately and dignified **majestically** adverb

majesty noun majesties
1 the title of a king or queen 2 majesty is the quality of being stately and dignified

major adjective
1 more important; main *Use the major roads.* 2 of the musical scale that has a semitone between the 3rd and 4th notes and between the 7th and 8th notes

major noun majors
an army officer above captain in rank

majority (say ma-**jo**-ri-ti) noun majorities
1 the greatest part of a group of people or things; more than half *The majority of the class wanted a quiz.* 2 the amount by which the winner in an election beats the loser *She had a majority of 25 over her opponent.* 3 the

age at which a person becomes legally an adult, now usually 18

make verb makes, making, made
1 to make something is to build or produce it *They are making a raft out of logs.* 2 to make someone or something do something is to cause it to happen *The bang made him jump.* 3 to make money is to get it or earn it *She makes £30,000 a year.* 4 in a game, to make a score is to achieve it *He has made 20 runs so far.* 5 to make a certain point is to reach it *The swimmer just made the shore.* 6 to make something is to estimate it or reckon it *What do you make the time?* 7 several numbers make a total when they add up to it *4 and 6 make 10.* 8 to make (for example) a suggestion or promise is to give it to someone 9 to make a bed is to tidy it or arrange it for use **to make someone's day** is to cause them to be happy or successful **to make do** is to manage with something that is not what you really want **to make for a place** is to go towards it **to make off** is to leave quickly **to make something** or **someone out** is to manage to see or hear or understand them **to make something up** is to invent a false story or excuse **to make up** is to be friendly again after a disagreement **to make up for something** is to give or do something in return for a loss or difficulty **to make up your mind** is to decide

make noun makes
1 how something is made 2 a brand of goods; something made by a particular firm *What make of car is that?*

make-believe noun
make-believe is pretending or imagining things

maker noun makers
the person or firm that has made something

makeshift adjective
used because you have nothing better *We'll use the bed as a makeshift table.*

make-up noun
1 make-up is creams and powders for making your skin look beautiful or different 2 a person's make-up is their character

A
B
C
D
E
F
G
H
I
J
K
L
M
N
O
P
Q
R
S
T
U
V
W
X
Y
Z

malaria (say ma-**lair**-i-a) noun
malaria is a tropical disease spread by
mosquito bites, that causes fever

male adjective
belonging to the sex that produces young
by fertilizing the female's egg cells
male noun males
a male person or animal

malevolent (say ma-**lev**-o-lent)
adjective
wanting to harm other people 'A bad
idea, Professor Lockhart,' said Snape,
gliding over like a large and malevolent
bat. — J. K. Rowling, Harry Potter and the
Chamber of Secrets **malevolently** adverb
malevolence noun

malice noun
malice is a desire to harm other people

malicious adjective
intending to do harm **maliciously** adverb
in a malicious way Inspector Hole grinned
maliciously. 'Well, it looks like you two are
out of a job,' he sniggered. — Jeremy Strong,
Viking at School

mall noun malls
a large covered shopping centre

mallet noun mallets
a large wooden hammer

malnutrition noun
malnutrition is bad health caused
by not having enough food
malnourished adjective

malt noun
malt is dried barley used in brewing and
making vinegar

mammal noun mammals
any animal of which the female gives birth
to live young and can feed them with her
own milk

mammoth noun mammoths
an extinct kind of hairy elephant with long
curved tusks
mammoth adjective
huge

man noun men
1 a man is a grown-up male human being
2 a man is also any individual person
No man is perfect. **3** man is all the people in
the world **4** a man is one of the pieces used
in a board game
man verb mans, manning, manned
to man something is to supply people to
work it Man the pumps!

manage verb manages, managing,
managed
1 to manage something is to be able to
do it although it is difficult **2** to manage a
shop or factory or other business is to be in
charge of it

manageable adjective
able to be managed or done

management noun
1 management is being in charge of
something **2** the management of a business
is the people in charge of it

manager noun managers
a person who manages a business or part
of it

manageress noun manageresses
a woman manager of a shop or restaurant

mane noun manes
the long hair along the back of the neck of
a horse or lion

manger (say **mayn**-jer) noun mangers
a trough in a stable for animals to
feed from

mangle verb mangles, mangling,
mangled
to mangle something is to crush or twist it
so it is badly damaged

mango noun mangoes
a juicy tropical fruit with yellow pulp

manhandle verb manhandles,
manhandling, manhandled
to manhandle someone or something is to
handle them or move them roughly

manhole noun manholes
a hole, usually with a cover, through which

a person can get into a sewer or boiler to inspect or repair it

mania noun manias
1 mania is violent madness 2 a mania is a strong enthusiasm *They have a mania for sport.*

maniac noun maniacs
a person who acts in a violent and wild way

manic adjective
manic behaviour is busy and excited

manifesto noun manifestos
a public statement of a group's or person's policy or principles

manipulate verb manipulates, manipulating, manipulated
1 to manipulate something is to handle it skilfully 2 to manipulate someone is to get them to do what you want by treating them cleverly **manipulation** noun

mankind noun
mankind is all the people in the world *This is a discovery for the good of all mankind.*

manly adjective manlier, manliest
1 strong or brave 2 suitable for a man **manliness** noun

manner noun manners
the way that something happens or is done

manners plural noun
a person's manners are how they behave with other people; behaving politely

manoeuvre (say ma-**noo**-ver) noun manoeuvres
a skilful or clever action

manoeuvre verb manoeuvres, manoeuvring, manoeuvred
1 to manoeuvre something is to move it skilfully into position 2 to manoeuvre is to move skilfully or cleverly

manor noun manors
a large important house in the country

mansion noun mansions
a large stately house

manslaughter (say **man**-slaw-ter) noun
manslaughter is the crime of killing someone without meaning to

mantelpiece noun mantelpieces
a shelf above a fireplace

mantle noun mantles
1 (old use) a cloak 2 a covering *There was a mantle of snow on the hills.*

manual adjective
manual work is work you do with your hands; manual equipment is equipment used with your hands **manually** adverb

manual noun manuals
a handbook or book of instructions

manufacture verb manufactures, manufacturing, manufactured
to manufacture things is to make them with machines, usually in a factory

manufacture noun
manufacture is the process of making things with machines, especially in large quantities for sale **manufacturer** noun

manure noun
manure is animal dung added to the soil to make it more fertile

manuscript noun manuscripts
something written or typed before it has been printed

Manx adjective
to do with the Isle of Man

Manx cat noun Manx cats
a breed of cat without a tail

many determiner more, most
large in number *There were many people at the party. How many potatoes do you want?*

many pronoun
a large number of people or things *Many were found.*

Maori (say **mow**-ri) noun Maoris
1 a member of the aboriginal people of New Zealand 2 their language

map noun maps
a diagram of part or all of the earth's

A
B
C
D
E
F
G
H
I
J
K
L

M

N
O
P
Q
R
S
T
U
V
W
X
Y
Z

surface, showing features such as towns, mountains, and rivers **to put a place on the map** is to do something that makes it famous

map verb **maps, mapping, mapped**
to map an area is to make a map of it **to map something out** is to arrange it or organize it

maple noun **maples**
a tree with broad leaves

mar verb **mars, marring, marred**
to mar something is to spoil it

marathon noun **marathons**
a long-distance running race on roads, usually 26 miles long

marauder noun **marauders**
marauders are people who attack a place and steal things from it

marble noun **marbles**
1 a marble is a small glass ball used in games 2 marble is a hard kind of limestone that is polished and used for building or sculpture

March noun
the third month of the year

march verb **marches, marching, marched**
1 to march is to walk with regular steps 2 to march someone is to make them walk somewhere *He marched them up the hill.*

march noun **marches**
1 a march is a large group of people marching, sometimes to protest about something 2 a march is also a piece of music suitable for marching to

mare noun **mares**
a female horse or donkey

margarine (say mar-ja-**reen**) noun
margarine is a soft creamy substance used like butter, made from animal or vegetable fats

margin noun **margins**
1 the empty space between the edge of a page and the writing or pictures 2 the small

difference between two scores or prices *She won by a narrow margin.*

marginal adjective
a marginal difference is a very small or slight one *The difference in price is marginal.*

marigold noun **marigolds**
a yellow or orange garden flower

marina (say ma-**ree**-na) noun **marinas**
a harbour for yachts and motor boats

marine (say ma-**reen**) adjective
to do with the sea

marine noun **marines**
a soldier trained to serve on land and sea

mariner noun **mariners** (old use)
a sailor

marionette noun **marionettes**
a puppet that you work by strings or wires

mark noun **marks**
1 a spot, dot, line, or stain on something 2 a number or letter put on a piece of work to show how good it is 3 a distinguishing feature or sign of something *They kept a minute's silence as a mark of respect.* 4 the place from which you start a race *On your marks, get set, go!*

mark verb **marks, marking, marked**
1 to mark something is to put a mark on it 2 to mark a piece of work is to give it a number or letter to show how good it is 3 in football or hockey, to mark a player on the other team is to keep close to them to stop them getting the ball 4 to mark something said is to take note of it *Mark my words!*

market noun **markets**
1 a place where things are bought and sold, usually from stalls in the open air 2 a demand for goods *There is hardly any market for typewriters now.*

market verb **markets, marketing, marketed**
to market a product is to put it on sale

marksman noun **marksmen**
an expert in shooting at a target

marmalade noun
marmalade is jam made from oranges
or lemons

maroon[1] verb maroons, marooning,
marooned
to maroon someone is to abandon them
in a place far away from other people *'It
sounds thrilling!' said George, picturing them
all marooned by fierce storms, waiting to
be rescued from peril and starvation! –* Enid
Blyton, *Five Go to Demon's Rocks*

maroon[2] adjective
dark red

marquee (say mar-**kee**) noun marquees
a large tent used for a party or
exhibition

marriage noun marriages
1 marriage is the state of being married
2 a marriage is a wedding

marrow noun marrows
1 a marrow is a large green or yellow
vegetable with a hard skin **2** marrow is the
soft substance inside your bones

marry verb marries, marrying, married
1 to marry someone is to become their
husband or wife **2** to marry two people is to
perform a marriage ceremony

marsh noun marshes
a low-lying area of very wet ground
marshy adjective

marshal noun marshals
1 an official who supervises a contest or
ceremony **2** a high-ranking officer *He is a
Field Marshal.* **3** a police official in
the USA

marshmallow noun marshmallows
marshmallow is a soft spongy sweet

marsupial (say mar-**soo**-pi-al) noun
marsupials
an animal such as a kangaroo, wallaby, or
koala. The female has a pouch for carrying
her young

martial adjective
to do with war or fighting

martial arts plural noun
martial arts are fighting sports such as
karate and judo

Martian noun Martians
in stories, a creature from the planet Mars

martin noun martins
a bird rather like a swallow

martyr (say mar-ter) noun martyrs
someone who is killed or suffers because of
their beliefs **martyrdom** noun

marvel noun marvels
a wonderful thing

marvel verb marvels, marvelling,
marvelled
to marvel at something is to be filled with
wonder or astonishment by it

marvellous adjective
wonderful **marvellously** adverb

marzipan noun
marzipan is a soft sweet food made from
almonds and sugar, sometimes put on the
top of cakes

mascot noun mascots
a person, animal, or object that is believed
to bring good luck

masculine adjective
1 to do with men or like men; suitable for
men **masculinity** noun

mash verb mashes, mashing, mashed
to mash something is to crush it into a
soft mass

mash noun (informal)
mashed potatoes

mask noun masks
a covering that you wear over your face to
disguise or protect it

mask verb masks, masking, masked
1 to mask your face is to cover it with a
mask **2** to mask something is to hide it

mason noun masons
someone who builds or works with stone

masonry noun
masonry is the stone parts of a building

a
b
c
d
e
f
g
h
i
j
k
l
m
n
o
p
q
r
s
t
u
v
w
x
y
z

Mass noun Masses
the Communion service in a Roman Catholic church

mass noun masses
1 a large amount of something 2 a lump or heap 3 (in science) the amount of matter in an object, measured in grams **the masses** the ordinary people

mass verb masses, massing, massed
to mass is to collect into a mass *People were massing in the square.*

massacre (say **mas**-a-ker) verb
massacres, massacring, massacred
to massacre people is to kill a large number of them

massacre noun massacres
the killing of a large number of people

massage (say **mas**-ahzh) verb
massages, massaging, massaged
to massage the body is to rub and press it to make it less stiff or less painful

massage noun
massaging someone's body

massive adjective
very big; large and heavy **massively** adverb hugely

mast noun masts
a tall pole that holds up a ship's sails or a flag or aerial

master noun masters
1 a man who is in charge of something 2 a male teacher 3 someone who is very good at what they do, such as a great artist or composer 4 something from which copies are made **Master** (old use) a title put before a boy's name

master verb masters, mastering, mastered
1 to master a subject or skill is to learn it completely 2 to master a fear or difficulty is to control it *She succeeded in mastering her fear of heights.*

masterly adjective
very clever or skilful

mastermind noun masterminds
1 a very clever person 2 someone who organizes a scheme or crime

masterpiece noun masterpieces
1 an excellent piece of work 2 someone's best piece of work

mastery noun
mastery is complete control or knowledge of something *He has a complete mastery of the art of fencing.*

mat noun mats
1 a small piece of material that partly covers a floor 2 a small piece of material put on a table to protect the surface

matador noun matadors
someone who fights and kills the bull in a bullfight

match[1] noun matches
a small thin stick with a small amount of chemical at one end that gives a flame when rubbed on something rough

match[2] noun matches
1 a game or contest between two teams or players 2 one person or thing that is equal or similar to another *Can you find a match for this sock?* 3 a marriage

match verb matches, matching, matched
1 to match another person or thing is to be equal to them 2 one thing matches another when it goes well with it *Your jacket matches your shoes.* 3 to match one person with another is to put them in competition

mate[1] noun mates
1 a friend or companion 2 one of a pair of animals that produce young together 3 one of the officers on a ship

mate verb mates, mating, mated
1 to mate is to come together in order to have offspring 2 to mate animals is to put them together so that they will have offspring

mate[2] noun mates
checkmate in chess

material noun materials
1 anything used for making something else *Iron and steel are the best materials for magnets.* **2** cloth or fabric

materialistic adjective
liking possessions and money more than anything else

maternal adjective
to do with a mother; motherly

maternity noun
maternity is having a baby; motherhood

mathematical adjective
1 a mathematical problem or calculation is one you need mathematics to work out **2** mathematical ability is being able to do mathematics

mathematician (say math-em-a-tish-an) noun mathematicians
an expert in mathematics

mathematics noun
mathematics is the study of numbers, measurements, and shapes

maths noun (informal)
maths is mathematics

matinee (say mat-i-nay) noun matinees
an afternoon performance at a theatre or cinema

matrimony (say mat-ri-mo-ni) noun
matrimony is marriage
matrimonial adjective

matt adjective
not shiny *The wall was decorated with matt paint.*

matted adjective
tangled

matter noun matters
1 something you need to think about or do *It is a serious matter.* **2** a substance *Peat consists mainly of vegetable matter.* **a matter of fact** something true **no matter** it is not important **what's the matter?** what is wrong?

matter verb matters, mattering, mattered
to matter is to be important

matting noun
matting is mats; rough material for covering a floor

mattress noun mattresses
a thick layer of soft or springy material covered in cloth and used on a bed

mature adjective
1 fully grown or developed **2** behaving in a sensible adult manner

mature matures, maturing, matured
to become fully grown or developed

maturity noun
1 maturity is being fully grown **2** maturity is also behaving in a sensible adult manner

mauve (say mohv) adjective
pale purple

maximum noun maxima
the greatest number or amount possible *The maximum is 10.*

maximum adjective
the greatest possible *The maximum speed is 60 miles per hour.*

May noun
the fifth month of the year

may verb past tense might
1 may means to be allowed to *May I have a sweet?* **2** may also means that something will possibly happen or has possibly happened *He may come tomorrow. He might have missed the train.*

maybe adverb
perhaps

mayday noun maydays
an international radio signal calling for help

May Day noun
the first day of May, often celebrated with sport and dancing

mayonnaise (say may-on-ayz) noun
mayonnaise is a creamy sauce made from eggs, oil, and vinegar, and used on salads

a
b
c
d
e
f
g
h
i
j
k
l
m
n
o
p
q
r
s
t
u
v
w
x
y
z

A
B
C
D
E
F
G
H
I
J
K
L
M
N
O
P
Q
R
S
T
U
V
W
X
Y
Z

mayor noun mayors
the person in charge of the council in a town or city

mayoress noun mayoresses
a woman who is a mayor

maypole noun maypoles
a decorated pole which people dance round on May Day

maze noun mazes
a complicated arrangement of paths or lines to follow through as a game or puzzle

me pronoun
a word used for *I*, usually when it is the object of a sentence, or when it comes after a preposition *She likes me. She gave it to me.*

meadow noun meadows
a field of grass

meagre (say **meeg**-er) adjective
very little; barely enough *The Rev. John Whittier was the pastor of this small mission church, and had a very meagre salary.* — Eleanor H. Porter, *Pollyanna*

meal[1] noun meals
a meal is the food eaten at one time, such as breakfast, lunch, or dinner

meal[2] noun
meal is grain ground to a coarse powder

mean[1] verb means, meaning, meant
1 to mean something is to have that as its explanation or equivalent, or to have that as its sense *What does this word mean?* **2** to mean to do something is to intend to do it *I meant to tell him, but I forgot.*

mean[2] adjective meaner, meanest
1 not generous; selfish *What a mean man.* **2** unkind or spiteful *That was a mean trick.* **meanly** adverb **meanness** noun

meander (say mee-**an**-der) verb
meanders, meandering, meandered
a river or road meanders when it takes a winding course, with a lot of bends

meaning noun meanings
what something means

meaningful adjective
a meaningful look is one that expresses a meaning *A meaningful glance passed between my parents.* **meaningfully** adverb

meaningless adjective
something is meaningless when it has no meaning or purpose

means noun
a means of doing something is a way or method of doing it **by all means** certainly **by no means** not at all

means plural noun
money or other resources for doing things

meantime noun
in the meantime meanwhile

meanwhile adverb
while something else is happening *I'll cut the cake up; meanwhile, you get the plates out.*

measles plural noun
measles is an infectious disease that causes small red spots on the skin

measly adjective measlier, measliest (informal)
very small or poor *All I got was a measly T-shirt.*

measure verb measures, measuring, measured
1 to measure something is to find out how big it is **2** to measure (for example) six feet is to be six feet long

measure noun measures
1 a unit used for measuring something **2** a device used for measuring **3** the size of something **4** something done for a particular purpose; a law or rule

measurement noun measurements
1 a measurement is the size or length of something **2** measurement is when you measure something

meat noun meats
meat is animal flesh that is cooked as food

mechanic noun mechanics
someone who maintains and repairs machinery

mechanical adjective
1 to do with machines 2 done without thinking about it **mechanically** adverb

mechanics noun
1 mechanics is the study of movement and force 2 mechanics is also the study or use of machines

mechanism noun **mechanisms**
1 the moving parts of a machine 2 the way a machine works

medal noun **medals**
a piece of metal shaped like a coin, star, or cross, given to someone for bravery or for achieving something *She won two Olympic gold medals.*

medallist noun **medallists**
a winner of a medal

meddle verb **meddles, meddling, meddled**
to meddle in something is to interfere in it **meddlesome** adjective a meddlesome person likes to interfere

media (say **mee**-di-a) plural noun
a plural of **medium**²
the media newspapers, radio, television and the Internet, which provide information about current events to the public

medical adjective
to do with the treatment of disease **medically** adverb

medicine noun **medicines**
1 a medicine is a substance, usually swallowed, used to try to cure an illness 2 medicine is the treatment of disease and injuries **medicinal** adjective

medieval (say med-i-**ee**-val) adjective
to do with the Middle Ages

mediocre (say meed-i-**oh**-ker) adjective
not very good, only fairly good **mediocrity** noun

meditate verb **meditates, meditating, meditated**
to meditate is to think deeply and seriously, usually in silence **meditation** noun

Mediterranean (say med-i-ter-**ay**-ni-an) adjective
to do with the Mediterranean Sea, which is between Europe and Africa, or the countries round it

medium¹ adjective
average; of middle size

medium² noun **media** or **mediums**
1 a thing in which something exists, moves, or is expressed *Air is the medium in which sound travels.* 2 someone who claims to communicate with the dead

meek adjective **meeker, meekest**
quiet and obedient **meekly** adverb **meekness** noun

meet verb **meets, meeting, met**
1 to meet is to come together from different places *We all met in London.* 2 to meet someone is to come face to face with them, especially for the first time or by arrangement *I met her at a party. I'll meet you at the station.* 3 to meet a bill or cost is to be able to pay it

meeting noun **meetings**
a time when people come together for a special purpose, often to discuss something

megabyte noun **megabytes**
(in computing) a unit that measures data or memory, roughly equal to one million bytes

megaphone noun **megaphones**
a funnel-shaped device for making someone's voice sound louder

melancholy adjective
sad and gloomy *By and by there was to be heard a sound at once the most musical and the most melancholy in the world: the mermaids calling to the moon.* — J. M. Barrie, *The Adventures of Peter Pan*

mellow adjective **mellower, mellowest**
having a soft rich sound or colour

a
b
c
d
e
f
g
h
i
j
k
l
m
n
o
p
q
r
s
t
u
v
w
x
y
z

melodic adjective
a melodic piece of music has a tune that is pleasant to listen to

melodious adjective
sounding sweet; pleasant to listen to

melodrama noun melodramas
a play full of excitement and emotion
melodramatic adjective

melody noun melodies
a tune, especially one that is pleasant to listen to

melon noun melons
a large juicy fruit with yellow or green skin

melt verb melts, melting, melted
1 to melt something solid is to make it liquid by heating it 2 to melt is to become liquid by heating 3 to melt, or to melt away, is to go away or disappear slowly *The crowd gradually melted away.*

member noun members
someone who belongs to a society or group
membership noun

Member of Parliament noun
Members of Parliament
someone who has been elected by the people of an area to speak for them in Parliament

membrane noun membranes
a thin skin or covering

memoirs plural noun
a famous person's account of their own life and experiences

memorable adjective
1 worth remembering *It was a memorable holiday.* 2 easy to remember *He has a memorable name.* **memorably** adverb

memorial noun memorials
something set up to remind people of a person or an event *They passed a war memorial in the High Street.*

memorize verb memorizes, memorizing, memorized
to memorize something is to learn it and remember it exactly

memory noun memories
1 memory is the ability to remember things 2 a memory is something that you remember, usually something interesting or special 3 a computer's memory is the part where information is stored **to do something in memory of someone** or **something** is to do it in order to remind people of a person or an event

men
plural of man noun

menace verb menaces, menacing, menaced
to menace someone is to threaten them with harm or danger *Rabbits avoid close woodland, where the ground is shady, damp and grassless and they feel menaced by the undergrowth.* – Richard Adams, *Watership Down*

menace noun menaces
1 something that threatens people with harm or danger 2 an annoying person or thing

menagerie (say min-aj-er-i) noun menageries
a small zoo

mend verb mends, mending, mended
to mend something that is broken or damaged is to make it as good as it was before **to be on the mend** is to be getting better after an illness

menstruation noun
menstruation is the natural flow of blood from a woman's womb, normally happening every 28 days **menstrual** adjective

–ment suffix
used to make nouns, as in *amusement* and *oddments*

mental adjective
to do with the mind *mental arithmetic*

mentally adverb
1 you do something mentally when you do it in your head *Edward mentally crossed his fingers.* 2 someone who is mentally ill is ill in their mind

A B C D E F G H I J K L **M** N O P Q R S T U V W X Y Z

mention verb mentions, mentioning, mentioned
to mention someone or something is to speak about them briefly

mention noun mentions
when someone or something is mentioned *Our school got a mention in the local paper.*

menu (say **men**-yoo) noun menus
1 a list of the food that is available in a restaurant or served at a meal 2 (in computing) a list of possible actions, displayed on a screen, from which you choose what you want a computer to do

MEP
short for *Member of the European Parliament*

mercenary adjective
interested only in the money you can get for the work you do

mercenary noun mercenaries
a soldier hired to fight for a foreign country

merchandise noun
merchandise is goods for buying or selling

merchant noun merchants
someone involved in trade

merchant navy noun merchant navies
the ships and sailors that carry goods for trade

merciful adjective
showing mercy **mercifully** adverb

merciless adjective
showing no mercy; cruel **mercilessly** adverb

mercury noun
mercury is a heavy silvery metal that is usually liquid, used in thermometers

mercy noun mercies
1 mercy is kindness or pity shown towards someone instead of harming them or punishing them 2 a mercy is something to be thankful for *Thank goodness for small mercies.*

mere adjective
not more than *He's a mere child.*

merely adverb
only; simply *She was merely joking.*

merge verb merges, merging, merged
1 to merge things is to combine or blend them 2 to merge is to be combined

merger noun mergers
a merger is when two businesses or companies join together into one

meridian (say mer-**rid**-i-an) noun meridians
a line on a map or globe from the North Pole to the South Pole

meringue (say mer-**rang**) noun meringues
a crisp cake made from the whites of eggs mixed with sugar and baked

merit noun merits
1 to have merit is to be good or excellent 2 a merit is something that deserves praise *I can see the merits of this plan.*

merit verb merits, meriting, merited
to merit something is to deserve something good

mermaid noun mermaids
a mythical sea creature with a woman's body and a fish's tail instead of legs

merry adjective merrier, merriest
happy and cheerful **merrily** adverb

merry-go-round noun merry-go-rounds
a large roundabout with horses and other things to ride on

mesh noun meshes
mesh is material made like a net, with open spaces between the wire or threads

mess noun messes
1 something untidy or dirty 2 a difficult or confused situation 3 a place where soldiers or sailors eat their meals **to make a mess of something** is to do it very badly

a
b
c
d
e
f
g
h
i
j
k
l
m
n
o
p
q
r
s
t
u
v
w
x
y
z

metamorphosis

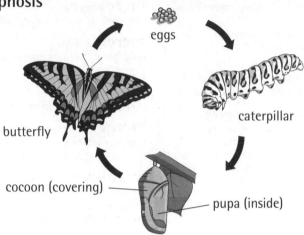

eggs

butterfly

caterpillar

cocoon (covering)

pupa (inside)

A B C D E F G H I J K L **M** N O P Q R S T U V W X Y Z

mess verb messes, messing, messed
to mess about is to waste time behaving stupidly or doing things slowly *Stop messing about and give me a hand.* **to mess something up** is to do it very badly

message noun messages
a question or piece of information that one person sends to another

messenger noun messengers
someone who carries a message

Messiah (say mi-**sy**-a) noun
1 the person that the Jews expect to come as their saviour **2** Jesus Christ, who Christians believe was their saviour.

messy adjective messier, messiest
1 untidy or dirty **2** difficult or complicated *I'm afraid it's a messy situation.*
messily adverb

met
past tense and past participle of meet *I met my friends after school. Most people I've met have been nice.*

metal noun metals
a hard substance that melts when it is heated, such as gold, silver, copper, and iron
metallic adjective made of metal or shining like metal

metamorphosis noun
metamorphoses
a complete change made by some living things, such as a caterpillar changing into a butterfly

metaphor (say **met**-a-fer) noun
metaphors
using words in a way that describes one thing as if it were something else, as in *the lion, the king of beasts*, in which *king* is a metaphor **metaphorical** adjective

meteor (say **meet**-i-er) noun meteors
a piece of rock or metal that moves through space and burns up as it enters the earth's atmosphere

meteoric adjective
very fast and sudden, like a meteor *They've had a meteoric rise to fame.*

meteorite (say **meet**-i-er-ryt) noun
meteorites
the remains of a meteor that has landed on the earth

meteorology (say meet-i-er-**ol**-o-ji)
noun
meteorology is the study of the weather **meteorological** adjective
meteorologist noun

meter noun meters
a device for measuring something, such as how much gas or electricity has been used

methane noun
methane is an inflammable gas produced when plants rot away, found mainly in mines and marshes

method noun methods
1 a method is a way of doing something
2 method is good organization or orderly behaviour *There is method in everything she does.*

methodical (say mi-**thod**-i-kal) adjective
done carefully and in a logical way
methodically adverb

Methodist noun Methodists
someone who believes in Methodism, a Christian religious movement started by John and Charles Wesley in the 18th century

meticulous adjective
very careful and precise
meticulously adverb

metre (say **meet**-er) noun metres
1 the main unit of length in the metric system, equal to about 39½ inches 2 a particular type of rhythm in poetry

metric adjective
1 to do with the metric system 2 to do with metre in poetry

metric system noun
a measuring system based on decimal units (the metre, litre, and gram)

metronome (say **met**-ro-nohm) noun metronomes
a device that makes a regular clicking noise to help you keep in time when practising music

mettle noun
to be on your mettle is to be ready to do your best

mew verb mews, mewing, mewed
to make a sound like a cat

miaow (say mee-**ow**) verb miaows, miaowing, miaowed
to make a sound like a cat

mice
plural of mouse

microbe (say **my**-krohb) noun microbes
a tiny organism that can only be seen with a microscope

microchip noun microchips
a very small piece of silicon working as an electric circuit, used in computers

microphone noun microphones
an electrical device that picks up sound waves for recording them or making them louder

microprocessor noun microprocessors
a set of microchips that form the central processing unit of a computer

microscope (say **my**-kro-skohp) noun microscopes
a device with lenses that make tiny objects appear larger so you can study them

microscopic (say my-kro-**skop**-ik) adjective
too small to be seen without a microscope; tiny

microwave noun microwaves
1 energy moving in very short waves
2 a kind of oven which heats things quickly by using energy in very short waves

microwave verb microwaves, microwaving, microwaved
to microwave food is to cook it in a microwave oven

mid adjective
in the middle of *The holiday is from mid-July to mid-August.*

midday noun
the middle of the day; noon

middle noun middles
1 the middle of something is the place or part that is at the same distance from all

a b c d e f g h i j k l **m** n o p q r s t u v w x y z

A

its sides or edges or from both its ends
2 someone's waist

middle adjective
placed in the middle

B

middle–aged adjective
aged between about forty and sixty

C

D

Middle Ages noun
the period in history from about AD 1100
to 1500

E

F

middle class noun or
middle classes plural noun
the class of people between the upper
class and the working class, including
business and professional people such
as teachers, doctors, and lawyers
middle–class adjective

G

H

I

J

Middle East noun
the countries to the east of the
Mediterranean Sea, from Egypt to Iran

K

L

middle school noun middle schools
a school for children aged from about 9
to 13

M

N

midge noun midges
a small insect like a gnat

O

midget noun midgets
an unusually short person

P

midland adjective
of the middle part of a country; of the
middle part of England

Q

R

Midlands plural noun
the central part of England

S

T

midnight noun
twelve o'clock at night

U

midst noun
to be in the midst of something is to be
in the middle of it

V

W

midsummer noun
the middle of summer, about 21 June in the
northern hemisphere

X

Y

midway adverb
halfway

Z

midwife noun midwives
a person trained to look after a woman who
is giving birth to a baby

might[1]
past tense of may *He sounded as if he might
be about to cry.*

might[2] noun
great power or strength

mighty adjective mightier, mightiest
very strong or powerful

migraine (say **mee**-grayn) noun
migraines
a severe kind of headache

migrant (say **my**-grant) noun migrants
1 a person who moves from one place
to another, usually to find work **2** a bird
or animal that moves from one region
to another

migrate (say my-**grayt**) verb migrates,
migrating, migrated
1 to migrate is to move from one place to
another, usually to find work **2** birds migrate
when they fly to a warmer region for the
winter **migration** noun **migratory** adjective
migratory birds migrate every year

mike noun mikes (informal)
a microphone

mild adjective milder, mildest
gentle; not harsh or severe *Miss Jennifer
Honey was a mild and quiet person who never
raised her voice and was seldom seen to smile.*
— Roald Dahl, *Matilda* **mildness** noun

mildly adverb
to be mildly surprised or interested is to be
slightly surprised or interested

mile noun miles
a measure of distance, equal to 1,760 yards
or about 1.6 kilometres

mileage noun mileages
the number of miles you have travelled

milestone noun milestones
1 a stone of a kind that used to be placed
beside a road to mark the distance between

towns **2** an important event in history or in a person's life

militant adjective
aggressive; eager to fight

military adjective
to do with soldiers or the armed forces

milk noun
milk is a white liquid that female mammals produce in their bodies to feed to their young
milk verb milks, milking, milked
to milk a cow or other animal is to get milk from it

milkman noun milkmen
a man who delivers milk to people's houses

milk shake noun milk shakes
a frothy drink of milk mixed with a sweet flavouring

milk tooth noun milk teeth
one of the first set of teeth a child or animal has, which are later replaced by adult teeth

milky adjective milkier, milkiest
1 like milk; white **2** made with a lot of milk

Milky Way noun
a faintly shining band of light from the stars in our galaxy

mill noun mills
1 a building with machinery for grinding corn to make flour **2** a factory for making materials, such as a paper mill or a steel mill **3** a machine for grinding something such as coffee or pepper
mill verb mills, milling, milled
1 to mill something is to grind or crush it in a mill **2** people mill or mill about when they move in a confused crowd

millennium noun millenniums
a period of 1,000 years

miller noun millers
someone who runs a flour mill

millet noun
a kind of cereal with tiny seeds

milligram noun milligrams
one thousandth of a gram

millilitre noun millilitres
one thousandth of a litre

millimetre noun millimetres
one thousandth of a metre

million noun millions
a thousand thousands (1,000,000)
millionth adjective, noun

millionaire noun millionaires
an extremely rich person who has at least a million pounds or dollars

millstone noun millstones
a large heavy stone used in grinding corn **a millstone round someone's neck** a heavy burden or responsibility

milometer (say my-**lom**-it-er) noun
milometers
a device for measuring how far a vehicle has travelled

mime verb mimes, miming, mimed
to mime is to tell a story by using movements of the body without speaking
mime noun mimes
mime is the art of telling a story by using movements of the body without speaking

mimic verb mimics, mimicking, mimicked
to mimic someone is to imitate them, especially to make people laugh
mimicry noun
mimic noun mimics
a person who is good at imitating other people

minaret noun minarets
a tall tower on a mosque

mince noun
mince is meat that has been cut up into very small pieces
mince verb minces, mincing, minced
to mince food is to cut it up into very small pieces **not to mince words** is to speak frankly

a
b
c
d
e
f
g
h
i
j
k
l
m
n
o
p
q
r
s
t
u
v
w
x
y
z

A
B
C
D
E
F
G
H
I
J
K
L
M
N
O
P
Q
R
S
T
U
V
W
X
Y
Z

mincemeat noun
mincemeat is a sweet mixture of currants, raisins, and chopped fruit, used in pies

mince pie noun mince pies
a pie containing mincemeat

mind noun minds
the function of the brain to think, feel, understand, and remember; your thoughts and feelings **to change your mind** is to have a new opinion or intention about something **to have a good mind to do something** is to intend to do it

mind verb minds, minding, minded
1 to mind something is to be sad or upset about it *I don't mind missing the party.* 2 to mind someone or something is to look after them for a time *He was minding the baby.*
3 to mind, or to mind out, is to be careful or watch out for something *Mind the doors!*

mindless adjective
done without thinking; stupid or pointless

mine[1] pronoun
belonging to me *That book is mine.*

mine[2] noun mines
1 a place where coal, metal, or precious stones are dug out of the ground 2 a type of bomb hidden under the ground or in the sea that explodes when people or things touch it

mine verb mines, mining, mined
1 to mine something is to dig it from a mine 2 to mine a place is to lay explosives in it

minefield noun minefields
1 an area where explosive mines have been laid 2 you can say that an activity is a minefield when it has many dangers

miner noun miners
someone who works in a mine

mineral noun minerals
1 a hard substance that can be dug out of the ground, such as coal and iron ore
2 a cold fizzy drink

mineral water noun
mineral water is water that comes from a natural spring. It can be fizzy or still

mingle verb mingles, mingling, mingled
1 things mingle when they become mixed together 2 to mingle things is to mix or blend them

mingy (say **min**-ji) adjective mingier, mingiest (informal)
mean or stingy

miniature (say **min**-i-cher) adjective
very small, especially copying something larger *When, what to my wondering / eyes should appear, / But a miniature sleigh, / and eight tiny reindeer.* — Clement Moore, *The Night Before Christmas*

TOP TIPS
There is a tricky bit in **miniature** —there is an **a** in the middle.

minibeast noun minibeasts
a very small creature such as an insect or spider

minibus noun minibuses
a small bus with seats for about ten people

minim noun minims
a musical note equal to two crotchets or half a semibreve, written ♩

minimal adjective
very little; as little as possible

minimize verb minimizes, minimizing, minimized
to minimize something is to make it as small as possible

minimum noun minima
the smallest number or amount possible *We want the minimum of fuss.*

minimum adjective
least or smallest *The minimum number is 3.*

minister noun ministers
1 a member of the government who is in charge of a department 2 a member of the clergy

ministry noun ministries
1 a government department *the Ministry of Defence* 2 the work of a minister in the church

mink noun minks
1 a mink is a small animal rather like a stoat
2 mink is this animal's valuable brown fur

minnow noun minnows
a tiny freshwater fish

minor adjective
1 not very important, especially when compared to something else 2 of the musical scale that has a semitone between the 2nd and 3rd notes

minority (say myn-**o**-ri-ti) noun minorities
1 the smaller part of a group of people or things *There was a minority who wanted to leave.* 2 a small group that is different from others

minstrel noun minstrels
a travelling singer and musician in the Middle Ages

mint[1] noun
1 mint is a green plant with sweet-smelling leaves used for flavouring 2 a mint is a sweet flavoured with peppermint

mint[2] noun mints
a place where a country's coins are made **to be in mint condition** is to be as new, as if it had just been made
mint verb mints, minting, minted
to mint coins is to make them

minus preposition
1 less; with the next number taken away *Eight minus two equals six (8-2 = 6).* 2 less than zero *The temperature is minus 5 degrees.*

minute[1] (say **min**-it) noun minutes
1 one-sixtieth of an hour 2 (informal) a short time *I'll be ready in a minute!*

minute[2] (say my-**newt**) adjective
1 tiny *The insect was minute.* 2 very detailed *He gave it a minute examination.*

miracle noun miracles
a wonderful or magical happening that is unexpected

miraculous adjective
something miraculous is wonderful or magical *By lunchtime, the whole place was a seething mass of men, women, and children all pushing and shoving to get a glimpse of this miraculous fruit.* – Roald Dahl, *James and the Giant Peach* **miraculously** adverb

mirage (say **mi**-rahzh) noun mirages
something that seems to be visible but is not really there, like a lake in a desert

mirror noun mirrors
a glass or metal surface that reflects things clearly

mirth noun
mirth is laughter or fun

mis– prefix
meaning 'wrong or wrongly', as in *misbehave* and *misunderstanding*

misbehave verb misbehaves, misbehaving, misbehaved
to misbehave is to behave badly **misbehaviour** noun

miscarriage noun miscarriages
a woman has a miscarriage when she gives birth to a baby before it is old enough to survive

miscellaneous (say mis-el-**ay**-ni-us) adjective
a miscellaneous group is one that is made up of different kinds of things

miscellany (say mis-**el**-an-ee) noun miscellanies
a mixture of different things

mischief noun
mischief is naughty or troublesome behaviour

mischievous adjective
naughty or troublesome

miser noun misers
someone who stores money away and spends as little as they can **miserly** adjective

miserable adjective
1 very unhappy *He felt miserable.*

A

2 unpleasant *What miserable weather!*
miserably adverb

B

misery noun miseries
1 misery is great unhappiness or suffering
2 (informal) a misery is someone who is
always unhappy or complaining

C

D

misfire verb misfires, misfiring, misfired
1 a gun misfires when it fails to fire **2** a plan
or idea or joke misfires when it goes wrong

E

F

misfit noun misfits
someone who does not fit in well with
other people

G

H

misfortune noun misfortunes
1 a misfortune is an unlucky event or an
accident **2** misfortune is bad luck

I

mishap (say **mis**-hap) noun mishaps
an unfortunate accident

J

K

misjudge verb misjudges, misjudging, misjudged
to misjudge someone or something is to
form a wrong idea or opinion about them

L

M

N

mislay verb mislays, mislaying, mislaid
to mislay something is to lose it for a
short time

O

mislead verb misleads, misleading, misled
to mislead someone is to give them a wrong
idea or impression deliberately

P

Q

R

misprint noun misprints
a mistake in printing, such as a
spelling mistake

S

Miss noun Misses
a title you put before the name of a girl or
unmarried woman

T

U

miss verb misses, missing, missed
1 to miss something is to fail to hit, reach,
catch, see, hear, or find it **2** to miss someone
or something is to be sad because they are
not with you *I missed my sister when she was
in hospital.* **3** to miss a train, bus, or plane
is to arrive too late to catch it **4** to miss a
lesson or other activity is to fail to attend it
How many classes have you missed? **5** to miss

V

W

X

Y

Z

something is also to notice that it is not
where it should be *When did you first miss
your wallet?*

miss noun misses
not hitting, reaching, or catching something
Was that shot a hit or a miss?

missile noun missiles
1 a weapon that is fired a long distance and
explodes when it lands **2** an object thrown
at someone

missing adjective
something is missing when it is lost or not
in the proper place

mission noun missions
1 an important job that someone is sent to
do or that someone feels they must do
2 a place or building where
missionaries work

missionary noun missionaries
someone who goes to another country to
spread a religious faith

misspell verb misspells, misspelling, misspelt or misspelled
to misspell a word is to spell it wrongly

mist noun mists
1 damp cloudy air like a thin fog
2 condensed water vapour on a window
or mirror

mistake noun mistakes
something done or said wrongly

mistake verb mistakes, mistaking, mistook, mistaken
to mistake one person or thing for another
is to confuse them

mistaken adjective
to be mistaken is to be incorrect or
wrong *You are mistaken if you believe that.*
mistakenly adverb

mister noun
1 Mr **2** (informal) sir *Can you tell me the
time, mister?*

mistletoe noun
mistletoe is a plant with green leaves and
white berries in winter

mistreat verb mistreats, mistreating, mistreated
to mistreat someone is to treat them badly or unfairly **mistreatment** noun

mistress noun mistresses
1 a woman who is in charge of something **2** a woman who teaches in a school **3** the woman owner of a dog or other animal

mistrust verb mistrusts, mistrusting, mistrusted
to mistrust someone or something is not to trust them

misty adjective mistier, mistiest
1 if it is misty outside there is a lot of mist **2** misty eyes are full of tears

misunderstand verb misunderstands, misunderstanding, misunderstood
to misunderstand something is to get a wrong idea or impression about it *You misunderstood what I said.*
misunderstanding noun

misuse (say mis-**yooz**) verb misuses, misusing, misused
to misuse something is to use it in the wrong way or treat it badly
misuse (say mis-**yooss**) noun
misuse is using something in the wrong way

mite noun mites
1 a tiny insect found in food **2** a small child

mitre (say **my**-ter) noun mitres
1 the tall tapering hat that a bishop wears **2** a joint of two tapering pieces of wood or cloth, forming a right angle

mitten noun mittens
a kind of glove without separate parts for the fingers

mix verb mixes, mixing, mixed
1 to mix different things is to stir or shake them together to make one thing **2** to mix is to get on well with other people *She mixes well.* **to mix up people** or **things** is to confuse them **mixer** noun

mixed adjective
containing two or more kinds of things or people

mixture noun mixtures
something made of different things mixed together

mix-up noun mix-ups
a muddle or confused situation, especially one that ruins a plan

mm
short for **millimetre** or **millimetres**

mnemonic (say nim-**on**-ik) noun mnemonics
a verse or saying that helps you to remember something

moan noun moans
1 a long low sound, usually of suffering **2** a complaint or grumble
moan verb moans, moaning, moaned
1 to moan is to make a long low sound **2** to moan is also to complain or grumble

moat noun moats
a deep ditch round a castle, usually filled with water

mob noun mobs
1 a large disorderly crowd of people **2** a gang
mob verb mobs, mobbing, mobbed
people mob someone when they crowd round them *The singer was mobbed by her fans.*

mobile adjective
able to be moved or carried about easily
mobility noun
mobile noun mobiles
1 a decoration made to be hung up from threads so that it moves about in the air **2** a mobile phone

mobile phone noun mobile phones
a telephone you can carry around with you

mobilize verb mobilizes, mobilizing, mobilized
to mobilize people or things is to get them

a
b
c
d
e
f
g
h
i
j
k
l
m
n
o
p
q
r
s
t
u
v
w
x
y
z

A

ready for a particular purpose, especially for war **mobilization** noun

moccasin (say **mok**-a-sin) noun
moccasins
a soft leather shoe like those worn by Native Americans

mock verb mocks, mocking, mocked
to mock someone or something is to make fun of them **mockery** noun

mock adjective
not real or genuine *They fought a mock battle.*

mode noun modes
1 the way that something is done *Flying is the fastest mode of transport.* **2** what is fashionable

model noun models
1 a small copy of an object *He makes models of aircraft.* **2** a particular version or design of something *We saw the latest models at the motor show.* **3** someone who displays clothes by wearing them or who poses for an artist or photographer **4** someone or something worth copying or imitating

model adjective
1 being a small copy of something *I'd like a model railway.* **2** being a good example for people to follow *She was a model pupil.*

model verb models, modelling, modelled
1 to model something is to make a small copy of it **2** to model one thing on another is to use the second thing as a pattern for the first *The building is modelled on an Egyptian temple.* **3** to model, or to model clothes, is to work as an artist's model or a fashion model

modem noun modems (in computing)
a piece of equipment that links a computer to a telephone line

moderate (say **mod**-er-at) adjective
1 a moderate amount or level is not too little and not too much **2** moderate opinions are not extreme **moderately** adverb **moderation** noun

moderate (say mod-er-ayt) verb
moderates, moderating, moderated
to moderate something is to make it less strong or severe

modern adjective
belonging to the present day or recent times

modernize verb modernizes, modernizing, modernized
to modernize something is to make it modern, or suitable for modern tastes **modernization** noun

modest adjective
1 not thinking or talking too much about how good you are **2** quite small in amount *Their needs were modest.* **modestly** adverb **modesty** noun

modify verb modifies, modifying, modified
to modify something is to change it slightly **modification** noun

module (say **mod**-yool) noun modules
1 a separate section or part of something larger, such as a spacecraft or building **2** one of the parts that make up a course of learning *This term I'm doing a Maths module.*

moist adjective
slightly wet

moisten (say **moi**-sen) verb moistens, moistening, moistened
1 to moisten something is to make it slightly wet **2** to moisten is to become slightly wet

moisture noun
moisture is tiny drops of water in the air or on a surface

molar (say **moh**-ler) noun molars
one of the wide teeth at the back of your mouth

mole noun moles
1 a small furry animal that digs holes under the ground **2** a small dark spot on the skin

molecule (say **mol**-i-kewl) noun
molecules (in science)
the smallest part into which a substance
can be divided without changing its
chemical nature; a group of atoms
molecular adjective

molehill noun molehills
a small pile of earth thrown up by a mole
to make a mountain out of a molehill is
to give something too much importance

mollusc noun molluscs
an animal with a soft body and usually a
hard shell, such as a snail or an oyster

molten adjective
molten rock or metal has been made into
liquid by great heat *Molten lava flowed down
the side of the volcano.*

moment noun moments
1 a very short period of time *Wait a
moment.* **2** a particular time *At that moment,
all the lights went out.* **at the moment** now

momentary (say **moh**-men-
ter-i) adjective
lasting for only a moment
momentarily adverb

momentous (say moh-**ment**-us)
adjective
very important

momentum (say moh-**ment**-um) noun
momentum is the amount or force of
movement *The stone gained momentum as it
rolled down the hill.*

monarch noun monarchs
a king, queen, emperor, or empress ruling
a country

monarchy noun monarchies
1 monarchy is rule by a monarch
2 a monarchy is a country ruled by
a monarch

monastery (say **mon**-a-ster-i) noun
monasteries
a building where monks live and work

Monday noun Mondays
the second day of the week

money noun
money is coins and notes used by people to
buy things

mongoose noun mongooses
a small animal like a large weasel, that can
kill snakes

mongrel (say **mung**-rel) noun mongrels
a dog of mixed breeds

monitor noun monitors
1 a device used for checking how
something is working **2** a computer or
television screen **3** a pupil who is given a
special job to do at school

monitor verb monitors, monitoring,
monitored
to monitor something or someone is
to watch or test them to see how they
are working

monk noun monks
a member of a religious community of men

monkey noun monkeys
1 an animal with long arms, hands with
thumbs, and a tail **2** a mischievous person,
especially a child

mono- prefix
meaning 'having one of something', as
in *monorail*

monogram noun monograms
a design made up of a letter or a group
of letters

monologue (say **mon**-o-log) noun
monologues
a long speech by one person or performer

monopolize verb monopolizes,
monopolizing, monopolized
to monopolize something is to have
complete control of it and keep out
everyone else

monopoly noun monopolies
control of a business or activity by one
person or group

monorail noun monorails
a railway that runs on a single rail

a
b
c
d
e
f
g
h
i
j
k
m
n
o
p
q
r
s
t
u
v
w
x
y
z

monotonous (say mon-**ot**-on-us) adjective
boring because it does not change *This is monotonous work. The sky became quite grey and, along with it, the whole countryside seemed to lose its colour and assume the same monotonous tone.* – Norton Juster, *The Phantom Tollbooth* **monotonously** adverb **monotony** noun

monsoon noun **monsoons**
a strong wind in and around the Indian Ocean, bringing heavy rain in summer

monster noun **monsters**
a huge frightening creature

monster adjective (informal)
huge

monstrosity noun **monstrosities**
a monstrosity is a dreadful or shocking thing

monstrous adjective
1 like a monster; huge 2 very shocking or cruel *It was a monstrous crime.*

month noun **months**
one of the twelve parts into which a year is divided

monthly adjective, adverb
something happens monthly when it happens every month

monument noun **monuments**
a statue, building, or column put up to remind people of some person or event

monumental adjective
1 built as a monument 2 great or huge *It was a monumental achievement.*

moo verb **moos, mooing, mooed**
to make the sound of a cow

mood noun **moods**
the way someone feels at a particular time *She is in a cheerful mood.*

moody adjective **moodier, moodiest**
1 gloomy 2 likely to have sudden changes of mood **moodily** adverb **moodiness** noun

moon noun **moons**
1 the natural satellite which orbits the earth and shines in the sky at night 2 a similar object which orbits another planet

moonlight noun
moonlight is the light reflected from the moon **moonlit** adjective

moor[1] noun **moors**
an area of rough land covered with bracken and bushes

moor[2] verb **moors, mooring, moored**
to moor a boat is to tie it up to the land

moorhen noun **moorhens**
a small water bird

mooring noun **moorings**
a place where a boat can be moored

moose noun **moose**
a North American elk

mop noun **mops**
a piece of soft material on the end of a stick, used for cleaning floors or dishes

mop verb **mops, mopping, mopped**
to mop something is to clean it with a mop **to mop something up** is to clear away spilt liquid

mope verb **mopes, moping, moped**
to mope is to be miserable and not interested in doing anything *'Eeyore, who is a friend of mine, has lost his tail. And he's moping about it. So could you very kindly tell me how to find it for him?'* – A. A. Milne, *Winnie-the-Pooh*

moped (say **moh**-ped) noun **mopeds**
a kind of small motorcycle with pedals

moral adjective
1 to do with people's behaviour and what is right and wrong 2 being or doing good and what is right *We are expected to lead moral lives.* **morality** noun **morally** adverb to behave morally is to behave in a good and right way

moral noun **morals**
a lesson taught by a story or event

A
B
C
D
E
F
G
H
I
J
K
L
M
N
O
P
Q
R
S
T
U
V
W
X
Y
Z

morale (say mo-**rahl**) noun
morale is confidence or courage

morals plural noun
standards of behaviour

morbid adjective
thinking about gloomy or unpleasant things such as death **morbidly** adverb

more determiner
greater in number or amount *We need more money.*

more pronoun
a larger number or amount *I want more.*

more adverb
1 to a greater extent *You must work more.*
2 again *I'll tell you once more.* **more or less** almost; approximately *I've more or less finished the work. The repairs cost £100, more or less.*

moreover adverb
also; in addition to what has been said

Mormon noun **Mormons**
a member of a religious group founded in the USA

morning noun **mornings**
the early part of the day before noon

moron noun **morons** (informal)
a stupid person **moronic** adjective

morose adjective
bad-tempered and miserable

morris dance noun **morris dances**
a traditional English dance performed by people in costume with ribbons and bells

Morse code noun
a code for sending radio signals, using dots and dashes to represent letters and numbers

morsel noun **morsels**
a small piece of food

mortal adjective
1 certain to die *All men are mortal.*
2 causing death *He received a mortal wound.*
mortally adverb

mortality noun
1 mortality can be used to talk about the number of people who die over a period of time *There is a low rate of infant mortality.*
2 mortality is also being mortal

mortar noun **mortars**
1 mortar is a mixture of sand, cement, and water used in building to stick bricks together **2** a mortar is a small thick bowl for pounding food with a tool called a pestle **3** a mortar is also a small cannon

mortgage (say **mor**-gij) noun **mortgages**
an arrangement to borrow money to buy a house, repaid over many years

Morse code

A .‑

B ‑...

C ‑.‑.

D ‑..

E .

F ..‑.

0 ‑‑‑‑‑

1 .‑‑‑‑

2 ..‑‑‑

3 ...‑‑

A
B
C
D
E
F
G
H
I
J
K
L
M
N
O
P
Q
R
S
T
U
V
W
X
Y
Z

mortuary noun mortuaries
a place where dead bodies are kept before they are buried or cremated

mosaic (say moh-**zay**-ik) noun mosaics
a picture or design made from small coloured pieces of glass or stone

mosque (say mosk) noun mosques
a building where Muslims worship

mosquito (say mos-**kee**-toh) noun mosquitoes
an insect that sucks blood and carries disease

moss noun mosses
a plant that grows in damp places and has no flowers

most determiner
greatest in number or amount *Most people came by bus.*

most pronoun
the greatest number or amount *They've eaten most of the food.*

most adverb
1 more than any other *I liked this book most.* **2** very; extremely *It was most amusing.*

mostly adverb
mainly

MOT or **MOT test** noun
MOTs, MOT tests
a safety check that has to be made every year on road vehicles

motel (say moh-**tel**) noun motels
a hotel near a main road, with parking and rooms for motorists

moth noun moths
an insect rather like a butterfly, that usually flies around at night

mother noun mothers
your female parent

motherhood noun
motherhood is being a mother and looking after children

mother-in-law noun
mothers-in-law
the mother of your husband or wife

motherly adjective
kind or tender like a mother

motion noun motions
a way of moving; movement **to go through the motions** is to do or say something because you have to, without much interest

motionless adjective
not moving; still

motivate verb motivates, motivating, motivated
to motivate someone is to make them keen to achieve something *She is good at motivating her team.*

motive noun motives
a person's motive is what makes them do something

motor noun motors
a machine that provides power to drive machinery

motorbike noun motorbikes
a motorcycle

motor boat noun motor boats
a boat driven by a motor

motor car noun motor cars
a motor vehicle that can carry several people inside it

motorcycle noun motorcycles
a motor vehicle with two wheels and a saddle for the riders **motorcyclist** noun

motorist noun motorists
someone who drives a motor car

motorway noun motorways
a wide road for fast long-distance traffic

mottled adjective
marked with spots or patches of colour

motto noun mottoes
1 a short saying used as a guide for behaviour *His motto was 'Do your best'.* **2** a short verse or riddle found inside a cracker

mould¹ noun moulds
a mould is a container for making things like jelly or plaster set in a special shape

mould verb moulds, moulding, moulded
to mould something is to make it have a particular shape or character

mould² noun moulds
mould is a furry growth that appears on some moist surfaces, especially on something decaying

mouldy adjective mouldier, mouldiest
something is mouldy when it has mould on it

moult (say mohlt) verb moults, moulting, moulted
animals or birds moult when they lose hair or feathers

mound noun mounds
a pile of earth or stones; a small hill

mount verb mounts, mounting, mounted
1 to mount a horse or bicycle is to get on it so that you can ride it 2 to mount is to increase in amount *The cost of running a car is mounting.* 3 to mount a picture or photograph is to put it in a frame or album in order to display it

mount noun mounts
1 a mountain, especially in names such as *Mount Everest* 2 something on which a picture or photograph is mounted 3 an animal for someone to ride on

mountain noun mountains
1 a very high hill 2 a large amount *We've got a mountain of work to do.*

mountaineer noun mountaineers
someone who climbs mountains

mountaineering noun
mountaineering is the sport of climbing mountains

mourn verb mourns, mourning, mourned
to mourn is to be sad, especially because someone has died **mourner** noun mourners
are the people who go to a funeral

mournful adjective
sad and sorrowful *Paddington sank down on to his case looking very mournful. Even the pom-pom on his hat seemed limp.*
— Michael Bond, *A Bear Called Paddington*
mournfully adverb

mouse noun mice
1 a small animal with a long tail and a pointed nose 2 (in computing) a small device that you move around on a mat to control the movements of the cursor on the computer screen

mousetrap noun mousetraps
a trap for catching and killing mice

mousse (say mooss) noun mousses
1 a creamy pudding flavoured with chocolate or fruit 2 a frothy creamy substance used for holding hair while styling it

moustache (say mus-**tahsh**) noun moustaches
a strip of hair that a man grows above his upper lip

mousy adjective mousier, mousiest
1 mousy hair is light brown in colour 2 a mousy person is timid and feeble

mouth noun mouths
1 the part of your face that opens for eating and speaking 2 the place where a river flows into the sea 3 an opening or outlet

mouthful noun mouthfuls
an amount of food you put in your mouth

mouth organ noun mouth organs
a small musical instrument you play by blowing and sucking while passing it along your lips

mouthpiece noun mouthpieces
the part of a musical instrument or other device that you put to your mouth

movable adjective
able to be moved

a
b
c
d
e
f
g
h
i
j
k
l
m
n
o
p
q
r
s
t
u
v
w
x
y
z

A
B
C
D
E
F
G
H
I
J
K
L
M
N
O
P
Q
R
S
T
U
V
W
X
Y
Z

move verb moves, moving, moved
1 to move something is to take it from one place to another **2** to move is to go from one place to another **3** to move someone is to affect their feelings *Their story moved us deeply.*

move noun moves
1 a movement **2** a player's turn in a game **to get a move on** (informal) is to hurry up **to be on the move** is to be moving or making progress

movement noun movements
1 movement is moving or being moved **2** a movement is a group of people working together to achieve something **3** in music, a movement is one of the main parts of a long piece such as a symphony

movie noun movies
a cinema film

moving adjective
causing someone to feel strong emotion, especially sadness or pity

mow verb mows, mowing, mowed, mown
to mow grass is to cut it with a machine **to mow people down** is to knock them down and kill them

MP
short for **Member of Parliament**

MP3 player noun MP3 players
a small portable device for playing sound files downloaded from the Internet

m.p.h.
short for *miles per hour*

Mr (say **mis**-ter) noun Messrs
a title you put before a man's name

Mrs (say **mis**-iz) noun Mrs or Mesdames
a title you put before a married woman's name

Ms (say miz) noun
a title you put before a woman's name

much adjective
existing in a large amount *There is much work to do.*

much pronoun
a large amount of something *£5 is not very much.*

much adverb
1 greatly; considerably *They came, much to my surprise.* **2** about; approximately *It's much the same.*

muck noun
1 muck is farmyard manure **2** (informal) muck is dirt or filth

muck verb mucks, mucking, mucked
(informal) **to muck about** or **muck around** is to behave stupidly or idly **to muck something up** is to do it very badly

mucky adjective muckier, muckiest
dirty or messy

mud noun
mud is wet soft earth

muddle verb muddles, muddling, muddled
1 to muddle things is to mix them up **2** to muddle someone is to confuse them

muddle noun muddles
a confusion or mess *I've got these papers in a bit of a muddle.*

muddy adjective muddier, muddiest
covered in mud

mudguard noun mudguards
a curved cover fixed over a bicycle wheel to stop mud and water being thrown up on to the rider

muesli (say **mooz**-li) noun
muesli is a breakfast food made of cereals, nuts, and dried fruit

muezzin noun muezzins
a man who calls Muslims to prayer from a minaret

muffle verb muffles, muffling, muffled
1 to muffle something is to cover or wrap it to protect it or keep it warm **2** to muffle a sound is to deaden it or reduce it

mug noun mugs
a large cup, usually used without a saucer

mug verb mugs, mugging, mugged
to mug someone is to attack and rob them
in the street **mugger** noun

muggy adjective muggier, muggiest
a muggy day is unpleasantly warm
and damp

mule noun mules
an animal that is the offspring of a donkey
and a mare

multi– prefix
meaning 'having many of something',
as in *multiracial*

multiple adjective
having many parts

multiple noun multiples
a number that can be divided exactly by
another number *30 and 50 are multiples
of 10.*

multiplication noun
multiplication is when you multiply numbers

multiply verb multiplies, multiplying,
multiplied
1 to multiply a number is to add it to itself
a certain number of times *Five multiplied
by four equals twenty (5 x 4 = 20).* **2** to
multiply is to increase or become many
His doubts started to multiply.

multiracial (say mul-ti-**ray**-shal)
adjective
a multiracial area has people living there of
many different races

multitude noun multitudes
a very large number of people or
things

mum noun mums (informal)
mother

mumble verb mumbles, mumbling,
mumbled
to speak softly and unclearly

mummify verb mummifies,
mummifying, mummified
in ancient Egypt, to mummify a dead body
was to prepare it as a mummy

mummy[1] noun mummies (informal)
mother

mummy[2] noun mummies
in ancient Egypt, a dead body wrapped in
cloth and treated with oils for burial

mumps noun
mumps is an infectious disease that makes
the neck swell painfully

munch verb munches, munching,
munched
to munch food is to chew it noisily

mundane adjective
ordinary or dull

municipal (say mew-**nis**-i-pal)
adjective
to do with a town or city

mural noun murals
a picture painted on a wall

murder verb murders, murdering,
murdered
to murder someone is to kill
them deliberately

murder noun murders
1 murder is the deliberate killing of
someone **2** (informal) you can say
something is murder when it is very difficult
or unpleasant *It was murder changing the
wheel in the dark.*

murderer noun murderers
someone who commits murder

murderous adjective
likely to commit murder; showing you are
very angry

murky adjective murkier, murkiest
dark and gloomy *The sea was murky and
choppy and uninviting. I didn't want to go
in, not one bit. – Michael Morpurgo, The
Sleeping Sword*

murmur noun murmurs
a low or soft continuous sound, especially
of people speaking

murmur verb murmurs, murmuring,
murmured
to murmur is to speak softly with a low

a
b
c
d
e
f
g
h
i
j
k
l
m
n
o
p
q
r
s
t
u
v
w
x
y
z

A
B
C
D
E
F
G
H
I
J
K
L

M

N
O
P
Q
R
S
T
U
V
W
X
Y
Z

continuous sound *The afternoon sun was getting low as the Rat sculled gently homewards in a dreamy mood, murmuring poetry-things over to himself, and not paying much attention to Mole.* — Kenneth Grahame, *The Wind in the Willows*

muscle noun muscles
a bundle of fibres that can stretch to cause movement of a part of the body

muscle verb muscles, muscling, muscled
to muscle in on something (informal) is to try to take part in something that does not concern you

 TOP TIPS
There is a tricky bit in **muscle**—the *s* sound is spelt **sc.**

muscular adjective
having a lot of muscles; powerful

museum noun museums
a place where interesting old or valuable objects are displayed for people to see

mushroom noun mushrooms
a fast-growing edible fungus with a dome-shaped top

mushroom verb mushrooms, mushrooming, mushroomed
things mushroom when they grow or appear suddenly like mushrooms *Blocks of flats mushroomed in the city.*

music noun
1 music is pleasant or interesting sounds made by instruments or by the voice **2** music is also a system of printed or written symbols for making this kind of sound

musical adjective
1 to do with music **2** good at music or interested in it **musically** adverb

musical noun musicals
a play or film with music and songs

musician noun musicians
someone who plays a musical instrument, especially for a living

musket noun muskets
an old type of rifle

musketeer noun musketeers
a soldier armed with a musket

Muslim (say **muuz**-lim) noun Muslims
someone who follows the religion of Islam

muslin noun
fine cotton cloth

mussel noun mussels
a black shellfish, often found sticking to rocks

must verb
a word used with another verb to show
1 that someone has to do something *I must go home soon.* **2** that something is certain *You must be joking!*

mustard noun
mustard is a yellow paste or powder used to give food a hot taste

muster verb musters, mustering, mustered
to muster something is to assemble it or gather it together

musty adjective mustier, mustiest
smelling or tasting mouldy or stale

mutation noun mutations
a change in the form of a living creature because of changes in its genes

mute adjective
not speaking or able to speak

mute noun mutes
1 a person who cannot speak **2** a device fitted to a musical instrument to soften the sound

muted adjective
silent or quiet *She gave a muted reply.*

mutilate verb mutilates, mutilating, mutilated
to mutilate something is to damage it by breaking or cutting off part of it
mutilation noun

mutineer (say mew-tin-**eer**) noun
mutineers
someone who takes part in a mutiny

mutiny (say **mew**-tin-i) noun mutinies
a rebellion by sailors or soldiers against
their officers

mutiny (say **mew**-tin-i) verb mutinies,
mutinying, mutinied
to mutiny is to take part in a mutiny

mutter verb mutters, muttering,
muttered
to murmur or grumble in a low voice
*Mildred muttered the spell under her breath –
and Ethel vanished. In her place stood a small
pink and grey pig.* – Jill Murphy, *The Worst
Witch*

mutton noun
mutton is meat from an adult sheep

mutual (say **mew**-tew-al) adjective
given or done to each other *They
have mutual respect for one another.*
mutually adverb

muzzle noun muzzles
1 an animal's nose and mouth **2** a cover put
over an animal's nose and mouth so that it
cannot bite **3** the open end of a gun

muzzle verb muzzles, muzzling,
muzzled
1 to muzzle an animal is to put a muzzle on
it **2** to muzzle someone is to prevent them
from saying what they think

my determiner
belonging to me *This is my book.*

myself pronoun
me and nobody else, used to refer back
to the person who is speaking *I have hurt
myself.* **by myself** on my own; alone *I did the
work all by myself.*

mysterious adjective
full of mystery; strange and puzzling

mysteriously adverb
something happens mysteriously
when what happens is difficult to
explain or understand. *My watch
mysteriously disappeared.*

mystery noun mysteries
something strange or puzzling *Exactly why
the ship sank is a mystery.*

mystify verb mystifies, mystifying,
mystified
to mystify someone is to puzzle them very
much **mystification** noun

myth noun myths
1 an old story about gods and heroes in
ancient times **2** an untrue story or belief *It
is a myth that carrots make you see better.*

mythical adjective
imaginary; only found in myths

mythology noun
mythology is the study of myths
mythological adjective mythological
creatures or characters are found in myths

Nn

nab verb nabs, nabbing, nabbed
(informal)
to nab someone is to catch or grab them

nag[1] verb nags, nagging, nagged
to nag someone is to keep criticizing them
or complaining to them

nag[2] noun nags (informal)
a horse

nail noun nails
1 the hard covering on the end of one of
your fingers or toes **2** a small, sharp piece of
metal used to fix pieces of wood together

nail verb nails, nailing, nailed
1 to nail something is to fasten it with a
nail or nails **2** to nail someone is to catch or
trap them

naive (say ny-**eev**) adjective
1 too ready to believe what you are told;
showing a lack of experience **2** innocent
and trusting **naively** adverb **naivety** noun

a
b
c
d
e
f
g
h
i
j
k
l
m
n
o
p
q
r
s
t
u
v
w
x
y
z

A

naked (say nay-kid) adjective
without any clothes or coverings on **to look at something with the naked eye** is to look at it with your eyes without the help of a telescope or microscope **nakedness** noun

B

C

D

name noun names
what you call a person or thing

name verb names, naming, named
1 to name someone or something is to give them a name 2 to name someone or something is to say what they are called *Can you name these plants?*

E

F

G

nameless adjective
1 not having a name 2 not named or identified *The culprit shall be nameless.*

H

I

namely adverb
that is to say *I will invite two friends, namely Vicky and Tom.*

J

K

nanny noun nannies
1 a woman whose job is to look after small children 2 (informal) a grandmother

L

M

nanny goat noun nanny goats
a female goat

N

nap noun naps
a short sleep

O

napkin noun napkins
a piece of cloth or paper to keep your clothes clean or wipe your lips at meals

P

Q

nappy noun nappies
a piece of cloth or a paper pad put round a baby's bottom

R

S

narcissus (say nar-sis-us) noun narcissi
a garden flower like a daffodil

T

narrate verb narrates, narrating, narrated
to narrate a story or experience is to tell it to someone *She narrated her adventures in South America.* **narration** noun

U

V

W

narrative noun narratives
a story or account that someone tells

X

Y

narrator noun narrators
the person who is telling a story

Z

narrow adjective narrower, narrowest
1 not wide 2 with only a small margin of error or safety *We all had a narrow escape.* **narrowly** adverb you say that something narrowly happens when it only just happens *She narrowly escaped injury.*

narrow-minded adjective
not liking or understanding other people's ideas or beliefs

nasal adjective
to do with the nose

nasturtium (say na-ster-shum) noun nasturtiums
a garden flower with round leaves

nasty adjective nastier, nastiest
not pleasant; unkind **nastily** adverb **nastiness** noun

nation noun nations
1 a large number of people who have the same history, language, and customs, and live in the same part of the world under one government 2 a country and the people who live there

national adjective
to do with a nation or country **nationally** adverb something happens nationally when it happens all over the country

nationalism noun
supporting your country and wanting it to be independent **nationalist** noun

nationality noun nationalities
the nation someone belongs to *What is her nationality?*

nationalize verb nationalizes, nationalizing, nationalized
to nationalize an industry or organization is to put it under government control **nationalization** noun

nationwide adjective, adverb
over the whole of a country

native noun natives
a person born in a particular place *He is a native of Sweden.*

native to nearby

native adjective
of the country where you were born *English is my native language.*

Native American noun Native Americans
one of the original inhabitants of North or South America

nativity (say na-**tiv**-i-ti) noun **nativities**
someone's birth **the Nativity** the birth of Jesus Christ

natural adjective
1 made or done by nature, not by people or machines **2** normal; not surprising **3** belonging to someone from birth *He has plenty of natural ability.* **4** in music, not sharp or flat

natural noun **naturals**
1 a natural note in music; a sign ♮ that shows a note is natural **2** someone who is naturally good at something *She's a natural at juggling.*

naturalist noun **naturalists**
someone who studies natural history

naturally adverb
1 in a natural way *The gas is produced naturally.* **2** as you would expect *Naturally I will pay your train fare.*

nature noun **natures**
1 nature is everything in the world that was not made by people, such as plants and animals **2** a person's or thing's nature is the qualities or characteristics they have *She has a loving nature.* **3** a nature is a kind or sort of thing *He likes insects and things of that nature.*

nature trail noun nature trails
a path in the country with signs telling you about the plants and wildlife you can see there

naughty adjective **naughtier, naughtiest**
not behaving as you should; disobedient or rude **naughtily** adverb **naughtiness** noun

nausea noun
nausea is a feeling of sickness or disgust

nautical adjective
connected with ships or sailors

naval adjective
to do with a navy

nave noun **naves**
the main central part of a church

navel noun **navels**
the small hollow at the front of your stomach

navigable adjective
a navigable river is suitable for ships to sail in

navigate verb **navigates, navigating, navigated**
1 to navigate is to make sure that an aircraft, ship, or vehicle is going in the right direction **2** to navigate a sea or river is to sail a ship on it

navigation noun
navigation is making sure that an aircraft, ship, or vehicle is going in the right direction

navigator noun **navigators**
the person who makes sure that an aircraft, ship, or vehicle is going in the right direction

navy noun **navies**
1 a fleet of ships and the people trained to use them **2** navy blue

navy blue noun, adjective
very dark blue

near adverb, adjective **nearer, nearest**
not far away **near by** at a place not far away *They live near by.*

near preposition
not far away from something *She lives near the town.*

near verb **nears, nearing, neared**
to near a place is to come close to it *The ships were nearing the harbour.*

nearby adjective
near; not far away *We live in a nearby town.*

a
b
c
d
e
f
g
h
i
j
k
l
m
n
o
p
q
r
s
t
u
v
w
x
y
z

339

A
B
C
D
E
F
G
H
I
J
K
L
M
N
O
P
Q
R
S
T
U
V
W
X
Y
Z

nearly adverb
1 almost *It was nearly midnight.* **2** closely *They are nearly related.*

neat adjective **neater, neatest**
1 tidy and carefully arranged **2** skilfully done *That was a neat goal.* **3** without water added *They were drinking neat orange juice.* **neatly** adverb **neatness** noun

necessarily adverb
for certain; definitely *It won't necessarily cost you a lot.*

necessary adjective
needed very much; essential

 TOP TIPS Double up the **s** in **necessary** (but the **c** stays single)!

necessity noun **necessities**
1 necessity is need *There is no necessity for you to come too.* **2** a necessity is also something needed *We have brought all the necessities for a picnic.*

neck noun **necks**
1 the part of the body that joins the head to the shoulders **2** a narrow part of something, especially of a bottle **to be neck and neck** is to be almost exactly together in a race or contest

necklace noun **necklaces**
a piece of jewellery you wear round your neck

nectar noun
nectar is a sweet liquid collected by bees from flowers

nectarine noun **nectarines**
a kind of peach with a smooth skin

need verb **needs, needing, needed**
1 to need something is to be without it when you should have it **2** to need to do something is to have to do it *I needed to get a haircut.*

need noun **needs**
1 a need is something that you need **2** need is a situation in which something is necessary *There's no need to shout.* **to be in need** is to need money or help

needle noun **needles**
1 a very thin pointed piece of metal used for sewing **2** something long, thin, and sharp, such as a knitting needle or a pine needle **3** the pointer of a meter or compass

needless noun
not necessary *That was a needless waste of time.* **needlessly** adverb

needlework noun
needlework is sewing or embroidery

needy adjective **needier, neediest**
needy people are very poor and do not have what they need to live properly

negative adjective
1 a negative statement or answer is one that says 'no' **2** not definite or confident *Ellie is always negative about herself.* **3** a negative number is one that is less than nought **4** a negative electric charge is one that carries electrons **negatively** adverb

negative noun **negatives**
1 something that means 'no' **2** a photograph or film with the dark parts light and the light parts dark, from which prints are made

neglect verb **neglects, neglecting, neglected**
1 to neglect something or someone is to fail to look after them or deal with them **2** to neglect to do something is to fail to do it

neglect noun
neglect is failing to look after someone or do something

neglectful adjective
tending not to do things you should

negligent adjective
not taking proper care or paying enough attention *The cleaners had been negligent and left the windows open.* **negligence** noun

negotiate (say nig-**oh**-shi-ayt) verb **negotiates, negotiating, negotiated**
1 to negotiate is to try to reach an agreement about something by discussing it **2** to negotiate an obstacle or difficulty is to get past it or over it **negotiations** plural noun

neigh verb neighs, neighing, neighed
to make a high-pitched cry like a horse

neigh noun neighs
the sound of a horse neighing

neighbour noun neighbours
someone who lives next door or near to you **neighbouring** adjective

neighbourhood noun neighbourhoods
the surrounding district

neighbourly adjective
someone is neighbourly when they are friendly and helpful to people who live near them

neither (say **ny**-ther or **nee**-ther) determiner, pronoun
not either *Neither parent was there. Neither of them likes cabbage.*

neither conjunction
neither ... nor ... not one thing and not the other *I neither know nor care.*

neon (say **nee**-on) noun
neon is a gas that glows when electricity passes through it, used in street lighting and signs

nephew noun nephews
the son of a person's brother or sister

nerve noun nerves
1 a nerve is one of the fibres inside your body that carry messages to and from your brain, so that parts of your body can feel and move **2** nerve is courage and calmness in a dangerous situation *Don't lose your nerve.* **3** (informal) nerve is cheek or impudence *He had the nerve to ask for more.*
to get on someone's nerves is to irritate them **nerves** nervousness *I always suffer from nerves before an exam.*

nerve-racking adjective
difficult and worrying *We had a nerve-racking time trying to get out.*

nervous adjective
1 easily upset or agitated; timid **2** to do with the nerves **nervously** adverb **nervousness** noun

nest noun nests
1 the place where a bird lays its eggs and feeds its young **2** a warm place where some small animals live

nest verb nests, nesting, nested
birds or animals nest when they make or have a nest *Gulls were nesting on the cliffs.*

nestle verb nestles, nestling, nestled
to curl up comfortably *Moomintroll stood on his doorstep and watched the valley nestle beneath its winter blanket.* — Tove Jansson, *Finn Family Moomintroll*

nestling noun nestlings
a young bird before it is old enough to leave the nest

net[1] noun nets
1 net is material made of pieces of thread, cord, or wire joined together in a criss-cross pattern with holes between **2** a net is a piece of this material **3** the net is the Internet

net[2] adjective
left over after everything has been taken away *The net weight, without the box, is 100 grams.*

netball noun
netball is a game in which two teams try to throw a ball through a high net hanging from a ring

nettle noun nettles
a wild plant with leaves that sting when you touch them

network noun networks
1 a criss-cross arrangement of lines **2** a system with many connections or parts, such as a railway or broadcasting or computer system

neuter (say **new**-ter) adjective
neither male nor female

neuter (say **new**-ter) verb neuters, neutering, neutered
to neuter an animal is to remove its sexual organs so that it cannot breed

neutral (say **new**-tral) adjective
1 not supporting either side in a war

a
b
c
d
e
f
g
h
i
j
k
l
m
n
o
p
q
r
s
t
u
v
w
x
y
z

neutral (continued) or quarrel **2** not distinct or distinctive *The room was painted in neutral colours.* **neutrality** noun

neutralize verb neutralizes, neutralizing, neutralized
to neutralize something is to take away its use or effect

never adverb
at no time; not ever; not at all

nevertheless adverb
in spite of this; although that is a fact *It's difficult. Nevertheless, I think you'll manage.*

new adjective newer, newest
1 not existing before; just bought, made, or received **2** different or unfamiliar *That's a new idea.* **newly** adverb recently **newness** noun

newcomer noun newcomers
someone who has recently arrived in a place

new moon noun new moons
the moon at the beginning of its cycle, when it appears as a thin crescent

news noun
1 news is new information about people or recent events *I've got some good news.* **2** news is also a radio or television report about important events

newsagent noun newsagents
a shopkeeper who sells newspapers and magazines

newsletter noun newsletters
a short informal report sent regularly to members of an organization or club

newspaper noun newspapers
1 a newspaper is a daily or weekly publication of large sheets of printed paper folded together, containing news reports and articles **2** newspaper is the paper these are printed on *Wrap it in newspaper.*

newt noun newts
a small animal rather like a lizard, that lives near or in water

New Testament noun
the second part of the Bible, which describes the life and teachings of Jesus Christ

next adjective
the nearest; following immediately after

next adverb
1 in the nearest place **2** at the nearest time *What comes next?*

nib noun nibs
the pointed metal part at the end of a pen

nibble verb nibbles, nibbling, nibbled
to nibble something is to take small or gentle bites at it

nice adjective nicer, nicest
1 pleasant or kind **2** attractive *She has nice hair.* **nicely** adverb **niceness** noun

nicety noun niceties
a small detail or feature

nick noun nicks
a small cut or notch **in the nick of time** only just in time

nick verb nicks, nicking, nicked
1 to nick something is to make a small cut in it **2** (informal) to nick something is to steal it

nickel noun nickels
1 a silver-white metal **2** (in America) a 5-cent coin

nickname noun nicknames
an informal name given to someone instead of their real name

nicotine (say **nik**-o-teen) noun
nicotine is a poisonous substance found in tobacco

niece noun nieces
the daughter of a person's brother or sister

night noun nights
the time when it is dark, between sunset and sunrise

nightdress noun nightdresses
a loose light dress that girls and women wear in bed

nightfall noun
nightfall is the time when it becomes dark just after sunset

nightingale noun nightingales
a small brown bird that sings sweetly

nightly adjective
happening every night

nightmare noun nightmares
1 a frightening or unpleasant dream
2 a terrifying experience
nightmarish adjective terrifying

nil noun
nothing *We lost three-nil.*

nimble adjective nimbler, nimblest
moving quickly or easily *As soon as the King and his huntsmen saw the Roe with the golden collar they all rode off after it, but it was far too quick and nimble for them.* — Andrew Lang, *The Red Fairy Book*

nine noun nines
the number 9

nineteen noun nineteens
the number 19 **nineteenth** adjective, noun

ninety noun nineties
the number 90 **ninetieth** adjective, noun

ninth adjective, noun
the next after the eighth **ninthly** adverb in the ninth place; as the ninth one

nip verb nips, nipping, nipped
1 to nip someone is to pinch or bite them sharply 2 (informal) to nip somewhere is to go quickly there *I'll just nip into the supermarket.*

nip noun nips
1 a quick pinch or bite 2 a cold feeling *There's a nip in the air.*

nipple noun nipples
one of the two small parts that stick out at the front of a person's chest

nippy adjective nippier, nippiest
(informal)
1 quick or nimble 2 cold

nit noun nits
a louse or its egg

nit-picking noun
pointing out small faults or mistakes

nitrogen (say **ny**-tro-jen) noun
nitrogen is a gas that makes up about four-fifths of the air

no interjection
a word you use to refuse something or say that you do not agree

no determiner, adverb
not any *We have no money. She is no better.*

nobility noun
1 the nobility is the nobles or the aristocracy 2 nobility is being noble

noble adjective nobler, noblest
1 of high social rank; aristocratic 2 having a good and generous nature *He is a noble king.* 3 stately or impressive *It was a noble building.*

noble noun nobles
a person of high social rank

nobleman or
noblewoman noun
noblemen, noblewomen
a man or woman of high rank

nobody pronoun
no person; not anyone *Nobody knows.*

nobody noun nobodies
an unimportant person *He's just a nobody.*

nocturnal (say nok-**ter**-nal) adjective
1 active at night *Badgers are nocturnal animals.* 2 happening at night

nod verb nods, nodding, nodded
to nod, or nod your head, is to move your head up and down as a way of agreeing with someone or as a greeting

noise noun noises
a loud sound, especially one that is unpleasant or unwanted

noiseless adjective
something is noiseless when it does not make any noise **noiselessly** adverb

a
b
c
d
e
f
g
h
i
j
k
l
m
n
o
p
q
r
s
t
u
v
w
x
y
z

A
B
C
D
E
F
G
H
I
J
K
L
M

N

O
P
Q
R
S
T
U
V
W
X
Y
Z

noisily adverb
you noisily do something when you make a lot of noise doing it

noisy adjective **noisier, noisiest**
making a lot of noise

nomad (say **noh**-mad) noun **nomads**
a member of a tribe that moves from place to place looking for pasture for their animals **nomadic** adjective

nominate verb **nominates, nominating, nominated**
to nominate someone is to suggest that they should be a candidate in an election or should be given a job or award **nomination** noun

non– prefix
meaning 'not', as in *non-existent*

none pronoun
not any; not one *None of us went.*

none adverb
not at all *He's none too pleased.* **none the less** nevertheless

non-existent adjective
not existing

non-fiction noun
non-fiction is writings that are not fiction; books about real things and true events

nonsense noun
1 nonsense is words that do not mean anything or make any sense **2** nonsense is also absurd or silly ideas or behaviour **nonsensical** adjective

non–stop adverb, adjective
1 not stopping *They talked non-stop all morning.* **2** not stopping until the end of a journey *There's a non-stop train to London.*

noodles plural noun
pasta made in narrow strips, used in soups

noon noun
twelve o'clock midday

no one pronoun
no person; not anyone

noose noun **nooses**
a loop in a rope that gets smaller when the rope is pulled

nor conjunction
and not *She cannot do it; nor can I.*

normal adjective
1 usual or ordinary *It's normal to want a holiday.* **2** natural and healthy; not suffering from an illness **normality** noun

normally adverb
1 usually *The journey normally takes an hour.* **2** in the usual way *Just breathe normally.*

north noun
1 north is the direction to the left of a person facing east **2** north is also the part of a country or city that is in this direction

north adjective, adverb
1 towards the north or in the north **2** coming from the north *A north wind was blowing.*

north–east noun, adjective, adverb
midway between north and east

northerly adjective
a northerly wind is one that blows from the north

northern adjective
from or to do with the north

northerner noun **northerners**
someone who lives in the north of a country

northward or **northwards** adjective, adverb
towards the north

north–west noun, adjective, adverb
midway between north and west

nose noun **noses**
1 the part of your face that you use for breathing and smelling **2** the front part of something, especially a vehicle or aircraft

nose verb **noses, nosing, nosed**
to nose forward or through is to make progress cautiously *The ship nosed through the ice.* **to nose about** or **nose around** is to pry or interfere in someone else's affairs

nosedive noun nosedives
a steep dive, especially in an aircraft
nosedive verb nosedives, nosediving, nosedived
to go suddenly downward

nostalgia (say nos-**tal**-ja) noun
you feel nostalgia when you fondly remember something that made you happy in the past **nostalgic** adjective

nostril noun nostrils
each of the two openings in your nose

nosy adjective nosier, nosiest (informal)
always wanting to know other people's business **nosiness** noun

not adverb
a word you use to change the meaning of something to its opposite

notable adjective
remarkable or famous **notably** adverb especially or remarkably

notch noun notches
a small V-shaped cut or mark

note noun notes
1 something you write down as a reminder or help **2** a short letter **3** a single sound in music **4** a sound or tone that indicates something *There was a note of anger in his voice.* **5** a banknote *Have you got a five-pound note?* **to take note of something** is to listen to it and understand it
note verb notes, noting, noted
to note something is to pay attention to it, or to write it down as a reminder or help

notebook noun notebooks
1 a book in which you write things down **2** a small computer that you can carry around with you

notepaper noun
notepaper is paper for writing letters

nothing noun
nothing is not anything

notice noun notices
1 a notice is something written or printed

and displayed for people to see **2** to take notice of something is to pay attention to it *It escaped my notice.* **3** a warning that something is going to happen
notice verb notices, noticing, noticed
to notice something is to see it or become aware of it

noticeable adjective
easy to see or notice **noticeably** adverb

noticeboard noun noticeboards
a board on which notices can be displayed

notion noun notions
an idea, especially one that is vague or uncertain *The notion that the earth is flat was disproved long ago.*

notoriety noun
notoriety is being well known for doing something bad

notorious (say noh-**tor**-i-us) adjective
well-known for doing something bad *He was a notorious criminal.*
notoriously adverb

nougat (say **noo**-gah) noun
nougat is a chewy sweet made from nuts and sugar or honey

nought (say nawt) noun noughts
1 the figure 0 **2** nothing

noun noun nouns
a word that stands for a person, place, or thing

nourish verb nourishes, nourishing, nourished
to nourish someone is to give them enough good food to keep them alive and well

nourishment noun
nourishment is the food someone needs to keep them alive and well

novel noun novels
a story that fills a whole book
novel adjective
unusual *What a novel idea.*

novelist (say **nov**-el-ist) noun novelists
someone who writes novels

a
b
c
d
e
f
g
h
i
j
k
l
m
n
o
p
q
r
s
t
u
v
w
x
y
z

A
B
C
D
E
F
G
H
I
J
K
L
M
N
O
P
Q
R
S
T
U
V
W
X
Y
Z

novelty noun **novelties**
1 novelty is being new or unusual *The novelty of living in a cave soon wore off.*
2 a novelty is something new and unusual
3 a novelty is also a cheap toy or ornament

November noun
the eleventh month of the year

novice noun **novices**
a beginner

now adverb
1 at this time *I am now living in Glasgow.*
2 without any delay *Do it now!* **for now** until a later time *Goodbye for now.* **now and again** or **now and then** occasionally; sometimes

now conjunction
since or as *I do remember, now you mention it.*

now noun
this moment *They should be home by now.*

nowadays adverb
at the present time

nowhere adverb
not anywhere; in no place or to no place

nozzle noun **nozzles**
the part at the end of a hose or pipe from which something flows

nuclear (say **new**-kli-er) adjective
1 to do with a nucleus, especially of an atom 2 using the energy that is created by the splitting of atoms *nuclear weapons*

nucleus (say **new**-kli-us) noun **nuclei**
1 the central part of an atom or cell 2 the part in the centre of something, round which other things are grouped *The queen bee is the nucleus of the hive.*

nude adjective
not wearing any clothes

nude noun **nudes**
a nude person, especially in a work of art

nudge verb **nudges, nudging, nudged**
to nudge someone is to touch or push them with your elbow

nugget noun **nuggets**
a rough lump of gold from the ground

nuisance noun **nuisances**
an annoying person or thing

numb adjective
part of your body is numb when you cannot feel anything in it **numbness** noun

number noun **numbers**
1 a symbol or word that tells you how many of something there are 2 a quantity of people or things *Do you know the number of bones in your body?* 3 a person's number is their telephone number 4 a song or piece of music

number verb **numbers, numbering, numbered**
1 to number things is to count them or mark them with numbers 2 to number a certain amount is to reach it *The crowd numbered 10,000.*

numeracy noun
numeracy is the ability to understand and work with numbers

numeral noun **numerals**
a symbol or figure that stands for a number

numerator noun **numerators**
the number above the line in a fraction. In ¼ the 1 is the numerator.

numerical adjective
to do with numbers

numerous adjective
many *There are numerous kinds of cat.*

nun noun **nuns**
a member of a religious community of women

nurse noun **nurses**
a person trained to look after people who are ill or injured

nurse verb **nurses, nursing, nursed**
1 to nurse someone is to look after them when they are ill or injured 2 to nurse someone or something is to hold them carefully in your arms *He was nursing a puppy.*

nursery noun **nurseries**
1 a place where young children are looked after or play **2** a place where young plants are grown and usually offered for sale

nursery rhyme noun **nursery rhymes**
a simple poem or song that young children like

nursery school noun **nursery schools**
a school for very young children

nursing home noun **nursing homes**
a small or private hospital

nurture verb **nurtures, nurturing, nurtured**
to nurture children is to look after them and educate them

nut noun **nuts**
1 a fruit with a hard shell **2** the part of this fruit that you can eat *a bag of mixed nuts* **3** a small piece of metal for screwing on to a bolt **4** (informal) the head **5** (informal) a mad or eccentric person

nutcrackers plural noun
pincers for cracking the shells of nuts

nutmeg noun **nutmegs**
a hard seed that is made into a powder and used as a spice

nutrient (say **new**-tri-ent) noun **nutrients**
a substance that is needed to keep a plant or animal alive and to help it to grow

nutrition (say new-**trish**-on) noun
nutrition is the food someone needs to keep them alive and well **nutritional** adjective

nutritious (say new-**trish**-us) adjective
nutritious food helps you to grow and keep well *They ate a nutritious meal.*

nutshell noun **nutshells**
the shell of a nut **to put something in a nutshell** is to state it very briefly

nutty adjective **nuttier, nuttiest**
1 tasting of nuts or full of nuts *nutty*

chocolate spread **2** (informal) mad or eccentric

nuzzle verb **nuzzles, nuzzling, nuzzled**
to nuzzle someone is to rub gently against them with the nose, in the way that some animals do *Bella lowered her head and turned to nuzzle Irina's hair with her warm velvety nose, then she trotted off into the barn and stood quietly in her corner on the straw.* — Magdalen Nabb, *The Enchanted Horse*

nylon noun
nylon is a lightweight synthetic cloth or fibre

nymph noun **nymphs**
in myths, a young goddess living in trees or rivers or the sea

Oo

oak noun **oaks**
a large tree that produces seeds called acorns

oar noun **oars**
a pole with a flat blade at one end, used for rowing a boat

oarsman or **oarswoman** noun **oarsmen, oarswomen**
a man or woman who rows a boat

oasis (say oh-**ay**-sis) noun **oases**
a fertile place with water and trees in a desert

oath noun **oaths**
1 a solemn promise to do something or that something is true **2** a swear word

oatmeal noun
oatmeal is ground oats

oats plural noun
a cereal used to make food for humans and animals

a
b
c
d
e
f
g
h
i
j
k
l
m
n
o
p
q
r
s
t
u
v
w
x
y
z

obedience noun
obedience is doing what you are told

obedient adjective
doing what someone tells you to do; willing to obey **obediently** adverb

obey verb obeys, obeying, obeyed
1 to obey someone is to do what they tell you 2 to obey a rule or law is to do what it says

obituary (say o-**bit**-yoo-er-i) noun
obituaries
an announcement in a newspaper that someone has died, often with a short account of their life

object (say **ob**-jikt) noun objects
1 something that can be seen or touched 2 the purpose of something 3 (in grammar) the word naming the person or thing that the action of the verb affects, for example *him* in the sentence *I chased him*

object (say ob-**jekt**) verb objects, objecting, objected
to object to something or someone is to say that you do not like them or do not agree with them

objection noun objections
1 objection is objecting to something 2 an objection is a reason for objecting *I have three objections to your plan.*

objectionable adjective
unpleasant or nasty

objective noun objectives
what you are trying to reach or do; an aim

objective adjective
not influenced by your own beliefs or ideas *He gave an objective account of the incident.*

obligation noun obligations
a duty

obligatory adjective
something is obligatory when you must do it because of a rule or law *Games are obligatory.*

oblige verb obliges, obliging, obliged
1 to oblige someone to do something is to force them to do it 2 to oblige someone is to help and please them *Always oblige your customers.* **to be obliged to someone** is to be grateful to them for helping you

oblique (say o-**bleek**) adjective
1 an oblique line slants at an angle 2 not straightforward or direct *They gave an oblique reply.*

oblong noun oblongs
a rectangle that is longer than it is wide
oblong adjective
having the shape of an oblong

obnoxious adjective
really horrible

oboe (say **oh**-boh) noun oboes
a high-pitched woodwind instrument
oboist noun

obscure adjective obscurer, obscurest
1 difficult to see or understand; very unclear 2 not well-known **obscurely** adverb **obscurity** noun

observance noun observances
obeying a law or keeping a custom

observant adjective
quick at noticing things *Paddington was a very observant bear, and since he had arrived in London he'd noticed lots of these shop windows. — Michael Bond, A Bear Called Paddington* **observantly** adverb

observation noun observations
1 observation is noticing or watching something carefully 2 an observation is a comment or remark *He made a few observations about the weather.*

observatory (say ob-**zerv**-a-ter-i) noun observatories
a building equipped with telescopes for looking at the stars or weather

observe verb observes, observing, observed
1 to observe someone or something is to watch them carefully 2 to observe something is to notice it 3 to observe a law or custom is to obey it or keep it 4 to observe a fact is to state it *She observed*

A
B
C
D
E
F
G
H
I
J
K
L
M
N
O
P
Q
R
S
T
U
V
W
X
Y
Z

that she did not like ice in her drinks.
observer noun

obsessed adjective
always thinking about something *He is obsessed with his work.*

obsession noun obsessions
an obsession is something that someone thinks about too much

obsolete adjective
not used any more; out of date

obstacle noun obstacles
something that gets in your way or makes it difficult for you to do something

obstinate adjective
not willing to change your ideas or ways, even though they may be wrong
obstinacy noun **obstinately** adverb

obstruct verb obstructs, obstructing, obstructed
to obstruct someone or something is to stop them from getting past, or to hinder them
obstruction noun

obtain verb obtains, obtaining, obtained
to obtain something is to get it or be given it **obtainable** adjective

obtuse adjective obtuser, obtusest
1 slow to understand; stupid **2** an obtuse angle is an angle of between 90 and 180 degrees

obvious adjective
easy to see or understand

obviously adverb
it is obvious that; clearly *Obviously we don't want to lose.*

occasion noun occasions
1 the time when something happens *On this occasion, we will not take any action.* **2** a special event *The wedding was a marvellous occasion.*

occasional adjective
happening from time to time, but not often and not regularly

occasionally adverb
something happens occasionally when it happens from time to time

occupant noun occupants
someone who occupies a place

occupation noun occupations
1 a person's occupation is their job or profession **2** the occupation of a country or territory is when an army captures it and stays there

occupy verb occupies, occupying, occupied
1 to occupy a place or building is to live in it **2** to occupy a space or position is to fill it **3** in a war, to occupy territory is to capture it and keep an army in it **4** to occupy someone is to keep them busy or interested

occur verb occurs, occurring, occurred
1 an event occurs when it happens or takes place *An earthquake occurred on the island in 1953.* **2** something occurs when it exists or is found somewhere *These plants occur in ponds.* **3** something occurs to you when it suddenly comes into your mind *Just then an idea occurred to me.*

occurrence noun occurrences
something that happens or exists

ocean noun oceans
1 the ocean is the area of salt water surrounding the land of the earth **2** an ocean is a large part of this water, such as the Pacific Ocean

o'clock adverb
by the clock *Lunch is at one o'clock.*

octagon noun octagons
a flat shape with eight sides
octagonal adjective

octave noun octaves
1 the interval between one musical note and the next note of the same name above or below it **2** these two notes played together

October noun
the tenth month of the year

a
b
c
d
e
f
g
h
i
j
k
l
m
n
o
p
q
r
s
t
u
v
w
x
y
z

octopus noun octopuses
a sea creature with eight arms
(called *tentacles*)

odd adjective odder, oddest
1 strange or unusual 2 an odd number is
one that cannot be divided by 2, such as 5
and 31 3 left over or spare *I've got an odd
sock.* 4 of various kinds; occasional *He's
doing odd jobs.* **oddness** noun being odd

oddly adverb
to behave oddly is to behave in a
strange way

oddments plural noun
small things of various kinds

odds plural noun
1 the chances that something will happen
2 the proportion of money that you will win
if a bet is successful *When the odds are 10
to 1, you will win £10 if you bet £1.* **odds and
ends** small things of various kinds

odour noun odours
a smell, usually an unpleasant one
odorous adjective

of preposition
1 belonging to *She is the mother of the child.*
2 coming from *He is a native of Italy.* 3 away
from *The supermarket is two miles north
of the town.* 4 about; concerning *Is there
any news of your father?* 5 from; out of *The
house is built of stone.*

off adverb
1 not on; away *His hat blew off.* 2 not
working or happening *The heating is off. The
match is off because of snow.* 3 behind or
at the side of a stage *There were noises off.*
4 beginning to go bad *I think the milk is off.*

off preposition
1 not on; away or down from *He fell off his
chair.* 2 not taking or wanting *She is off her
food.* 3 taken away from *There is £5 off the
normal price.*

offence noun offences
1 an offence is a crime or something illegal
When was the offence committed? 2 offence
is a feeling of annoyance or hurt

offend verb offends, offending,
offended
1 to offend someone is to hurt their
feelings or be unpleasant to them 2 to
offend is to break a law or do something
wrong **offender** noun

offensive adjective
1 insulting or causing offence 2 used
for attacking *He was arrested for carrying
an offensive weapon.* **offensively** adverb

offer verb offers, offering, offered
1 to offer something is to hold it out so
that someone can take it if they want it
2 to offer to do something is to say that
you are willing to do it 3 to offer a sum of
money is to say how much you are willing
to pay for something

offer noun offers
1 the action of offering something *Thank
you for your offer of help.* 2 an amount
of money that you are willing to pay
for something

offhand adjective
1 said without much thought 2 rude
or abrupt

office noun offices
1 a room or building where people work,
often at desks 2 a place where you can
go for tickets, information, or some
other purpose *a lost property office* 3 an
important job or position *He was honoured
to hold the office of President.*

officer noun officers
1 someone who is in charge of other people,
especially in the armed forces 2 a policeman
or policewoman

official adjective
1 done or said by someone with authority
2 connected with the job of someone in a
position of authority *The prime minister will
make an official visit to Australia next month.*
officially adverb

official noun officials
someone who does a job of authority
or trust

officious (say o-**fish**-us) adjective
too ready to order people about; bossy and
unpleasant **officiously** adverb

offset verb offsets, offsetting, offset
one thing offsets another when it
balances it out *The failures were offset by
some successes.*

offshore adjective, adverb
1 from the land towards the sea *There
is an offshore breeze.* **2** in the sea some
distance from the shore *They swam to an
offshore island.*

offside adjective (in sport)
in a position which is not allowed by
the rules

offspring noun offspring
a child or young animal

often adverb
many times; in many cases

ogre noun ogres
1 a cruel giant in stories
2 a frightening person

oh interjection
a cry of surprise, pain, or delight

oil noun oils
1 an oil is a thick slippery liquid that
does not mix with water **2** oil is a kind of
petroleum used as fuel

oil verb oils, oiling, oiled
to oil something is to put oil on it to make it
work smoothly

oilfield noun oilfields
an area where oil is found under the ground
or under the sea

oil painting noun oil paintings
a painting done using paints made with oil

oil rig noun oil rigs
a structure set up to support the equipment
used for drilling for oil

oilskin noun oilskins
a waterproof piece of clothing worn
especially by fishermen

oil well noun oil wells
a hole drilled in the ground or under the sea
to get oil

oily adjective oilier, oiliest
1 like oil or covered in oil **2** unpleasantly
over-polite *She didn't like his oily manner.*

ointment noun ointments
a cream that you put on sore skin and cuts

OK adverb, adjective (informal)
all right

a
b
c
d
e
f
g
h
i
j
k
l
m
n
o
p
q
r
s
t
u
v
w
x
y
z

oil rig

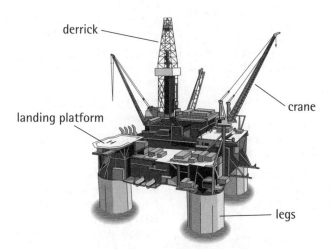

derrick

crane

landing platform

legs

351

old adjective **older, oldest**
1 not new; born or made a long time ago
2 of a particular age *I'm ten years old.*
3 former or original *I liked my old school better than the one I go to now.*

old age noun
old age is the time when a person is old

old-fashioned adjective
of the kind that was usual a long time ago; out of date

Old Testament noun
the first part of the Bible, which is the holy book of the Jewish and Christian religions

olive noun **olives**
1 an evergreen tree with a small bitter fruit
2 the fruit of this tree, used for eating and to make olive oil

Olympic Games (say o-**lim**-pik) or **Olympics** plural noun
a series of international sports contests held every four years in different countries

omelette (say **om**-lit) noun **omelettes**
eggs beaten together and fried, often with a filling or flavouring

omen noun **omens**
an event that some people see as a sign that something is going to happen

ominous adjective
suggesting that trouble is coming *In winter the dragons were hibernating and the cliff fell silent, except for the ominous, low rumble of their snores. — Cressida Cowell, How to Train Your Dragon* **ominously** adverb

omission noun **omissions**
something left out or not done

omit verb **omits, omitting, omitted**
1 to omit something is to leave it out 2 to omit to do something is to fail to do it

omnivorous adjective
an omnivorous animal is one that feeds on plants as well as the flesh of animals

on preposition
1 at or over the top or surface of something *Sit on the floor.* 2 at the time of *Come on Monday.* 3 about; concerning *We went to a talk on butterflies.* 4 towards or near *They advanced on the town.*

on adverb
1 so as to be on something *Put your hat on.*
2 forwards *Move on.* 3 working; in action *Is the heater on?*

once adverb
1 at one time *I once lived in Leeds.* 2 one time only *I've only met him once.*

once conjunction
as soon as *We can get out once I open this door.* **at once** immediately

one noun **ones**
the smallest whole number, 1

one pronoun
a person or thing on their own *One likes to help. One of my friends is ill.* **one another** each other

one adjective
single *I have one packet left.*

oneself pronoun
one's own self; yourself *One should not always think of oneself.*

one-sided adjective
a one-sided contest is one where one side has a big advantage *It will be a very one-sided game.*

one-way adjective
a one-way street is one where traffic is only allowed to go in one direction

ongoing adjective
continuing to exist or make progress *It's an ongoing project.*

onion noun **onions**
a round vegetable with a strong flavour

onlooker noun **onlookers**
a spectator

only adjective
being the one person or thing of a kind *He's the only person we can trust.*

only adverb
no more than *There are only three cakes.*

only conjunction
but then; however *I want to come, only I'm busy that day.*

onomatopoeia (say on-om-at-o-**pee**-a) noun
onomatopoeia is forming or using words that sound like the thing they describe, such as *cuckoo, hiss,* and *plop*
onomatopoeic adjective

onset noun
the onset of (for example) winter or war is the beginning of it

onshore adjective
from the sea towards the land *There is an onshore breeze.*

onto preposition
to a position on *They fell onto the floor.*

onward or **onwards** adverb
forward or forwards

ooze verb oozes, oozing, oozed
a thick liquid oozes when it flows out slowly, especially through a narrow opening *Blood oozed from his wound.*

opaque (say oh-**payk**) adjective
something that is opaque does not allow light through and so cannot be seen through

open adjective
1 allowing people or things to pass through; not shut *The door is open. The bottles need to be open.* 2 not enclosed *There were miles of open land.* 3 not folded; spread out *She greeted us with open arms.* 4 honest; not secret or secretive *We all want open government.* 5 not settled or finished *That is still an open question.* **in the open air** outdoors; not inside a house or building

open verb opens, opening, opened
1 to open something is to make it open 2 to open is to become open 3 to open is also to start *The jumble sale opens at 2 o'clock.* 4 a shop opens when it starts business for the day *What time do you open?*

opener noun openers
a device for opening a bottle or can

opening noun openings
1 a space or gap in something 2 the beginning of something 3 an opportunity, especially for a job

openly adverb
to do something openly is to do it for all to see, not secretly

open-minded adjective
ready to listen to other people's ideas and opinions; not having fixed ideas

opera noun operas
opera, or an opera, is a form of drama in which the characters sing all or most of the words, with an orchestra **operatic** adjective

operate verb operates, operating, operated
1 to operate something is to make it work 2 to operate is to work or be in action 3 to operate on someone is to perform a surgical operation on them

operation noun operations
1 something done to a patient's body by a surgeon to remove or repair a part of it 2 a carefully planned activity **to be in operation** is to be working *The new rules are now in operation.*

opinion noun opinions
what you think of something; a belief or judgement

opponent noun opponents
someone who is against you in a contest, war, or argument

opportunity noun opportunities
a good time to do something

oppose verb opposes, opposing, opposed
to oppose someone or something is to be against them or disagree with them **as opposed to** in contrast with *fact, as opposed to fiction*

opposite adjective, adverb
1 on the other side; facing *She lives on the opposite side of the road to me. I'll sit opposite.* 2 completely different *They went in opposite directions.*

A
B
C
D
E
F
G
H
I
J
K
L
M
N

O

P
Q
R
S
T
U
V
W
X
Y
Z

opposite noun opposites
something that is completely different from something else *'Happy' is the opposite of 'sad'.*

opposition noun
opposition is opposing something; resistance **the Opposition** the chief political party opposing the one that has formed the government

oppress verb oppresses, oppressing, oppressed
1 to oppress people is to govern them or treat them cruelly or unjustly 2 to oppress someone is to trouble them with worry or sadness **oppression** noun **oppressor** noun

oppressive adjective
1 harsh and cruel *They live under an oppressive regime.* 2 hot and tiring *The weather can be very oppressive in July.*

opt verb opts, opting, opted
to opt for something or to do something is to choose it *I opted for the cash prize. We opted to go abroad.* **to opt out of something** is to decide not to join in with it

optical adjective
to do with sight or the eyes

optical illusion noun optical illusions
something you think you see that is not really there

optician (say op-**tish**-an) noun opticians
someone who tests your eyesight and makes and sells glasses and contact lenses

optimist noun optimists
someone who usually expects things to turn out well **optimism** noun the feeling that things will turn out well

optimistic adjective
expecting things to turn out well **optimistically** adverb

option noun options
1 one of the things that you can choose *Your options are to travel by bus or by train.*

2 the right to choose; choice *You have the option of staying.*

optional adjective
something is optional when you can choose whether to do it or not

opulent (say **op**-yoo-lent) adjective
1 made or decorated with expensive things; luxurious 2 very rich **opulence** noun

or conjunction
used to show that there is a choice or alternative *Do you want a cake or a biscuit?*

oral adjective
1 spoken, not written 2 to do with the mouth or using your mouth **orally** adverb

orange noun oranges
1 a round juicy fruit with thick reddish-yellow peel 2 a red-yellow colour

orange adjective
reddish-yellow

orangeade noun orangeades
a drink with a flavour of oranges

orang-utan (say o-rang-u-**tan**) noun orang-utans
a large kind of ape

oration noun orations
a long formal speech

orator (say **o**-ra-ter) noun orators
someone who makes formal speeches

orbit noun orbits
the curved path taken by something moving round a planet or other body in space

orbit verb orbits, orbiting, orbited
to orbit a planet or other body in space is to move round it *The satellite orbited the earth.* **orbital** adjective

orchard noun orchards
a piece of ground with fruit trees

orchestra noun orchestras
a group of musicians playing various instruments together **orchestral** adjective

orchid (say **or**-kid) noun orchids
a type of brightly coloured flower

ordeal noun ordeals
a difficult or unpleasant experience

order noun orders
1 a command 2 a request for something to be supplied *The waiter came to take our order.* 3 the way things are arranged *The words are in alphabetical order.* 4 obedience or good behaviour *Can we have some order please?* 5 tidiness or neatness 6 a kind or sort of thing *They showed courage of the highest order.* 7 a group of religious monks, priests, or nuns **in order that** or **in order to** for the purpose of **to be out of order** is to be broken or not working

order verb orders, ordering, ordered
1 to order someone to do something is to tell them to do it 2 to order something is to ask for it to be supplied to you

orderly adjective
1 arranged tidily or well; methodical
2 well-behaved; obedient

ordinal number noun ordinal numbers
a number that shows where something comes in a series, for example 1st, 2nd, 3rd (compare *cardinal number*)

ordinarily adverb
something ordinarily happens when it is what normally happens *Stanley Lambchop had noticed in the lift that Mr Dart, who was ordinarily a cheerful man, had become quite gloomy. — Jeff Brown, Flat Stanley*

ordinary adjective
normal or usual; not special

ore noun ores
rock with metal in it, such as iron ore

organ noun organs
1 a musical instrument from which sounds are produced by air forced through pipes, played by keys and pedals 2 a part of your body with a particular function, for example the digestive organs

organic adjective
1 organic food is grown or produced without using artificial chemicals to act as fertilizers or pesticides 2 made by or found in living things

organism noun organisms
a living animal or plant

organist noun organists
someone who plays the organ

organization noun organizations
1 an organization is a group of people who work together to do something
2 organization is planning or arranging things such as getting people together to do something

organize verb organizes, organizing, organized
1 to organize people is to get them together to do something 2 to organize something is to plan or arrange it *We organized a picnic.* 3 to organize things is to put them in order **organizer** noun

oriental adjective
to do with the countries east of the Mediterranean Sea, especially China and Japan

orienteering (say or-i-en-**teer**-ing) noun
orienteering is the sport of finding your way across rough country with a map and compass

origami (say o-ri-**gah**-mi) noun
origami is folding pieces of paper to make decorative shapes

origin noun origins
the start of something; the point where something began *a book about the origins of life on earth*

original adjective
1 existing from the start; earliest *They were the original inhabitants.* 2 new; not a copy or an imitation *It is an original design.* 3 producing new ideas; inventive *He was an original thinker.* **originally** adverb what happened originally is what happened in the beginning *My family came from Pakistan originally.* **originality** noun

a
b
c
d
e
f
g
h
i
j
k
l
m
n
o
p
q
r
s
t
u
v
w
x
y
z

originate verb originates, originating, originated
1 to originate something is to create it or develop it **2** to originate is to start in a certain way *Pumpkins are believed to have originated in North America.* **originator** noun

ornament noun ornaments
an object you wear or display as a decoration **ornamental** adjective

ornithology (say or-ni-**thol**-o-ji) noun
ornithology is the study of birds
ornithologist noun

orphan noun orphans
a child whose parents are dead

orphanage noun orphanages
a home for orphans

orthodox adjective
having beliefs that are correct or generally accepted

Orthodox Church noun
the Christian Churches of eastern Europe

ostrich noun ostriches
a large long-legged bird that can run fast but cannot fly

other determiner
not the same as this; different *Play some other tune. Try the other shoe.* **other than** except *They have no belongings other than what they are carrying.* **the other day** or **the other week** a few days or weeks ago

other pronoun others
the other person or thing *Where are the others?*

otherwise adverb
1 if you do not; if things happen differently *Write it down, otherwise you'll forget it.* **2** in other ways *It rained a lot but otherwise the holiday was good.* **3** differently *We could not do otherwise.*

otter noun otters
an animal with thick fur, webbed feet, and a flat tail, that lives near water

ouch interjection
a cry of pain

ought verb
used with other words to show
1 what you should or must do *You ought to do your music practice.* **2** what is likely to happen *With all these dark clouds it ought to rain.*

ounce noun ounces
a unit of weight equal to $\frac{1}{16}$ of a pound or about 28 grams

our determiner
belonging to us *This is our house.*

ours pronoun
belonging to us *This house is ours.*

TOP TIPS
Oops! There is no apostrophe in **ours**: *Those sweets are ours.*

ourselves pronoun
us and nobody else, used to refer back to the subject of a verb *We have hurt ourselves.* **by ourselves** on our own; alone *We did the work all by ourselves.*

out adverb
1 away from a place or not in it; not at home **2** into the open or outdoors *Are you going out today?* **3** not burning or working *The fire has gone out.* **4** loudly *She cried out.* **5** completely *They have sold out.* **6** dismissed from a game *Another batsman is out.* **to be out for something** is to want it badly **to be out of something** is to have no more of it left **out of date** old-fashioned; not used any more **out of doors** in the open air **out of the way** remote or distant

out and out adjective
complete or thorough *He is an out and out villain.*

outback noun
the remote inland areas of Australia

outbreak noun outbreaks
the sudden start of a disease, war, or show of anger

outburst noun outbursts
the sudden beginning of anger or laughter

356

outcast noun outcasts
someone who has been rejected by their family, friends, or society

outcome noun outcomes
the result of what happens or has happened

outcry noun outcries
a strong protest from many people

outdated adjective
out of date

outdo verb outdoes, outdoing, outdid, outdone
to outdo someone else is to do better than them

outdoor adjective
done or used outside *You'll need your outdoor clothes.*

outdoors adverb
in the open air *It is cold outdoors.*

outer adjective
nearer the outside; external

outer space noun
outer space is the universe beyond the earth's atmosphere

outfit noun outfits
1 a set of clothes you wear together **2** a set of things you need for doing something

outgrow verb outgrows, outgrowing, outgrew, outgrown
1 to outgrow something such as clothes or a habit is to grow too big or too old for them **2** to outgrow someone is to grow faster or taller than them

outhouse noun outhouses
a small building attached to a larger building or close to it

outing noun outings
a trip or short journey you make for pleasure

outlast verb outlasts, outlasting, outlasted
to outlast something else is to last longer than it

outlaw noun outlaws
a robber or bandit who is hiding to avoid being caught and is not protected by the law

outlaw verb outlaws, outlawing, outlawed
to outlaw something is to make it illegal

outlet noun outlets
1 a way for something to get out *The tank has an outlet at the bottom.* **2** a place to sell goods *We need to find fresh outlets for our products.*

outline noun outlines
1 a line round the outside of something; a line showing the shape of a thing **2** a summary

outline verb outlines, outlining, outlined
1 to outline something is to draw a line round it to show its shape **2** to outline a story or account is to summarize or describe it briefly

outlook noun outlooks
1 a view on which people look out **2** a person's outlook is the way that they look at and think about things *She has a serious outlook on life.* **3** what seems likely to happen in the future *The outlook is bright.*

outlying adjective
far from a town or city *We need to visit the outlying districts.*

outnumber verb outnumbers, outnumbering, outnumbered
to outnumber something else is to be greater in number than it *The girls outnumber the boys in our team.*

outpatient noun outpatients
a patient who visits a hospital for treatment but does not stay there overnight

outpost noun outposts
a distant settlement

output noun outputs
1 the amount produced, especially by a factory or business **2** (in computing) information produced by a computer

a
b
c
d
e
f
g
h
i
j
k
l
m
n
o
p
q
r
s
t
u
v
w
x
y
z

A
B
C
D
E
F
G
H
I
J
K
L
M
N

O

P
Q
R
S
T
U
V
W
X
Y
Z

output verb outputs, outputting, output (in computing)
to output information is to get it from a computer

outrage noun outrages
1 outrage is the anger you feel when something shocking happens **2** an outrage is something very shocking or cruel

outrage verb outrages, outraging, outraged
to outrage someone is to make them very shocked and angry *The Scarecrow was outraged. He waved his road sign, he opened and shut his umbrella, and he stamped with fury.* – Philip Pullman, *The Scarecrow and his Servant*

outrageous adjective
shocking or dreadful

outright adverb
1 completely *We won outright.*
2 immediately; instantly *They were killed outright.*

outset noun
at or **from the outset** at or from the beginning of something

outside noun outsides
the outer side or surface of a thing; the part furthest from the middle

outside adjective
1 on or coming from the outside **2** slight or remote *There is an outside chance that he will come.*

outside adverb, preposition
on or to the outside of something *Go outside. It's outside the house.*

outsider noun outsiders
1 someone who is not a member of a particular group of people **2** a horse or person that people think has no chance of winning a race or contest

outskirts plural noun
the parts on the outside edge of an area, especially of a town or city

outspoken adjective
speaking frankly even though it might offend people

outstanding adjective
1 extremely good or distinguished *She is an outstanding athlete.* **2** not yet dealt with *He has outstanding bills to pay.*

outward adjective
1 going outwards **2** on the outside

outwardly adverb
on the outside; for people to see *They were outwardly calm.*

outwards adverb
towards the outside

outweigh verb outweighs, outweighing, outweighed
to outweigh something is to be more important than it *The advantages of the plan outweigh the disadvantages.*

outwit verb outwits, outwitting, outwitted
to outwit someone is to deceive or defeat them by being more clever

oval adjective
shaped like an egg or a number 0

oval noun ovals
an oval shape

ovary noun ovaries
1 part of a female body where egg cells are produced **2** the part of a flowering plant that produces seeds

oven noun ovens
a closed space in which things are cooked or heated

over adverb
1 down or sideways; out and down from the top or edge *He fell over.* **2** across to a place *We walked over to the house.* **3** so that a different side shows *Turn it over.* **4** finished *The lesson is over.* **5** left or remaining *There are a few apples over.* **6** through or thoroughly *Think it over.* **over and over** repeatedly; many times

over preposition
1 above or covering *There's a light over the door. I'll put a cloth over the table.* **2** across *They ran over the road.* **3** more than *The house is over a mile away.* **4** concerning; about *They quarrelled over money.* **5** during *We can talk over dinner.* **6** being better than *They won a victory over their opponents.*

over noun **overs**
in cricket, a series of six balls bowled by one person

over– prefix
meaning 'too much', as in *over-excited*

overall adjective, adverb
including everything; total *What is the overall cost?*

overalls plural noun
a piece of clothing that you wear over your other clothes to protect them when you are working

overarm adjective, adverb
with the arm lifted above shoulder level and coming down in front of the body

overboard adverb
to fall or jump overboard is to go over the side of a boat into the water

overcast adjective
covered with cloud *The sky is grey and overcast.*

overcoat noun **overcoats**
a warm outdoor coat

overcome verb **overcomes, overcoming, overcame, overcome**
1 to overcome a problem or difficulty is to succeed in dealing with it or controlling it *He overcame injury to win a gold medal.* **2** to be overcome by something is to become helpless from it *She was overcome by the fumes.* **3** to overcome someone is to beat them

overdo verb **overdoes, overdoing, overdid, overdone**
1 to overdo something is to do it too much **2** to overdo food is to cook it for too long

overdose noun **overdoses**
too large a dose of a drug or medicine

overdue adjective
something is overdue when it is later than it should be *The train is overdue.*

overflow verb **overflows, overflowing, overflowed**
to overflow is to flow over the edges or limits of something

overgrown adjective
a place is overgrown when it is thickly covered with weeds or unwanted plants

overhang verb **overhangs, overhanging, overhung**
to overhang something is to stick out beyond and above it *The branches of the tree overhung the pond.*

overhaul verb **overhauls, overhauling, overhauled**
1 to overhaul a machine or vehicle is to check it thoroughly and repair it if necessary **2** to overhaul someone or something is to overtake them

overhead adjective, adverb
above your head; in the sky

overhear verb **overhears, overhearing, overheard**
to overhear something is to hear it accidentally or without the speaker knowing

overland adjective, adverb
over the land, not by sea or air *an overland expedition, We travelled overland to Italy.*

overlap verb **overlaps, overlapping, overlapped**
one thing overlaps another when it lies across part of it *The carpet overlapped the fireplace.*

overlook verb **overlooks, overlooking, overlooked**
1 to overlook something is not to notice it **2** to overlook a mistake or offence is not to punish it **3** to overlook a place is to have a view over it *The hotel overlooks the city park.*

A

overnight adverb, adjective
of or during a night *We stayed overnight in a hotel. There will be an overnight stop in Paris.*

B

overpower verb overpowers, overpowering, overpowered
to overpower someone is to defeat them because you are stronger

C

D

overpowering adjective
very strong *The smell of the cheese was overpowering.*

E

F

overrun verb overruns, overrunning, overran, overrun
1 to overrun an area is to spread quickly over it *The place is overrun with mice.*
2 something overruns when it goes on longer than it should *The programme overran by ten minutes.*

G

H

I

J

overseas adverb
abroad *They travelled overseas.*

K

overseas adjective
from abroad; foreign *We met some overseas students.*

L

M

oversight noun oversights
a mistake you make by not noticing something

N

O

oversleep verb oversleeps, oversleeping, overslept
to sleep longer than you intended to

P

Q

overtake verb overtakes, overtaking, overtook, overtaken
to overtake a moving vehicle or person is to catch them up and pass them in the same direction

R

S

T

overthrow verb overthrows, overthrowing, overthrew, overthrown
to overthrow a government is to remove it from power by force

U

V

overthrow noun overthrows
the overthrow of a government is when it is forced out of power

W

X

overtime noun
overtime is time someone spends working outside their normal hours

Y

Z

overture noun overtures
a piece of music played at the start of a concert, opera, or ballet **overtures** a friendly attempt to start a discussion with someone

overturn verb overturns, overturning, overturned
1 to overturn something is to make it turn over or fall over 2 to overturn is to turn over *The car went out of control and overturned.*

overweight adjective
too heavy

overwhelm verb overwhelms, overwhelming, overwhelmed
1 to overwhelm someone is to have a very strong effect on them *I was overwhelmed by everyone's kindness.* 2 to overwhelm someone is to defeat them completely

overwork verb overworks, overworking, overworked
to overwork is to become exhausted from working too hard

overwork noun
overwork is too much work, causing exhaustion

owe verb owes, owing, owed
1 to owe something, especially money, is to have a duty to pay or give it to someone *I owe you a pound.* 2 to owe something to someone is to have it thanks to them *They owed their lives to the pilot's skill.* **owing to something** because of it *The train was late owing to leaves on the line.*

owl noun owls
a bird of prey with large eyes and a short beak, usually flying at night

own adjective
belonging to yourself or itself **to get your own back** (informal) is to have your revenge **on your own** by yourself; alone *I did it all on my own. I sat on my own in the empty room.*

own verb owns, owning, owned
to own something is to have it as your property **to own up to something** (informal) is to admit that you did it

owner noun **owners**
the person who owns something
ownership noun

ox noun **oxen**
a bull kept for its meat and for pulling carts

oxygen noun
oxygen is one of the gases in the air that people need to stay alive

oyster noun **oysters**
a kind of shellfish whose shell sometimes contains a pearl

oz.
short for **ounce** or **ounces**

ozone noun
ozone is a strong-smelling gas that is a form of oxygen

ozone layer noun
a layer of ozone high in the atmosphere, that absorbs harmful radiation from the sun

Pp

p
short for **penny** or **pence**

pa noun **pas** (informal)
father

pace noun **paces**
1 one step in walking, marching, or running **2** speed *He set a fast pace.*

pace verb **paces, pacing, paced**
to pace is to walk up and down with slow or regular steps *The rat, in the dungeon below, was pacing and muttering in the darkness, waiting to take his revenge on the princess.* — Kate DiCamillo, *The Tale of Despereaux*
to pace something out is to measure a distance in paces

pacemaker noun **pacemakers**
1 a person who sets the speed for someone else in a race **2** an electrical device put into

a person by surgery, that keeps the heart beating regularly

pacifist (say **pas**-i-fist) noun **pacifists**
someone who believes that war is always wrong **pacifism** noun

pacify (say **pas**-i-fy) verb **pacifies, pacifying, pacified**
to pacify someone is to calm them down

pack noun **packs**
1 a bundle or collection of things wrapped or tied together **2** a set of playing cards **3** a strong bag carried on your back **4** a group of hounds, wolves, or other animals **5** a group of people, especially a group of Brownies or Cub Scouts

pack verb **packs, packing, packed**
1 to pack a suitcase, bag, or box is to put things in it so that you can store them or take them somewhere **2** to pack a room or building is to fill it *The hall was packed.*

package noun **packages**
1 a parcel or packet **2** a number of things offered or accepted together

packet noun **packets**
a small parcel

pad[1] noun **pads**
1 a number of sheets of blank or lined paper joined together along one edge **2** a piece of soft material used to protect or shape something **3** a piece of soft material that you wear to protect your leg in cricket and other games **4** a flat surface from which helicopters take off or rockets are launched

pad verb **pads, padding, padded**
to pad something is to put a piece of soft material on it or into it in order to protect or shape it **to pad something out** is to make a book or story longer than it needs to be

pad[2] verb **pads, padding, padded**
to pad is to walk softly

padding noun
padding is soft material used to protect or shape things

a b c d e f g h i j k l m n o p q r s t u v w x y z

A
B
C
D
E
F
G
H
I
J
K
L
M
N
O
P
Q
R
S
T
U
V
W
X
Y
Z

paddle verb paddles, paddling, paddled
1 to paddle is to walk about with bare feet in shallow water 2 to paddle a boat is to move it along with a short oar

paddle noun paddles
1 a time spent paddling in water 2 a short oar with a broad blade

paddock noun paddocks
a small field for keeping horses

paddy noun paddies
a field where rice is grown

padlock noun padlocks
a lock with a metal loop that you can use to fasten a gate or lock a bicycle

pagan noun pagans (old use)
a person who does not believe in any of the world's main religions

page noun pages
a piece of paper that is part of a book or newspaper; one side of this piece of paper

pageant (say **paj**-ent) noun pageants
1 a play or entertainment about historical events and people 2 a procession of people in costume **pageantry** noun

pagoda (say pa-**goh**-da) noun pagodas
a Buddhist tower or Hindu temple in the Far East

paid
past tense and past participle of **pay** She paid for the magazine and left the shop. Have you paid for those sweets yet?

pail noun pails
a bucket

pain noun pains
1 pain or a pain is an unpleasant feeling caused by injury or disease Are you in pain? 2 pain is also mental suffering

pain verb pains, paining, pained
to pain someone is to cause them pain, usually mental pain

painful adjective
causing you pain My ankle is too painful to walk on.

painfully adverb
1 in a way that causes you pain He grasped my arm in a painfully tight grip. 2 to be (for example) painfully thin or painfully slow is to be extremely thin or extremely slow

painkiller noun painkillers
a drug that reduces pain

painless adjective
not causing any pain

painstaking adjective
making a careful effort Rebecca sat down carefully, smoothing her dress under her with painstaking precision. – Kate Douglas Wiggin, Rebecca of Sunnybrook Farm

paint noun paints
a liquid substance put on something to colour or cover it

paint verb paints, painting, painted
1 to paint something is to put paint on it 2 to paint a picture is to make it with paints 3 to paint someone or something is to make a picture of them using paint

paintbox noun paintboxes
a box of coloured paints used in art

paintbrush noun paintbrushes
a brush used in painting

painter noun painters
1 an artist who paints pictures 2 a person whose job is painting walls and houses

painting noun paintings
1 painting is using paints to make a picture She likes painting. 2 a painting is a painted picture

pair noun pairs
1 two things or people that go together or are the same kind I need a new pair of shoes. 2 something made of two parts joined together Have you got a pair of scissors?

pal noun pals (informal)
a friend

palace noun palaces
a large and splendid house where a king or queen or other important person lives

palate (say **pal**-at) noun **palates**
1 the roof of your mouth 2 a person's sense of taste *We have food to suit every palate.*

pale adjective **paler, palest**
1 almost white *He had a pale face.* 2 not bright in colour; faint *The sky was a pale blue.* **paleness** noun

palette (say **pal**-it) noun **palettes**
a board on which an artist mixes colours

pall verb **palls, palling, palled**
something palls when it becomes dull or uninteresting after a time *The novelty of the new computer game soon began to pall.*

pallid adjective
pale, especially because of illness

pallor noun
pallor is paleness in a person's face, especially because they are ill

palm noun **palms**
1 the inner part of your hand, between your fingers and wrist 2 a tropical tree with large leaves and no branches

palm verb **palms, palming, palmed**
to palm something off on someone is to fool them into taking something they do not want

palmistry noun
palmistry is fortune-telling by looking for signs in the lines of a person's hand

Palm Sunday noun
the Sunday before Easter, when Christians celebrate Christ's entry into Jerusalem on a path of palm leaves

paltry adjective
not very much or not very valuable *His reward was a paltry 50 pence.*

pampas plural noun
pampas are wide grassy plains in South America

pamper verb **pampers, pampering, pampered**
to pamper someone is to go to a lot of trouble to make someone feel comfortable and let them have whatever they want

pamphlet noun **pamphlets**
a thin book with a paper cover

pan noun **pans**
a pot or dish with a flat base, used for cooking

pancake noun **pancakes**
a flat round cake of batter fried on both sides

panda noun **pandas**
a large black and white bear-like animal found in China

pandemonium noun
you say there is pandemonium when there is a loud noise or disturbance *At this pandemonium broke loose. All the men leaped to their feet and shouted and waved their cudgels and guns.* — Elizabeth Goudge, *The Little White Horse*

pander verb **panders, pandering, pandered**
to pander to someone is to let them have whatever they want

pane noun **panes**
a sheet of glass in a window

panel noun **panels**
1 a long flat piece of wood, metal, or other material that is part of a door, wall, or piece of furniture 2 a group of people appointed to discuss or decide something *The winner of the contest will be decided by a panel of judges.*

pang noun **pangs**
a sudden feeling of pain or strong emotion

panic noun
panic is sudden fear that makes you behave wildly

panic verb **panics, panicking, panicked**
to panic is to be overcome with fear or anxiety and behave wildly

pannier noun **panniers**
a bag or basket hung on one side of a bicycle or horse

panorama noun **panoramas**
a view or picture of a wide area *I know not*

a
b
c
d
e
f
g
h
i
j
k
l
m
n
o
p
q
r
s
t
u
v
w
x
y
z

363

A B C D E F G H I J K L M N O **P** Q R S T U V W X Y Z

how to describe the glorious panorama which unfolded itself to our gaze.
– H. Rider Haggard, *King Solomon's Mines*
panoramic adjective

pansy noun **pansies**
a small brightly-coloured garden flower

pant verb **pants, panting, panted**
you pant when you take short quick breaths, usually after running or working hard

panther noun **panthers**
a leopard

pantomime noun **pantomimes**
a Christmas entertainment based on a fairy tale

pantry noun **pantries**
a cupboard or small room for storing food

pants plural noun
1 (informal) underpants or knickers
2 (in America) trousers

paper noun **papers**
1 paper is a thin substance made in sheets and used for writing or printing or drawing on, or for wrapping things **2** a paper is a newspaper **3** papers are documents

paper verb **papers, papering, papered**
to paper a wall or room is to cover it with wallpaper

paperback noun **paperbacks**
a book with thin flexible covers

papier mâché (say pap-yay **mash-ay**) noun
papier mâché is a mixture of paper pulp and glue you use to make models or ornaments

papyrus (say pa-**py**-rus) noun **papyri**
1 papyrus is a kind of paper made from the stems of reeds, used in ancient Egypt **2** a papyrus is a document written on this paper

parable noun **parables**
a story told to teach people something, especially one of the stories told by Jesus Christ

parachute noun **parachutes**
an umbrella-shaped device on which people

or things can float slowly down to the ground from an aircraft **parachutist** noun

parade noun **parades**
1 a line of people or vehicles moving forward through a place as a celebration **2** soldiers are on parade when they assemble for inspection or drill **3** a public square or row of shops

parade verb **parades, parading, paraded**
1 to parade is to move forward through a place as a celebration **2** soldiers parade when they assemble for inspection or drill

paradise noun
1 paradise is heaven or, in the Bible, the Garden of Eden **2** you can describe a wonderful or perfect place as a paradise

paradox (say **pa**-ra-doks) noun **paradoxes**
a statement which, because it has two opposite ideas in it, does not seem to make sense but may still be true, for example *'More haste, less speed'*

paradoxical adjective
a paradoxical statement seems to contradict itself but may still be true
paradoxically adverb

paraffin noun
paraffin is a kind of oil used as fuel

paragraph noun **paragraphs**
one of the group of sentences that a piece of writing is divided into, beginning on a new line

parallel adjective
parallel lines are lines that are the same distance apart for their whole length, like railway lines

TOP TIPS Double up the first **l** in **parallel** (but the last **l** stays single)!

parallelogram noun **parallelograms**
a four-sided figure with its opposite sides parallel to each other and equal in length

paralyse verb **paralyses, paralysing, paralysed**
1 to paralyse someone is to make them

unable to feel anything or to move *A few children whimpered and clung to each other; but most just stared at the lion, paralysed with terror.* — Michael Morpurgo, *Tom's Sausage Lion* **2** to paralyse something is to make it unable to move or work properly *Train services were paralysed by the strike.*

paralysis (say pa-**ral**-i-sis) noun
paralysis is the loss of the ability to move or feel anything

parapet noun **parapets**
a low wall along the edge of a balcony, bridge, or roof

paraphernalia (say pa-ra-fer-**nay**-li-a) noun
paraphernalia is various pieces of equipment or small possessions

paraphrase verb **paraphrases, paraphrasing, paraphrased**
to paraphrase something that has been said or written is to give its meaning by using different words

parasite noun **parasites**
an animal or plant that lives in or on another and gets its food from it
parasitic adjective

parasol noun **parasols**
a lightweight umbrella you use to shade yourself from the sun

paratroops plural noun
troops trained to be dropped from aircraft by parachute **paratrooper** noun

parcel noun **parcels**
something wrapped up to be posted or carried

parched adjective
very dry or thirsty

parchment noun
parchment is a kind of heavy paper originally made from animal skins

pardon verb **pardons, pardoning, pardoned**
to pardon someone is to forgive or excuse them

pardon noun **pardons**
1 forgiveness; an act of pardoning someone **2** used as an exclamation to mean 'I didn't hear or understand what you said', or 'I apologize'

pardonable adjective
a pardonable mistake is one that can be forgiven

parent noun **parents**
your parents are your father and mother
parental adjective

parentage noun
your parentage is who your parents are

parenthesis (say pa-**ren**-thi-sis) noun
parentheses
1 something extra put in a sentence between brackets or dashes **2** one of a pair of brackets (like these) used in the middle of a sentence

parish noun **parishes**
a district that has its own church
parishioner noun a parishioner of a church is a person who regularly goes to that church

park noun **parks**
1 a large area with grass and trees, for public use **2** a piece of ground belonging to a large country house

park verb **parks, parking, parked**
to park a vehicle is to leave it somewhere for a time

parka noun **parkas**
a warm jacket with a hood attached

parking meter noun **parking meters**
a device that shows how long a vehicle has been parked in a street

parliament noun **parliaments**
the group of people that make a country's laws **parliamentary** adjective

parody noun **parodies**
a play or poem that makes fun of people or things by imitating them

a
b
c
d
e
f
g
h
i
j
k
l
m
n
o
p
q
r
s
t
u
v
w
x
y
z

parole (say pa-**rohl**) noun
parole is letting someone out of prison before they have finished their sentence, on condition that they behave well *He was on parole.*

parrot noun **parrots**
a brightly-coloured bird with a curved beak, that can learn to repeat words or sounds

parsley noun
parsley is a plant with crinkled green leaves used to flavour and decorate food

parsnip noun **parsnips**
a pale yellow vegetable

part noun **parts**
1 some but not all of a thing or a number of things; anything that belongs to something bigger **2** the character played by an actor or actress; the words spoken by a character in a play *She has a good part in the school play.*

part verb **parts, parting, parted**
1 to part people or things is to separate them or divide them **2** to part is to separate **3** to part hair is to divide it so that it goes in two different directions **to part with something** is to give it away or get rid of it

partial adjective
1 not complete or total *There will be a partial eclipse of the sun.* **2** unfairly showing more support for one person or side than another **to be partial to something** is to like it **partiality** noun to have a partiality for something is to like it **partially** adverb

participant noun **participants**
someone who participates in something

participate verb **participates, participating, participated**
to participate in something is to take part in it **participation** noun

participle noun **participles**
a word formed from a verb and used as part of the verb or as an adjective, for example 'going', 'gone', 'sailed', 'sailing'

particle noun **particles**
a very small piece or amount

particular adjective
1 only this one and no other; special; individual *Are you looking for a particular book?* **2** fussy; hard to please *He is very particular about his clothes.* **in particular** especially; chiefly

particular noun **particulars**
a detail or single fact

particularly adverb
you can say something is (for example) particularly good or useful when it is especially good or useful

parting noun **partings**
1 leaving or separation **2** the line where hair is combed in different directions

partition noun **partitions**
1 partition is dividing something into parts **2** a partition is a thin dividing wall

partly adverb
not completely; in some ways

partner noun **partners**
1 one of a pair of people who do something together, especially dancing, running a business, or playing a game **2** someone's partner is the person they are married to or live with **partnership** noun

part of speech noun **parts of speech**
each of the groups (also called **word classes**) into which words can be divided in grammar: noun, adjective, verb, pronoun, adverb, preposition, conjunction, interjection

partridge noun **partridges**
a game bird with brown feathers

part-time adjective, adverb
working for only some of the normal hours

party noun **parties**
1 a time when people get together to enjoy themselves *Come to my birthday party.* **2** a group of people working or travelling together *They organized a search party.* **3** an organized group of people with similar political beliefs *The Labour Party* **4** a person

who is involved in an action or legal case *He is the guilty party.*

pass verb **passes, passing, passed**
1 to pass something or someone is to go past them 2 to pass in a certain direction is to move or go that way *They passed over the bridge.* 3 to pass something to someone is to give it or hand it to them *Can you pass the butter, please?* 4 to pass an examination is to be successful in it 5 to pass time is to use time doing something 6 to pass is to finish or no longer be there *His opportunity passed.* 7 to pass a law or rule is to approve or accept it

pass noun **passes**
1 when a ball is kicked, hit, or thrown from one player to another in a game 2 a success in an examination 3 a card or ticket that allows you to go in or out of a place 4 a narrow way between mountains

passable adjective
just about acceptable or all right

passage noun **passages**
1 a corridor or narrow space between two walls 2 a section of a piece of writing or music 3 a journey by sea or air 4 passing *the passage of time*

passageway noun **passageways**
a passage or way through, especially between buildings

passenger noun **passengers**
someone who is travelling in a car or other vehicle and is not the driver or a member of the crew

passer–by noun **passers-by**
someone who is going past by chance when something happens

passion noun **passions**
1 passion is strong feeling or emotion 2 a passion is a great enthusiasm for something

passionate adjective
full of passion or strong feeling
passionately adverb

passive adjective
1 not active; not resisting or fighting

against something 2 (in grammar) describing a verb in which the subject receives the action, for example in the sentence *She was hit by a car* the subject is *She* and *was hit* is a passive verb
passively adverb

Passover noun
Passover is a Jewish religious festival, celebrating the escape of the ancient Jews from slavery in Egypt.

passport noun **passports**
an official document that allows you to travel abroad

password noun **passwords**
a secret word or phrase that you need to know to be allowed to go somewhere or to gain access to a computer system

past noun
the time gone by *Try to forget the past.*

past adjective
of the time gone by *He was thinking about his past achievements.*

past preposition
1 beyond *Go past the school and turn right.* 2 later than *It is past midnight.*

pasta noun
pasta is an Italian food made as a dried paste of flour, water, and often eggs, formed into various shapes such as spaghetti and lasagne
Please see illustration on following page.

paste noun **pastes**
a soft and moist or gluey substance

paste verb **pastes, pasting, pasted**
to paste something is to stick it to a surface with paste

pastel noun **pastels**
1 a crayon that is like a slightly greasy chalk 2 a light delicate colour

pasteurize (say **pahs**-cher-ryz) verb
pasteurizes, pasteurizing, pasteurized
to pasteurize milk is to purify it by heating and then cooling it

pastille noun **pastilles**
a small flavoured sweet that you suck

a b c d e f g h i j k l m n o **p** q r s t u v w x y z

A
B
C
D
E
F
G
H
I
J
K
L
M
N
O
P
Q
R
S
T
U
V
W
X
Y
Z

pasta

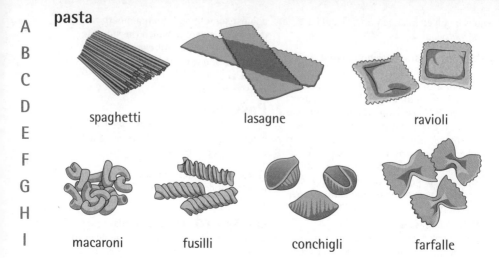

spaghetti   lasagne   ravioli

macaroni   fusilli   conchigli   farfalle

pastime noun **pastimes**
something you do to pass time pleasantly; a hobby or game

pastoral adjective
to do with the country

past participle noun **past participles**
a form of a verb used after *has, have, had, was, were,* to describe an action that happened at a time before now, for example *done, overtaken,* and *written*

pastry noun **pastries**
1 pastry is dough made from flour, fat, and water rolled flat and baked **2** a pastry is a cake made from this dough

past tense noun
a form of a verb used to describe an action that happened at a time before now, for example *took* is the past tense of *take*

pasture noun **pastures**
land covered with grass that cattle, sheep, or horses can eat

pasty[1] (say **pas**-ti) noun **pasties**
a pastry filled with meat and vegetables, like a small pie

pasty[2] (say **pay**-sti) adjective **pastier, pastiest**
looking pale and unhealthy

pat verb **pats, patting, patted**
to pat something or someone is to tap them gently with your open hand or with something flat

pat noun **pats**
1 a patting movement or sound **2** a small piece of butter

patch noun **patches**
1 a piece of material put over a hole or damaged place **2** an area that is different from its surroundings *We have a black cat with a white patch on its chest.* **3** a small area of land **4** a small piece of something *There are patches of ice on the road.*

patch verb **patches, patching, patched**
to patch something is to put a piece of material on it to repair it **to patch something up** is to repair it roughly **to patch things up** is to be friendly again after a quarrel

patchwork noun
patchwork is needlework using small pieces of different cloth which are sewn together

patchy adjective **patchier, patchiest**
occurring in some areas but not others; uneven *There may be some patchy rain.*

patent (say **pay**-tent or **pat**-ent) noun
patents
the official right given to someone to make
something they have invented and to stop
other people from copying it

patent (say **pay**-tent) adjective
obvious *What they say is a patent lie.*

patent (say **pay**-tent or **pat**-ent) verb
patents, patenting, patented
to patent an idea or invention is to get a
patent for it

patent leather noun
patent leather is leather with a special
glossy surface

patently adverb
clearly; obviously *They were patently lying.*

paternal adjective
to do with a father, or like a father

path noun **paths**
1 a narrow way to walk or ride along 2 the
line along which something moves *They
were tracing the path of the meteor.*

pathetic adjective
1 sad and pitiful 2 sadly or comically weak
or useless *He made a pathetic attempt to
climb the tree.* **pathetically** adverb

patience (say **pay**-shens) noun
1 patience is the ability to stay calm,
especially when you have to wait for a long
time 2 patience is also a card game for
one person

patient (say **pay**-shent) adjective
1 able to wait for a long time without
getting anxious or angry 2 able to bear pain
or trouble

patient (say **pay**-shent) noun **patients**
a person who is getting treatment from a
doctor or dentist

patiently adverb
you do something patiently when you do
it in a patient way *He waited patiently for
his turn.*

patio (say **pat**-i-oh) noun **patios**
a paved area beside a house

patriot (say **pay**-tri-ot or **pat**-ri-ot) noun
patriots
someone who loves and supports their
country **patriotic** adjective **patriotism** noun

patrol verb **patrols, patrolling,
patrolled**
to walk or travel regularly round a place or
a thing to guard it and make sure that all
is well

patrol noun **patrols**
1 a group of people or vehicles patrolling a
place 2 a group of Scouts or Guides **to be
on patrol** is to be patrolling a place

patron (say **pay**-tron) noun **patrons**
1 someone who supports a person or
cause with money or encouragement 2 a
regular customer of a shop or business
patronage noun

patronize verb **patronizes,
patronizing, patronized**
1 to patronize someone is to treat them as
an inferior 2 to patronize a shop or business
is to be one of its regular customers

patron saint noun **patron saints**
a saint who is thought of as protecting a
place or activity

patter[1] noun **patters**
a series of light tapping sounds

patter verb **patters, pattering,
pattered**
to patter is to make light tapping sounds
The rain was pattering on the glass roof.

patter[2] noun
patter is the quick talk of a performer
or salesperson

pattern noun **patterns**
1 a decorative arrangement of lines or
shapes 2 a thing that you copy so that
you can make something, such as a piece
of clothing

pause noun **pauses**
a short stop before continuing
with something

pause verb **pauses, pausing, paused**
1 to pause is to make a short stop before

A
B
C
D
E
F
G
H
I
J
K
L
M
N
O
P
Q
R
S
T
U
V
W
X
Y
Z

continuing with something **2** to pause (for example) a DVD player or CD player is to make the disc stop for a short time

pave verb **paves, paving, paved**
to pave a road or path is to put a hard surface on it **to pave the way** is to prepare for something

pavement noun **pavements**
a path with a hard surface, along the side of a street

pavilion noun **pavilions**
a building at a sports ground for players and spectators to use

paw noun **paws**
an animal's foot

paw verb **paws, pawing, pawed**
an animal paws something when it touches or scrapes it clumsily with its paw

pawn noun **pawns**
1 one of the sixteen pieces in chess that are at the front on each side and are the least valuable **2** a person who is controlled by someone else

pawn verb **pawns, pawning, pawned**
to pawn something is to leave it with a pawnbroker while borrowing money *He had to pawn his watch.*

pawnbroker noun **pawnbrokers**
a shopkeeper who lends money to people in return for objects that they leave and which are sold if the money is not paid back

pay verb **pays, paying, paid**
1 to pay for something is to give money in return for it *Have you paid for your lunch?* **2** to pay someone is to give them money for something they have done *Wash my car and I'll pay you £5.* **3** to pay is to be profitable or worthwhile *It pays to be honest.* **4** to pay (for example) attention or a compliment is to give someone your attention or a compliment **5** to pay for something you have done wrong is to suffer for it *I'll make you pay for this!* **to pay someone back 1** is to pay money that you owe them **2** is to get revenge on them

pay noun
pay is the money you earn when you work

payment noun **payments**
1 payment is when you pay someone or are paid for something **2** a payment is money you pay

PC
short for *personal computer* or *police constable*

PE
short for **physical education**

pea noun **peas**
a small round green seed of a climbing plant, growing inside a pod and used as a vegetable

peace noun
1 peace is a time when there is no war or violence *At last the country was at peace.* **2** peace is also quiet and calm

peaceful adjective
1 quiet and calm **2** not involving violence
peacefully adverb

peach noun **peaches**
a soft round juicy fruit with a slightly furry skin and a large stone

peacock noun **peacocks**
a large male bird with a long brightly coloured tail that it can spread out like a fan

peak noun **peaks**
1 the top of a mountain **2** the highest or best point of something *Traffic reaches its peak at 5 o'clock.* **3** the part of a cap that sticks out in front

peak verb **peaks, peaking, peaked**
to reach the highest point or amount *Prices peaked in March.*

peal verb **peals, pealing, pealed**
bells peal when they make a loud ringing sound

peal noun **peals**
a loud ringing sound made by bells

peanut noun peanuts
a small round nut that grows in a pod in the ground

peanut butter noun
peanut butter is a paste made from crushed roasted peanuts

pear noun pears
a juicy fruit that gets narrower near the stalk

pearl noun pearls
a small shiny white ball found in the shells of some oysters and used as a jewel **pearly** adjective

peasant noun peasants
a person who belongs to a farming community, especially in poor areas of the world

peat noun
peat is rotted plant material that can be dug out of the ground and used as fuel or fertilizer

pebble noun pebbles
a small round stone found on the beach

peck verb pecks, pecking, pecked
when a bird pecks something, it bites it or eats it with its beak
peck noun pecks
1 a short sharp bite with a bird's beak
2 (informal) a quick kiss

peckish adjective (informal)
hungry

peculiar adjective
strange or unusual **to be peculiar to someone** or **something** is to be restricted to them *This species of bird is peculiar to Asia.* **peculiarly** adverb more than usually; strangely *He is peculiarly fond of brightly coloured socks.*

peculiarity noun peculiarities
something peculiar or special

pedal noun pedals
a lever that you press with your foot to operate a bicycle, car, or machine, or to play some musical instruments

pedal verb pedals, pedalling, pedalled
to pedal is to push or turn the pedals of a bicycle or other device

peddle verb peddles, peddling, peddled
to peddle things is to sell them

pedestal noun pedestals
the base that supports a statue or pillar

pedestrian noun pedestrians
someone who is walking

pedigree noun pedigrees
a list of a person's or animal's ancestors, especially to show how well an animal has been bred

peel noun peels
the skin of some fruit and vegetables
peel verb peels, peeling, peeled
1 to peel a piece of fruit or a vegetable is to remove the peel or covering from it
2 to peel is to lose a covering or skin *My skin is peeling.*

peep verb peeps, peeping, peeped
1 to look quickly or secretly, or through a narrow opening 2 to peep or peep out is to come slowly or briefly into view *The moon peeped out through the clouds.*
peep noun peeps
a quick look

peer¹ verb peers, peering, peered
to peer at something or someone is to look at them closely or with difficulty

peer² noun peers
1 a noble 2 your peers are the people who are the same age as you

peewit noun peewits
a kind of wading bird

peg noun pegs
a clip or pin for fixing things in place or for hanging things on
peg verb pegs, pegging, pegged
to peg something is to fix it with pegs *We pegged out the tent.*

a
b
c
d
e
f
g
h
i
j
k
l
m
n
o
p
q
r
s
t
u
v
w
x
y
z

A
B
C
D
E
F
G
H
I
J
K
L
M
N
O

P

Q
R
S
T
U
V
W
X
Y
Z

Pekingese (say peek-i-**neez**) or
Pekinese noun Pekingese, Pekinese
a small breed of dog with short legs and
long silky hair

pelican noun pelicans
a large bird with a pouch in its long beak
for storing fish

pelican crossing noun pelican
crossings
a place where pedestrians can cross a street
by operating lights that signal the traffic
to stop

pellet noun pellets
a tiny ball of metal, food, wet paper, or
other substance

pelt¹ verb pelts, pelting, pelted
1 to pelt someone with things is to throw
a lot of things at them *We pelted him with
snowballs.* **2** it pelts down when it is raining
very hard **3** to pelt is to run fast

pelt² noun pelts
an animal skin, especially with the fur or
hair still on it

pelvis noun pelvises
your pelvis is the large bowl-shaped bone at
your hips, to which the bones of your legs
are attached

pen¹ noun pens
a device with a metal point for writing
with ink

pen² noun pens
an enclosure for cattle or other animals

penalize verb penalizes, penalizing,
penalized
1 to penalize someone is to punish them
2 in a game, to penalize someone is to
award a penalty against them

penalty noun penalties
1 a punishment **2** a point or advantage
given to one side in a game when a member
of the other side breaks a rule

pence plural noun
pennies

pencil noun pencils
a device for drawing or writing, made of
a thin stick of graphite or coloured chalk
inside a cylinder of wood or metal

pencil verb pencils, pencilling,
pencilled
to pencil something is to write it or mark it
with a pencil *I'll pencil that date in
my diary.*

pendant noun pendants
a piece of jewellery hung round the neck on
a long chain or string

pendulum noun pendulums
a weight hung at the end of a rod so that
it swings to and fro, especially to keep a
clock working

penetrate verb penetrates,
penetrating, penetrated
to penetrate something is to find a way
through it or into it **penetration** noun

penfriend noun penfriends
someone in another country you write to,
usually without meeting them

penguin noun penguins
an Antarctic sea bird that cannot fly but
uses its wings as flippers for swimming

penicillin noun
penicillin is a drug that kills bacteria, made
from mould

peninsula noun peninsulas
a long piece of land that is almost
surrounded by water **peninsular** adjective

penis noun penises
the part of the body with which a male
person or animal passes water from
the body

penitent adjective
sorry for what you have done
penitence noun

penknife noun penknives
a small folding knife

pennant noun pennants
a long pointed flag

penniless adjective
having no money; very poor

penny noun pennies or pence
a British coin worth a hundredth of
a pound

pension noun pensions
an income of regular payments made to
someone who has retired

pensioner noun pensioners
someone who receives a pension

pentagon noun pentagons
a flat shape with five sides
pentagonal adjective

pentathlon (say pent-**ath**-lon) noun
pentathlons
a sports competition that has five
different events

peony (say **pee**-o-ni) noun peonies
a plant with large round red, pink, or
white flowers

people plural noun
1 people are human beings; men, women,
and children 2 the people of a particular
country or area are the men, women, and
children who live there

people noun peoples
a people is a community or nation *They are
a peaceful people.*

pepper noun peppers
1 pepper is a hot-tasting powder used to
flavour food 2 a pepper is a bright green,
red, or yellow vegetable **peppery** adjective

peppermint noun peppermints
1 peppermint is a kind of mint used for
flavouring 2 a peppermint is a sweet
flavoured with this mint

per preposition
for each *The charge is £2 per person.*

perceive verb perceives, perceiving,
perceived
to perceive something is to see or notice it
or understand it

per cent adverb
for every hundred *We pay interest at 5 per
cent (5%).*

percentage noun percentages
an amount or rate expressed as a
proportion of 100

perceptible adjective
able to be seen or noticed
perceptibly adverb

perception noun
perception is the ability to see, notice, or
understand something

perceptive adjective
quick to notice or understand things *It was
very perceptive of you to spot that.*

perch¹ noun perches
a place where a bird sits or rests

perch verb perches, perching, perched
to perch is to sit or stand on the edge of
something or on something small *Matilda,
who was perched on a tall stool at the
kitchen table, ate her bread and jam slowly.
— Roald Dahl, Matilda*

perch² noun perch
a freshwater fish used for food

percolator noun percolators
a pot for making coffee with ground
coffee beans

percussion noun
percussion is musical instruments that you
play by hitting them or shaking them, such
as drums and cymbals **percussionist** noun

perennial adjective
lasting or occurring for many years

perennial noun perennials
a plant that lives for many years

perfect (say **per**-fikt) adjective
1 so good that it cannot be made any
better; without any faults 2 complete *The
man is a perfect stranger.* **perfection** noun

perfect noun
a form of a verb that describes a completed
action or event in the past, in English

formed with *has* and *have*, for example
I have lost my pen

perfect (say per-**fekt**) verb **perfects,
perfecting, perfected**
to perfect something is to make it perfect

perfectly adverb
1 completely *She stood perfectly still.*
2 without any faults *The toaster works
perfectly now.*

perforate verb **perforates,
perforating, perforated**
to perforate something is to make tiny holes
in it, especially so that it can be torn off
easily **perforations** plural noun perforations
are the tiny holes made in something so
that it can be torn off easily

perform verb **performs, performing,
performed**
1 to perform something is to present it in
front of an audience *They performed a play
in the school hall.* **2** to perform something
is also to do something you have to do
or ought to do *The surgeon performed the
operation on Tuesday.*

performance noun **performances**
the showing of something in front of
an audience

performer noun **performers**
someone who performs an entertainment

perfume noun **perfumes**
1 a sweet-smelling liquid that people put on
their skin **2** a sweet or pleasant smell

perhaps adverb
it may be; possibly

peril noun **perils**
peril is danger *She was in great peril.*

perilous adjective
a perilous journey or adventure is a
dangerous one *It was a perilous climb. The
rocks were slippery with snow and the other
boys were thoroughly over-excited, making
the ascent far too quickly.* – Cressida Cowell,
How to Train Your Dragon **perilously** adverb
dangerously *We came perilously close to
disaster.*

perimeter (say per-**im**-it-er) noun
perimeters
1 a boundary *A fence marks the perimeter
of the park.* **2** the distance round the edge
of something

period noun **periods**
1 a length of time **2** the time every month
when a woman or girl bleeds from her
womb in menstruation

periodic adjective
occurring at regular intervals
periodically adverb something happens
periodically when it happens from time to
time

periodical noun **periodicals**
a magazine published regularly, for example
once a month

periscope noun **periscopes**
a device with a tube and mirrors that lets
you see things at a higher level, used for
example in submarines

perish verb **perishes, perishing,
perished**
1 to perish is to die or be destroyed *Many
sailors perished in the shipwreck.* **2** to
perish is also to rot *The tyres have perished.*
3 (informal) to be perished is to feel
extremely cold *I was perished after the long
walk in the hills.*

perm noun
treatment of the hair with chemicals to give
it long-lasting waves
perm verb **perms, perming, permed**
to perm hair is to treat it with chemicals to
give it long-lasting waves

permanent adjective
lasting for ever or for a long time
Will there be any permanent damage?
permanence noun **permanently** adverb

permissible adjective
something is permissible when it is allowed

permission noun
you have permission to do something when
you are allowed to do it

A B C D E F G H I J K L M N O **P** Q R S T U V W X Y Z

permit (say per-**mit**) verb permits, permitting, permitted
1 to permit someone to do something is to allow them to do it **2** to permit something is to allow it to be done

permit (say **per**-mit) noun permits
a written or printed statement that says you are allowed to do something

perpendicular adjective
upright, or at a right angle to a line or surface

perpetual adjective
lasting for ever or for a long time
perpetually adverb continually

perplex verb perplexes, perplexing, perplexed
to perplex someone is to puzzle them very much **perplexity** noun

persecute verb persecutes, persecuting, persecuted
to persecute someone is to be continually cruel to them, especially because you disagree with their beliefs
persecution noun **persecutor** noun

persevere verb perseveres, persevering, persevered
to persevere is to go on with something even though it is difficult
perseverance noun

persist verb persists, persisting, persisted
1 to persist is to keep on firmly or obstinately doing something *She persists in breaking the rules.* **2** to persist is also to last for a long time *The rain persisted all afternoon.* **persistence** noun you show persistence when you keep on doing something without giving up

persistent adjective
1 refusing to give up **2** lasting for a long time *The rain was persistent.*
persistently adverb

person noun persons or people
1 a human being; a man, woman, or child
2 (in grammar) each of the parts of a verb and the pronouns that go with the verb. The **first person** (*I, me, we, us*) refers to the person or people speaking; the **second person** (*you*) refers to the person or people spoken to; and the **third person** (*he, him, she, her, it, they, them*) refers to the person or people spoken about

personal adjective
1 belonging to, done by, or concerning a particular person *The stars of the film will be making a personal appearance at the première.* **2** private *I can't tell you about that because it's personal.*

personal computer noun personal computers
a small computer designed for a single user

personality noun personalities
1 your personality is your nature and character *She has a cheerful personality.*
2 a well-known person *There were several TV personalities at the party.*

personally adverb
1 in person; being actually there *The head thanked me personally.* **2** as far as I am concerned *Personally, I'd rather stay here.*

personnel (say per-so-**nel**) noun
the personnel in a business or organization are the people who work there

perspective noun perspectives
1 perspective is the impression of depth and space in a picture or scene **2** your perspective on a situation is your point of view **in perspective** giving a balanced view of things *Try to see the problem in perspective.*

perspire verb perspires, perspiring, perspired
to perspire is to sweat **perspiration** noun

persuade verb persuades, persuading, persuaded
to persuade someone is to get them to agree about something

persuasion noun
persuasion is when you persuade someone to do or believe something

a
b
c
d
e
f
g
h
i
j
k
l
m
n
o
p
q
r
s
t
u
v
w
x
y
z

A
B
C
D
E
F
G
H
I
J
K
L
M
N
O
P
Q
R
S
T
U
V
W
X
Y
Z

persuasive adjective
a persuasive person is good at persuading people

perverse (say per-**verss**) adjective
obstinate or unreasonable in what you do or say **perversely** adverb **perversity** noun

Pesach noun
Pesach is the Hebrew name for Passover.

pessimist noun **pessimists**
someone who usually expects things to turn out badly **pessimism** noun pessimism is the feeling that things will turn out badly

pessimistic adjective
expecting things to turn out badly **pessimistically** adverb

pest noun **pests**
1 a destructive insect or animal, such as a locust or a mouse **2** a nuisance

pester verb **pesters, pestering, pestered**
to pester someone is to annoy them with frequent questions or interruptions

pesticide noun **pesticides**
a chemical used to kill insects and grubs

pet noun **pets**
1 a tame animal that you keep at home **2** a person treated as a favourite *She seems to be teacher's pet.*

petal noun **petals**
each of the separate coloured outer parts of a flower

petition noun **petitions**
a written request for something, usually signed by a large number of people

petrify verb **petrifies, petrifying, petrified**
to petrify someone is to make them so terrified that they cannot move

petrochemical noun
petrochemicals
a chemical substance made from petroleum or natural gas

petrol noun
petrol is a liquid made from petroleum, used as a fuel for engines

petroleum (say pi-**troh**-li-um) noun
petroleum is an oil found underground that is purified to make petrol, diesel oil, and other fuels

petticoat noun **petticoats**
a piece of women's clothing worn under a skirt or dress

petty adjective **pettier, pettiest**
1 minor and unimportant *There are some petty regulations.* **2** mean and small-minded **pettily** adverb **pettiness** noun

pew noun **pews**
one of the long wooden seats in a church

pewter noun
pewter is a grey alloy of tin and lead

phantom noun **phantoms**
a ghost

pharmacy noun **pharmacies**
a shop that sells medicines

phase noun **phases**
a stage in the progress or development of something

phase verb **phases, phasing, phased**
to phase a plan or operation is to carry it out in stages

pheasant (say **fez**-ant) noun **pheasants**
a game bird with a long tail

phenomenal (say fin-**om**-in-al) adjective
amazing or remarkable **phenomenally** adverb

phenomenon noun **phenomena**
an event or fact, especially one that is remarkable or unusual

philosopher noun **philosophers**
someone who studies philosophy

philosophical adjective
1 to do with philosophy **2** calmly accepting disappointment or suffering

He was philosophical about losing.
philosophically adverb

philosophy (say fil-**os**-o-fi) noun
philosophies
1 philosophy is the study of truths about life and human behaviour **2** a philosophy is a way of thinking or a system of beliefs

phobia (say **foh**-bi-a) noun **phobias**
a great or unusual fear of something

phoenix (say **fee**-niks) noun **phoenixes**
a mythical bird that was said to burn itself to death on a fire and be born again from the ashes

phone noun **phones**
a telephone
phone verb **phones, phoning, phoned**
to phone someone is to telephone them

phone-in noun **phone-ins**
a radio or TV programme in which people telephone the studio and take part in a discussion

phosphorescent adjective
shining or glowing in the dark
phosphorescence noun

photo noun **photos** (informal)
a photograph

photocopier noun **photocopiers**
a machine that makes photocopies

photocopy noun **photocopies**
a copy of a document or page made by a machine that photographs it on special paper
photocopy verb **photocopies, photocopying, photocopied**
to photocopy a document is to make a copy of it with a photocopier

photograph noun **photographs**
a picture made on film, using a camera
photograph verb **photographs, photographing, photographed**
to photograph someone or something is to take a photograph of them

photographer noun
someone who takes photographs

photography noun
photography is taking photographs with a camera **photographic** adjective

photosynthesis noun
photosynthesis is the process by which green plants use sunlight to make their food from carbon dioxide and water

phrase noun **phrases**
1 a group of words that form a unit smaller than a clause, for example *in the garden* in the sentence *The Queen was in the garden.* **2** a short section of a tune
phrase verb **phrases, phrasing, phrased**
to phrase an idea or thought is to put it into words

physical adjective
1 to do with the body rather than the mind or feelings **2** to do with things you can touch or see **physically** adverb

physical education noun
physical education is gymnastics or other exercises that you do to keep your body healthy

physician noun **physicians**
a doctor

physics noun
physics is the study of matter and energy, including movement, heat, light, and sound **physicist** noun

physiology (say fiz-i-**ol**-o-ji) noun
physiology is the study of the body and how it works **physiological** adjective

pianist noun **pianists**
someone who plays the piano

piano noun **pianos**
a large musical instrument with a row of black and white keys on a keyboard

pick[1] verb **picks, picking, picked**
1 to pick something or someone is to choose them *Pick a card from this pack.* **2** to pick flowers or fruit is to cut or pull them off the plant or tree **3** to pick someone's pocket is to steal from it **4** to pick a lock is to open it without using a key **5** to pick bits off or out of something is to pull them

a
b
c
d
e
f
g
h
i
j
k
l
m
n
o
p
q
r
s
t
u
v
w
x
y
z

A
B
C
D
E
F
G
H
I
J
K
L
M
N
O
P
Q
R
S
T
U
V
W
X
Y
Z

away from it **to pick on someone** is to keep criticizing or bothering them **to pick someone up** is to give them a lift in a vehicle **to pick something up 1** is to take it from the ground or a surface **2** is to collect it *I'll pick up my bags from the station.* **to pick up** is to improve or recover

pick noun
1 a choice *Take your pick.* **2** the pick of a group of things is the best things in it

pick² noun **picks**
a pickaxe

pickaxe noun **pickaxes**
a heavy pointed tool with a long handle, used for breaking up concrete or hard ground

picket noun **pickets**
a group of strikers who try to persuade other people not to go into a place of work during a strike

picket verb **pickets, picketing, picketed**
a group of people picket a place of work when they stand outside and try to persuade other people not to go in during a strike

pickle noun **pickles**
1 a strong-tasting food made of vegetables preserved in vinegar **2** (informal) a difficulty *Now we're in a real pickle!*

pickle verb **pickles, pickling, pickled**
to pickle food is to preserve it in vinegar or salt water

pickpocket noun **pickpockets**
a thief who steals from people's pockets or bags

pick-up noun **pick-ups**
an open truck for carrying small loads

picnic noun **picnics**
a meal eaten in the open air away from home

picnic verb **picnics, picnicking, picnicked**
to picnic is to have a picnic
picnicker noun

pictogram noun **pictograms**
a picture or symbol that stands for a word or a phrase

pictorial adjective
with or using pictures

picture noun **pictures**
a painting, drawing, or photograph

picture verb **pictures, picturing, pictured**
1 to picture someone or something is to show them in a picture **2** to picture someone or something in your mind is to imagine them

picturesque (say pik-cher-**esk**) adjective
a picturesque place is attractive or charming *We drove through a picturesque village.*

pie noun **pies**
a baked dish of meat or fruit covered with pastry

piece noun **pieces**
1 a part of something; a bit **2** a work of art or writing or music *They played a piece of piano music.* **3** one of the objects you use on a board to play a game *a chess piece* **4** a coin *a 20p piece* **to be in one piece** is to be not broken or injured **piece by piece** gradually; one bit at a time

piece verb **pieces, piecing, pieced**
to piece things together is to join them to make something

TOP TIPS
To remember the spelling, remember you can have a **pie**ce of **pie**!

piecemeal adverb
you do something piecemeal when you do it gradually, a bit at a time

pie chart noun **pie charts**
a diagram in the form of a circle divided into slices, showing how a quantity or amount is divided up

pier noun **piers**
1 a long structure built out into the sea for people to walk on **2** a pillar supporting a bridge or arch

pierce verb pierces, piercing, pierced
to pierce something is to make a hole through it

piercing adjective
1 a piercing sound is loud and high-pitched *We heard a piercing shriek.* 2 something piercing seems to go right through you *The wind was cold and piercing.*

pig noun pigs
a fat animal with short legs and a blunt snout, kept for its meat

pigeon noun pigeons
a common grey bird with a small head and large chest

pigeon-hole noun pigeon-holes
a small compartment for holding papers and letters, for someone to collect

piggy noun piggies (informal)
a little pig

piggyback noun piggybacks
a ride on someone's back

pig-headed adjective
obstinate; stubborn

piglet noun piglets
a young pig

pigment noun pigments
a substance that colours something

pigmy noun pigmies
another spelling of pygmy

pigsty noun pigsties
1 a place for keeping pigs 2 (informal) you can describe a very untidy room or place as a pigsty

pigtail noun pigtails
a single plait of hair worn hanging at the back of the head

pike noun pikes
1 a large fish that lives in rivers and lakes 2 a heavy spear

pilchard noun pilchards
a small sea fish

pile noun piles
a number of things on top of one another

pile verb piles, piling, piled
to pile things is to put them into a pile **to pile up** is to become very much or very many *The work was piling up.*

pilfer verb pilfers, pilfering, pilfered
to pilfer small or unimportant things is to steal them

pilgrim noun pilgrims
someone who goes on a journey to a holy place

pilgrimage noun pilgrimages
a journey to a holy place

pill noun pills
a small piece of medicine that you swallow

pillage verb pillages, pillaging, pillaged
to pillage a place is to seize things from it by force and carry them off, especially in a war

pillar noun pillars
a tall stone or wooden post

pillar box noun pillar boxes
a postbox standing in a street

pillion noun pillions
a seat for a passenger behind the driver's seat on a motorcycle

pillow noun pillows
a cushion to rest your head on in bed

pillowcase noun pillowcases
a cloth cover for a pillow

pilot noun pilots
1 someone who flies an aircraft 2 someone who helps to steer a ship in and out of a port or through a difficult stretch of water

pilot verb pilots, piloting, piloted
to pilot an aircraft is to be the pilot of it

pimple noun pimples
a small round swelling on your skin

pin noun pins
1 a short piece of metal with a sharp point and a rounded head, used to fasten pieces of paper or cloth together 2 a pointed

a
b
c
d
e
f
g
h
i
j
k
l
m
n
o
p
q
r
s
t
u
v
w
x
y
z

device for fixing or marking something
pins and needles a tingling feeling in
the skin

pin verb pins, pinning, pinned
1 to pin something is to fasten it with a pin
2 to pin someone or something in a place is
to keep them fixed or trapped there *He was
pinned under the wreckage for hours.*

pinafore noun pinafores
a large apron

pincer noun pincers
the claw of a shellfish such as a lobster

pincers plural noun
a tool for gripping and pulling things,
especially for pulling out nails

pinch verb pinches, pinching, pinched
1 to pinch something is to squeeze it tightly
between two things, especially between
the finger and thumb **2** (informal) to pinch
something is to steal it

pinch noun pinches
1 a firm squeezing movement **2** the amount
you can pick up between the tips of your
finger and thumb *Take a pinch of salt.*

pincushion noun pincushions
a small pad into which needles and pins are
stuck to keep them ready for use

pine[1] noun pines
an evergreen tree with leaves shaped
like needles

pine[2] verb pines, pining, pined
1 to pine for someone or something is to
feel a strong longing for them **2** to pine, or
pine away, is to become weak or ill through
sorrow or yearning

pineapple noun pineapples
a large tropical fruit with yellow flesh and
prickly leaves and skin

ping-pong noun
ping-pong is table tennis

pink adjective pinker, pinkest
pale red

pink noun pinks
a pink colour

pint noun pints
a measure of liquid, an eighth of a gallon or
about 568 millilitres

pioneer noun pioneers
one of the first people to go to a place or
do something new

pious adjective
very religious or devout **piously** adverb

pip noun pips
1 a small hard seed of a fruit such as
an apple, orange, or pear **2** a short
high-pitched sound *She heard the six pips of
the time signal on the radio.*

pipe noun pipes
1 a tube for carrying water, gas, or oil from
one place to another **2** a short tube with
a small bowl at one end, used to smoke
tobacco **3** a tubular musical instrument

pipe verb pipes, piping, piped
1 to pipe something is to send it along pipes
or wires **2** to pipe is to play music on a pipe
or the bagpipes **to pipe down** (informal) is
to be quiet **to pipe up** (informal) is to start
saying something

pipeline noun pipelines
a pipe for carrying oil, water, or gas over a
long distance **to be in the pipeline** is to be
planned and ready to happen soon

piper noun pipers
someone who plays a pipe or the bagpipes

piping adjective
high-pitched; shrill **piping hot** very hot,
ready to eat

piping noun
piping is a length of pipes or material used
for making pipes

piracy noun
1 attacking and robbing ships at sea
2 making copies of films or records without
permission, to sell or pass on

pirate noun pirates
a sailor who attacks and robs other ships

A
B
C
D
E
F
G
H
I
J
K
L
M
N
O
P
Q
R
S
T
U
V
W
X
Y
Z

pistil noun **pistils**
the part of a flower that produces the seed

pistol noun **pistols**
a small gun held in the hand

piston noun **pistons**
a disc that moves up and down inside a cylinder in an engine or pump

pit noun **pits**
1 a deep hole or hollow 2 a coal mine 3 the part of a race circuit where cars are refuelled and serviced during a race

pit verb **pits, pitting, pitted**
1 to pit something is to make deep holes or hollows in it *The surface of the planet was pitted with craters.* 2 to pit one person against another is to arrange for them to compete with one another *In the final he was pitted against the champion.*

pitch¹ noun **pitches**
1 a pitch is a piece of ground marked out for cricket, football, or another game 2 pitch is how high or low a voice or musical note is 3 the pitch of something is also its intensity or strength *Excitement was at a high pitch.*

pitch verb **pitches, pitching, pitched**
1 to pitch something is to throw or fling it 2 to pitch a tent is to set it up 3 to pitch is to fall heavily *He tripped over the doorstep and pitched headlong.* 4 a ship pitches when it moves up and down on a rough sea 5 to pitch something is to set it at a particular level *We are pitching our hopes high.* **to pitch in** is to join in and help with something *Everyone pitched in with ideas.*

pitch² noun
pitch is a black sticky substance like tar

pitch-black or
pitch-dark adjective
completely black or dark, with no light at all

pitfall noun **pitfalls**
a hidden danger or difficulty

pitiful adjective
1 making you feel pity *It was a pitiful sight.*

2 inadequate; feeble *He made a pitiful attempt to make us laugh.* **pitifully** adverb

pitiless adjective
having or showing no pity **pitilessly** adverb

pitta bread noun
pitta bread is a flat, round piece of bread that you can open and fill with food

pity noun
1 pity is the feeling of being sorry because someone is in pain or in trouble *I feel pity for homeless people.* 2 a pity is something that you regret *It's a pity we can't meet.* **to take pity on someone** is to help someone who is in trouble

pity verb **pities, pitying, pitied**
to pity someone is to feel sorry for them

pivot noun **pivots**
a point on which something turns or balances

pivot verb **pivots, pivoting, pivoted**
to pivot is to turn on a pivot or balance

pixel noun **pixels**
each of the tiny dots on a computer screen from which the image is formed

pixie or **pixy** noun **pixies**
a small fairy or elf

pizza (say **peet**-sa) noun **pizzas**
an Italian food made as a layer of dough covered with cheese, vegetables, and spices and baked

placard noun **placards**
a large poster or notice put up on a wall or carried at a demonstration

place noun **places**
1 a particular part of space, especially where something belongs; an area or position 2 a position in a race or competition 3 a seat *Save me a place.* 4 a person's duty or function *It's not my place to interfere.* **in place** in the proper position **in place of something** or **someone** instead of them **out of place** 1 in the wrong position 2 unsuitable *Jeans and sandals are out of place in a smart restaurant.*

place verb places, placing, placed
to place something somewhere is to put it in a particular place

placid adjective
calm and gentle; peaceful *a placid horse.*
placidly adverb

plague noun plagues
1 a dangerous illness that spreads very quickly **2** a large number of pests *The crops were devastated by a plague of locusts.*

plague verb plagues, plaguing, plagued
to plague someone is to pester or annoy them continuously *They have been plagued with complaints.*

plaice noun plaice
a flat sea fish used for food

plaid (say plad) noun plaids
cloth with a tartan or chequered pattern

plain adjective plainer, plainest
1 simple; not decorated **2** not pretty **3** easy to understand or see **4** frank; straightforward *I'll be quite plain with you.*
plainness noun

plain noun plains
a large area of flat country without trees

plainly adverb
1 clearly or obviously *The clock tower was plainly visible in the distance.* **2** simply *She was plainly dressed.*

plaintive adjective
sounding sad *We heard a plaintive cry.*
plaintively adverb in a plaintive way *'Will somebody please tell me what all this is about?' the Hemulen asked plaintively.* – Tove Jansson, *Finn Family Moomintroll*

plait (say plat) noun plaits
a length of hair or rope with several strands twisted together

plait (say plat) verb plaits, plaiting, plaited
to plait hair or rope is to make it into a plait

plan noun plans
1 a way of doing something that you think out in advance **2** a drawing showing how the parts of something are arranged **3** a map of a town or district

plan verb plans, planning, planned
1 to plan something is to think out in advance how you are going to do it **2** to plan to do something is to intend to do it
planner noun

plane[1] noun planes
1 an aeroplane **2** a tool for making wood smooth **3** a flat or level surface

plane verb planes, planing, planed
to plane wood is to smooth it with a plane

plane[2] noun planes
a tall tree with broad leaves

planet noun planets
one of the bodies that move in an orbit round the sun. The main planets of the solar system are Mercury, Venus, Earth, Mars, Jupiter, Saturn, Uranus, and Neptune. *Please see illustration on following page.*
planetary adjective

plank noun planks
a long flat piece of wood

plankton noun
plankton is made up of tiny creatures that float in the sea and lakes

plant noun plants
1 a living thing that grows out of the ground, including flowers, bushes, trees, and vegetables **2** a factory or its equipment

plant verb plants, planting, planted
1 to plant something such as a tree or flower is to put it in the ground to grow **2** to plant something is also to put it firmly in place *He planted his feet on the ground and took hold of the rope.* **3** to plant something such as a piece of evidence is to put it where it will be found, usually to mislead people or to cause trouble

plantation noun plantations
an area of land where a crop such as tobacco, tea, or rubber is planted

plaque (say plak or plahk) noun plaques
1 a plaque is a metal or porcelain plate fixed on a wall as a memorial or an ornament **2** plaque is a substance that forms a thin

A
B
C
D
E
F
G
H
I
J
K
L
M
N
O
P
Q
R
S
T
U
V
W
X
Y
Z

planet

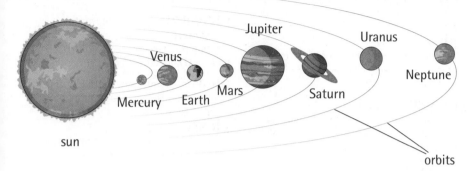

layer on your teeth, allowing bacteria to develop

plasma (say **plaz**-ma) noun
1 plasma is the colourless liquid part of blood, which carries the corpuscles **2** a plasma television screen uses a special type of gas to show the colours on the screen

plaster noun **plasters**
1 a plaster is a small covering you put over your skin around a cut or wound to protect it **2** plaster is a mixture of lime, sand, and water, used to cover walls and ceilings
plaster verb **plasters, plastering, plastered**
1 to plaster a surface is to cover it with plaster **2** to plaster a surface with something is to cover it thickly *His clothes were plastered with mud.*

plaster of Paris noun
plaster of Paris is a white paste used for making moulds and for casts round a broken leg or arm

plastic noun **plastics**
a strong light synthetic substance that can be moulded into different shapes
plastic adjective
made of plastic *I need a plastic bag.*

Plasticine noun (trademark)
Plasticine is a soft and easily shaped substance used for making models.

plastic surgery noun
plastic surgery is work done by a surgeon to alter or mend parts of someone's body

plate noun **plates**
1 a dish that is flat or almost flat, used for eating **2** a thin flat sheet of metal, glass, or other hard material **3** one of the large areas of rock that make up the earth's crust
plate verb **plates, plating, plated**
to plate metal is to cover it with a thin layer of gold, silver, tin, or other soft metal

plateau (say **plat**-oh) noun **plateaux**
a flat area of high land

plateful noun **platefuls**
as much as you can put on a plate

platform noun **platforms**
1 a flat raised area along the side of the line at a railway station **2** a small stage in a hall

platinum noun
platinum is a silver-coloured metal that does not lose its brightness

platoon noun **platoons**
a small unit of soldiers

platypus noun **platypuses**
an Australian animal with a beak and feet like those of a duck

play verb **plays, playing, played**
1 to play, or play a game, is to take part in a game or other amusement **2** to play music, or a musical instrument, is to make music

a
b
c
d
e
f
g
h
i
j
k
l
m
n
o
p
q
r
s
t
u
v
w
x
y
z

or sound with it **3** to play a part in a film or play is to perform it **4** to play a CD or DVD is to put it in a machine and listen to it or watch it

play noun **plays**
1 a play is a story acted on a stage or broadcast on radio or television **2** play is playing or having fun

player noun **players**
someone who plays a game or a musical instrument *a football player, He's an excellent piano player.*

playful adjective
1 wanting to play; full of fun **2** not serious **playfully** adverb **playfulness** noun

playground noun **playgrounds**
a place out of doors where children can play

playgroup noun **playgroups**
a group of very young children who play together regularly, with adults to supervise them

playing card noun **playing cards**
each of a set of cards (usually 52) used for playing games

playing field noun **playing fields**
a grassy field for outdoor games

playmate noun **playmates**
someone that you play games with

play-off noun **play-offs**
an extra match played to decide a draw or tie

playtime noun **playtimes**
the time when young schoolchildren go out to play

playwright noun **playwrights**
someone who writes plays

plea noun **pleas**
1 a request or appeal **2** a statement of 'guilty' or 'not guilty' made in a law court by someone accused of a crime

plead verb **pleads, pleading, pleaded**
to plead with someone is to beg them to do something **to plead guilty** or **not guilty** is

to state in a law court that you are guilty or not guilty of a crime

pleasant adjective **pleasanter, pleasantest**
pleasing or enjoyable or friendly
pleasantly adverb

please verb **pleases, pleasing, pleased**
to please someone is to make them happy or satisfied

please adverb
used when you want to ask something politely *Please shut the door.* **as you please** as you like *Do as you please.*

pleasurable adjective
causing pleasure; enjoyable

pleasure noun **pleasures**
1 pleasure is being pleased **2** a pleasure is something that pleases you **with pleasure** gladly; willingly

pleat noun **pleats**
a permanent fold made in the cloth of a piece of clothing **pleated** adjective

pledge noun **pledges**
a solemn promise

pledge verb **pledges, pledging, pledged**
to pledge something is to promise it

plentiful adjective
large in amount *a plentiful crop of fruit*
plentifully adverb

plenty noun
to have plenty of something is to have a lot of it or more than enough *We have plenty of chairs.*

pliable adjective
easy to bend; flexible

pliers plural noun
pincers with flattened jaws for gripping something or for breaking wire

plight noun **plights**
a difficult and sad situation *The programme examines the plight of the homeless.*

plod verb **plods, plodding, plodded**
1 to plod is to walk slowly and with heavy

steps *We plodded back through the rain.*
2 to plod, or plod away, is to work slowly but steadily

plop noun **plops**
the sound of something dropping into a liquid

plop verb **plops, plopping, plopped**
to plop is to fall into a liquid with a plop

plot noun **plots**
1 a secret plan, especially to do something illegal or bad **2** what happens in a story, film, or play **3** a piece of land for a house or garden

plot verb **plots, plotting, plotted**
1 to plot is to make a secret plan to do something **2** to plot a chart or graph is to make it, marking all the points on it

plotter noun **plotters**
plotters are people who take part in a plot

plough (say plow) noun **ploughs**
a device used on farms for turning over the soil

plough verb **ploughs, ploughing, ploughed**
1 to plough the soil is to turn it over with a plough **2** to plough through something is to go through it with effort or difficulty *He ploughed through the book.*

plover (say **pluv**-er) noun **plovers**
a long-legged wading bird

pluck verb **plucks, plucking, plucked**
1 to pluck a bird is to pull the feathers off it to prepare it for cooking **2** to pluck a flower or fruit is to pick it **3** to pluck something is to pull it or pull it out *I'll try and pluck out your splinter.* **4** in music, to pluck a string is to pull it and let it go again **to pluck up courage** is to be brave and overcome fear

pluck noun
pluck is courage or bravery

plucky adjective **pluckier, pluckiest**
brave or courageous *Emil was past fourteen and a plucky fellow, so he challenged Dan to a fight.* — Louisa May Alcott, *Little Men*
pluckily adverb

plug noun **plugs**
1 something used to stop up a hole, especially in a sink or bath **2** a device that is used to connect a piece of electric equipment to a socket

plug verb **plugs, plugging, plugged**
1 to plug a hole is to stop it up **2** (informal) to plug an event or product is to publicize it **to plug something in** is to connect it to an electric socket by means of a plug

plum noun **plums**
a soft juicy fruit with a stone in the middle

plumage (say **ploo**-mij) noun
a bird's plumage is its feathers

plumb verb **plumbs, plumbing, plumbed**
1 to plumb a river or the sea is to measure how deep it is **2** to plumb a mystery or puzzle is to find out what it means

plumber noun **plumbers**
someone who fits and mends water pipes in a building

plumbing noun
1 plumbing is the work of a plumber **2** the plumbing in a building is all the water pipes and water tanks

plume noun **plumes**
1 a large feather **2** something shaped like a feather *We saw a plume of smoke in the distance.*

plump adjective **plumper, plumpest**
rounded or slightly fat

plump verb **plumps, plumping, plumped**
to plump for something or **someone** is to choose them

plunder verb **plunders, plundering, plundered**
to plunder a place or person is to rob them violently, especially in a time of war or disorder *The chief brigand counted out the jewels and gold coins they'd plundered and divided them all into twenty heaps.* — Philip Pullman, *The Scarecrow and his Servant*

a b c d e f g h i j k l m n o **p** q r s t u v w x y z

plunder noun
1 plunder is plundering a person or place
2 plunder is also goods taken by plundering

plunge verb plunges, plunging, plunged
1 to plunge into water is to jump or dive into it with force 2 to plunge something into a liquid or something soft is to put it in with force

plunge noun plunges
a sudden fall or dive

plural noun plurals
the form of a word meaning more than one person or thing, such as *cakes* and *children*

plural adjective
in the plural; meaning more than one *'Mice' is a plural noun.*

plus preposition
with the next number or thing added *2 plus 2 equals 4 (2 + 2 = 4).*

plywood noun
plywood is board made from thin sheets of wood glued together

p.m.
short for Latin *post meridiem*, which means 'after midday'

pneumatic (say new-**mat**-ik) adjective
filled with air or worked by compressed air *a pneumatic tyre, a pneumatic drill*

pneumonia (say new-**moh**-ni-a) noun
pneumonia is a serious disease of the lungs

poach verb poaches, poaching, poached
1 to poach food, especially fish or an egg taken out of its shell, is to cook it in or over boiling water 2 to poach animals is to hunt them illegally on someone else's land **poacher** noun

pocket noun pockets
1 part of a piece of clothing shaped like a small bag, for keeping things in 2 a small area in which something happens *There will be pockets of rain in the south.* 3 a person's pocket is their supply of money *The cost is well beyond my pocket.* **to be out of pocket** is to have spent more money than you got back

pocket adjective
small enough to carry in your pocket *Use a pocket calculator.*

pocket verb pockets, pocketing, pocketed (informal)
to pocket something is to steal it

pocketful noun pocketfuls
an amount you can put in your pocket

pocket money noun
pocket money is money given to a child to spend

pod noun pods
a long seed-container on a pea or bean plant

podgy adjective podgier, podgiest
short and fat

poem noun poems
a piece of writing arranged in short lines, often with a particular rhythm and sometimes rhyming

poet noun poets
someone who writes poetry

poetic or **poetical** adjective
like poetry; using the language of poetry
poetically adverb

poetry noun
poetry is poems as a form of literature *Do you write poetry?*

point noun points
1 the narrow or sharp end of something *Don't hold the knife by its point.* 2 a written dot *Put in a decimal point.* 3 a single mark in a game or quiz *How many points did I get?* 4 a particular place or time *They gave up at this point.* 5 something that someone says during a discussion *That's a very good point.* 6 a detail or special feature *He has some good points.* 7 purpose or advantage *There's no point in hurrying.* 8 the points on a railway line are the movable parts that allow trains to change from one track to another

to come to the point is to mention the thing you really want to say

point verb **points, pointing, pointed**
1 to point to something is to show where it is, especially by holding out your finger towards it **2** to point something is to aim it or direct it *She pointed a gun at us.* **to point something out** is to show it or explain it

point-blank adjective, adverb
1 close to the target **2** directly and completely *He refused point-blank.*

pointed adjective
1 a pointed object has a point at the end **2** a pointed remark is clearly directed at a person, especially to criticize them *He made a pointed remark about working hard.*

pointer noun **pointers**
1 a stick or device you use to point at something **2** a dog that points with its muzzle at birds which it scents **3** a hint or piece of guidance *He gave us a few pointers on the best way to make a campfire.*

pointless adjective
something is pointless when it has no purpose or meaning **pointlessly** adverb

point of view noun **points of view**
1 a way of looking or thinking of something **2** the way that a writer chooses to tell a story, for example by telling it through the experiences of one of the characters

poise noun
poise is a dignified and self-confident manner

poise verb **poises, poising, poised**
1 to poise something is to balance it or keep it steady **2** to be poised to do something is to be ready to do it

poison noun **poisons**
a substance that can kill or harm living things

poison verb **poisons, poisoning, poisoned**
1 to poison someone is to kill or harm them with poison **2** to poison something is to put poison in it

poisonous adjective
1 a poisonous chemical, gas, or plant can kill or harm you if you swallow it or breathe it in **2** poisonous animals or insects can kill or harm you with poison if they bite you *a poisonous snake*

poke verb **pokes, poking, poked**
to poke something or someone is to push or jab them hard with your finger or a pointed object **to poke out** is to stick out

poke noun **pokes**
a prod or jab

poker noun **pokers**
1 a poker is a metal rod for stirring a fire **2** poker is a card game in which the players bet on who has the best cards

polar adjective
to do with the North or South Pole, or near one of them

polar bear noun **polar bears**
a powerful white bear living in Arctic regions

pole[1] noun **poles**
a long thin piece of wood or metal

pole[2] noun **poles**
1 each of the two points at the ends of the earth's axis, the **North Pole** and the **South Pole 2** each end of a magnet

pole vault noun
the pole vault is an athletic contest in which you jump over a high bar with the help of a long springy pole

police noun
the police are the people whose job is to catch criminals and make sure that people obey the law

policeman or policewoman noun
policemen, policewomen
a man or woman member of the police

police officer noun **police officers**
a member of the police

policy noun **policies**
1 the aims or plans of a person or group

a
b
c
d
e
f
g
h
i
j
k
l
m
n
o
p
q
r
s
t
u
v
w
x
y
z

of people **2** a plan of action *Honesty is the best policy.*

polio (say **poh**-li-oh) noun
polio is a disease that paralyses the body. Polio is short for *poliomyelitis*

polish (say **pol**-ish) verb **polishes, polishing, polished**
to polish something is to make its surface shiny or smooth **to polish something off** (informal) is to finish it quickly

polish (say **pol**-ish) noun **polishes**
1 polish is a substance used in polishing **2** a polish is a shine got by polishing *He gave his shoes a good polish.*

polished adjective
1 shiny **2** well practised or rehearsed *The choir gave a polished performance.*

polite adjective **politer, politest**
having good manners; respectful and thoughtful towards other people **politely** adverb **politeness** noun

political adjective
to do with the governing of a country **politically** adverb

politician noun **politicians**
someone who is involved in politics

politics noun
politics is political matters; the business of governing a country

polka noun **polkas**
a lively dance

poll noun **polls**
1 a round of voting at an election **2** an estimate of what people think, made by questioning a certain number of them

pollen noun
pollen is yellow powder found inside flowers, containing male seeds for fertilizing other flowers

pollinate verb **pollinates, pollinating, pollinated**
to pollinate a flower or plant is to put pollen into it so that it becomes fertilized **pollination** noun

pollute verb **pollutes, polluting, polluted**
to pollute a place or thing is to make it dirty or impure

pollution noun
pollution is the process of making the air, water, and soil dirty or impure

polo noun
polo is a game rather like hockey, with players on horseback using long mallets

polo neck noun **polo necks**
a high rounded collar that is turned over at the top

poltergeist (say **pol**-ter-gyst) noun **poltergeists**
a noisy mischievous ghost that damages things *Peeves was the school poltergeist, a grinning, airborne menace who lived to cause havoc and distress.* – J. K. Rowling, *Harry Potter and the Chamber of Secrets*

poly– prefix
meaning 'many', as in *polygon*

polygon noun **polygons**
a figure or shape with many sides, such as a hexagon or octagon

polystyrene (say pol-i-**sty**-reen) noun
polystyrene is a kind of plastic used for insulating or packing things

polythene (say pol-i-theen) noun
polythene is a lightweight plastic used to make bags and wrappings

pomp noun
pomp is the dignified and solemn way in which an important ceremony is carried out

pompous adjective
someone is being pompous when they are thinking too much of their own importance **pompously** adverb

pond noun **ponds**
a small lake

ponder verb **ponders, pondering, pondered**
to ponder something is to think carefully and seriously about it

ponderous adjective
1 heavy and awkward **2** dull and not easy to follow *He writes in a ponderous style.* **ponderously** adverb

pony noun **ponies**
a small horse

ponytail noun **ponytails**
a bunch of long hair tied at the back of the head

pony-trekking noun
pony-trekking is travelling across country on ponies for pleasure

poodle noun **poodles**
a dog with long curly hair

pool¹ noun **pools**
1 a pond **2** a puddle **3** a swimming pool

pool² noun **pools**
1 a group of things shared by several people **2** the fund of money that can be won in a gambling game **3** pool is a game similar to snooker but played on a smaller table
pool verb **pools, pooling, pooled**
to pool things is to put them all together so that everyone can share them

poor adjective **poorer, poorest**
1 having very little money *He came from a poor family.* **2** not good or adequate *This is poor work.* **3** unfortunate *Poor fellow!*

poorly adverb
not adequately *They arrived poorly dressed.*
poorly adjective
unwell *I'm feeling poorly today.*

pop¹ noun **pops**
1 a pop is a small explosive sound **2** pop is a fizzy drink
pop verb **pops, popping, popped**
1 to pop is to make a small explosive sound **2** (informal) to pop somewhere is to go there quickly *I'm just popping out to the shops.* **3** to pop something somewhere is to put it there quickly *Will you pop the potatoes in the oven?*

pop² noun
pop is modern popular music

popcorn noun
popcorn is maize heated till it bursts and forms light fluffy balls for eating

Pope noun **Popes**
the Pope is the leader of the Roman Catholic Church

poplar noun **poplars**
a tall straight tree

poppadom or **poppadam** noun
poppadoms, poppadams
a thin crisp pancake that you eat with Indian food

poppy noun **poppies**
a plant with large red flowers

popular adjective
liked or enjoyed by a lot of people
popularly adverb something is (for example) popularly believed when it is believed by a large number of people

popularity noun
popularity is being liked or enjoyed by a lot of people

popularize verb **popularizes, popularizing, popularized**
to popularize something is to make it known and liked by a lot of people

populated adjective
a place is populated when it has people living there *The land is thinly populated.*

population noun **populations**
the population of a particular place is all the people who live there; the total number of people who live there *What's the population of London?*

populous adjective
a populous place is inhabited by a lot of people

porcelain (say **por**-se-lin) noun
porcelain is a fine kind of china

porch noun **porches**
a small roofed area outside the door of a building

a
b
c
d
e
f
g
h
i
j
k
l
m
n
o
p
q
r
s
t
u
v
w
x
y
z

porcupine noun **porcupines**
a small animal covered with long prickles

pore¹ noun **pores**
one of the tiny openings in your skin which sweat can pass through

pore² verb **pores, poring, pored**
to pore over something is to study it closely

pork noun
pork is meat from a pig

porous adjective
something is porous when it allows liquid or air to pass through *Sandy soil is porous.*

porpoise (say **por**-pus) noun **porpoises**
a sea animal rather like a small whale

porridge noun
porridge is a food made by boiling oatmeal to make a thick paste

port¹ noun **ports**
1 a port is a harbour **2** a port is also a city or town with a harbour **3** port is the left-hand side of a ship or aircraft when you are facing forward

port² noun
port is a strong red Portuguese wine

portable adjective
able to be carried easily

portcullis noun **portcullises**
a heavy grating that can be lowered to block the gateway to a castle

porter noun **porters**
1 someone whose job is to carry luggage or goods **2** someone whose job is to look after the entrance to a large building

porthole noun **portholes**
a small round window in the side of a ship or aircraft

portion noun **portions**
a part or share given to someone

portly adjective **portlier, portliest**
rather fat *By dinner-time we arrived at Porlock, and dined with my old friend, Master Pooke, now growing rich and portly.* – R. D. Blackmore, *Lorna Doone*

portrait noun **portraits**
a picture of a person

portray verb **portrays, portraying, portrayed**
1 to portray someone is to make a portrait of them **2** to portray something or someone is to describe or show them in a certain way *The play portrays the king as a kind man.* **portrayal** noun

pose noun **poses**
1 a way of standing or sitting for a portrait or photograph to be made of you *Just hold that pose for a second.* **2** a pretence; unnatural behaviour to impress people

pose verb **poses, posing, posed**
1 to pose is to put your body into a special position **2** to pose someone is to put them in a particular position to be painted or photographed **3** to pose as someone is to pretend to be them *The man posed as a police officer.* **4** to pose a question or problem is to present it *Icy weather poses a problem to motorists.*

posh adjective **posher, poshest** (informal)
1 very smart; high-class *They stayed at a posh hotel.* **2** of a high social class *She spoke with a posh accent.*

position noun **positions**
1 the place where something is or should be **2** the way in which someone or something is placed or arranged *He was sleeping in an uncomfortable position.* **3** a person's place in a race or competition **4** a situation or condition *I am in no position to help you.* **5** a regular job

position verb **positions, positioning, positioned**
to position something somewhere is to place it there

positive adjective
1 sure or definite *I am positive I saw him. We need positive proof.* **2** agreeing or saying 'yes' *We received a positive answer.* **3** a positive number is one that is greater than nought **4** a positive electric charge

is one that does not carry electrons
positively adverb

posse (say **poss**-i) noun **posses**
a group of people that helps a sheriff in
the USA

possess verb **possesses, possessing,
possessed**
to possess something is to own or have it
possessor noun

possessed adjective
someone is possessed when they are
behaving as if they are controlled by an
outside force *He fought like a man possessed.*

possession noun **possessions**
1 a possession is something that you own
2 possession is owning something *They
gained possession of a piece of land.*

possessive adjective
1 you are being possessive when you
want to get and keep things for yourself
2 (in grammar) showing that someone
owns something *'His' and 'yours' are
possessive pronouns.*

possibility noun **possibilities**
1 possibility is being possible *Is there
any possibility of changing your mind?* **2** a
possibility is something that is possible
There are many possibilities.

possible adjective
able to exist, happen, be done, or be used

possibly adverb
1 in any way *That cannot possibly be right.*
2 perhaps *I will arrive at six o'clock, or
possibly earlier.*

post^1 noun **posts**
1 an upright piece of wood, concrete, or
metal fixed in the ground **2** the starting
point or finishing point of a race *He was left
at the post.*
post verb **posts, posting, posted**
to post a notice or poster is to put it in a
public place

post^2 noun **posts**
1 the post is the collecting and delivering
of letters and parcels **2** post is letters and

parcels carried by post; mail **3** a post is a
collection or delivery of mail at a particular
time *The last post is at 4 p.m.*
post verb **posts, posting, posted**
to post a letter or parcel is to send it to
someone by post

post^3 noun **posts**
1 a regular job **2** the place where a sentry
stands **3** a place occupied by soldiers
or traders
post verb **posts, posting, posted**
to be posted somewhere is to be sent there
for a time as part of your job

post– prefix
meaning 'after', as in *post-war*

postage noun
postage is the cost of sending a letter or
parcel by post

postage stamp noun **postage
stamps**
a stamp for putting on letters and parcels,
showing the amount paid

postal adjective
to do with the post; by post

postbox noun **postboxes**
a box into which you put letters to be sent
by post

postcard noun **postcards**
a card that you can write a message on and
post without an envelope

postcode noun **postcodes**
a group of letters and numbers included in
an address to help in sorting the post

poster noun **posters**
a large public notice having information or
advertising something

postman noun **postmen**
someone who collects and delivers letters
and parcels

postmark noun **postmarks**
an official mark stamped on something
sent by post, showing when and where it
was posted

a
b
c
d
e
f
g
h
i
j
k
l
m
n
o
p
q
r
s
t
u
v
w
x
y
z

A
B
C
D
E
F
G
H
I
J
K
L
M
N
O

P

Q
R
S
T
U
V
W
X
Y
Z

post office noun post offices
a place where you can post letters and parcels and buy stamps, postal orders, and other official documents

postpone verb postpones, postponing, postponed
to postpone a meeting or event is to arrange for it to take place later than was originally planned *The match has been postponed for two weeks.* **postponement** noun

postscript noun postscripts
something extra added at the end of a letter or book

posture noun postures
the way that a person stands, sits, or walks

posy noun posies
a small bunch of flowers

pot noun pots
1 a deep round container 2 a flowerpot

pot verb pots, potting, potted
1 to pot a plant is to put it into a flowerpot 2 to pot a ball in a game such as snooker or pool is to hit it into a pocket

potato noun potatoes
a vegetable that grows underground

potent adjective
powerful *Anne got Marilla a glassful of her potent currant wine.* – L. M. Montgomery, *Anne of Avonlea* **potency** noun **potently** adverb

potential adjective
capable of happening or becoming important or useful in the future *She is a potential star.* **potentially** adverb

potential noun
to have potential is to be capable of becoming important or useful in the future

pothole noun potholes
1 a deep natural hole in the ground 2 a hole in a road

potholing noun
potholing is exploring underground caves by climbing down potholes **potholer** noun

potion (say **poh**-shon) noun potions
a drink containing medicine or poison

potter[1] noun potters
someone who makes pottery

potter[2] verb potters, pottering, pottered
to potter, or potter about, is to spend time doing little jobs in a relaxed way

pottery noun potteries
1 pottery is pots, cups, plates, and other things made of baked clay 2 pottery is also the craft of making pottery 3 a pottery is a place where a potter works

potty[1] adjective pottier, pottiest (informal)
mad or silly

potty[2] noun potties (informal)
a small bowl used by young children as a lavatory

pouch noun pouches
1 a small bag or pocket 2 a fold of skin in which a kangaroo keeps its young

poultry noun
poultry are birds such as chickens, geese, and turkeys, kept for their eggs and meat

pounce verb pounces, pouncing, pounced
to pounce on someone or something is to jump on them or attack them suddenly *The Pelican opened his gigantic beak and immediately the policemen pounced upon the burglar who was crouching inside.* – Roald Dahl, *The Giraffe and the Pelly and Me*

pound[1] noun pounds
1 a unit of money, in Britain equal to 100 pence 2 a unit of weight equal to 16 ounces or about 454 grams

pound[2] verb pounds, pounding, pounded
1 to pound something is to hit it repeatedly to crush it 2 to pound, or pound along, is to walk with heavy steps 3 your heart is pounding when it beats heavily, making a dull thumping sound *My heart was pounding with the excitement.*

pour verb **pours, pouring, poured**
1 to pour a liquid is to make it flow out of a container **2** to pour is to flow in a large amount *Blood was pouring from the wound on her leg.* **3** it is pouring when it is raining heavily **4** to pour in or out is to come or go in large numbers or amounts *After the programme, letters of complaint poured in. The fans poured out of the stadium.*

pout verb **pouts, pouting, pouted**
you pout when you stick out your lips because you are annoyed or sulking

poverty noun
poverty is being poor

powder noun **powders**
1 a mass of tiny pieces of something dry, like flour or dust **2** make-up in the form of powder **powdery** adjective
powder verb **powders, powdering, powdered**
to powder something is to put powder on it *She powdered her face.*

power noun **powers**
1 power is strength or great energy **2** power is also control over other people **3** the power to do something is the ability to do it *Humans have the power of speech.*
4 a power is a powerful country **5** power is also electricity or another form of energy

powerful adjective
having a lot of power or influence
powerfully adverb

powerless adjective
someone is powerless if they are unable to act or control things

power station noun **power stations**
a building where electricity is produced

practicable adjective
possible or able to be done *That is not a practicable plan.*

practical adjective
1 someone is practical when they are able to do or make useful things *She is a very practical person.* **2** something is practical when it is likely to be useful

That is a practical idea. **3** concerned with doing or making things *He has had practical experience.*

practical noun **practicals**
a lesson or examination in which you actually do or make something rather than reading or writing about it

practical joke noun **practical jokes**
a trick played on someone

practically adverb
1 in a practical way *He is practically skilled.*
2 almost *It's practically ready now.*

practice noun **practices**
1 practice is doing something often and regularly so that you get better at it *I must do my piano practice.* **2** practice is also actually doing something rather than thinking or talking about it *I hope my plan works in practice.* **3** a practice is the business of a doctor or lawyer

practise verb **practises, practising, practised**
1 to practise something is to do it often so that you get better at it **2** to practise an activity or custom is to do it regularly *She practises yoga.* **3** to practise (for example) medicine or law is to work as a doctor or lawyer

prairie noun **prairies**
a large area of flat grass-covered land in North America

praise verb **praises, praising, praised**
to praise someone or something is to say that they are good or have done well
praise noun **praises**
praise is words that praise someone or something

pram noun **prams**
a small open carriage for a baby, pushed by a person walking

prance verb **prances, prancing, pranced**
to prance, or prance about, is to jump about in a lively or happy way *The Scarecrow leaped all over the room, capering and*

a
b
c
d
e
f
g
h
i
j
k
l
m
n
o
p
q
r
s
t
u
v
w
x
y
z

skipping and prancing like a goat. – Philip Pullman, *The Scarecrow and his Servant*

prank noun pranks
a trick played on someone for mischief

prawn noun prawns
a shellfish like a large shrimp, used for food

pray verb prays, praying, prayed
1 to pray is to talk to God 2 to pray is also to ask earnestly or hope for something *We are praying for good weather.*

prayer noun prayers
1 prayer is praying 2 a prayer is what you say when you pray

pre– prefix
meaning 'before', as in *pre-war*

preach verb preaches, preaching, preached
to preach is to give a talk about religion or about right and wrong **preacher** noun

precarious (say pri-**kair**-i-us) adjective
not at all safe or secure *That vase is in a precarious position.* **precariously** adverb in a precarious way *Somehow a porter managed to wheel Eddie's huge trunk, with Lady Constance's bags balanced precariously on top, out of the busy station.* – Philip Ardagh, *Terrible Times*

precaution noun precautions
something you do to prevent trouble or danger in the future

precede verb precedes, preceding, preceded
one thing precedes another when it comes or goes in front of the other thing *The film was preceded by a short cartoon.*

precinct (say **pree**-sinkt) noun precincts
1 a part of a town where traffic is not allowed *The town has a large shopping precinct.* 2 the area round a cathedral

precious adjective
very valuable or loved *Remembering her precious cordial, Lucy poured a few drops*

into her brother's mouth. – C. S. Lewis, *The Lion, The Witch and the Wardrobe*

precipice noun precipices
the steep face of a mountain or cliff

precise adjective
1 clear and accurate *I gave them precise instructions.* 2 exact *At that precise moment, the doorbell rang.* **precisely** adverb **precision** noun

predator (say **pred**-a-ter) noun predators
an animal that hunts other animals **predatory** adjective

predecessor (say **pree**-di-ses-er) noun predecessors
an earlier person or thing, such as an ancestor or someone who once did the job you do now

predict verb predicts, predicting, predicted
to predict something is to say that it will happen in the future

predictable adjective
something is predictable when you are able to say what will happen before it actually happens **predictably** adverb

prediction noun predictions
a prediction is something that someone predicts

predominant adjective
most important or largest in size or number **predominance** noun **predominantly** adverb

predominate verb predominates, predominating, predominated
to predominate is to be the largest in size or number, or the most important *Girls predominate in our class.*

preen verb preens, preening, preened
a bird preens when it smooths and cleans its feathers using its beak

preface (say **pref**-ass) noun prefaces
an introduction at the beginning of a book

prefect noun prefects
1 a school pupil who is given authority

to help to keep order **2** a local official in some countries

prefer verb prefers, preferring, preferred
to prefer one thing to another is to like it better than the other thing

preferable (say **pref**-er-a-bul) adjective
something is preferable to something else when it is better or you like it more **preferably** adverb you use preferably to say what you would prefer *Meet me tomorrow, preferably before school.*

preference noun preferences
your preference is what you prefer

prefix noun prefixes
a word or syllable joined to the front of a word to change or add to its meaning, as in *dis*order, *out*stretched, and *un*happy

pregnant adjective
a pregnant woman has an unborn baby growing inside her womb **pregnancy** noun

prehistoric adjective
belonging to a very long time ago, before written records were kept

prejudice noun prejudices
a prejudice is when you make up your mind that you do not like someone or something without a good reason or without thinking about it **prejudiced** adjective

preliminary adjective
coming before something or preparing for it

premature adjective
happening or coming before the proper time *a premature baby*

premier (say **prem**-i-er) noun premiers
the leader of a government

premiere (say **prem**-yair) noun premieres
the first public performance of a play or showing of a film

premises plural noun
an organization's or business's premises are the building and land it uses

premium (say **pree**-mi-um) noun premiums
an amount paid regularly to an insurance company **to be at a premium** is to be valued highly and perhaps expensive because of this

premonition noun premonitions
a feeling that something bad is going to happen

preoccupied adjective
you are preoccupied when you are thinking hard about something and do not notice other things **preoccupation** noun something you think about most of the time

preparation noun preparations
1 preparation is getting something ready **2** preparations are things you do in order to get ready for something *We were making last-minute preparations.*

preparatory (say pri-**pa**-ra-ter-i) adjective
preparing for something

prepare verb prepares, preparing, prepared
to prepare something is to get it ready **to be prepared to do something** is to be ready or willing to do it

preposition noun prepositions
a word you put in front of a noun or pronoun to show how the noun or pronoun is connected with another word, for example *on* in the sentence *Put the flowers on the table* and *with* in the sentence *I'd like some sauce with my food*

prep school noun prep schools
a preparatory school

prescribe verb prescribes, prescribing, prescribed
1 to prescribe a medicine for a patient is to instruct them to take it and give them a prescription for it **2** to prescribe a method or solution is to say what must be done

prescription noun prescriptions
a doctor's order for a medicine to be prepared for a patient

a b c d e f g h i j k l m n o p q r s t u v w x y z

395

A
B
C
D
E
F
G
H
I
J
K
L
M
N
O
P
Q
R
S
T
U
V
W
X
Y
Z

presence noun
your presence somewhere is the fact that you are there *Your presence is expected.*

present¹ (say **prez**-ent) adjective
1 in a particular place; here *Nobody else was present.* **2** existing or happening now *Who is the present Queen?*

present (say **prez**-ent) noun
the present is the time now *Our teacher is away at present.*

present² (say **prez**-ent) noun **presents**
something that you give to someone or receive from them

present (say pri-**zent**) verb **presents, presenting, presented**
1 to present something to someone is to give it to them, especially with a ceremony *Who will present the prizes this year?* **2** to present a play or other entertainment is to perform it or arrange for it to be performed **3** to present a radio or television programme is to introduce it to the audience **4** to present something you have done or made is to show it formally to people *We are here to present our latest products.*

presentation noun **presentations**
1 a formal talk showing or demonstrating something **2** a ceremony in which someone is given a gift or prize *I'd like to make a little presentation.*

presenter noun **presenters**
someone who presents something, especially a radio or television programme

presently adverb
soon; in a while

present participle noun **present participles**
a form of a verb used after *am, are* and *is* to describe an action that is happening now, or used after *was, were, has been, have been* and *had been* to describe an action that went on for some time in the past, for example *looking* in the sentences *I am looking at the pictures* and *I was looking at the pictures*

present tense noun
a form of a verb used to describe something that is happening now, for example *likes* in the sentence *He likes swimming*

preservative noun **preservatives**
a substance added to food to preserve it

preserve verb **preserves, preserving, preserved**
to preserve something is to keep it safe or in good condition **preservation** noun

preside (say pri-**zyd**) verb **presides, presiding, presided**
to preside over a meeting or other occasion is to be in charge of it

president noun **presidents**
1 the head of a country that is a republic **2** the person in charge of a society, business, or club **presidency** noun **presidential** adjective

press verb **presses, pressing, pressed**
1 to press something is to push it firmly or squeeze it *Press the red button.* **2** to press clothes is to make them flat and smooth with an iron **3** to press someone for something is to urge them to do or give it *She's pressing me for a decision.*

press noun **presses**
1 the action of squeezing or pushing on something *Give the bell another press.* **2** the press are newspapers and journalists **3** a machine for printing things **4** a business that prints or publishes books **5** a device for flattening and smoothing things *a trouser press*

press–up noun **press–ups**
an exercise in which you lie face downwards and push down with your hands to lift your body

pressure noun **pressures**
1 pressure is continuous pushing or squeezing *Apply pressure to the cut to stop it bleeding.* **2** pressure is also the force with which a liquid or gas pushes against something **3** there is pressure on you when someone is trying to persuade or force you to do something

pressurize verb **pressurizes, pressurizing, pressurized**
1 to pressurize a place or compartment is to keep it at the same air pressure all the time *The cabin of the aeroplane is pressurized.* 2 to pressurize someone is to try to force them to do something

prestige (say pres-**tee**zh) noun
prestige is the respect something has because it is important or of a high quality **prestigious** adjective

presumably adverb
probably; I suppose

presume verb **presumes, presuming, presumed**
to presume something is to suppose it *I presumed that he was dead.*

presumption noun
1 presumption is supposing that something is probably true 2 presumption is also being too bold or confident

presumptuous adjective
too bold or confident

pretence noun **pretences**
a pretence is an attempt to pretend something

pretend verb **pretends, pretending, pretended**
1 to pretend is to behave as if something untrue or imaginary is true 2 to pretend something is to claim it dishonestly *They pretended they were policemen.*

pretender noun **pretenders**
someone who claims the right to be a king or queen of a country

pretty adjective **prettier, prettiest**
pleasant to look at or hear; attractive **prettily** adverb **prettiness** noun

pretty adverb (informal)
quite; moderately *It's pretty cold outside.*

prevail verb **prevails, prevailing, prevailed**
1 to prevail is to be most frequent or general *The prevailing view is that we were*
wrong. 2 to prevail is also to be successful in a battle, contest, or game

prevalent adjective
most frequent or common; widespread

prevent verb **prevents, preventing, prevented**
1 to prevent something is to stop it from happening or make it impossible 2 to prevent someone is to stop them from doing something **prevention** noun **preventive** adjective something that is preventive is meant to help prevent something *preventive medicine*

preview noun **previews**
a showing of a film or play before it is shown to the public

previous adjective
coming before this; preceding *I was in London the previous week.*

previously adverb
to happen previously is to happen before or earlier *He looked back over the work he had done previously.*

prey (say pray) noun
an animal that is hunted or killed by another animal for food

prey (say pray) verb **preys, preying, preyed**
to prey on something is to hunt and kill an animal for food *Owls prey on mice and other small animals.*

price noun **prices**
1 the amount of money for which something is sold 2 what you have to give or do to get something *What is the price of peace?* **at any price** at any cost

price verb **prices, pricing, priced**
to price something is to decide its price **pricey** adjective expensive

priceless adjective
1 very valuable 2 (informal) very amusing

prick verb **pricks, pricking, pricked**
1 to prick something is to make a tiny hole in it 2 to prick someone is to hurt them with something sharp or pointed

a
b
c
d
e
f
g
h
i
j
k
l
m
n
o
p
q
r
s
t
u
v
w
x
y
z

prick noun pricks
a prick is a pricking feeling

prickle noun prickles
a sharp point on a plant or animal
prickly adjective something prickly is
covered in prickles or feels like prickles
prickle verb prickles, prickling,
prickled
to prickle is to make your skin feel as
though lots of little sharp points are
sticking into it *This jumper is prickling me.*

pride noun prides
1 pride is a feeling of being very pleased
with yourself or with someone else who
has done well *My heart swelled with pride.*
2 pride is also being too satisfied because of
who you are or what you have done
3 a pride is something that makes you
feel proud *This stamp is the pride of my
collection.* **4** a pride is also a group
of lions

priest noun priests
1 a member of the clergy **2** someone
who conducts religious ceremonies; a
religious leader

priestess noun priestesses
a female priest in a non-Christian religion

prig noun prigs
someone who is smug and self-righteous
priggish adjective

prim adjective primmer, primmest
liking things to be correct, and easily
shocked by anything rude **primly** adverb
primness noun

primarily adverb
mainly or most importantly

primary adjective
first; most important

primary colour noun primary
colours
one of the colours from which all other
colours can be made by mixing: red, yellow,
and blue for paint, and red, green, and
violet for light

primary school noun primary
schools
a school for the first stage of a child's
education, between the ages of 5 and 11

primate noun primates
1 an animal of the group that includes
human beings, apes, and monkeys
2 an archbishop

prime adjective
1 chief or most important *The weather was
the prime cause of the accident.* **2** of the
best quality

prime noun primes
the best part or stage of something *He was
in the prime of life.*

prime verb primes, priming, primed
1 to prime something is to get it ready for
use *Pour water into the pump to prime it.*
2 to prime a surface is to put a special
liquid on it before painting it

prime minister noun prime
ministers
the leader of a government

prime number noun prime
numbers
a number that can only be divided exactly
by itself and the number one, for example 2,
3, 5, 7, and 11

primeval (say pry-**mee**-val) adjective
belonging to the earliest times of the
world; ancient

primitive adjective
1 at an early stage of development or
civilization *Primitive humans were hunters
rather than farmers.* **2** basic or simple *Our
accommodation was fairly primitive.*

primrose noun primroses
a pale yellow flower that comes out
in spring

prince noun princes
1 the son of a king or queen **2** a man or boy
in a royal family

princess noun princesses
1 the daughter of a king or queen

2 a woman or girl in a royal family 3 the wife of a prince

principal adjective
chief or most important *Name the principal cities of Britain.* **principally** adverb chiefly or mainly

principal noun **principals**
the head of a college or school

principle noun **principles**
1 a general rule or truth *the principles of mathematics* 2 someone's principles are the basic rules and beliefs they have about how they should behave **in principle** in general, not in detail *I agree with your plan in principle.*

print verb **prints, printing, printed**
1 to print words or pictures is to put them on paper with a machine 2 to print letters is to write them separately and not joined together 3 to print a photograph is to make it from a negative

print noun **prints**
1 print is printed words or pictures
2 a print is a mark made by something pressing on a surface *Her thumb left a print on the glass.* 3 a print is also a printed photograph, picture, or design

printer noun **printers**
1 a machine that prints on paper from data in a computer 2 someone who prints books or newspapers

printout noun **printouts**
the information printed on paper from data in a computer

priority (say pry-o-ri-ti) noun **priorities**
1 a priority is something that is more urgent or important than other things and needs to be dealt with first *Repairing the roof is a priority.* 2 priority is the right to go first or be considered before other things *People in need of urgent medical help will have priority.*

prise verb **prises, prising, prised**
to prise something open is to force or lever it open *He prised open the lid with a screwdriver. Woken by Latch's gargling*

tooth-brushing sounds, Titus prised his eyes open. — Debi Gliori, *Pure Dead Wicked*

prism noun **prisms**
1 a piece of glass that breaks up light into the colours of the rainbow
2 (in mathematics) a solid object with parallel ends that are equal triangles or polygons

prison noun **prisons**
a place where criminals are kept as a punishment

prisoner noun **prisoners**
someone who is kept in a prison or who is a captive

privacy noun
privacy is being private or away from other people *Our new garden fence will give us more privacy.*

private adjective
1 belonging to a particular person or group of people *This is a private road.* 2 meant to be kept secret *These letters are private.* 3 away from other people *Is there a private place to swim?* **in private** where only particular people can see or hear; not in public

private noun **privates**
a soldier of the lowest rank

privately adverb
to do something privately is to do it away from other people *Can we speak privately?*

privatize verb **privatizes, privatizing, privatized**
to privatize a public business or organization is to sell it to private owners to run **privatization** noun

privet noun
privet is an evergreen shrub with small leaves, used to make hedges

privilege noun **privileges**
a special right or advantage given to one person or group of people **privileged** adjective

prize noun **prizes**
1 something you get for winning a game

a
b
c
d
e
f
g
h
i
j
k
l
m
n
o
p
q
r
s
t
u
v
w
x
y
z

399

A
B
C
D
E
F
G
H
I
J
K
L
M
N
O

P

Q
R
S
T
U
V
W
X
Y
Z

or competition, or for doing well in an examination **2** something taken from an enemy

prize verb prizes, prizing, prized
to prize something is to value it highly

pro noun pros (informal)
a professional

pro– prefix
meaning 'in favour of' or 'supporting', as in *pro-government*

probability noun probabilities
the probability of something is how likely it is to happen

probable adjective
likely to be true or to happen

probably adverb
you say that something will probably happen or is probably true when you think it is likely to happen or be true

probation noun
probation is a time when someone is tried out in a new job to make sure they are suitable for the work **on probation** if you are on probation, you are being watched to see if you behave properly

probe noun probes
1 a long thin instrument used to look closely at something such as a wound **2** an investigation

probe verb probes, probing, probed
1 to probe something is to look at it with a probe **2** to probe is to investigate

problem noun problems
something difficult to answer or deal with

procedure noun procedures
a fixed or special way of doing something

proceed (say pro-**seed**) verb proceeds, proceeding, proceeded
to proceed is to go on or continue

proceedings plural noun
1 things that happen; activities **2** a dispute that has been brought to a law court

proceeds (say **proh**-seedz) plural noun
the proceeds of a sale or event are the money made from it

process noun processes
a series of actions for making or doing something **to be in the process of doing something** is to be in the middle of doing it

process verb processes, processing, processed
to process something is to treat it or deal with it by a process so that it can be used *Oil can be processed into petrol and diesel.*

procession noun processions
a number of people or vehicles moving steadily forwards

proclaim verb proclaims, proclaiming, proclaimed
to proclaim something is to announce it officially or publicly **proclamation** noun

prod verb prods, prodding, prodded
to prod something or someone is to poke or jab them

prodigal adjective
wasteful or extravagant

produce (say pro-**dewss**) verb produces, producing, produced
1 to produce something is to make or create it **2** to produce something that is hidden or put away is to bring it out so that people can see it **3** to produce a play or film or other entertainment is to organize the performance of it

produce (say **prod**-yewss) noun
produce is things produced, especially by farmers

producer noun producers
someone who produces a play or film

product noun products
1 something someone makes or produces for sale **2** the result of multiplying two numbers *12 is the product of 4 and 3.*

production noun productions
1 production is the process of making or creating something *The factory is engaged in car production.* **2** production is also

the amount someone produces or makes *Oil production increased last year.* **3** a production is a version of a play or film

productive adjective
producing a lot of good or useful things

productivity noun
productivity is the rate at which someone works or produces something

profession noun professions
a type of work for which you need special knowledge and training, for example medicine, law, or teaching

professional adjective
1 doing a certain type of work to earn money *He became a professional tennis player.* **2** to do with a profession **3** you can describe something done with great skill and to a high standard as professional **professionally** adverb

professional noun professionals
someone doing a certain type of work to earn money

professor noun professors
a teacher of the highest rank in a university

proficient (say pro-**fish**-ent) adjective
to be proficient at something is to be able to do it well **proficiency** noun **proficiently** adverb

profile noun profiles
1 a person's profile is a side view of their face **2** a short description of a person's life or character

profit noun profits
1 the extra money got by selling something for more than it cost to buy or make **2** an advantage or benefit

profit verb profits, profiting, profited
to profit from something is to get an advantage from it

profitable adjective
making a profit; bringing in money **profitably** adverb

profound adjective
1 very deep or intense *The film had a profound effect on us all.* **2** showing or

needing great knowledge or thought *The poem she wrote was quite profound.* **profoundly** adverb

profuse (say pro-**fewss**) adjective
produced in large amounts; plentiful *He offered his profuse thanks.* **profusely** adverb

program noun programs
a series of coded instructions for a computer to carry out

program verb programs, programming, programmed
to program a computer is to prepare or control it by means of a program

programme noun programmes
1 a show, play, or talk on radio or television **2** a list of a planned series of events **3** a leaflet or pamphlet that gives details of a play, concert, or other event

progress (say proh-gress) noun
1 progress is forward movement *The march made slow progress.* **2** progress is also development or improvement *You have made a lot of progress this term.*

progress (say pro-gress) verb progresses, progressing, progressed
1 to progress is to move forward **2** to progress is also to develop or improve **progression** noun **progressive** adjective developing steadily

prohibit verb prohibits, prohibiting, prohibited
to prohibit something is to forbid it, especially by law *Smoking is prohibited.* **prohibition** noun

project (say proj-ekt) noun projects
1 a planned task in which you find out as much as you can about something and write about it **2** a plan or scheme

project (say pro-jekt) verb projects, projecting, projected
1 to project is to stick out **2** to project your voice is to speak loudly and clearly so that it carries a long way **3** to project a picture or film is to show it with a projector on a screen

a
b
c
d
e
f
g
h
i
j
k
l
m
n
o
p
q
r
s
t
u
v
w
x
y
z

A
B
C
D
E
F
G
H
I
J
K
L
M
N
O
P
Q
R
S
T
U
V
W
X
Y
Z

projection noun projections
1 projection is showing a picture or film on a screen with a projector 2 a projection is a part of something that sticks out

projector noun projectors
a machine for showing films or photographs on a screen

prologue (say **proh**-log) noun prologues
an introduction to a poem or play or long story

prolong verb prolongs, prolonging, prolonged
to prolong something is to make it last longer

promenade (say prom-en-**ahd**) noun promenades
1 a place suitable for walking, especially beside the seashore 2 a leisurely walk

prominent adjective
1 easily seen; standing out *She has prominent teeth.* 2 important **prominence** noun **prominently** adverb

promise noun promises
1 a promise is a statement that you will definitely do or not do something 2 something shows promise when it shows signs that it will be successful in the future

promise verb promises, promising, promised
to promise to do something is to say that you will definitely do it

promising adjective
likely to be good or successful *We have several promising pupils.*

promontory (say **prom**-on-ter-i) noun promontories
a piece of high land sticking out into the sea *Beyond the promontory was a wide bay with deep beds of rushes on either side of it.* – Arthur Ransome, *Swallows and Amazons*

promote verb promotes, promoting, promoted
1 to be promoted is to be given a more senior or more important job or rank

2 a sports team is promoted when it moves to a higher division or league 3 to promote a product or cause is to make people more aware of it *He has done much to promote the cause of peace.* **promoter** noun

promotion noun promotions
1 promotion is when someone is given a more senior or more important job or rank 2 promotion is also when a sports team moves to a higher division or league 3 a promotion is a piece of publicity or advertising

prompt adjective prompter, promptest
happening soon or without delay *We need a prompt reply.* **promptly** adverb **promptness** noun

prompt verb prompts, prompting, prompted
1 to prompt someone to do something is to cause or encourage them to do it 2 to prompt an actor is to remind them of their words if they forget them during a play

prone adjective
lying face downwards **to be prone to something** is to be likely to do it or suffer from it *He is prone to jealousy.*

prong noun prongs
one of the pointed spikes at the end of a fork

pronoun noun pronouns
a word used instead of a noun, such as *he, her, it, them, those*

pronounce verb pronounces, pronouncing, pronounced
1 to pronounce a word is to say it in a particular way *'Too' and 'two' are pronounced the same.* 2 to pronounce something is to declare it formally *I now pronounce you husband and wife.*

pronounced adjective
noticeable; definite *This street has a pronounced slope.*

pronouncement noun pronouncements
something said formally; a declaration

pronunciation (say pro-nun-si-**ay**-shon) noun **pronunciations**
the way a word is pronounced

proof noun **proofs**
1 proof is a fact which shows that something is true or exists *There is no proof that she stole the money.* **2** a proof is a printed copy of something, made for checking before other copies are printed

proof adjective
giving protection against something *They wore bullet-proof jackets.*

prop[1] noun **props**
a support, especially one made of a long piece of wood or metal

prop verb **props, propping, propped**
to prop something somewhere is to lean it there so that it does not fall over *The ladder was propped up against the wall.*

prop[2] noun **props**
a piece of furniture or other object used on stage in a theatre

propaganda noun
propaganda is information, especially false information, that is spread around to make people believe something

propel verb **propels, propelling, propelled**
to propel something is to move it rapidly forward

propeller noun **propellers**
a device with blades that spin round to drive an aircraft or ship

proper adjective
1 suitable or right *This is the proper way to hold a bat.* **2** respectable *You must behave in a proper fashion.*

proper fraction noun **proper fractions**
a fraction that is less than 1, such as ½ or ⅗

properly adverb
to do something properly is to do it in a way that is correct or suitable

proper noun noun **proper nouns**
the name given to one person or thing, such as *Mary* or *Tokyo*, and written with a capital first letter

property noun **properties**
1 a person's property is a thing, or all the things, that belong to them **2** a property is buildings or land belonging to someone **3** a property is also a quality or characteristic that something has *Rubber has elastic properties.*

prophecy (say **prof**-i-si) noun **prophecies**
1 a prophecy is something that someone has said will happen in the future
2 prophecy is saying what will happen in the future

prophesy (say **prof**-i-sy) verb **prophesies, prophesying, prophesied**
to prophesy something is to say that it will happen in the future

prophet noun **prophets**
1 someone who makes prophecies
2 a religious teacher who is believed to speak the word of God **the Prophet** a name for Muhammad, the founder of the Muslim faith

prophetic adjective
saying or showing what will happen in the future

proportion noun **proportions**
1 a fraction or share of something *Water covers a large proportion of the earth's surface.* **2** the proportion of one thing to another is how much there is of one compared to the other **3** the correct relationship between the size, amount, or importance of two things *You've drawn the head out of proportion with the body.*
proportions size or scale *It is a ship of large proportions.*

proportional or **proportionate** adjective
in proportion; according to a ratio
proportionally or **proportionately** adverb
in proportion

a
b
c
d
e
f
g
h
i
j
k
l
m
n
o
p
q
r
s
t
u
v
w
x
y
z

A
B
C
D
E
F
G
H
I
J
K
L
M
N
O

P

Q
R
S
T
U
V
W
X
Y
Z

proposal noun **proposals**
1 a suggestion 2 when someone asks another person to marry them

propose verb **proposes, proposing, proposed**
1 to propose an idea or plan is to suggest it 2 to propose to someone is to ask them to marry you

proprietor (say pro-**pry**-et-er) noun **proprietors**
the owner of a shop or business

propulsion noun
propulsion is propelling something or driving it forward

prose noun
prose is writing that is like ordinary speech, not poetry or verse

prosecute verb **prosecutes, prosecuting, prosecuted**
to prosecute someone is to make them go to a law court to be tried for a crime
prosecution noun

prospect (say **pros**-pekt) noun **prospects**
1 a possibility or hope; what may happen in the future *There's not much prospect of the weather improving.* 2 a wide view *We saw a vast prospect from the top of the hill.*

prospect (say pro-**spekt**) verb **prospects, prospecting, prospected**
to prospect is to search for gold or some other mineral

prosper verb **prospers, prospering, prospered**
to prosper is to be successful or do well

prosperity noun
prosperity is being successful or rich

prosperous adjective
successful or rich

protect verb **protects, protecting, protected**
to protect someone or something is to keep them safe

protection noun
protection is keeping someone or something safe

protective adjective
1 a person is protective when they want to protect someone or something 2 a thing is protective when it is meant to protect something

protector noun **protectors**
a protector is a person who protects someone or something

protein (say **proh**-teen) noun **proteins**
protein is a substance found in some types of food, for example meat, eggs, and cheese. Your body needs protein to help you grow and be healthy

protest (say **proh**-test) noun **protests**
something you say or do because you disapprove of someone or something

protest (say pro-**test**) verb **protests, protesting, protested**
to protest about something is to say publicly that you think it is wrong
protester noun

Protestant (say **prot**-is-tant) noun **Protestants**
a member of a western Christian Church other than the Roman Catholic Church

prototype (say **proh**-to-typ) noun **prototypes**
the first example of something, used as a model for making others

protractor noun **protractors**
a device in the shape of a semicircle, used for measuring and drawing angles on paper

protrude verb **protrudes, protruding, protruded**
to protrude is to stick out *He had protruding eyes.* **protrusion** noun

proud adjective **prouder, proudest**
1 very pleased with yourself or with someone else who has done well *I am proud of my sister.* 2 too satisfied because of who you are or what you have done *They were too proud to ask for help.* **proudly** adverb

prove verb proves, proving, proved
1 to prove something is to show that it is true **2** to prove to be something is to turn out to be that way *The forecast proved to be correct.*

proverb noun proverbs
a short well-known saying that states a truth or gives advice, for example *many hands make light work*

proverbial adjective
1 occurring in a proverb **2** familiar or well-known, like a proverb

provide verb provides, providing, provided
1 to provide something is to supply it **2** to provide for something is to prepare for it *They have provided for all possible disasters.* **provided** or **providing** on condition; on condition that *The jungle, you should know, / Can be a thrilling place to go. / Provided that you do not sin / Against the beasts that live therein.*
— Dick King-Smith, *Jungle Jingles*

province noun provinces
1 a region or division of a country **2** an area of knowledge or skill **the provinces** the part of a country outside the capital **provincial** adjective in a part of a country away from the capital

provision noun provisions
provision is providing something *the provision of free meals for old people*

provisional adjective
arranged or agreed on for the time being, but not yet definite *They have set a provisional date for the wedding.*

provisions plural noun
supplies of food and drink

provocation noun
provocation is saying or doing something to deliberately make someone angry

provocative adjective
likely to make someone angry *That was a provocative remark.*

provoke verb provokes, provoking, provoked
1 to provoke someone is to deliberately make them angry **2** to provoke a feeling is to arouse or cause it *His statement provoked a great deal of criticism.*

prow noun prows
the front end of a ship

prowl verb prowls, prowling, prowled
to prowl is to move about quietly and secretly, as some animals do when they are hunting

proximity noun
to be in the proximity of something is to be near it

prudent (say **proo**-dent) adjective
wise and careful; not taking risks
prudence noun **prudently** adverb

prune¹ noun prunes
a dried plum

prune² verb prunes, pruning, pruned
to prune a tree or bush is to cut off unwanted parts from it

pry verb pries, prying, pried
to pry is to snoop in someone else's business

PS
short for **postscript**

psalm (say sahm) noun psalms
a religious song, especially one from the Book of Psalms in the Bible

pseudonym (say s'**yoo**-do-nim) noun pseudonyms
a false name that an author uses

psychiatrist (say sy-**ky**-a-trist) noun psychiatrists
a doctor who treats mental illness

psychiatry (say sy-**ky**-a-tree) noun
psychiatry is the treatment of mental illness
psychiatric adjective

psychic (say **sy**-kik) adjective
someone is psychic when they can tell the future or read other people's minds

A
B
C
D
E
F
G
H
I
J
K
L
M
N
O

P

Q
R
S
T
U
V
W
X
Y
Z

psychologist (say sy-**kol**-o-jist) noun psychologists
someone who studies how the mind works

psychology noun
psychology is the study of the mind and the way people behave **psychological** adjective

PTA
short for *Parent-Teacher Association*, an organization that arranges discussions between teachers and parents about school business, and raises money for the school

pub noun pubs (informal)
a building where people can buy and drink alcoholic drinks

puberty (say **pew**-ber-ti) noun
puberty is the time when a young person starts to become an adult and their body starts to change

public adjective
1 belonging to everyone or able to be used by everyone *I often use public transport.*
2 to do with people in general *Newspapers can influence public opinion.* **publicly** adverb in public

public noun
the public is people in general **in public** openly; where anyone can see or take part

publication noun publications
1 a publication is a book or magazine that is printed and sold **2** publication is printing and selling books or magazines

publicity noun
publicity is information or advertising that makes people know about someone or something

publicize (say **pub**-li-syz) verb publicizes, publicizing, publicized
to publicize something is to make people know about it

public school noun public schools
1 (in England and Wales) a secondary school that charges fees **2** (in Scotland and America) a school run by the State or by a local authority

publish verb publishes, publishing, published
1 to publish books or magazines is to print and sell them **2** to publish information is to make it known publicly **publisher** noun

puck noun pucks
a hard rubber disc used in ice hockey

pucker verb puckers, puckering, puckered
to pucker is to form into wrinkles

pudding noun puddings
1 a food made in a soft mass, especially with a mixture of flour and other ingredients **2** the sweet course of a meal

puddle noun puddles
a small pool, especially of rainwater

puff verb puffs, puffing, puffed
1 to puff smoke or steam is to blow it out
2 you puff when you breathe with difficulty *She was puffing when she got to the top of the hill.* **3** to puff something, or to puff it out, is to inflate or swell it *He puffed out his chest.*

puff noun puffs
a small amount of breath, wind, smoke, or steam *He vanished in a puff of smoke.*

puffin noun puffins
a sea bird with a large striped beak

pull verb pulls, pulling, pulled
1 to pull something is to get hold of it and make it come towards you or follow behind you **2** to pull is to move with an effort *She tried to grab the boy but he pulled away.*
to pull a face is to twist your face into a strange expression **to pull in 1** a car pulls in when it stops at the side of the road
2 a train pulls in when it comes into a station and stops **to pull out** is to decide to stop taking part in something *He had to pull out of the race after he twisted his ankle.*
to pull someone's leg is to tease them
to pull something off is to achieve it
to pull through is to recover from an illness
to pull up is to stop *A car pulled up and two men got out.* **to pull yourself together** is to become calm or sensible

pull noun **pulls**
a pull is an action of pulling *Give the handle a good pull.*

pulley noun **pulleys**
a wheel with a groove round it to take a rope, used for lifting heavy things

pullover noun **pullovers**
a knitted piece of clothing for the top half of your body, that you put on over your head

pulp noun **pulps**
a soft wet mass of something, especially for making paper

pulp verb **pulps, pulping, pulped**
to pulp something is to make it into a pulp

pulpit noun **pulpits**
a raised platform in a church, from which the preacher speaks to the congregation

pulse¹ noun **pulses**
1 your pulse is the regular beat as your heart pumps your blood through your arteries. You can feel your pulse in your wrist or neck **2** a regular vibration or movement *The music had a throbbing pulse.*

pulley

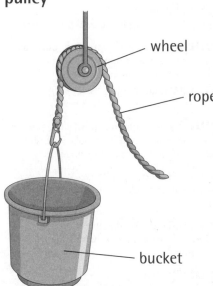

wheel

rope

bucket

pulse² noun **pulses**
pulses are the edible seeds of certain plants, such as peas, beans, and lentils

pulverize verb **pulverizes, pulverizing, pulverized**
to pulverize something is to crush it into a powder

puma noun **pumas**
a large wild cat of North and South America

pumice (say **pum**-iss) noun
pumice is a kind of soft sponge-like stone rubbed on hard surfaces to clean or polish them

pump noun **pumps**
1 a device that forces air or liquid into or out of something, or along pipes
2 a lightweight shoe *She took off her pumps.*

pump verb **pumps, pumping, pumped**
to pump air or liquid is to force it into or out of something with a pump **to pump something up** is to fill something like a balloon or tyre with air or gas

pumpkin noun **pumpkins**
a large round fruit with a hard yellow skin

pun noun **puns**
a joke made by using a word with two different meanings, or two words that sound the same, as in *Choosing where to bury him was a grave decision.*

pun verb **puns, punning, punned**
to pun is to make a pun

punch¹ verb **punches, punching, punched**
1 to punch someone is to hit them with your fist **2** to punch a hole is to make a hole in something *The guard checked and punched our tickets. The builder punched a hole in the wall.*

punch noun **punches**
1 a punch is a blow or hit with the fist **2** a punch is also a device for making holes in paper, metal, or other things

punch² noun **punches**
punch is a hot alcoholic drink

a
b
c
d
e
f
g
h
i
j
k
l
m
n
o
p
q
r
s
t
u
v
w
x
y
z

punchline noun **punchlines**
the last part of a joke or story, that makes it funny

punctual adjective
you are punctual when you arrive exactly on time, not late **punctuality** noun **punctually** adverb

punctuate verb **punctuates, punctuating, punctuated**
to punctuate a piece of writing is to put the commas, full stops, and other punctuation in it

punctuation noun
punctuation is the set of marks such as commas, full stops, and brackets put into a piece of writing to make it easier to understand

puncture noun **punctures**
a small hole made in a tyre by accident

pungent adjective
smelling or tasting very strong or sharp

punish verb **punishes, punishing, punished**
to punish someone is to make them suffer in some way because they have done something wrong

punishment noun **punishments**
a way of punishing someone

punk noun **punks**
punk is a kind of loud, simple rock music

punt noun **punts**
a flat-bottomed boat moved by pushing a pole against the bottom of a river while standing in the punt

punt verb **punts, punting, punted**
to punt is to use a pole to push a boat along

puny (say **pew**-ni) adjective **punier, puniest**
small and weak *'Our tribes, if we just whistle them up, will far outnumber your puny forces; so resistance is useless.'* – Edith Nesbit, *Five Children and It*

pup noun **pups**
a puppy

pupa (say pew-pa) noun **pupae**
an insect at the stage of development between a larva and an adult insect; a chrysalis

pupil noun **pupils**
1 someone who is being taught by a teacher
2 the opening in the centre of your eye

puppet noun **puppets**
a kind of doll that can be made to move by fitting it over your fingers or hand or by pulling strings or wires attached to it

puppy noun **puppies**
a young dog

purchase verb **purchases, purchasing, purchased**
to purchase something is to buy it

purchase noun **purchases**
1 a purchase is something you have bought
2 purchase is the fact of buying something *Keep the receipt as proof of purchase.*
3 a purchase is a firm hold or grip *It was hard to get a purchase on the slippery rocks.*

pure adjective **purer, purest**
1 not mixed with anything else *Use pure olive oil.* 2 clean or clear *They washed in a pure cold mountain stream.*

purely adverb
only, simply *They did it purely for the money.*

purge verb **purges, purging, purged**
to purge people or things is to get rid of them when they are not wanted

purge noun **purges**
an act of purging

purify verb **purifies, purifying, purified**
to purify something is to make it pure **purification** noun **purifier** noun

puritan noun **puritans**
someone who believes in leading a strictly moral life

puritanical adjective
extremely strict in your behaviour and morals

purity noun
purity is the state of being pure

purple noun, adjective
a deep reddish-blue

purpose noun **purposes**
the reason why you do something; what something is for **to do something on purpose** is to do it deliberately

purr verb **purrs, purring, purred**
a cat purrs when it makes a gentle murmuring sound because it is pleased

purse noun **purses**
a small bag for holding money

pursue verb **pursues, pursuing, pursued**
1 to pursue someone or something is to chase them **2** to pursue an activity is to continue to do it or work at it *She pursued her studies at college.*

pursuit noun **pursuits**
1 pursuit is the action of chasing someone **2** a pursuit is something you spend a lot of time doing

pus noun
pus is a thick yellow substance produced in boils and other sore places on your body

push verb **pushes, pushing, pushed**
to push something is to move it away from you by pressing against it **to push off** (informal) is to go away

push noun **pushes**
a pushing movement

pushchair noun **pushchairs**
a small folding chair with wheels, in which a child can be pushed along

puss or **pussy** noun
pusses or **pussies** (informal)
a cat

put verb **puts, putting, put**
1 to put something in a place is to move it there *Put it over there. Where shall I put it?* **2** to put also means to affect someone or something in a particular way *They've put me in a bad mood.* **3** to put an idea in a certain way is to express it in words of a special kind *She put it very tactfully.* **to put someone off** is to make them less keen on

something *Seeing you eat so much has put me off my food.* **to put someone up** is to give them a place to sleep *Can we put them up for the night?* **to put something off** is to decide to do it later instead of now *We'll have to put off the party if you're ill.* **to put something on 1** is to switch on an electrical device, for example a light or a television **2** is to start wearing a piece of clothing *I'll just put on my coat.* **to put something out** is to stop something like a fire or light from burning or shining **to put something up** is to raise it or make it upright *Let's put up the tent.* **to put up with something** is to be willing to accept it without complaining

putt verb **putts, putting, putted**
to putt a golf ball is to tap it gently towards the hole

putt noun **putts**
when a golfer taps the ball gently towards the hole

putter noun **putters**
a golf club used to putt the ball

putty noun
putty is a soft paste that sets hard, used by builders to fit windows in their frames

puzzle noun **puzzles**
1 a tricky game that you have to solve **2** a difficult question; a problem

puzzle verb **puzzles, puzzling, puzzled**
1 to puzzle someone is to give them a problem that is hard to understand **2** to puzzle over something is to think hard about it

pygmy (say **pig**-mi) noun **pygmies**
an unusually small person or animal

pyjamas plural noun
a loose lightweight set of jacket and trousers that you wear in bed

pylon noun **pylons**
a metal tower for supporting electric cables

pyramid noun **pyramids**
1 an object with a square base and four sloping sides coming to a point **2** an ancient Egyptian monument shaped like this. They

a b c d e f g h i j k l m n o p q r s t u v w x y z

A B C D E F G H I J K L M N O P Q R S T U V W X Y Z

were massive and were usually built of huge stone blocks

python noun pythons
a large snake that crushes its prey

Qq

quack noun quacks
the harsh loud sound made by a duck

quack verb quacks, quacking, quacked
a duck quacks when it makes a harsh loud sound

quad noun quads (informal)
1 a quadrangle **2** a quadruplet

quadrangle noun quadrangles
a rectangular courtyard with large buildings round it

quadrant noun quadrants
a quarter of a circle

quadrilateral noun quadrilaterals
a flat shape with four straight sides

quadruple adjective
1 four times as much or as many **2** having four parts

quadruple verb quadruples, quadrupling, quadrupled
1 to quadruple something is to make it four times as much or as many **2** to quadruple is to become four times as much or as many

quadruplet noun quadruplets
each of four children born to the same mother at one time

quail[1] noun quails
a bird that looks like a small partridge

quail[2] verb quails, quailing, quailed
to feel or show fear

quaint adjective quainter, quaintest
attractive in an unusual or old-fashioned way

quake verb quakes, quaking, quaked
to tremble or shake

Quaker noun Quakers
a member of a religious group called the Society of Friends, founded by George Fox in the 17th century

qualification noun qualifications
1 a skill or ability to do a job **2** an examination you have passed or a course you have completed that shows you have a skill or ability

qualify verb qualifies, qualifying, qualified
1 to qualify for something such as a job is to be suitable for it or show you have gained the abilities you need to do it *She qualified as a doctor last year.* **2** to qualify for a competition is to reach a high enough standard to take part in it

quality noun qualities
1 the quality of something is how good or bad it is **2** what something is like *The paper had a shiny quality.*

quantity noun quantities
how much there is of something, or how many things there are of one sort

quarantine (say **kwo**-ran-teen) noun
quarantine is a period when a person or animal is kept apart from others to prevent a disease from spreading

quarrel noun quarrels
a strong or angry argument

quarrel verb quarrels, quarrelling, quarrelled
to quarrel with someone is to argue fiercely with them

quarrelsome adjective
fond of quarrelling or often quarrelling

quarry noun quarries
1 a place where stone or slate is dug out of the ground **2** an animal that is being hunted

quart (say kwort) noun quarts
a measure of liquid, a quarter of a gallon or about 1.136 litres

quarter noun **quarters**
1 each of four equal parts into which something is divided or can be divided **2** three months, one-fourth of a year **at close quarters** close together *They fought at close quarters.*

quarters plural noun
where someone lives for a time; lodgings

quartet (say kwor-**tet**) noun **quartets**
1 a group of four musicians **2** a piece of music for four musicians

quartz (say kworts) noun
quartz is a hard mineral, used in making accurate electronic watches and clocks

quaver verb **quavers, quavering, quavered**
to quaver is to tremble

quaver noun **quavers**
1 a trembling sound **2** a musical note equal to half a crotchet, written ♪

quay (say kee) noun **quays**
a harbour wall or pier where ships can be tied up for loading and unloading

queasy adjective **queasier, queasiest**
you feel queasy when you feel slightly sick

queen noun **queens**
1 a woman who has been crowned as the ruler of a country **2** a king's wife **3** a female bee or ant that produces eggs **4** a piece in chess, the most powerful on the board **5** a playing card with a picture of a queen

queen mother noun
a king's widow who is the mother of the present king or queen

queer adjective **queerer, queerest**
1 strange or odd **2** ill or unwell *I feel a bit queer.*

quench verb **quenches, quenching, quenched**
1 to quench your thirst is to drink until you are not thirsty any more **2** to quench a fire is to put it out

query (say **kweer**-i) noun **queries**
1 a question **2** a question mark

query verb **queries, querying, queried**
to query something is to question whether it is true or correct

quest noun **quests**
a long search, especially for something precious or valuable

question noun **questions**
1 something you ask *I will try to answer your question.* **2** a problem or subject for discussion *The question is, where can we go on holiday?* **to be out of the question** is to be impossible or not even worth considering

question verb **questions, questioning, questioned**
1 to question someone is to ask them questions **2** to question something is to be doubtful about it

questionable adjective
causing doubt; not certainly true or correct

question mark noun **question marks**
the punctuation mark (?) put at the end of a question

questionnaire (say kwes-chon-**air**) noun **questionnaires**
a set of questions asked to get information for a survey

queue (say kew) noun **queues**
a line of people or vehicles waiting for something

queue (say kew) verb **queues, queueing, queued**
people queue, or queue up, when they wait in a queue

TOP TIPS
Queue can be tricky to spell—the letter **u** appears twice!

quibble verb **quibbles, quibbling, quibbled**
to quibble is to argue or complain about minor details

quibble noun **quibbles**
a quibble is a trivial complaint or objection

quiche (say keesh) noun **quiches**
an open tart with a savoury filling

a
b
c
d
e
f
g
h
i
j
k
l
m
n
o
p
q
r
s
t
u
v
w
x
y
z

A
B
C
D
E
F
G
H
I
J
K
L
M
N
O
P
Q
R
S
T
U
V
W
X
Y
Z

quick adjective quicker, quickest
1 taking only a short time *You were quick.*
2 done in a short time *She gave a quick answer.* 3 able to learn or think quickly
quickly adverb

quicken verb quickens, quickening, quickened
1 to quicken something is to make it quicker *She quickened her pace.* 2 to quicken is to become quicker

quicksand noun quicksands
quicksand is an area of loose wet sand that sucks in anything that falls into it

quid noun quid (informal)
a pound (£1)

quiet adjective quieter, quietest
1 silent 2 not loud *He spoke in a quiet voice.* 3 calm and peaceful *They lead a quiet life.*
quietly adverb
quiet noun
quiet is a time when it is calm and peaceful *Let's have a bit of quiet now.*

quieten verb quietens, quietening, quietened
1 to quieten something or someone is to make them quiet 2 to quieten is to become quiet

quill noun quills
1 a bird's quills are its large feathers 2 a pen made from a large feather 3 a porcupine's quills are its long spines

quilt noun quilts
a thick soft cover for a bed

quintet noun quintets
1 a group of five musicians 2 a piece of music for five musicians

quit verb quits, quitting, quitted or quit
1 to quit something is to leave or abandon it 2 (informal) to quit doing something is to stop it *Quit teasing him!*

quite adverb
1 rather or fairly *He's quite a good swimmer.*
2 completely or entirely *I am quite all right.*

quiver[1] verb quivers, quivering, quivered
to tremble *He was quivering with excitement.*

quiver[2] noun quivers
a container for arrows

quiz noun quizzes
a series of questions, especially as an entertainment or competition
quiz verb quizzes, quizzing, quizzed
to quiz someone is to ask them a lot of questions

quota (say kwoh-ta) noun quotas
a fixed share or amount *Each school has its quota of equipment.*

quotation noun quotations
1 quotation is the action of repeating words that were first written or spoken by someone else 2 a quotation is a set of words taken from a book or speech

quotation marks plural noun
inverted commas, used to mark a quotation

quote verb quotes, quoting, quoted
1 to quote words is to use them in a quotation 2 to quote someone is to quote words first used by them

Rr

rabbi (say rab-I) noun rabbis
a Jewish religious leader

rabbit noun rabbits
a furry animal with long ears that digs burrows

rabid (say rab-id) adjective
1 a rabid animal is affected with rabies
2 you can say someone is rabid when they are fiercely enthusiastic about something

rabies (say ray-beez) noun
rabies is a fatal disease involving madness

that affects dogs and cats and can be passed to humans

raccoon noun **raccoons**
a small North American meat-eating animal with grey-brown fur and a bushy, striped tail

race¹ noun **races**
a competition to be the first to reach a particular place or to do something

race verb **races, racing, raced**
1 to race someone is to have a race against them 2 to race is to move very fast *The train raced along the track.* **racer** noun

race² noun **races**
a large group of people who have the same ancestors, and share certain physical features such as the colour of their skin and hair

racecourse noun **racecourses**
a place where horse races are run

racial adjective
to do with a person's race or with different races

racism (say **ray**-sizm) noun
racism is believing that one race of people is better than all the others and treating people unfairly because they belong to a different race

racist noun **racists**
someone who treats other people unfairly because they belong to a different race

racist adjective
a racist attitude or remark is one that shows racism

rack noun **racks**
1 a framework used as a shelf or container *a plate rack* 2 an ancient device for torturing people by stretching them

rack verb **racks, racking, racked**
to rack your brains is to think hard to remember something or solve a problem

racket¹ noun **rackets**
a bat with strings stretched across a frame, used in tennis and similar games

racket² noun **rackets**
1 to make a racket is to make a loud noise
2 (informal) a dishonest business; a swindle

radar (say **ray**-dar) noun
radar is a system that uses radio waves to show the position of ships or aircraft which cannot be seen because of distance or poor visibility

radiant adjective
1 radiating light or heat 2 you can say someone is radiant when they look happy and beautiful **radiance** noun **radiantly** adverb

radiate verb **radiates, radiating, radiated**
1 to radiate heat, light, or other energy is to send it out in rays 2 to radiate is to spread out like the spokes of a wheel *The city's streets radiate from the central square.*

radiation noun
1 radiation is heat, light, or other energy given out by something 2 radiation is also energy or particles sent out by something radioactive

radiator noun **radiators**
1 a device that gives out heat, especially a metal container through which steam or hot water flows 2 a device that cools the engine of a motor vehicle

radical adjective
1 thorough and complete; going right to the roots of something *The new head teacher made radical changes.* 2 wanting to make changes or reforms *He is a radical politician.* **radically** adverb

radical noun **radicals**
someone who is radical

radii noun
plural of **radius**

radio noun **radios**
1 radio is sending or receiving sound by means of electrical waves 2 a radio is an apparatus for receiving broadcast sound programmes, or for receiving and sending messages

a
b
c
d
e
f
g
h
i
j
k
l
m
n
o
p
q
r
s
t
u
v
w
x
y
z

radioactive adjective
radioactive substances have atoms that break up and send out radiation which produces electrical and chemical effects **radioactivity** noun

radish noun **radishes**
a small hard red vegetable with a hot taste, eaten raw in salads

radius noun **radii**
1 a straight line from the centre of a circle to the circumference 2 the length of this line

raffle noun **raffles**
a way of raising money by selling numbered tickets, some of which win prizes

raffle verb **raffles, raffling, raffled**
to raffle something is to give it as a prize in a raffle

raft noun **rafts**
a floating platform of logs or barrels tied together

rafter noun **rafters**
each of the long sloping pieces of wood that hold up a roof

rag noun **rags**
1 an old or torn piece of cloth 2 to be dressed in rags is to be wearing very old, torn clothes

rage noun **rages**
great or violent anger **to be all the rage** (informal) is to be very fashionable or popular

rage verb **rages, raging, raged**
1 to rage is to be very angry 2 to rage is also to be violent or noisy *The storm was raging outside. Rain lashed against the windows, the wind howled through the telegraph wires.* – Catherine MacPhail, *Granny Nothing*

ragged (say **rag**-id) adjective
1 torn or frayed 2 wearing torn or old clothes *a ragged beggar* 3 not smooth *They gave a ragged performance.*

raid noun **raids**
1 a sudden attack 2 an unexpected visit from police to search a place or arrest people

raid verb **raids, raiding, raided**
to raid a place is to make a raid on it
raider noun

rail noun **rails**
1 a bar or rod that you can hang things on or that form part of a fence or banisters 2 a long metal strip that is part of a railway track **by rail** on a train

railings plural noun
a fence made of metal bars

railway noun **railways**
1 the parallel metal strips that trains travel on 2 a system of transport using rails

rain noun
rain is drops of water that fall from the sky

rain verb **rains, raining, rained**
1 to rain is to come down like rain *After the explosion fragments of glass rained on them from above.* 2 to rain something is to send it down like rain *They rained blows on him.* **it is raining** when rain is falling

rainbow noun **rainbows**
a curved band of colours that you can sometimes see in the sky when the sun shines through rain

raincoat noun **raincoats**
a waterproof coat

raindrop noun **raindrops**
a single drop of rain

rainfall noun
rainfall is the amount of rain that falls in a particular place or time

rainforest noun **rainforests**
a dense tropical forest in an area of very heavy rainfall

raise verb **raises, raising, raised**
1 to raise something is to move it to a higher place or to an upright position 2 to raise an amount or number is to increase it *They raised our pay by 20%.* 3 to raise money is to succeed in collecting it *They raised £1,000 for the appeal.* 4 to raise your voice is to speak loudly 5 to raise a subject or idea is

to mention it for people to think about
6 to raise young children is to bring them up and educate them **7** to raise animals is to breed them **8** to raise a laugh or smile is to make people laugh or smile

raisin noun **raisins**
a dried grape

rake noun **rakes**
a gardening tool with a row of short spikes fixed to a long handle

rake verb **rakes, raking, raked**
1 to rake something is to move it or smooth it with a rake **2** to rake, or rake around, is to search *I raked around in my desk for the letter.*

rally noun **rallies**
1 a large public meeting **2** a competition to test skill in driving **3** a series of strokes and return strokes of the ball in tennis or squash

rally verb **rallies, rallying, rallied**
1 to rally people is to bring them together for a united effort **2** to rally, or rally round, is to come together to support someone **3** to rally is to revive or recover after an illness or setback *The team rallied when they realized they could win.*

RAM
short for *random-access memory*, a type of computer memory with parts that can be located directly

ram noun **rams**
a male sheep

ram verb **rams, ramming, rammed**
to ram something is to push one thing hard against another

Ramadan (say ram-a-**dan**) noun
Ramadan is the ninth month of the Muslim year, when Muslims do not eat or drink during the day.

ramble noun **rambles**
a long walk in the country

ramble verb **rambles, rambling, rambled**
1 to ramble is to go for a long walk in the country **2** to ramble is also to say a lot without keeping to a subject **rambler** noun

ramp noun **ramps**
a slope joining two different levels

rampage (say ram-**payj**) verb
rampages, rampaging, rampaged
to rampage is to rush about wildly or violently

rampage noun
to go on the rampage is to rush about violently

ran
past tense of **run** verb *I panicked and ran off.*

ranch noun **ranches**
a large cattle-farm in America

random noun
at random by chance; without any purpose or plan

random adjective
done or taken at random *They took a random sample.*

rang
past tense of **ring**² verb *My mobile rang again.*

range noun **ranges**
1 a collection of different things of the same type *The shop sells a wide range of games and puzzles.* **2** the limits of something, from the highest to the lowest *Most of the children here are in the 8-11 age range.* **3** a line of hills or mountains **4** the distance that a gun can shoot, or an aircraft can fly, or a sound can be heard **5** a place with targets for shooting practice **6** a kitchen fireplace with ovens

range verb **ranges, ranging, ranged**
1 to range between two limits is to extend from one to the other *Prices ranged from £1 to £50.* **2** to range people or things is to arrange them in a line *Crowds were ranged along the streets, hoping to see the Queen go by.* **3** to range is to wander or move over a wide area *Hens ranged all over the farm.*

Ranger noun **Rangers**
a senior member of the Guides

a
b
c
d
e
f
g
h
i
j
k
l
m
n
o
p
q
r
s
t
u
v
w
x
y
z

A
B
C
D
E
F
G
H
I
J
K
L
M
N
O
P
Q
R
S
T
U
V
W
X
Y
Z

ranger noun **rangers**
1 someone who looks after a park or forest
2 a mounted police officer in a remote area

rank noun **ranks**
1 a position in a series of people or things
He was promoted to the rank of captain.
2 a line of people or things
rank verb **ranks, ranking, ranked**
to rank is to have a certain rank or place
She ranks among the greatest writers.

ransack verb **ransacks, ransacking, ransacked**
to ransack a place is to search it thoroughly, looking for something to steal, and leave it in a mess

ransom noun **ransoms**
money paid so that someone who has been kidnapped can be set free **to hold someone to ransom** is to keep them prisoner and demand a ransom
ransom verb **ransoms, ransoming, ransomed**
to ransom someone who has been kidnapped is to free them by paying a ransom

rap verb **raps, rapping, rapped**
to rap is to knock quickly and loudly
rap noun **raps**
1 a rap is a rapping movement or sound
2 rap is a kind of pop music in which you speak words rapidly in rhythm

rapid adjective
moving or working at speed **rapidity** noun
rapidly adverb

rapids plural noun
part of a river where the water flows very fast

rare adjective **rarer, rarest**
unusual; not often found or experienced
She died of a rare disease.

rarely adverb
something happens rarely when it doesn't happen very often

rarity noun **rarities**
a rarity is a person or thing that is unusual

rascal noun **rascals**
a dishonest or mischievous person

rash[1] adjective **rasher, rashest**
you are rash when you do something quickly without thinking properly about it
By the time Hallowe'en arrived, Harry was regretting his rash promise to go to the Deathday Party. — J. K. Rowling, *Harry Potter and the Chamber of Secrets*

rash[2] noun **rashes**
1 an outbreak of red spots or patches on the skin **2** a number of unwelcome things happening about the same time *A late winter storm caused a rash of accidents in the city.*

rasher noun **rashers**
a slice of bacon

raspberry noun **raspberries**
a small soft red fruit

Rastafarian (say ras-ta-**fair**-i-an)
noun **Rastafarians**
a member of a religious group that started in Jamaica

rat noun **rats**
1 an animal like a large mouse **2** you can describe a nasty or treacherous person as a rat

rate noun **rates**
1 how fast or how often something happens
The train moved at a great rate. **2** a charge or payment *What is the rate for a letter to Italy?*
at any rate anyway *I don't want to go, not yet at any rate.*
rate verb **rates, rating, rated**
to rate something or someone is to regard them in a certain way or as having a certain value *Drivers rate the new car very highly. He rated me among his best friends.*

rather adverb
1 slightly; somewhat *It was rather dark.*
2 you would rather do one thing than another thing if you would prefer to do it *I think I'd rather do this later.* **3** more truly or correctly *He lay down, or rather fell, on the bed.* **4** (informal) as an answer: definitely, yes *'Will you come?' 'Rather!'*

ratio (say **ray**-shi-oh) noun **ratios**
the relationship between two numbers; how many times one number goes into another *In a group of 2 girls and 10 boys, the ratio of girls to boys is 1 to 5.*

ration (say **rash**-on) noun **rations**
the amount of something one person is allowed to have

ration (say **rash**-on) verb **rations, rationing, rationed**
to ration something is to give it out in fixed amounts because there is not a lot of it to share

rational (say **rash**-o-nal) adjective
reasonable or sensible *No rational person would do such a thing.* **rationally** adverb

rattle verb **rattles, rattling, rattled**
1 to rattle is to make a series of short sharp hard sounds 2 to rattle something is to make it rattle 3 (informal) to rattle someone is to make them nervous and confused

rattle noun **rattles**
1 a rattling sound 2 a baby's toy that rattles

rattlesnake noun **rattlesnakes**
a poisonous American snake that makes rattling sounds with its tail

rave verb **raves, raving, raved**
1 to be raving is to be talking wildly 2 to rave about something is to talk very enthusiastically about it

raven noun **ravens**
a large black bird

ravenous (say **rav**-e-nus) adjective
very hungry **ravenously** adverb in a ravenous way *The starving dog ate and drank ravenously, then at once settled to sleep.* – Dodie Smith, *The Hundred and One Dalmatians*

ravine (say ra-**veen**) noun **ravines**
a very deep narrow gorge

ravioli noun
ravioli is small squares of pasta filled with meat and served with a sauce

raw adjective **rawer, rawest**
1 raw food is not cooked 2 raw (for example) cotton or sugar is in its natural state before being processed *What raw materials do you need?* 3 you can say someone is raw when they don't have any experience *They are just raw beginners.* 4 with the skin removed *He had a raw wound on his leg.* 5 cold and damp *There was a raw wind.*

ray[1] noun **rays**
a thin line of light, heat, or other energy

ray[2] noun **rays**
a large sea fish with a flat body and a long tail

razor noun **razors**
a device with a very sharp blade, used for shaving

reach verb **reaches, reaching, reached**
1 to reach a place is to go as far as it and arrive there 2 to reach, or reach out, is to stretch out your hand to get or touch something

reach noun **reaches**
1 the distance you can reach with your hand 2 a distance that you can easily travel *My uncle lives within reach of the sea.*

react verb **reacts, reacting, reacted**
to react is to act in response to another person or thing

reaction noun **reactions**
an action or feeling caused by another person or thing

reactor noun **reactors**
an apparatus for producing nuclear power

read verb **reads, reading, read**
1 to read something written or printed is to look at it and understand it or say it aloud 2 a gauge or instrument reads a certain amount when that is what it shows *The thermometer reads 20°.*

readable adjective
1 a readable book is enjoyable to read 2 readable writing is clear and easy to read

a
b
c
d
e
f
g
h
i
j
k
l
m
n
o
p
q
r
s
t
u
v
w
x
y
z

A
B
C
D
E
F
G
H
I
J
K
L
M
N
O
P
Q

R

S
T
U
V
W
X
Y
Z

reader noun **readers**
1 someone who reads 2 a book that helps you learn to read

readily adverb
1 willingly or eagerly *She readily agreed to help.* 2 quickly and without any difficulty *All the ingredients you need are readily available.*

readiness noun
readiness is being ready for something

reading noun **readings**
1 reading is the action of reading a book, magazine, or newspaper 2 a reading is an amount shown on a gauge or instrument

ready adjective **readier, readiest**
1 able or willing to do something or to be used at once; prepared 2 quick *He always has ready answers.* **at the ready** ready for action or ready to be used

ready–made adjective
made already, and not made specially

real adjective
1 true or existing; not imaginary 2 genuine; not a copy *Are those pearls real?*

realism noun
realism is seeing or showing things as they really are

realist noun **realists**
someone who tries to see things as they really are

realistic adjective
1 true to life *It is a very realistic painting.* 2 seeing things as they really are *She is realistic about her chances of winning.* **realistically** adverb you say realistically when you are talking about what you think can actually be achieved *Realistically, I don't think we have much hope of winning.*

reality noun **realities**
1 reality is what is real 2 a reality is something that is real *Cold and hunger are the realities of being homeless.*

realize verb **realizes, realizing, realized**
to realize something is to understand it or accept that it is true **realization** noun

really adverb
truly; certainly; in fact

realm (say relm) noun **realms**
1 a kingdom 2 an area of knowledge or activity

reap verb **reaps, reaping, reaped**
1 to reap corn is to cut it down and gather it in when it is ripe 2 to reap a benefit is to gain it

reappear verb **reappears, reappearing, reappeared**
to reappear is to appear again **reappearance** noun

rear[1] adjective
placed or found at the back *She had a car with a rear engine.*
rear noun **rears**
the back part of something

rear[2] verb **rears, rearing, reared**
1 to rear young children or animals is to bring them up or help them grow 2 a horse or other animal rears, or rears up, when it rises up on its hind legs so that its front legs are in the air

rearrange verb **rearranges, rearranging, rearranged**
to rearrange something is to arrange it differently **rearrangement** noun

reason noun **reasons**
1 the reason for something is why it happens 2 reason is thinking in a clear and logical way *He wouldn't listen to reason.*
reason verb **reasons, reasoning, reasoned**
1 to reason is to think in a logical way 2 to reason with someone is to try to persuade them of something

reasonable adjective
1 sensible or logical 2 fair or moderate *These are reasonable prices for what you get.*

reasonably adverb
1 in a reasonable way; sensibly *They were behaving quite reasonably.* 2 fairly; somewhat *It had taken Mildred several weeks of falling off and crashing before she could*

ride the broomstick reasonably well. — Jill Murphy, *The Worst Witch*

reassure verb reassures, reassuring, reassured
to reassure someone is to take away their doubts or fears **reassurance** noun

rebel (say ri-**bel**) verb rebels, rebelling, rebelled
to rebel is to refuse to obey someone in authority, especially the government

rebel (say **reb**-el) noun rebels
someone who refuses to obey or fights against someone in authority

rebellion noun rebellions
1 rebellion is when people refuse to obey or fight against someone in authority 2 a rebellion is a fight against someone in authority, especially the government

rebellious adjective
someone is rebellious when they refuse to obey authority or are likely to rebel

rebuild verb rebuilds, rebuilding, rebuilt
to rebuild something is to build it again after it has been destroyed

recall verb recalls, recalling, recalled
1 to recall someone or something is to remember them 2 to recall someone is to tell them to come back

recap verb recaps, recapping, recapped (informal)
to recap is to summarize what has been said

recapture verb recaptures, recapturing, recaptured
to recapture something or someone is to capture them again, especially after they have escaped

recede verb recedes, receding, receded
1 to recede is to go back *The floods have receded.* 2 a man's hair is receding when he starts to go bald at the front

receipt (say ri-**seet**) noun receipts
1 a receipt is a written statement saying that a payment has been received or

goods have been delivered 2 receipt is receiving something

receive verb receives, receiving, received
1 to receive something is to get it when it is given or sent to you 2 to receive visitors is to greet them formally *The President was received at Buckingham Palace.*

TOP TIPS
In **receive**, **e** before **i** is the right way round.

receiver noun receivers
1 someone who receives something 2 someone who buys and sells stolen goods 3 an official who takes charge of a bankrupt person's property 4 a radio or television set 5 the part of a telephone that you hold to your ear

recent adjective
made or happening a short time ago

recently adverb
something happened recently when it happened only a short time ago

receptacle noun receptacles
something for holding what is put into it; a container

reception noun receptions
1 the sort of welcome that someone gets *We were given a friendly reception.* 2 a formal party to receive guests *a wedding reception* 3 a place in a hotel or office where visitors report or check in 4 the quality of the signals your radio or television set receives *We don't get good reception here.*

receptionist noun receptionists
someone whose job is to receive and welcome visitors to a hotel or office

recess noun recesses
1 an alcove 2 a time when work or business is stopped for a while

recession noun recessions
a reduction in trade or in the wealth of a country

a
b
c
d
e
f
g
h
i
j
k
l
m
n
o
p
q
r
s
t
u
v
w
x
y
z

A
B
C
D
E
F
G
H
I
J
K
L
M
N
O
P
Q

R

S
T
U
V
W
X
Y
Z

recipe (say **ress**-i-pi) noun **recipes**
a list of ingredients and instructions for
preparing or cooking food

recital (say ri-**sy**-tal) noun **recitals**
a performance of music or poetry by a small
number of people

recite verb **recites, reciting, recited**
to recite something such as a poem is to say
it aloud

reckless adjective
someone is reckless when they do
things without thinking or caring about
what might happen **recklessly** adverb
recklessness noun

reckon verb **reckons, reckoning,
reckoned**
1 to reckon something is to calculate or
count it 2 to reckon something is to think
it or have an opinion about it *I reckon it's
about to rain.*

reclaim verb **reclaims, reclaiming,
reclaimed**
1 to reclaim land is to make it suitable for
farming or building on again by clearing or
draining it 2 to reclaim something is to get
it back, especially after losing it *I reclaimed
my umbrella from the lost property office.*

recline verb **reclines, reclining,
reclined**
to lean or lie back

recognition noun
recognizing someone or something *When he
saw me, a smile of recognition appeared on
his face.*

recognize verb **recognizes,
recognizing, recognized**
1 to recognize someone or something
is to know who they are because you
have seen them before 2 to recognize
a fault or mistake is to admit to it *We
recognize that we may have acted unfairly.*
recognizable adjective

recoil verb **recoils, recoiling, recoiled**
to recoil is to move backwards suddenly *He
recoiled in horror.*

recollect verb **recollects,
recollecting, recollected**
to recollect something is to remember it

recollection noun **recollections**
1 recollection is being able to remember
something *I have no recollection of seeing
her before.* 2 a recollection is something
you remember

recommend verb **recommends,
recommending, recommended**
1 to recommend something is to suggest it
because you think it is good or suitable
I recommend the strawberry ice cream.
2 to recommend an action is to advise
someone to do it *We recommend that
you wear strong shoes on the walk.*
recommendation noun

reconcile verb **reconciles,
reconciling, reconciled**
1 to be reconciled with someone is to
become friendly with them again after
quarrelling or fighting with them 2 you
are reconciled to something when you
are persuaded to put up with it *He soon
became reconciled to wearing glasses.*
reconciliation noun

reconstruction noun
reconstructions
1 reconstruction is building something up
again 2 a reconstruction is acting out an
event that took place in the past *They did a
reconstruction of the bank robbery.*

record (say **rek**-ord) noun **records**
1 a disc with recorded sound on it
2 the best performance in a sport or the
most remarkable event of its kind *She broke
the record for swimming 100 metres.* 3 a set
of facts or information about something
that you write down and keep *Keep a
record of all the birds you see in the garden.*
recordings noun

record (say ri-**kord**) verb **records,
recording, recorded**
1 to record music or sound or a television
programme is to store it on a tape or disc
2 to record things that have happened is to
put them down in writing

recorder noun **recorders**
1 a video recorder, DVD recorder, or other machine for recording sounds and pictures 2 a wooden musical instrument that you play by blowing into one end and covering holes with your fingers 3 someone who records something

record player noun **record players**
a machine that plays records

recount verb **recount, recounting, recounted**
to tell someone about something true that has happened *We recounted our adventures.*

recover verb **recovers, recovering, recovered**
1 to recover is to get better after being ill 2 to recover something is to get it back after losing it

recovery noun
1 you make a recovery when you get better after being ill 2 the recovery of something is getting it back after it was lost

recreation noun **recreations**
a game, hobby, or other enjoyable pastime you do in your spare time **recreational** adjective

recruit noun **recruits**
someone who has just joined the armed forces or a business or club

recruit verb **recruits, recruiting, recruited**
to recruit someone is to get them to join something you belong to

rectangle noun **rectangles**
a shape with four straight sides and four right angles **rectangular** adjective

recuperate verb **recuperates, recuperating, recuperated**
to recuperate is to get better after you have been ill

recur verb **recurs, recurring, recurred**
something recurs when it happens again **recurrence** noun

recycle verb **recycles, recycling, recycled**
to recycle waste material is to treat it so that it can be used again *Waste paper can be recycled to make cardboard.*

red adjective **redder, reddest**
1 of the colour of blood 2 red hair is orange-brown in colour

red noun **reds**
a red colour **to see red** is to become suddenly angry

redden verb **reddens, reddening, reddened**
to redden is to become red *He reddened with embarrassment.*

reddish adjective
fairly red

redeem verb **redeems, redeeming, redeemed**
1 to redeem something is to get it back by paying for it or handing over a voucher 2 to redeem yourself is to do something good to make up for an earlier mistake 3 to redeem someone is to save them from evil, as in some religions

redemption noun
redemption is redeeming or saving someone

red-handed adjective
to catch someone red-handed is to catch them while they are actually committing a crime or doing something wrong

redhead noun **redheads**
a person with reddish-brown hair

red herring noun **red herrings**
something that takes attention away from the real point or answer; a false clue

reduce verb **reduces, reducing, reduced**
1 to reduce something is to make it smaller or less 2 to be reduced to something is to be forced to do it *He was reduced to asking for more money.*

reduction noun **reductions**
1 there is a reduction in something when it becomes smaller or less 2 the amount by

a
b
c
d
e
f
g
h
i
j
k
l
m
n
o
p
q
r
s
t
u
v
w
x
y
z

A

which something is reduced *They gave us a reduction of £5.*

B

redundant adjective
1 to be redundant is to be no longer needed
2 someone is made redundant when they lose their job because it is no longer needed
redundancy noun

C

D

E

reed noun **reeds**
1 a plant that grows in or near water 2 a thin strip that vibrates to make the sound in some wind instruments, such as a clarinet, saxophone, or oboe

F

G

H

reef noun **reefs**
a line of rocks or sand near the surface of the sea

I

J

reef knot noun **reef knots**
a symmetrical double knot for tying two cords together

K

reek verb **reeks, reeking, reeked**
to reek is to have a strong unpleasant smell

L

M

reel noun **reels**
1 a round device on which cotton or thread is wound 2 a lively Scottish dance
reel verb **reels, reeling, reeled**
to stagger *He reeled back in shock.* **to reel something off** is to say a lot very quickly

N

O

P

Q

refer verb **refers, referring, referred**
1 to refer to someone or something is to mention them or speak about them 2 to refer to (for example) a dictionary is to look at it so that you can find something out
3 to refer a question or problem to someone else is to give it to them to deal with

R

S

T

referee noun **referees**
someone who makes sure that people keep to the rules of a game
referee verb **referees, refereeing, refereed**
to referee a game is to act as referee in it

U

V

W

reference noun **references**
1 a mention of something 2 a place in a book or file where information can be found 3 a description of the work someone has done and how well they have done it, used especially when someone is applying for a

X

Y

Z

job **in** or **with reference to something** or **someone** concerning them or about them

referendum (say ref-er-**en**-dum)
noun **referendums**
a vote on a particular question by all the people in a country

refill verb **refills, refilling, refilled**
to refill something is to fill it again
refill noun **refills**
a container used to replace something that has been used up *My pen needs a refill.*

refine verb **refines, refining, refined**
to refine something is to purify or improve it

refined adjective
1 refined (for example) sugar or oil has been made pure by taking other substances out of it 2 someone is refined when they have good manners and are well educated

refinement noun **refinements**
1 refinement is the process of refining something 2 a refinement is something special that improves a thing

refinery noun **refineries**
a factory for refining a product, such as oil

reflect verb **reflects, reflecting, reflected**
1 something reflects light or heat or sound when it sends it back from a surface
2 a mirror or other shiny surface reflects something when it forms an image of it
3 you reflect on something when you think seriously about it

reflection noun **reflections**
the image you can see in a mirror or other shiny surface

reflective adjective
1 sending back light *The traffic policeman wore a reflective waistcoat.* 2 suggesting or showing serious thought *The music has a reflective quality.*

reflex (say **ree**-fleks) noun **reflexes**
a movement or action that you do without any conscious thought

reflex angle noun reflex angles
an angle of between 180 and 360
degrees

reform verb reforms, reforming,
reformed
1 to reform a person or thing is to
improve them by getting rid of their faults
2 someone reforms when they improve
their behaviour

reform noun reforms
1 reform is changing something to improve
it 2 a reform is a change made for this
reason **reformation** noun

reformer noun reformers
someone who makes reforms

refrain¹ verb refrains, refraining,
refrained
to refrain from something is to keep
yourself from doing it *Please refrain
from talking.*

refrain² noun refrains
the chorus of a song

refresh verb refreshes, refreshing,
refreshed
to refresh someone who is tired is to make
them feel fresh and strong again

refreshments plural noun
food and drink

refrigerate verb refrigerates,
refrigerating, refrigerated
to refrigerate something is to freeze
it so that it keeps in good condition
refrigeration noun

refrigerator noun refrigerators
a cabinet in which you can store food at a
low temperature to keep it fresh

refuel verb refuels, refuelling,
refuelled
to refuel a ship or aircraft is to supply it
with more fuel

refuge noun refuges
a place where someone can go to be safe
from danger

refugee (say ref-yoo-**jee**) noun
refugees
someone who has had to leave their home
or country because of war or persecution
or disaster

refund (say ri-**fund**) verb refunds,
refunding, refunded
to refund money is to pay it back

refund (say **ree**-fund) noun refunds
money that is paid back to you

refusal noun refusals
refusal, or a refusal, is when someone
refuses something

refuse (say ri-**fewz**) verb refuses,
refusing, refused
to refuse something, or to do something,
is to say that you will not accept it or do it
They refuse to help.

refuse (say **ref**-yooss) noun
rubbish or waste material

regain verb regains, regaining,
regained
to regain something is to get it back

regard verb regards, regarding,
regarded
1 to regard someone or something as
something is to think of them in a certain
way *I regard her as a friend.* 2 to regard
someone or something is also to look at
them closely

regard noun
regard is consideration or respect *They acted
without regard for our safety.* **with regard
to something** about it; in connection with
it

regarding preposition
on the subject of; about *There are rules
regarding use of the library.*

regardless adjective
paying no attention to something *Buy it,
regardless of the cost.*

regards plural noun
kind wishes you send in a message *Give your
parents my regards.*

a
b
c
d
e
f
g
h
i
j
k
l
m
n
o
p
q
r
s
t
u
v
w
x
y
z

regatta (say ri-**gat**-a) noun **regattas**
a meeting for boat or yacht races

reggae (say **reg**-ay) noun
reggae is a West Indian style of music with a strong beat

regiment noun **regiments**
an army unit consisting of two or more battalions **regimental** adjective

region noun **regions**
1 a part of a country **2** a part of the world *These plants only grow in tropical regions.* **regional** adjective belonging to a particular region

register noun **registers**
1 an official list of names or information, especially of people present each day at a school **2** the range of a voice or musical instrument

register verb **registers, registering, registered**
1 to register something or someone is to put their name on an official list **2** a gauge or instrument registers a certain amount when that is what it shows *The thermometer registered 25°.* **3** to register a letter or parcel is to have it officially recorded for sending with special care

registration noun
registration is making an official record of something

regret noun **regrets**
you feel regret when you feel sorry or sad about something

regret verb **regrets, regretting, regretted**
to regret something is to feel sorry or sad about it

regretful adjective
feeling sorry or sad about something **regretfully** adverb

regrettable adjective
you say something is regrettable when you wish it hadn't happened

regular adjective
1 always happening at certain times *You*
need regular meals. **2** even or symmetrical *She has beautiful regular teeth.* **3** normal or correct *Do you want a regular or large coffee?* **4** a regular soldier belongs to a country's permanent army **regularity** noun **regularly** adverb

regulate verb **regulates, regulating, regulated**
to regulate something is to adjust or control it

regulation noun **regulations**
1 a regulation is a rule or law **2** regulation is the adjusting or controlling of something

rehearsal noun **rehearsals**
a rehearsal is when you practise something before performing it

rehearse verb **rehearses, rehearsing, rehearsed**
to rehearse (for example) a play or piece of music is to practise it before you perform it

reign verb **reigns, reigning, reigned**
1 to reign is to be king or queen **2** something reigns when it is the most noticeable or important thing *Silence reigned for a while.*

reign noun **reigns**
the time when someone is king or queen

rein noun **reins**
a strap used by a rider to guide a horse

reindeer noun **reindeer**
a kind of deer that lives in Arctic regions

reinforce verb **reinforces, reinforcing, reinforced**
to reinforce something is to strengthen it

reinforcement noun **reinforcements**
a thing that strengthens something **reinforcements** extra troops or equipment sent to strengthen a military force

reject (say ri-**jekt**) verb **rejects, rejecting, rejected**
1 to reject something or someone is to refuse to accept them *They have rejected my offer of help.* **2** to reject something is to

get rid of it *Faulty parts are rejected at the factory.* **rejection** noun

reject (say **ree**-jekt) noun **rejects**
a thing that is got rid of, especially because it is faulty or poorly made

rejoice verb **rejoices, rejoicing, rejoiced**
to rejoice is to be very happy or pleased

relate verb **relates, relating, related**
1 things relate to each other when there is a connection between them 2 to relate one thing with another is to compare them 3 to relate a story is to tell it

related adjective
1 two people are related when they belong to the same family 2 two things are related when they are connected or linked in some way

relation noun **relations**
1 a relation is someone who is related to you 2 relation is the way that one thing is connected or compared with another

relationship noun **relationships**
1 the way people or things are connected with each other 2 the way people get on with one another *There is a good relationship between the teachers and the children.* 3 a close friendship or connection between two people

relative noun **relatives**
your relatives are the people who are related to you

relative adjective
1 connected or compared with something 2 compared with the average *They live in relative comfort.*

relatively adverb
compared with other people or things; more or less *Books are relatively cheap.*

relative pronoun noun **relative pronouns**
one of the words *who, what, which,* or *that,* placed in front of a clause to connect it with an earlier clause. In the sentence *we saw the man who had stolen the car,* the relative pronoun is 'who'

relax verb **relaxes, relaxing, relaxed**
1 to relax is to become less anxious or worried 2 to relax is also to rest or stop working 3 to relax a part of you is make it less stiff or tense *Try to relax your arm.* **relaxation** noun

relay verb **relays, relaying, relayed**
to relay a message or broadcast is to pass it on

relay noun **relays**
1 a race between two teams in which each member of the team runs part of the distance 2 a fresh group taking the place of another *The firemen worked in relays.* 3 a device for passing on a broadcast

release verb **releases, releasing, released**
1 to release something or someone is to set them free or unfasten them 2 to release a film or record is to make it available to the public

release noun **releases**
1 release is being released 2 a release is something released, especially a new film or piece of recorded music 3 a release is a device that unfastens something *The seatbelt has a quick release.*

relegate (say **rel**-i-gayt) verb **relegates, relegating, relegated**
1 a sports team is relegated when it goes down into a lower division of a league 2 to relegate something is to put it into a lower group or position than before **relegation** noun

relent verb **relents, relenting, relented**
to relent is to be less angry or severe than you were going to be

relentless adjective
1 never stopping or letting up *Their criticism was relentless.* 2 showing no pity *They faced a relentless enemy.* **relentlessly** adverb

relevant (say **rel**-i-vant) adjective
connected with what you are discussing or dealing with **relevance** noun

reliable adjective
able to be trusted or depended on

a
b
c
d
e
f
g
h
i
j
k
l
m
n
o
p
q
r
s
t
u
v
w
x
y
z

reliability noun **reliably** adverb you are reliably informed about something when you are told it by someone you trust

reliant adjective
you are reliant on someone or something when you rely on them and cannot do without them **reliance** noun

relic noun relics
something that has survived from an ancient time

relief noun reliefs
1 a good feeling you get because something unpleasant has stopped or is not going to happen *It was such a relief when we reached dry land.* **2** relief is the ending or lessening of pain or suffering **3** aid given to people in need *The charity is involved in famine relief.* **4** a relief is also a person or thing that takes over or helps with a job **5** relief is also a method of making a map or design that stands out from a flat surface *The model shows hills and valleys in relief.*

relieve verb relieves, relieving, relieved
to relieve pain or suffering is to end or lessen it **to relieve someone of something** is to take it from them

relieved adjective
feeling good because something unpleasant has stopped or is not going to happen

religion noun religions
what people believe about God or gods, and how they worship

religious adjective
1 to do with religion **2** someone is religious when they they believe in a religion and follow it carefully

religiously adverb
to do something religiously is to do it with great attention or care *He wrote up his diary religiously every night.*

reluctant adjective
you are reluctant to do something when you do not want to do it **reluctance** noun **reluctantly** adverb

rely verb relies, relying, relied
to rely on someone or **something** is to trust them or need them to help or support you

remain verb remains, remaining, remained
1 to remain is to continue in the same place or condition *It will remain cloudy all day.* **2** to remain is also to be left over *A lot of food remained after the party.*

remainder noun remainders
1 something left over **2** (in mathematics) the amount that is left over when you divide one number into another

remains plural noun
1 something left over **2** ruins or relics **3** a dead body

remark verb remarks, remarking, remarked
to remark on something is to say something that you have thought or noticed

remark noun remarks
something you say

remarkable adjective
so unusual or impressive that you notice or remember it **remarkably** adverb

remedy noun remedies
a cure for an illness or problem

remedy verb remedies, remedying, remedied
to put something right

remember verb remembers, remembering, remembered
1 to remember something is to keep it in your mind, or bring it into your mind when you need to **2** to remember someone is to be thinking about them

remembrance noun
you do something in remembrance of someone or something when you do it as a way of remembering them

remind verb reminds, reminding, reminded
to remind someone is to help or make them

remember something *The girl in that painting reminds me of you.*

reminder noun reminders
a reminder of a person or thing is something that makes you think about or remember them

reminisce (say rem-in-iss) verb
reminisces, reminiscing, reminisced
to think or talk about things you remember
reminiscent adjective to be reminiscent of something is to remind you of it
reminiscences noun a person's memories of their past life

remnant noun remnants
a small piece of something left over

remorse noun
remorse is deep regret for something wrong you have done

remorseful adjective
feeling remorse **remorsefully** adverb

remorseless adjective
relentless; not stopping or ending
remorselessly adverb

remote adjective remoter, remotest
1 far away *He lived on a remote island.*
2 unlikely or slight *Their chances of winning were remote.* **remotely** adverb something is not (for example) remotely funny when it is not even slightly funny **remoteness** noun

remote control noun remote controls
1 remote control is controlling something from a distance, usually by means of radio or electricity **2** a remote control is a device for doing this

removal noun removals
removing or moving something

remove verb removes, removing, removed
to remove something is to take it away or take it off

render verb renders, rendering, rendered
1 to render someone (for example)

speechless or unconscious is to put them in that condition *The shock rendered her speechless.* **2** to render help or a service is to provide it

rendezvous (say ron-day-voo) noun rendezvous
1 a meeting with someone **2** a meeting place *Exactly one hour later, Pronto arrived in a hired van at the agreed rendezvous.*
— Debi Gliori, *Pure Dead Magic*

renew verb renews, renewing, renewed
to renew something is to make it as it was before or replace it with something new
renewal noun

renewable adjective
able to be renewed or replaced; never completely used up

renown noun
fame *He is a man of great renown.*
renowned adjective famous *She is renowned for her generosity.*

rent noun rents
a regular payment for the use of something, especially a house or flat

rent verb rents, renting, rented
to rent something is to pay money for the use of it

repair verb repairs, repairing, repaired
to repair something is to mend it

repair noun repairs
1 repair is mending something *The car is in for repair.* **2** a repair is a mended place *You can hardly see the repair.* **to be in good repair** is to be in good condition

repay verb repays, repaying, repaid
1 to repay money is to pay it back
2 to repay someone's kindness is to do something for them in return
repayment noun

repeat verb repeats, repeating, repeated
to repeat something is to say it or do it again

repeat noun repeats
something that is repeated, especially a television programme

a
b
c
d
e
f
g
h
i
j
k
l
m
n
o
p
q
r
s
t
u
v
w
x
y
z

A
B
C
D
E
F
G
H
I
J
K
L
M
N
O
P
Q
R
S
T
U
V
W
X
Y
Z

repeatedly adverb
several times; again and again

repel verb repels, repelling, repelled
1 to repel someone or something is to drive or force them away or apart 2 to repel someone is to make them disgusted **repellent** adjective disgusting

repent verb repents, repenting, repented
to repent is to be sorry for what you have done **repentance** noun **repentant** adjective

repetition noun repetitions
1 repeating or doing something again
2 something repeated

repetitive adjective
something is repetitive when it is repeated too much and so becomes boring

replace verb replaces, replacing, replaced
1 to replace something is to put it back in its place 2 to replace someone or something is to take their place 3 to replace something is to put a new thing in the place of it *We will have to replace the old engine with a new one.*

replacement noun replacements
1 replacement is when something or someone is replaced for another
2 a replacement is something used or given in place of another

replay noun replays
1 a football match played for a second time after the first match has ended in a draw 2 the playing or showing again of a recording

replay verb replays, replaying, replayed
to replay a tape is to play it again

replica (say rep-li-ka) noun replicas
an exact copy

reply noun replies
something you say or write to deal with what someone else has asked or said

reply verb replies, replying, replied
to reply is to give a reply

report verb reports, reporting, reported
1 to report something is to describe something that has happened or something you have studied 2 to report someone is to complain about them to those in charge of them 3 to report to someone is to tell them you have arrived or are available

report noun reports
1 a description or account of something
2 a regular statement of how someone has worked or behaved, especially at school
3 an explosive sound *We heard the report of a gun.*

reported speech noun
reported speech is when you report someone's words in a changed form, as in *He said that he would come* (reporting that someone has said the words 'I will come')

reporter noun reporters
someone whose job is to collect news for a newspaper or for radio or television

represent verb represents, representing, represented
1 to represent something or someone is to be a picture or model or symbol of them 2 to represent something is also to be a typical example of it 3 to represent someone is to support them by speaking or acting on their behalf

representation noun representations
a representation of a thing is something that shows or describes it

representative noun
a person or thing that represents others

representative adjective
typical of a group

repress verb represses, repressing, repressed
to repress something or someone is to control or restrain them by force **repression** noun **repressive** adjective

reprieve (say ri-preev) noun reprieves
someone is given a reprieve when their

reptile

crocodile

snake

tortoise

punishment is postponed or cancelled, especially the death penalty

reprieve verb reprieves, reprieving, reprieved
to reprieve someone is to cancel or postpone their punishment

reprimand verb reprimands, reprimanding, reprimanded
to reprimand someone is to scold them or tell them off

reprimand noun reprimands
a telling-off

reprisal (say ri-**pry**-zal) noun reprisals
an act of revenge

reproach verb reproaches, reproaching, reproached
to reproach someone is to blame them for something and show you are disappointed with them

reproach noun
reproach is blame or criticism *His behaviour was beyond reproach.*

reproduce verb reproduces, reproducing, reproduced
1 to reproduce something is to make it be heard or seen again *Sound can be reproduced by discs or tapes.* **2** to reproduce something is also to copy it **3** animals and people reproduce when they produce offspring

reproduction noun reproductions
1 reproduction is the process of producing offspring **2** a reproduction is a copy of something **reproductive** adjective to do with producing offspring

reptile noun reptiles
a cold-blooded animal that creeps or crawls, such as snakes and lizards

republic noun republics
a country ruled by a president and government that are chosen by the people

republican noun republicans
someone who supports the idea of a republic

repulsion noun
1 repulsion is a feeling of disgust **2** repulsion is also repelling something

repulsive adjective
disgusting

reputation noun reputations
what most people think about a person or thing *He has a reputation for being honest.*

request verb requests, requesting, requested
to request something is to ask politely or formally for it

a b c d e f g h i j k l m n o p q r s t u v w x y z

A
B
C
D
E
F
G
H
I
J
K
L
M
N
O
P
Q

R

S
T
U
V
W
X
Y
Z

request noun requests
1 the action of asking for something 2 what someone asks for

require verb requires, requiring, required
1 to require something is to need or want it 2 you are required to do something when you have to do it *Pedestrians are required to walk on the pavements.*

requirement noun requirements
a requirement is something that is needed

reread verb rereads, rereading, reread
to reread something is to read it again

rescue verb rescues, rescuing, rescued
to rescue someone is to save them from danger or capture
rescue noun rescues
when someone is rescued **rescuer** noun

research noun researches
research is careful study or investigation to learn more about a subject **researcher** noun

resemblance noun resemblances
there is a resemblance between two or more things when they are similar

resemble verb resembles, resembling, resembled
to resemble someone or something is to look or sound like them

resent verb resents, resenting, resented
to resent something is to feel hurt or angry about it

resentful adjective
hurt and angry about something

resentment noun
to feel resentment is to feel hurt and angry about something

reservation noun reservations
1 arranging for (for example) a restaurant table or seat on a train to be kept for you 2 an area of land kept for a special purpose 3 you have reservations about something when you feel doubtful or uneasy about it *I had reservations about the excuses he made.*

reserve verb reserves, reserving, reserved
to reserve something is to keep it or order it for a particular person or for a special use
reserve noun reserves
1 a person kept ready to be used if necessary, especially an extra player in a sports team 2 an area of land kept for a special purpose *This island is a nature reserve.*

reserved adjective
1 kept for someone *These seats are reserved.* 2 someone is reserved when they are shy or unwilling to show their feelings

reservoir (say rez-er-vwar) noun reservoirs
a place where water is stored, especially an artificial lake

reside verb resides, residing, resided
to reside in a place is to live there

residence noun residences
a place where someone lives

resident noun residents
someone who lives in a particular place

resign verb resigns, resigning, resigned
to give up your job or position **to resign yourself to something** is to accept a difficulty without complaining or arguing

resignation noun resignations
1 resignation is accepting a difficulty without complaining 2 a resignation is a letter saying you are resigning a job or position

resin (say rez-in) noun resins
resin is a sticky substance that comes from plants or is made artificially

resist verb resists, resisting, resisted
to resist someone or something is to oppose them or try to stop them

resistance noun
resistance is fighting back or taking action against someone or something *The troops came up against armed resistance.*
resistant adjective to be resistant to

something is not to be affected or damaged by it

resolute (say rez-o-loot) adjective
determined or firm **resolutely** adverb

resolution noun resolutions
1 resolution is being determined or firm 2 a resolution is something you have decided to do 3 the resolution of a story is the last part where we find out how the story comes to an end and how some of the difficulties faced by the characters are sorted out

resolve verb resolves, resolving, resolved
1 to resolve to do something is to decide to do it 2 to resolve doubts or disagreements is to deal successfully with them

resort noun resorts
a place where people go for a holiday, especially by the sea **the last resort** the only thing you can do when everything else has failed

resort verb resorts, resorting, resorted
to resort to something is to make use of it, especially when everything else has failed *In the end they resorted to violence.*

resound verb resounds, resounding, resounded
to resound is to fill a place with sound or to echo

resource noun resources
resources are things that you have and are able to use *The land is rich in natural resources.*

respect noun respects
1 respect is admiration for someone's good qualities or achievements 2 respect is also consideration or concern *Have respect for people's feelings.* 3 a respect is a detail or aspect *In some respects, he is like his sister.*

respect verb respects, respecting, respected
to respect someone is to have respect for them

respectable adjective
1 a respectable person has good manners and character 2 something respectable is of a good size or standard **respectability** noun **respectably** adverb

respectful adjective
showing respect; polite **respectfully** adverb

respecting preposition
concerning; to do with

respective adjective
belonging to each one of several *We went to our respective rooms.*

respectively adverb
in the same order as the people or things already mentioned *Emma and I went to London and Paris respectively.*

respiration noun
respiration is breathing **respiratory** adjective to do with breathing

respirator noun respirators
a mask or machine for helping with people's breathing

respond verb responds, responding, responded
to respond to someone or something is to reply or react to them

response noun responses
your response is how you reply or react to something

responsibility noun responsibilities
1 responsibility is being responsible for something 2 a responsibility is something for which you are responsible

responsible adjective
1 looking after something and likely to take the blame if anything goes wrong 2 able to be trusted 3 important and needing trust *She has a responsible job.* 4 to be responsible for something is to be the cause of it *Faulty wiring was responsible for the fire.* **responsibly** adverb

rest[1] noun rests
1 a time when you can sleep or relax 2 a support for something

rest verb rests, resting, rested
1 to rest is to sleep or relax 2 to rest on

a
b
c
d
e
f
g
h
i
j
k
l
m
n
o
p
q
r
s
t
u
v
w
x
y
z

A B C D E F G H I J K L M N O P Q **R** S T U V W X Y Z

or against something is to lean on it *The ladder is resting against the wall.* **3** to rest something is to lean or support it somewhere *Rest the ladder on the roof.*

rest² noun
the rest the part that is left; the others

restaurant noun **restaurants**
a place where you can buy a meal and eat it

restful adjective
giving a feeling of rest

restless adjective
you are restless when you can't relax or keep still **restlessly** adverb
restlessness noun

restore verb **restores, restoring, restored**
to restore something is to put it back as it was or make it new again
restoration noun

restrain verb **restrains, restraining, restrained**
to restrain someone or something is to hold them or keep them tightly controlled

restraint noun
self-control *Show a little restraint.*

restrict verb **restricts, restricting, restricted**
to restrict someone or something is to keep them within certain limits or stop them from acting freely **restriction** noun
restrictive adjective

result noun **results**
1 a thing that happens because something else has happened **2** the score or situation at the end of a game or competition or race **3** the answer to a sum or problem

result verb **results, resulting, resulted**
to result is to happen as a result **to result in something** is to have it as a result *The game resulted in a draw.*

resume verb **resumes, resuming, resumed**
to resume, or to resume something, is to start again after stopping

resuscitate (say ri-**suss**-it-ate) verb
resuscitates, resuscitating, resuscitated
to resuscitate someone is to revive them after they have been unconscious

retail noun
retail is the business of selling goods to the public **retailer** noun

retain verb **retains, retaining, retained**
1 to retain something is to keep it *Retain your tickets for inspection.* **2** to retain something is to hold it in place

retina (say **ret**-i-na) noun **retinas**
a layer at the back of your eyeball that is sensitive to light

retire verb **retires, retiring, retired**
1 someone retires when they give up regular work at a certain age **2** to retire is also to retreat or withdraw, or to go to bed *He was so exhausted he had to retire from the race.* **retirement** noun

retiring adjective
a retiring person is shy and avoids company

retort verb **retorts, retorting, retorted**
to retort is to reply quickly or angrily
'Swallows can't read, silly,' said Peter. 'Silly yourself,' retorted Phyllis; 'how do you know?'
— Edith Nesbit, *The Railway Children*

retort noun **retorts**
a quick or angry reply

retrace verb **retraces, retracing, retraced**
to retrace your steps is to go back the way you came

retreat verb **retreats, retreating, retreated**
to go back when you are attacked or defeated

retrieve verb **retrieves, retrieving, retrieved**
to retrieve something is to get it back or find it again **retrievable** adjective
retrieval noun

retriever noun **retrievers**
a dog that can find and bring back birds and animals that have been shot

return to revolt

return verb returns, returning, returned
1 to return is to come or go back to a place
2 to return something is to give it or send it back

return noun returns
1 when you come back to a place
2 something that is given or sent back
3 profit *He gets a good return on his savings.*
4 a return ticket *Do you want a single or return?*

return ticket noun return tickets
a ticket for a journey to a place and back again

reunion noun reunions
a meeting of people who have not met for some time

rev verb revs, revving, revved (informal)
to rev an engine is to make it run quickly

rev noun revs (informal)
a revolution of an engine

Rev.
short for Reverend

reveal verb reveals, revealing, revealed
to reveal something is to show it or make it known

revelation noun revelations
a surprising fact that is made known

revenge noun
revenge is harming someone because they have done harm to you

revenue (say rev-e-nyoo) noun revenues
revenue is money that a business or organization receives

revere (say ri-veer) verb reveres, revering, revered
to revere someone or something is to respect them deeply or religiously

reverence noun
reverence is great respect or awe, especially towards God or holy things
reverent adjective

Reverend noun
the title of a member of the clergy *This is the Reverend John Smith.*

reverse noun
the opposite way or side **in reverse** going in the opposite direction

reverse verb reverses, reversing, reversed
1 to reverse something is to turn it round
2 to reverse is to go backwards in a vehicle
3 to reverse a decision is to cancel it
reversal noun

reversible adjective
1 a reversible change or decision can be easily changed back 2 reversible clothing can be worn with either side on the outside

review noun reviews
1 a published description and opinion of a book or film or play, or a piece of music
2 an inspection or survey of something

review verb reviews, reviewing, reviewed
1 to review a book or play or film, or a piece of music, is to write a review of it 2 to review something is to inspect or survey it
reviewer noun

revise verb revises, revising, revised
1 before you do an examination, you revise when you go over work that you have already done 2 to revise something is to correct or change it

revision noun revisions
1 a revision is a change or correction
2 revision is learning work before you do an examination

revival noun revivals
a revival is when something becomes popular again

revive verb revives, reviving, revived
1 to revive something is to start using it again 2 to revive someone is to make them conscious again after fainting

revolt verb revolts, revolting, revolted
1 to revolt is to rebel 2 something revolts you when it disgusts or horrifies you

433

A
B
C
D
E
F
G
H
I
J
K
L
M
N
O
P
Q
R
S
T
U
V
W
X
Y
Z

revolt noun **revolts**
a rebellion

revolting adjective
something is revolting when it is very unpleasant or disgusting *What a revolting smell.*

revolution noun **revolutions**
1 a rebellion that overthrows the government 2 a complete change 3 one turn of a wheel or engine

revolutionary adjective
1 to do with a revolution 2 completely new or original

revolutionize verb **revolutionizes, revolutionizing, revolutionized**
to revolutionize something is to change it completely

revolve verb **revolves, revolving, revolved**
something revolves when it goes round in a circle

revolver noun **revolvers**
a pistol that has a revolving store for bullets so that it can be fired several times without having to be loaded again

reward noun **rewards**
something given to a person in return for something they have done

reward verb **rewards, rewarding, rewarded**
to reward someone is to give them a reward

rewarding adjective
pleasing or satisfying

rewind verb **rewinds, rewinding, rewound**
to rewind a cassette or videotape is to wind it back to the beginning

rewrite verb **rewrites, rewriting, rewrote, rewritten**
to rewrite something is to write it again or differently

rheumatism (say **roo**-ma-tizm) noun
rheumatism is a disease that causes pain and stiffness in the joints and muscles **rheumatic** adjective

rhinoceros (say ry-**noss**-er-os) noun **rhinoceroses** or **rhinoceros**
a large heavy animal with a horn or two horns on its nose

rhododendron (say roh-do-**den**-dron) noun **rhododendrons**
an evergreen shrub with large flowers

rhombus noun **rhombuses**
a shape with four equal sides and no right angles, like a diamond on a playing card

rhubarb noun
rhubarb is a plant with pink or green stalks used as food

rhyme noun **rhymes**
1 similar sounds in the endings of words, as in *bat* and *mat*, *batter* and *matter* 2 a short rhyming poem

rhyme verb **rhymes, rhyming, rhymed**
1 a poem rhymes when it has rhymes at the ends of its lines 2 one word rhymes with another word when it forms a rhyme with it *Bat rhymes with hat.*

TOP TIPS
Keep it quiet! There is a silent **h** in **rhyme** and in **rhythm**.

rhythm noun **rhythms**
a regular pattern of beats, sounds, or movements in music and poetry **rhythmic** or **rhythmical** adjective something is rhythmic or rhythmical when it has a rhythm **rhythmically** noun

rib noun **ribs**
your ribs are the curved bones above your waist

ribbon noun **ribbons**
a strip of nylon, silk, or other material

rice noun
rice is white seeds from a cereal plant, used as food

rich adjective **richer, richest**
1 someone is rich when they have a lot of money or property 2 something is rich when it is full of goodness, quality, or

strength **3** costly or luxurious *The house has rich furnishings.* **richness** noun

riches plural noun
wealth

richly adverb
thoroughly, completely *They richly deserved their punishment.*

rickety adjective
a rickety (for example) bridge or chair is unsteady and likely to break or fall down

rickshaw noun **rickshaws**
a two-wheeled carriage pulled by one or more people, used in the Far East

ricochet (say **rik**-o-shay) verb **ricochets, ricocheting, ricocheted**
to bounce off something *The bullets ricocheted off the wall.*

rid verb **rids, ridding, rid**
to rid a person or place of something unwanted is to free them from it *He rid the town of rats.* **to get rid of something** or **someone** is to cause them to go away *I wish I could get rid of these spots.*

riddance noun
good riddance used to show that you are glad that something or someone has gone

riddle noun **riddles**
a puzzling question, especially as a joke

ride verb **rides, riding, rode, ridden**
1 to ride a horse or bicycle is to sit on it and be carried along on it **2** to ride is to travel in a vehicle

ride noun **rides**
a journey on a horse or bicycle, or in a vehicle

rider noun **riders**
someone who rides a horse

ridge noun **ridges**
a long narrow part higher than the rest of something *a mountain ridge*

ridicule verb **ridicules, ridiculing, ridiculed**
to ridicule someone or something is to make fun of them

ridiculous adjective
extremely silly or absurd
ridiculously adverb

rifle noun **rifles**
a long gun. You hold it against your shoulder to fire it

rift noun **rifts**
1 a crack or split **2** a disagreement or a break in a friendship

rig verb **rigs, rigging, rigged**
1 to rig a ship is to fit it with rigging, sails, and other equipment **2** to rig an election or competition is to control the result dishonestly **to rig something up** is to make it quickly

rigging noun
rigging is the ropes that support a ship's masts and sails

right adjective
1 on or towards the east if you think of yourself as facing north **2** correct *Is this sum right?* **3** fair or honest *It's not right to cheat.* **4** conservative; not in favour of political reforms

right adverb
1 on or towards the right *Turn right.* **2** completely *Turn right round.* **3** exactly *She stood right in the middle.* **4** straight; directly *Go right ahead.* **right away** immediately

right noun **rights**
1 the right side **2** what is fair or just; something that people ought to be allowed *They fought for their rights.*

right verb **rights, righting, righted**
1 to right something is to make it upright *They learned how to right their canoe.* **2** to right something is also to put it right *The fault might right itself.*

right angle noun **right angles**
an angle of 90 degrees, like angles in a rectangle

righteous adjective
morally right or good; doing the right thing **righteously** adverb
righteousness noun

a
b
c
d
e
f
g
h
i
j
k
l
m
n
o
p
q
r
s
t
u
v
w
x
y
z

A
B
C
D
E
F
G
H
I
J
K
L
M
N
O
P
Q

R

S
T
U
V
W
X
Y
Z

rightful adjective
deserved or proper *The bike was returned to its rightful owner.* **rightfully** adverb

right–hand adjective
on the right side of something

right–handed adjective
using the right hand more than the left hand

rightly adverb
correctly or fairly

rightness noun
the rightness of (for example) a decision is the fact that it is correct or fair

rigid (say **rij**-id) adjective
1 firm or stiff 2 strict or harsh *The rules are rigid.* **rigidity** noun **rigidly** adverb to rigidly keep to a rule is to strictly keep to it

rim noun **rims**
the outer edge of a cup or wheel or other round object

rind noun **rinds**
the tough skin on bacon, cheese, or fruit

ring¹ noun **rings**
1 something in the shape of a circle *The children sat in a ring around the clown.*
2 a thin circular piece of metal you wear on a finger 3 the place where a boxing match or other contest is held 4 the space where a circus performs

ring verb **rings, ringing, ringed**
to ring something is to put a ring round it *Ring the answer that you think is the right one.*

ring² verb **rings, ringing, rang, rung**
1 to ring a bell is to make it sound 2 a bell rings when it makes a clear musical sound 3 to ring someone is to telephone them *She rang her brother last night.*

ring noun **rings**
a ringing sound **to give someone a ring** (informal) is to telephone them

ringleader noun **ringleaders**
someone who leads other people in rebellion or mischief or crime

ringlet noun **ringlets**
a long curled piece of hair

ringmaster noun **ringmasters**
the person who is in charge of a performance in the circus ring

ring road noun **ring roads**
a road that goes right round a town

rink noun **rinks**
a place made for skating

rinse verb **rinses, rinsing, rinsed**
to rinse something is to wash it in clean water without soap

rinse noun **rinses**
a wash in clean water without soap

riot noun **riots**
wild or violent behaviour by a crowd of people in a public place

riot verb **riots, rioting, rioted**
people riot when they run wild and behave violently in a public place

riotous adjective
wild or unruly

rip verb **rips, ripping, ripped**
to rip something is to tear it roughly

rip noun **rips**
a torn place

ripe adjective **riper, ripest**
ready to be harvested or eaten
ripeness noun

ripen verb **ripens, ripening, ripened**
1 to ripen something is to make it ripe 2 to ripen is to become ripe

ripple noun **ripples**
a small wave on the surface of water

ripple verb **ripples, rippling, rippled**
water ripples when it forms small waves on the surface

rise verb **rises, rising, rose, risen**
1 to rise is to go upwards *Smoke was rising from the fire. The sun rises in the east.* 2 to rise is also to get larger or more *Prices rose this year.* 3 a person rises when they get up from sleeping or sitting *They all rose as she*

came in. **4** people rise, or rise up, when they rebel *The army rose against the government.*

rise noun rises
1 an increase, especially in wages **2** an upward slope **to give rise to something** is to cause it

risk verb risks, risking, risked
to risk something is to take a chance of damaging or losing it *They risked their lives during the rescue.*

risk noun risks
a chance that something bad will happen *There's a risk that the river might flood.*

risky adjective riskier, riskiest
dangerous or involving risk

risotto noun
risotto is an Italian dish of rice cooked with vegetables and often with meat

rite noun rites
a ceremony or ritual

ritual noun rituals
a regular ceremony or series of actions

rival noun rivals
a person or thing that competes with another or tries to do the same thing

rival verb rivals, rivalling, rivalled
to rival someone or something is to be as good as they are *Nothing can rival the taste of home-made ice cream.*

rivalry noun rivalries
a rivalry is when two people compete against each other

river noun rivers
a large natural stream of water flowing along a channel

rivet noun rivets
a strong metal pin for holding pieces of metal together

rivet verb rivets, riveting, riveted
1 to rivet something is to fasten it with rivets **2** to rivet someone is to hold them still *She stood riveted to the spot.* **3** to be riveted by something is to be fascinated by it *The children were riveted by his story.*
riveting adjective fascinating

road noun roads
a level way with a hard surface made for traffic to go along

roadside noun roadsides
the side of a road

roadway noun roadways
the middle part of the road, used by traffic

roam verb roams, roaming, roamed
to roam is to wander *They roamed about the city. For many months, close to starvation, I roamed the hills and glens of the Highlands, hunting and scavenging for my food like some wild beast.* – Michael Morpurgo, *The Last Wolf*

roar noun roars
a loud deep sound of the kind that a lion makes

roar verb roars, roaring, roared
to roar is to make a loud deep sound

roast verb roasts, roasting, roasted
1 to roast food is to cook it in an oven or over a fire **2** you say you are roasting when you are very hot

rob verb robs, robbing, robbed
to rob someone or a place is to steal something from them *He robbed me of my watch. The bank's been robbed.*

robber noun robbers
someone who steals something

robbery noun robberies
a robbery is when something is stolen

robe noun robes
a long loose piece of clothing

robin noun robins
a small brown bird with a red breast

robot noun robots
a machine that imitates the movements of a person or does the work of a person

robust adjective
tough and strong

rock[1] noun rocks
1 a rock is a large stone **2** rock is a large mass of stone **3** rock is also a hard sweet

a
b
c
d
e
f
g
h
i
j
k
l
m
n
o
p
q
r
s
t
u
v
w
x
y
z

A

usually shaped like a stick and sold at the seaside

rock² verb **rocks, rocking, rocked**
1 to rock is to move gently backwards and forwards or from side to side **2** to rock something is to make it do this

rock noun **rocks**
rock music

rocker noun **rockers**
1 a rocking chair **2** a curved support for a chair or cradle

rockery noun **rockeries**
part of a garden where people grow flowers between rocks

rocket noun **rockets**
1 a firework that shoots high into the air **2** a pointed tube-shaped vehicle pushed into the air by hot gases, especially as a spacecraft or weapon

rocking chair noun **rocking chairs**
a chair which can be rocked by the person sitting in it

rock music noun
rock music is popular music with a heavy beat

rocky adjective **rockier, rockiest**
1 a rocky place is full of rocks **2** unsteady or shaky

rod noun **rods**
1 a long thin stick or bar **2** a rod with a line attached for fishing

rode
past tense of **ride** verb *The prince rode in on his horse.*

rodent noun **rodents**
an animal that has large front teeth for gnawing things, such as a rat, mouse, or squirrel

rodeo (say roh-**day**-oh or **roh**-di-oh) noun **rodeos**
a display or contest of cowboys' skill in riding and in controlling cattle

rogue noun **rogues**
a dishonest or mischievous person

role noun **roles**
1 the part that an actor plays in a play, film, or story **2** the purpose something has *Computers have a role in teaching.*

roll verb **rolls, rolling, rolled**
1 to roll is to move along by turning over and over, like a ball or wheel **2** to roll something is to make it do this **3** to roll something, or roll something up, is to form it into the shape of a cylinder or ball **4** to roll something soft, such as dough, is to flatten it by moving a round heavy object over it **5** a ship rolls when it sways from side to side **6** drums roll when they make a long rumbling sound

roll noun **rolls**
1 a cylinder made by rolling something up **2** a small loaf of bread shaped like a bun **3** a list of names **4** the rumbling sound of drums

roller noun **rollers**
1 a cylinder-shaped object, especially one used for flattening things **2** a long swelling wave in the sea

Rollerblade noun **Rollerblades** (trademark)
Rollerblades are boots with a line of small wheels fitted underneath, so that you can move smoothly over the ground.

roller skate noun **roller skates**
roller skates are boots with two pairs of wheels fitted underneath, so that you can move smoothly over the ground

rolling pin noun **rolling pins**
a heavy cylinder you roll over pastry dough to flatten it

ROM
short for *read-only memory*, a type of computer memory with information that can be accessed but not changed by the user

Roman noun **Romans**
a person who lived in ancient Rome
Roman adjective
to do with ancient Rome

R

A B C D E F G H I J K L M N O P Q R S T U V W X Y Z

Roman Catholic noun Roman Catholics
a member of the Church with the Pope in Rome at its head

romance noun romances
1 romance is experiences and feelings connected with love 2 a romance is a love affair or a love story

Roman numerals plural noun
letters that represent numbers, as used by the ancient Romans (compare *Arabic figures*): I = 1, V = 5, X = 10, L = 50, C = 100, and M = 1000

romantic adjective
1 to do with love or romance 2 to do with emotions or imagination
romantically adverb

romp verb romps, romping, romped
to romp is to play in a lively way
romp noun romps
a spell of lively play

rompers plural noun
a piece of clothing for a young child, covering the body and legs

roof noun roofs
1 the part that covers the top of a building, shelter, or vehicle 2 the upper part of your mouth

rook noun rooks
1 a black bird that looks like a crow 2 a piece in chess, also called a *castle*

room noun rooms
1 a room is a part of a building with its own walls and ceiling 2 room is space for someone or something *Is there room for me?*

roomful adjective roomfuls
the amount or number a room will hold

roomy adjective roomier, roomiest
somewhere is roomy when there is plenty of room or space inside

roost noun roosts
the place where a bird rests

root noun roots
1 the part of a plant that grows under the ground 2 a source or basis of something *People say that money is the root of all evil.* 3 a number in relation to the number it produces when multiplied by itself *9 is the square root of 81.* **to take root** is to grow roots or to become established *The custom never took root in other countries.*

root verb roots, rooting, rooted
1 to root is to take root in the ground 2 to root someone is to fix them firmly *Fear rooted him to the spot.* **to root something out** is to find it and get rid of it

rope noun ropes
a strong thick cord made of strands twisted together **to show someone the ropes** is to show them how to do a job

rose¹ noun roses
a scented flower with a long thorny stem

rose²
past tense of rise verb *Clouds of smoke rose from the building.*

rosette noun rosettes
a large circular badge made of ribbons

rosy adjective rosier, rosiest
1 pink 2 hopeful or cheerful *The future looks rosy.*

rot verb rots, rotting, rotted
to rot is to go soft or bad so that it is useless *This wood has rotted.*
rot noun
1 rot is decay 2 (informal) rot is also nonsense *Don't talk such rot.*

rota noun rotas
a list of people who have to do tasks

rotate verb rotates, rotating, rotated
1 to rotate is to go round like a wheel 2 to rotate is to take turns at something *The job of running the tuck shop rotates.* **rotation** noun

rotor noun rotors
the part of a machine that goes round, especially the large horizontal propeller of a helicopter

a
b
c
d
e
f
g
h
i
j
k
l
m
n
o
p
q
r
s
t
u
v
w
x
y
z

rotten adjective
1 rotted or decayed *There was rotten fruit on the ground.* **2** (informal) nasty or very bad *We had rotten weather.* **rottenness** noun

Rottweiler noun **Rottweilers**
a large dog with short black and tan hair, often kept as a guard dog

rough adjective **rougher, roughest**
1 not smooth; uneven **2** violent; not gentle *He is a rough boy.* **3** not exact; done quickly *It's only a rough guess.* **roughness** noun

roughage noun
roughage is fibre in food, which helps you to digest it

roughen verb **roughens, roughening, roughened**
to roughen something is to make it rough

roughly adverb
1 approximately; not exactly *There were roughly a hundred people there.* **2** in a rough way; not gently *She pushed him roughly out of the way.*

round adjective **rounder, roundest**
1 shaped like a circle or ball or cylinder **2** full or complete *We bought a round dozen.* **3** a round trip is one that returns to the start

round adverb
1 in a circle or curve; by a longer route *Go round to the back of the house.* **2** in every direction or to every person *Hand the cakes round.* **3** in a new direction *Turn your chair round.* **4** to someone's house or place of work *Come round at lunchtime.*

round preposition
1 on all sides of *We'll put a fence round the field.* **2** in a curve or circle about *The earth moves round the sun.* **3** to every part of *Show them round the house.*

round noun **rounds**
1 each stage in a competition *The winners go on to the next round.* **2** a series of visits or calls made by a doctor, postman, or other person **3** a whole slice of bread, or a sandwich made from two whole slices of bread **4** a shot or series of shots from a gun; a piece of ammunition **5** a song in which people sing the same words but start at different times

round verb **rounds, rounding, rounded**
to round a place is to travel round it *A large car rounded the corner.* **to round a number down** is to decrease it to the nearest lower number *123.4 may be rounded down to 123.* **to round a number up** is to increase it to the nearest higher number *123.7 may be rounded up to 124.* **to round something off** is to finish it **to round up people or things** is to gather them together

roundabout noun **roundabouts**
1 a road junction at which traffic has to pass round a circular island **2** a merry-go-round

roundabout adjective
not using the shortest or most direct way *We went by a roundabout route.*

rounded adjective
round in shape

rounders noun
rounders is a game in which players try to hit a ball and run round a circuit

roundly adverb
thoroughly or severely *We were roundly told off for being late.*

rouse verb **rouses, rousing, roused**
to rouse someone is to wake them up or make them excited *I had eaten my hay and was lying down in my straw fast asleep, when I was suddenly roused by the stable bell ringing very loud.* — Anna Sewell, *Black Beauty*

rout (say rowt) verb **routs, routing, routed**
to rout an enemy is to defeat them and chase them away

rout (say rowt) noun **routs**
a disorderly retreat after being defeated in a battle

route (say root) noun **routes**
the way you have to go to get to a place

routine (say roo-**teen**) noun **routines**
a regular or fixed way of doing things

rove verb roves, roving, roved
to roam or wander *The Trunchbull's dangerous glittering eyes roved around the classroom.* – Roald Dahl, *Matilda*
rover noun

row[1] (rhymes with **go**) noun rows
a line of people or things

row[2] (rhymes with **go**) verb rows, rowing, rowed
to row a boat is to use oars to make it move
rower noun

row[3] (rhymes with **cow**) noun rows
1 a great noise or disturbance 2 a quarrel; a noisy argument or scolding

row (rhymes with **cow**) verb rows, rowing, rowed
people row when they have a noisy argument

rowdy adjective rowdier, rowdiest
noisy and disorderly **rowdily** adverb
rowdiness noun

rowing boat noun rowing boats
a small boat that you move forward by using oars

royal adjective
to do with a king or queen

royalty noun
1 royalty is being royal 2 royalty is also a royal person or royal people *We will be in the presence of royalty.*

rub verb rubs, rubbing, rubbed
to rub something is to move it backwards and forwards while pressing it on something else *He rubbed his hands together.* **to rub something off** or **out** is to make it disappear by rubbing it
rub noun rubs
when you rub something *Give it a quick rub.*

rubber noun rubbers
1 rubber is a strong elastic substance used for making tyres, balls, hoses, and other things 2 a rubber is a piece of rubber or soft plastic for rubbing out pencil marks
rubbery adjective

rubbish noun
1 rubbish is things that are not wanted or needed 2 rubbish is also nonsense

rubble noun
rubble is broken pieces of brick or stone

ruby noun rubies
a red jewel

rucksack noun rucksacks
a bag with shoulder straps that you carry on your back

rudder noun rudders
a flat hinged device at the back of a ship or aircraft, used for steering it

ruddy adjective ruddier, ruddiest
red and healthy-looking *He had a ruddy face.*

rude adjective ruder, rudest
1 not polite; not showing respect for other people *It was rude of me to push in.* 2 indecent or improper *a rude joke* 3 roughly made *a rude shelter* **rudely** adverb
rudeness noun

ruffian noun ruffians
a violent brutal person

ruffle verb ruffles, ruffling, ruffled
1 to ruffle something is to disturb its smoothness *The bird ruffled its feathers.* 2 to ruffle someone is to annoy them or upset them

rug noun rugs
1 a thick piece of material that partly covers a floor 2 a thick blanket

rugby or **rugby football** noun
rugby is a kind of football game using an oval ball that players may kick or carry

rugged (say **rug**-id) adjective
something rugged has a rough or uneven surface or outline *His face was rugged. It has a rugged coastline.*

ruin verb ruins, ruining, ruined
to ruin something is to spoil it or destroy it completely

a
b
c
d
e
f
g
h
i
j
k
l
m
n
o
p
q
r
s
t
u
v
w
x
y
z

441

A
B
C
D
E
F
G
H
I
J
K
L
M
N
O
P
Q
R
S
T
U
V
W
X
Y
Z

ruin noun ruins
1 a ruin is a building that has been so badly damaged that it has almost all fallen down **2** ruin is when something is ruined or destroyed **to be in ruins** is to be destroyed *My plans were in ruins.*

rule noun rules
1 a rule is something that people have to obey **2** rule is ruling or governing *The country used to be under French rule.*
as a rule usually; normally
rule verb rules, ruling, ruled
1 to rule people is to govern them; to rule is to be a ruler **2** to rule something is to make a decision *The referee ruled that it was a foul.* **3** to rule a line is to draw a straight line with a ruler or other straight edge

ruler noun rulers
1 someone who governs a country **2** a strip of wood, plastic, or metal with straight edges, used for measuring and drawing straight lines

ruling noun rulings
a judgement or decision *I will give my ruling tomorrow.*

rum noun rums
rum is a strong alcoholic drink made from sugar cane

rumble verb rumbles, rumbling, rumbled
to rumble is to make a deep heavy sound like thunder *His stomach was rumbling.*
rumble noun rumbles
a long deep heavy sound *There was a rumble of thunder in the distance.*

rummage verb rummages, rummaging, rummaged
to turn things over or move them about while looking for something

rummy noun
rummy is a card game in which players try to form sets or sequences of cards

rumour noun rumours
something that a lot of people are saying, although it may not be true

rump noun rumps
the back part of an animal, above its hind legs

run verb runs, running, ran, run
1 to run is to move with quick steps and with both feet off the ground for a time **2** to run is also to move or go or travel *Tears ran down his cheeks.* **3** a tap or your nose runs when liquid flows from it **4** an engine or machine runs when it is working or functioning *The engine was running smoothly.* **5** to run something is to manage it or organize it *She runs a corner shop.* **6** to run someone somewhere is to give them a lift there **to run a risk** is to take a chance **to run away** is to leave a place quickly or secretly **to run into someone** is to meet them unexpectedly **to run out of something** is to have used up a supply of it **to run someone over** is to knock them down with a car or bicycle
run noun runs
1 a spell of running *Let's go for a run.* **2** a point scored in cricket or baseball **3** a series of damaged stitches in a pair of tights or other piece of clothing **4** a continuous series of events *They've had a run of good luck.* **5** a place with a fence round it for keeping animals **to be on the run** is to be running away, especially from the police

runaway noun runaways
someone who has run away from home

rung¹ noun rungs
each of the short crossbars on a ladder

rung²
past participle of ring² verb *Has grandma rung yet?*

runner noun runners
1 a person or animal that runs in a race **2** the part of a sledge that slides along the ground

runner bean noun runner beans
a kind of climbing bean

runner-up noun runners-up
someone who comes second in a race or competition

runny adjective **runnier, runniest**
flowing or moving like liquid

runway noun **runways**
a long strip with a hard surface for aircraft to take off and land

rural adjective
to do with the countryside; in the country

rush[1] verb **rushes, rushing, rushed**
1 to rush is to hurry 2 to rush someone is to attack or capture them by surprise
rush noun
a rush is a hurry *I can't stop—I'm in a rush.*

rush[2] noun **rushes**
rushes are plants with thin stems that grow in wet or marshy places

rusk noun **rusks**
a kind of hard dry biscuit for babies to chew

rust noun
rust is a red or brown substance formed on metal that is exposed to air and dampness
rust verb **rusts, rusting, rusted**
metal rusts when it develops rust

rustic adjective
to do with the countryside

rustle verb **rustles, rustling, rustled**
1 to rustle is to make a gentle sound like dry leaves being blown by the wind 2 to rustle horses or cattle is to steal them **to rustle something up** (informal) is to collect it or provide it quickly

rusty adjective **rustier, rustiest**
1 coated with rust 2 not as good as it used to be because you have not had enough practice *My French is a bit rusty.*

rut noun **ruts**
a deep groove made by wheels in soft ground **to be in a rut** is to have a dull life with no changes

ruthless adjective
someone is ruthless when they are determined to get what they want and do not care if they hurt other people
ruthlessly adverb **ruthlessness** noun

rye noun
rye is a cereal used to make bread and biscuits

Ss

sabbath noun **sabbaths**
the sabbath is the weekly day for rest and prayer, Saturday for Jews, Sunday for Christians

sabotage (say **sab**-o-tahzh) noun
sabotage is deliberately damaging machinery or equipment
sabotage verb **sabotages, sabotaging, sabotaged**
to sabotage machinery or equipment is to damage it deliberately

sac noun **sacs**
any bag-like part of an animal or plant

saccharin (say **sak**-a-rin) noun
saccharin is a very sweet substance used as a substitute for sugar

sachet (say **sash**-ay) noun **sachets**
a small sealed packet of something such as shampoo or sugar

sack[1] noun **sacks**
a large bag made of strong material **to get the sack** (informal) is to be dismissed from your job
sack verb **sacks, sacking, sacked** (informal)
to sack someone is to dismiss them from their job

sack[2] verb **sacks, sacking, sacked**
to sack a place is to plunder and destroy it in war

sacred adjective
to do with God or a god; holy

sacrifice noun **sacrifices**
1 giving up a thing that you value so that something good may happen *If you want to*

a
b
c
d
e
f
g
h
i
j
k
l
m
n
o
p
q
r
s
t
u
v
w
x
y
z

save some money you might have to make a few sacrifices. **2** killing an animal or person as an offering to a god **sacrificial** adjective offered as a sacrifice

sacrifice verb sacrifices, sacrificing, sacrificed
1 to sacrifice something is to give it up so that something good may happen **2** to sacrifice an animal or person is to kill them as an offering to a god

sad adjective sadder, saddest
unhappy; showing sorrow or causing it **sadly** adverb **sadness** noun

sadden verb saddens, saddening, saddened
something saddens you when it makes you sad or unhappy

saddle noun saddles
1 a seat that you put on the back of a horse or other animal so that you can ride it **2** the seat of a bicycle

saddle verb saddles, saddling, saddled
to saddle an animal is to put a saddle on its back **to be saddled with something** is to have it as a burden or problem

safari (say sa-**far**-i) noun safaris
an expedition to see wild animals or hunt them

safari park noun safari parks
a large park where wild animals can roam around freely and visitors can watch them from their cars

safe adjective safer, safest
1 free from danger; protected **2** not causing danger *Drive at a safe speed.*

safe noun safes
a strong cupboard or box in which valuable things can be locked away safely

safeguard noun safeguards
something that protects you against danger

safeguard verb safeguard, safeguards, safeguarded
to safeguard something is to protect it from danger

safely adverb
to do something safely is to do it without risk or danger *The plane landed safely.*

safety noun
safety is being safe; protection *We listened to a talk on road safety.*

safety belt noun safety belts
a belt to hold someone securely in a seat

safety pin noun safety pins
a curved pin made with a clip that closes to cover the point

sag verb sags, sagging, sagged
something sags when it sinks slightly in the middle because something heavy is pressing on it

saga noun sagas
a long story with many adventures

said
past tense and past participle of say verb *'Look out,' said Jamie. I didn't hear what she had said.*

sail noun sails
1 a large piece of strong cloth attached to a mast to make a boat move **2** a short voyage *We went for a sail around the island.* **3** an arm of a windmill **to set sail** is to start on a voyage in a ship

sail verb sails, sailing, sailed
1 to sail somewhere is to travel there in a ship **2** a ship or boat sails when it starts out on a voyage *What time does the ferry sail?* **3** to sail a ship or boat is to control it

sailor noun sailors
1 a member of a ship's crew **2** someone who sails

saint noun saints
a holy or very good person **saintly** adjective

sake noun
for the sake of something in order to do it or get it *He'll do anything for the sake of money.* **for someone's sake** in order to help them or please them *She went to great trouble for his sake.*

salaam interjection
a word used by Muslims to greet someone

salad noun salads
a mixture of vegetables eaten cold and often raw

salami noun salamis
salami is a kind of strong spicy sausage

salary noun salaries
a regular wage, usually paid every month

sale noun sales
1 the selling of something 2 a time when a shop sells things at reduced prices **for sale** or **on sale** able to be bought

salesperson or **salesman** or **saleswoman** noun
salespeople, salesmen, saleswomen
someone whose job is to sell things

saline adjective
containing salt

saliva (say sa-**ly**-va) noun
saliva is the natural liquid in your mouth

sally verb sallies, sallying, sallied
to sally forth or **sally out** is to rush forward or rush ahead

salmon noun salmon
a large fish with pink flesh, used for food

salon noun salons
a room or shop where a hairdresser or a beauty specialist works

saloon noun saloons
1 a motor car with a hard roof 2 a bar in a public house

salt noun
salt is the white substance that gives sea water its taste and is used for flavouring food **salty** adjective

salt verb salts, salting, salted
to salt food is to use salt to flavour or preserve it

salute verb salutes, saluting, saluted
to salute is to raise your hand to your forehead as a sign of respect or greeting

salute noun salutes
1 the act of saluting 2 when guns are fired as a sign of respect on an official occasion

salvage verb salvages, salvaging, salvaged
to salvage something such as a damaged ship is to save or rescue it or parts of it *Jan's treasure box was one of the few things which they had salvaged from the wrecked canoes.* – Ian Serraillier, *The Silver Sword*

salvation noun
salvation is saving someone or something

same adjective
not different; exactly equal or alike *We are the same age. Look, these two leaves are exactly the same.*

sample noun samples
a small amount that shows what something is like

sample verb samples, sampling, sampled
1 to sample something is to take a sample of it *Scientists sampled the lake water.* 2 to sample something is also to try part of it *She sampled the cake.*

sanctuary noun sanctuaries
1 a safe place, especially for someone who is being chased or attacked 2 a place where wildlife is protected *We visited a bird sanctuary.*

sand noun
sand is the tiny grains of rock that you find on beaches and in deserts

sand verb sands, sanding, sanded
to sand a surface is to smooth or polish it with sandpaper or rough material

sandal noun sandals
a lightweight shoe with straps that go round your foot

sandbag noun sandbags
sandbags are bags filled with sand, used to build defences against flood water or bullets

a
b
c
d
e
f
g
h
i
j
k
l
m
n
o
p
q
r
s
t
u
v
w
x
y
z

sandpaper noun
sandpaper is strong paper coated with hard grains, rubbed on rough surfaces to make them smooth

sands plural noun
a beach or sandy area

sandstone noun
sandstone is rock made of compressed sand

sandwich noun sandwiches
slices of bread with meat, cheese, or some other filling between them

sandy adjective sandier, sandiest
1 made of sand; covered with sand 2 sandy hair is yellow-red

sane adjective saner, sanest
having a healthy mind; not mad

sang
past tense of sing We sang all our favourite songs.

sanitary adjective
free from germs and dirt; hygienic

sanitation noun
sanitation is arrangements for drainage and the disposal of sewage

sanity noun
sanity is being sane

sank
past tense of sink verb My heart sank when I heard the news.

sap noun
sap is the juice inside a tree or plant

sap verb saps, sapping, sapped
to sap someone's strength or energy is to use it up or weaken it gradually The heat had sapped all my energy.

sapling noun saplings
a young tree

sapphire noun sapphires
a bright blue jewel

sarcastic noun
you are being sarcastic when you mock someone or something by saying the opposite of what you mean She said she liked the music I was playing but I think she was being sarcastic. **sarcasm** noun **sarcastically** adverb

sardine noun sardines
a small sea fish, usually sold packed tightly in tins

sari (say **sar**-i) noun saris
a long length of cloth worn as a dress, especially by Indian women and girls

sash noun sashes
a strip of cloth worn round the waist or over one shoulder

sat
past tense and past participle of sit
We sat at our desks. Jack had sat at the back of the class.

satchel noun satchels
a bag you wear over your shoulder or on your back, especially for carrying books to and from school

satellite noun satellites
1 a spacecraft sent into space to move in an orbit round a planet, in order to get and send information 2 a moon that moves in orbit round a planet
Please see illustration on following page.

satellite dish noun satellite dishes
a dish-shaped aerial for receiving television signals sent by satellite

satellite television noun
satellite television is television programmes that are broadcast using a satellite

satin noun
satin is a silky material that is shiny on one side

satisfaction noun
1 satisfaction is the feeling of being satisfied 2 satisfaction is also giving someone what they need or want

satisfactory adjective
good enough; acceptable
satisfactorily adverb

A B C D E F G H I J K L M N O P Q R **S** T U V W X Y Z

satellite

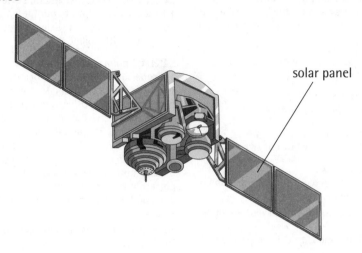

solar panel

satisfy verb satisfies, satisfying, satisfied
1 to satisfy someone is to give them what they need or want **2** to be satisfied is to be sure of something *I am satisfied that you have done your best.*

saturate verb saturates, saturating, saturated
1 to be saturated is to be soaking wet *My clothes are saturated with rain.* **2** to saturate a place is to make it take in as much as possible or too much of something *The town is saturated with tourists in the summer.*
saturation noun

Saturday noun Saturdays
the seventh day of the week

sauce noun sauces
a sauce is a thick liquid served with food to add flavour

saucepan noun saucepans
a metal cooking pan with a long handle

saucer noun saucers
a small curved plate for a cup to stand on

saucy adjective saucier, sauciest
rude or cheeky

sauna (say **saw**-na or **sow**-na) noun saunas
a room filled with steam where people sit and sweat a lot, used as a kind of bath

saunter verb saunters, sauntering, sauntered
to walk about in a leisurely way

sausage noun sausages
a tube of edible skin or plastic stuffed with minced meat and other ingredients

sausage roll noun sausage rolls
a small short roll of pastry filled with meat

savage adjective
wild and fierce; cruel **savagely** adverb

savage verb savages, savaging, savaged
an animal savages someone when it attacks them and bites or scratches them fiercely

savannah (say sa-**van**-a) noun savannahs
a grassy plain in a hot country, with few trees

save verb saves, saving, saved
1 to save someone or something is to free them from danger or harm **2** to save something, especially money, is to keep it so that it can be used later **3** to save computer

a
b
c
d
e
f
g
h
i
j
k
l
m
n
o
p
q
r
s
t
u
v
w
x
y
z

data is to instruct the computer to keep it on its hard disk **4** in football, to save a ball is to stop it going into your goal **saver** noun

savings plural noun
your savings are the money that you have saved

saviour noun **saviours**
a person who saves someone

savoury adjective
savoury food is tasty but not sweet

saw¹ noun **saws**
a tool with sharp teeth for cutting wood or other hard materials

saw verb **saws, sawing, sawed, sawn** or **sawed**
to saw something is to cut it with a saw

saw²
past tense of **see**

sawdust noun
sawdust is powder that comes from wood when it is cut with a saw

saxophone noun **saxophones**
a wind instrument with a tube that curves upward and a reed in the mouthpiece

say verb **says, saying, said**
to say something is to make words with your voice

say noun
to have a say or **have your say** is to be able to speak or give your opinion

saying noun **sayings**
a well-known phrase or proverb

scab noun **scabs**
a hard crust that forms over a cut or graze while it is healing

scabbard noun **scabbards**
a cover for a sword or dagger

scaffold noun **scaffolds**
a platform on which criminals are executed

scaffolding noun
scaffolding is a structure of poles and planks for workers to stand on when building or repairing a house

scald verb **scalds, scalding, scalded**
1 to scald your skin is to burn it with very hot liquid or steam **2** to scald something is to clean it with boiling water

scale¹ noun **scales**
1 a series of units or marks for measuring something *This ruler has one scale in centimetres and another in inches.* **2** the relationship between the size of something on a map or model and the actual size of the thing in the real world *The scale of this map is one inch to the mile.* **3** a series of musical notes going up or down in a fixed pattern **4** the relative size or importance of something *He painted pictures on a huge scale.*

scale verb **scales, scaling, scaled**
to scale something is to climb up it

scale² noun **scales**
1 a scale is one of the thin overlapping parts on the outside of fish, snakes, and other animals **2** scale is the coating that forms on the inside of kettles and pans

scales plural noun
a device for weighing things

scalp noun **scalps**
the skin on the top of your head

scalp verb **scalps, scalping, scalped**
to scalp someone is to cut off their scalp

scaly adjective
scaly skin is covered in scales

scamper verb **scampers, scampering, scampered**
to run quickly with short steps *A harvest mouse goes scampering by, / With silver claws and silver eye.* — Walter de la Mare, *Silver*

scampi plural noun
scampi are large prawns

scan verb **scans, scanning, scanned**
1 to scan something is to look at every part of it **2** to scan a piece of writing is to look over it quickly **3** to scan an area, or a part of the body, is to sweep a radar or electronic beam over it in order to find

something **4** poetry scans when it has a fixed rhythm

scan noun scans
a search or examination using a scanner

scandal noun scandals
1 a scandal is a shameful or disgraceful action **2** scandal is gossip that damages someone's reputation **scandalous** adjective

Scandinavian adjective
to do with Scandinavia (Norway, Sweden, and Denmark, and sometimes Finland and Iceland)

scanner noun scanners
1 a machine used to examine part of the body, using an electronic beam **2** a machine that converts print and pictures into data that can be read by a computer

scanty adjective scantier, scantiest
hardly big enough; small

scapegoat noun scapegoats
someone who gets all the blame for something that other people have done

scar noun scars
a mark left on your skin by a cut or burn after it has healed

scar verb scars, scarring, scarred
an injury scars you when it leaves a permanent mark on your skin

scarce adjective scarcer, scarcest
not enough to supply people *Wheat was scarce because of the bad harvest.* **to make yourself scarce** (informal) is to go away or keep out of the way

scarcely adverb
hardly; only just *She could scarcely walk. So it was that I found myself at scarcely twelve years of age wandering the world alone and quite destitute.* — Michael Morpurgo, *The Last Wolf*

scarcity noun
there is a scarcity of something when there is not enough of it

scare verb scares, scaring, scared
to scare someone is to frighten them

scare noun scares
a scare is a fright *You gave me quite a scare.*

scarecrow noun scarecrows
a figure of a person dressed in old clothes, that farmers put in a field to frighten birds away from crops

scarf noun scarves
a strip of material that you wear round your neck or head

scarlet adjective
bright red

scary adjective scarier, scariest (informal)
frightening

scatter verb scatters, scattering, scattered
1 to scatter things is to throw them in all directions **2** to scatter is to move quickly in all directions *The crowd scattered when the police arrived.*

scavenge verb scavenges, scavenging, scavenged
an animal or bird scavenges when it eats dead animals that have been killed by another animal **scavenger** noun

scene noun scenes
1 the place where something happens *Here is the scene of the crime.* **2** a part of a play or film **3** a view someone sees **4** an angry or noisy outburst *They made a scene about the money.*

scenery noun
1 scenery is the natural features of an area *We were admiring the scenery.* **2** scenery is also things put on a stage to make it look like a place

scent (say sent) noun scents
1 a pleasant smell or perfume **2** an animal's smell, that other animals can follow **scented** adjective

scent verb scents, scenting, scented
to scent something is to discover it by its scent

A
B
C
D
E
F
G
H
I
J
K
L
M
N
O
P
Q
R
S
T
U
V
W
X
Y
Z

sceptic (say **skep**-tik) noun **sceptics**
someone who does not believe things easily or readily

sceptical (say **skep**-tik-al) adjective
you are sceptical when you do not believe things easily or readily

schedule (say **shed**-yool) noun
schedules
a timetable of things that have to be done
to be on schedule is to be on time; not late

scheme noun **schemes**
a plan of what to do

scheme verb **schemes, scheming, schemed**
to scheme is to make secret plans

scholar noun **scholars**
1 someone who studies a subject thoroughly **2** someone who has been given a scholarship

scholarly adjective
showing knowledge and learning

scholarship noun **scholarships**
1 a scholarship is a grant of money given to someone for their education **2** scholarship is knowledge and learning

school[1] noun **schools**
1 a place where children go to be taught **2** the children who go there *The whole school had a holiday.*

school[2] noun **schools**
a group of whales or fish

schoolchild noun **schoolchildren**
a child who goes to school

schoolteacher noun
schoolteachers
a teacher at a school

schooner (say **skoo**-ner) noun
schooners
a sailing ship with two or more masts

science noun
science is the study of objects and happenings in the world that can be observed and tested

science fiction noun
science fiction is stories about imaginary worlds, especially in space and in the future

scientific adjective
1 to do with science **2** studying things carefully and logically

scientist noun **scientists**
someone who studies science or is an expert in science

scissors plural noun
a cutting device made of two movable blades joined together

TOP TIPS
There is a tricky bit in **scissors**—it begins with **sc.**

scoff verb **scoffs, scoffing, scoffed**
to scoff at someone or something is to make fun of them

scold verb **scolds, scolding, scolded**
to scold someone is to tell them off harshly

scone (say skon or skohn) noun **scones**
a small plain cake, usually eaten with butter and jam

scoop noun **scoops**
1 a deep spoon for serving soft food such as ice cream or mashed potato **2** a deep shovel **3** (informal) an important piece of news that only one newspaper prints

scoop verb **scoops, scooping, scooped**
to scoop something, or to scoop it out, is to take it out with a scoop or the palm of your hand

scooter noun **scooters**
1 a kind of motor cycle with small wheels **2** a simple type of bicycle for a child, with two wheels and a narrow platform. You stand on the platform and push on the ground with one foot

scope noun
1 opportunity or possibility for something *There is scope for improvement.* **2** the range or extent of something *Chemistry is outside the scope of the syllabus for this year.*

scorch verb scorches, scorching, scorched
to scorch something is to make it go brown by slightly burning it

scorching adjective
very hot

score noun scores
1 the number of points or goals made in a game *What's the score?* 2 (old use) a score is twenty *He reached the age of four-score (= 80) years.*

score verb scores, scoring, scored
1 to score a goal or point in a game is to get it 2 to score is to keep a count of the score in a game *I thought you were scoring.* 3 to score a surface is to scratch it **scorer** noun

scorn noun
scorn is treating a person or thing with contempt

scorn verb scorns, scorning, scorned
to scorn someone or something is to have contempt for them

scornful adjective
to be scornful is to be full of contempt and show no respect **scornfully** adverb

scorpion noun scorpions
an animal related to the spider, with pincers and a poisonous sting in its curved tail

Scot noun Scots
a person from Scotland

Scotch adjective
Scottish

Scottish adjective
to do with Scotland

scoundrel noun scoundrels
a wicked or dishonest person

scour verb scours, scouring, scoured
1 to scour (for example) a pan or bath is to rub it hard with something rough until it is clean and bright 2 to scour an area is to search it thoroughly

Scout noun Scouts
a member of the Scout Association, an organization for boys

scout noun scouts
someone sent out ahead of a group in order to collect information

scowl verb scowls, scowling, scowled
to scowl is to look bad-tempered

scowl noun scowls
an angry look

scramble verb scrambles, scrambling, scrambled
1 to scramble is to move quickly and clumsily *The women and children scrambled down the hill to get a good view of the standing stones. – Clive King, Stig of the Dump* 2 to scramble eggs is to cook them by mixing them and heating them in a pan 3 to scramble for something is to struggle to do it or get it

scramble noun scrambles
1 a climb or walk over rough ground 2 a struggle to get something *There was a scramble for the best seats.* 3 a motorcycle race across rough country

scrap[1] noun scraps
1 a scrap is a small piece of something 2 scrap is rubbish, especially unwanted metal

scrap verb scraps, scrapping, scrapped
to scrap something is to get rid of it when you do not want it

scrap[2] noun scraps (informal)
a fight

scrap verb scraps, scrapping, scrapped
to scrap is to fight or quarrel

scrape verb scrapes, scraping, scraped
1 to scrape something is to rub it with something rough, hard, or sharp 2 to scrape past or through is to only just get past or succeed *She scraped through her exams.* 3 to scrape something together is to collect it with difficulty *They scraped together enough money for a holiday.*

scrape noun scrapes
1 a scraping movement or sound 2 a mark made by scraping something 3 (informal) an awkward situation *He's always getting into scrapes.*

a
b
c
d
e
f
g
h
i
j
k
l
m
n
o
p
q
r
s
t
u
v
w
x
y
z

A

scrappy adjective **scrappier, scrappiest**
done carelessly or untidily

B

scratch verb **scratches, scratching, scratched**
1 to scratch a surface is to damage it by rubbing something sharp over it 2 you scratch your skin when you rub it with your fingers because it itches

C

D

E

scratch noun **scratches**
1 a mark or cut made by scratching 2 the action of scratching *I need to have a scratch.* **to start from scratch** is to begin at the very beginning **to be up to scratch** is to be up to the proper standard

F

G

H

scrawl noun **scrawls**
untidy writing *Can you read my scrawl?*

I

scrawl verb **scrawls, scrawling, scrawled**
to scrawl something is to write it in a hurried or careless way

J

K

L

scream noun **screams**
1 a loud high-pitched cry of pain or fear or anger 2 (informal) you can say something is a scream when it is very amusing

M

N

scream verb **screams, screaming, screamed**
to scream is to make a loud high-pitched cry

O

P

screech noun **screeches**
a harsh high-pitched sound *There was a screech of tyres as the car sped off.*

Q

screech verb **screeches, screeching, screeched**
to screech is to make a harsh high-pitched sound *Baby Thomas screeched. His eyes crossed in horror. Baths were his worst nightmare.* – Catherine MacPhail, *Granny Nothing*

R

S

T

U

screen noun **screens**
1 a surface on which films or television programmes or computer data are shown 2 a movable panel used to hide or protect something 3 a windscreen

V

W

X

screen verb **screens, screening, screened**
1 to screen a film or television programme is to show it 2 to screen something is to

Y

Z

hide it or protect it with a screen 3 to screen people is to test them to find out if they have a disease

screw noun **screws**
1 a metal pin with a spiral ridge round it, which holds things by being twisted into them 2 a propeller

screw verb **screws, screwing, screwed**
1 to screw something is to fix it with screws 2 to screw something in or on is to fit it by turning it *Screw the lid on to the jar. I screwed in the light-bulb.* **to screw something up** is to twist or squeeze it into a tight ball

screwdriver noun **screwdrivers**
a tool for putting in or taking out screws

scribble verb **scribbles, scribbling, scribbled**
to write untidily or carelessly, or to make meaningless marks

script noun **scripts**
1 the words of a play, film, or broadcast 2 handwriting 3 something you write, especially the answers you write to exam questions

scripture noun **scriptures**
a sacred book, especially the Bible

scroll noun **scrolls**
a roll of paper or parchment with writing on it

scroll verb **scrolls, scrolling, scrolled**
you scroll up or down on a computer screen when you move the text up or down on the screen to see what comes before or after

scrounge verb **scrounges, scrounging, scrounged** (informal)
to scrounge something is to get it without paying for it *He scrounged a meal from us.* **scrounger** noun

scrub¹ verb **scrubs, scrubbing, scrubbed**
to scrub something is to rub it with a hard brush

scrub noun
the action of scrubbing *You'll need to give your face a good scrub.*

scrub² noun
scrub is low trees and bushes, or land covered with them

scruffy adjective **scruffier, scruffiest**
shabby and untidy

scrum or **scrummage** noun
scrums or **scrummages** (in rugby football) a group of players from each side who push against each other and try to win the ball with their feet

scrumptious adjective
delicious

scrutinize verb **scrutinizes, scrutinizing, scrutinized**
to scrutinize something is to examine it or look at it closely

scrutiny noun
scrutiny is examining or looking at something closely

scuba diving noun
scuba diving is swimming underwater, breathing air from a supply carried on your back

scuffle noun **scuffles**
a confused struggle or fight
scuffle verb **scuffles, scuffling, scuffled**
people scuffle when they fight in a confused way

sculptor noun **sculptors**
someone who makes sculptures

sculpture noun **sculptures**
1 a sculpture is something carved or shaped out of a hard material such as stone, clay, or metal 2 sculpture is the art or work of a sculptor

scum noun
scum is froth or dirt on the top of a liquid

scurry verb **scurries, scurrying, scurried**
to scurry is to run or hurry with short steps *Then a snout appeared, the tip of a tail, and within moments a complete and perfect tiny crocodile had scurried out on to the sand.*

— Alexander McCall Smith, *Akimbo and the Crocodile Man*

scurvy noun
scurvy is a disease caused by lack of fresh fruit and vegetables

scuttle¹ noun **scuttles**
a container for coal, kept by a fireplace

scuttle² verb **scuttles, scuttling, scuttled**
to scuttle a ship is to sink it deliberately by making holes in the side or bottom

scuttle³ verb **scuttles, scuttling, scuttled**
to run with short quick steps *'Oh! Oh! Oh!' said Mrs Crabbity, and she turned and scuttled into her cottage like a small frightened spider.* — Vivian French, *Under the Moon*

scythe (say syth) noun **scythes**
a tool with a long curved blade for cutting grass or corn

sea noun **seas**
1 the salt water that covers most of the earth's surface 2 a large lake or area of water, such as the Mediterranean Sea 3 a large area of something *Across the table we saw a sea of faces.* **at sea 1** on the sea 2 unable to understand something or cope with it *He's completely at sea in his new job.*

seabed noun
the seabed is the bottom of the sea

seafaring adjective, noun
travelling or working on the sea
seafarer noun

seafood noun
seafood is fish or shellfish from the sea eaten as food

seagull noun **seagulls**
a sea bird with long wings

seahorse noun **seahorses**
a small fish that swims upright, with a head rather like a horse's head

seal¹ noun **seals**
a furry sea animal that breeds on land

a b c d e f g h i j k l m n o p q r **s** t u v w x y z

seal² noun seals
1 something designed to close an opening and stop air or liquid getting in or out 2 a design pressed into a soft substance such as wax or lead

seal verb seals, sealing, sealed
to seal something is to close it by sticking two parts together *He sealed the envelope.*

sea level noun
sea level is the level of the sea halfway between high and low tide *The mountain rises 1,000 metres above sea level.*

sea lion noun sea lions
a large kind of seal. The male has a kind of mane

seam noun seams
1 the line where two edges of cloth join together 2 a layer of coal in the ground

seaman noun seamen
a sailor

seaplane noun seaplanes
an aeroplane that can land on water and take off from water

seaport noun seaports
a port on the coast

search verb searches, searching, searched
1 to search for something or someone is to look very carefully for them 2 to search a person or place is to look very carefully for something they may have

search noun searches
1 a very careful look for someone or something 2 when you look for information in a computer database or on the Internet *Let's do a search for 'Roald Dahl'.*

search engine noun search engines
a computer program that helps you find information on the Internet

searching adjective
a searching question or look is a thorough one that is trying to find out the truth about something

searchlight noun searchlights
a light with a strong beam that can be turned in any direction

search party noun search parties
a group of people organized to look for someone or something

seashore noun
the seashore is the land close to the sea

seasick adjective
someone is seasick when they are sick because of the movement of a ship
seasickness noun

seaside noun
the seaside is a place by the sea where people go on holiday

season noun seasons
1 one of the four main parts of the year: spring, summer, autumn, and winter
2 the time of year when a sport or other activity happens *When does the football season start?*

season verb seasons, seasoning, seasoned
to season food is to put salt, pepper, or other strong-tasting things on it to flavour it

seasonal adjective
happening only at certain times of the year *Fruit-picking is seasonal work.*

seasoning noun seasonings
seasoning is something strong-tasting like salt and pepper, used to season food

season ticket noun season tickets
a ticket that you can use as often as you like for a certain period

seat noun seats
1 a piece of furniture for sitting on
2 a place in parliament or on a council or a board of a business 3 the place where something is located *London is the seat of government.*

seat verb seats, seating, seated
a place seats a certain number of people when it has that many seats for them *The theatre seats 3,000.*

A B C D E F G H I J K L M N O P Q R **S** T U V W X Y Z

seat belt noun **seat belts**
a strap to hold a person securely in the seat of a vehicle or aircraft

seaward or **seawards** adverb
towards the sea

seaweed noun **seaweeds**
seaweed is plants that grow in the sea

secateurs (say **sek**-a-terz) plural noun
clippers used for pruning plants

secluded adjective
a secluded place is away from large numbers of people; quiet and hidden *They found a secluded beach for their picnic.*

seclusion noun
seclusion is being private or hidden *She lived in seclusion in the countryside.*

second adjective, noun
the next after the first **to have second thoughts** is to wonder whether your decision was really right

second noun **seconds**
1 a very short period of time, one-sixtieth of a minute **2** a person or thing that is second **3** seconds are products that are not of the best quality

second verb **seconds, seconding, seconded**
1 to second a proposal or motion is to support it formally **2** to second a fighter is be the person who helps and supports them in a fight

secondary adjective
coming second; not original or essential *This is of secondary importance.*

secondary school noun **secondary schools**
a school for children who are about 11 years old and older

second-hand adjective, adverb
1 bought or used after someone else has used it *I can only afford a second-hand car.* **2** that sells used goods *She runs a second-hand shop.*

secondly adverb
as the second thing *Secondly, I'd like to thank my parents.*

secrecy noun
secrecy is being secret

secret adjective
1 that must not be told or shown to other people **2** that is not known by everyone

secret noun **secrets**
something that is secret **to do something in secret** is to do it secretly

secretary (say **sek**-re-tri) noun **secretaries**
1 someone whose job is to type letters, keep files, answer the telephone, and make business arrangements for a person or organization **2** the chief assistant of a government minister

secrete (say si-**kreet**) verb **secretes, secreting, secreted**
1 to secrete something is to hide it carefully **2** to secrete a substance in the body is to release it *Saliva is secreted in the mouth.*

secretive (say **seek**-rit-iv) adjective
liking or trying to keep things secret **secretively** adverb **secretiveness** noun

secretly adverb
you secretly do something when you do it without telling other people *Jilly had always secretly thought how marvellous it would be to have a dragon as a pet.* – Helen Cresswell, *Dragon Ride*

secret service noun
a country's secret service is the government department in charge of spies and espionage

sect noun **sects**
a group of people who have special or unusual religious opinions or beliefs

section noun **sections**
a part of something *Our school library has a large history section. The tail section of the plane broke off.*

sector noun **sectors**
1 a part of an area or activity **2** a part of a

a
b
c
d
e
f
g
h
i
j
k
l
m
n
o
p
q
r
s
t
u
v
w
x
y
z

A
B
C
D
E
F
G
H
I
J
K
L
M
N
O
P
Q
R

S

T
U
V
W
X
Y
Z

circle made by drawing two straight lines from the centre to the circumference

secure adjective
1 firm and safe *Is that ladder secure?* 2 not likely to be lost *I need a secure job.* 3 made safe or protected from attack *Check that all the doors and windows are secure.*
securely adverb

secure verb secures, securing, secured
1 to secure something is to make it safe or firmly fixed 2 to secure something is also to get hold of it *She secured two tickets for the show.*

security noun
1 security is being secure or safe 2 security is also measures taken to prevent theft, spying, or terrorism

sedate (say si-**dayt**) adjective
calm and dignified **sedately** adverb

sediment noun
sediment is solid matter that settles at the bottom of a liquid

sedimentary (say sed-i-**ment**-er-i) adjective
sedimentary rock is formed from layers of sand, stones, or mud that have settled on the bottom of a lake or river

see verb sees, seeing, saw, seen
1 to see something or someone is to use your eyes to notice them or be aware of them 2 to see someone is to meet or visit them *See me after class.* 3 to see something is to understand it *I see what you mean.* 4 to see someone as something is to imagine them being it *Can you see yourself as a teacher?* 5 to see that something happens is to make sure of it *See that the windows are shut.* 6 to see someone somewhere is to escort or lead them *I'll see you to the door.*
to see through something or **someone** is not to be deceived by them **to see to something** is to deal with it

seed noun seeds
a tiny part of a plant that can grow in the ground to make a new plant

seedling noun seedlings
a very young plant

seek verb seeks, seeking, sought
1 to seek a person or thing is to try to find them 2 to seek something is to try to achieve it *She is seeking fame.*

seem verb seems, seeming, seemed
to seem to be something or to have some quality is to appear that way or give that impression *They seem happy in their new house.*

seemingly adverb
you can say that (for example) a road is seemingly endless or a question is seemingly stupid when it appears that way but in fact might not be *It was a single arch of grey stone, and lying flat upon the bridge was a scarlet alligator, seemingly fast asleep.*
— L. Frank Baum, *The Emerald City of Oz*

seen
past participle of see *I have seen him before.*

seep verb seeps, seeping, seeped
a liquid or gas seeps when it flows slowly through or into or out of something *Water was seeping into the cellar.*

see-saw noun see-saws
a plank balanced in the middle so that people can sit at each end and make it go up and down

seethe verb seethes, seething, seethed
1 a liquid seethes when it boils or bubbles 2 you are seething when you are very angry or excited

segment noun segments
a part that is cut off or can be separated from the rest of something *He ate a few segments of an orange.*

segregate (say **seg**-ri-gayt) verb segregates, segregating, segregated
to segregate people of different races or religions is to keep them apart and make them live separately **segregation** noun

seize (say seez) verb seizes, seizing, seized
to seize someone or something is to take

hold of them suddenly or firmly **to seize up** is to become jammed or stuck

seizure noun seizures
a seizure is a sudden attack of an illness

seldom adverb
not often *I seldom cry.*

select verb selects, selecting, selected
to select a person or thing is to choose them carefully

select adjective
small and carefully chosen *They have a select group of friends.*

self noun selves
the type of person you are; your individual nature *You'll soon be feeling your old self again.*

self-centred adjective
selfish; thinking about yourself too much

self-confident adjective
confident in what you can do
self-confidence noun

self-conscious adjective
embarrassed or shy because you know people are watching you

self-contained adjective
having everything you need in one place *a self-contained flat*

self-control noun
self-control is the ability to control your own behaviour or feelings

self-defence noun
1 you act in self-defence when you do something defending yourself against attack **2** self-defence is also skill in defending yourself if someone attacks you

self-evident adjective
clear or obvious and not needing proof

self-important adjective
pompous or haughty

selfish adjective
having or doing what you want without thinking of other people **selfishly** adverb
selfishness noun

selfless adjective
thinking of other people rather than yourself; not selfish

self-raising flour noun
self-raising flour is flour that makes cakes and pastry rise during cooking

self-respect noun
self-respect is the feeling that you are behaving and thinking in the proper way

self-righteous adjective
if you are self-righteous, you are smug because you are sure that you are a good person

self-service adjective
a self-service shop or restaurant is one where customers serve themselves with goods and pay a cashier for what they have taken

self-sufficient adjective
able to provide what you need without help from others

sell verb sells, selling, sold
to sell goods or services is to offer them in exchange for money **to sell out** is to sell all your stock of something

semaphore noun
semaphore is a system of signalling by holding flags out with your arms in positions to indicate letters or numbers
Please see illustration on following page.

semi- prefix
meaning 'half', as in *semicircle*

semibreve (say **sem**-i-breev) noun
semibreves
the longest musical note normally used, written o

semicircle noun semicircles
half a circle **semicircular** adjective

semicolon noun semicolons
a punctuation mark (;), marking a more definite break in a sentence than a comma does

a
b
c
d
e
f
g
h
i
j
k
l
m
n
o
p
q
r
s
t
u
v
w
x
y
z

A
B
C
D
E
F
G
H
I
J
K
L
M
N
O
P
Q
R
S
T
U
V
W
X
Y
Z

semaphore

A

B

C

D

E

F

semi-detached adjective
a semi-detached house is one that is joined to another house on one side

semi-final noun semi-finals
a match played to decide who will take part in the final **semi-finalist** noun

semitone noun semitones
half a tone in music

semolina noun
semolina is a milk pudding made with grains of wheat

senate (say **sen**-at) noun
1 the governing council in ancient Rome
2 the higher-ranking section of the parliament in France, the USA, and some other countries

senator noun senators
a member of a senate

send verb sends, sending, sent
1 to send something somewhere is to arrange for it to be taken there 2 to send someone somewhere is to tell them to go there **to send someone up** (informal) is to make fun of them

senior adjective
1 older than someone else 2 higher in rank *He is a senior officer in the navy.*
senior noun seniors
someone is your senior when they are older or higher in rank than you are

senior citizen noun senior citizens
an elderly person, especially a pensioner

sensation noun sensations
1 a feeling *We had a sensation of warmth.* 2 a very exciting event or the excitement caused by it *The news caused a great sensation.*

sensational adjective
causing great excitement or shock

sense noun senses
1 the ability to see, hear, smell, touch, or taste things 2 the ability to feel or appreciate something *She has a good sense of humour.* 3 the power to think or make

good judgements *He hasn't got the sense to come in out of the rain.* **4** meaning *The word 'set' has many senses.* **to make sense** is to have a meaning you can understand

sense verb **senses, sensing, sensed**
1 to sense something is to feel it or be aware of it *I sensed that she did not like me.*
2 to sense something is also to detect it *This device senses radioactivity.*

senseless adjective
1 stupid; not sensible **2** unconscious

sensible adjective
wise; having or showing common sense
sensibly adverb

sensitive adjective
1 affected by the sun or chemicals or something else physical *I have sensitive skin.* **2** easily offended or upset *She is very sensitive about her age.* **3** aware of other people's feelings **sensitively** adverb

sensitivity noun **sensitivities**
1 sensitivity is being sensitive **2** a sensitivity is something you are sensitive about

sensor noun **sensors**
a device or instrument for detecting something physical such as heat or light

sent
past tense and past participle of **send** *I sent the letter yesterday. I would have sent you home if I'd known you were ill.*

sentence noun **sentences**
1 a group of words that express a complete thought and form a statement or question or command **2** the punishment given to a convicted person in a law court
sentence verb **sentences, sentencing, sentenced**
to sentence someone is to give them a sentence in a law court *They were sentenced to two years in prison.*

sentiment noun **sentiments**
1 a sentiment is a feeling or opinion
2 sentiment is a show of feeling or emotion

sentimental adjective
showing or making you feel emotion,

especially too much sad emotion
That love story is too sentimental.
sentimentality noun **sentimentally** adverb

sentinel noun **sentinels**
a sentry *The six black queens stood like silent sentinels on the rocks watching us go.*
– Michael Morpurgo, *The Sleeping Sword*

sentry noun **sentries**
a soldier guarding something

separable adjective
able to be separated from each other

separate (say **sep**-er-at) adjective
1 not joined to anything; on its own **2** not together; not with other people *They lead separate lives.*
separate (say **sep**-er-ayt) verb
separates, separating, separated
1 to separate things or people is to take them away from others **2** to separate is to become separate or move away from each other **3** two people separate when they stop living together as a couple

TOP TIPS There is a tricky bit in **separate** –there is an **a** in the middle.

separately adverb
people do something separately when they do it on their own, not together *They arrived together but left separately.*

separation noun
separation is when people or things move apart or are taken away from each other

September noun
the ninth month of the year

septic adjective
a wound goes septic when it becomes infected with harmful bacteria

sequel (say **see**-kwel) noun **sequels**
1 a book or film that continues the story of an earlier one **2** something that results from an earlier event

sequence (say **see**-kwenss) noun **sequences**
1 a series of things **2** the order in which things should follow each other *Arrange*

these playing cards in sequence, the highest first.

sequin (say **see**-kwin) noun **sequins**
sequins are tiny bright discs sewn on clothes to decorate them

serene adjective
calm and peaceful **serenely** adverb **serenity** noun

sergeant (say **sar**-jent) noun **sergeants**
a soldier or police officer who is in charge of others

sergeant major noun **sergeant majors**
a soldier who is one rank higher than a sergeant

serial noun **serials**
a story that is presented in separate parts over a period, for example week by week

series noun **series**
1 a number of things following each other or connected with each other 2 a set of television or radio programmes with the same title

serious adjective
1 not funny; important *We need a serious talk.* 2 thoughtful or solemn *His face was serious.* 3 very bad *They've had a serious accident.* **seriously** adverb **seriousness** noun

sermon noun **sermons**
a talk given by a preacher

serpent noun **serpents**
a snake

servant noun **servants**
a person whose job is to work in someone else's house

serve verb **serves, serving, served**
1 to serve people in a shop is to help them find the things they want to buy 2 to serve food or drink is to give it to people at a meal 3 to serve a person or organization is to work for them 4 to serve is to be suitable for a purpose *This tree stump will serve as a table.* 5 (in tennis) to serve is to start play by

hitting the ball to your opponent *it serves you right* you deserve it **server** noun

serve noun **serves**
the action of serving in tennis

service noun **services**
1 service is working for someone or something 2 a service is something that helps people or supplies what they want *There is a good bus service into town.* 3 a service is also a religious ceremony in a church 4 a service, or dinner service, is a set of crockery 5 a vehicle or machine has a service when someone spends time repairing and maintaining it 6 (in tennis) a service is a serve **the services** the armed forces of a country

service verb **services, servicing, serviced**
to service a vehicle or machine is to repair and maintain it

service station noun **service stations**
a place beside the road where you can buy petrol

serviette noun **serviettes**
a piece of cloth or paper for use at meals

session noun **sessions**
1 a time spent doing one thing *They were in the middle of a recording session.* 2 a meeting or series of meetings *The Queen will open the next session of Parliament.*

set verb **sets, setting, set**
This word has many meanings, depending on the words that go with it:
1 to set something somewhere is to put or place it there *Set the vase on the table.* 2 to set a device is to make it ready to work *Have you set the alarm?* 3 to set is to become solid or hard *The jelly has set now.* 4 the sun sets when it goes down towards the horizon 5 to set someone doing something is to start them doing it *The news set me thinking.* 6 to set someone a task or problem is to give it to them to do or solve *Has the teacher set your homework?* **to set about something** is to start doing it **to set off** or **set out** is to begin a journey **to set something out** is to

display it or make it known *She set out her reasons for leaving.* **to set something up** is to place it in position or get it started *We want to set up a playgroup.*

set noun sets
1 a group of people or things that belong together 2 a radio or television receiver 3 (in mathematics) a collection of things that you treat as a group because they have something in common, such as being odd numbers 4 a series of games in a tennis match 5 the scenery on a stage

set square noun set squares
a device in the shape of a triangle, used for drawing parallel lines and to draw angles

sett noun setts
the underground burrow of a badger

settee noun settees
a sofa

setting noun settings
1 the setting of a story is the place and time in which it happens 2 the land and buildings around something *The house stood in a rural setting.* 3 a set of cutlery or crockery for one person

settle verb settles, settling, settled
1 to settle a problem, difficulty, or argument is to solve it or decide about it 2 to settle, or settle down, is to become relaxed or make yourself comfortable *He settled down in the armchair.* 3 to settle somewhere is to go and live there *The family settled in Canada.* 4 something light such as dust or snow settles when it comes to rest on something *The dust was settling on the books. A bird flew down and settled on the fence.* 5 to settle a bill or debt is to pay it

settlement noun settlements
1 a settlement is a group of people or houses in a new area 2 a settlement is also an agreement to end an argument

settler noun settlers
one of the first people to settle in a new area

seven noun sevens
the number 7

seventeen noun seventeens
the number 17 **seventeenth** adjective, noun

seventh adjective, noun
the next after the sixth **seventhly** adverb in the seventh place; as the seventh one

seventy noun seventies
the number 70 **seventieth** adjective, noun

sever verb severs, severing, severed
to sever something is to cut or break it off

several determiner, pronoun
more than two but not many

severe adjective severer, severest
1 strict or harsh; not gentle or kind *The Mathematical Master frowned and looked very severe, for he did not approve of children dreaming. — Oscar Wilde, The Happy Prince* 2 very bad or serious *a severe cold, We're in for some severe weather.*

severely adverb
to be severely punished is to be harshly punished

severity noun
the severity of something is its extreme seriousness

sew (say so) verb sews, sewing, sewed, sewn or sewed
1 to sew cloth or other soft material is to use a needle and thread to join it or form it into clothing 2 to sew is to work with a needle and thread or with a sewing machine

sewage (say soo-ij) noun
sewage is waste matter carried away in drains

sewer (say soo-er) noun sewers
an underground drain that carries away sewage

sewing machine noun sewing machines
a machine for sewing things

sex noun sexes
1 a sex is each of the two groups, male or female, that people and animals belong to 2 sex is the instinct that causes members of the two sexes to be attracted to one

a
b
c
d
e
f
g
h
i
j
k
l
m
n
o
p
q
r
s
t
u
v
w
x
y
z

another **3** to have sex is to come together to have offspring

sextet noun sextets

1 a group of six musicians **2** a piece of music for six musicians

shabby adjective shabbier, shabbiest

1 very old and worn *The stranger was wearing an extremely shabby set of wizard's robes which had been darned in several places. – J. K. Rowling, Harry Potter and the Prisoner of Azkaban* **2** mean or unfair *What a shabby trick.* **shabbily** adverb **shabbiness** noun

shack noun shacks

a roughly-built hut

shade noun shades

1 shade is an area sheltered from bright sunlight *We sat down in the shade.* **2** a shade is a colour, or how light or dark a colour is **3** a shade is also a device that decreases or shuts out bright light **4** a shade of something is a slight difference or amount *He played a shade better than anybody else.*

shade verb shades, shading, shaded

1 to shade something or someone is to shelter them from bright light **2** to shade a drawing is to make parts of it darker than the rest

shadow noun shadows

1 a shadow is a dark shape that falls on a surface when something is between it and the light **2** shadow is an area that is dark because the light is blocked *His face was in shadow.* **shadowy** adjective

shadow verb shadows, shadowing, shadowed

1 to shadow someone is to follow them secretly **2** to shadow something is to cast a shadow on it

shady adjective shadier, shadiest

1 giving shade *We sat under a shady tree.* **2** situated in the shade *Find a shady spot.* **3** dishonest or suspect *It was a shady deal.*

shaft noun shafts

1 a long thin rod or straight part of something **2** a deep narrow hole in a mine

or building *They found an old mine shaft. a lift shaft* **3** a beam of light

shaggy adjective shaggier, shaggiest

having long untidy hair

shake verb shakes, shaking, shook, shaken

1 to shake something is to move it quickly up and down or from side to side *Have you shaken the bottle?* **2** to shake is to move in this way **3** to shake someone is to shock or upset them *The news shook her.* **4** to shake is to tremble *His voice was shaking.* **to shake hands** is to clasp someone's right hand as a greeting or as a sign that you agree

shake noun shakes

a quick movement up and down or from side to side *Give the bottle a shake.*

shaky adjective shakier, shakiest

shaking or likely to fall down
shakily adverb

shall verb past tense should

used with *I* and *we* to refer to the future *We shall arrive tomorrow. We told them we should arrive the next day.*

shallow adjective shallower, shallowest

not deep *The stream is quite shallow here. We were playing in the shallow end of the pool.*

sham noun shams

a person or thing that is not genuine or what they claim to be

shamble verb shambles, shambling, shambled

to walk in an awkward way, dragging your feet along the ground

shambles noun

you say something is a shambles when it is in great disorder or in a mess

shame noun

1 shame is a feeling of great sorrow or guilt because you have done something wrong **2** you say something is a shame when it is something that you regret or are sorry about *What a shame you won't be able to come.*

shame verb shames, shaming, shamed
to shame someone is to make them
feel ashamed

shameful adjective
causing shame; disgraceful
shamefully adverb

shameless adjective
feeling or showing no shame
shamelessly adverb

shampoo noun shampoos
shampoo is liquid soap for washing things,
especially your hair or a carpet

shampoo verb shampoos,
shampooing, shampooed
to shampoo something is to wash it
with shampoo

shamrock noun
shamrock is a small plant rather like clover,
with leaves divided in three

shan't
short for *shall not*

shanty[1] noun shanties
a sailor's traditional song

shanty[2] noun shanties
a roughly-built hut

shape noun shapes
1 the outline of something or the way it
looks **2** something that has a definite or
regular form, such as a square, circle, or
triangle **3** the condition that something is
in *The garden isn't in very good shape.*
to be out of shape is to no longer have
the normal shape *The front wheel was
twisted out of shape.* **to take shape** is to
start to develop properly

shape verb shapes, shaping, shaped
to shape something is to give it a shape
to shape up is to develop well

shapeless adjective
having no definite shape *With these words
the Witch fell down in a brown, melted,
shapeless mass and began to spread over the
clean boards of the kitchen floor.*
— L. Frank Baum, *The Wizard of Oz*

shapely adjective shapelier, shapeliest
having an attractive shape

share noun shares
1 one of the parts into which something is
divided between several people or things
2 part of a company's money, lent by
someone who is then given part of the
profits in return

share verb shares, sharing, shared
1 to share something, or share it out, is to
divide it between several people or things
2 to share something is to use it when
someone else is also using it *She shared a
room with me.*

shark noun sharks
a large sea fish with sharp teeth

sharp adjective sharper, sharpest
1 a sharp object has an edge or point that
can cut or make holes *This is a sharp knife.*
2 quick to learn or notice things *She has
sharp eyes. It was sharp of you to spot that
mistake.* **3** sudden or severe *We came to a
sharp bend in the road. I felt a sharp pain
in my side.* **4** slightly sour *The apples taste
sharp.* **5** above the proper musical pitch
sharpness noun

sharp adverb
1 with a sudden change of direction *Now
turn sharp right.* **2** punctually; exactly *Be
there at six o'clock sharp.*

sharp noun sharps
the note that is a semitone above a
particular musical note; the sign that
indicates this is #

sharpen verb sharpens, sharpening,
sharpened
to sharpen something is to make it sharp or
pointed **sharpener** noun

sharply adverb
to say something sharply is to say it in a
critical or severe way

shatter verb shatters, shattering,
shattered
1 to shatter is to break suddenly into lots
of tiny pieces **2** to shatter something is
to break it in this way **3** to shatter hopes
or dreams is to show they are unreal

a
b
c
d
e
f
g
h
i
j
k
l
m
n
o
p
q
r
s
t
u
v
w
x
y
z

4 someone is shattered when they are very upset by something *We were shattered by the news.*

shave verb shaves, shaving, shaved
1 someone shaves when they scrape hair from their skin with a razor **2** to shave something is to cut or scrape a thin slice off it **shaver** noun

shave noun shaves
the act of shaving the face *Dad was having a shave.* **a close shave** (informal) a narrow escape

shawl noun shawls
a large piece of material for covering the shoulders or wrapping a baby

she pronoun
a female person or animal: used as the subject of a verb

sheaf noun sheaves
1 a bundle of papers **2** a bundle of corn stalks tied together after reaping

shear verb shears, shearing, sheared, shorn or sheared
to shear a sheep is to cut the wool from it **shearer** noun **to shear off** is to break off

shears plural noun
a tool like a very large pair of scissors for trimming grass and bushes or for shearing sheep

sheath noun sheaths
1 a cover for the blade of a sword or dagger **2** a cover that fits something closely

sheathe verb sheathes, sheathing, sheathed
1 to sheathe a sword is to put it into its sheath **2** to sheathe something is to put a protective covering on it

shed¹ noun sheds
a simply-made building used for storing things or sheltering animals, or as a workshop

shed² verb sheds, shedding, shed
to shed something is to let it fall or flow *The trees are shedding their leaves. He was so badly hurt he was shedding blood.*

she'd
short for *she had, she should,* or *she would*

sheen noun
a soft shine on a surface

sheep noun sheep
a grass-eating animal kept by farmers for its wool and meat

sheepdog noun sheepdogs
a dog trained to guard and control sheep

sheepish adjective
someone looks sheepish when they look shy or embarrassed **sheepishly** adverb

sheer adjective sheerer, sheerest
1 complete or total *There was a look of sheer misery on his face.* **2** extremely steep; vertical *To the right of the road there was a sheer drop.* **3** sheer material is so thin that you can see through it

sheet noun sheets
1 a large piece of lightweight material put on a bed **2** a whole flat piece of paper, glass, or metal *You will need two sheets of newspaper.* **3** a wide area of water, snow, ice, or flame

sheikh (say shayk) noun sheikhs
the leader of an Arab tribe or village

shelf noun shelves
1 a flat piece of hard material fitted to a wall or in a piece of furniture so that you can put things on it **2** a flat level surface that sticks out from a cliff or under the sea

shell noun shells
1 the hard outer covering round a nut or egg, or round an animal such as a snail or tortoise **2** a metal case filled with explosive, fired from a large gun **3** the walls or framework of a building or ship

shell verb shells, shelling, shelled
1 to shell something is to take it out of its shell **2** to shell a building or ship or town is to fire explosive shells at it

she'll
short for *she will*

shellfish noun shellfish
a sea animal that has a shell

shelter noun shelters
1 a shelter is a place that protects people from danger or from the weather 2 shelter is being protected from danger or from the weather *We found shelter from the rain.*

shelter verb shelters, sheltering, sheltered
1 to shelter somewhere is to stay there because you are protected from danger or from the weather *We sheltered under the trees.* 2 to shelter something or someone is to protect or cover them *The hill shelters the house from the wind.*

shelve verb shelves, shelving, shelved
1 to shelve something is to put it on a shelf or shelves 2 to shelve an idea or piece of work is to reject or postpone it

shepherd noun shepherds
someone whose job is to look after sheep

 TOP TIPS Keep it quiet! There is a silent **h** in **shepherd**.

shepherd's pie noun shepherd's pies
a baked dish of minced meat covered with mashed potato

sherbet noun sherbets
a fizzy sweet powder or drink

sherry noun sherries
a kind of strong wine

she's
short for *she is* and (before a verb in the past tense) *she has*

shield noun shields
1 a large piece of metal or wood a person carries to protect their body in fighting 2 a design or trophy in the shape of a shield 3 a protection from harm *The spacecraft's heat shield protects it as it enters the planet's atmosphere.*

shield verb shields, shielding, shielded
to shield someone or something is to protect them *I was shielded from the wind. She shielded her eyes from the sun.*

shift noun shifts
1 a change of position or condition 2 a group of workers who start work as another group finishes; the time when they work *He's on the night shift this month.* 3 a woman's lightweight dress that hangs loosely

shift verb shifts, shifting, shifted
1 to shift something is to move it 2 to shift is to change position

shilling noun shillings
an old British coin that was worth a twentieth of a pound (now 5 pence)

shimmer verb shimmers, shimmering, shimmered
to shine with a quivering light *The sea shimmered in the sunlight. Before them the water shimmered, satin smooth and silver grey.* – L. M. Montgomery, *Anne of the Island*

shin noun shins
the front of your leg between your knee and your ankle

shine verb shines, shining, shone or, in 'polish' sense, shined
1 to shine is to give out or reflect bright light 2 to shine a torch or light somewhere is to point the light in that direction 3 to shine something is to polish it *Have you shined your shoes?* 4 to shine is to do well or be excellent *He does not shine in maths.*

shine noun
1 shine is brightness 2 a shine is an act of polishing *Give your shoes a good shine.*

shingle noun
shingle is pebbles on a beach

shiny adjective shinier, shiniest
bright or glossy

ship noun ships
a large boat, especially one that goes to sea

ship verb ships, shipping, shipped
to ship something is to send it on a ship

shipping noun
1 shipping is all the ships of a country 2 shipping is also the business of carrying goods by ship

a
b
c
d
e
f
g
h
i
j
k
l
m
n
o
p
q
r
s
t
u
v
w
x
y
z

465

shipwreck noun shipwrecks
1 when a ship is wrecked in a storm or accident at sea **2** the remains of a wrecked ship **shipwrecked** adjective

shipyard noun shipyards
a dockyard

shire noun shires
a county

shirk verb shirks, shirking, shirked
you shirk a task or duty when you avoid doing it

shirt noun shirts
a piece of clothing you wear on the top half of the body, with a collar and sleeves **to be in your shirtsleeves** is to be wearing a shirt but not a jacket over it

shiver verb shivers, shivering, shivered
you shiver when you tremble with cold or fear **shivery** adjective

shiver noun shivers
an act of shivering *I felt a shiver down my spine.*

shoal noun shoals
a large number of fish swimming together

shock¹ noun shocks
1 a shock is a sudden unpleasant surprise **2** a shock is also a violent knock or jolt **3** shock is weakness caused by severe pain or injury **4** a shock, or electric shock, is a painful effect caused by a strong electric current passing through your body

shock verb shocks, shocking, shocked
1 to shock someone is to give them a shock **2** to shock someone is also to make them feel disgusted or appalled

shock² noun shocks
a shock of hair is a bushy mass of it

shocking adjective
1 horrifying or disgusting **2** very bad *The weather's been shocking today.*

shoddy adjective shoddier, shoddiest
of poor quality *This is shoddy work.*

shoe noun shoes
1 a strong covering you wear on your foot **2** a horseshoe

shoelace noun shoelaces
a cord for fastening a shoe

shoestring noun
to do something on a shoestring is to do it with only a small amount of money

shone
past tense and past participle of shine verb *Jamie shone his torch down the tunnel. The sun has shone all day.*

shook
past tense of shake verb *He shook with fear.*

shoot verb shoots, shooting, shot
1 to shoot a gun or other weapon is to fire it **2** to shoot a person or animal is to fire a gun at them **3** to shoot somewhere is to move very fast *The car shot past.* **4** (in football) to shoot is to kick or hit a ball at a goal **5** to shoot a film or scene is to film or photograph it *The film was shot in Africa.*

shoot noun shoots
a young branch or new growth of a plant

shooting star noun shooting stars
a meteor

shop noun shops
1 a building where people buy things **2** a workshop

shop verb shops, shopping, shopped
to shop is to go and buy things at shops

shopkeeper noun shopkeepers
someone who owns or looks after a shop

shoplifter noun shoplifters
someone who steals from shops
shoplifting noun

shopper noun shoppers
someone who goes shopping

shopping noun
1 shopping is buying things at shops *I like shopping.* **2** shopping is also things that you have bought in shops *Let me help you carry your shopping.*

shore noun **shores**
1 the seashore **2** the land along the edge of a lake

shorn
past participle of **shear** *The farmer had shorn the sheep.*

short adjective **shorter, shortest**
1 not long; not lasting long *I went for a short walk.* **2** not tall *He is a short man.* **3** not sufficient; scarce *Water is short.* **4** bad-tempered *He was rather short with me.* **5** short pastry is rich and crumbly, and contains a lot of fat **for short** as a shorter form of something *Joanna is called Jo for short.* **short for something** a shorter form of something *Jo is short for Joanna.* **to be short of something** is to not have enough of it *We seem to be short of chairs.*
shortness noun

short adverb
1 before reaching the point aimed at *My ball fell just short of the hole.* **2** suddenly *The horse stopped short.*

shortage noun **shortages**
there is a shortage when there is not enough of something

shortbread noun
shortbread is a rich sweet biscuit made with butter

shortcake noun **shortcakes**
1 shortbread **2** a light cake usually served with fruit

short circuit noun **short circuits**
a fault in an electrical circuit in which current flows along a shorter route than the normal one

shortcoming noun **shortcomings**
a fault or failure *He has many shortcomings.*

short cut noun **short cuts**
a route or method that is quicker than the usual one

shorten verb **shortens, shortening, shortened**
1 to shorten something is to make it shorter **2** to shorten is to become shorter

shorthand noun
shorthand is a set of special signs for writing words down as quickly as people say them

short-handed adjective
to be short-handed is to not have enough people to help you

shortly adverb
1 soon *I'll be there shortly.* **2** briefly or sharply *'Go away,' she said shortly.*

shorts plural noun
trousers with legs that stop at or above the knee

short-sighted adjective
1 unable to see things clearly when they are further away **2** not thinking enough about what may happen in the future

shot[1] noun **shots**
1 a shot is the firing of a gun or other weapon **2** shot is lead pellets fired from small guns **3** a good or bad shot is a person judged by their skill in shooting *She is a great shot.* **4** a shot is a stroke in a game with a ball, such as tennis or snooker **5** a shot is also an injection **6** in photography, a shot is a photograph or filmed sequence **7** a shot is a heavy metal ball thrown as a sport **8** a shot at something is an attempt to do it *Have a shot at this puzzle.*

shot[2]
past tense and past participle of **shoot** verb *He shot me a furious look. I have never shot a gun.*

shotgun noun **shotguns**
a gun for firing small lead pellets over a short distance

should verb
used to express:
1 what someone ought to do *You should have told me.* **2** what someone expects *They should be here soon.* **3** what might happen *If you should happen to see him, tell him to come.*

a
b
c
d
e
f
g
h
i
j
k
l
m
n
o
p
q
r
s
t
u
v
w
x
y
z

shoulder noun **shoulders**
the part of your body between your neck and your arm

shoulder verb **shoulders, shouldering, shouldered**
1 to shoulder something is to put it or rest it on your shoulder or shoulders 2 to shoulder blame or responsibility is to accept it

shoulder blade noun **shoulder blades**
each of the two large flat bones at the top of your back

shout verb **shouts, shouting, shouted**
to shout is to speak or call very loudly

shout noun **shouts**
a loud cry or call

shove (say shuv) verb **shoves, shoving, shoved**
to shove something is to push it hard **to shove off** (informal) is to go away

shovel (say **shuv**-el) noun **shovels**
a tool like a spade with the sides turned up, for lifting and moving coal, earth, sand, snow, and other things

shovel verb **shovels, shovelling, shovelled**
to shovel (for example) earth or snow is to move it or clear it with a shovel

show verb **shows, showing, showed, shown**
1 to show something is to let people see it *She showed me her new bike.* 2 to show something to someone is to explain it to them *Can you show me how to do it?* 3 to show someone somewhere is to guide or lead them there *I'll show you to your seat.* 4 to show is to be visible *That stain won't show.* **to show off** is to try to impress people **to show something off** is to be proud of letting people see it

show noun **shows**
1 an entertainment *She loves TV game shows.* 2 a display or exhibition *Have you been to the flower show?*

show business noun
show business is the entertainment business; the theatre, films, radio, and television

shower noun **showers**
1 a brief fall of rain or snow *It's only a shower.* 2 a lot of small things coming or falling like rain *They were met by a shower of stones.* 3 a device or cabinet for spraying water to wash the body; a wash in this

shower verb **showers, showering, showered**
1 to shower is to fall like rain 2 to shower someone with things is to give a lot of them *He showered her with presents.* 3 to shower is to wash under a shower

showery adjective
raining occasionally

showjumping noun
showjumping is a competition in which riders make their horses jump over fences and other obstacles **showjumper** noun

showman noun **showmen**
1 someone who presents entertainments 2 someone who is good at attracting attention or at entertaining

show-off noun **show-offs**
someone who is trying to impress other people

showroom noun **showrooms**
a large room where goods are displayed for people to look at and to buy

showy adjective **showier, showiest**
likely to attract attention; bright or highly decorated **showily** adverb **showiness** noun

shrank
past tense of **shrink** *My jumper shrank in the wash.*

shrapnel noun
shrapnel is pieces of metal scattered from an exploding shell

shred noun **shreds**
1 a tiny strip or piece torn or cut off something *His cloak had been ripped to shreds.* 2 a very small amount of something *There's not a shred of evidence for what you say.*

shred verb shreds, shredding, shredded
to shred something is to tear or cut it into tiny strips or pieces

shrew noun shrews
a small animal rather like a mouse

shrewd adjective shrewder, shrewdest
having common sense and showing good judgement **shrewdly** adverb **shrewdness** noun

shriek noun shrieks
a shrill cry or scream

shriek verb shrieks, shrieking, shrieked
to shriek is to give a shrill cry or scream

shrill adjective
a shrill sound is very high and loud
There was a shrill blast of the whistle.
shrilly adverb **shrillness** noun

shrimp noun shrimps
a small shellfish

shrine noun shrines
an altar or chapel or other sacred place

shrink verb shrinks, shrinking, shrank, shrunk
1 to shrink is to become smaller *My dress has shrunk.* **2** to shrink something is to make it smaller, usually by washing it *Their jeans have been shrunk.* **3** to shrink from something is to avoid it because you are afraid or embarrassed *He shrank from meeting strangers.*

shrinkage noun
shrinkage is the amount that something shrinks

shrivel verb shrivels, shrivelling, shrivelled
to become wrinkled and dry

shroud noun shrouds
a sheet in which a dead body is wrapped

shroud verb shrouds, shrouding, shrouded
1 to shroud a dead body is to wrap it in a shroud **2** to shroud something is to cover or conceal it *The mountain was shrouded in mist.*

Shrove Tuesday noun
the day before Ash Wednesday, when people eat pancakes

shrub noun shrubs
a bush or small tree

shrubbery noun shrubberies
an area where shrubs are grown

shrug verb shrugs, shrugging, shrugged
you shrug when you raise your shoulders slightly as a sign that you do not care or do not know

shrug noun shrugs
the act of shrugging

shrunk
past participle of shrink *My jumper has shrunk in the wash.*

shrunken adjective
smaller than it used to be because it has shrunk

shudder verb shudders, shuddering, shuddered
you shudder when you shake because you are cold or afraid

shudder noun shudders
the act of shuddering

shuffle verb shuffles, shuffling, shuffled
1 to shuffle is to drag your feet along the ground as you walk **2** to shuffle playing cards is to mix them by sliding them over each other several times

shuffle noun shuffles
the act of shuffling *Give the cards a quick shuffle.*

shunt verb shunts, shunting, shunted
to shunt a railway train or wagons is to move them from one track to another

shut verb shuts, shutting, shut
1 to shut a door or window, or a lid or cover, is to move it so that it blocks up an opening **2** to shut is to become closed *The door shut suddenly.* **to shut down** is to stop work or business **to shut up** (informal) is to stop talking

a
b
c
d
e
f
g
h
i
j
k
l
m
n
o
p
q
r
s
t
u
v
w
x
y
z

A

shut adjective
closed *Keep your eyes shut.*

shutter noun shutters
1 a panel or screen that can be closed over a window 2 the device in a camera that opens and closes to let light fall on the film

shuttle noun shuttles
1 a train or bus or aircraft that makes frequent short journeys between two places 2 a space shuttle 3 the part of a loom that carries the thread from side to side

shuttlecock noun shuttlecocks
a small rounded piece of cork or plastic with a ring of feathers fixed to it, that you use in the game of badminton

shy adjective shyer, shyest
timid and afraid to meet or talk to other people **shyly** adverb **shyness** noun

sibling noun siblings
your siblings are your brothers and sisters

sick adjective sicker, sickest
1 ill or unwell *He looks after sick animals.* 2 you feel sick when you feel that you are going to vomit; you are sick when you vomit **to be sick of something** or **someone** is to be tired of them or fed up with them

sicken verb sickens, sickening, sickened
1 to sicken someone is to disgust them 2 to sicken is to start feeling ill

sickly adjective sicklier, sickliest
1 often ill; unhealthy *a sickly child* 2 making people feel sick *There was a sickly taste.*

sickness noun sicknesses
an illness or disease

side noun sides
1 a flat surface, especially one that joins the top and bottom of something 2 a line that forms the edge of a shape *A triangle has three sides.* 3 the outer part of something that is not the front or the back *The instructions are on the side of the box.* 4 a position or space to the left or right of something *There's a window on either side of the door.* 5 your sides are the parts of your body from your armpits to your hips *I've*

got a pain down my right side. 6 a group of people playing, arguing, or fighting against another group *They are on our side.*

side verb sides, siding, sided
to side with someone is to support them in a quarrel or argument

sideboard noun sideboards
a long heavy piece of furniture with drawers and cupboards and a flat top

sidecar noun sidecars
a small compartment for a passenger, fixed to the side of a motorcycle

sideline noun sidelines
something that you do in addition to your normal work or activity

sideshow noun sideshows
a small entertainment forming part of a large show, especially at a fair

sideways adverb, adjective
1 to or from the side *Crabs walk sideways.* 2 with one side facing forward *We sat sideways in the bus.*

siding noun sidings
a short railway line leading off the main line

siege (say seej) noun sieges
when an army surrounds a place until the people inside surrender

sieve (say siv) noun sieves
a device made of mesh or perforated metal or plastic, used to separate harder or larger parts from liquid

sift verb sifts, sifting, sifted
1 to sift a fine or powdery substance is to pass it through a sieve 2 to sift facts or information is to examine or select them

sigh noun sighs
a sound you make by breathing out heavily when you are sad, tired, or relieved

sigh verb sighs, sighing, sighed
to sigh is to make a sigh

sight noun sights
1 sight is the ability to see *She has very good sight.* 2 a sight is something that you see *That sunset is a sight I'll never forget.*

3 the sights of a place are the interesting places worth seeing there *Visit the sights of Paris.* **4** you can describe something silly or ridiculous to look at as a sight *What a sight you are!* **5** a sight on a gun is a device that helps you to aim it **to be in sight** is to be able to be seen **to be out of sight** is to be no longer able to be seen

sight verb sights, sighting, sighted
to sight something is to see it or observe it

sightseeing noun
sightseeing is going round looking at interesting places **sightseer** noun

sign noun signs
1 a mark or symbol that stands for something *a minus sign* **2** a board or notice that tells or shows people something **3** something that shows that a thing exists *There are signs of rust.* **4** an action or signal giving information or a command *She made a sign to them to be quiet.*

sign verb signs, signing, signed
1 you sign your name when you write your signature on something **2** to sign is to make a sign or signal *He signed to them to follow him.* **3** to sign someone is to give them a contract for a job, especially in a professional sport *They have signed three new players.*

signal noun signals
1 a device or gesture or sound or light that gives information or a message **2** a series of radio waves sent out or received

signal verb signals, signalling, signalled
to signal to someone is to give them a signal **signaller** noun

signal box noun signal boxes
a building from which railway signals and points are controlled

signalman noun signalmen
a person who controls railway signals

signature noun signatures
your name written by yourself

signature tune noun signature tunes
a special tune used to introduce a

well-known person on radio or television, or to begin or end a programme

significance noun
the significance of something is its meaning or importance

significant adjective
something is significant when it has a meaning or importance **significantly** adverb

signify verb signifies, signifying, signified
to signify something is to mean it or indicate it

signing or **sign language** noun
signing is a way of communicating by using movements of your hands instead of sounds, used by deaf people

signpost noun signposts
a sign at a road junction showing the names and distances of the places that each road leads to

Sikh (say seek) noun Sikhs
someone who believes in **Sikhism**, a religion of India having one God and some Hindu and Islamic beliefs

silence noun silences
silence is when no sound can be heard

silence verb silences, silencing, silenced
to silence someone or something is to make them silent

silencer noun silencers
a device designed to reduce the sound made by an engine or a gun

silent adjective
without any sound; not speaking **silently** adverb

silhouette (say sil-oo-**et**) noun silhouettes
a dark outline of something seen against a light background

silicon noun
silicon is a substance found in many rocks and used in making microchips

471

A
B
C
D
E
F
G
H
I
J
K
L
M
N
O
P
Q
R
S
T
U
V
W
X
Y
Z

silk noun
1 silk is a fine soft thread produced by silkworms for making their cocoons 2 silk is also smooth shiny cloth made from this thread **silken** adjective

silkworm noun silkworms
a kind of caterpillar that covers itself with a cocoon of fine threads when it is ready to turn into a moth

silky adjective silkier, silkiest
silky hair or fur is soft, smooth, and shiny like silk

sill noun sills
a strip of stone or wood or metal underneath a window or door

silly adjective sillier, silliest
foolish **silliness** noun

TOP TIPS There is no adverb *sillily*, because it would be too difficult to say!

silver noun
1 silver is a shiny white precious metal 2 silver is also coins made of this metal or a metal that looks like it 3 silver is also a grey-white colour

silver wedding noun silver weddings
the 25th anniversary of a wedding

similar adjective
one thing is similar to another when it is like it in some ways but not exactly the same **similarly** adverb

similarity noun similarities
1 the similarity between two things is the fact that they are similar 2 a similarity between two things is a way in which they are similar

simile (say **sim**-i-li) noun similes
a kind of expression in which you describe something by comparing it with something else, such as *bold as brass* or *as brave as a lion*

simmer verb simmers, simmering, simmered
food simmers when it boils very gently over a low heat **to simmer down** is to become calm after being anxious or angry

simple adjective simpler, simplest
1 easy *That's a simple question to answer.* 2 not complicated *It was a simple plan, but it worked.* 3 plain *She was wearing a simple dress.* 4 not having much sense or intelligence *Do you think I'm simple or something?* **simplicity** noun

simplify verb simplifies, simplifying, simplified
to simplify something is to make it simple or easy to understand

simply adverb
1 in a simple way *Explain it simply.* 2 completely *It's simply marvellous.* 3 only or merely *It's simply a question of time.*

simulate verb simulates, simulating, simulated
1 to simulate something is to reproduce the conditions for it *The machine simulates a space flight.* 2 to simulate a feeling or state is to pretend to have it *He simulated illness.* **simulation** noun **simulator** noun

simultaneous (say sim-ul-**tay**-ni-us) adjective
two things are simultaneous when they happen at the same time **simultaneously** adverb

sin noun sins
a wicked act that breaks a religious or moral law

sin verb sins, sinning, sinned
to sin is to commit a sin **sinner** noun

since conjunction
1 from the time when *Where have you been since I last saw you?* 2 because *Since we have missed the bus, we must walk home.*

since preposition
from a certain time *I have been here since Christmas.*

since adverb
between then and now *He has not been seen since.*

sincere adjective sincerer, sincerest
you are being sincere when you mean

what you say and express your true feelings *I gave them my sincere good wishes.* **sincerely** adverb **sincerity** noun

sinew noun sinews
strong tissue that joins a muscle to a bone

sinful adjective
wicked; guilty of sin **sinfully** adverb **sinfulness** noun

sing verb sings, singing, sang, sung
1 to sing is to make musical sounds with your voice **2** birds and insects sing when they make musical sounds

singe (say sinj) verb singes, singeing, singed
to singe something is to burn it slightly

singer noun singers
someone who sings

single adjective
1 only one; not double **2** designed for one person *The bedroom had two single beds.* **3** not married **4** for a journey in one direction only

single noun singles
1 a single ticket **2** a recording with one song or short piece of music on it **3** you play singles in tennis when you play against only one other person

single verb singles, singling, singled
to single someone out is to pick them from other people

single file noun
in single file in a line, one behind the other

single-handed adjective
by your own efforts; without any help

single-minded adjective
thinking only about one thing you are determined to achieve

single parent noun single parents
a person who is bringing up a child or children without a partner

single ticket noun single tickets
a ticket for a journey you make to a place but not back again

singly adverb
one at a time or one by one *These stamps are available singly or in books of twelve.*

singular noun singulars
the form of a word meaning only one person or thing, such as *cake* and *child*

singular adjective
1 in the singular; meaning only one *'Mouse' is a singular noun.* **2** extraordinary *She is a woman of singular courage.*

sinister adjective
looking or seeming evil or harmful

sink verb sinks, sinking, sank or sunk, sunk
1 to sink is to go under water *The ship sank in a storm.* **2** to sink something is to make it go under water *They fired on the ship and sank it.* **3** to sink, or to sink down, is to go or fall down to the ground *He sank to his knees.* **to sink in** is to be gradually understood

sink noun sinks
a fixed basin with taps to supply water

sinus (say sy-nus) noun sinuses
your sinuses are the hollows in the bones of your skull, connected with your nose *My sinuses are blocked.*

sip verb sips, sipping, sipped
to sip a drink is to drink it slowly in small mouthfuls

siphon noun siphons
a bent tube used for transferring liquid from one container to another at a lower level

siphon verb siphons, siphoning, siphoned
to siphon liquid is to transfer it with a siphon

sir noun
a word sometimes used when speaking politely to a man, instead of his name *Can I help you, sir?* **Sir** the title given to a knight *Sir Francis Drake.*

siren noun sirens
a device that makes a loud hooting or screaming sound, usually as a warning signal

a
b
c
d
e
f
g
h
i
j
k
l
m
n
o
p
q
r
s
t
u
v
w
x
y
z

A B C D E F G H I J K L M N O P Q R **S** T U V W X Y Z

sister noun sisters
1 your sister is a woman or girl who has the same parents as you 2 a senior nurse in a hospital

sister-in-law noun sisters-in-law
a person's sister-in-law is the sister of their husband or wife, or the wife of their brother

sit verb sits, sitting, sat
1 to sit is to rest on your bottom, as you do when you are on a chair 2 to sit someone, or to sit someone down, is to put them in a sitting position 3 to sit an examination or test is to do it *We sit our end-of-year exam this afternoon.* 4 to sit somewhere is to be situated or positioned there *The house sits on top of a hill.* 5 to sit for someone is to act as a babysitter

site noun sites
1 the place where something has been built or will be built *They crossed a building site.* 2 a place used for something or where something happened *We stayed at a camping site. This is the site of a famous battle.*

site verb sites, siting, sited
to site something somewhere is to locate or build it there

sit-in noun sit-ins
a protest in which a lot of people sit down in a place and refuse to move

sitting room noun sitting rooms
a room with comfortable chairs for sitting in

situated adjective
to be situated in a particular place or position is to be placed there *They lived in a town situated in a valley.*

situation noun situations
1 a place or position; where something is 2 all the things that are happening to someone at a particular time; the way things are *We're now in a difficult situation because we've run out of money.* 3 a job or employment

six noun sixes
the number 6

sixpence noun sixpences
an old British coin that was worth half a shilling

sixteen noun sixteens
the number 16 **sixteenth** adjective, noun

sixth adjective, noun
the next after the fifth **sixthly** adverb in the sixth place; as the sixth one

sixty noun sixties
the number 60 **sixtieth** adjective, noun

size noun sizes
1 how big a person or thing is 2 the measurement something is made in *I wear a size eight shoe.*

size verb sizes, sizing, sized
to size something or **someone up** (informal) is to form an opinion about them

sizeable adjective
fairly large

sizzle verb sizzles, sizzling, sizzled
to make a crackling and hissing sound *The bacon sizzled in the pan.*

skate[1] noun skates
1 a boot with a steel blade attached to the sole, used for sliding smoothly over ice 2 a roller skate

skate verb skates, skating, skated
to skate is to move around on skates **skater** noun

skate[2] noun skate
a large flat sea fish used for food

skateboard noun skateboards
a small board with wheels, used for standing and riding on **skateboarding** noun

skeleton noun skeletons
1 the framework of bones in a person's or animal's body 2 the framework or shell of a new building **skeletal** adjective
Please see illustration on following page.

sketch noun sketches
1 a quick or rough drawing 2 a short amusing play

skeleton

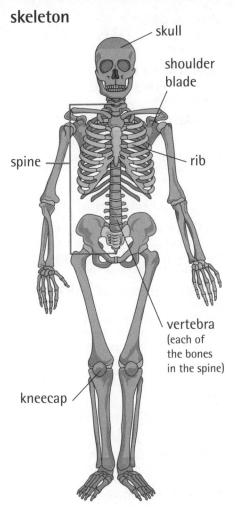

skull

shoulder blade

spine

rib

vertebra
(each of the bones in the spine)

kneecap

sketch verb sketches, sketching, sketched
to sketch something or someone is to make a sketch of them

sketchy adjective sketchier, sketchiest
roughly drawn or described, without any detail *Reports of what happened are sketchy at the moment.*

skewer noun skewers
a long wooden or metal or plastic pin that you push through meat to hold it together while it is being cooked

ski (say skee) noun skis
a long flat strip of wood or metal or plastic, fastened to each foot for moving quickly over snow
ski verb skis, skiing, skied or ski'd
to ski is to travel on snow wearing skis
skier noun

skid verb skids, skidding, skidded
to skid is to slide accidentally, especially in a vehicle
skid noun skids
a skidding movement *The car went into a skid on the icy road.*

skilful adjective
having or showing a lot of skill
skilfully adverb

skill noun skills
1 to do something with skill is to do it well 2 a type of work or ability that you learn through training and practice *He's been learning some new football skills.*
skilled adjective

skim verb skims, skimming, skimmed
1 to skim is to move quickly over a surface 2 to skim something is to remove it from the surface of a liquid, especially to take the cream off milk

skimmed adjective
skimmed milk has had the cream removed

skimp verb skimps, skimping, skimped
to use or provide less than is needed for something

skimpy adjective skimpier, skimpiest
skimpy clothes do not cover much of your body

skin noun skins
1 the outer covering of a person's or animal's body 2 the outer covering of a fruit or vegetable 3 a thin firm layer that has formed on the surface of a liquid
skin verb skins, skinning, skinned
to skin something is to take the skin off it

skinny adjective skinnier, skinniest
very thin

a
b
c
d
e
f
g
h
i
j
k
l
m
n
o
p
q
r
s
t
u
v
w
x
y
z

475

A
B
C
D
E
F
G
H
I
J
K
L
M
N
O
P
Q
R
S
T
U
V
W
X
Y
Z

skip[1] verb skips, skipping, skipped
1 to skip is to jump or move along by hopping from one foot to the other 2 to skip is also to jump with a skipping rope 3 to skip something is to miss it out or ignore it *You can skip the last chapter.*

skip noun skips
a skipping movement

skip[2] noun skips
a large metal container for taking away builders' rubbish

skipper noun skippers
the captain of a ship or team

skipping rope noun skipping ropes
a length of rope, usually with a handle at each end, that you swing over your head and under your feet as you jump

skirt noun skirts
a piece of clothing for a woman or girl that hangs down from her waist

skirt verb skirts, skirting, skirted
to skirt something is to go round the edge of it

skirting or **skirting board** noun skirtings, skirting boards
a narrow board round the wall of a room, close to the floor

skit noun skits
a play or sketch or poem that makes fun of something by imitating it

skittish adjective
lively and excitable

skittle noun skittles
a piece of wood or plastic shaped like a bottle, that people try to knock down with a ball in a game of **skittles**

skull noun skulls
the framework of bones in your head which contains your brain

skunk noun skunks
a black and white furry animal from North America that can make an unpleasant smell

sky noun skies
the space above the earth, where you can see the sun, moon, and stars

skylark noun skylarks
a small brown bird that sings as it hovers high in the air

skylight noun skylights
a window in a roof

skyscraper noun skyscrapers
a very tall building

slab noun slabs
a thick flat piece of something

slack adjective slacker, slackest
1 loose; not pulled tight *The rope was slack.* 2 lazy; not busy or working hard
slackly adverb **slackness** noun

slacken verb slackens, slackening, slackened
1 to slacken something is to loosen it 2 to slacken is to become slower or less busy *Her pace gradually slackened.*

slacks plural noun
loose-fitting casual trousers

slain
past participle of **slay** *George had slain the dragon.*

slam verb slams, slamming, slammed
1 to slam (for example) a door is to shut it hard or loudly 2 to slam something is to hit it with great force *He slammed the ball into the net.*

slang noun
slang is a kind of colourful language used in less formal writing and speaking

slant verb slants, slanting, slanted
1 to slant is to slope or lean 2 to slant news or information is to present it from a particular point of view

slant noun slants
1 a sloping or leaning position *The caravan floor was at a slant.* 2 a way of presenting news or information from a particular point of view

slap verb slaps, slapping, slapped
1 to slap someone is to hit them with the palm of your hand 2 to slap something somewhere is to put it there forcefully or carelessly *We slapped paint on the walls.*

slap noun slaps
to give someone a slap is to slap them

slapstick noun
slapstick is noisy lively comedy, with people hitting each other, throwing things, and falling over

slash verb slashes, slashing, slashed
1 to slash something is to make large cuts in it 2 to slash prices or costs is to reduce them a lot

slash noun slashes
1 a large cut 2 a sloping line (/) used to separate words or letters

slat noun slats
a thin strip of wood or plastic, usually arranged to overlap with others, for example in a blind or screen

slate noun slates
1 slate is a kind of grey rock that is easily split into flat plates 2 slates are flat pieces of this rock used to cover a roof

slaughter (say **slor**-ter) verb slaughters, slaughtering, slaughtered
1 to slaughter an animal is to kill it for food 2 to slaughter people or animals is to kill a lot of them

slaughter noun
slaughter is the killing of a lot of people or animals

slaughterhouse noun slaughterhouses
a place where animals are killed for food

slave noun slaves
a person who is owned by someone else and has to work for them without being paid

slave verb slaves, slaving, slaved
to slave over something is to work very hard

slavery noun
slavery is being a slave or the system of having slaves

slay verb slays, slaying, slew, slain (old or poetic use)
to slay someone is to kill them

sledge or **sled** noun sledges, sleds
a vehicle for travelling over snow, with strips of metal or wood instead of wheels

sledgehammer noun sledgehammers
a very large heavy hammer

sleek adjective sleeker, sleekest
smooth and shiny *She has lovely sleek hair.*

sleep noun
1 sleep is the condition in which your eyes are closed, your body is relaxed, and your mind is unconscious *You need some sleep.* 2 a sleep is a time when you are sleeping *Did you have a good sleep?*

sleep verb sleeps, sleeping, slept
to sleep is to have a sleep

sleeper noun sleepers
1 someone who is asleep 2 each of the wooden or concrete beams on which a railway line rests 3 a railway carriage equipped for sleeping in

sleeping bag noun sleeping bags
a warm padded bag for sleeping in, especially when you are camping

sleepless adjective
unable to sleep; without sleep *We've had a sleepless night.*

sleepwalker noun sleepwalkers
someone who walks around while they are asleep **sleepwalking** noun

sleepy adjective sleepier, sleepiest
feeling tired and wanting to go to sleep **sleepily** adverb **sleepiness** noun

sleet noun
sleet is a mixture of rain with snow or hail

sleeve noun sleeves
the part of a piece of clothing that covers your arm

a b c d e f g h i j k l m n o p q r **s** t u v w x y z

A
B
C
D
E
F
G
H
I
J
K
L
M
N
O
P
Q
R

S

T
U
V
W
X
Y
Z

sleeveless adjective
a sleeveless (for example) jumper or dress is one without sleeves

sleigh (say slay) noun **sleighs**
a large sledge pulled by horses

slender adjective **slenderer, slenderest**
1 slim or thin 2 slight or small *Their chances of winning are slender.*

slept
past tense and past participle of **sleep** verb *I slept until ten o'clock. The baby has slept all night.*

slew
past tense of **slay** *George slew the dragon.*

slice noun **slices**
a thin flat piece cut off something
slice verb **slices, slicing, sliced**
to slice something is to cut it into slices

slick adjective **slicker, slickest**
done quickly and in a clever way, without obvious effort
slick noun **slicks**
a large patch of oil floating on water

slide verb **slides, sliding, slid**
1 to slide is to move smoothly over a flat or polished or slippery surface *She loved sliding down the bannister.* 2 to slide somewhere is to move there quickly or secretly *The thief slid behind a bush.*
slide noun **slides**
1 a sliding movement 2 a structure for children to play on, with a smooth slope for sliding down 3 a type of photograph that lets light through and that can be shown on a screen 4 a small glass plate on which you can examine things under a microscope 5 a fastener for keeping your hair tidy

slight adjective **slighter, slightest**
very small; not serious or important

slightly adverb
in a slight way; not seriously *They were slightly hurt.*

slim adjective **slimmer, slimmest**
1 thin and graceful 2 small; hardly enough *We have a slim chance of winning.*
slim verb **slims, slimming, slimmed**
to slim is to try to make yourself thinner, especially by dieting

slime noun
slime is unpleasant wet slippery stuff *There was slime on the pond.*

slimy adjective **slimier, slimiest**
covered in slime, or like slime

sling verb **slings, slinging, slung**
1 to sling something somewhere is to throw it there roughly or carelessly *You can sling your wet clothes into the washing machine.* 2 to sling something is also to hang it up or support it so that it hangs loosely *He had slung the bag round his neck.*
sling noun **slings**
1 a piece of cloth tied round your neck to support an injured arm 2 a device for throwing stones

slink verb **slinks, slinking, slunk**
to slink somewhere is to move there slowly and quietly because you feel guilty or don't want to be noticed *He slunk off to bed.*

slip verb **slips, slipping, slipped**
1 to slip is to slide without meaning to or to fall over 2 to slip somewhere is to move there quickly and quietly *He slipped out of the house before anyone was awake.* 3 to slip something somewhere is to put it there quickly without being seen *She slipped the letter into her pocket.* 4 to slip something is to escape from it *The dog slipped its leash.*
to slip up is to make a mistake
slip noun **slips**
1 an accidental slide or fall *One slip and you could fall into the river.* 2 a small mistake 3 a small piece of paper 4 a piece of women's underwear like a thin dress or skirt **to give someone the slip** is to escape from them or avoid them

slipper noun **slippers**
a soft comfortable shoe for wearing indoors

slippery adjective
smooth or wet so that it is difficult to stand on or hold

slipshod adjective
a slipshod piece of work is careless or badly done

slit noun slits
a long narrow cut or opening
slit verb slits, slitting, slit
to slit something is to make a slit in it

slither verb slithers, slithering, slithered
to slip or slide along, often unsteadily *The snake slithered away. We were slithering around on the ice.*

sliver (say **sli**-ver) noun slivers
a thin strip of wood, glass, or other material

slog verb slogs, slogging, slogged
1 to slog something is to hit it hard or wildly 2 to slog is to work hard *I'm slogging away at my essay.* 3 to slog is also to walk with effort *We slogged through the snow.*
slog noun
a piece of hard work or effort *Climbing up that hill was a real slog.*

slogan noun slogans
a short catchy phrase used to advertise something or to sum up an idea

slop verb slops, slopping, slopped
1 to slop liquid is to spill it over the edge of its container 2 liquid slops when it spills in this way

slope verb slopes, sloping, sloped
to slope is to go gradually downwards or upwards or to have one end higher than the other
slope noun slopes
1 a sloping surface 2 the amount by which a surface slopes *The hill has a slope of 30°.* 3 the side of a mountain

sloppy adjective sloppier, sloppiest
1 liquid and spilling easily 2 careless or badly done *Their work is sloppy.* 3 (informal) too sentimental or romantic *What a sloppy story.* **sloppily** adverb **sloppiness** noun

slops plural noun
liquid waste matter

slosh verb sloshes, sloshing, sloshed (informal)
you slosh liquid, or it sloshes, when it gets splashed in a messy or careless way

slot noun slots
a narrow opening to put things in

sloth (rhymes with **both**) noun sloths
1 sloth is laziness 2 a sloth is a long-haired South American animal that lives in trees and moves very slowly

slouch verb slouches, slouching, slouched
to move or stand or sit in a lazy way, especially with your head and shoulders bent forwards

slovenly (say **sluv**-en-li) adjective
careless or untidy

slow adjective slower, slowest
1 not quick; taking more time than usual 2 a clock or watch is slow when it shows a time earlier than the correct time
slow adverb
at a slow rate; slowly *Go slow.*
slowness noun
slow verb slows, slowing, slowed
1 to slow, or to slow down, is to go slower 2 to slow something, or to slow it down, is to make it go slower

slowcoach noun slowcoaches (informal)
someone who moves or works slowly

slowly adverb
at a slow rate or speed

sludge noun
sludge is thick sticky mud

slug noun slugs
1 a small slimy animal like a snail without its shell 2 a pellet for firing from a gun

slum noun slums
an area of dirty and crowded houses in a city

a
b
c
d
e
f
g
h
i
j
k
l
m
n
o
p
q
r
s
t
u
v
w
x
y
z

slumber noun
slumber is peaceful sleep

slumber verb slumbers, slumbering, slumbered
to slumber is to sleep peacefully

slump verb slumps, slumping, slumped
to slump is to fall heavily or suddenly

slump noun slumps
a slump is a sudden fall in prices or trade

slung
past tense and past participle of sling verb
She slung the sack over her shoulder. Mum was angry because he had slung his clothes on the floor.

slunk
past tense and past participle of slink *She slunk out the door. The thieves had slunk off.*

slur noun slurs
something that harms a person's reputation; an insult

slush noun
slush is snow that is melting on the ground
slushy adjective

sly adjective slyer, slyest
cunning or mischievous **slyly** adverb
slyness noun

smack verb smacks, smacking, smacked
to smack someone is to slap them with your hand, especially as a punishment

smack noun smacks
a slap with your hand

small adjective smaller, smallest
not large; less than the normal size

smallpox noun
smallpox is a serious disease that causes a fever and produces spots that leave scars on the skin

smart adjective smarter, smartest
1 neat and well dressed 2 clever and quick-thinking 3 fast *We'll need to walk at a smart pace.* **smartness** noun

smart verb smarts, smarting, smarted
to smart is to feel a stinging pain

smarten verb smartens, smartening, smartened
1 to smarten something or someone is to make them smarter *You need to smarten yourself up a bit.* 2 to smarten is to become smarter

smartly adverb
1 to be smartly dressed is to have nice clothes on 2 to move smartly is to do so quickly

smash verb smashes, smashing, smashed
1 to smash is to break into pieces noisily and violently; to smash something is to break it in this way 2 to smash into something is to hit it with great force *The lorry left the road and smashed into a wall.* 3 (informal) to smash something or someone is to destroy them or defeat them completely

smash noun smashes
1 the act or sound of smashing 2 a collision between vehicles

smashing adjective (informal)
excellent

smear verb smears, smearing, smeared
to smear something dirty or greasy is to rub it thickly over a surface

smear noun smears
a dirty or greasy mark made by smearing

smell verb smells, smelling, smelt or smelled
1 you smell something when you use your nose to sense it 2 to smell is to give out a smell *The cheese smells funny.*

smell noun smells
1 a smell is something you can smell, especially something unpleasant 2 smell is the ability to smell things *I have a good sense of smell.*

smelly adjective smellier, smelliest
having an unpleasant smell

smelt verb smelts, smelting, smelted
to smelt ore is to melt it in order to get metal from it

A
B
C
D
E
F
G
H
I
J
K
L
M
N
O
P
Q
R
S
T
U
V
W
X
Y
Z

smile noun smiles
an expression on your face that shows you are pleased or amused, with your lips stretched and turning upwards at the ends
smile verb smiles, smiling, smiled
to smile is to give a smile

smith noun smiths
someone who makes things out of metal

smithereens plural noun
something is smashed or blown to smithereens when it is broken into lots of tiny fragments

smock noun smocks
a loose piece of clothing like a very long shirt

smog noun
smog is a mixture of smoke and fog

smoke noun
1 smoke is the grey or blue mixture of gas and particles that rises from a fire 2 to have a smoke is to spend time smoking a cigarette *He wants a smoke.*
smoke verb smokes, smoking, smoked
1 something smokes when it gives out smoke *The fire is smoking.* 2 someone is smoking when they have a lit cigarette in their mouth and are breathing in the smoke from it **smoker** noun

smokeless adjective
smokeless fuel burns without giving off much smoke

smooth adjective smoother, smoothest
1 having an even surface without any marks or roughness 2 a smooth liquid or substance has no lumps in it 3 moving without bumps or jolts *We had a smooth ride.* 4 not harsh; flowing easily *She spoke in a smooth voice.*
smoothness noun
smooth verb smooths, smoothing, smoothed
to smooth something is to make it smooth and flat

smoothie noun smoothies
a thick, smooth drink made from crushed fruit

smoothly adverb
1 something flows smoothly when it does so easily and evenly 2 an event goes smoothly when it happens without any problems

smother verb smothers, smothering, smothered
1 to smother someone is to cover their face so that they can't breathe 2 to smother something is to cover it thickly *He brought in a cake smothered in icing.* 3 to smother a fire is to put it out by covering it

smoulder verb smoulders, smouldering, smouldered
to burn slowly without a flame

smudge noun smudges
a dirty or messy mark made by rubbing something
smudge verb smudges, smudging, smudged
to smudge paint or ink is to touch it while it is still wet and make it messy

smug adjective smugger, smuggest
too pleased with yourself **smugly** adverb **smugness** noun

smuggle verb smuggles, smuggling, smuggled
to smuggle something is to bring it into a country secretly and illegally **smuggler** noun

snack noun snacks
a quick light meal

snag noun snags
an unexpected difficulty or obstacle
snag verb snags, snagging, snagged
to snag something you are wearing is to catch it on something sharp

snail noun snails
a small animal with a soft body in a hard shell

snake noun snakes
a reptile with a long narrow body and no legs

snap verb snaps, snapping, snapped
1 something snaps when it breaks suddenly

a
b
c
d
e
f
g
h
i
j
k
l
m
n
o
p
q
r
s
t
u
v
w
x
y
z

with a sharp noise **2** an animal snaps when it bites suddenly or quickly *The dog snapped at me.* **3** to snap something is to say it quickly and angrily *There's no need to snap.* **4** to snap your fingers is to make a sharp snapping sound with them **5** to snap something or someone is to take a quick photograph of them

snap noun **snaps**
1 a snap is the act or sound of snapping **2** a snap is also an informal photograph taken quickly **3** snap is a card game in which players shout 'Snap!' when they spot two cards of the same value

snappy adjective **snappier, snappiest**
quick and lively

snapshot noun **snapshots**
an informal photograph taken quickly

snare noun **snares**
a trap for catching animals

snare verb **snares, snaring, snared**
to snare an animal is to catch it in a snare

snarl[1] verb **snarls, snarling, snarled**
an animal snarls when it growls angrily

snarl noun **snarls**
a snarling sound

snarl[2] verb
to be snarled up is to become tangled or jammed *The motorway was snarled up for several miles.*

snatch verb **snatches, snatching, snatched**
to snatch something is to grab it quickly *He snatched the bag from me.*

snatch noun **snatches**
1 a short piece of conversation or music **2** (informal) a robbery or theft

sneak verb **sneaks, sneaking, sneaked**
1 to sneak somewhere is to move there quietly and secretly **2** (informal) to sneak on someone is to tell tales about them

sneak noun **sneaks** (informal)
a person who tells tales

sneaky adjective **sneakier, sneakiest**
dishonest or deceitful

sneer verb **sneers, sneering, sneered**
to speak or behave in a scornful way

sneeze verb **sneezes, sneezing, sneezed**
you sneeze when you push air through your nose suddenly and uncontrollably *She was sneezing a lot because of her cold.*

sneeze noun **sneezes**
the action or sound of sneezing

sniff verb **sniffs, sniffing, sniffed**
1 to sniff is to make a noise by drawing air in through your nose **2** to sniff something is to smell it with a sniff

sniff noun **sniffs**
the action or sound of sniffing or smelling something

sniffle verb **sniffles, sniffling, sniffled**
to keep sniffing because you have a cold or are crying

snigger verb **sniggers, sniggering, sniggered**
to snigger is to give a quiet sly laugh

snigger noun **sniggers**
a quiet sly laugh

snip verb **snips, snipping, snipped**
to snip something is to cut a small piece or pieces off it

snip noun **snips**
an act of snipping something

sniper noun **snipers**
someone who shoots at people from a hiding place

snippet noun **snippets**
a short piece of news or information

snivel verb **snivels, snivelling, snivelled**
to snivel is to cry or complain in a whining way

snob noun **snobs**
someone who despises people who have not got wealth or power or particular tastes or interests **snobbery** noun **snobbish** adjective

snooker noun
snooker is a game played with long sticks (called *cues*) and 22 balls on a cloth-covered table

snoop verb snoops, snooping, snooped
to pry or try to find out about someone else's business

snore verb snores, snoring, snored
to breathe noisily while you are sleeping

snorkel noun snorkels
a tube with one end above the water, worn by an underwater swimmer to get air

snort verb snorts, snorting, snorted
to snort is to make a loud noise by forcing air out through your nose

snort noun snorts
a snorting noise

snout noun snouts
an animal's snout is the front part sticking out from its head, with its nose and mouth

snow noun
snow is frozen drops of water falling from the sky as small white flakes

snow verb snows, snowing, snowed
it is snowing when snow is falling

snowball noun snowballs
snow pressed into the shape of a ball for throwing

snowboard noun snowboards
a board like a short, broad ski, used for riding downhill on snow
snowboarding noun

snowdrop noun snowdrops
a small white flower that blooms in early spring

snowflake noun snowflakes
a flake of snow

snowman noun snowmen
a figure of a person made of snow

snowplough noun snowploughs
a vehicle or device for clearing snow from a road or railway track

snowshoe noun snowshoes
snowshoes are broad frames with a mesh, that you can attach to your feet so that you can walk over deep snow without sinking in

snowstorm noun snowstorms
a storm with snow falling

snowy adjective snowier, snowiest
1 with snow falling *We're expecting snowy weather.* 2 covered with snow *The roofs looked snowy.* 3 brightly white

snub verb snubs, snubbing, snubbed
to snub someone is to treat them in a scornful or unfriendly way

snub-nosed adjective
having a short turned-up nose

snuff noun
snuff is powdered tobacco that is taken into the nose by sniffing

snug adjective snugger, snuggest
warm and cosy *We found a snug corner by the fire.* **snugly** adverb

snuggle verb snuggles, snuggling, snuggled
to curl up in a warm comfortable place *She snuggled down in bed.*

so adverb
1 in this way; to such an extent *Why are you so cross?* 2 very *Cricket is so boring.* 3 also *I was wrong but so were you.* **and so on** and other similar things *They took food, water, spare clothing, and so on.* **or so** or about that number *We need about fifty or so.* **so as to** in order to **so far** up to now **so what?** (informal) what does that matter?

so conjunction
for that reason *They threw me out, so I came here.*

soak verb soaks, soaking, soaked
to soak someone or something is to make them very wet or leave them in water **to soak something up** is to take in a liquid in the way that a sponge does

so-and-so noun so-and-so's (informal)
1 a person whose name you don't know or can't remember *Old so-and-so told me.* 2 an unpleasant person *He's a real so-and-so.*

soap noun soaps
1 soap is a substance you use with water for

a b c d e f g h i j k l m n o p q r s t u v w x y z

483

washing and cleaning things **2** (informal) a soap is a soap opera **soapy** adjective

soap opera noun **soap operas**
a television serial about the day-to-day life of a group of imaginary people

soar verb **soars, soaring, soared**
1 to soar is to rise or fly high in the air **2** to soar is also to increase a lot *Prices were soaring.*

sob verb **sobs, sobbing, sobbed**
to sob is to cry with gasping noises
sob noun **sobs**
a sound of sobbing

sober adjective
1 not drunk **2** calm and serious *She had a sober expression.* **3** not bright or showy *The room was painted in sober colours.* **soberly** adverb

so-called adjective
named in what may be the wrong way *Even the so-called experts couldn't solve the problem.*

soccer noun
soccer is a game played by two teams which try to kick an inflated ball into their opponents' goal

sociable (say **soh**-sha-bul) adjective
sociable people are friendly and like to be with other people

social (say **soh**-shal) adjective
1 to do with people meeting one another in their spare time *Let's join a social club.* **2** living in groups, not alone *Bees are social insects.* **3** to do with society or a community *They were writing a social history of the area.* **socially** adverb

society noun **societies**
1 a society is a community of people; society is people living together in a group or nation **2** a society is also a group of people organized for a particular purpose *He's joined a dramatic society.* **3** society is also company or companionship *We enjoy your society.*

sociology (say soh-si-**ol**-o-ji) noun
sociology is the study of how people behave in different societies **sociologist** noun

sock[1] noun **socks**
a soft piece of clothing that covers your foot and the lower half of your leg **to pull your socks up** (informal) is to try to do better

sock[2] verb **socks, socking, socked** (informal)
to sock someone is to hit or punch them hard *He socked me on the jaw.*

socket noun **sockets**
a device or hole that something fits into, especially the place where an electric plug or bulb is put to make a connection

soda noun
1 soda is a substance made from sodium, such as baking soda **2** soda is also soda water

soda water noun
soda water is fizzy water used in drinks

sodium (say **soh**-di-um) noun
sodium is a soft silver-white metal

sofa noun **sofas**
a long soft seat with sides and a back

soft adjective **softer, softest**
1 not hard or firm; easily pressed or cut into a new shape **2** smooth; not rough or stiff **3** gentle; not loud *He spoke in a soft voice.* **softness** noun

soft drink noun **soft drinks**
a drink that does not contain alcohol

soften verb **softens, softening, softened**
1 to soften something is to make it softer **2** to soften is to become softer

softly adjective
1 in a gentle way *She closed the door softly behind her.* **2** to speak softly is to speak quietly

software noun (in computing)
software is programs and data, which are

A
B
C
D
E
F
G
H
I
J
K
L
M
N
O
P
Q
R
S
T
U
V
W
X
Y
Z

not part of the machinery (the *hardware*) of a computer

soggy adjective **soggier, soggiest**
very wet and heavy

soil[1] noun
soil is the loose earth that plants grow in

soil[2] verb **soils, soiling, soiled**
to soil something is to make it dirty

solar adjective
to do with the sun or powered by the sun's energy

solar panel noun **solar panels**
a panel that absorbs the sun's rays in order to generate heat or electricity, built into the side of a building

solar system noun
the solar system is the sun and the planets that revolve round it

sold
past tense and past participle of **sell** *He sold his bike. Shops have sold thousands of copies of the book.*

solder noun
solder is a soft alloy that is melted to join pieces of metal together
solder verb **solders, soldering, soldered**
to solder two pieces of metal is to join them together with solder

soldier noun **soldiers**
a member of an army

sole[1] noun **soles**
1 the bottom part of a shoe or foot **2** a flat sea fish used for food

sole[2] adjective
single or only *She was the sole survivor.*
solely adverb

solemn adjective
serious and dignified *The children could hardly look into the Lion's royal, solemn eyes, for he was both good and terrible at the same time.* – C. S. Lewis, *The Lion, The Witch and the Wardrobe* **solemnity** noun

solemnly adverb
to do something solemnly is to do it in a serious and dignified way *'In that case,' said the Dodo solemnly, rising to its feet, 'I move that the meeting adjourn.'* – Lewis Carroll, *Alice's Adventures in Wonderland*

solicitor noun **solicitors**
a lawyer who advises clients and prepares legal documents

solid adjective
1 keeping its shape; not a liquid or gas **2** not hollow; with no space inside *These bars are made of solid steel.* **3** firm or strongly made *The house is built on solid foundations.* **4** strong and reliable *They gave solid support.* **solidity** noun
solid noun **solids**
1 a solid thing **2** a three-dimensional shape, such as a cube, sphere, or cone

solidify verb **solidifies, solidifying, solidified**
1 to solidify is to change from a liquid into a solid **2** to solidify something is to make it solid

solidly adverb
1 something is solidly built when it is firmly and strongly built **2** to rain solidly is to rain continuously

solitary adjective
1 alone; on your own *He lived a solitary life.*
2 single *This is a solitary example.*

solitude noun
solitude is being on your own

solo noun **solos**
something sung or performed by one person alone

soloist noun **soloists**
someone who plays or sings a solo

solstice noun **solstices**
either of the two times in the year when the sun is at its furthest point north or south of the equator. The **summer solstice** is about 21 June, and the **winter solstice** is about 22 December, in the northern hemisphere *Please see illustration on following page.*

a
b
c
d
e
f
g
h
i
j
k
l
m
n
o
p
q
r
s
t
u
v
w
x
y
z

solstice

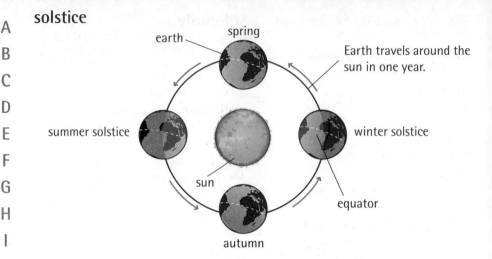

earth · spring · Earth travels around the sun in one year. · summer solstice · winter solstice · sun · equator · autumn

soluble adjective
1 a soluble substance is able to be dissolved
2 a soluble problem or puzzle is able to be solved

solution noun solutions
1 the answer to a problem or puzzle
2 a liquid with something dissolved in it

solve verb solves, solving, solved
to solve a problem or puzzle is to find an answer to it

solvent noun solvents
a liquid in which other substances can be dissolved

solvent adjective
to be solvent is to have enough money to pay your debts

sombre adjective
gloomy or dark *From their feet the land dropped away into a shallow vale, then rose again to sombre moors inland.* – Rosemary Sutcliff, *Beowulf: Dragonslayer*

some determiner
1 a few or a little *I'd like some biscuits and some sugar.* 2 a certain amount of *Would you like some cake?* 3 an unknown person or thing *Some fool left the window open.*

some pronoun
a certain or unknown number or amount *Some of them were late.*

somebody pronoun
someone; some person

somehow adverb
in some way *We must finish the work somehow.*

someone pronoun
some person

somersault (say sum-er-solt) noun somersaults
a movement in which you turn head over heels and land on your feet

something pronoun
a certain or unknown thing

sometime adverb
at some time *I saw her sometime last year.*

sometimes adverb
at some times but not always *We sometimes walk to school.*

somewhat adverb
to some extent; rather *He was somewhat annoyed.*

somewhere adverb
in or to some place

son noun sons
a boy or man who is someone's child

sonar noun
sonar is a system using the echo from sound waves to locate objects underwater

song noun songs
1 a song is a tune with words for singing 2 a bird's song is the musical sounds it makes 3 song is singing *He burst into song.*

songbird noun songbirds
a bird that sings sweetly

sonic adjective
to do with sound or sound waves

sonnet noun sonnets
a kind of poem with 14 lines

soon adverb sooner, soonest
1 in a short time from now 2 not long after something *She became ill, but was soon better.* 3 early or quickly *You spoke too soon.* **as soon** as willingly *I'd just as soon stay at home.* **sooner or later** at some time in the future

soot noun
soot is the black powder left by smoke in a chimney or on a building
sooty adjective

soothe verb soothes, soothing, soothed
1 to soothe someone is to make them calm 2 to soothe a pain or ache is to ease it

sophisticated (say sof-**iss**-ti-kay-tid) adjective
1 someone is sophisticated when they are used to a fashionable or cultured life and have experienced a lot of different things 2 something is sophisticated when it is complicated and highly developed *It is a sophisticated machine.* **sophistication** noun

sopping adjective
very wet; soaked

soppy adjective soppier, soppiest (informal)
sentimental or silly

soprano (say so-**prah**-noh) noun sopranos
a woman or young boy with a high singing voice

sorcerer noun sorcerers
someone who can do magic

sorceress noun sorceresses
a woman who can do magic

sorcery noun
magic or witchcraft

sore adjective sorer, sorest
1 painful or smarting *I've got a sore throat.* 2 (informal) annoyed or upset
soreness noun

sore noun sores
a red and painful place on your skin

sorely adverb
seriously; very *I was sorely tempted to run away.*

sorrow noun sorrows
sorrow is sadness or regret
sorrowful adjective feeling sorrow
sorrowfully adverb

sorry adjective sorrier, sorriest
1 you are sorry that you did something when you regret doing it or want to apologize *I'm sorry I forgot to send you a birthday card.* 2 you feel sorry for someone when you feel pity for them or are sad that something bad has happened to them *I'm sorry you've been ill.*

sort noun sorts
1 a group of things or people that are similar; a kind *What sort of fruit do you like?* 2 (in computing) putting data in a particular order *Can you help me do an alphabetical sort of these names?*

sort verb sorts, sorting, sorted
to sort things is to arrange them in groups or kinds **to sort something out** is to organize it or arrange it

SOS noun
an SOS is an urgent appeal for help from someone whose life is in danger

A B C D E F G H I J K L M N O P Q R **S** T U V W X Y Z

sought
past tense and past participle of seek *We sought a place to hide. Police had sought the criminal everywhere.*

soul noun souls
a person's invisible spirit that some people believe goes on living after the body has died

sound¹ noun sounds
1 sound is vibrations in the air that you can detect with your ear 2 a sound is something that you can hear

sound verb sounds, sounding, sounded
1 to sound is to make a sound *The trumpets sounded.* 2 to sound something is to make a sound with it *Don't forget to sound your horn.* 3 to sound a certain way is to give that impression when heard *You sound in a good mood. The car sounds as if it needs a service.*

sound² verb sounds, sounding, sounded
to sound a river or sea is to test the depth of it **to sound someone out** is to try to find out what they think or feel about something

sound³ adjective sounder, soundest
1 not damaged; in good condition 2 healthy 3 reasonable or correct *His ideas are sound.* 4 reliable or secure *a building on sound foundations* 5 thorough or deep *She has a sound knowledge of history. I am a sound sleeper.* **soundness** noun

sound⁴ noun sounds
a narrow passage of water

soundly adverb
1 you sleep soundly when you sleep deeply 2 to be soundly beaten is to be completely or thoroughly beaten

soundtrack noun soundtracks
the sound or music that goes with a film or television programme

soup noun soups
a liquid food made from vegetables or meat

sour adjective sourer, sourest
1 having a sharp taste like vinegar or lemons 2 unpleasant or bad-tempered **sourly** adverb **sourness** noun

source noun sources
1 the place where something comes from 2 the place where a river starts

south noun
1 the direction to the right of a person facing east 2 the part of a country or city that is in this direction

south adjective, adverb
1 towards the south or in the south 2 coming from the south *A south wind was blowing.*

south–east noun, adjective, adverb
midway between south and east

southerly (say suth-er-lee) adjective
a southerly wind is one that blows from the south

southern (say suth-ern) adjective
from or to do with the south

southerner (say suth-er-ner) noun southerners
someone who lives in the south of a country

southward or southwards adjective, adverb
towards the south

south–west noun, adjective, adverb
midway between south and west

souvenir (say soo-ven-eer) noun souvenirs
something that you buy or keep to remind you of a person, place, or event

sovereign (say sov-rin) noun sovereigns
1 a king or a queen 2 an old British gold coin that was worth £1

sow¹ (rhymes with go) verb sows, sowing, sowed, sown or sowed
to sow seeds is to put them into the ground so that they will grow into plants

sow[2] (rhymes with **cow**) noun **sows**
a female pig

soya bean noun **soya beans**
a kind of bean from which edible oil and
flour are made

space noun **spaces**
1 space is the whole area outside the earth,
where the stars and planets are 2 space is
also an area or volume *There isn't enough
space for a car.* 3 a space is an empty area
or gap *There is a space at the back of the
cupboard. Leave a space for your name and
address.* 4 a space is also a period of time
*They moved house twice in the space of
a year.*

space verb **spaces, spacing, spaced**
to space things, or space things out, is to
arrange them with gaps or periods of time
between them

spacecraft noun **spacecraft**
a vehicle for travelling in outer space

spaceman noun **spacemen**
a man who travels in a spacecraft

spaceship noun **spaceships**
a spacecraft

space station noun **space stations**
a satellite which orbits the earth and is used
as a base by scientists and astronauts

spacewoman noun **spacewomen**
a woman who travels in a spacecraft

spacious adjective
large and roomy *a spacious kitchen*
spaciously adverb **spaciousness** noun

spade noun **spades**
1 a tool with a long handle and a wide
blade for digging 2 a playing card with
black shapes like upside-down hearts on it

spaghetti (say spa-**get**-i) noun
spaghetti is pasta made in long thin strips

 TOP TIPS
Keep it quiet! There is a silent **h** in
spaghetti.

span noun **spans**
1 the length from one end of something

to the other 2 the distance between the
tips of your thumb and little finger when
your hand is spread out 3 a part of a bridge
between two supports 4 a period of time

span verb **spans, spanning, spanned**
to span something is to reach from one side
or end of it to the other *A wooden bridge
spanned the river.*

spaniel noun **spaniels**
a breed of dog with long ears and
silky fur

spank verb **spanks, spanking, spanked**
to spank someone is to smack them several
times on the bottom as a punishment

spanner noun **spanners**
a tool for tightening or loosening a nut

spar[1] noun **spars**
a strong pole used for a mast or boom on
a ship

spar[2] verb **spars, sparring, sparred**
to spar is to practise boxing *He was my
sparring partner.*

spare verb **spares, sparing, spared**
1 to spare something is to afford it or be
able to give it to someone *Can you spare
a moment?* 2 to spare someone is to avoid
harming them or making them suffer
something unpleasant 3 to spare something
is to use it or treat it economically *No
expense will be spared.*

spare adjective
1 not used but kept ready in case it is
needed; extra *Where's the spare wheel? What
do you do in your spare time?* 2 thin or lean

spare noun **spares**
a spare thing or part *The local garage
sells spares.*

sparing adjective
careful or economical, especially
with money

spark noun **sparks**
1 a tiny flash of electricity 2 a tiny glowing
piece of something hot

spark verb **sparks, sparking, sparked**
to spark is to give off sparks

A
B
C
D
E
F
G
H
I
J
K
L
M
N
O
P
Q
R
S
T
U
V
W
X
Y
Z

sparkle verb sparkles, sparkling, sparkled
to shine with a lot of tiny flashes of bright light *The sea sparkled in the sunlight.*

sparkler noun sparklers
a firework that sparkles

sparrow noun sparrows
a small brown bird

sparse adjective sparser, sparsest
small in number or amount; thinly scattered *Vegetation on the island is sparse.* **sparsely** adverb **sparseness** noun

spat
past tense and past participle of **spit**[1] verb *She spat out her reply. After he had spat out the food, he had a drink of water.*

spatter verb spatters, spattering, spattered
to spatter something is to splash it or scatter it in small drops or pieces *The lorry spattered mud all over the pavement.*

spawn noun
spawn is the eggs of frogs, fish, and other water animals

spawn verb spawns, spawning, spawned
frogs, fish, and other water animals spawn when they lay their eggs

speak verb speaks, speaking, spoke, spoken
1 to speak is to say something *I spoke to them this morning.* 2 to speak a language is to be able to talk in it *Do you speak German?* **to speak up** is to say something more clearly or loudly

speaker noun speakers
1 a person who is speaking or making a speech 2 the part of (for example) a radio, CD player, or computer that the sound comes out of

spear noun spears
a long pole with a sharp point, used as a weapon

spear verb spears, spearing, speared
to spear something is to pierce it with a spear or something pointed

special adjective
1 different from other people or things; unusual 2 meant for a particular person or purpose *You'll need special training.*

specialist noun specialists
an expert in a particular subject

speciality noun specialities
1 something that someone specializes in *Dr Dandiffer is an ethnobotanist. His speciality is the medicinal use of tropical plants.* — Michael Hoeye, *Time Stops for No Mouse* 2 a special product, especially a food

specialize verb specializes, specializing, specialized
to specialize is to give particular attention to one subject or thing *She is specializing in biology.* **specialization** noun

specially adverb
for a special purpose *I came specially to see you.*

species (say spee-shiz) noun species
a group of animals or plants that have similar features and can breed with each other

specific adjective
1 definite or precise 2 to do with a particular thing *The money was given for a specific purpose.*

specifically adverb
1 in a special way or for a special purpose *The car is designed specifically for disabled people.* 2 clearly and precisely *I specifically said we had to go.*

specification noun specifications
a detailed list or description of something

specify verb specifies, specifying, specified
to specify a person or thing is to name or mention them precisely *The recipe specified brown sugar, not white.*

specimen noun specimens
1 a small amount or sample of something
2 an example of one kind of plant, animal, or thing *We saw a fine specimen of an oak.*

speck noun specks
1 a tiny piece of something 2 a tiny mark or spot

speckled adjective
covered with small spots

spectacle noun spectacles
1 an exciting sight or display
2 a ridiculous sight

spectacles plural noun
a pair of lenses in a frame, worn over your eyes to help improve your eyesight

spectacular adjective
exciting to see *The exhibition was quite spectacular. They went to the Palace of Engineering first, as this was what Grandad wanted to see.* — Theresa Breslin, *Kezzie*

spectator noun spectators
a person who watches a game or show

spectre (say **spek**-ter) noun spectres
a ghost *'Ghost of the Future,' he exclaimed, 'I fear you more than any spectre I have seen.'* — Charles Dickens, *A Christmas Carol*

spectrum noun spectra
1 the band of colours like those in a rainbow 2 a range of things or ideas *She has a broad spectrum of interests.*

speech noun speeches
1 speech is the ability to speak or a person's way of speaking 2 a speech is a talk given to a group of people

speechless adjective
unable to speak, especially because you are surprised or angry *For a second, Lloyd was speechless. Then he whirled round. 'It's the Headmaster!' he hissed. 'He's almost here!'* — Gillian Cross, *The Revenge of the Demon Headmaster*

speech marks plural noun
inverted commas, used to show that someone is speaking

speed noun speeds
1 the speed of something is the rate at which it moves or happens 2 speed is being quick or fast

speed verb speeds, speeding, sped or speeded
to speed is to go very fast or too fast *Drivers can be fined for speeding.* **to speed up** is to become quicker

speedboat noun speedboats
a fast motor boat

speedometer (say spee-**dom**-it-er) noun speedometers
a device in a vehicle that shows its speed

speedy adjective speedier, speediest
quick or fast *We need a speedy reply.*
speedily adverb

spell[1] verb spells, spelling, spelt or spelled
to spell a word is to give its letters in the right order

spell[2] noun spells
1 a period of time *We're having a cold spell.*
2 a period of activity *I must do a spell of work now.*

spell[3] noun spells
a set of words that is supposed to have magic power

spellchecker or **spellcheck** noun spellcheckers, spellchecks
a computer program you use to check your writing to see if your spelling is correct

spelling noun spellings
1 the way in which letters are put together to form words 2 how well someone can spell *Her spelling is poor.*

spend verb spends, spending, spent
1 to spend money is to use it to pay for things 2 to spend time is to pass it doing something *He spent the weekend painting his bedroom.* 3 to spend energy or effort is to use it up *She spends all her spare energy on gardening.*

sphere noun spheres
1 a perfectly round solid shape; a globe

a
b
c
d
e
f
g
h
i
j
k
l
m
n
o
p
q
r
s
t
u
v
w
x
y
z

491

A
B
C
D
E
F
G
H
I
J
K
L
M
N
O
P
Q
R
S
T
U
V
W
X
Y
Z

or ball **2** an area of activity or interest
spherical adjective

spice noun spices
a strong-tasting substance used to flavour
food, often made from the dried parts
of plants

spicy adjective spicier, spiciest
spicy food tastes strongly of spices

spider noun spiders
a small animal with eight legs that spins
webs to catch insects on which it feeds

spied
past tense and past participle of **spy** verb
*They spied a ship on the horizon. I think they
have spied us.*

spike noun spikes
a pointed piece of metal; a sharp point

spiky adjective spikier, spikiest
something is spiky when it is full of spikes
or sharp points *She has short spiky hair.*

spill verb spills, spilling, spilt or spilled
1 to spill something is to let it fall out of
a container by accident *Careful or you'll
spill your juice.* **2** to spill is to fall out of a
container *The coins came spilling out.*

spill noun spills
when something gets spilt *There's been an
oil spill at sea.*

spin verb spins, spinning, spun
1 to spin is to turn round and round quickly
2 to spin something is to make it spin **3** to
spin is also to make pieces of wool or cotton
into thread by twisting them **4** to spin a
web or cocoon is to make it out of threads
The spider spun a web.

spin noun spins
1 a spinning movement **2** a short outing in
a car

spinach noun
spinach is a vegetable with dark
green leaves

spinal adjective
a spinal injury is one affecting a
person's spine

spin-drier noun spin-driers
a machine for drying clothes by spinning
them round in a drum at high speed

spine noun spines
1 the line of bones down the middle of
your back **2** a sharp point on an animal or
plant *This cactus has sharp spines.* **3** the
back part of a book where the pages are
joined together

spine-chilling adjective
frightening and exciting *We heard a
spine-chilling ghost story.*

spinning wheel noun spinning
wheels
a machine for spinning thread out of wool
or cotton

spin-off noun spin-offs
something extra produced while you are
making something else

spinster noun spinsters
a woman who has not married

spiral adjective
going round and round a central point,
getting further from it with each turn

spiral noun spirals
something with a spiral shape

spire noun spires
a tall pointed part on top of a church
tower

spirit noun spirits
1 a person's spirit is their soul or their
deepest thoughts and feelings **2** a spirit is a
ghost or other supernatural being **3** spirit is
courage or liveliness **4** a person's spirits are
their mood or the way they feel *She was in
good spirits after the exam.* **5** a spirit is also
a strong alcoholic drink

spiritual adjective
1 to do with the human soul and with a
person's deepest thoughts and feelings **2** to
do with religious beliefs **spiritually** adverb

spiritual noun spirituals
a religious song originally sung by
African Americans

492

spit[1] verb spits, spitting, spat
1 to spit is to send drops of liquid forcibly out of your mouth *He spat into the basin.* **2** (informal) to spit is to rain lightly *It's only spitting.*

spit noun
saliva that has been spat out

spit[2] noun spits
1 a long thin metal spike put through meat to hold it while it is roasted **2** a narrow strip of land sticking out into the sea

spite noun
spite is a desire to hurt or annoy someone **in spite of something** although something has happened or is happening *They went out in spite of the rain.*

spiteful adjective
behaving unkindly in order to hurt or annoy someone **spitefully** adverb

spittle noun
saliva, especially when it is spat out

splash verb splashes, splashing, splashed
1 to splash liquid is to make it fly about, as you do when you jump into water **2** to splash is to fly about in drops *The water splashed all over me.* **3** to splash someone or something is to make them wet by sending drops of liquid towards them *The bus splashed us as it went past.*

splash noun splashes
the action or sound of splashing

splendid adjective
magnificent; very fine **splendidly** adverb

splendour noun
splendour is a brilliant display or appearance *The children stood for some minutes, held by the splendour of the view.* — Alan Garner, *The Weirdstone of Brisingamen*

splint noun splints
a straight piece of wood or metal that is tied to a broken arm or leg to hold it firm

splinter noun splinters
a small sharp piece of wood or glass broken off a larger piece

splinter verb splinters, splintering, splintered
to splinter is to break into splinters

split verb splits, splitting, split
1 to split is to break into parts **2** to split something is to divide it into parts **to split up 1** is to divide into parts **2** is to separate after being together for some time

split noun splits
a crack or tear in something, where it has split **the splits** a movement in gymnastics with your legs stretched widely in opposite directions

splutter verb splutters, spluttering, spluttered
1 to splutter is to make a quick series of spitting or coughing sounds *The smoke from the bonfire made him splutter.* **2** to splutter is also to speak quickly and unclearly

spoil verb spoils, spoiling, spoilt or spoiled
1 to spoil something is to damage it and so make it less good or useful *The rain spoilt our holiday.* **2** to spoil someone is to make them selfish by always letting them have what they want

spoils plural noun
valuable things taken by invaders in war

spoilsport noun spoilsports
someone who spoils other people's fun

spoke[1] noun spokes
each of the rods or bars that go from the centre of a wheel to the rim

spoke[2]
past tense of speak *None of the other children spoke to her.*

spoken
past participle of speak *She hadn't spoken for ages.*

spokesman or spokeswoman
noun spokesmen, spokeswomen
a man or woman who speaks on behalf of other people

a
b
c
d
e
f
g
h
i
j
k
l
m
n
o
p
q
r
s
t
u
v
w
x
y
z

A
B
C
D
E
F
G
H
I
J
K
L
M
N
O
P
Q
R
S
T
U
V
W
X
Y
Z

spokesperson noun **spokespersons**
someone who speaks on behalf of a group
of people

sponge noun **sponges**
1 a lump of soft material containing lots
of tiny holes, used for washing 2 a sea
creature from which this kind of material is
made 3 a soft lightweight cake or pudding

sponge verb **sponges, sponging,
sponged**
1 to sponge something is to wash it with
a sponge 2 (informal) to sponge is to get
money from people without doing anything
for them *He was always sponging off
his relatives.*

spongy adjective **spongier, spongiest**
soft and absorbent like sponge

sponsor verb **sponsors, sponsoring,
sponsored**
1 to sponsor someone is to promise to give
them money if they do something difficult
and give the money to charity 2 to sponsor
something or someone is to provide money
to support them

sponsor noun **sponsors**
someone who provides money to support a
person or thing, or who supports someone
who sets out to do something for charity
sponsorship noun

spontaneous (say spon-**tay**-ni-
us) adjective
happening or done without being planned;
not forced or suggested by someone else
*The assembled company—including young
Eddie Dickens—burst into spontaneous
applause.* – Philip Ardagh, *Awful End*
spontaneously adverb **spontaneity** noun

spooky adjective **spookier, spookiest**
(informal)
strange and quite frightening; haunted
by ghosts

spool noun **spools**
a rod or reel for winding on something such
as thread or film or tape

spoon noun **spoons**
a piece of metal or wood or plastic

consisting of a small bowl with a handle,
used for lifting food to your mouth or for
stirring or measuring

spoon verb **spoons, spooning, spooned**
to spoon something is to lift it or take it
with a spoon

spoonful noun **spoonfuls**
as much as a spoon will hold

sport noun **sports**
1 a sport is a game that exercises your body,
especially a game you play out of doors
What sports do you play? 2 sport is games of
this sort *Are you keen on sport?* 3 (informal)
a sport is someone who plays or behaves
fairly and unselfishly *Come on, be a sport.*

sporting adjective
1 connected with sport; interested in sport
2 behaving fairly and unselfishly

sports car noun **sports cars**
an open low-built fast car

sportsman or
sportswoman noun
sportsmen, sportswomen
a man or woman who takes part
in sport

sportsmanship noun
sportsmanship is behaving fairly and
generously in sport and in other ways

spot noun **spots**
1 a small round mark 2 a pimple on your
skin 3 a small amount of something *We've
had a spot of bother.* 4 a place *This is a nice
spot.* **on the spot** immediately; there and
then *We can repair your bike on the spot.*

spot verb **spots, spotting, spotted**
1 to spot someone or something is to notice
them or see them *I suddenly spotted my
friend Alex in the crowd.* 2 to be spotted is to
be marked with spots

spotless adjective
perfectly clean

spotlight noun **spotlights**
a strong light with a beam that shines on a
small area

spotter noun **spotters**
someone who goes to watch or study things that interest them for a hobby *They are keen trainspotters.*

spotty adjective **spottier, spottiest**
marked with spots

spout noun **spouts**
1 a pipe or opening from which liquid can pour 2 a jet of liquid

spout verb **spouts, spouting, spouted**
1 to spout is to come out in a jet of liquid 2 (informal) to spout is also to speak for a long time

sprain verb **sprains, spraining, sprained**
you sprain your ankle or wrist when you injure it by twisting it

sprain noun **sprains**
an injury by spraining

sprang
past tense of **spring** verb *The soldiers sprang into action.*

sprawl verb **sprawls, sprawling, sprawled**
1 you sprawl when you sit or lie with your arms and legs spread out 2 to be sprawled is to be spread out loosely or untidily *There were newspapers sprawled all over the floor.*

spray verb **sprays, spraying, sprayed**
to spray liquid is to scatter it in tiny drops over something; to spray something is to cover it with liquid in this way

spray noun **sprays**
1 tiny drops of liquid sprayed on something 2 a device for spraying liquid

spray noun **sprays**
a small bunch of flowers

spread verb **spreads, spreading, spread**
1 to spread something is to lay or stretch it out to its full size *The bird spread its wings and flew away.* 2 to spread something over a surface is to make it cover the surface *He spread a thick layer of jam on his toast.* 3 to spread news or information is to make it widely known 4 news or information spreads when it becomes widely known *The story spread quickly round the village.*

spread noun **spreads**
1 something you can spread on bread 2 the breadth or extent of something 3 (informal) a large meal

sprightly adjective **sprightlier, sprightliest**
lively and energetic

spring noun **springs**
1 spring is the season of the year when most plants start to grow, between winter and summer 2 a spring is a coil of wire that goes back to its original shape when you bend it or squeeze it and let it go 3 a spring is also a sudden upward movement 4 a spring is also a place where water rises out of the ground and becomes a stream

spring verb **springs, springing, sprang, sprung**
1 to spring is to move quickly or suddenly *He sprang to his feet.* 2 to spring, or spring up, is to develop or come from something *This squabble has sprung from a misunderstanding.* 3 to spring something on someone is to surprise them with it

springboard noun **springboards**
a springy board from which people jump or dive

spring-clean verb **spring-cleans, spring-cleaning, spring-cleaned**
to spring-clean a house is to clean it thoroughly, usually in spring

springy adjective **springier, springiest**
able to spring back to its original position when you bend it or squeeze it and let it go *'I'd like to lie down on this springy heather and watch the stars gradually come sparkling into the sky,' said Anne.* — Enid Blyton, *Five On a Secret Trail*

sprinkle verb **sprinkles, sprinkling, sprinkled**
to sprinkle liquid or powder is to make tiny drops or pieces of it fall on something **sprinkler** noun

sprint verb **sprints, sprinting, sprinted**
to sprint is to run very fast for a short distance **sprinter** noun

a
b
c
d
e
f
g
h
i
j
k
l
m
n
o
p
q
r
s
t
u
v
w
x
y
z

A
B
C
D
E
F
G
H
I
J
K
L
M
N
O
P
Q
R
S
T
U
V
W
X
Y
Z

sprint noun sprints
a short fast race

sprout verb sprouts, sprouting, sprouted
1 a plant sprouts when it starts to produce leaves or shoots 2 to grow or start appearing *When Artemis smiled, as he did now, one almost expected vampire fangs to sprout from his gums.* – Eoin Colfer, *Artemis Fowl*

sprout noun sprouts
a Brussels sprout

spruce[1] noun spruces
a kind of fir tree

spruce[2] adjective srucer, srucest
neat and smart *Jeff looked spruce in a shirt and tie.*

sprung
past participle of **spring** verb *A friendship had sprung up between the two.*

spud noun spuds (informal)
a potato

spun
past tense and past participle of **spin** verb *He spun round. She sold all the wool she had spun.*

spur noun spurs
1 a sharp device that a rider wears on the heel of their boot to urge a horse to go faster 2 a ridge that sticks out from a mountain **on the spur of the moment** on an impulse; without planning

spur verb spurs, spurring, spurred
to spur someone, or to spur someone on, is to encourage them

spurt verb spurts, spurting, spurted
a liquid spurts when it gushes out or up *Blood was spurting from the cut.*

spurt noun spurts
1 a jet of liquid 2 a sudden increase in speed *He put on a spurt and caught us up.*

spy noun spies
someone who works secretly to find out things about another country or person

spy verb spies, spying, spied
1 to spy is to be a spy or to watch secretly *He was spying on us.* 2 to spy someone or something is to see them or notice them *We spied a house in the distance.*

squabble verb squabbles, squabbling, squabbled
people squabble when they quarrel about something unimportant

squabble noun squabbles
a quarrel or argument

squad noun squads
a small group of people working or being trained together

squadron noun squadrons
part of an army, navy, or air force

squalid adjective
dirty and unpleasant *He lived in a squalid little flat.* **squalor** noun

squall noun squalls
1 a sudden storm or strong wind 2 a baby's loud cry **squally** adjective

squander verb squanders, squandering, squandered
to squander money or time is to waste it

square noun squares
1 a shape with four equal sides and four right angles 2 in a town, an area surrounded by buildings 3 the result of multiplying a number by itself *9 is the square of 3.*

square adjective
1 shaped like a square 2 forming a right angle or having right angles 3 used for units of measurement that give an area, such as a square metre and a square foot. For example, a square metre is the size of a square with each side one metre long 4 equal or even *The teams are all square with six points each. If you pay for lunch, we'll be square.*

square verb squares, squaring, squared
1 to square something is to make it have square edges and corners 2 to square a number is to multiply it by itself *3 squared is 9.* 3 to square with something is to match

it or agree with it *His story doesn't square with yours.*

squarely adverb
directly or exactly *The ball hit him squarely in the mouth.*

square root noun **square roots**
the number that gives a particular number if it is multiplied by itself *3 is the square root of 9.*

squash verb **squashes, squashing, squashed**
1 to squash something is to squeeze it so that it loses its shape 2 to squash a person or thing into something is to force them into it when there is not much space *We squashed ourselves into the minibus.*

squash noun **squashes**
1 a squash is when people or things are pressed together because there is not enough space *There was a tremendous squash outside the stadium.* 2 squash is a fruit-flavoured drink 3 squash is also a game played with rackets and a small ball in a special indoor court

squat verb **squats, squatting, squatted**
1 to squat is to sit back on your heels 2 to squat in an unoccupied house is to live there without permission **squatter** noun

squat adjective **squatter, squattest**
short and fat

squawk verb **squawks, squawking, squawked**
to squawk is to make a loud harsh cry

squawk noun **squawks**
a loud harsh cry

squeak verb **squeaks, squeaking, squeaked**
to make a short high-pitched sound or cry

squeak noun **squeaks**
a short high-pitched sound or cry

squeaky adjective **squeakier, squeakiest**
something is squeaky when it makes squeaks *a squeaky floorboard*

squeal verb **squeals, squealing, squealed**
to squeal is to make a long shrill sound

squeal noun **squeals**
a long shrill sound

squeeze verb **squeezes, squeezing, squeezed**
1 to squeeze something is to press it from opposite sides, especially so that you get liquid out of it 2 to squeeze somewhere is to force a way into or through a place or gap *We squeezed into the car.*

squeeze noun **squeezes**
1 the action of squeezing 2 a tight fit *We all got on the bus but it was a bit of a squeeze.* 3 a time when money is difficult to get or borrow

squelch verb **squelches, squelching, squelched**
to squelch is to make a sound like someone treading in thick mud

squelch noun **squelches**
a squelching sound

squid noun **squid or squids**
a sea animal with eight short arms and two long ones

squiggle noun **squiggles**
a short curly or wavy line

squint verb **squints, squinting, squinted**
1 to squint at something is to peer at it or look at it with half-shut eyes 2 to squint is to have eyes that look in different directions

squint noun **squints**
a fault in someone's eyesight that makes them squint

squirm verb **squirms, squirming, squirmed**
to wriggle about, especially when you feel awkward or embarrassed

squirrel noun **squirrels**
a small animal with grey or red fur and a bushy tail, that lives in trees and eats nuts

squirt verb **squirts, squirting, squirted**
to squirt something is to send it out in a

a
b
c
d
e
f
g
h
i
j
k
l
m
n
o
p
q
r
s
t
u
v
w
x
y
z

A
B
C
D
E
F
G
H
I
J
K
L
M
N
O
P
Q
R
S
T
U
V
W
X
Y
Z

strong jet of liquid; to squirt is to come out like this *The orange juice squirted in his eye.*

St. or St
short for **Saint** or **Street**

stab verb stabs, stabbing, stabbed
to stab someone is to pierce or wound them with something sharp *She stabbed him with a knife.*

stab noun stabs
1 the action of stabbing 2 a sudden sharp pain

stability noun
stability is being stable or firm

stabilize verb stabilizes, stabilizing, stabilized
1 to stabilize something is to make it stable 2 to stabilize is to become stable

stabilizer noun stabilizers
a device for keeping a vehicle or ship steady

stable¹ adjective stabler, stablest
steady or firmly fixed **stably** adverb

stable² noun stables
a building where horses are kept

stack noun stacks
1 a neat pile of things 2 a haystack 3 a large amount of something *I've got a stack of work to do.* 4 a single small chimney

stack verb stacks, stacking, stacked
to stack things is to pile them up neatly

stadium noun stadiums or stadia
a sports ground surrounded by seats for spectators

staff noun staffs
1 the people who work in an office or shop 2 the teachers in a school or college 3 a thick stick for walking with 4 a set of five lines on which music is written

stag noun stags
a male deer

stage noun stages
1 a platform for performances in a theatre or hall 2 the point that you have reached in a process or journey *Now for the final stage.*

stage verb stages, staging, staged
1 to stage a performance is to present it on a stage 2 to stage an event is to organize it *They decided to stage a protest.*

stagecoach noun stagecoaches
a horse-drawn coach of a kind that used to travel regularly along the same route

stagger verb staggers, staggering, staggered
1 to stagger is to walk unsteadily 2 to stagger someone is to amaze or shock them *I was staggered at the price.* 3 to stagger events is to arrange them so that they do not all happen at the same time *We stagger our holidays so that someone is always here.* **staggering** adjective

stagnant adjective
stagnant water is not flowing or fresh *The pond is stagnant.*

stain noun stains
1 a dirty mark that is difficult to remove 2 something bad in someone's character or past record

stain verb stains, staining, stained
1 to stain something is to make a stain on it *The juice has stained my dress.* 2 to stain material or wood is to colour it

stainless adjective
without stains

stainless steel noun
stainless steel is steel that does not rust easily

stair noun stairs
each of a series of steps that take you from one floor to another in a building

staircase noun staircases
a set of stairs

stake noun stakes
1 a thick pointed stick to be driven into the ground 2 the thick post to which people used to be tied for execution by being burnt alive 3 an amount of money you bet on something **to be at stake** is to be at risk of being lost

stake verb stakes, staking, staked
to stake money is to use it on a bet **to stake a claim** is to claim something or get a right to it

stalactite noun stalactites
a stony spike hanging like an icicle from the roof of a cave

stalagmite noun stalagmites
a stony spike standing like a pillar on the floor of a cave

stale adjective staler, stalest
no longer fresh *This bread has gone stale. The air in here smells stale.*

stalk¹ noun stalks
the main part of a plant, from which the leaves and flowers grow

stalk² verb stalks, stalking, stalked
1 to stalk a person or animal is to follow or hunt them stealthily **2** to stalk is to walk in a proud or stiff way

stall¹ noun stalls
1 a table or small open-fronted shop where things are sold, usually in the open air **2** a place for one animal in a stable or shed

stall verb stalls, stalling, stalled
a vehicle stalls when the engine stops suddenly *The car stalled at the traffic lights.*

stall² verb stalls, stalling, stalled
to stall is to delay or hold things up to give yourself more time

stallion noun stallions
a male horse

stalls plural noun
the seats on the ground floor of a theatre or cinema

stamen (say **stay**-men) noun stamens
the part of a flower that produces pollen

stamina (say **stam**-in-a) noun
stamina is the strength and energy you need to keep doing something for a long time *Does she have the stamina to run a marathon?*

stammer verb stammers, stammering, stammered
to stammer is to keep repeating the sounds at the beginning of words

stammer noun stammers
a tendency to stammer

stamp noun stamps
1 a small piece of gummed paper with a special design on it; a postage stamp **2** when you bang your foot on the ground **3** a small block with raised letters for printing words or marks on something; the words or marks made with this

stamp verb stamps, stamping, stamped
1 to stamp is to bang your foot heavily on the ground **2** to stamp an envelope or parcel is to put a postage stamp on it **3** to stamp something is also to put marks on it with a stamp *The librarian stamped my books.*

stampede noun stampedes
a sudden rush of animals or people

stampede verb stampedes, stampeding, stampeded
animals or people stampede when they rush in a stampede

stand verb stands, standing, stood
1 to stand is to be on your feet without moving *She stood at the back of the hall.* **2** to stand something somewhere is to put it upright there *Stand the vase on the table.* **3** something stands somewhere when that is where it is *The castle stood on the top of a hill.* **4** something stands when it stays unchanged *My offer still stands.* **5** to stand a difficulty or hardship is to be able to bear it *I can't stand the heat.* **it stands to reason** it is reasonable or obvious **to stand by** is to be ready for action **to stand for something 1** is to tolerate it or put up with it *She won't stand for any arguments.* **2** is to mean something *'Dr' stands for 'Doctor'.* **to stand in for someone** is to take their place **to stand out** is to be clear or obvious **to stand up for someone** is to support them or defend them

stand noun stands
1 something made for putting things on *Use*

a music stand. **2** a stall where things are sold or displayed **3** a building at a sports ground, that is open at the front with rows of seats for spectators **4** when someone resists an attack or defends their opinion *She was determined to make a stand for her rights.*

standard noun standards
1 how good something is *They reached a high standard of work.* **2** a thing used to measure or judge something else *The metre is the standard for length.* **3** a special flag, especially one used by an army
standard adjective
of the usual or ordinary kind

standardize verb standardizes, standardizing, standardized
to standardize something is to make it a standard size or type

standard lamp noun standard lamps
a lamp on an upright pole that stands on the floor

standby noun standbys
something or someone kept to be used if they are needed

standstill noun
a complete stop *The blizzard brought traffic to a standstill.*

stank
past tense of **stink** verb *The shed stank of old wood.*

stanza noun stanzas
a group of lines in a poem

staple¹ noun staples
1 a tiny piece of metal used to fasten pieces of paper together **2** a U-shaped nail
stapler noun
staple verb staples, stapling, stapled
to fasten pieces of paper together with a staple

staple² adjective
main or normal *Rice is their staple food.*

star noun stars
1 a large mass of burning gas that you see as a bright speck of light in the sky at night

2 one of the main performers in a film or show; a famous entertainer **3** a shape with five or six points

star verb stars, starring, starred
1 to star in a film or show is to be one of the main performers **2** a film or show stars someone when it has them as a main performer

starboard noun
starboard is the right-hand side of a ship or aircraft when you are facing forward

starch noun starches
1 starch is a white carbohydrate in bread, potatoes, and other food **2** starch is also a form of this substance used to stiffen clothes

stare verb stares, staring, stared
to look continuously at someone or something without moving your eyes
stare noun stares
a long fixed look *I gave him a hard stare.*

starfish noun starfish or starfishes
a sea animal shaped like a star with five points

starling noun starlings
a noisy black or brown speckled bird

starry adjective
a starry sky or night is full of stars

start verb starts, starting, started
1 to start something is to take the first steps in doing it **2** to start, or start out, is to begin a journey **3** to start is also to make a sudden movement of surprise *They all started at the noise outside.*
start noun starts
1 the act of starting; the point or place where something starts **2** an advantage that someone starts with *We gave the young ones 10 minutes' start.* **3** a sudden movement of surprise *It gave me quite a start when the hooter sounded.*

starter noun starters
1 someone who starts a race **2** a device for starting the engine of a vehicle

A B C D E F G H I J K L M N O P Q R **S** T U V W X Y Z

startle verb startles, startling, startled
to startle a person or animal is to surprise or alarm them

starve verb starves, starving, starved
1 someone starves when they suffer or die because they do not have enough food **2** to starve someone is to make them suffer or die in this way *The prisoners had been starved to death.* **3** to starve someone of something they need is to deprive them of it *She was starved of love.* **4** (informal) to be starving is to be very hungry
starvation noun

state noun states
1 the quality of a person or thing or their circumstances; the way they are **2** a nation **3** a division of a country **4** you can refer to a government and its officials as the state
to be in a state (informal) is to be upset

state verb states, stating, stated
to state something is to say it clearly or formally

stately adjective statelier, stateliest
grand and dignified **stateliness** noun

stately home noun stately homes
a large and splendid house that a noble family has owned for many years

statement noun statements
1 words that state something **2** a formal account of something that happened *A witness to the robbery has given a statement to the police.* **3** a report made by a bank about the money in a person's account

state school noun state schools
a school which gets its money from the government and does not charge fees

statesman or
stateswoman noun
statesmen, stateswomen
someone who is important or skilled in governing a state

static adjective
not moving or changing

static electricity noun
static electricity is electricity which is

present in something but does not flow as a current

station noun stations
1 a set of buildings where people get on or off trains or buses **2** a building for police, firemen, or other workers who serve the public **3** a place from which radio or television broadcasts are made

station verb stations, stationing, stationed
to station a person somewhere is to place them there for a particular purpose *He was stationed at the door to take the tickets.*

stationary adjective
not moving; still *The car was stationary when the van hit it.*

stationery noun
stationery is paper, envelopes, and other things used for writing or word processing

statistic noun statistics
a piece of information expressed as a number *These statistics show that the population has doubled.*

statistics noun
statistics is the study of information that is expressed as numbers

statue noun statues
a model made of stone or metal to look like a person or animal

status noun statuses
1 a person's status is their position or rank in relation to other people *What is your status in the company?* **2** status is high rank or prestige

staunch adjective
firm and loyal *They are the team's most staunch supporters.*

stave noun staves
a set of five lines on which music is written

stave verb staves, staving, staved or stove
to stave something is to make a hole or dent in it *The collision stove in the front of the ship.* **to stave something off** is to keep something unwelcome away or delay it *I ate a banana to stave off my hunger.*

A
B
C
D
E
F
G
H
I
J
K
L
M
N
O
P
Q
R
S
T
U
V
W
X
Y
Z

stay verb stays, staying, stayed
1 to stay somewhere is to continue to be there or to remain there **2** to stay somewhere or with someone is to spend time as a visitor *We stayed in a little hotel near the sea.*

stay noun stays
a period of time spent somewhere *We didn't have time for a long stay.*

steady adjective steadier, steadiest
1 not shaking or moving; firm **2** regular or constant; not changing much *They kept up a steady pace.*

steady verb steadies, steadying, steadied
to steady something is to make it steady
steadily adverb

steak noun steaks
a thick slice of meat or fish

steal verb steals, stealing, stole, stolen
1 to steal something is to take and keep it when it does not belong to you **2** to steal somewhere is to move there stealthily *He stole out of the room.*

stealthy adjective stealthier, stealthiest
moving or doing something secretly and quietly so that you are not noticed
stealth noun **stealthily** adverb

steam noun
steam is the gas or vapour that comes from boiling water **to run out of steam** (informal) is to have no energy left

steam verb steams, steaming, steamed
1 to steam is to give out steam **2** to steam somewhere is to move using the power of steam *The boat steamed down the river.* **3** to steam food is to cook it with steam *Let's have a steamed pudding.* **to steam up** is to be covered with mist or condensation *The windows have steamed up.*

steam engine noun steam engines
an engine driven by steam

steamer noun steamers
a steamship

steamroller noun steamrollers
a heavy vehicle with wide metal wheels, used to flatten surfaces when making roads

steamship noun steamships
a ship driven by steam

steed noun steeds (old or poetic use)
a horse

steel noun
steel is a strong metal made from iron and carbon

steel verb steels, steeling, steeled
to steel yourself is to find courage to do something difficult

steel band noun steel bands
a West Indian band of musicians who play instruments made from oil drums

steely adjective steelier, steeliest
someone is steely when they behave in a strong, hard way, like steel *She had a steely look in her eyes.*

steep adjective steeper, steepest
rising or sloping sharply **steeply** adverb
steepness noun

steeple noun steeples
a church tower with a spire

steer[1] verb steers, steering, steered
to steer a vehicle is to make it go in the direction you want

steer[2] noun steers
a young bull kept for its beef

steering wheel noun steering wheels
a wheel for steering a vehicle

stem noun stems
1 the main central part of a plant or tree; a stalk **2** (in grammar) the main part of a word, to which different endings are attached. For example, *call* is the stem of the words *caller, called, calls,* and *calling*

stem verb stems, stemming, stemmed
to stem from something is to start there or come from it *The problem stems from lack of money.*

stench noun stenches
a very unpleasant smell

stencil noun stencils
a piece of card or metal or plastic with
pieces cut out of it, used to produce a
picture or design

step noun steps
1 a movement you make with your foot
when you are walking, running, or dancing
2 the sound of a person putting down
their foot when walking **3** each of the level
surfaces on a stair or ladder **4** each of a
series of actions
step verb steps, stepping, stepped
to step is to tread or walk **to step
something up** is to increase it

stepchild noun stepchildren
a child that someone's husband or wife has
from an earlier marriage. A boy is a **stepson**
and a girl is a **stepdaughter**.

stepfather noun stepfathers
a man who is married to your mother but is
not your own father

stepladder noun stepladders
a folding ladder with flat treads

stepmother noun stepmothers
a woman who is married to your father but
is not your own mother

stepping stone noun stepping
stones
stepping stones are a line of stones put
in a river or stream to help people
walk across

stereo adjective
stereophonic
stereo noun stereos
1 stereo is stereophonic sound or recording
2 a stereo is a stereophonic radio or
record player

stereophonic (say ste-ri-o-**fon**-ik)
adjective
using sound that comes from two different
directions to give a natural effect

sterile adjective
1 clean and free from germs **2** not able
to have children or reproduce
sterility noun

sterilize verb sterilizes, sterilizing,
sterilized
1 to sterilize something is to make it free
from germs **2** to sterilize a person or animal
is to make them unable to bear young
sterilization noun

sterling noun
sterling is British money *Tourists paid for
their meals in sterling.*

stern[1] adjective sterner, sternest
strict and severe **sternly** adverb in a stern
way *The Lady frowned. 'Is that how you
address a queen?' she asked sternly. — C. S.
Lewis, The Lion, The Witch and the Wardrobe*
sternness noun

stern[2] noun sterns
the back part of a ship

stethoscope (say **steth**-o-skohp)
noun stethoscopes
a device used by doctors for listening to a
patient's heartbeat or breathing

stew verb stews, stewing, stewed
to stew food is to cook it slowly in liquid
stew noun stews
a dish of meat and vegetables cooked slowly
in liquid

steward noun stewards
1 a man whose job is to look after the
passengers on a ship or aircraft **2** an official
who looks after the arrangements at a
public event

stewardess noun stewardesses
a woman whose job is to look after the
passengers on a ship or aircraft

stick[1] noun sticks
1 a long thin piece of wood **2** a walking
stick **3** the long thin piece of wood used
to hit the ball in hockey, polo, or other ball
games **4** a long thin piece of something *I
must get a stick of rock.*

a
b
c
d
e
f
g
h
i
j
k
l
m
n
o
p
q
r
s
t
u
v
w
x
y
z

A
B
C
D
E
F
G
H
I
J
K
L
M
N
O
P
Q
R
S
T
U
V
W
X
Y
Z

stick² verb **sticks, sticking, stuck**
1 to stick something sharp into a thing is to push it in roughly or carelessly *He stuck a pin in her finger.* **2** to stick things is to fasten or join them **3** something sticks when it becomes fixed or jammed *The door keeps sticking.* **4** (informal) you can't stick something when you can't bear it *I can't stick it any longer.* **to stick out** is to come out from a surface or be noticeable **to stick up for someone** (informal) is to support them or defend them

sticker noun **stickers**
a label or sign for sticking on something

stick insect noun **stick insects**
an insect with a long thin body that looks like a twig

sticky adjective **stickier, stickiest**
1 able or likely to stick to things
2 (informal) unpleasant or nasty *He came to a sticky end.* **stickily** adverb **stickiness** noun

stiff adjective **stiffer, stiffest**
1 not able to bend or change its shape easily **2** difficult *We had a stiff test.*
3 formal; not friendly **4** strong or severe *There's a stiff wind outside.* **stiffly** adverb **stiffness** noun

stiffen verb **stiffens, stiffening, stiffened**
1 to stiffen something is to make it stiff **2** to stiffen is to become stiff

stifle verb **stifles, stifling, stifled**
1 to be stifled is to find it difficult or impossible to breathe **2** to stifle something is to stop it happening *She stifled a yawn. John clapped his hands on the ill-fated pirate's mouth to stifle the dying groan.* — J. M. Barrie, *The Adventures of Peter Pan*

stile noun **stiles**
an arrangement of steps or bars for people to climb over a fence

still adjective **stiller, stillest**
1 not moving **2** silent *In the night, the streets are still.* **3** not fizzy **stillness** noun

still adverb
1 up to this or that time *He was still there.*
2 even; yet; in a greater amount *They wanted still more food.* **3** however *They lost. Still, they have another game.*

still verb **stills, stilling, stilled**
to still something is to make it still

stilts plural noun
1 a pair of poles on which you can walk high above the ground **2** supports for a house built over water

stimulate verb **stimulates, stimulating, stimulated**
1 to stimulate someone is to make them excited or interested **2** to stimulate something is to encourage it to develop *His new book stimulated an interest in wildlife.* **stimulation** noun

stimulus noun **stimuli**
something that encourages a thing to develop or produces a reaction

sting noun **stings**
1 the part of an insect or plant that can cause pain or a wound **2** a painful area or wound caused by an insect or plant

sting verb **stings, stinging, stung**
1 an insect or plant stings you when it wounds or hurts you with a sting *She was stung by a wasp.* **2** part of your body stings when you feel a sharp or throbbing pain there *My back is stinging from sunburn.*

stingy (say **stin**-ji) adjective **stingier, stingiest**
mean; not generous

stink noun **stinks**
1 an unpleasant smell **2** (informal) an unpleasant fuss or complaint

stink verb **stinks, stinking, stank** or **stunk, stunk**
to stink is to have an unpleasant smell

stir verb **stirs, stirring, stirred**
1 to stir something liquid or soft is to move it round and round, especially with a spoon
2 to stir is to move slightly or start to move after sleeping or being still *She didn't stir all afternoon.* **to stir something up** is to excite or arouse it *They are always stirring up trouble.*

stir noun stirs
1 an act of stirring *Give it a stir.* 2 a fuss or disturbance *The news caused a stir.*

stirrup noun stirrups
a metal loop that hangs down on each side of a horse's saddle to support the rider's foot

stitch noun stitches
1 a loop of thread made in sewing or knitting 2 a sudden pain in your side caused by running

stoat noun stoats
an animal rather like a weasel, also called an ermine

stock noun stocks
1 a stock of things is an amount of them kept ready to be sold or used 2 stock is a collection of farm animals, also called livestock 3 a person's stock is the line of their ancestors 4 stock is a liquid used in cooking, made from the juices you get by stewing meat, fish, or vegetables 5 stock is also a number of shares in a company's capital 6 stock is also a garden flower with a sweet smell

stock verb stocks, stocking, stocked
1 a shop stocks goods when it keeps a supply of them to sell 2 to stock a place is to provide it with a stock of things *The explorers stocked their base camp with tinned food.* **to stock up** is to buy a large supply of something

stockade noun stockades
a fence made of large stakes

stock car noun stock cars
an ordinary car strengthened for use in races in which cars are allowed to bump each other

stocking noun stockings
a piece of clothing that covers the whole of someone's leg and foot

stockpile noun stockpiles
a large stock of things kept in reserve

stocks plural noun
a wooden framework with holes for people's legs and arms, in which criminals were locked as a punishment

stocky adjective stockier, stockiest
short and solidly built

stodgy adjective stodgier, stodgiest
1 thick and heavy; not easy to digest *The pudding's very stodgy.* 2 dull and boring *What a stodgy book.*

stoke verb stokes, stoking, stoked
to stoke a furnace or fire is to add fuel to it

stole[1] noun stoles
a wide piece of material worn round the shoulders by women

stole[2]
past tense of steal *He stole his aunt's purse.*

stolen
past participle of steal *Someone has stolen my packed lunch.*

stomach noun stomachs
1 the part of your body where food starts to be digested 2 the front part of your body that contains your stomach; your abdomen

stomach verb stomachs, stomaching, stomached
to stomach something is to tolerate it or put up with it *I can't stomach their awful jokes.*

stone noun stones or, for the unit of weight, stone
1 stone is the hard solid mineral of which rocks are made 2 a stone is a piece of this mineral 3 a stone is also a jewel 4 a stone is also the hard seed in the middle of some fruits, such as a cherry, plum, or peach 5 a stone is also a unit of weight equal to 14 pounds or about 6.35 kilograms *She weighs 6 stone.*

stone verb stones, stoning, stoned
1 to stone someone is to throw stones at them 2 to stone fruit is to take the stones out of it

stone-cold adjective
extremely cold

stony adjective stonier, stoniest
1 stony ground is full of stones 2 hard like

a b c d e f g h i j k l m n o p q r **s** t u v w x y z

stone **3** unfriendly or hostile *Our question was met by a stony silence.*

stood
past tense and past participle of **stand** verb *A man stood up to speak. We should have stood up to those bullies.*

stool noun stools
a small seat without a back

stoop verb stoops, stooping, stooped
1 to stoop is to bend your body forwards and downwards **2** to stoop to doing something is to lower your standards of behaviour *I didn't think he'd stoop to cheating.*

stop verb stops, stopping, stopped
1 to stop something is to finish doing it, or make it finish **2** to stop is to be no longer moving or working or to come to an end **3** to stop something is to prevent it happening or continuing *I must go out and stop that noise.* **4** to stop a hole or gap, or stop it up, is to fill it **5** to stop at a place is to stay there briefly

stop noun stops
1 when something stops or ends *She brought the car to a stop.* **2** a place where a bus or train stops regularly

stoppage noun stoppages
1 an interruption in the work of a business or factory **2** a blockage in something

stopper noun stoppers
something that fits into the top of a bottle or jar to close it

stopwatch noun stopwatches
a watch that you can start or stop, used for timing races

storage noun
storage is the storing of things

store verb stores, storing, stored
to store things is to keep them until they are needed

store noun stores
1 a place where things are stored **2** things kept for future use **3** a shop, especially a large one **to be in store** is to be waiting to happen soon *There is a treat in store for you.*

storey noun storeys
one whole floor of a building

stork noun storks
a large bird with long legs and a long beak

storm noun storms
1 a period of bad weather with strong winds, rain or snow, and often thunder and lightning **2** a violent attack or outburst *There was a storm of protest.* **a storm in a teacup** a big fuss over something unimportant

storm verb storms, storming, stormed
1 to storm is to move or shout angrily *He stormed out of the room.* **2** soldiers or police storm a place when they attack it suddenly *They stormed the castle.*

stormy adjective stormier, stormiest
1 likely to end in a storm *The weather is stormy today.* **2** loud and angry *We had a stormy meeting.*

story noun stories
1 an account of real or imaginary events **2** (informal) a lie *Don't tell stories!*

stout adjective stouter, stoutest
1 rather fat **2** thick and strong *She carried a stout stick.* **3** brave *The defenders put up a stout resistance.* **stoutly** adverb **stoutness** noun

stove¹ noun stoves
a device that produces heat for warming a room or cooking

stove²
past tense and past participle of **stave** verb *The collision stove in the front of the ship.*

stow verb stows, stowing, stowed
to stow something is to pack it or store it away *The witch stowed her knitting in her pocket and got up. She followed Lizzie to the mill door and peered in.* – Helen Cresswell, *Lizzie Dripping* **to stow away** is to hide on a ship or aircraft so that you can travel without paying

stowaway noun **stowaways**
someone who stows away on a ship or aircraft

straddle verb **straddles, straddling, straddled**
1 to straddle something is to sit or stand with your legs either side of it 2 to straddle something is also to be built across it *A long bridge straddles the river.*

straggle verb **straggles, straggling, straggled**
1 to straggle is to walk too slowly and not keep up with the rest of a group
2 to straggle is also to grow or move in an untidy way *Brambles straggled across the path.* **straggler** noun someone who does not keep up with the rest of a group **straggly** adjective straggly hair grows or hangs untidily

straight adjective **straighter, straightest**
1 going continuously in one direction; not curving or bending 2 level *Is this picture straight?* 3 tidy; in proper order 4 honest or frank *Give me a straight answer.*

straight adverb
1 in a straight line *Go straight on, then turn left.* 2 at once; directly *I came straight here.*

straightaway adverb
immediately; at once

straighten verb **straightens, straightening, straightened**
1 to straighten something is to make it straight 2 to straighten is to become straight

straightforward adjective
1 easy to understand or do; not complicated 2 honest or frank

strain verb **strains, straining, strained**
1 to strain something is to stretch it or push it or pull it hard or too hard 2 to strain a muscle is to damage it by using it too much 3 to strain is to make a great effort to do something 4 to strain liquid is to put it through a sieve to take out any lumps or other things in it

strain noun **strains**
1 the strain on something is when it is stretched or pulled too hard *The rope broke under the strain.* 2 a strain is an injury caused by straining 3 strain is the effect on someone of too much work or worry

strainer noun **strainers**
a device for straining liquids

strait noun **straits**
a narrow stretch of water connecting two seas

strait

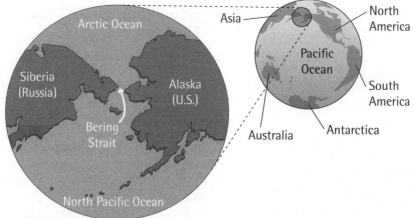

A B C D E F G H I J K L M N O P Q R **S** T U V W X Y Z

straits plural noun
to be in dire straits is to have severe difficulties

strand noun strands
1 each of the threads or wires twisted together to make a rope or cable 2 a lock of hair

stranded adjective
1 left on sand or rocks in shallow water *We could see a stranded ship.* 2 left in a difficult or lonely position *They were stranded in the desert.*

strange adjective stranger, strangest
1 unusual or surprising 2 not known or experienced before **strangely** adverb **strangeness** noun

stranger noun strangers
1 a person you do not know 2 a person who is in a place they do not know

strangle verb strangles, strangling, strangled
to strangle someone is to kill them by pressing their throat and so prevent them breathing **strangulation** noun

strap noun straps
a flat strip of leather or cloth or plastic for fastening things together or holding them in place
strap verb straps, strapping, strapped
to strap something is to fasten it with a strap or straps

strategy noun strategies
1 a strategy is a plan to achieve or win something 2 strategy is planning a war or military campaign **strategic** adjective

stratum (say strah-tum) noun strata
a layer or level *You can see several strata of rock in the cliffs.*

straw noun straws
1 straw is dry cut stalks of corn 2 a straw is a narrow tube that you can drink through

strawberry noun strawberries
a small red juicy fruit, with its seeds on the outside

stray verb strays, straying, strayed
to wander or become lost
stray adjective
1 wandering around lost *We found a stray cat.* 2 out of place; separated from all the others *a stray hair*
stray noun strays
a stray dog or cat

streak noun streaks
1 a long thin line or mark 2 a streak of something is a trace or sign of it *He has a cruel streak.*
streak verb streaks, streaking, streaked
1 to streak something is to mark it with streaks 2 to streak somewhere is to move there very quickly

streaky adjective streakier, streakiest
marked with streaks

stream noun streams
1 a narrow river or brook 2 liquid flowing in one direction 3 a number of things moving in the same direction, such as traffic
stream verb streams, streaming, streamed
1 to stream is to move in a strong or fast flow *Traffic streamed across the junction.* 2 to stream is also to produce a flow of liquid *Blood was streaming from her cut hand.*

streamer noun streamers
a long strip of paper or ribbon

streamline verb streamlines, streamlining, streamlined
1 to streamline a vehicle or object is to give it a smooth shape that helps it to move easily through air or water 2 to streamline an activity or operation is to make it work more efficiently

street noun streets
a road with houses beside it in a city or town

strength noun strengths
1 strength is how strong a person or thing is 2 a person's strengths are their good

points or the things they are good at
Patience is your greatest strength.

 TOP TIPS Keep it quiet! There is a silent **g** in **strength**.

strengthen verb **strengthens, strengthening, strengthened**
1 to strengthen something or someone is to make them stronger **2** to strengthen is to become stronger

strenuous adjective
needing or using great effort and determination **strenuously** adverb

stress noun **stresses**
1 a stress is a force or pressure that pulls or pushes or twists something **2** stress is the effect on someone of too much work or worry or pressure **3** stress is also emphasis, especially the extra force with which you pronounce part of a word or phrase

stress verb **stresses, stressing, stressed**
1 to stress part of a word or phrase is to pronounce it with extra emphasis **2** to stress a point or idea is to emphasize it **3** to stress someone is to make them suffer stress

stretch verb **stretches, stretching, stretched**
1 to stretch something is to pull it so that it becomes longer or wider **2** something stretches when it becomes longer or wider when it is pulled **3** you stretch, or stretch out, when you reach out with your arms or extend your arms and legs fully **4** to stretch somewhere is to extend or continue there *The wall stretches all the way round the park.* **stretchy** adjective

stretch noun **stretches**
1 the action of stretching something *I got up and had a good stretch.* **2** a continuous period of time or area of land or water

stretcher noun **stretchers**
a framework like a light folding bed with handles at each end, for carrying a sick or injured person

strew verb **strews, strewing, strewed, strewn** or **strewed**
to strew things is to scatter them over a surface *Flowers were strewn over the path.*

stricken adjective
overcome or strongly affected by a feeling or illness

strict adjective **stricter, strictest**
1 demanding that people obey rules and behave well *The teachers are all fairly strict.* **2** complete or exact *He's not really a hero in the strict sense of the word.* **strictness** noun

strictly adverb
1 something is (for example) strictly forbidden when it is completely forbidden **2** you say something is not strictly true when it is not exactly true

stride verb **strides, striding, strode, stridden**
to walk with long steps

stride noun **strides**
a long step you take when walking or running **to take something in your stride** is to cope with it easily

strife noun
strife is fighting or quarrelling

strike verb **strikes, striking, struck**
1 to strike something or someone is to hit them **2** to strike people or a place is to attack them suddenly *Plague struck the village.* **3** to strike a match is to light it by rubbing it against something rough **4** a clock strikes (for example) seven when it rings seven chimes at seven o'clock **5** workers strike when they stop working as a protest against their pay or conditions **6** to strike oil or gold is to find it by drilling or mining **7** to strike someone in some way is to make them think that way *The film struck me as quite funny.* **to strike up** is to begin playing or singing

strike noun **strikes**
1 a hit **2** when workers refuse to work, as a way of making a protest **3** a find of oil or gold underground

a
b
c
d
e
f
g
h
i
j
k
l
m
n
o
p
q
r
s
t
u
v
w
x
y
z

striker noun strikers
1 a worker who is on strike 2 in football, an attacking player who tries to score goals

striking adjective
so impressive, interesting, or attractive that you can't help noticing it *And the most striking pup of all was one who had a perfect horse-shoe of spots on his back – and had therefore been named 'Lucky'.* – Dodie Smith, *The Hundred and One Dalmatians*

string noun strings
1 string is thin rope or cord for tying things; a string is a piece of thin rope 2 in music, a string is a piece of stretched wire or nylon used in an instrument to make sounds 3 a string of things is a line or series of them *There was a string of buses along the High Street.*

string verb strings, stringing, strung
1 to string something is to hang it on a string 2 to string pearls or beads is to thread them on a string 3 to string beans is to remove the tough fibre from them 4 to string a racket or musical instrument is to put strings on it **to string something out** is to spread or stretch it out

stringed adjective
in music, stringed instruments are ones that have strings, especially members of the violin family

strings plural noun
the stringed instruments in an orchestra

stringy adjective stringier, stringiest
1 long and thin like string 2 stringy meat contains tough fibres

strip¹ verb strips, stripping, stripped
1 to strip something is to take a covering off it 2 to strip is to take all your clothes off 3 to strip someone of something is to take it away from them

strip noun strips
the special outfit worn by a sports team

strip² noun strips
a long narrow piece of something

stripe noun stripes
1 a long narrow band of colour 2 something

worn on the sleeve of a uniform to show the rank of the person wearing it

striped or **stripy** adjective
something is striped or stripy if it has stripes

strive verb strives, striving, strove, striven
to strive to do something is to try hard to do it

strobe noun strobes
a light that flickers on and off continuously

strode
past tense of **stride** verb *He strode confidently into the room.*

stroke¹ noun strokes
1 a hit or movement made by swinging your arm 2 one of the styles you can use to swim 3 a line drawn by a pen or brush 4 a sudden illness that often causes someone to be paralysed

stroke² verb strokes, stroking, stroked
to stroke something is to move your hand gently along it

stroll verb strolls, strolling, strolled
to walk slowly

stroll noun strolls
a short leisurely walk

strong adjective stronger, strongest
1 having great power, energy, or effect 2 not easily broken or damaged *The gate was held by a strong chain.* 3 having a lot of flavour or smell *Do you like your tea strong?* 4 having a particular number or size *The game had a crowd 20,000 strong.*

strong adverb
to be going strong is to be making good progress

stronghold noun strongholds
a fortress or other place that is well defended

strongly adverb
1 in a strong way; with strength *They fought back strongly.* 2 very much *The room smelt strongly of perfume.*

strove
past tense of **strive** *He strove to learn more about space.*

struck
past tense and past participle of **strike** verb *The clock struck three. We raced for safety as the storm had struck.*

structure noun structures
1 a structure is something that has been built or put together 2 a thing's structure is the way that it is built or made **structural** adjective **structurally** adverb

struggle verb struggles, struggling, struggled
1 to struggle is to move your body about violently while you are fighting or trying to get free 2 to struggle to do something is to make strong efforts to do it

struggle noun struggles
1 fighting or trying to get free 2 a great effort

strum verb strums, strumming, strummed
to strum a guitar is to sound it by running your finger across its strings

strung
past tense and past participle of **string** verb *The archer strung his bow. His sister had strung along with him.*

strut verb struts, strutting, strutted
to walk proudly or stiffly *Hare began to strut about so that the moon should see what a fine figure of a creature was waiting for her.* — Ted Hughes, *How the Whale Became and Other Stories*

strut noun struts
1 a strutting walk 2 a bar of wood or metal that strengthens a framework

stub verb stubs, stubbing, stubbed
1 you stub your toe when you knock it against something hard 2 to stub, or to stub out, a cigarette or cigar is to put it out by pressing it against something hard

stub noun stubs
a short piece of something left after the rest has been used up or worn down

stubble noun
1 stubble is the short stalks of corn left in the ground after a harvest 2 stubble is also the short stiff hairs growing on a man's chin when he has not shaved

stubborn adjective
not willing to change your ideas or ways; obstinate **stubbornly** adverb **stubbornness** noun

stuck[1]
past tense and past participle of **stick**[2] *Edward stuck his hands in his pockets. Have you stuck a stamp on the envelope?*

stuck[2] adjective
unable to move or make progress *Is anyone stuck?*

stuck-up adjective (informal)
unpleasantly proud or snobbish

stud noun studs
a small metal button or knob fixed into something

student noun students
someone who studies, especially at a college or university

studio noun studios
1 a place where radio or television broadcasts are made 2 a place where cinema or television films are made 3 the room where an artist or photographer works

studious adjective
fond of studying; studying hard **studiously** adverb

study verb studies, studying, studied
1 to study is to spend time learning about something 2 to study something is to look at it carefully

study noun studies
1 study is the process of studying 2 a study is a room used for studying or writing

stuff noun
1 stuff is a substance or material *What's this stuff at the bottom of the glass?* 2 stuff is also a group of things or a person's

possessions *Will you move your stuff off the table?*

stuff verb stuffs, stuffing, stuffed
1 to stuff something is to fill it tightly, especially with stuffing *She stuffed the turkey.* 2 to stuff one thing inside another is to push it in carelessly *He stuffed the paper into his pocket.*

stuffing noun stuffings
1 stuffing is material used to fill the inside of something 2 stuffing is also a savoury mixture you put into meat or poultry before cooking it

stuffy adjective stuffier, stuffiest
1 a stuffy room is badly ventilated, without enough fresh air 2 formal and boring **stuffily** adverb **stuffiness** noun

stumble verb stumbles, stumbling, stumbled
1 to stumble is to lose your balance or fall over something 2 to stumble when you are speaking is to make mistakes or hesitate

stump noun stumps
1 the bottom of a tree trunk left in the ground when the tree has fallen or been cut down 2 (in cricket) each of the three upright sticks of a wicket

stump verb stumps, stumping, stumped
something stumps you when it is too difficult for you *The last question stumped everyone.*

stun verb stuns, stunning, stunned
1 to stun someone is to knock them unconscious 2 something stuns you when it shocks or confuses you *They were stunned by the news.*

stung
past tense and past participle of **sting** verb *Tears stung Alisha's eyes. He jumped as if he'd been stung by a bee.*

stunk
past tense and past participle of **stink** verb *The room stunk of smoke. The mouldy cheese had stunk for days in the fridge.*

stunt noun stunts
1 something daring or dangerous done in a film or as part of a performance 2 something unusual done to attract publicity or attention

stupendous adjective
amazing; tremendous *The Iron Man had had the most stupendous idea. The Iron Man would go out, as the champion of the earth, against this monster from space.* – Ted Hughes, *The Iron Man*

stupid adjective stupider, stupidest
without reason or common sense; not clever or thoughtful **stupidity** noun **stupidly** adverb

sturdy adjective sturdier, sturdiest
strong and solid **sturdily** adverb **sturdiness** noun

stutter verb stutters, stuttering, stuttered
to keep repeating the sounds at the beginning of words
stutter noun stutters
a tendency to stutter

sty¹ noun sties
a pigsty

sty² or **stye** noun sties, styes
a sore swelling on your eyelid

style noun styles
1 a style is the way that something is done, made, said, or written 2 style is being smart and elegant 3 a style is also a part of the pistil in a flower
style verb styles, styling, styled
to style something is to give it a special style

stylish adjective
fashionable and smart **stylishly** adverb

sub noun subs (informal)
1 a submarine 2 a subscription 3 a substitute, especially in sports

sub– prefix
meaning 'below', as in *submarine* and *substandard*

subcontinent noun subcontinents
a large area of land that forms part of a continent *the Indian subcontinent*

subdivide verb subdivides, subdividing, subdivided
to subdivide something that has already been divided is to divide it again into smaller parts

subdue verb subdues, subduing, subdued
1 to subdue someone is to overcome them or bring them under control 2 to subdue a person or animal is to make them quieter or gentler

subject (say sub-jikt) noun subjects
1 the person or thing that is being talked or written about 2 something that is studied 3 (in grammar) the person or thing that is doing the action stated by the verb in a sentence, for example *dog* in the sentence *the dog chewed a bone* 4 someone who must obey the laws of a particular ruler or government

subject adjective
subject to something depending on it or likely to be affected by it *The area is subject to storms.*

subject (say sub-jekt) verb subjects, subjecting, subjected
to subject someone to something is to make them experience or suffer it *They subjected him to a string of questions.*

subjective adjective
influenced by your own beliefs or ideas *His account of what happened is rather subjective.*

submarine noun submarines
a type of ship that can travel under water

submerge verb submerges, submerging, submerged
1 to submerge is to go under water 2 to submerge something or someone is to put them under water

submission noun submissions
1 submission is submitting to someone

2 a submission is something that you submit or offer to someone

submissive adjective
willing to obey

submit verb submits, submitting, submitted
1 to submit to someone is to give in to them or agree to obey them 2 to submit something to someone is to hand it in or offer it to be considered *I submitted an entry to the competition.*

subordinate (say sub-or-din-at) adjective
less important, or lower in rank

subordinate noun subordinates
someone who is subordinate to someone else

subordinate (say sub-or-din-ayt) verb subordinates, subordinating, subordinated
to subordinate something is to treat it as less important than something else
subordination noun

subscribe verb subscribes, subscribing, subscribed
to subscribe to something is to pay money to receive it regularly or to be a member of a club or society subscriber noun

subscription noun subscriptions
money you pay to subscribe to something

subsequent adjective
coming later or after something else *Subsequent events proved that she was right.*
subsequently adverb

subside verb subsides, subsiding, subsided
1 to subside is to sink *The house has subsided over the years.* 2 to subside is also to become quiet or normal *The noise subsided after midnight.*

subsidize verb subsidizes, subsidizing, subsidized
to subsidize someone or something is to give them money to support them or to keep prices low for their customers

a b c d e f g h i j k l m n o p q r s t u v w x y z

513

A
B
C
D
E
F
G
H
I
J
K
L
M
N
O
P
Q
R
S
T
U
V
W
X
Y
Z

subsidy noun subsidies
money paid to keep prices low or to support an industry or activity

substance noun substances
1 something that you can touch or see; what something is made of 2 the essential part of something

substantial adjective
1 large or important 2 strong and solid

substitute verb substitutes, substituting, substituted
to substitute one thing or person for another is to use the first one instead of the second *In this recipe you can substitute oil for butter.* **substitution** noun

substitute noun substitutes
a person or thing that is used instead of another

subtle (say **sut**-el) adjective subtler, subtlest
1 slight and delicate *a subtle flavour*
2 ingenious but not obvious *Your jokes are too subtle for me.* **subtly** adverb
subtlety noun

subtract verb subtracts, subtracting, subtracted
to subtract one amount from another is to take it away *If you subtract 2 from 7, you get 5.* **subtraction** noun

suburb noun suburbs
an area of houses on the edge of a city or large town **suburban** adjective

subway noun subways
an underground passage for pedestrians

succeed verb succeeds, succeeding, succeeded
1 to succeed is to do or get what you wanted or intended 2 to succeed someone is to be the next person to do what they did, especially to be king or queen

success noun successes
1 success is doing or getting what you wanted or intended 2 a success is a person or thing that does well *The plan was a complete success.*

TOP TIPS
Double up! There is double **c** and double **s** in **success**.

successful adjective
having success **successfully** adverb

succession noun successions
1 a series of people or things 2 the right to be the next person to do something, especially becoming king or queen

successive adjective
following one after another
successively adverb

successor noun successors
a person or thing that comes after another *My old teacher handed over to her successor.*

such adjective
1 of the same kind *Cakes and sweets and all such food is fattening.* 2 so great or so much *That was such fun!*

such–and–such adjective
one in particular but you are not saying which *He promises to come at such-and-such a time but is always late.*

suck verb sucks, sucking, sucked
1 to suck liquid or air is to take it in through your mouth *I sucked milk through a straw.*
2 to suck something is to move it around inside your mouth *She was sucking a sweet.*
3 to suck something is also to draw it in or absorb it *The boat was sucked into the whirlpool. He sucked in his cheeks.*

suck noun sucks
the action of sucking

suction noun
suction is producing a vacuum so that liquid or air is drawn in

sudden adjective
happening or done quickly and unexpectedly **suddenness** noun

suddenly adverb
quickly and unexpectedly

suds plural noun
froth on soapy water

sue verb sues, suing, sued
to sue someone is to start a claim in a law court to get money from them

suede (say swayd) noun
suede is leather with one side soft and velvety

suffer verb suffers, suffering, suffered
1 to suffer is to feel pain or misery 2 to suffer something unpleasant is to have to put up with it

suffering noun sufferings
suffering is pain or misery

sufficient adjective
enough *Have we sufficient food?*
sufficiently adverb to a sufficient degree *I got my breath back sufficiently to speak.*

suffix noun suffixes
a word or syllable joined to the end of a word to change or add to its meaning, as in forget*ful*, lion*ess*, and rust*y*

suffocate verb suffocates, suffocating, suffocated
1 to suffocate is to suffer or die because you cannot breathe 2 to suffocate someone is to make it impossible or difficult for them to breathe **suffocation** noun

sugar noun
sugar is a sweet food obtained from the juices of various plants, such as sugar beet or sugar cane

suggest verb suggests, suggesting, suggested
1 to suggest something is to offer it as an idea or possibility 2 to suggest something is also to give an idea or hint of something *Your smile suggests that you agree with me.*

suggestion noun suggestions
something that you mention to someone as an idea or possibility

suicide noun suicides
suicide is killing yourself deliberately *He committed suicide.*

suit noun suits
1 a matching set of jacket and trousers or jacket and skirt, that are meant to be worn together 2 a set of clothing for a particular activity *He wore a diving suit.* 3 each of the four sets in a pack of playing cards: spades, hearts, diamonds, and clubs 4 a case in a law court

suit verb suits, suiting, suited
1 to suit someone or something is to be suitable or convenient for them 2 a piece of clothing or hairstyle suits you when it looks good on you

suitable adjective
satisfactory or right for a particular person, purpose, or occasion **suitability** noun **suitably** adverb

suitcase noun suitcases
a container with a lid and a handle, for carrying clothes and other things on journeys

suite (say sweet) noun suites
1 a set of rooms in a hotel 2 a set of matching furniture 3 a set of short pieces of music

suitor noun suitors
a woman's suitor is a man who wants to marry her

sulk verb sulks, sulking, sulked
to be silent and bad-tempered because you are not pleased

sulky adjective sulkier, sulkiest
sulking or inclined to sulk **sulkily** adverb **sulkiness** noun

sullen adjective
sulking and gloomy **sullenly** adverb **sullenness** noun

sulphur noun
sulphur is a yellow chemical used in industry and medicine

sultan noun sultans
the ruler of certain Muslim countries

sultana noun sultanas
a raisin without seeds

sum noun sums
1 a total, or the amount you get when

a
b
c
d
e
f
g
h
i
j
k
l
m
n
o
p
q
r
s
t
u
v
w
x
y
z

you add numbers together **2** a problem in arithmetic **3** an amount of money

sum verb sums, summing, summed
to sum up is to give a summary at the end of a discussion or talk

summarize verb summarizes, summarizing, summarized
to summarize something is to give a short statement of its main points

summary noun summaries
a short statement of the main points of something said or written

summer noun summers
the warm season between spring and autumn

summit noun summits
1 the top of a mountain or hill **2** a meeting between the leaders of powerful countries

summon verb summons, summoning, summoned
to summon someone is to order them to come or appear **to summon something up** is to find it in yourself *He summoned up all his courage for the battle ahead.*

summons noun summonses
a command to someone to appear in a law court

sun noun
1 the star round which the earth travels, and from which it gets warmth and light **2** warmth and light from the sun *Shall we sit in the sun?*

sun verb suns, sunning, sunned
to sun yourself is to warm yourself in the sun

sunbathe verb sunbathes, sunbathing, sunbathed
to sit or lie in the sun to get a suntan

sunburn noun
sunburn is the redness of the skin someone gets if they are in the sun for too long
sunburned or **sunburnt** adjective

sundae (say sun-day) noun sundaes
a mixture of ice cream with fruit, nuts, and cream

Sunday noun Sundays
the first day of the week

sundial noun sundials
a device that shows the time by a shadow made by the sun

sunflower noun sunflowers
a tall flower with a large round yellow head

sung
past participle of **sing** *I've never sung this song before.*

sunglasses plural noun
dark glasses you wear to protect your eyes from strong sunlight

sunk
past tense and past participle of **sink** verb *The boat sunk in a storm. I hoped the lesson had sunk in.*

sunlight noun
sunlight is light from the sun
sunlit adjective

sunny adjective sunnier, sunniest
1 having a lot of sunshine *It's a sunny day.* **2** full of sunshine *What a sunny room.*

sunrise noun sunrises
sunrise is the time when the sun first appears; dawn *They left at sunrise.*

sunset noun sunsets
sunset is the time when the sun sets

sunshade noun sunshades
a parasol or other device to protect people from the sun

sunshine noun
sunshine is warmth and light that come from the sun

sunstroke noun
sunstroke is an illness caused by being in the sun for too long

suntan noun suntans
a brown colour of the skin caused by the sun **suntanned** adjective

super adjective (informal)
excellent or very good

super– prefix
meaning 'over' or 'beyond', as
in *superhuman*

superb adjective
magnificent or excellent **superbly** adverb

superficial adjective
1 on the surface *It's only a superficial
cut.* 2 not deep or thorough *His
knowledge of French is fairly superficial.*
superficially adverb

superfluous (say soo-**per**-floo-us)
adjective
not necessary; no longer needed

superhuman adjective
more than a human being is normally
capable of *He believed he had
superhuman powers.*

superintendent noun
superintendents
1 someone who is in charge 2 a police
officer above the rank of inspector

superior adjective
1 higher or more important than someone
else 2 better than another person or thing
3 showing that you think you are better
than other people *The mechanical toys
were very superior, and looked down upon
everyone else; they were full of modern ideas,
and pretended they were real.* – Margery
Williams, *The Velveteen Rabbit*

superior noun **superiors**
someone of higher rank or position than
another person

superiority noun
1 superiority is being better than something
else 2 superiority is also behaviour that
shows you think you are better than
other people

superlative (say soo-**per**-la-tiv)
adjective
of the highest quality

superlative noun **superlatives**
the form of an adjective or adverb that
expresses 'most' *The superlative of 'big'
is 'biggest', and the superlative of 'bad'
is 'worst'.*

supermarket noun **supermarkets**
a large self-service shop that sells food and
other goods

supernatural adjective
not belonging to the natural world or
having a natural explanation

supersonic adjective
faster than the speed of sound

superstition noun **superstitions**
a belief or action that is not based on
reason or evidence *It is a superstition
that 13 is an unlucky number.*
superstitious adjective

supervise verb **supervises,
supervising, supervised**
to supervise someone or something is to
be in charge of them **supervision** adjective
supervisor adjective

supper noun **suppers**
a meal or snack eaten in the
evening

supple adjective **suppler, supplest**
able to bend easily; flexible, not stiff
suppleness noun

supplement noun **supplements**
1 something added as an extra 2 an extra
section added to a book or newspaper
supplementary adjective

supplier noun **suppliers**
someone who gives or sells something
to people who need it *the school's
paper supplier*

supply verb **supplies, supplying,
supplied**
1 to supply something is to give or sell it to
people who need it 2 to supply someone is
to give them what they need

supply noun **supplies**
1 a supply of something is an amount of it
kept ready to be used when needed *We
keep a supply of paper in the cupboard.*
2 supplies are food, medicines, or
equipment needed by (for example) an
army or an expedition *The truck was
carrying medical supplies.*

A
B
C
D
E
F
G
H
I
J
K
L
M
N
O
P
Q
R

S

T
U
V
W
X
Y
Z

support verb supports, supporting, supported
1 to support something is to hold it so that it does not fall down **2** to support someone or something is to give them help or encouragement **3** to support a sports team is to like them and want them to do well *Which football team do you support?*

support noun supports
1 support is the action of supporting *You can rely on my support.* **2** a support is a person or thing that supports

supporter noun supporters
someone who gives support, especially to a sports team

suppose verb supposes, supposing, supposed
to suppose something is to think that it is likely or true **to be supposed to do something** is to have to do it as an order or duty

supposedly adverb
so people believe or think *They are supposedly millionaires.*

suppress verb suppresses, suppressing, suppressed
to suppress something is to keep it hidden or stop it happening *He managed to suppress a smile.* **suppression** noun

supremacy noun
supremacy is having more power or a higher position than anyone else

supreme adjective
highest or greatest; most important **supremely** adverb

sure adjective surer, surest
1 confident about something; having no doubts *Are you sure you locked the door?* **2** very likely to happen or do something *Don't worry, we're sure to win.* **3** completely true or known *One thing is sure: she is not here at the moment.* **4** reliable *Visiting places is a sure way of getting to know them.* **to make sure of something** is to find out that it is true or right

sure adverb (informal)
certainly; of course *Sure I'll come with you.*

surely adverb
1 certainly or definitely *'They are evil sailors,' said Jip, 'and their ship is very swift. They are surely the pirates of Barbary.'* – Hugh Lofting, *The Story of Doctor Dolittle* **2** it must be true; I feel sure *Surely I met you last year.*

surf noun
surf is the white foam of waves breaking on rocks or the seashore

surf verb surfs, surfing, surfed
1 to surf is to go surfing **2** to surf the Internet is to browse through it

surface noun surfaces
1 the outside of something **2** each of the sides of something, especially the top part

surface verb surfaces, surfacing, surfaced
1 to surface is to come up to the surface from under water *The submarine slowly surfaced.* **2** to surface a road or path is to give it a hard covering layer

surfboard noun surfboards
a board used in surfing

surfing noun
surfing is the sport of balancing yourself on a board that is carried towards the seashore by the waves **surfer** noun

surge verb surges, surging, surged
to move forwards or upwards like waves *Back and back retreated the water, surging over rocks, leaving the great steamship exposed to its keel and giant propeller.* – Alan Temperley, *The Brave Whale*

surge noun surges
a sudden rush forward or upward

surgeon noun surgeons
a doctor who deals with disease or injury by cutting or repairing the affected parts of the body

surgery noun surgeries
1 a surgery is a building or room where a doctor or dentist sees patients **2** surgery is the time when patients can see a doctor or

dentist *Surgery will close at 6 o'clock today.*
3 surgery is also the work of a surgeon

surgical adjective
to do with a surgeon or surgery
surgically adverb

surname noun **surnames**
your last name, which you share with other
members of your family

surpass verb **surpasses, surpassing,
surpassed**
to surpass someone is to do better or be
better than them

surplus noun **surpluses**
an amount left over after you have spent or
used what you need

surprise noun **surprises**
1 a surprise is something that you did
not expect **2** surprise is the feeling you
have when something unexpected
happens

surprise verb **surprises, surprising,
surprised**
1 to surprise someone is to be a surprise to
them **2** to surprise someone is also to catch
or attack them unexpectedly

surrender verb **surrenders,
surrendering, surrendered**
1 to surrender to someone is to stop
fighting them and admit that you have
been beaten **2** to surrender something to
someone is to give it over to them

surrender noun
when someone surrenders

surround verb **surrounds,
surrounding, surrounded**
to surround someone or something is to be
or come all round them *Soldiers surrounded
the village.*

surroundings plural noun
the things or conditions around a person
or place

survey (say **ser**-vay) noun **surveys**
1 a general look at a topic or activity
2 a detailed inspection or examination of a
building or area

survey (say ser-**vay**) verb **surveys,
surveying, surveyed**
to survey something is to inspect it or make
a survey of it

surveyor noun **surveyors**
someone whose job is to make close
inspections of buildings and land

survival noun
survival is staying alive

survive verb **survives, surviving,
survived**
1 to survive is to stay alive **2** to survive an
accident or disaster is to remain alive in
spite of it *Only two people survived the car
crash.* **3** to survive someone is to continue
living after they have died

survivor noun **survivors**
someone who survives, especially after an
accident or disaster

suspect (say su-**spekt**) verb **suspects,
suspecting, suspected**
1 to suspect something is to think that it is
likely or possible **2** to suspect someone is to
think that they have done something wrong
or are not to be trusted

suspect (say **sus**-pekt) noun **suspects**
someone who is thought to have done
something wrong

suspend verb **suspends, suspending,
suspended**
1 to suspend something that is happening is
to stop it for a time **2** to suspend someone
is to take away their job or position for a
time *He was suspended from the team for
bad behaviour.* **3** to suspend something is to
hang it up

suspense noun
suspense is an anxious or uncertain
feeling you have while you are waiting for
something to happen or for news about
something *Don't keep us in suspense—
who won?*

suspension noun **suspensions**
1 suspension is suspending something or
someone **2** a vehicle's suspension is the set

a
b
c
d
e
f
g
h
i
j
k
l
m
n
o
p
q
r
s
t
u
v
w
x
y
z

suspension bridge

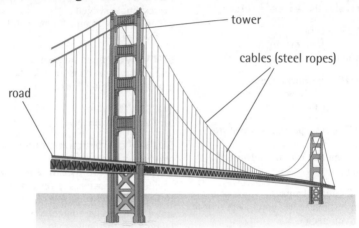

tower

cables (steel ropes)

road

of springs and other devices that make the ride more comfortable

suspension bridge noun
suspension bridges
a bridge supported by cables

suspicion noun suspicions
1 suspicion is feeling that someone has done something wrong or cannot be trusted **2** a suspicion is a slight or uncertain feeling about something or someone

suspicious adjective
1 making you suspect someone or something *There are suspicious footprints along the path.* **2** suspecting someone or something *I'm suspicious about what happened.* **suspiciously** adverb

sustain verb sustains, sustaining, sustained
1 to sustain something is to keep it going *It's difficult to sustain such an effort.* **2** to sustain someone is to give them energy or strength *We'd packed sandwiches to sustain us on our walk.* **3** to sustain an injury is to be injured

swagger verb swaggers, swaggering, swaggered
to walk or behave in a conceited way

Mr. Toad, arrayed in goggles, cap, gaiters, and enormous overcoat, came swaggering down the steps. — Kenneth Grahame, *The Wind in the Willows*

swallow¹ verb swallows, swallowing, swallowed
to swallow something is to make it go down your throat **to swallow something up** is to cover or hide it

swallow² noun swallows
a small bird with a forked tail and pointed wings

swam
past tense of swim verb *She swam to the other end of the pool.*

swamp verb swamps, swamping, swamped
1 to swamp something is to flood it **2** to be swamped is to be overwhelmed with a large number of things *They have been swamped with complaints.*

swamp noun swamps
a marsh

swan noun swans
a large white water bird with a long neck and powerful wings

520

swank verb **swanks, swanking, swanked** (informal)
to swagger or boast

swap verb **swaps, swapping, swapped** (informal)
to swap something is to exchange one thing for another *After the game they swapped jerseys.*

swap noun **swaps**
1 an act of swapping *Let's do a swap.*
2 something you swap for something else

swarm noun **swarms**
a large number of insects flying or moving about together

swarm verb **swarms, swarming, swarmed**
1 bees or other insects swarm when they move in a swarm 2 to be swarming is to be crowded with people *The town is swarming with tourists in summer.*

swastika (say **swos**-ti-ka) noun **swastikas**
a sign formed by a cross with its ends bent at right angles, used as a symbol by the Nazis in Germany

swat (say swot) verb **swats, swatting, swatted**
to swat a fly or other insect is to hit or crush it

sway verb **sways, swaying, swayed**
to move gently from side to side

swear verb **swears, swearing, swore, sworn**
1 to swear is to make a solemn promise *She swore to tell the truth.* 2 to swear someone to secrecy is to make them promise not to tell anyone 3 to swear is also to use very rude or offensive words **to swear by something** is to have a lot of confidence in it

swear word noun **swear words**
a word that is very rude or offensive, used especially by someone who is very angry

sweat (say swet) verb **sweats, sweating, sweated**
you sweat when you give off moisture through the pores of your skin, especially when you are hot or doing exercise

sweat (say swet) noun
sweat is moisture that you give off when you sweat

sweater (say **swet**-er) noun **sweaters**
a jersey or pullover

sweatshirt noun **sweatshirts**
a thick cotton jersey

sweaty adjective **sweatier, sweatiest**
covered or damp with sweat

swede noun **swedes**
a large kind of turnip with purple skin and yellow flesh

sweep verb **sweeps, sweeping, swept**
1 to sweep a room or floor is to clean or clear it with a broom or brush *He swept the floor.* 2 to sweep something away is to move or change it quickly *The flood has swept away the bridge.* 3 to sweep somewhere is to go there swiftly or proudly *She swept out of the room.*

sweep noun **sweeps**
1 a sweeping action or movement *Give this room a sweep.* 2 a chimney sweep

sweeper noun **sweepers**
1 a machine for sweeping floors
2 (in football) a defensive player at the back

sweet adjective **sweeter, sweetest**
1 tasting of sugar or honey 2 very pleasant *There was a sweet smell in the room.* 3 charming or delightful *What a sweet little cottage.* **sweetly** adverb **sweetness** noun

sweet noun **sweets**
1 a small shaped piece of sweet food made of sugar or chocolate 2 a pudding; the sweet course in a meal

sweetcorn noun
sweetcorn is the juicy yellow seeds of maize

a
b
c
d
e
f
g
h
i
j
k
l
m
n
o
p
q
r
s
t
u
v
w
x
y
z

sweeten verb sweetens, sweetening, sweetened
to sweeten something is to make it sweet

sweetheart noun sweethearts
a person you love very much

sweet pea noun sweet peas
a climbing plant with sweet-smelling flowers

swell verb swells, swelling, swelled, swollen or swelled
to get bigger or louder
swell noun swells
the rise and fall of the sea's surface

swelling noun swellings
a swollen place on your body

swelter verb swelters, sweltering, sweltered
to be uncomfortably hot

swept
past tense and past participle of sweep verb
She swept past him into the kitchen. After he had swept the floor, he washed the dishes.

swerve verb swerves, swerving, swerved
to move suddenly to one side *The car swerved to avoid the cyclist.*
swerve noun swerves
a swerving movement

swift adjective swifter, swiftest
quick; moving quickly and easily
swiftly adverb **swiftness** noun
swift noun swifts
a small bird rather like a swallow

swill verb swills, swilling, swilled
to swill something is to rinse or flush it
swill noun
swill is a sloppy mixture of waste food given to pigs

swim verb swims, swimming, swam, swum
1 to swim is to move yourself through the water or to be in the water for pleasure
2 to swim a stretch of water is to cross it by swimming *She has swum the Channel.* 3 to be swimming in liquid or with liquid is to be covered in it or full of it *Their eyes were swimming with tears.* 4 your head swims when you feel dizzy
swim noun swims
a spell of swimming *Let's go for a swim.*

swimmer noun swimmers
someone who swims *Are you a good swimmer?*

swimming bath or **swimming pool** noun
swimming baths, swimming pools
a specially built pool with water for people to swim in

swimming costume noun
swimming costumes
a piece of clothing for swimming in

swimsuit noun swimsuits
a one-piece swimming costume

swindle verb swindles, swindling, swindled
to swindle someone is to get money or goods from them dishonestly
swindler noun
swindle noun swindles
a trick to swindle someone

swine noun swine or swines
1 a pig 2 (informal) an unpleasant person or a difficult thing

swing verb swings, swinging, swung
1 to swing is to move to and fro or in a curve 2 to swing something is to turn it quickly or suddenly *He swung the car round to avoid the bus.*
swing noun swings
1 a swinging movement *He took a swing at the ball.* 2 a seat hung on chains or ropes so that it can move backwards and forwards **to be in full swing** is to be full of activity or working fully

swipe verb swipes, swiping, swiped
1 to swipe someone or something is to give them a hard hit 2 (informal) to swipe something is to steal it 3 to swipe a credit card is to pass it through a special electronic device that reads the details on it

swipe noun swipes
a hard hit

swirl verb swirls, swirling, swirled
to swirl is to move around quickly in circles;
to swirl something is to make it do this *The
water swirled down the plug hole.*

swirl noun swirls
a swirling movement

swish verb swishes, swishing, swished
to make a hissing or rustling sound

swish noun swishes
a swishing sound

switch noun switches
1 a device that you press or turn to start
or stop something working, especially by
electricity **2** a sudden change *a switch
of direction*

switch verb switches, switching,
switched
1 to switch a device on or off is to use a
switch to make it work or stop working **2** to
switch something is to change it suddenly

switchboard noun switchboards
a panel with switches for connecting
telephone lines

swivel verb swivels, swivelling,
swivelled
to turn round

swollen
past participle of swell verb *A large lump
had swollen in his throat.*

swollen adjective
something that has swelled a lot is
swollen *My wrist is still very swollen where I
bumped it.*

swoon verb swoons, swooning,
swooned (old use)
to faint from fear or weakness

swoop verb swoops, swooping,
swooped
1 to swoop is to dive or come down
suddenly *The post owls arrived, swooping
down through rain-flecked windows,
scattering everyone with droplets of water.*
— J. K. Rowling, *Harry Potter and the*

Half-Blood Prince **2** to swoop is also to make
a sudden attack or raid

swoop noun swoops
a sudden dive or attack

swop verb swops, swopping, swopped
(informal)
to swap

sword (say sord) noun swords
a weapon with a long pointed blade fixed in
a handle

swore
past tense of swear *He swore to tell
the truth.*

sworn
past participle of swear *She has sworn to tell
the truth.*

swot verb swots, swotting, swotted
(informal)
to study hard

swot noun swots (informal)
someone who swots

swum
past participle of swim verb *She had swum
the Channel in record time.*

swung
past tense and past participle of swing verb
*He sat up and swung his legs out of the bed.
The gate had swung open in the wind.*

sycamore noun sycamores
a tall tree with winged seeds

syllable noun syllables
a word or part of a word that has one
separate sound when you say it *'Cat' has
one syllable, 'el-e-phant' has three syllables.*
syllabic adjective

syllabus (say sil-a-bus) noun syllabuses
a list of things to be studied by a class or
for an examination

symbol noun symbols
1 a mark or sign with a special meaning
2 a thing that stands for something *The
crescent is a symbol of Islam.*

a
b
c
d
e
f
g
h
i
j
k
l
m
n
o
p
q
r
s
t
u
v
w
x
y
z

symbolic or **symbolical** adjective
acting as a symbol of something
symbolically adverb

symbolism noun
symbolism is the use of symbols to stand
for something

symbolize verb **symbolizes,
symbolizing, symbolized**
to symbolize something is to be a symbol of
it *Red symbolizes danger.*

symmetrical (say sim-**et**-rik-al)
adjective
able to be divided into two halves which
are exactly the same but the opposite way
round *Wheels and butterflies are symmetrical.*
symmetrically adverb

symmetry noun
something has symmetry when it can
be divided into two halves which are
exactly the same but the opposite
way round

sympathetic adjective
feeling sympathy or understanding for
someone **sympathetically** adverb

sympathize verb **sympathizes,
sympathizing, sympathized**
to sympathize with someone is to show or
feel sympathy for them

sympathy noun **sympathies**
1 sympathy is the sharing or understanding
of other people's feelings or opinions
2 sympathy is also the feeling of being
sorry for someone's unhappiness
or suffering

symphony noun **symphonies**
a long piece of music for an orchestra
symphonic adjective

symptom noun **symptoms**
something wrong with you that is a
sign that you have an illness *Red spots
are a symptom of measles.*
symptomatic adjective

synagogue (say **sin**-a-gog) noun
synagogues
a building where Jewish people meet
to worship

synchronize (say **sink**-ro-nyz) verb
synchronizes, synchronizing, synchronized
1 to synchronize things is to make them
happen at the same time **2** to synchronize
watches or clocks is to set them to show the
same time **synchronization** noun

synonym (say **sin**-o-nim) noun
synonyms
a word that means the same or nearly the
same as another word, such as *big* and *large*
synonymous adjective

synthesis noun **syntheses**
synthesis is when different things or parts
are combined into a whole thing or system

synthesize verb **synthesizes,
synthesizing, synthesized**
to synthesize something is to make it by
combining parts

synthesizer noun **synthesizers**
an electronic musical instrument that can
make many different sounds

synthetic adjective
artificially made; not natural
synthetically adverb

syringe noun **syringes**
a device for sucking in a liquid and squirting
it out

syrup noun **syrups**
a thick sweet liquid

system noun **systems**
1 a set of parts or things or ideas that work
together *the digestive system, the solar
system* **2** a well-organized way of doing
something *We have a new system for taking
books out of the library.*

systematic adjective
using a system; careful and well planned
systematically adverb

A B C D E F G H I J K L M N O P Q R S T U V W X Y Z

Tt

tab noun **tabs**
a small strip or flap that sticks out

tabby noun **tabbies**
a grey or brown cat with dark streaks in its fur

table noun **tables**
1 a piece of furniture with a flat top supported on legs **2** a list of facts or numbers arranged in rows and columns **3** a list of the results of multiplying a number by other numbers *Do you know your multiplication tables?*

tablecloth noun **tablecloths**
a cloth for covering a table

tablespoon noun **tablespoons**
a large spoon used for serving food

tablespoonful noun **tablespoonfuls**
as much as a tablespoon will hold

tablet noun **tablets**
1 a pill **2** a lump of soap **3** a flat piece of stone or wood with words carved or written on it

table tennis noun
table tennis is a game played on a table divided in the middle by a net, over which you hit a small ball with bats

tack¹ noun **tacks**
a short nail with a flat top

tack verb **tacks, tacking, tacked**
1 to tack something is to nail it with tacks **2** to tack material is to sew it together quickly with long stitches **3** to tack is to sail a zigzag course to get full benefit from the wind

tack² noun
tack is equipment for horses, such as harnesses and saddles

tackle verb **tackles, tackling, tackled**
1 to tackle a task is to start doing it **2** in football or hockey, to tackle a player is to try to get the ball from them or (in rugby) to bring them to the ground

tackle noun **tackles**
1 tackle is equipment, especially for fishing **2** a tackle is when you tackle someone in football or rugby or hockey

tacky adjective **tackier, tackiest**
1 sticky or not quite dry *The paint is still tacky.* **2** (informal) cheaply made and showing poor taste

tact noun
tact is skill in not offending or upsetting people

tactful adjective
careful not to offend or upset people by saying something unkind **tactfully** adverb

tactics plural noun
someone's tactics are the methods they use to achieve or win something **tactical** adjective

tactless adjective
likely to offend or upset people; having no tact **tactlessly** adverb

tadpole noun **tadpoles**
a young frog or toad at a stage when it has an oval head and a long tail and lives in water

tag¹ noun **tags**
1 a label tied or stuck to something **2** the metal or plastic part at the end of a shoelace

tag verb **tags, tagging, tagged**
to tag something is to fix a tag or label on it **to tag along** is to go along with other people

tag² noun
tag is a game in which one person chases the others

tail noun **tails**
1 the part that sticks out from the rear end of the body of an animal or bird **2** the part at the end or rear of something, such as an aircraft **3** the side of a coin opposite the head

a
b
c
d
e
f
g
h
i
j
k
l
m
n
o
p
q
r
s
t
u
v
w
x
y
z

tail verb tails, tailing, tailed
to tail someone is to follow them without them seeing you **to tail off** is to become less and less or smaller and smaller

tailback noun tailbacks
a long line of traffic stretching back from an obstruction

tailless adjective
not having a tail

tailor noun tailors
someone whose job is to make clothes

take verb takes, taking, took, taken
This word has many meanings, depending on the words that go with it:
1 to take something or someone is to get hold of them or bring them into your possession *He took a cake from the plate. Who do you think took the money? They took many prisoners.* 2 to take someone or something somewhere is to carry or drive or convey them there *Shall I take you to the station? Take this parcel to the post.* 3 to take something useful or pleasant is to make use of it *Do you take sugar? You must take a holiday this year. Do take a seat.* 4 to take someone or something is to need them for a purpose *It will take two people to lift the table.* 5 to take a piece of information is to make a note of it *Take their names and addresses.* 6 to take a class for a subject is to teach it to them *Who takes you for English?* 7 to take one number from another is to subtract it *Take two from ten and you get eight.* 8 to take an examination is to do it *I'm taking my maths exam today.* 9 to take a joke is to accept it well 10 to take a photograph or picture is to produce it with a camera **to take off** is to leave the ground at the beginning of a flight **to take part in something** is to share in doing it **to take place** is to happen **to take someone in** is to fool or deceive them **to take something over** is to take control of it **to take something up** is to start doing it *I've taken up swimming.*

takeaway noun takeaways
1 a place that sells cooked food for customers to take away 2 a meal from a takeaway

takings plural noun
money that has been received, especially by a shopkeeper

talcum powder or **talc** noun
talcum powder is a sweet-smelling powder put on the skin to dry it or make it smell pleasant

tale noun tales
a story

talent noun talents
a natural ability or skill to do something well *She has a talent for singing.*

talented adjective
someone is talented when they have the ability or skill to do something well

talk verb talks, talking, talked
to talk is to speak or have a conversation **talker** noun

talk noun talks
1 a conversation or discussion 2 a lecture

talkative adjective
someone is talkative when they talk a lot

tall adjective taller, tallest
1 higher than the average *They sat under a tall tree.* 2 measured from the bottom to the top *The bookcase is two metres tall.* **a tall story** is a story that is hard to believe

tally verb tallies, tallying, tallied
one thing tallies with another when they match or agree *Do your figures tally with mine? Their answers don't tally.*

Talmud noun
a collection of writings on Jewish religious law

talon noun talons
a strong claw, especially on a bird of prey

tambourine noun tambourines
a round musical instrument like a small drum with metal discs fixed around the edge so that it jingles when you shake it or hit it

tame adjective tamer, tamest
1 a tame animal is one that is gentle and not afraid of people **2** something is tame when it is dull or uninteresting **tamely** adverb **tameness** noun
tame verb tames, taming, tamed
to tame a wild animal is to make it used to being with people **tamer** noun

tamper verb tampers, tampering, tampered
to tamper with something is to interfere with it or change it so that it will not work properly

tan noun tans
1 a tan is a suntan **2** tan is a yellow-brown colour
tan verb tans, tanning, tanned
1 to tan your skin is to make it brown with a suntan **2** to tan the skin of a dead animal is to make it into leather

tandem noun tandems
a bicycle for two riders, one behind the other

tang noun
a strong flavour or smell

tangerine (say tan-jer-**een**) noun tangerines
a kind of small orange

tangle verb tangles, tangling, tangled
1 you tangle something, or it tangles, when it becomes twisted or muddled *My fishing line has tangled.* **2** something is tangled up when it is twisted together in an untidy mess *These computer cables are all tangled up.*
tangle noun tangles
a twisted or muddled mass of (for example) hair or wire

tank noun tanks
1 a large container for a liquid or gas **2** a heavy armoured vehicle used in war

tankard noun tankards
a large heavy mug for drinking from

tanker noun tankers
1 a large ship for carrying oil **2** a large lorry for carrying a liquid

tanner noun tanners
someone who tans animal skins to make leather

tantalize verb tantalizes, tantalizing, tantalized
to tantalize someone is to torment them by showing them something good that they cannot have

tantrum noun tantrums
an outburst of bad temper

tap¹ noun taps
a device for letting out liquid or gas in a controlled flow
tap verb taps, tapping, tapped
1 to tap a source of information or supplies is to make use of it **2** to tap a telephone is to fix a device to it so that you can hear someone else's conversation

tap² noun taps
1 a tap is a quick light hit, or the sound it makes *I gave him a tap on the shoulder.* **2** tap is tap-dancing
tap verb taps, tapping, tapped
to tap someone or something is to give them a tap or gentle hit *I tried tapping on the window.*

tap–dancing noun
tap-dancing is dancing in hard shoes that make sharp tapping sounds on the floor

tape noun tapes
1 tape is soft material such as cloth or paper or plastic in a thin strip; a tape is a piece of this **2** tape is also a narrow plastic strip coated with a magnetic substance and used for making recordings; a tape is a cassette *a video tape*
tape verb tapes, taping, taped
1 to tape something is to fasten it by sticking it or tying it with tape **2** to tape music or sound or a television programme is to record it on tape

tarantula

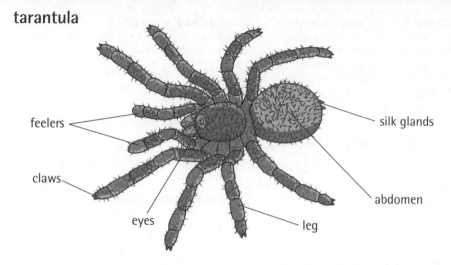

feelers

claws

eyes

silk glands

abdomen

leg

tape-measure noun
tape-measures
a long strip marked in centimetres or inches
for measuring things

taper verb **tapers, tapering, tapered**
something tapers when it gets narrower
towards one end
taper noun **tapers**
a piece of string thinly coated with wax, for
lighting things

tape recorder noun **tape recorders**
a machine for recording music or sound on
tape and playing it back

tapestry (say **tap**-i-stree) noun
tapestries
a piece of strong cloth with pictures
or patterns woven or embroidered
on it

tapeworm noun **tapeworms**
a long flat worm that can live as a
parasite in the intestines of people
and animals

tar noun
tar is a thick black sticky liquid made from
coal or wood and used in making roads
tar verb **tars, tarring, tarred**
to tar something is to cover it with tar

tarantula (say ta-**ran**-tew-la) noun
tarantulas
a large hairy poisonous spider found in
warm countries

target noun **targets**
something that you aim at and try to hit
or reach
target verb **targets, targeting,
targeted**
to target something or someone is to aim
at them

tarmac noun
1 (trademark) tarmac is a mixture of tar
and broken stone, used for making a hard
surface on roads and paths and open areas.
Tarmac is short for *tarmacadam* **2** the
tarmac is an area covered with tarmac,
especially on an airfield *The plane was
standing on the tarmac, waiting to take off.*

tarnish verb **tarnishes, tarnishing,
tarnished**
1 metal tarnishes when it becomes stained
and less shiny **2** to tarnish something is to
spoil it *The scandal tarnished his reputation.*

tarpaulin noun **tarpaulins**
a large sheet of waterproof canvas

tart[1] noun **tarts**
a pie containing fruit or jam

tart² adjective **tarter, tartest**
sour-tasting *The apples are tart.*

tartan noun **tartans**
a woollen cloth with a pattern of squares and stripes in different colours, especially as worn in the Scottish Highlands

task noun **tasks**
a piece of work that needs to be done **to take someone to task** is to tell them off for doing something wrong

task force noun **task forces**
a group of people, especially soldiers, given a special task to do

tassel noun **tassels**
a bundle of threads tied together at the top and used to decorate something

taste verb **tastes, tasting, tasted**
1 to taste food or drink is to eat or drink a small amount to see what it is like 2 food or drink tastes a certain way when it has a particular flavour *The milk tastes sour.*

taste noun **tastes**
1 the taste of something is the flavour it has when you taste it *The milk has a strange taste.* 2 taste is the ability to taste things 3 your tastes are the things you like or prefer *What are your tastes in music?* 4 you show taste when you are able to choose things that are of good quality or go together well *The way she dresses shows good taste.* 5 a taste is a tiny amount of food *Can I have a taste of your pudding?*

tasteful adjective
something that is tasteful is well chosen or of good quality *The decorations were very tasteful.* **tastefully** adverb

tasteless adjective
1 tasteless food has no flavour 2 a tasteless joke is unpleasant or vulgar **tastelessly** adverb

tasty adjective **tastier, tastiest**
tasty food has a strong pleasant taste

tattered adjective
tattered clothing is badly torn and ragged

tatters plural noun
in tatters badly torn

tattoo¹ noun **tattoos**
a picture or pattern made on someone's skin with a needle and dye
tattoo verb **tattoos, tattooing, tattooed**
someone is tattooed when they have a tattoo on their skin

tattoo² noun **tattoos**
1 a drumming sound *He beat a tattoo on the table with his fingers.* 2 an outdoor entertainment including military music and marching

tatty adjective **tattier, tattiest**
shabby and worn *The Viking Hotel was beginning to look a bit tatty. What it really needed was a good coat of paint.* – Jeremy Strong, *Viking at School*

taught
past tense and past participle of **teach** *My uncle taught me to play piano. I remembered everything she had taught me.*

taunt verb **taunts, taunting, taunted**
to taunt someone is to jeer at them or insult them
taunt noun **taunts**
an insulting or mocking remark

taut adjective **tauter, tautest**
stretched tightly **tautly** adverb **tautness** noun

tavern noun **taverns** (old use)
an inn or pub

tawny adjective **tawnier, tawniest**
brown-yellow

tax noun **taxes**
an amount of money that people and businesses have to pay to the government for public use
tax verb **taxes, taxing, taxed**
1 to tax someone is to charge them a tax 2 to tax goods or someone's income is to put a tax on them **taxation** noun

taxi noun taxis
a car with a driver which you can hire for journeys, with a meter for recording the distance

taxi verb taxis, taxiing, taxied
an aircraft taxis when it moves slowly along the ground before taking off or after landing

taxpayer noun taxpayers
someone who pays taxes

tea noun teas
1 tea is a drink made by pouring hot water on the dried leaves of an evergreen shrub 2 tea is also the dried leaves of this shrub 3 tea is also a meal eaten in the late afternoon or early evening

tea bag noun tea bags
a small bag of tea for making tea in a cup

teacake noun teacakes
a kind of bun, usually toasted and eaten with butter

teach verb teaches, teaching, taught
1 to teach someone is to show them how to do something or give them knowledge about something 2 to teach a subject is to give lessons in it *She taught us history last year.*

teacher noun teachers
someone who teaches people at a school or college

tea cloth or **tea towel** noun
tea cloths, tea towels
a cloth you use for drying washed dishes and cutlery

teacup noun teacups
a cup for drinking tea

teak noun
teak is a hard strong wood from Asia

team noun teams
1 a set of players who form one side in a game or sport 2 a group of people who work together

teapot noun teapots
a pot with a handle and spout, for making and pouring out tea

tear[1] (say tair) verb tears, tearing, tore, torn
1 to tear something is to make a split in it or to pull it apart 2 to tear something is also to pull or remove it with force *He tore the picture off the wall.* 3 to tear is to become torn *Paper tears easily.* 4 to tear somewhere is to move very quickly there *He tore down the street.*

tear (say tair) noun tears
a hole or split made by tearing something

tear[2] (say teer) noun tears
a drop of water that comes from your eye when you cry

tearful adjective
in tears; crying easily *He suddenly became very tearful. Signora Strega-Borgia bid the children a tearful farewell and set off to complete her degree in advanced witchcraft.* — Debi Gliori, *Pure Dead Magic*
tearfully adverb

tease verb teases, teasing, teased
to tease someone is to make fun of them and say things to make them annoyed

teaspoon noun teaspoons
a small spoon for stirring tea

teaspoonful noun teaspoonfuls
as much as a teaspoon will hold

teat noun teats
1 a nipple through which a baby drinks milk 2 the cap of a baby's feeding bottle

technical adjective
1 to do with technology or the way things work 2 using the words that only people who know a lot about a subject will understand *This book is full of technical words.*

technicality noun technicalities
a small detail of the law or a process

technically adverb
1 something is technically possible when

A B C D E F G H I J K L M N O P Q R S **T** U V W X Y Z

the technology exists to do it **2** something is technically allowed when it is allowed according to a set of rules

technician noun technicians
someone whose job is to look after scientific equipment and do practical work in a laboratory

technique (say tek-**neek**) noun techniques
a particular method of doing something skilfully

technology noun technologies
technology is the study of machinery and the way things work **technological** adjective

teddy bear noun teddy bears
a soft furry toy bear

tedious (say **tee**-di-us) adjective
slow or long; boring **tediously** adverb **tediousness** noun

tedium noun
tedium is a dull or boring time or experience *He hated the tedium of visiting his grandparents.*

teem verb teems, teeming, teemed
1 to teem with something is to be full of it *The river was teeming with fish.* **2** to teem, or teem down, is to rain very hard

teenage or **teenaged** adjective
in your teens; to do with teenagers

teenager noun teenagers
a person in their teens

teens plural noun
the time of your life between the ages of 13 and 19 *They started playing chess in their teens.*

teeth
plural of **tooth**

telecommunications plural noun
telecommunications is sending news and information over long distances by telephone, telegraph, fax, television, and radio

telegram noun telegrams
a message sent by telegraph

telegraph noun telegraphs
telegraph is a way of sending messages by using electric current along wires or by radio

telepathy (say til-**ep**-a-thee) noun
telepathy is communication of thoughts from one person's mind to another without speaking, writing, or gestures **telepathic** adjective

telephone noun telephones
a device using electric wires or radio to enable someone to speak to another person who is some distance away

telephone verb telephones, telephoning, telephoned
to telephone someone is to speak to them by telephone

telescope noun telescopes
a tube with lenses at each end, through which you can see distant objects more clearly because they look closer and larger

telescopic adjective
to do with telescopes

teletext noun
teletext is a system for displaying news and information on a television screen

televise verb televises, televising, televised
to televise an event is to film it and put it on television

television noun televisions
1 television is a system using radio waves to reproduce pictures on a screen **2** a television, or a television set, is a device for receiving these pictures

tell verb tells, telling, told
1 to tell something to someone is to give them information by speaking to them **2** to tell someone to do something is to order them to do it **3** to tell is to reveal a secret *Promise you won't tell.* **4** to tell something is to recognize it *Can you tell the difference between butter and margarine?* **all told** in

a
b
c
d
e
f
g
h
i
j
k
l
m
n
o
p
q
r
s
t
u
v
w
x
y
z

531

all, altogether *There are ten of them, all told.*
to tell someone off is to scold them **to tell tales** is to report someone else's bad behaviour

tell-tale noun tell-tales
someone who tells tales

tell-tale adjective
revealing something that is supposed to be secret *He had a tell-tale spot of jam on his chin.*

telly noun tellies (informal)
1 telly is television 2 a telly is a television set

temper noun tempers
1 a person's mood *He is in a good temper.* 2 an angry mood *She was in a temper.*
to lose your temper is to become very angry

temperate adjective
a temperate climate is neither extremely hot nor extremely cold

temperature noun temperatures
1 the temperature of something is how hot or cold it is 2 an unusually high body temperature *She's feverish and has a temperature.*

tempest noun tempests (old use)
a violent storm

temple¹ noun temples
a building where a god is worshipped

temple² noun temples
the part of your head between your forehead and your ear

tempo noun tempos
the tempo of a piece of music is its speed or rhythm

temporary adjective
only lasting or used for a short time *They were using a temporary classroom.*
temporarily adverb

tempt verb tempts, tempting, tempted
to tempt someone is to try to make them do something wrong or foolish

temptation noun temptations
temptation, or a temptation, is when someone is being tempted

tempting adjective
something is tempting when it is hard to resist

ten noun tens
the number 10

tenant noun tenants
someone who rents a house or building or a piece of land from a landlord **tenancy** noun

tend¹ verb tends, tending, tended
something tends to happen when it is likely to happen or is what usually happens *Prices tend to rise.*

tend² verb tends, tending, tended
to tend something or someone is to look after them *Lorna was in her favourite place, the little garden which she tended with such care and diligence.* – R. D. Blackmore, *Lorna Doone*

tendency noun tendencies
the way a person or thing is likely to behave *She has a tendency to be lazy.*

tender¹ adjective tenderer, tenderest
1 not tough or hard; easy to chew 2 delicate or sensitive *These are tender plants.* 3 gentle or loving *She gave a tender smile.*
tenderly adverb **tenderness** noun

tender² verb tenders, tendering, tendered
to tender something is to give it or offer it

tender noun tenders
an offer to do work or supply goods at an agreed price

tendon noun tendons
a piece of strong tissue in the body that joins a muscle to a bone

tendril noun tendrils
the part of a climbing plant that twists round something to support itself

tennis noun
tennis is a game played with rackets and a ball on a court with a net across the middle

tenor noun **tenors**
a male singer with a high voice

tenpin bowling noun
tenpin bowling is a game in which you knock down sets of ten skittles with a ball

tense¹ adjective **tenser, tensest**
1 tightly stretched *tense muscles* 2 to be tense is to be nervous and not able to relax 3 a tense situation makes people feel nervous and unable to relax **tensely** adverb

tense² noun **tenses**
a form of a verb that shows when something happens. The past tense of come is *came*; the present tense is *come*, and the future tense is *will come*

tension noun **tensions**
1 tension is a feeling of anxiety or nervousness about something about to happen 2 tension is also how tightly stretched a rope or wire is

tent noun **tents**
a shelter made of canvas or cloth supported by upright poles

tentacle noun **tentacles**
a long bending part of the body of an octopus and some other animals

tenth adjective, noun
the next after the ninth **tenthly** adverb in the tenth place; as the tenth one

tepid adjective
tepid liquid is only slightly warm; lukewarm

term noun **terms**
1 the time when a school or college is open for teaching 2 a definite period *He was sentenced to a term of imprisonment.* 3 a word or expression with a special meaning *I don't understand these technical terms.* 4 the terms of an agreement are the conditions offered or agreed *They won't agree to our terms.* **to be on good** or **bad terms** is to be friendly or unfriendly with someone

term verb **terms, terming, termed**
to term something is to give it a special name *This music is termed jazz.*

terminal noun **terminals**
1 a building where passengers arrive or depart *an airport terminal* 2 a place where a wire is connected to a battery or electric circuit 3 a computer keyboard and screen used for sending data to or from the main computer

terminal adjective
a terminal illness is one that cannot be cured and that the person will die from

terminate verb **terminates, terminating, terminated**
you terminate something, or it terminates, when it ends or stops *This train terminates here.* **termination** noun

terminus noun **termini**
the station at the end of a railway or bus route

termite noun **termites**
a small insect that eats wood and lives in large groups

terrace noun **terraces**
1 a row of houses joined together 2 a level area on a slope or hillside 3 a paved area beside a house

terrapin noun **terrapins**
a kind of small turtle that lives in water

terrible adjective
awful; very bad

terribly adverb
awfully; badly *I'm terribly sorry I kept you waiting. He was missing his parents terribly.*

terrier noun **terriers**
a kind of strong lively small dog

terrific adjective (informal)
1 very good or excellent *That's a terrific idea.* 2 very great *They went at a terrific speed.* **terrifically** adverb very; greatly

terrify verb **terrifies, terrifying, terrified**
to terrify a person or animal is to make them very frightened

territory noun **territories**
an area of land, especially an area

a b c d e f g h i j k l m n o **t** u v w x y z

A

that belongs to a country or person
territorial adjective

B

terror noun terrors
terror is great fear

C

terrorism noun
terrorism is when people use violence,
such as setting off bombs, to try to force
a government to do what they want
terrorist noun

D

E

F

terrorize verb terrorizes, terrorizing,
terrorized
to terrorize someone is to terrify them
with threats

G

H

test noun tests
1 a short set of questions to check
someone's knowledge, especially in school
2 a series of questions or experiments
to get information about someone or
something *They gave her a test to see if she
had diabetes.* 3 (informal) a test match in
cricket or rugby

I

J

K

L

test verb tests, testing, tested
1 to test someone is to give them a test
2 to test something is to use it so that you
can find out whether it works properly or
find out more about it

M

N

O

testament noun testaments
1 a written statement 2 each of the two
main parts of the Bible, the **Old Testament**
and the **New Testament**

P

Q

testify verb testifies, testifying,
testified
to testify is to give evidence or swear that
something is true

R

S

testimonial noun testimonials
a statement describing someone's abilities
and character

T

U

testimony noun testimonies
evidence; what someone testifies

V

test match noun test matches
a cricket or rugby match between teams
from different countries

W

X

Y

test tube noun test tubes
a tube of thin glass closed at one end, used
for experiments in chemistry

Z

testy adjective testier, testiest
irritable or slightly bad-tempered

tether verb tethers, tethering,
tethered
to tether an animal is to tie it up so that it
cannot move far

tether noun tethers
a rope for tying an animal **to be at the
end of your tether** is to be unable to stand
something any more

tetrahedron noun tetrahedrons
a solid shape that has four triangular
sides

text noun texts
1 the words of something printed or written
2 a text message

text verb texts, texting, texted
you text someone when you send them a
text message **texting** noun

textbook noun textbooks
a book that teaches you about a subject

textiles plural noun
kinds of cloth; fabrics

text message noun text messages
a written message sent using a
mobile phone

texture noun textures
the way that the surface of something feels
when you touch it *Silk has a smooth texture.*

than conjunction
compared with another person or thing *His
sister is taller than him. His sister is taller
than he is.*

thank verb thanks, thanking, thanked
to thank someone is to tell them you are
grateful for something they have given you
or done for you **thank you** words that you
say when you thank someone

thankful adjective
feeling glad that someone has done
something for you **thankfully** adverb you
say thankfully when you are pleased and
relieved about something *Thankfully no one
was hurt.*

thankless adjective
a thankless job or task is one that is not very enjoyable and that you are not likely to get any thanks for

thanks plural noun
1 words that thank someone **2** (informal) a short way of saying 'Thank you' **thanks to someone** or **something** because of them *Thanks to you, we succeeded.*

that determiner
the one there *Whose is that book?*
that conjunction
used to introduce a fact or statement or result *I hope that you are well. Do you know that it is one o'clock? The puzzle was so hard that no one could solve it.*
that pronoun
1 the one there *Whose book is that?* **2** which or who *This is the book that I wanted. Are you the person that I saw the other day?*

thatch noun
thatch is straw or reeds used to make a roof
thatch verb thatches, thatching, thatched
to thatch a roof is to make it with straw or reeds

thaw verb thaws, thawing, thawed
something thaws when it melts and is no longer frozen *The snow was beginning to thaw.*

the determiner (called the definite article)
a particular one; that or those

theatre noun theatres
1 a building where people go to see plays or shows **2** a special room where surgical operations are done

theatrical adjective
to do with plays or acting
theatrically adverb in an exaggerated or dramatic way *Danny sighed theatrically.*

thee pronoun (old use)
you, referring to one person and used as the object of a verb *I will allow thee one favour.*

theft noun thefts
theft is stealing

their determiner
belonging to them *This is their house.*

theirs pronoun
belonging to them *This house is theirs.*

them pronoun
a word used for *they* when it is the object of a verb, or when it comes after a preposition *I like them. I gave it to them.*

theme noun themes
1 a main idea or subject of (for example) a book or speech **2** a short tune or melody

theme park noun theme parks
an amusement park with rides and activities connected with a special subject or theme

themselves plural noun
them and nobody else, used to refer back to the subject of a verb *They have hurt themselves.* **by themselves** on their own; alone *They did the work all by themselves.*

then adverb
1 at that time *I lived in London then.* **2** after that; next *Then they came home.* **3** in that case; therefore *If you are going, then I can stay.*

theology noun
theology is the study of God and religion

theoretical adjective
based on theory and not on practice or experience

theory noun theories
1 a theory is an idea or set of ideas suggested to explain something **2** the theory of a subject is the ideas and principles behind it, rather than the practice **in theory** according to what should happen

therapy noun therapies
a way of treating an illness of the mind or the body, usually without using surgery or medicines **therapist** noun

there adverb
1 in or to that place **2** a word that you say to call attention to someone or something or to refer to them *There's a spider in the bath. There has been a mistake.*

a
b
c
d
e
f
g
h
i
j
k
l
m
n
o
p
q
r
s
t
u
v
w
x
y
z

thereabouts adverb
near there *They live in York or thereabouts.*

therefore adverb
for that reason; and so

thermal adjective
to do with heat; using heat

thermometer noun **thermometers**
a device for measuring temperature

Thermos noun **Thermoses** (trademark)
a kind of vacuum flask

thermostat noun **thermostats**
a device that automatically controls
the temperature of a room or piece
of equipment

thesaurus noun **thesauri** or
thesauruses
a kind of dictionary in which words with
similar meanings are listed in groups
together, instead of one long list in
alphabetical order

these determiner, pronoun
the people or things here *Whose are these
shoes? These are the ones I want.*

they pronoun
1 the people or things that someone is
talking about 2 people in general *They say
it's a very good film.*

they'd
short for *they had* or *they should* or
they would

they'll
short for *they will*

they're
short for *they are*

they've
short for *they have*

thick adjective **thicker, thickest**
1 measuring a lot from one side to the
other *He cut himself a thick slice of cake.*
2 measured from one side to the other
The wall is ten centimetres thick. 3 dense or
closely packed together *The town was in*
thick fog. 4 not very runny *I love thick gravy.*
5 (informal) stupid

thicken verb **thickens, thickening,
thickened**
you thicken something, or it thickens, when
it becomes thicker *As he stirred the sauce, it
started to thicken.*

thicket noun **thickets**
a group of trees and shrubs growing
close together

thickly adverb
1 to be thickly cut is to be cut in thick
pieces 2 to be thickly covered in something
is to be covered in a deep layer of it

thickness noun **thicknesses**
the thickness of something is how thick it is

thief noun **thieves**
someone who steals things

thigh noun **thighs**
the part of your leg above your knee

thimble noun **thimbles**
a metal or plastic cover that you put on the
end of your finger to protect it when you
are sewing

thin adjective **thinner, thinnest**
1 measuring a small amount from one
side to the other 2 not fat 3 not dense or
closely packed together 4 runny or watery
thinness noun

thin verb **thins, thinning, thinned**
1 to thin something, or thin something out,
is to make it less thick or less crowded 2 to
thin, or thin out, is to become less dense
or less crowded *The crowds had thinned by
late afternoon.*

thine adjective (old use)
yours (referring to one person) *All I have
is thine.*

thing noun **things**
an object; anything that can be touched or
seen or thought about

think verb **thinks, thinking, thought**
1 to think is to use your mind 2 to think
something is to have it as an idea or opinion

I think that's a good idea. **3** to be thinking of doing something is to be planning to do it

thinly adverb
1 to be thinly cut is to be cut in thin pieces
2 to be thinly covered in something is to be covered in a thin layer of it

third adjective, noun
the next after the second **thirdly** adverb as the third thing
third noun thirds
each of three equal parts into which something can be divided

Third World noun
the poor or developing countries of Asia, Africa, and South and Central America

thirst noun
thirst is the feeling that you need to drink

thirsty adjective thirstier, thirstiest
feeling that you need to drink

thirteen noun thirteens
the number 13 **thirteenth** adjective, noun

thirty noun thirties
the number 30 **thirtieth** adjective, noun

this determiner, pronoun
the one here *Take this pen. This is the one.*

thistle noun thistles
a wild plant with prickly leaves and purple or white or yellow flowers

thorax noun thoraces or thoraxes
1 the part of your body between your neck and your abdomen **2** the part of an insect's body between the head and abdomen, to which the legs and wings are joined

thorn noun thorns
a small pointed growth on the stem of roses and other plants

thorny adjective thornier, thorniest
1 full of thorns; prickly **2** a thorny problem is a difficult one that causes argument or disagreement

thorough adjective
1 done properly and carefully *This is a thorough piece of work.* **2** absolute or complete *Everything was in a thorough mess.*
thoroughness noun

thoroughly adverb
1 to do something thoroughly is to do it properly and carefully **2** to be thoroughly (for example) exhausted or bored is to be completely exhausted or bored

those determiner, pronoun
the ones there *Where are those cards? Those are the ones I want.*

thou pronoun (old use)
you (referring to one person) *Thou shalt get thy reward.*

though conjunction
in spite of the fact that; even if *It is not true, though he says it is.*
though adverb
however; all the same *She's right, though.*

thought noun thoughts
1 a thought is something that you think; an idea or opinion **2** thought is thinking *I'll give the question some thought.*
thought
past tense and past participle of **think**
I thought she looked nice. Have you thought about where you want to go?

thoughtful adjective
1 looking or sounding as if you are thinking a lot about something *There was a long and thoughtful silence and then Pooh, who had been frowning very hard for some minutes, said: 'I make it fifteen.'* — A. A. Milne, *Winnie-the-Pooh* **2** thinking of other people and what they would like
thoughtfully adverb **thoughtfulness** noun

thoughtless adjective
not thinking of other people and what they would like; reckless **thoughtlessly** adverb
thoughtlessness noun

thousand noun thousands
the number 1,000 **thousandth** adjective, noun

thrash verb thrashes, thrashing, thrashed
1 to thrash someone is to keep hitting them

a
b
c
d
e
f
g
h
i
j
k
l
m
n
o
p
q
r
s
t
u
v
w
x
y
z

three-dimensional

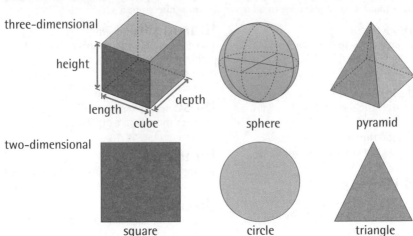

three-dimensional

height

depth

length

cube

sphere

pyramid

two-dimensional

square

circle

triangle

hard with a stick or whip **2** to thrash a person or team is to defeat them completely in a game or sport **3** to thrash, or thrash about, is to fling your arms and legs about wildly

thread noun **threads**
1 a long piece of cotton, wool, nylon, or other material used for sewing or weaving **2** a long thin piece of something **3** the spiral ridge round a screw or bolt

thread verb **threads, threading, threaded**
1 to thread a needle is to put a thread through its eye **2** to thread a long and thin material is to put it through or round something **3** to thread a piece of string is to put beads on it

threadbare adjective
clothes are threadbare when they are worn thin with threads showing

threat noun **threats**
1 a warning that you will punish or harm someone if they do not do what you want **2** a danger

threaten verb **threatens, threatening, threatened**
1 to threaten someone is to warn them that you will punish or harm them if they do not

do what you want **2** to threaten is to be a danger to someone or something *The clouds threatened a storm.*

three noun **threes**
the number 3

three-dimensional adjective
having three dimensions: length, width, height or depth

thresh verb **threshes, threshing, threshed**
to thresh corn is to beat it so that you separate the grain from the husks

threshold noun **thresholds**
1 a slab of stone or board under the doorway of a building; the entrance **2** the beginning of something important *We are on the threshold of a great discovery.*

threw
past tense of **throw** verb *Grandad threw the ball to me.*

thrift noun
thrift is being careful with money and not wasting it

thrifty adjective **thriftier, thriftiest**
careful with money and not wasting it
thriftily adverb

thrill noun thrills
1 a sudden feeling of excitement
2 something that gives you this feeling
thrill verb thrills, thrilling, thrilled
something thrills you when it gives you a sudden feeling of excitement

thriller noun thrillers
an exciting story or film, usually about crime or spying

thrilling adjective
very exciting

thrive verb thrives, thriving, thrived or throve, thrived or thriven
to prosper or grow strongly

throat noun throats
1 the front of your neck 2 the tube in your neck that takes food and air into your body

throb verb throbs, throbbing, throbbed
to beat or vibrate with a strong rhythm
The ship's engines throbbed quietly. He had a throbbing pain in his head.
throb noun throbs
a throbbing sound or feeling

throne noun thrones
1 a special chair for a king or queen 2 the position of being king or queen *The prince is heir to the throne.*

throng noun throngs
a large crowd of people

throttle verb throttles, throttling, throttled
to throttle someone is to squeeze their throat and strangle them
throttle noun throttles
a device to control the flow of fuel to an engine

through adverb, preposition
1 from one end or side to the other *I can't get through. Climb through the window.*
2 because of; by means of *We'll do it through hard work.* 3 (informal) finished *I'm through now.*
through adjective
1 travelling all the way to a place *I'm*

catching a through train to Dover. 2 having a way through *This is a no through road.*

throughout preposition, adverb
all the way through

throve
past tense of **thrive** *The baby throve and grew quickly.*

throw verb throws, throwing, threw, thrown
1 to throw something or someone is to send them through the air 2 to throw something somewhere is to put it there carelessly *He came in and threw his coat on the chair.* 3 to throw a part of your body is to move it quickly *She threw her head back and laughed.*
4 to throw someone into a certain state is to put them in that state *We were thrown into confusion.* **to throw something away** is to get rid of it
throw noun throws
a throwing action or movement *That was a good throw.*

thrush noun thrushes
a bird that has a white front with brown spots

thrust verb thrusts, thrusting, thrust
to thrust something somewhere is to push it there with a lot of force *He thrust his hands into his pockets.*

thud noun thuds
the dull sound of something heavy falling
thud verb thuds, thudding, thudded
to fall with a thud

thumb noun thumbs
the short thick finger at the side of each hand **to be under someone's thumb** is to be controlled or ruled by them

thump verb thumps, thumping, thumped
1 to thump someone or something is to hit them heavily 2 to thump is to make a dull heavy sound
thump noun thumps
an act or sound of thumping

a
b
c
d
e
f
g
h
i
j
k
l
m
n
o
p
q
r
s
t
u
v
w
x
y
z

A
B
C
D
E
F
G
H
I
J
K
L
M
N
O
P
Q
R
S
T
U
V
W
X
Y
Z

thunder noun
thunder is the loud rumbling noise that you hear with lightning during a storm

thunder verb **thunders, thundering, thundered**
1 to thunder is to make the noise of thunder 2 someone thunders when they speak with a loud booming voice

thunderous adjective
extremely loud *The curtain came down to thunderous applause.*

thunderstorm noun **thunderstorms**
a storm with thunder and lightning

Thursday noun **Thursdays**
the fifth day of the week

thus adverb
1 in this way *We did it thus.* 2 therefore *Thus, we must try again.*

thy adjective (old use)
your (referring to one person) *Thou shalt get thy reward.*

tick noun **ticks**
1 a small mark, usually ✓, made next to something when checking it as a sign that it is correct or has been done 2 each of the regular clicking sounds that a clock or watch makes 3 (informal) a moment *I won't be a tick.*

tick verb **ticks, ticking, ticked**
1 to tick something is to mark it with a tick *She ticked the correct answers.* 2 a clock or watch ticks when it makes regular clicking sounds **to tick someone off** (informal) is to scold them or tell them off

ticket noun **tickets**
a piece of paper or card that allows you to do something such as see a show or travel on a bus or train

tickle verb **tickles, tickling, tickled**
1 to tickle someone is to keep touching their skin lightly so that they get a tingling feeling that can make them laugh and wriggle 2 to tickle is to have a tickling or itching feeling *My throat is tickling.* 3 to tickle someone is also to please or amuse them

ticklish adjective
1 someone is ticklish when they are likely to laugh or wriggle if they are tickled 2 awkward or difficult *This is a ticklish situation.*

tidal adjective
to do with tides or affected by tides

tidal wave noun **tidal waves**
a huge sea wave moving with the tide

tiddler noun **tiddlers** (informal)
a very small fish

tiddlywink noun **tiddlywinks**
a small counter that you flip into a cup with another counter in the game of **tiddlywinks**

tide noun **tides**
the regular rising or falling of the sea, which usually happens twice a day

tide verb **tides, tiding, tided**
to tide someone over is to give them what they need, especially money, for the time being

tidy adjective **tidier, tidiest**
1 a tidy place is neat and orderly, with things in the right place *What a tidy room.* 2 a tidy person keeps things neat and in the right place 3 (informal) fairly large *That's a tidy sum of money.* **tidily** adverb **tidiness** noun

tidy verb **tidies, tidying, tidied**
to tidy a place is to make it neat by putting things away in the right place

tie verb **ties, tying, tied**
1 to tie something is to fasten it with string, rope, or ribbon 2 to tie a knot or bow is to make one in a strip of material such as a ribbon 3 two players or teams tie when they finish a game or competition with an equal score or position

tie noun **ties**
1 a thin strip of material tied round the collar of a shirt with a knot at the front 2 the result of a game or competition in which two players or teams have the same position or score 3 one of the matches in a competition

tie-break or **tie-breaker** noun
tie-breaks, tie-breakers
an extra game or part of a game, played
when the result so far is a tie

tiger noun **tigers**
a large wild animal of the cat family, with
yellow and black stripes

tight adjective **tighter, tightest**
1 fitting very closely or firmly fastened
These shoes are a bit tight. **2** fully stretched
Is this string tight enough? **3** (informal) mean
or stingy *He's a bit tight with his money.*
tightly adverb **tightness** noun
tight adverb
1 firmly *Hold on tight.* **2** fully stretched *Now
pull the string tight.*

tighten verb **tightens, tightening,
tightened**
1 to tighten something is to make it tighter
These screws need to be tightened. **2** to
tighten is to become tighter

tightrope noun **tightropes**
a tightly stretched rope above the ground,
for acrobats to perform on

tights plural noun
a piece of clothing that fits tightly over the
lower parts of the body including the legs
and feet

tigress noun **tigresses**
a female tiger

tile noun **tiles**
a thin piece of baked clay or other hard
material used in rows to cover roofs, walls,
or floors **tiled** adjective

till[1] preposition, conjunction
until

till[2] noun **tills**
a drawer or box for money in a shop;
a cash register

till[3] verb **tills, tilling, tilled**
to till soil or land is to plough it ready
for planting

tiller noun **tillers**
a handle used to turn a boat's rudder

tilt verb **tilts, tilting, tilted**
1 to tilt is to slope or lean **2** to tilt
something is to tip it or make it slope
tilt noun **tilts**
a sloping position

timber noun **timbers**
1 timber is wood used for building or
making things **2** a timber is a beam of
wood

time noun **times**
1 time is a measure of the continued
existence of everything in years, months,
days, and other units **2** you ask the time
when you want to know what point in the
day it is, as shown on a watch or clock
What's the time? **3** a time is a particular
moment or period of things existing or
happening *Come back another time. There
were fields here in past times.* **4** a time is also
an occasion *This is the first time I've been
here.* **5** a time is also a period that is suitable
or available for something *Is there time for
something to eat?* **6** time is the rhythm and
speed of a piece of music **at times** or **from
time to time** sometimes or occasionally **in
time** or **on time** soon or early enough; not
late *Make sure you get to the station in time.
The train left on time.*

time verb **times, timing, timed**
1 to time something is to measure how long
it takes **2** to time an event or activity is to
arrange the time when it will happen *You
timed your arrival perfectly.*

timer noun **timers**
a device for timing things

times plural noun
multiplied by *5 times 3 is 15 (5 x 3 = 15).*

timetable noun **timetables**
a list of the times when things happen, such
as buses and trains leaving and arriving, and
when school lessons take place

timid adjective
nervous and easily frightened
timidly adverb **timidity** noun

timing noun
timing is choosing the right time to do

a
b
c
d
e
f
g
h
i
j
k
l
m
n
o
p
q
r
s
t
u
v
w
x
y
z

A

something *Arriving at lunchtime was good timing.*

B

timpani (say **timp**-a-nee) plural noun
kettledrums

C

tin noun tins
1 tin is a soft white metal 2 a tin is a metal container for preserving food

D

tin verb tins, tinning, tinned
to tin food is to preserve it in tins

E

F

tingle verb tingles, tingling, tingled
part of your body tingles when you have a slight stinging or tickling feeling there *The cold water made my skin tingle.*

G

H

tingle noun tingles
a tingling feeling

I

J

tinker verb tinkers, tinkering, tinkered
to tinker with something is to try to mend or improve it, often without really knowing how to *He loves tinkering with old clocks.*

K

L

tinker noun tinkers (old use)
someone who travelled around mending pots and pans

M

N

tinkle verb tinkles, tinkling, tinkled
something tinkles when it makes a gentle ringing sound

O

tinkle noun tinkles
a tinkling sound

P

tinsel noun
tinsel is strips of glittering material used for decoration

Q

R

tint noun tints
a shade of a colour, especially a pale one

S

tint verb tints, tinting, tinted
to tint something is to colour it slightly

T

tiny adjective tinier, tiniest
very small

U

tip¹ noun tips
the part at the very end of something

V

tip verb tips, tipping, tipped
to tip something is to give it a tip *The parcel was tied in a red ribbon tipped with gold.*

W

X

tip² noun tips
1 a small amount of money given to thank

Y

Z

someone who has helped you 2 a quick piece of advice or useful information

tip verb tips, tipping, tipped
1 to tip someone is to give them a small amount of money to thank them for helping you 2 to tip someone or something is to name them as likely to win or succeed

tip³ verb tips, tipping, tipped
1 to tip something is to turn it upside down or tilt it *She tipped the water out of the bucket. He tipped his head back and laughed.* 2 to tip rubbish is to leave it somewhere

tip noun tips
1 a place where rubbish is left 2 a very untidy place

tiptoe verb tiptoes, tiptoeing, tiptoed
to walk on your toes very quietly or carefully

tiptoe noun
on tiptoe walking or standing on your toes

tire verb tires, tiring, tired
1 to tire someone is to make them tired 2 to tire is to become tired

tired adjective
feeling that you need to sleep or rest **to be tired of something** is to have had enough of it **tiredness** noun

tireless adjective
having a lot of energy; not tiring easily

tiresome adjective
annoying *Grown-ups never understand anything by themselves, and it is tiresome for children to be always and forever explaining things to them.* – Antoine de Saint-Exupéry, *The Little Prince*

tissue noun tissues
1 tissue, or tissue paper, is thin soft paper 2 a tissue is a piece of this 3 tissue is also the substance of which an animal or plant is made

tit¹ noun tits
a kind of small bird

tit² noun
tit for tat something equal given in return

titbit noun titbits
a small piece of something

title noun titles
1 the name of something such as a book, film, painting, or piece of music 2 a word that shows a person's position or profession, such as *Sir, Lady, Dr, Mrs.* 3 a legal right to something, especially land or property

titter verb titters, tittering, tittered
to giggle or laugh in a silly way

to preposition
1 towards *They set off to London.* 2 as far as; so as to reach *I am soaked to the skin.* 3 compared with; rather than *She prefers cats to dogs.*

to adverb
to the usual or closed position *Push the door to.* **to and fro** backwards and forwards

toad noun toads
an animal like a large frog, that lives on land

toadstool noun toadstools
a fungus that looks like a mushroom, and is often poisonous

toast verb toasts, toasting, toasted
1 to toast food is to cook it by heating it under a grill or in front of a fire 2 to toast someone or something is to have a drink in their honour

toast noun toasts
1 toast is toasted bread 2 a toast is when people are asked to toast someone or something with a drink *Let's drink a toast to the bride and groom.*

toaster noun toasters
an electrical device for toasting bread

tobacco noun
tobacco is the dried leaves of certain plants prepared for smoking in cigarettes, cigars, or pipes

tobacconist noun tobacconists
a shopkeeper who sells cigarettes, cigars, and tobacco

toboggan noun toboggans
a small sledge for sliding downhill
tobogganing noun

today noun
this day *Today is Monday.*
today adverb
1 on this day *I saw him today.* 2 nowadays *Today we don't have slaves.*

toddler noun toddlers
a young child who is just learning to walk

toe noun toes
1 each of the five separate parts at the end of each foot 2 the part of a shoe or sock that covers your toes

toffee noun toffees
1 toffee is a sticky sweet made from butter and sugar 2 a toffee is a piece of this

toga noun togas
a long loose piece of clothing worn by men in ancient Rome

together adverb
with another person or thing; with each other *They went to school together. Now glue the two parts together.*

toil verb toils, toiling, toiled
1 to toil is to work hard 2 to toil is also to move slowly and with difficulty *The village carpenter had fixed up a bench upon which panting grown-ups could sit and rest themselves after they had toiled up the hill.* — Elizabeth Goudge, *The Little White Horse*

toilet noun toilets
1 a large bowl with a seat that you use for getting rid of waste from your body 2 a room with a toilet in it

toilet paper noun
toilet paper is paper for cleaning yourself after you have used a toilet

token noun tokens
1 a card or voucher that you can exchange for goods in a shop 2 a piece of metal or plastic you use instead of money to pay for something 3 a sign or signal of something *These flowers are a small token of my gratitude.*

a
b
c
d
e
f
g
h
i
j
k
l
m
n
o
p
q
r
s
t
u
v
w
x
y
z

A B C D E F G H I J K L M N O P Q R **S** **T** U V W X Y Z

told
past tense and past participle of **tell** *I told the truth. I've told you ten times to stop doing that.*

tolerable adjective
able to be tolerated; bearable
tolerably adverb to do something tolerably well is to do it fairly well

tolerant adjective
accepting or putting up with other people's behaviour and opinions when you do not agree with them **tolerance** noun
tolerantly adverb

tolerate verb tolerates, tolerating, tolerated
to tolerate something is to allow it or put up with it although you do not approve of it

toll¹ noun tolls
1 a payment charged for using a bridge or road **2** an amount of loss or damage *The death toll in the earthquake is rising.*

toll² verb tolls, tolling, tolled
to toll a bell is to ring it slowly

tom or **tomcat** noun toms, tomcats
a male cat

tomahawk noun tomahawks
an axe used by Native Americans

tomato noun tomatoes
a soft round red fruit with seeds inside it, eaten as a vegetable

tomb (say toom) noun tombs
a place where a dead body is buried; a grave

tomboy noun tomboys
a girl who enjoys rough noisy games and activities

tombstone noun tombstones
a memorial stone set up over a grave

tomorrow noun, adverb
the day after today

TOP TIPS
Double up the **r** in **tomorrow** (but the **m** stays single)!

tom-tom noun tom-toms
a type of drum that you beat with the palms of your hands

ton noun tons
1 a unit of weight equal to 2,240 pounds or about 1,016 kilograms **2** (informal) a large amount *There's tons of room.*

tone noun tones
1 a sound in music or speech **2** each of the five larger intervals between two notes in a musical scale **3** a shade of a colour **4** the quality or character of something

tone verb tones, toning, toned
to tone something down is to make it softer or quieter **to tone in** is to blend or fit in well, especially in colour

tongs plural noun
a tool with two arms joined at one end, used to pick things up or hold them

tongue noun tongues
1 the long soft part that moves about inside your mouth **2** a language **3** the flap of material under the laces of a shoe **4** the part inside a bell that makes it ring

tongue-tied adjective
to be tongue-tied is to feel too shy or embarrassed to speak

tongue-twister noun tongue-twisters
a sentence or phrase that is very difficult to say

tonic noun tonics
something that makes a person healthier or stronger

tonight adverb, noun
this evening or night

tonne noun tonnes
a metric ton, a unit of weight equal to 1,000 kilograms

tonsillitis noun
tonsillitis is a disease that makes your tonsils extremely sore

tonsils plural noun
your tonsils are two small masses of soft flesh inside your throat

too adverb
1 also *Take the others too.* 2 more than is wanted or allowed or wise *Don't drive too fast.*

took
past tense of **take** *I took no notice of what he said.*

tool noun tools
a device that you use to help you do a particular job, such as a hammer or saw

tooth noun teeth
1 each of the hard white bony parts that grow in the gums, used for biting and chewing 2 each in a row of sharp points on a saw or comb **toothed** adjective

toothache noun
toothache is a pain in one of your teeth

toothbrush noun toothbrushes
a small brush on a long handle, for brushing your teeth

toothpaste noun toothpastes
toothpaste is a creamy paste for cleaning your teeth

top¹ noun tops
1 the highest part of something 2 the upper surface of something 3 the covering or stopper of a jar or bottle 4 a piece of clothing you wear on the upper part of your body
top adjective
highest or most important *They were travelling at top speed.*
top verb tops, topping, topped
1 to top something is to put a top on it *The cake was topped with icing.* 2 to top something is also to be at the top of it *She tops the class in maths.* **to top something up** is to fill it to the top when it is already partly full

top² noun tops
a toy that can be made to spin on its point

top hat noun top hats
a man's tall stiff black or grey hat worn with formal clothes

topic noun topics
a subject that you are writing or talking or learning about

topical adjective
to do with things that are happening or in the news now *The film we saw was very topical.* **topicality** noun

topless adjective
not wearing any clothes on the top half of your body

topmost adjective
highest *Jay, Magpie, and Parrot went along at dawn and sat in the topmost twigs of Cat's old tree.* – Ted Hughes, *How the Whale Became and Other Stories*

topping noun toppings
food that is put on the top of (for example) a cake or pizza

topple verb topples, toppling, toppled
1 to topple, or topple over, is to fall over 2 to topple something is to make it fall over 3 to topple someone in power is to overthrow them

top secret adjective
extremely secret

topsy-turvy adverb, adjective
upside down; muddled

torch noun torches
1 a small electric lamp that you hold in your hand 2 a stick with burning material on the end, used as a light

tore
past tense of **tear¹** verb *She tore open the parcel.*

torment verb torments, tormenting, tormented
1 to torment someone is to make them suffer or feel pain 2 to torment someone is also to keep annoying them deliberately **tormentor** noun

a
b
c
d
e
f
g
h
i
j
k
l
m
n
o
p
q
r
s
t
u
v
w
x
y
z

A

torment noun torments
torment is great suffering

B

torn
past participle of **tear¹** verb *The old house had been torn down.*

C

D

tornado (say tor-**nay**-doh) noun
tornadoes
a violent storm or whirlwind

E

F

torpedo noun torpedoes
a long tube-shaped missile sent under water to destroy ships and submarines

G

torpedo verb torpedoes, torpedoing, torpedoed
to torpedo a ship is to attack it with a torpedo

H

I

J

torrent noun torrents
a very strong stream or fall of water *Then a great storm came up, with thunder and lightning. The wind howled, the rain came down in torrents, and the waves got so high, they splashed right over the boat.* — Hugh Lofting, *The Story of Doctor Dolittle* **torrential** adjective

K

L

M

N

torso noun torsos
the main part of the human body, not including the head, arms, or legs

O

tortoise (say **tor**-tus) noun tortoises
a slow-moving animal with a shell over its body

P

Q

R

torture verb tortures, torturing, tortured
to torture someone is to make them feel great pain, especially so that they will give information

S

T

torture noun tortures
torture is something done to torture a person **torturer** noun

U

V

Tory noun Tories
a Conservative

W

toss verb tosses, tossing, tossed
1 to toss something is to throw it into the air 2 to toss a coin is to throw it in the air and see which side it lands on, as a way of deciding something 3 to toss is to move

X

Y

Z

about restlessly in bed *She was tossing and turning all night.*

total noun totals
the amount you get by adding everything together

total adjective
1 complete; including everything *What is the total amount?* 2 complete *There was total darkness outside.* **totally** adverb

total verb totals, totalling, totalled
1 to total something is to add it up 2 to total an amount is to reach it as a total *Sales totalled over £50,000 this month.*

totem pole noun totem poles
a large pole carved or painted by Native Americans

totter verb totters, tottering, tottered
to walk unsteadily or wobble

toucan noun toucans
a tropical bird with a large brightly-coloured beak

touch verb touches, touching, touched
1 you touch something when you feel it lightly with your hand or fingers 2 to touch something is to come into contact with it or hit it gently 3 to be touching something is to be next to it so that there is no space in between 4 to touch something is also to interfere or meddle with it *Don't touch anything in this room.* 5 to touch an amount is to just reach it *His temperature touched 100 degrees.* 6 to touch someone is to affect their emotions *We were touched by his sad story.* **to touch down** is to land in an aircraft or spacecraft **to touch something up** is to improve it by making small changes or additions

touch noun touches
1 a touch is an act of touching *You can find any train timetable you want at the touch of a button.* 2 touch is the ability to feel things by touching them 3 a touch is also a small thing that greatly improves something *We're just putting the finishing touches to it.* 4 touch is also communication with someone *We have lost touch with them.* 5 touch is also the part of a football

or rugby pitch outside the playing area *He kicked the ball into touch.*

touchy adjective **touchier, touchiest**
someone who is touchy is easily or quickly offended

tough adjective **tougher, toughest**
1 strong; hard to break or damage *You'll need tough shoes for the climb.* 2 tough food is hard to chew 3 rough or violent *The police were dealing with tough criminals.* 4 firm or severe *It's time to get tough with football hooligans.* 5 difficult *It was a tough decision.*
toughly adverb **toughness** noun

toughen verb **toughens, toughening, toughened**
to toughen someone or something, or toughen them up, is to make them tougher

tour noun **tours**
a journey in which you visit several places

tourism noun
tourism is travelling or being on holiday abroad

tourist noun **tourists**
someone who is travelling or on holiday abroad

tournament noun **tournaments**
a competition in which there is a series of games or contests

tow (rhymes with **go**) verb **tows, towing, towed**
to tow a vehicle or boat is to pull it behind you in another vehicle *They towed our car to a garage.*

tow noun
an act of towing

toward or **towards** preposition
1 in the direction of *She walked towards the sea.* 2 in relation to *He behaved kindly towards his children.* 3 as a contribution to *Put the money towards a new bicycle.*

towel noun **towels**
a piece of soft cloth that you use for drying yourself

towelling noun
towelling is material that towels are made of

tower noun **towers**
a tall narrow building or part of a building

tower verb **towers, towering, towered**
to tower above or over things is to be taller than them *The skyscrapers towered above the city.*

tower block noun **tower blocks**
a tall building containing offices or flats

town noun **towns**
a place with many houses, shops, schools, offices, and other buildings

town hall noun **town halls**
a building with offices for the local council and usually a hall for public events

toxic adjective
poisonous

toy noun **toys**
something to play with

toy verb **toys, toying, toyed**
to toy with an idea is to think about it casually or idly

trace noun **traces**
1 a mark or sign left by a person or thing *He vanished without a trace.* 2 a very small amount of something *They found traces of blood on the carpet.*

trace verb **traces, tracing, traced**
1 to trace someone or something is to find them after a search *Police are trying to trace one of the witnesses.* 2 to trace a picture or map is to copy it by drawing over it on thin paper you can see through

traceable adjective
able to be traced or found

track noun **tracks**
1 a path made by people or animals 2 tracks are marks left by a person or thing 3 a set of rails for trains or trams to run on 4 a road or area of ground prepared for racing 5 a metal belt used instead of wheels on a heavy vehicle such as a tank or tractor **to keep track of something** or **someone** is to know where they are or what they are doing

track verb tracks, tracking, tracked
1 to track a person or animal is to follow them by following the signs they leave **2** to track something is to follow or observe it as it moves

tracksuit noun tracksuits
a warm loose suit of a kind worn by athletes for jogging and warming up

tract¹ noun tracts
1 an area of land **2** a series of connected parts in the body

tract² noun tracts
a short pamphlet or essay, especially about religion

traction noun
1 traction is the ability of a vehicle to grip the ground *The car's wheels lost traction in the mud.* **2** traction is also a medical treatment in which an injured arm or leg is pulled gently for a long time by means of weights and pulleys

tractor noun tractors
a motor vehicle with large rear wheels, used for pulling farm machinery or heavy loads

trade noun trades
1 trade is the business of buying or selling or exchanging things **2** a trade is a job or occupation, especially a skilled craft

trade verb trades, trading, traded
to trade is to buy or sell or exchange things **to trade something in** is to give it towards the cost of something new *He traded in his motorcycle for a car.*

trademark noun trademarks
a symbol or name that only one manufacturer is allowed to use

trader noun traders
someone who buys and sells things in trade

tradesman noun tradesmen
someone who sells or delivers goods

trade union noun trade unions
an organization of workers in a particular industry, set up to help improve pay and work conditions

tradition noun traditions
1 tradition is the passing down of customs and beliefs from one generation to the next **2** a tradition is a custom or belief passed on in this way

traditional adjective
1 passed down from one generation to the next *It is a book of traditional stories from all round the world.* **2** of a kind that has existed for a long time *We go to a very traditional school.* **traditionally** adverb something is traditionally done a certain way when that is what has been done for generations

traffic noun
1 traffic is vehicles, ships, or aircraft moving along a route **2** traffic is also trade, especially in something illegal or wrong

traffic verb traffics, trafficking, trafficked
to traffic in something is to trade in it illegally

traffic lights plural noun
a set of coloured lights used to control traffic at road junctions and other hazards

traffic warden noun traffic wardens
an official whose job is to make sure that vehicles are parked legally

tragedy noun tragedies
1 a play with unhappy events or a sad ending **2** a very sad event

tragic adjective
1 very sad or distressing **2** to do with tragedy **tragically** adverb

trail noun trails
1 a path or track through the countryside or a forest **2** the scent and marks left behind by an animal as it moves **3** marks left behind by something that has passed

trail verb trails, trailing, trailed
1 to trail an animal is to follow the scent or marks it has left behind **2** you trail something, or it trails, when it drags along the ground behind you **3** to trail behind someone is to follow them more slowly or

at a distance *A few walkers trailed behind the others.* **4** to trail is also to hang down or float loosely *She wore a long trailing scarf.*

trailer noun trailers
1 a truck or other container that is pulled along by a car or lorry **2** a short film advertising a film or television programme that will soon be shown

train noun trains
1 a group of railway coaches or trucks joined together and pulled by an engine **2** a number of people or animals moving along together, especially in a desert *a camel train* **3** a series of things *The train of events began in London.* **4** a long part of a dress that trails on the ground

train verb trains, training, trained
1 to train someone is to give them skill or practice in something **2** to train is to learn how to do a job *He's training to be a doctor.* **3** to train is also to practise for a sporting event *She was training for the race.* **4** to train a plant is to make it grow in a particular direction *Roses can be trained up walls.* **5** to train a gun is to aim it at a target *He trained his rifle on the bridge.*

trainer noun trainers
1 a person who trains people or animals **2** a soft shoe with a rubber sole, worn for running and sport

traitor noun traitors
someone who betrays their country or friends

tram noun trams
a passenger vehicle that runs along rails set in the road

tramp noun tramps
1 a person without a home or job who walks from place to place **2** a long walk **3** the sound of heavy footsteps
tramp verb tramps, tramping, tramped
1 to tramp is to walk with heavy footsteps **2** to tramp is also to walk for a long distance

trample verb tramples, trampling, trampled
to trample something, or to trample on it, is to crush it by treading heavily on it

trampoline (say tramp-o-leen) noun trampolines
a large piece of canvas joined to a frame by springs, used by gymnasts for jumping on

trance noun trances
a dreamy or unconscious condition like sleep

tranquil adjective
quiet and peaceful **tranquillity** noun

tranquillizer noun tranquillizers
a drug used to make a person feel calm and relaxed

trans– prefix
meaning 'across' , as in *transatlantic*

transaction noun transactions
a piece of business that involves buying and selling something

transatlantic adjective
across the Atlantic Ocean or on the other side of it

transfer (say trans-**fer**) verb transfers, transferring, transferred
1 to transfer someone or something is to move them from one place to another **2** to transfer something is to give it or pass it on to someone else

transfer (say **trans**-fer) noun transfers
1 the process of moving a person or thing from one place to another **2** a piece of paper with a picture or design that can be transferred to another surface by soaking or heating the paper

transferable adjective
a ticket is transferable when it can be used by someone other than the person who bought it

transform verb transforms, transforming, transformed
to transform a person or thing is to change their form or appearance to something

a
b
c
d
e
f
g
h
i
j
k
l
m
n
o
p
q
r
s
t
u
v
w
x
y
z

A

quite different *The caterpillar is transformed into a butterfly.* **transformation** noun

B

transformer noun **transformers**
a device used to change the voltage of an electric current

C

D

transfusion noun **transfusions**
putting blood taken from one person into another person's body

E

F

transistor noun **transistors**
1 a tiny electronic device that controls a flow of electricity 2 a portable radio that uses transistors to strengthen the signal it receives

G

H

I

transition noun **transitions**
a change from one thing to another

J

transitive adjective (in grammar)
a verb is transitive when it is used with a direct object, for example *ran* in *they ran a paper shop* (but not in *they ran away*)

K

L

translate verb **translates, translating, translated**
to translate something said or written in one language is to say or write it in another language **translation** noun **translator** noun

M

N

O

translucent adjective
something is translucent when it allows light to shine through, without being fully transparent

P

Q

transmission noun **transmissions**
1 transmission is transmitting something 2 a transmission is a radio or television broadcast

R

S

T

transmit verb **transmits, transmitting, transmitted**
1 to transmit a broadcast or signal is to send it out 2 to transmit something is to send it or pass it from one person or place to another

U

V

W

transmitter noun **transmitters**
a device for transmitting radio signals

X

Y

transparency noun **transparencies**
1 transparency is being transparent 2 a transparency is a type of transparent

Z

photograph that you can project on a screen

transparent adjective
something is transparent when you can see through it

transpire verb **transpires, transpiring, transpired**
1 to transpire is to become known *It transpired that she had known nothing about it.* 2 to transpire is also to happen *This is what transpired.* 3 plants and animals transpire when they emit moisture through their leaves or skin

transplant verb **transplants, transplanting, transplanted**
1 to transplant a body organ is to remove it from one person and put it in another 2 to transplant a plant is to move it from one place to another **transplantation** noun

transplant noun **transplants**
1 when a body organ is removed from one person and put in another *a heart transplant* 2 something that is transplanted

transport (say trans-**port**) verb **transports, transporting, transported**
to transport people or things is to take them from one place to another **transportation** noun

transport (say **trans**-port) noun
1 transport is the process of transporting people or things 2 transport is also vehicles used to do this

transporter noun **transporters**
a heavy vehicle for transporting large objects, such as cars

trap noun **traps**
1 a device for catching and holding animals 2 a plan or trick to capture, detect, or cheat someone 3 a two-wheeled carriage pulled by a horse 4 a bend in a pipe, filled with liquid to prevent air or gas escaping

trap verb **traps, trapping, trapped**
1 to trap a person or animal is to catch them in a trap 2 to trap someone is to capture, detect, or cheat them 3 to be trapped is to be stuck in a dangerous

situation you can't escape from *They were trapped in the burning building.*

trapdoor noun trapdoors
a door in a floor or ceiling or roof

trapeze noun trapezes
a bar hanging from two ropes, used as a swing by acrobats

trapezium noun trapeziums
a four-sided figure that has only two parallel sides, which are of different length

trapezoid noun trapezoids
a four-sided figure with no two sides parallel

trash noun
trash is rubbish or nonsense

travel verb travels, travelling, travelled
to travel is to go from one place to another

travel noun
travel is going on journeys *Do you enjoy travel?*

travel agent noun travel agents
a person or business whose job is to arrange travel and holidays for people

traveller noun travellers
1 someone who is travelling or who often travels 2 a person who lives in a vehicle and does not settle in one place

trawler noun trawlers
a fishing boat that pulls a large net behind it

tray noun trays
a flat piece of wood or metal or plastic, used for carrying food, cups, plates, and other household things

treacherous adjective
1 betraying someone; not loyal 2 dangerous *The snow was deep and treacherous, with a thick, shiny crust of ice on top.* — Neil Gaiman, *Odd and the Frost Giants*
treacherously adverb

treachery noun
treachery is doing something that betrays someone

treacle noun
treacle is a thick sweet sticky liquid made from purified sugar

tread verb treads, treading, trod, trodden
to tread on something is to walk on it or put your foot on it

tread noun treads
1 the sound someone makes when they walk *He had a heavy tread.* 2 the part of a staircase or ladder that you put your foot on 3 the part of a tyre that touches the ground

treason noun
treason is betraying your country

treasure noun treasures
1 treasure is a collection of valuable things like jewels or money 2 a treasure is a precious thing

treasure verb treasures, treasuring, treasured
to treasure something is to think that it is very precious

treasure hunt noun treasure hunts
a game in which people try to find a hidden object

treasurer noun treasurers
an official who is in charge of the money of an organization or club

treasury noun treasuries
a place where treasure is stored **the Treasury** the government department in charge of a country's income

treat verb treats, treating, treated
1 to treat someone or something in a certain way is to behave towards them in that way *She treats her friends very kindly.* 2 to treat a person or animal is to give them medical care *He was treated for sunstroke.* 3 to treat someone is to pay for their food or drink or entertainment *I'll treat you to an ice cream.*

treat noun treats
1 something special that gives someone pleasure 2 the act of treating someone by paying for them *This is my treat.*

a b c d e f g h i j k l m n o p q r s t u v w x y z

treatment noun treatments
1 your treatment of someone is the way you treat them 2 treatment is medical care

treaty noun treaties
a formal agreement between two or more countries

treble adjective
three times as much or three times as many

treble noun trebles
1 treble the amount of something is three times as much or as many 2 a treble is a boy with a high singing voice

treble verb trebles, trebling, trebled
1 to treble something is to make it three times as big 2 to treble is to become three times as big

tree noun trees
a tall plant with leaves, branches, and a thick wooden stem called a trunk

trek verb treks, trekking, trekked
to make a long walk or journey

trek noun treks
a long walk or journey

trellis noun trellises
a framework of crossing wooden or metal bars, used to support climbing plants

tremble verb trembles, trembling, trembled
to shake gently, especially because you are afraid

tremble noun trembles
a trembling movement or sound

tremendous adjective
1 very large or very great *A tremendous banging noise was coming from inside the Pelican's beak. It sounded as though someone was using a sledgehammer against it from the inside.* – Roald Dahl, *The Giraffe and the Pelly and Me* 2 excellent **tremendously** adverb

tremor noun tremors
1 a shaking or trembling 2 a small earthquake

trench noun trenches
a long hole or ditch dug in the ground

trend noun trends
the general direction in which something is going or developing

trendy adjective trendier, trendiest (informal)
fashionable; trying to be up to date
trendily adverb **trendiness** noun

trespass verb trespasses, trespassing, trespassed
to trespass is to go on someone's land or property without their permission *The sign said 'No Trespassing'.* **trespasser** noun

trestle noun trestles
each of a set of supports on which you place a board to make a table

trial noun trials
1 trying or testing something to see how well it works 2 the process of hearing all the evidence about a crime in a law court in order to find out whether someone is guilty of it **on trial** being tried out, or being tried in a law court

triangle noun triangles
1 a flat shape with three straight sides and three angles 2 a percussion instrument made from a metal rod bent into a triangle

triangular adjective
in the shape of a triangle

tribe noun tribes
a group of families living together, ruled by a chief **tribal** adjective

tribesman noun tribesmen
a man who belongs to a particular tribe

tributary noun tributaries
a river or stream that flows into a larger river or a lake

tribute noun tributes
1 something said or done as a mark of respect or admiration for someone 2 money that people in one country used to have to pay a powerful ruler in another country

trick noun tricks
1 something done to deceive or fool

someone **2** a clever or skilful action *a card trick*

trick verb **tricks, tricking, tricked**
to trick someone is to deceive or fool them **trickery** noun **trickster** noun someone who plays tricks on people

trickle verb **trickles, trickling, trickled**
liquid trickles when it flows slowly in small quantities

trickle noun **trickles**
a slow gradual flow

tricky adjective **trickier, trickiest**
1 difficult or awkward *There were a couple of tricky questions in the quiz.* **2** cunning or deceitful

tricycle noun **tricycles**
a vehicle like a bicycle with three wheels

tried
past tense and past participle of **try** verb *He tried to cover up his laugh with a cough. I have tried to be patient with you.*

trifle noun **trifles**
1 a pudding made of sponge cake covered with custard, fruit, and cream **2** a very small amount of something **3** something that has little importance or value

trifle verb **trifles, trifling, trifled**
to trifle with someone or something is to treat them without seriousness or respect

trifling adjective
very small or unimportant

trigger noun **triggers**
a lever that is pulled to fire a gun

trigger verb **triggers, triggering, triggered**
to trigger something, or trigger it off, is to start it happening

trillion noun **trillions**
a million million (1,000,000,000,000)

trilogy noun **trilogies**
a group of three books or films about the same characters

trim adjective **trimmer, trimmest**
neat and tidy

trim verb **trims, trimming, trimmed**
1 you trim something when you cut the edges or unwanted parts from it **2** to trim clothing is to decorate its edges *The gown was trimmed with fur.* **3** in a boat, to trim the sails is to arrange them to suit the wind

trim noun
an act of trimming *My hair needs a quick trim.*

Trinity noun
the Trinity in Christianity, the union of Father, Son, and Holy Spirit in one God

trio noun **trios**
1 three people or things **2** a group of three musicians **3** a piece of music for three musicians

trip verb **trips, tripping, tripped**
1 to trip, or trip over, is to catch your foot on something and fall or stumble **2** to trip someone, or trip them up, is to make them fall or stumble **3** to trip, or trip along, is to move with quick gentle steps

trip noun **trips**
1 a short journey or outing **2** the action of tripping or stumbling

tripe noun
1 tripe is part of the stomach of an ox used as food **2** (informal) tripe is also nonsense

triple adjective
1 three times as much or three times as many **2** consisting of three parts or involving three people or groups

triple verb **triples, tripling, tripled**
to triple something is to make it three times as big

triplet noun **triplets**
each of three children or animals born at the same time to the same mother

tripod (say **try**-pod) noun **tripods**
a stand with three legs, for supporting a camera or other instrument

triumph noun **triumphs**
1 a triumph is a great success or victory **2** triumph is a feeling of victory or success *They returned home in triumph.*

a
b
c
d
e
f
g
h
i
j
k
l
m
n
o
p
q
r
s
t
u
v
w
x
y
z

A
B
C
D
E
F
G
H
I
J
K
L
M
N
O
P
Q
R
S
T
U
V
W
X
Y
Z

triumph verb triumphs, triumphing, triumphed
to triumph is to win or succeed

triumphant adjective
enjoying a victory or celebrating one
triumphantly adverb in a triumphant way
'Now do you believe in witches?' cried Lizzie's witch triumphantly. – Helen Cresswell, Lizzie Dripping

trivial adjective
not important or valuable **trivially** adverb
triviality noun

trod
past tense of **tread** verb *Laura trod in something slippery.*

trodden
past participle of **tread** verb *Many other people had trodden this path.*

troll noun trolls
a creature in Scandinavian mythology, either a dwarf or a giant

trolley noun trolleys
1 a basket on wheels, used in supermarkets 2 a small table on wheels, used for serving food and drink

trombone noun trombones
a large brass musical instrument with a sliding tube
Please see illustration on following page.

troop noun troops
an organized group of people, especially soldiers or Scouts

troop verb troops, trooping, trooped
people troop when they move along in large numbers

troops plural noun
soldiers

trophy noun trophies
a cup or other prize you get for winning a competition

tropic noun tropics
a line of latitude about 23½° north of the equator (**Tropic of Cancer**) or about 23½° south of the equator (**Tropic of Capricorn**)
the tropics the hot regions between these two latitudes

tropical adjective
a tropical (for example) plant, bird, or rainforest is one found in the tropics

trot verb trots, trotting, trotted
1 a horse trots when it runs gently without cantering or galloping 2 a person trots when they run gently with short steps

trot noun trots
a trotting run **on the trot** (informal) one after another

trouble noun troubles
trouble is something that causes worry or difficulty **to be in trouble** is to be likely to get punished because of something you have done **to take trouble** is to take great care in doing something

trouble verb troubles, troubling, troubled
1 to trouble someone is to cause them worry or difficulty 2 to trouble someone is also to bother or disturb them *Sorry to trouble you, but can you spare a minute?* 3 to trouble to do something is to make an effort to do it *Nobody troubled to ask us what we wanted.*

troublesome adjective
causing trouble or worry

trough (say trof) noun troughs
1 a long narrow box for animals to eat or drink from 2 an area of low pressure between two areas of high pressure

trousers plural noun
a piece of clothing worn over the lower half of your body, with two parts to cover your legs

trout noun trout
a freshwater fish

trowel noun trowels
1 a tool for digging small holes or lifting plants 2 a tool with a flat blade for spreading cement or mortar

truant noun truants
a child who stays away from school

trumpet

trumpet

tuba

trombone

without permission **to play truant** is to stay away from school without permission **truancy** noun

truce noun **truces**
an agreement to stop fighting for a while

truck noun **trucks**
1 a lorry **2** an open railway wagon for carrying goods **3** a cart

trudge verb **trudges, trudging, trudged**
to walk slowly and heavily

true adjective **truer, truest**
1 real or correct; telling what actually exists or happened *This is a true story.* **2** genuine or proper *He was the true heir.* **3** loyal and faithful *You are a true friend.* **to come true** is to actually happen *I hope your dreams come true.*

truly adverb
1 truthfully **2** sincerely or genuinely *We are truly grateful.* **3** loyally or faithfully

 TOP TIPS **Truly** can be tricky to spell—it has no e!

trump noun **trumps**
a playing card of a suit that ranks above the others for one game or round of play

trump verb **trumps, trumping, trumped**
to trump a card is to beat it by playing a trump

trumpet noun **trumpets**
a brass musical instrument with a narrow tube that widens at the end
trumpeter noun

trumpet verb **trumpets, trumpeting, trumpeted**
1 an elephant trumpets when it makes a loud sound **2** to trumpet something is to shout it out or announce it loudly

truncheon noun **truncheons**
a short thick stick carried as a weapon by a police officer

trundle verb **trundles, trundling, trundled**
to move along heavily, especially on wheels *A lorry trundled across the bridge.*

trunk noun **trunks**
1 the main stem of a tree **2** an elephant's long flexible nose **3** a large box with a hinged lid, for carrying or storing clothes and other things **4** the human body except for the head, legs, and arms

trunks plural noun
shorts worn by men and boys for swimming, boxing, and other activities

A
B
C
D
E
F
G
H
I
J
K
L
M
N
O
P
Q
R
S
T
U
V
W
X
Y
Z

trust verb **trusts, trusting, trusted**
1 to trust someone or something is to believe that they are good or truthful or reliable **2** to trust that something is so is to hope it *I trust that you are well.*

trust noun
1 trust is the feeling that a person or thing can be trusted **2** trust is also responsibility or being trusted *Our pet dog was left in the trust of our next-door neighbour.*

trustful adjective
trusting people **trustfully** adverb

trustworthy adjective
able to be trusted; reliable

trusty adjective **trustier, trustiest**
trustworthy or reliable

truth noun **truths**
1 truth is the quality of being true; the facts about something **2** a truth is something that is true

truthful adjective
1 telling the truth *They are truthful children.* **2** true *They gave a truthful account of what happened.* **truthfully** adverb **truthfulness** noun

try verb **tries, trying, tried**
1 to try to do something is to make an effort to do it or to see if you can do it *Try to keep still.* **2** to try something is to use it to see if it works or taste it to see if you like it *Try this can opener.* **3** to try someone in a law court is to find out whether they are guilty of a crime, by hearing all the evidence about it **4** to try someone is also to annoy them over a long time *You really do try me with your constant complaining.* **to try something on** is to put on clothes to see if they fit or look good **to try something out** is to use it to see if it works

try noun **tries**
1 a go at trying something; an attempt *Have another try.* **2** (in rugby football) putting the ball down on the ground behind your opponents' goal to score points

T-shirt noun **T-shirts**
a shirt or vest with short sleeves

tsunami (say soo-**nah**-mi) noun
tsunami or **tsunamis**
a huge sea wave caused by an earthquake

tub noun **tubs**
a round container for liquids or soft stuff such as ice cream

tuba (say **tew**-ba) noun **tubas**
a large brass musical instrument that makes a deep sound
Please see illustration on previous page.

tube noun **tubes**
1 a tube is a long thin hollow piece of material such as metal, plastic, rubber, or glass **2** a tube is also a long hollow container for something soft such as toothpaste **3** the tube is the underground railway in London *She goes to work by tube.*

tuber noun **tubers**
a thick rounded plant root or stem that produces buds

tubing noun
tubing is a length or piece of tube

tubular adjective
shaped like a tube

tuck verb **tucks, tucking, tucked**
to tuck something somewhere is to push a loose edge of it there so that it is tidy or hidden *Now tuck in the flap of the envelope. She tucked her hair under her cap.* **to tuck in** (informal) is to eat heartily **to tuck someone up** is to put the bedclothes snugly round them

tuck noun **tucks**
a tuck is a flat fold stitched into clothing

tuck shop noun **tuck shops**
a shop that sells snacks to children

Tuesday noun **Tuesdays**
the third day of the week

tuft noun **tufts**
a bunch of soft or fluffy things such as threads, grass, hair, or feathers, held or growing together

tug verb **tugs, tugging, tugged**
to tug something is to pull it hard

tug noun tugs
1 a hard or sudden pull 2 a small powerful boat used for towing ships

tug–of–war noun tugs of war
a contest between two teams pulling a rope from opposite ends

tulip noun tulips
a large bright cup-shaped flower that grows on a tall stem from a bulb

tumble verb tumbles, tumbling, tumbled
1 to tumble is to fall over or fall down clumsily 2 to tumble to something is to suddenly realize it or be aware of it

tumble noun tumbles
a clumsy fall

tumble–drier noun tumble-driers
a machine that dries washing in a rotating drum with heated air passing through

tumbler noun tumblers
1 a drinking glass with no stem or handle 2 an acrobat

tummy noun tummies (informal)
your stomach

tumour (say tew-mer) noun tumours
an abnormal growth on or in your body

tumult (say tew-mult) noun
an uproar or state of great confusion

tumultuous adjective
noisy and excited *The teams walked onto the pitch to tumultuous applause. — J. K. Rowling, Harry Potter and the Chamber of Secrets*

tuna (say tew-na) noun tuna or tunas
a large sea fish used for food

tundra noun
tundra is a large area of flat land in cold regions (especially northern Canada and Siberia) with no trees and with soil that is frozen for most of the year

tune noun tunes
a short piece of music; a pleasant series of musical notes **to be in tune** is to be at the correct musical pitch

tune verb tunes, tuning, tuned
1 to tune a musical instrument is to adjust it to be in tune 2 to tune a radio or television is to adjust it to receive a particular broadcasting station 3 to tune an engine is to adjust it so that it works smoothly

tuneful adjective
having a pleasant tune **tunefully** adverb

tunic (say tew-nik) noun tunics
1 a jacket that is part of some uniforms 2 a loose piece of clothing with no sleeves

tunnel noun tunnels
a passage made underground or through a hill

tunnel verb tunnels, tunnelling, tunnelled
to tunnel is to make a tunnel

turban noun turbans
a covering for the head made by wrapping a long strip of cloth round it, worn especially by Sikh, Hindu, or Muslim men

turbine noun turbines
a machine or motor that is driven by a flow of water or gas or wind

turbulent adjective
moving violently; heaving *The seas in March can be turbulent.* **turbulence** noun

turf noun turfs or turves
1 turf is short grass with the soil it is growing in 2 a turf is a piece of grass and soil cut out of the ground

turkey noun turkeys
a large bird kept for its meat

turmoil noun
turmoil is a great disturbance or confusion

turn verb turns, turning, turned
1 to turn is to move round or move to a new direction; to turn something is to make it move in this way 2 to turn (for example) pale is to change appearance and become pale 3 to turn into something is to change into it *The frog turned into a prince.* 4 to turn

a
b
c
d
e
f
g
h
i
j
k
l
m
n
o
p
q
r
s
t
u
v
w
x
y
z

A
B
C
D
E
F
G
H
I
J
K
L
M
N
O
P
Q
R
S
T
U
V
W
X
Y
Z

something into something else is to change it *You can turn milk into cheese.* **5** to turn a device on or off is to use a switch to make it work or stop working; to turn (for example) a radio or television up or down is to make it louder or quieter **to turn out** is to happen a certain way *The weather's turned out fine.* **to turn something down** is to refuse it **to turn up** is to appear or arrive suddenly or unexpectedly

turn noun turns
1 the action of turning; a turning movement *Give the key three turns.* **2** a place where a road bends; a junction *Take the next turn on the left.* **3** a task or duty that people do one after the other *It's your turn to wash up.* **4** a short performance in a show **5** (informal) an attack of illness; a nervous shock *It gave me a nasty turn.* **a good turn** is a favour you do for someone **in turn** first one and then the other; following one after another

turncoat noun turncoats
someone who changes sides or changes what they believe

turnip noun turnips
a plant with a large round white root used as a vegetable

turnover noun turnovers
a small pie made of pastry folded over fruit or jam

turnstile noun turnstiles
a revolving gate that lets one person through at a time

turntable noun turntables
a revolving platform or support, especially the part of a record player that you put the record on

turpentine (say ter-pen-tyn) noun
turpentine is a kind of oil used to make paint thinner and to clean paintbrushes

turquoise (say ter-kwoiz) noun
1 a sky-blue or green-blue colour **2** a blue jewel

turret noun turrets
1 a small tower in a castle **2** a revolving structure containing a gun

turtle noun turtles
a sea animal that looks like a tortoise **to turn turtle** is to capsize

tusk noun tusks
one of a pair of long pointed teeth that stick out of the mouth of an elephant or walrus or boar

tussle noun tussles
a hard struggle or fight

tussle verb tussles, tussling, tussled
to struggle or fight over something

tutor noun tutors
a teacher who teaches one person or a small group at a time

TV
short for **television**

tweak verb tweaks, tweaking, tweaked
to tweak something is to twist it or pull it sharply

tweak noun tweaks
a tweaking movement

tweed noun
tweed is a thick rough woollen cloth

tweezers plural noun
a small tool for gripping or picking up small things like stamps and hairs

twelve noun twelves
the number 12 **twelfth** adjective, noun

TOP TIPS
Twelfth can be tricky to spell—it has an **f**!

twenty noun twenties
the number 20 **twentieth** adjective, noun

twice adverb
1 two times; on two occasions **2** double the amount

twiddle verb twiddles, twiddling, twiddled
to twiddle something is to turn it round

or over and over in an idle way *He was twiddling a knob on the radio.*

twiddle noun twiddles
a twiddling movement

twig¹ noun twigs
a short thin branch or shoot

twig² verb twigs, twigging, twigged (informal)
to twig something is to realize what it means *I suddenly twigged what she was talking about.*

twilight noun
twilight is the time of dim light just after sunset

twin noun twins
1 each of two children or animals born at the same time from one mother **2** each of two things that are exactly alike

twin verb twins, twinning, twinned
one city or town is twinned with one in another country when they have an arrangement involving exchange visits and other cultural events that they do together

twine noun
twine is strong thin string

twinge noun twinges
a sudden pain or unpleasant feeling

twinkle verb twinkles, twinkling, twinkled
to sparkle or shine with flashes of bright light

twinkle noun twinkles
a twinkling light

twirl verb twirls, twirling, twirled
to twirl is to turn round and round quickly; to twirl something is to make it do this

twirl noun twirls
a twirling movement

twist verb twists, twisting, twisted
1 to twist something is to turn its ends in opposite directions **2** to twist is to turn round or from side to side *The road twisted through the hills.* **3** to twist something is to bend it out of its proper shape *My bicycle's*

front wheel is twisted. I think I've twisted my ankle.

twist noun twists
a twisting movement or action

twitch verb twitches, twitching, twitched
to twitch is to jerk or move suddenly and quickly; to twitch something is to make it do this

twitch noun twitches
a twitching movement

twitter verb twitters, twittering, twittered
birds twitter when they make quick chirping sounds

two noun twos
the number 2

two-dimensional adjective
having two dimensions: length and width; flat

two-faced adjective
dishonest or deceitful

tying
present participle of tie verb *Tom is tying his shoelaces.*

type noun types
1 a type is a group or class of similar people or things; a kind or sort **2** type is letters and figures designed for use in printing

type verb types, typing, typed
to type something is to write it with a typewriter or computer

typewriter noun typewriters
a machine with keys that you press to print letters or figures on a sheet of paper
typewritten adjective written with a typewriter

typhoon noun typhoons
a violent windy storm

typical adjective
1 having the usual qualities or features of a particular type of person or thing *They are typical schoolchildren.* **2** as you would expect from a particular person or thing

She worked with typical thoroughness.
typically adverb

typist noun typists
a person who types, especially as their job

tyranny (say ti-ra-nee) noun tyrannies
tyranny is a cruel or unjust way of ruling
people **tyrannical** adjective

tyrant (say ty-rant) noun tyrants
someone who rules people cruelly
or unjustly

tyre noun tyres
a covering of rubber fitted round the rim
of a wheel to make it grip the road and
run smoothly

Uu

udder noun udders
the bag-like part of a cow, goat, or ewe,
from which milk is taken

UFO noun UFOs
short for *unidentified flying object*

ugly adjective uglier, ugliest
1 not beautiful; unpleasant to look at
2 threatening or dangerous *The crowd was
in an ugly mood.* **ugliness** noun

ulcer noun ulcers
a sore on the inside or outside of your body

ultimate adjective
furthest in a series of things; final
ultimately adverb finally or eventually

ultra– prefix
meaning 'beyond', as in *ultraviolet*

ultraviolet adjective
ultraviolet light is light beyond the violet
end of the spectrum, that causes your skin
to tan

umbrella noun umbrellas
a mushroom-shaped piece of cloth

stretched over a folding frame, which you
open to protect yourself from rain

umpire noun umpires
someone who makes sure that people keep
to the rules in cricket, tennis, and some
other games

un– prefix
meaning 'not', as in *uncommon*, or added
to verbs to make the action of the verb
opposite to normal, as in *undo*

unable adjective
not able *She was unable to hear.*

unaided adjective
without any help

unanimous (say yoo-nan-i-mus)
adjective
a unanimous decision or vote is one where
everyone agrees **unanimously** adverb

unarmed adjective
without weapons *unarmed combat*

unavoidable adjective
not able to be avoided; bound to happen
unavoidably adverb

unaware adjective
not knowing about something *Blissfully
unaware that his fate was being decided,
Paddington was sitting in the middle of the
bathroom floor drawing a map of South
America with a tube of Mr Brown's shaving
cream. – Michael Bond, A Bear Called
Paddington*

unawares adverb
unexpectedly; without someone knowing
His question caught me unawares.

unbearable adjective
something is unbearable when it is so
painful or unpleasant that you cannot bear
or endure it **unbearably** adverb

unbelievable adjective
1 difficult to believe **2** amazing
unbelievably adverb

unborn adjective
not yet born

uncalled for adjective
not justified or necessary *Your rudeness is uncalled for.*

uncanny adjective **uncannier, uncanniest**
strange and mysterious *There was an uncanny silence.*

uncertain adjective
1 not certain *He is uncertain about what to do.* **2** not reliable *The weather is uncertain at the moment.* **uncertainly** adverb
uncertainty noun

uncle noun **uncles**
1 the brother of your father or mother **2** your aunt's husband

unclear adjective
not clear; not easy to see or understand **unclearly** adverb

uncomfortable adjective
not comfortable **uncomfortably** adverb

uncommon adjective
not common; unusual

unconscious adjective
1 not awake or knowing what is happening around you because you have fainted or been knocked out **2** not aware of something *I was unconscious of doing anything wrong.* **unconsciously** adverb
unconsciousness noun

uncontrollable adjective
unable to be controlled
uncontrollably adverb

uncountable adjective
unable to be counted; too many to count

uncouth (say un-**koo**th) adjective
rude and rough in manner

uncover verb **uncovers, uncovering, uncovered**
1 to uncover something is to take the cover or top off it **2** to uncover a secret or something unknown is to discover it

undecided adjective
you are undecided about something when you have not made up your mind about it

undeniable adjective
impossible to deny; certainly true
undeniably adverb

under preposition
1 lower than; below *Hide it under the desk.* **2** less than *They are under 5 years old.* **3** ruled or controlled by *The army is under his command.* **4** in the process of; undergoing *The road is under repair.* **5** using; moving by means of *The machine moves under its own power.*

under adverb
in or to a lower place *Slowly the diver went under.*

underarm adjective, adverb
with the arm kept below shoulder level and moving forward and upwards

undercarriage noun
undercarriages
an aircraft's undercarriage is its landing wheels and the parts that support them

underclothes plural noun or
underclothing noun
underwear

underdog noun **underdogs**
the person or team in a contest that is expected to lose

underdone adjective
not properly done or cooked

underfoot adverb
1 on the ground where you are walking *It was slippery underfoot.* **2** under someone's feet *The flag fell to the ground and was trampled underfoot.*

undergo verb **undergoes, undergoing, underwent, undergone**
to undergo something is to experience something or be subjected to it *He underwent an operation on his leg.*

underground adjective, adverb
1 under the ground **2** done or working in secret
underground noun **undergrounds**
a railway that runs through tunnels under the ground

a
b
c
d
e
f
g
h
i
j
k
l
m
n
o
p
q
r
s
t
u
v
w
x
y
z

undergrowth noun
undergrowth is bushes and other plants growing closely under tall trees

underhand adjective
secret and deceitful

underlie verb underlies, underlying, underlay, underlain
to underlie something is to be the cause or basis of it *Hard work underlies the team's success this season.*

underline verb underlines, underlining, underlined
1 to underline something you have written is to draw a line under it 2 to underline a fact is to emphasize it or show it clearly *This accident underlines the need to be careful.*

undermine verb undermines, undermining, undermined
1 to undermine someone's efforts or plans is to weaken them gradually 2 to undermine something is to make a hollow or tunnel beneath it

underneath preposition, adverb
below or beneath

underpants plural noun
a piece of men's underwear worn under trousers

underpass noun underpasses
a place where one road or path goes under another

understand verb understands, understanding, understood
1 to understand something is to know what it means or how it works 2 to understand something is also to have heard about it *I understand you've not been well.* 3 to understand someone is to know what they are like and why they behave the way they do

understandable adjective
1 able to be understood 2 reasonable or normal *He replied with understandable delight.* **understandably** adverb

understanding noun
1 understanding is the power to understand or think; intelligence 2 an understanding is when people have an agreement 3 understanding is also sympathy or tolerance

understanding adjective
sympathetic and helpful *He was very understanding when I was ill.*

understudy noun understudies
an actor who learns a part in a play so that they can play the part if the usual actor isn't able to perform

undertake verb undertakes, undertaking, undertook, undertaken
to undertake something is to agree or promise to do it

undertaker noun undertakers
someone whose job is to arrange funerals

undertaking noun undertakings
something that someone agrees to do

underwater adjective
placed or used or done below the surface of water

underwear noun
underwear is clothes you wear next to your skin, under other clothes

underworld noun
1 in legends, the underworld is the place for the spirits of the dead; hell 2 the underworld is also people who are regularly involved in crime

undesirable adjective
not wanted or liked

undeveloped adjective
not yet developed

undo verb undoes, undoing, undid, undone
1 to undo something is to unfasten or unwrap it *Can you undo this knot?* 2 to undo something already done is to cancel the effect of it *He has undone all our careful work.* 3 when you undo a change you have made on a computer, you change it back

undoubted adjective
definite or certain **undoubtedly** adverb

A
B
C
D
E
F
G
H
I
J
K
L
M
N
O
P
Q
R
S
T
U
V
W
X
Y
Z

undress verb undresses, undressing, undressed
1 to undress is to take your clothes off 2 to undress someone is to take their clothes off

unearth verb unearths, unearthing, unearthed
1 to unearth something is to dig it up 2 to unearth something is also to find it after searching for it

unearthly adjective
supernatural; strange and frightening

uneasy adjective uneasier, uneasiest
anxious or worried *Noah had been studying the sky since dawn yesterday, and he had looked uneasy all morning.* — Richard Platt, *Pirate Diary* **uneasily** adverb

unemployed adjective
to be unemployed is to be without a job
unemployment noun

uneven adjective
1 not level, flat, or regular *The path was uneven.* 2 not of the same quality throughout *It was an uneven performance.*
unevenly adverb **unevenness** noun

unexpected adjective
not expected; surprising
unexpectedly adverb

unfair adjective
not fair; unjust **unfairly** adverb
unfairness noun

unfaithful adjective
not faithful or loyal

unfamiliar adjective
not familiar

unfasten verb unfastens, unfastening, unfastened
to unfasten something is to open it when it has been fastened

unfavourable adjective
not favourable or helpful
unfavourably adverb

unfinished adjective
not finished

unfit adjective
1 someone is unfit when they are not fit or fully healthy 2 to be unfit for something is to be not suitable *Next day there was a dead calm, most unfit for war.* — Arthur Ransome, *Swallows and Amazons*

unfold verb unfolds, unfolding, unfolded
1 to unfold something is to open it or spread it out *She unfolded the map.* 2 to unfold a story or plan is to make it known gradually 3 a story unfolds when it becomes known gradually

unforgettable adjective
impossible to forget

unforgivable adjective
not able to be forgiven

unfortunate adjective
1 unlucky 2 you say something is unfortunate when you wish it hadn't happened; regrettable *It was an unfortunate remark.* **unfortunately** adverb you say unfortunately when you are sad about something *Unfortunately he wasn't able to come to the party.*

unfriendly adjective
not friendly **unfriendliness** noun

ungrateful adjective
not grateful **ungratefully** adverb

unhappy adjective unhappier, unhappiest
1 not happy or pleased 2 you say something is unhappy when you wish it hadn't happened; regrettable *It was an unhappy choice of words.* **unhappily** adverb
unhappiness noun

unhealthy adjective unhealthier, unhealthiest
1 not in good health 2 not good for you *She has an unhealthy diet.*

unheard-of adjective
never heard or done before; extraordinary

unicorn (say **yoo**-ni-korn) noun unicorns
an imaginary animal in stories, like a horse

a
b
c
d
e
f
g
h
i
j
k
l
m
n
o
p
q
r
s
t
u
v
w
x
y
z

with a long straight horn growing out of the front of its head

uniform noun **uniforms**
the special clothes worn by members of an army or school or organization

uniform adjective
always the same; not changing

uniformed adjective
wearing a uniform

unify verb **unifies, unifying, unified**
to unify several things, especially countries, is to join them into one thing; to unify is to join together

unimportant adjective
not important **unimportance** noun

uninhabited adjective
a place is uninhabited when there is nobody living there

unintentional adjective
not done deliberately
unintentionally adverb

uninterested adjective
not interested

uninteresting adjective
not interesting

union noun **unions**
1 the joining of things together; a united thing 2 a trade union

Union Jack noun **Union Jacks**
the flag of the United Kingdom

unique (say yoo-**neek**) adjective
something is unique when it is the only one of its kind *Everyone's fingerprints are unique. This jewel is unique.* **uniquely** adverb **uniqueness** noun

unisex adjective
designed to be suitable for either men or women

unison (say yoo-ni-son) noun
in unison said or done by people together at the same time

unit noun **units**
1 an amount used in measuring or counting, such as a centimetre or a pound 2 a single person or thing 3 a group of people or things that belong together

unite verb **unites, uniting, united**
1 to unite several people or things is to form them into one thing or group 2 people or things unite when they join together

unity noun **unities**
1 unity is being united or having agreement 2 a unity is a complete thing

universal adjective
including everyone and everything
universally adverb to be universally accepted is to be accepted by everyone

universe noun
the universe is everything that exists, including the earth and living things and all the stars and planets

university noun **universities**
a place where people go to study for degrees after they have left school

unjust adjective
not fair or just **unjustly** adverb

unkind adjective **unkinder, unkindest**
cruel and not kind **unkindly** adverb
unkindness noun

unknown adjective
not known

unleaded adjective
unleaded petrol does not contain lead

unless conjunction
except when; if not *We cannot go unless we are invited.*

unlike preposition
not like *Unlike me, she enjoys sport.*
unlike adjective
not alike; different *The two children are very unlike.*

unlikely adjective **unlikelier, unlikeliest**
not likely to happen or be true

unload verb unloads, unloading, unloaded
to unload a container or vehicle is to take off the things it carried

unlock verb unlocks, unlocking, unlocked
to unlock a door or container is to open it with a key

unlucky adjective unluckier, unluckiest
not lucky **unluckily** adverb as the result of bad luck

unmistakable adjective
not likely to be mistaken for something or someone else; clear and definite **unmistakably** adverb

unnatural adjective
not natural or normal **unnaturally** adverb

unnecessary adjective
not needed **unnecessarily** adverb

unoccupied adjective
a house is unoccupied when it is empty, with no one living there

unpack verb unpacks, unpacking, unpacked
to unpack a suitcase or bag is to take out the things in it

unpleasant adjective
not pleasant **unpleasantly** adverb **unpleasantness** noun

unplug verb unplugs, unplugging, unplugged
to unplug an electrical device is to disconnect it by taking its plug out of the socket

unpopular adjective
not liked or enjoyed by people **unpopularity** noun

unravel verb unravels, unravelling, unravelled
1 to unravel something is to unwind it or take the knots from it 2 to unravel a problem or mystery is to investigate it and solve it

unreal adjective
not real; existing only in the imagination

unreasonable adjective
not reasonable or fair

unrest noun
unrest is a discontented feeling among a group of people, or the trouble caused by it

unroll verb unrolls, unrolling, unrolled
to unroll something is to open it when it has been rolled up

unruly (say un-**roo**-lee) adjective unrulier, unruliest
badly behaved and difficult to control **unruliness** noun

unsafe adjective
not safe; dangerous

unscrew verb unscrews, unscrewing, unscrewed
to unscrew something is to undo it by turning it or by removing screws

unseemly adjective
not proper or suitable; indecent

unseen adjective
not seen or noticed *He managed to slip out of the room unseen.*

unselfish adjective
not selfish; not thinking only about yourself **unselfishly** adverb **unselfishness** noun

unsightly adjective unsightlier, unsightliest
not pleasant to look at; ugly

unsteady adjective unsteadier, unsteadiest
shaking or wobbling or likely to fall **unsteadily** adverb **unsteadiness** noun

unsuccessful adjective
not successful **unsuccessfully** adverb

unsuitable adjective
not suitable **unsuitably** adverb

unthinkable adjective
too bad or unlikely to be worth thinking about

A
B
C
D
E
F
G
H
I
J
K
L
M
N
O
P
Q
R
S
T
U
V
W
X
Y
Z

untidy adjective untidier, untidiest
messy and not tidy **untidily** adverb
untidiness noun

untie verb unties, untying, untied
to untie something is to undo it when it has
been tied

until preposition, conjunction
up to a particular time or event *The shop
is open until 8 o'clock. We will stay with you
until the train comes.*

TOP TIPS
Select a single! There is only one **I**
in **until**.

untimely adjective untimelier,
untimeliest
happening too soon or at an unsuitable time

unto preposition (old use)
to

untold adjective
too great to be counted or measured *The
hurricane caused untold damage.*

untoward adjective
inconvenient or unfortunate *I hope nothing
untoward happens.*

untrue adjective
not true

untruthful adjective
not telling the truth **untruthfully** adverb

unused (say un-**yoozd**) adjective
not yet used **unused to something**
(say un-**yoost**) not familiar with something
He is unused to eating meat.

unusual adjective
different from what is usual or normal;
strange or rare **unusually** adverb

unwanted adjective
not wanted

unwell adjective
not well; ill

unwilling adjective
you are unwilling to do something when
you don't want to do it **unwillingly** adverb
unwillingness noun

unwind (rhymes with **find**) verb unwinds,
unwinding, unwound
1 to unwind something is to unroll it **2** to
unwind is to become unrolled **3** (informal)
to unwind is also to relax after you have
been working hard

unworthy adjective unworthier,
unworthiest
not deserving something; not good enough
for something

unwrap verb unwraps, unwrapping,
unwrapped
to unwrap something is to take it out of
its wrapping

unzip verb unzips, unzipping, unzipped
to unzip something is to undo it when it is
zipped up

up adverb
1 in or to a standing or upright position
Stand up. **2** in or to a high or higher place or
level *Put it up on the shelf. Prices are going
up.* **3** completely *Eat up your carrots.* **4** out
of bed *It's time to get up.* **5** finished *Your
time is up.* **6** (informal) happening
Something is up. **ups and downs** changes
of luck, sometimes good and sometimes
bad **to be up to something** is to be doing
something mysterious or suspicious *What
are they up to?* **up to date 1** modern or
fashionable **2** having the latest
information *Keep me up to date with
what happens.*

up preposition
in or to a higher position on something *Let's
climb up the mountain.*

upbringing noun upbringings
your upbringing is the way you have been
brought up

update verb updates, updating,
updated
to update something is to bring it up
to date

upgrade verb upgrades, upgrading,
upgraded
to upgrade a machine is to improve it by
installing new parts in it

upheaval noun upheavals
a sudden violent change or disturbance

uphill adjective, adverb
1 sloping upwards; going up a slope
2 difficult *It was an uphill job.*

uphold verb upholds, upholding, upheld
to uphold a decision or belief is to support it or agree with it

upholstery noun
upholstery is covers and padding for furniture

upkeep noun
the upkeep of something is the cost of looking after it and keeping it in good condition

uplands plural noun
the highest part of a country or region

upload verb uploads, uploading, uploaded (in computing)
to upload data is to transfer it from a smaller system to a larger one

upload noun uploads
data that has been uploaded

upon preposition
on

upper adjective
higher in position or rank

upper case noun
upper case is capital letters

upper class noun or
upper classes plural noun
the highest class in society, especially the aristocracy **upper-class** adjective

upright adjective
1 standing straight up; vertical 2 honest
upright noun uprights
an upright post or support

uprising noun uprisings
a rebellion or revolt against the government

uproar noun
uproar is a loud or angry noise or disturbance *The room was in uproar.*

upset (say up-set) adjective
unhappy or anxious about something

upset (say up-set) verb upsets, upsetting, upset
1 to upset someone is to make them unhappy or anxious 2 to upset something is to knock it over and spill its contents

upset (say up-set) noun upsets
1 a slight illness *He's got a stomach upset.*
2 an unexpected result or setback *Losing the game on Saturday was a real upset.*

upshot noun
what happens in the end *The upshot was that we had to stay behind.*

upside down adjective, adverb
1 with the upper part underneath instead of on top; the wrong way up 2 in disorder or confusion *The thieves turned the place upside down.*

upstairs adverb, adjective
to or on a higher floor in a house or other building

upstart noun upstarts
someone who quickly reaches a position of power and behaves in an arrogant way

upstream adjective, adverb
in the direction opposite to the flow of a river or stream

uptake noun
to be quick on the uptake is to be quick to understand **to be slow on the uptake** is to be slow to understand

uptight adjective (informal)
upset or nervous about something

up-to-date adjective
1 modern or fashionable 2 having the latest information *up-to-date news*

upward adjective, adverb
going towards what is higher
upwards adverb

a
b
c
d
e
f
g
h
i
j
k
l
m
n
o
p
q
r
s
t
u
v
w
x
y
z

urban adjective
to do with a town or city

urchin noun urchins
a dirty or mischievous child

Urdu noun
Urdu is a language related to Hindi, spoken in northern India and Pakistan.

urge verb urges, urging, urged
1 to urge someone to do something is to try to persuade them to do it 2 to urge people or animals is to drive them forward

urge noun urges
a sudden strong desire or wish *She felt an urge to go for a swim.*

urgent adjective
needing to be done or dealt with immediately **urgency** noun
urgently adverb

urine (say **yoor**-in) noun
urine is the waste liquid that collects in your bladder and is passed out of your body

urn noun urns
1 a large metal container with a tap, in which water is heated 2 a kind of large vase for holding the ashes of a person who has been cremated

US or **USA**
short for *United States of America*

us pronoun
a word used for *we*, usually when it is the object of a sentence, or when it comes after a preposition *She likes us. She gave it to us.*

usable adjective
able to be used *We looked around for usable chairs.*

usage (say **yoo**-sij) noun usages
the way that something is used, especially the way that words and language are used

use (say **yooz**) verb uses, using, used
to use something is to perform an action

or job with it *Are you using my pen?* **used to** did in the past *I used to live in Glasgow.*
to be used to something or **someone** is to know them well or be familiar with them *We're used to hard work.* **to use something up** is to use all of it, so that none is left

use (say **yooss**) noun uses
1 the action of using something or being used 2 the purpose or value of something *Can you find a use for this box? This knife is no use to us.*

used (say **yoozd**) adjective
not new; second-hand *We're buying a used car.*

useful adjective
able to be used a lot or do something that needs doing **usefully** adverb
usefulness noun

useless adjective
1 not having any use 2 (informal) not very good at something *I'm useless at drawing.*
uselessly adverb **uselessness** noun

user noun users
someone who uses something

user-friendly adjective
user-friendlier, user-friendliest
designed to be easy to use

usher noun ushers
someone who shows people to their seats in a church or cinema or theatre

usher verb ushers, ushering, ushered
to usher someone is to lead them in or out of a place *Hal ushered the children inside a dim room with a low ceiling—so low that Hal's grey hair almost brushed against the top.*
— Lemony Snicket, *A Series of Unfortunate Events*

usherette noun usherettes
a woman who shows people to their seats in a cinema or theatre

usual adjective
as happens often or all the time; expected *He sat in his usual chair by the fire. She was late as usual.*

A B C D E F G H I J K L M N O P Q R S T U V W X Y Z

Vv

usually adverb
something usually happens when it happens on most occasions or normally

usurp (say yoo-**zerp**) verb usurps, usurping, usurped
to usurp power or a position is to take it by force from someone else

utensil (say yoo-**ten**-sil) noun utensils
a tool or device, especially one you use in the house

utilize verb utilizes, utilizing, utilized
to utilize something is to make use of it

utmost adjective
greatest *Look after it with the utmost care.*

Utopia noun Utopias
an imaginary place where everyone is happy and everything is perfect

utter[1] verb utters, uttering, uttered
to utter something is to say it clearly, or to make a sound with your mouth *He uttered a loud yell.*

utter[2] adjective
complete or absolute *It was utter misery. Sheltered under a clump of Scots pine, the beasts gazed up at the moonlit sky in a state of utter contentment.*
— Debi Gliori, *Pure Dead Wicked*

utterance noun utterances
an utterance is something that someone says

utterly adverb
to be (for example) utterly different or ridiculous is to be completely different or ridiculous

U-turn noun U-turns
1 a turn a vehicle makes when it is driven round in one movement to face the opposite direction 2 a complete change of ideas or opinions

vacancy noun vacancies
a job, or a room in a guest house, that is available and not taken

vacant adjective
1 empty; not filled or occupied *There were no vacant seats.* 2 not showing any expression *He gave a vacant stare.* **vacantly** adverb

vacate verb vacates, vacating, vacated
to vacate a place is to leave it empty

vacation (say vay-**kay**-shon) noun vacations
a holiday, especially between the terms at a university

vaccinate (say **vak**-si-nayt) verb vaccinates, vaccinating, vaccinated
to vaccinate someone is to protect them from a disease by injecting them with a vaccine **vaccination** noun

vaccine (say **vak**-seen) noun vaccines
a type of medicine injected into people to protect them from disease

vacuum noun vacuums
a completely empty space; a space without any air in it

vacuum verb vacuums, vacuuming, vacuumed
to clean something using a vacuum cleaner

vacuum cleaner noun vacuum cleaners
an electrical device that sucks up dust and dirt from the floor

vacuum flask noun vacuum flasks
a container with double walls that have a vacuum between them, for keeping liquids hot or cold

vagina (say va-**jy**-na) noun vaginas
the passage in a woman's body that leads from the outside of her body to her womb

A
B
C
D
E
F
G
H
I
J
K
L
M
N
O
P
Q
R
S
T
U
V
W
X
Y
Z

vague adjective **vaguer, vaguest**
not definite or clear *I only have a vague memory of his face.* **vaguely** adverb **vagueness** noun

vain adjective **vainer, vainest**
1 too proud of yourself, especially of how you look **2** unsuccessful or useless *They made vain attempts to save him.* **in vain** with no result; without success *I tried in vain to call for help.* **vainly** adverb

valentine noun **valentines**
1 a card sent on St Valentine's Day (14 February) to someone you love **2** the person you send a valentine to

valiant adjective
brave or courageous **valiantly** adverb

valid adjective
able to be used or accepted; legal *Your passport is not valid.* **validity** noun

valley noun **valleys**
an area of low land between hills

valour noun
valour is bravery, especially in a battle

valuable adjective
1 worth a lot of money **2** very useful or important *She gave me valuable advice.*

valuables plural noun
things that are worth a lot of money

value noun **values**
1 the amount of money that something could be sold for **2** how useful or important something is

value verb **values, valuing, valued**
1 to value something is to think that it is important or worth having *I value her friendship.* **2** to value something is also to work out how much it could be sold for

valueless adjective
having no value

valve noun **valves**
a device used to control the flow of gas or liquid

vampire noun **vampires**
in stories, a creature that sucks people's blood

van noun **vans**
1 a small lorry with a covered area for goods at the back **2** a railway carriage used for goods or for the train's guard

vandal noun **vandals**
someone who deliberately breaks or damages things, especially buildings **vandalism** noun

vane noun **vanes**
1 a pointer that shows which way the wind is blowing **2** the blade or surface of a propeller, sail of a windmill, or other device that moves through air or water

vanilla noun
vanilla is a flavouring made from the pods of a tropical plant

vanish verb **vanishes, vanishing, vanished**
to disappear completely

vanity noun
vanity is being too proud of yourself, especially of how you look

vanquish verb **vanquishes, vanquishing, vanquished**
to vanquish someone is to win a victory over them

vaporize verb **vaporizes, vaporizing, vaporized**
to turn into vapour

vapour noun **vapours**
a visible gas, such as mist or steam, which some liquids and solids can be turned into by heat

variable adjective
able or likely to change

variable noun **variables**
a variable is something that varies or can vary

variation noun **variations**
1 a variation in something is a change in it *There have been slight variations in*

temperature. **2** variation is the process of changing something **3** a variation is a different form of something

varied adjective
of various kinds; full of variety *She has varied interests.*

variety noun **varieties**
1 a variety is a number of different kinds of the same thing *There was a variety of cakes to choose from.* **2** a variety is a particular kind of something *There are many varieties of butterfly.* **3** variety is a situation where things are not always the same *Their lives are full of variety.* **4** variety is also a form of entertainment made up of short performances of singing, dancing, and comedy

various adjective, determiner
1 of different kinds *They came for various reasons.* **2** several *We met various people.*
variously adverb

varnish noun **varnishes**
a liquid that dries to form a hard shiny surface on wood or other surfaces
varnish verb **varnishes, varnishing, varnished**
to varnish wood or another surface is to put varnish on it

vary verb **varies, varying, varied**
1 to vary is to keep changing *The weather varies a lot here.* **2** things vary when they are different from each other *The cars are the same, although the colours vary.* **3** to vary something is to make changes to it

vase (say vahz) noun **vases**
a jar used for holding flowers or as an ornament

vast adjective
very large or wide *Vast stretches of land flashed by; grassland, mountains, grassland again. Naledi suddenly felt very small.* — Beverley Naidoo, *Journey to Jo'burg*
vastly adverb **vastness** noun

VAT
short for *value-added tax*, a tax on things you buy

vat noun **vats**
a very large container for holding liquid

vault verb **vaults, vaulting, vaulted**
you vault something, or vault over it, when you jump over it, using your hands to support you or with the help of a pole
vault noun **vaults**
1 a jump done by vaulting **2** an arched roof **3** an underground room for storing money and valuables

veal noun
veal is the meat from a calf

Veda plural noun
the ancient writings of the Hindu religion

veer verb **veers, veering, veered**
to swerve or change direction suddenly *No sooner had we returned to the deck when the wind veered rapidly round.* — Richard Platt, *Pirate Diary*

vegan (say **vee**-gan) noun **vegans**
someone who does not use or eat any products made from animals

vegetable noun **vegetables**
a plant that can be used as food

vegetarian (say vej-i-**tair**-i-an) noun **vegetarians**
someone who does not eat meat

vegetation noun
vegetation is plants that are growing

vehicle noun **vehicles**
a means of carrying people or things, especially on land. Cars, buses, trains, and lorries are vehicles

veil noun **veils**
a piece of thin material to cover a woman's face or head
veil verb **veils, veiling, veiled**
1 to veil something is to cover it with a veil **2** to veil something such as a hint or a threat is to suggest it without being clear about it

vein noun **veins**
1 your veins are the tubes in your body that carry blood towards your heart **2** a line or

A
B
C
D
E
F
G
H
I
J
K
L
M
N
O
P
Q
R
S
T
U
V
W
X
Y
Z

Venn diagram

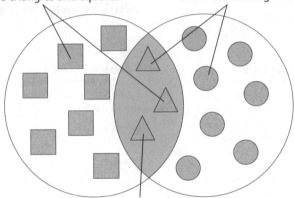

set 1 blue triangles and squares

set 2 blue triangles and circles

things that belong in both sets blue triangles

streak on a leaf or rock or insect's wing
3 a long deposit of a mineral in the middle
of rock

velocity (say vil-**os**-i-tee) noun
velocities
velocity is speed in a particular
direction

velvet noun
velvet is a soft material with short furry
fibres on one side

vendetta noun **vendettas**
a long-lasting quarrel or feud

vending machine noun **vending
machines**
a machine that you can buy food, drinks, or
other things from

vendor noun **vendors**
someone who is selling something

venerable adjective
worthy of respect or honour because of
being so old

vengeance noun
vengeance is harming or punishing someone
because they have done harm to you
with a vengeance very strongly or
effectively

vengeful adjective
a vengeful person wants to punish someone
who has harmed them

venison noun
venison is the meat from a deer

Venn diagram noun **Venn diagrams**
(in mathematics)
a diagram using circles to show how sets of
things relate to one another

venom noun
1 venom is the poison of snakes **2** venom is
also a feeling of bitter hatred for someone
venomous adjective

vent noun **vents**
an opening in something, especially to
let out smoke or gas **to give vent to
something** is to express your feelings
openly *He gave vent to his anger.*

ventilate verb **ventilates, ventilating,
ventilated**
to ventilate a place is to let fresh air come
into it and move around it **ventilation** noun

ventilator noun **ventilators**
1 a device that brings in and moves air
around a place **2** a machine that helps
someone to breathe

ventriloquist (say ven-**tril**-o-kwist) noun **ventriloquists**
an entertainer who speaks without moving their lips, making it appear that a dummy is speaking **ventriloquism** noun

venture noun **ventures**
something new that you decide to do that is risky or daring

venture verb **ventures, venturing, ventured**
to venture somewhere is to go there even though you know it might be dangerous or difficult

venue noun **venues**
a place where an event is held

veranda (say ver-**an**-da) noun **verandas**
an open terrace with a roof along the outside of a house

verb noun **verbs**
a word that shows what someone or something is doing, such as *be, go, sing, take*

 TOP TIPS Did you know that every sentence must have a verb? No verb, no sentence!

verbal adjective
spoken rather than written *We had a verbal agreement.* **verbally** adverb

verdict noun **verdicts**
the decision reached by a judge or jury about whether someone is guilty of a crime

verge noun **verges**
a strip of grass beside a road or path

verge verb **verges, verging, verged**
to verge on something is to be nearly something *His reply verged on impertinent.*

verify verb **verifies, verifying, verified**
to verify something is to find or show whether it is true or correct

vermin noun
vermin are animals or insects that damage crops or food or carry disease, such as rats and fleas

verruca (say ver-**oo**-ka) noun **verrucas**
a kind of wart on the sole of your foot

versatile (say **ver**-sa-tyl) adjective
able to do or be used for many different things **versatility** noun

verse noun **verses**
1 verse is writing in the form of poetry
2 a verse is a group of lines in a poem or song

version noun **versions**
1 someone's account of something that has happened *His version of the accident is different from mine.* **2** a different form of a thing *I don't like their version of the song.*

versus preposition
against or competing with, especially in sport *The final will be Brazil versus Germany.*

vertebra (say **ver**-ti-bra) noun **vertebrae**
each of the bones that form your backbone

vertebrate (say **ver**-ti-brit) noun **vertebrates**
an animal with a backbone

vertex noun **vertices**
the highest point of a hill, or of a cone or triangle

vertical adjective
going directly upwards, at right angles to something level or horizontal **vertically** adverb

vertigo noun
vertigo is feeling dizzy because you are high up

very adverb
to a great amount; extremely *It is very cold.*

very adjective
1 exact or actual *That's the very thing we need!* **2** extreme *We've reached the very end.*

Vesak (say **ves**-ak) noun
Vesak is an important festival of Buddhism, held in April to May.

vessel noun **vessels**
1 a boat or ship **2** a container for liquids

a b c d e f g h i j k l m n o p q r s t u **v** w x y z

A

3 a tube inside an animal or plant, carrying blood or some other liquid

B

vest noun vests
a piece of underwear you wear on the top half of your body

C

vestment noun vestments
a piece of outer clothing worn by the clergy or choir at a church service

D

E

vestry noun vestries
a room in a church where the vestments are kept and the clergy and choir prepare for a service

F

G

vet noun vets
a person trained to treat sick animals

H

I

veteran noun veterans
1 a person with long experience of something 2 a soldier who has returned from a war

J

K

veterinary (say **vet**-rin-ree) adjective
to do with the medical treatment of animals

L

M

veto (say **vee**-toh) noun vetoes
1 a refusal to let something happen 2 the right to stop something from happening

N

veto verb vetoes, vetoing, vetoed
to veto something is to refuse to let it happen

O

P

vex verb vexes, vexing, vexed
to vex someone is to annoy them or cause them worry **vexation** noun

Q

via (say **vy**-a) preposition
going through; stopping at *This train goes from Edinburgh to London via York.*

R

S

T

viaduct (say **vy**-a-dukt) noun viaducts
a long bridge with many arches, carrying a road or railway over low ground

U

vibrate verb vibrates, vibrating, vibrated
to move quickly from side to side and with small movements *Every time a train went past the walls vibrated.* **vibration** noun

V

W

X

vicar noun vicars
a member of the clergy who is in charge of a parish

Y

Z

vicarage noun vicarages
the house of a vicar

vice¹ noun vices
1 a vice is a bad or evil habit 2 vice is evil or wickedness

vice² noun vices
a device with jaws for holding something tightly in place while you work on it

vice-president noun vice-presidents
a deputy to a president

vice versa (say vys-**ver**-sa) adverb
the other way round *'We talk about them and vice versa' means 'We talk about them and they talk about us'.*

vicinity noun vicinities
the area near or surrounding a particular place *Are there any parks in the vicinity?*

vicious (say **vish**-us) adjective
1 cruel and aggressive 2 severe or violent *a vicious storm* **viciously** adverb **viciousness** noun

victim noun victims
1 a person who suffers from something *victims of fever* 2 someone who is killed, injured, or robbed *The thief lay in wait for his victim.*

victimize verb victimizes, victimizing, victimized
to victimize someone is to pick them out and treat them unfairly

victor noun victors
the winner of a battle or contest

Victorian adjective
belonging to the time when Queen Victoria reigned (1837-1901)

victorious adjective
someone is victorious when they win a battle or contest or game

victory noun victories
winning a battle or contest or game

video (say **vid**-i-oh) noun videos
1 video is the recording on tape of pictures

and sound **2** a video is a video recorder **3** a video is also a television programme or a film recorded on a video cassette

video verb videoes, videoing, videoed
to video something is to record it on videotape

video recorder or
video cassette recorder noun
video recorders, video cassette recorders
a machine for recording television programmes and playing them back

videotape noun videotapes
videotape is tape used for video recording

view noun views
1 what you can see from one place *There's a fine view from the top of the hill.* **2** someone's opinion *She has strong views about smoking.* **in view of something** because of it **on view** shown for people to see

view verb views, viewing, viewed
1 to view something is to look at it carefully **2** to view something or someone in a certain way is to think about them in that way *He viewed us with suspicion.*

viewer noun viewers
someone who watches something, especially a television programme

viewpoint noun viewpoints
your viewpoint is your opinion about something

vigilant (say vij-i-lant) adjective
someone is vigilant when they are watching carefully for something **vigilance** noun **vigilantly** adverb

vigorous adjective
full of strength and energy **vigorously** adverb

vigour noun
vigour is strength and energy

Viking noun Vikings
a Scandinavian pirate or trader in the 8th to 10th centuries

vile adjective viler, vilest
disgusting or bad *What a vile smell.*

villa noun villas
a house, especially a large one in its own grounds, or one used for holidays abroad

village noun villages
a group of houses and other buildings in the country, smaller than a town

villager noun villagers
someone who lives in a village

villain noun villains
a wicked person or criminal **villainy** noun wickedness

vine noun vines
a plant on which grapes grow

vinegar noun
vinegar is a sour liquid used to flavour food

vineyard (say vin-yard) noun vineyards
an area of land where vines are grown to produce grapes for making wine

vintage noun vintages
1 all the grapes that are harvested in one season, or the wine made from them **2** something's vintage is the period from which it comes

vintage adjective
from a period in the past *vintage clothes*

vinyl (say vy-nil) noun
vinyl is a kind of plastic

viola (say vee-oh-la) noun violas
a stringed instrument rather like a violin but slightly larger and with a lower pitch

violate verb violates, violating, violated
1 to violate a rule or law is to break it **2** to violate a person or place is to treat them without respect **violation** noun

violence noun
1 violence is when someone uses force to hurt or kill people **2** violence is also force that damages things *We weren't prepared for the violence of the storm.*

violent adjective
1 to be violent is to use force to hurt people **2** something such as a storm or a dislike

A B C D E F G H I J K L M N O P Q R S T U **V** W X Y Z

is violent when it is strong and forceful **violently** adverb

violet noun violets
1 a blue-purple colour **2** a small plant that usually has purple flowers

violin noun violins
a musical instrument with four strings, played with a bow **violinist** noun

VIP
short for *very important person*

viper noun vipers
a small poisonous snake

virtual adjective
1 amounting to the real thing in effect *His red face was a virtual admission of guilt.* **2** using virtual reality *Click here to go on a virtual tour of the gallery.*

virtually adverb
in effect; nearly *She virtually admitted it.*

virtual reality noun
virtual reality is an image or environment created by a computer that imitates the real world and that you can be part of

virtue noun virtues
1 a virtue is a good quality in a person's character *Honesty is a virtue.* **2** virtue is moral goodness

virtuous adjective
a virtuous person behaves in a very good way **virtuously** adverb

virus (say **vy**-rus) noun viruses
1 a microscopic creature that can cause disease **2** a disease caused by a virus *The doctor said I had a virus.* **3** a hidden set of instructions in a computer program that is designed to destroy data

visa noun visas
an official mark put on someone's passport by officials of a foreign country to show that the holder of the passport has permission to enter that country

visibility noun
visibility is how far you can see clearly *Visibility is down to 20 metres.*

visible adjective
able to be seen *The ship was visible on the horizon.* **visibly** adverb

vision noun visions
1 vision is the ability to see **2** a vision is something that you see or imagine, especially in a dream **3** vision is also imagination and understanding *They need a leader with vision.*

visit verb visits, visiting, visited
to visit a place or person is to go to see them or stay there

visit noun visits
a short stay at a place or with a person

visitor noun visitors
someone who is visiting or staying at a place

visor (say **vy**-zer) noun visors
the clear part of a helmet that closes over the face

visual adjective
to do with seeing; used for seeing **visually** adverb

visual display unit noun visual display units
a screen on which a computer displays information

visualize verb visualizes, visualizing, visualized
to visualize something is to form an image of it in your mind

vital adjective
1 extremely important; essential *It is vital that we get there on time.* **2** connected with life; needed in order to live **vitally** adverb
something is vitally important when it is extremely important

vitality noun
vitality is liveliness or energy

vitamin noun vitamins
each of several substances which are present in some foods and which you need to stay healthy

vivid adjective
bright and clear *The colours are very vivid.*
She gave a vivid description of the storm.
vividly adverb to remember something
vividly is to remember it very clearly
vividness noun

vivisection noun
vivisection is doing experiments on live
animals as part of scientific research

vixen noun **vixens**
a female fox

vocabulary noun **vocabularies**
1 the vocabulary of a language is all the
words used in it 2 a person's vocabulary is
the words that they know and use

vocal adjective
to do with the voice; using your voice
vocally adverb

vocalist noun **vocalists**
a singer in a band

vocation noun **vocations**
1 a job or activity that you feel strongly you
want to do 2 a strong feeling that you want
to do a particular job **vocational** adjective
teaching you the skills you need for a
particular job *vocational training*

vodka noun **vodkas**
vodka is a strong alcoholic drink especially
popular in Russia

voice noun **voices**
1 the sound you make when you speak or
sing 2 the ability to speak or sing *She has
lost her voice.*
voice verb **voices, voicing, voiced**
to voice something is to say it clearly and
strongly *He voiced the objections to the plan.*

voicemail noun
a system that lets you leave spoken
messages for someone on their phone

volcano noun **volcanoes**
a mountain with a hole at the top formed
by molten lava which has burst through the
earth's crust **volcanic** adjective

vole noun **voles**
a small animal rather like a rat

volley noun **volleys**
1 a number of bullets or shells fired at
the same time 2 in ball games, hitting or
kicking the ball back before it touches
the ground

volleyball noun
volleyball is a game in which two teams
hit a large ball to and fro over a net with
their hands

volt noun **volts**
a unit for measuring the force of an
electric current

voltage noun **voltages**
voltage is electric force measured in volts

volume noun **volumes**
1 the amount of space filled by something
2 the strength or power of sound *Turn down
the volume!* 3 an amount *The volume of work
has increased.* 4 a book, especially one of
a set

voluntary adjective
done or doing something because you want
to, not for pay **voluntarily** adverb

volunteer verb **volunteers,
volunteering, volunteered**
1 to volunteer is to offer to do something
that you do not have to do 2 to volunteer
(for example) information or time is to
provide it willingly without being asked
for it *Several people generously volunteered
their time.*
volunteer noun **volunteers**
someone who volunteers to do something

vomit verb **vomits, vomiting, vomited**
to bring food back from the stomach
through your mouth

vote verb **votes, voting, voted**
1 to vote for someone or something is to
show which you prefer by putting up your
hand or making a mark on a piece of paper
2 to vote to do something is to say that you
want to do it *I vote we go away this weekend.*

a
b
c
d
e
f
g
h
i
j
k
l
m
n
o
p
q
r
s
t
u
v
w
x
y
z

vote noun votes
1 a way of choosing someone or something by getting people to put up their hand or make a mark on a piece of paper **2** a choice you make by voting **3** the right to vote

voter noun voters
someone who votes, especially in an election

vouch verb vouches, vouching, vouched
to vouch for something or **someone** is to say they are genuine or reliable

voucher noun vouchers
a piece of paper showing that you are allowed to pay less for something or that you can get something in exchange

vow verb vows, vowing, vowed
to make a solemn promise to do something
vow noun vows
a solemn promise

vowel noun vowels
any of the letters a, e, i, o, u, and sometimes y

voyage noun voyages
a long journey by ship or in a spacecraft
voyager noun

vulgar adjective
rude; without good manners

vulgar fraction noun vulgar fractions
a fraction shown by numbers above and below a line (such as ½ and ⅞), not a decimal fraction

vulnerable adjective
able to be harmed or attacked easily

vulture noun vultures
a large bird that eats dead animals

Ww

wad noun wads
a pad or bundle of soft material or pieces of paper

waddle verb waddles, waddling, waddled
to walk with short steps, rocking from side to side, like a duck *Aunt Sponge, fat and pulpy as a jellyfish, came waddling up behind her sister to see what was going on.* – Roald Dahl, *James and the Giant Peach*
waddle noun waddles
a waddling walk

wade verb wades, wading, waded
to wade through water or mud is to walk through it

wafer noun wafers
a thin kind of biscuit, often eaten with ice cream

waffle noun waffles
1 a waffle is a crisp square pancake with a pattern of squares on it **2** waffle is talking for a long time without saying anything important or interesting

wag verb wags, wagging, wagged
1 a dog wags its tail when it moves it quickly from side to side because it is happy or excited **2** you wag your finger when you move it up and down or from side to side
wag noun wags
a wagging movement

wage noun or **wages** plural noun
the money paid to someone for the job they do
wage verb wages, waging, waged
to wage a war or campaign is to fight it

wager (say **way**-jer) noun wagers
a bet
wager verb wagers, wagering, wagered
to wager someone is to make a bet with them

waggle verb waggles, waggling, waggled
to waggle something is to move it quickly to and fro

wagon noun wagons
1 a cart with four wheels, pulled by a horse or ox **2** an open railway truck

wail verb wails, wailing, wailed
to make a long sad cry
wail noun wails
a sound of wailing

waist noun waists
the narrow part in the middle of your body

waistcoat noun waistcoats
a close-fitting jacket without sleeves, worn over a shirt and under a jacket

wait verb waits, waiting, waited
1 to wait, or to wait for someone or something, is to stay in a place or situation until something happens **2** to wait is also to be a waiter
wait noun waits
a time spent waiting *We had a long wait for the bus.*

waiter noun waiters
a man who serves people with food in a restaurant or hotel

waiting room noun waiting rooms
a room provided for people who are waiting for something

waitress noun waitresses
a woman who serves people with food in a restaurant or hotel

waive verb waives, waiving, waived
to waive a right or privilege is to say you do not need it *She waived her right to a first-class seat.*

wake¹ verb wakes, waking, woke, woken
1 you wake, or wake up, when you stop sleeping **2** to wake someone, or wake them up, is to make them stop sleeping *You have woken the baby.*

wake² noun wakes
1 the trail left on the water by a ship or boat **2** what is left when something is gone, or when something unusual has happened *The storm left a lot of damage in its wake.*

waken verb wakens, wakening, wakened
to waken someone is to wake them

walk verb walks, walking, walked
to move along on your feet at an ordinary speed
walk noun walks
1 a journey on foot **2** the way that someone walks *He has a funny walk.* **3** a path or route for walking *There are some lovely walks near here.*

walkabout noun walkabouts
an informal stroll among a crowd by an important visitor

walker noun walkers
someone who goes for a walk, especially a long one

walkie-talkie noun walkie-talkies
a small portable radio transmitter and receiver

walking stick noun walking sticks
a stick a person carries or uses as a support while walking

wall noun walls
1 a structure built of brick or stone and forming one of the sides of a building or room, or going round a garden or other space **2** the outer surface of something, such as the stomach
wall verb walls, walling, walled
to wall something, or wall it in, is to surround or enclose it with a wall

wallaby (say wol-a-bee) noun wallabies
a kind of small kangaroo

wallet noun wallets
a small flat folding case for holding banknotes, credit cards, and small documents

a
b
c
d
e
f
g
h
i
j
k
l
m
n
o
p
q
r
s
t
u
v
w
x
y
z

A
B
C
D
E
F
G
H
I
J
K
L
M
N
O
P
Q
R
S
T
U
V
W
X
Y
Z

wallop verb wallops, walloping, walloped (informal)
to wallop someone is to hit or beat them

wallow verb wallows, wallowing, wallowed
1 to wallow is to roll about in water or mud
2 to wallow in something is to get great pleasure from it *They are wallowing in luxury.*

wallpaper noun wallpapers
wallpaper is paper used to cover the walls of rooms

walnut noun walnuts
a kind of nut with a wrinkled surface

walrus noun walruses
a large Arctic sea animal that looks like a large seal and has two long tusks

waltz noun waltzes
a dance with three beats to a bar
waltz verb waltzes, waltzing, waltzed
to waltz is to dance a waltz

wand noun wands
a short thin rod used by a magician, wizard, or fairy

wander verb wanders, wandering, wandered
1 to wander is to go about without trying to reach a particular place 2 to wander, or wander off, is to stray or get lost *Don't let the sheep wander.* **wanderer** noun

wane verb wanes, waning, waned
1 the moon wanes when its bright area gets gradually smaller 2 to wane is to become less or smaller or less strong *His popularity was waning.*

wangle verb wangles, wangling, wangled (informal)
to wangle something is to get it or arrange it by trickery or clever planning *I'll see if I can wangle you a ticket to the match.*

want verb wants, wanting, wanted
1 to want something is to feel that you would like to have it or do it 2 to want something is also to need it *Your hair wants cutting.*

want noun wants
1 a want is a wish to have something
2 want of something is a lack of it *They died for want of water.*

wanted adjective
someone is wanted when they are being looked for by the police as a suspected criminal *He was a wanted man.*

war noun wars
1 war is fighting between nations or armies; a war is a period of fighting 2 a war is also a serious struggle or effort against something bad such as crime or disease

warble verb warbles, warbling, warbled
to sing gently, the way some birds do
warble noun warbles
a warbling sound

ward noun wards
1 a long room with beds for patients in a hospital 2 a child looked after by a guardian
ward verb wards, warding, warded
to ward something off is to keep it away *He put his arms up to ward off the blows.*

–ward or **–wards** suffix
an ending for words such as *backward* and *homewards*, which show direction

warden noun wardens
1 an official in charge of a hostel or college, or who supervises something
2 a traffic warden

warder noun warders
an official in charge of prisoners in a prison

wardrobe noun wardrobes
1 a cupboard to hang your clothes in
2 a stock of clothes or costumes

warehouse noun warehouses
a large building where goods are stored

wares plural noun
goods offered for sale

warfare noun
warfare is fighting or waging war

warhead noun **warheads**
the explosive head of a missile

warlike adjective
warlike people are fond of fighting or are likely to start a war

warm adjective **warmer, warmest**
1 fairly hot; not cold or cool **2** warm clothes are thick and keep you warm **3** a warm person is enthusiastic or friendly *They gave us a warm welcome.* **4** (informal) close to the right answer, or to something hidden *You're getting warm now.*

warm verb **warms, warming, warmed**
1 to warm something or someone is to make them warm **2** to warm, or warm up, is to become warm **to warm up** is to do gentle exercises to prepare yourself before playing sport

warmly adverb
1 you are warmly dressed when you are dressed in warm clothes **2** to warmly welcome or greet someone is to do it in a very friendly way

warmth noun
1 warmth is being warm or keeping warm *The cattle huddled together for warmth.* **2** warmth is also being friendly and enthusiastic *She was touched by the warmth of their welcome.*

warn verb **warns, warning, warned**
to warn someone is to tell them about a danger or difficulty that might affect them

warning noun **warnings**
something said or written to warn someone

warp (say worp) verb **warps, warping, warped**
1 to warp, or be warped, is to become bent or twisted out of shape because of dampness or heat **2** to warp someone's ideas or judgement is to distort them *Jealousy warped his mind.*

warrant noun **warrants**
a document that gives the police the right to arrest someone or search a place

warrant verb **warrants, warranting, warranted**
to warrant something is to justify or deserve it *Nothing warrants such rudeness.*

warren noun **warrens**
a piece of ground where there are many rabbit burrows

warrior noun **warriors**
someone who fights in battles; a soldier

warship noun **warships**
a ship designed for use in war

wart noun **warts**
a small hard lump on your skin

wary adjective **warier, wariest**
cautious and careful *I gave the tiger a wary glance.* **warily** adverb **wariness** noun

was
1st and 3rd person singular past tense of be *I was very angry. She was a brave soldier.*

wash verb **washes, washing, washed**
1 to wash something is to clean it with water **2** you wash when you clean yourself with water **3** to wash is to flow over or against something *Waves washed over the beach.* **4** to be washed somewhere is to be carried along by the force of moving water *The boxes were washed overboard.* **5** (informal) an explanation or excuse won't wash when it is not acceptable or believable *That story just won't wash.* **to wash up** is to wash the dishes and cutlery after a meal

wash noun **washes**
1 the action of washing **2** the disturbed water behind a moving ship **3** a thin coating of colour or paint

washable adjective
able to be washed without being damaged

washbasin noun **washbasins**
a small basin with taps, holding water for washing your hands and face

washer noun **washers**
1 a small ring of metal or rubber placed between two surfaces, especially under a bolt or screw, to fit them tightly together **2** a washing machine

a
b
c
d
e
f
g
h
i
j
k
l
m
n
o
p
q
r
s
t
u
v
w
x
y
z

A
B
C
D
E
F
G
H
I
J
K
L
M
N
O
P
Q
R
S
T
U
V
W
X
Y
Z

washing noun
washing is clothes that need to be washed or have been washed

washing machine noun washing machines
a machine for washing clothes

washing-up noun
washing-up is washing the dishes and cutlery after a meal

wash-out noun wash-outs (informal)
a complete failure

wasn't
short for *was not*

wasp noun wasps
a stinging insect with black and yellow stripes across its body

wastage noun
wastage is losing something by waste

waste verb wastes, wasting, wasted
1 to waste something is to use more of it than you need to, or to use it without getting much value from it 2 to waste something is also to fail to use it *You are wasting a good opportunity.* **to waste away** is to become thinner and weaker

waste adjective
1 left over or thrown away because it is not wanted *What shall we do with all this waste paper?* 2 not used or usable *We came to an area of waste land.*

waste noun wastes
1 a waste is wasting something or not using it well *It's a waste of time.* 2 waste is things that are not wanted or used 3 a waste is also an area of desert or frozen land *We flew over the wastes of Alaska.*

wasteful adjective
wasting things or not using them well
wastefully adverb

watch verb watches, watching, watched
1 to watch someone or something is to look at them for some time 2 to watch, or watch out, is to be on guard or ready for something to happen *Watch for the light to change.* 3 to watch something is also to take care of it *His job is to watch the sheep.*

watch noun watches
1 a device like a small clock, usually worn on a person's wrist 2 a period of being on guard or on duty

watchdog noun watchdogs
a dog kept to guard buildings

watchful adjective
alert and watching carefully
watchfully adverb **watchfulness** noun

watchman noun watchmen
someone whose job is to guard a building at night

water noun waters
1 water is a transparent colourless liquid that is a compound of hydrogen and oxygen 2 a water is a sea or lake 3 water is also the state of the tide *The sea is at high water.*

water verb waters, watering, watered
1 to water a plant is to sprinkle water over it *Have you watered the flowers?* 2 to water an animal is to give it water to drink 3 your eyes or mouth water when they produce tears or saliva *The smell of toast makes my mouth water.* **to water something down** is to dilute it or make it weaker

watercolour noun watercolours
1 a paint that can be mixed with water 2 a painting done with this kind of paint

watercress noun
a kind of cress that grows in water

water cycle noun
the process by which water falls to the ground as rain and snow, runs into rivers and lakes, flows into the sea, evaporates into the air and forms clouds, and then falls to the ground again
Please see illustration on following page.

waterfall noun waterfalls
a place where a river or stream flows over a cliff or large rock

watering can noun watering cans
a container with a long spout, for watering plants

water cycle

cloud
rain
snow
lake
river
sun
evaporation
sea

waterlogged adjective
waterlogged ground is so wet it cannot soak up any more water

watermark noun **watermarks**
1 a mark showing the level of water 2 a faint design in some types of paper, which you can see if you hold it up to the light

waterproof adjective
able to keep water out *a waterproof jacket*

water–skiing noun
the sport of skimming over the surface of water on flat boards (**water-skis**) while being towed by a motor boat

watertight adjective
1 made so that water cannot get into it 2 a watertight (for example) excuse or plan is carefully prepared so that it has no mistakes or weaknesses

waterway noun **waterways**
a river or canal that ships can travel on

waterworks noun
a place with pumping machinery for supplying water to a district

watery adjective
1 like water 2 full of water *You have watery eyes.*

watt noun **watts**
a unit of electric power

wave verb **waves, waving, waved**
1 to wave is to move your hand from side to side, usually to say hello or goodbye 2 you wave something, or it waves, when it moves from side to side or up and down *Flags were waving in the wind.* 3 to wave hair is to make it curl

wave noun **waves**
1 a moving ridge on the surface of water, especially on the sea 2 a curling piece of hair 3 (in science) one of the to-and-fro movements in which sound and light and electricity travel 4 the action of waving your hand *He gave us a little wave.* 5 a sudden build-up of something strong *She felt a wave of anger.*

wavelength noun **wavelengths**
the size of a sound wave or electric wave

waver verb **wavers, wavering, wavered**
1 to waver is to be unsteady or uncertain *They wavered between two choices.* 2 to waver is also to move unsteadily

wavy adjective **wavier, waviest**
full of waves or curves

a b c d e f g h i j k l m n o p q r s t u v **w** x y z

A B C D E F G H I J K L M N O P Q R S T U V **W** X Y Z

wax¹ noun waxes
wax is a soft substance that melts easily, used for making candles, crayons, and polish **waxy** adjective

wax verb waxes, waxing, waxed
to wax something is to cover it with wax

wax² verb waxes, waxing, waxed
the moon waxes when its bright area gets gradually larger

waxwork noun waxworks
a model made of wax, especially a full-size model of a person

way noun ways
1 how something is done; a method or manner 2 the way to a place is how you get there 3 a road or path leading from one place to another 4 a distance *Is it a long way?* 5 a respect *It's a good idea in some ways.* 6 a condition or state *Things are in a bad way.* **to get your own way** is to make people let you have what you want **in the way** blocking something or stopping something from progressing **no way** (informal) that is impossible; that is not true

WC
short for **water closet**, used especially on a plan or a sign showing where a lavatory is

we pronoun
a word used by someone to mean 'I and someone else' or 'I and others'

weak adjective weaker, weakest
1 without much strength or energy 2 easy to break, bend, or defeat 3 poor at doing something **weakly** adverb

weaken verb weakens, weakening, weakened
1 to weaken something is to make it weaker 2 to weaken is to become weaker

weakling noun weaklings
a weak person

weakness noun weaknesses
1 weakness is being weak 2 a weakness a person has is one of their faults or something they don't do well 3 a weakness

is also something you cannot help liking *Chocolate is my weakness.*

wealth noun
1 wealth is a lot of money or property 2 a wealth of something is a lot of it *The book has a wealth of illustrations.*

wealthy adjective wealthier, wealthiest
someone is wealthy when they have a lot of money or property

weapon noun weapons
something used to harm or kill people in a battle or fight

wear verb wears, wearing, wore, worn
1 to wear something is to be dressed in it 2 to wear something is to damage it by rubbing or using it; to wear is to become damaged like this *The carpet has worn thin.* 3 to last *This cloth wears well.* **to wear off** is to become less strong or intense **to wear out** is to become weak or useless **to wear someone out** is to make them very tired **wearer** noun

wear noun
1 wear is clothes *Where can I find children's wear?* 2 wear is gradual damage done by rubbing or using something

weary adjective wearier, weariest
very tired **wearily** adverb **weariness** noun

weasel noun weasels
a small fierce animal with a slender body

weather noun
weather is the rain, snow, wind, sunshine, and temperature at a particular time or place **to be under the weather** is to feel ill or depressed

weather verb weathers, weathering, weathered
1 to weather is to become worn because of being exposed to the weather 2 to weather something is to make it suffer the effects of the weather *The wind and rain have weathered the cliffs.* 3 you weather a difficulty when you come through it successfully *They weathered the storm.*

weave verb weaves, weaving, wove, woven
1 to weave material or baskets is to make them by crossing threads or strips over and under each other **2** to weave is to twist and turn *He wove skilfully through the traffic.* **weaver** noun

web noun webs
1 a net of thin sticky threads that spiders spin to catch insects **2** something complicated *We were caught up in a web of lies.* **3** a computer network, especially the Internet

webbed adjective
webbed feet have toes joined by pieces of skin, as ducks' feet do

webcam noun webcams
a camera that films things that are happening and broadcasts them live over the Internet

website noun websites
a place on the Internet where you can get information

wed verb weds, wedding, wedded or wed
to wed someone is to marry them

we'd
short for *we had* or *we should* or *we would*

wedding noun weddings
the ceremony when a man and woman get married

wedge noun wedges
1 a piece of wood or metal or plastic that is thick at one end and thin at the other, pushed between things to force them apart or to hold them tight **2** something shaped like a wedge *a wedge of cheese*

wedge verb wedges, wedging, wedged
to wedge something is to hold it in place, especially with a wedge

Wednesday noun Wednesdays
the fourth day of the week

 TOP TIPS
There is a tricky bit in **Wednesday** —there is an **e** in the middle.

weed noun weeds
a wild plant that grows where it is not wanted

weed verb weeds, weeding, weeded
to weed the ground is to remove weeds from it

weedy adjective weedier, weediest
1 full of weeds **2** thin and weak

week noun weeks
1 a period of seven days, especially from Sunday to the following Saturday **2** the part of the week that doesn't include the weekend

weekday noun weekdays
any day except Saturday and Sunday

weekend noun weekends
Saturday and Sunday

weekly adjective, adverb
every week

weep verb weeps, weeping, wept
to cry or shed tears

weeping willow noun weeping willows
a kind of willow tree that has drooping branches

weigh verb weighs, weighing, weighed
1 to weigh something is to find out how heavy it is **2** to weigh a certain amount is to have that as its weight *How much do you weigh?* **to weigh someone down** is to make them unhappy or trouble them **to weigh something down** is to hold it down with something heavy **to weigh something up** is to think about it carefully before deciding what to do

weight noun weights
1 weight is the measure of how heavy something is **2** a weight is a piece of metal of known weight, used on scales to weigh things **3** a weight is also a heavy object, used to hold things down

weightless adjective
astronauts in spacecraft are weightless when they float around because there is no gravity **weightlessness** noun

a
b
c
d
e
f
g
h
i
j
k
l
m
n
o
p
q
r
s
t
u
v
W
x
y
z

A
B
C
D
E
F
G
H
I
J
K
L
M
N
O
P
Q
R
S
T
U
V
W
X
Y
Z

weightlifting noun
weightlifting is the sport or exercise of lifting heavy weights

weighty adjective weightier, weightiest
1 heavy **2** important *These are weighty matters.*

weir (say weer) noun weirs
a small dam across a river or canal to control the flow of water

weird (say weerd) adjective weirder, weirdest
very strange or unnatural **weirdly** adverb **weirdness** noun

 TOP TIPS
In **weird**, **e** before **i** is the right way round.

welcome noun welcomes
a kind or friendly greeting or reception
welcome adjective
1 that you are glad to get or see *This is a welcome surprise.* **2** allowed or free to do or take something *You are welcome to use my bicycle.*
welcome verb welcomes, welcoming, welcomed
to welcome someone or something is to show that you are pleased when they arrive

weld verb welds, welding, welded
to weld pieces of metal or plastic together is to join them by using heat or pressure **welder** noun

welfare noun
welfare is people's health, happiness, and comfort

welfare state noun
a system of paying for health care and other social services from public funds

well¹ noun wells
a deep hole dug or drilled to get water or oil out of the ground

well² adverb better, best
1 in a good or successful way *He can play the piano quite well now.* **2** thoroughly *Wash your hands well.* **3** actually; probably *It may*

well be our last chance. **as well** also **to be well off** is to be fairly rich or fortunate
well adjective
1 in good health *She is not well.* **2** good or satisfactory *All is well.*

we'll
short for *we shall* or *we will*

well–being noun
well-being is health or happiness

wellington boots or wellingtons plural noun
rubber or plastic waterproof boots

well–known adjective
known to many people

well–mannered adjective
having good manners

went
past tense of **go** verb *I went out to the cinema.*

wept
past tense and past participle of **weep** *She wept bitterly when she left. I could have wept with pride.*

were
plural and 2nd person singular past tense of **be** *My brothers were very helpful. You were a lovely baby.*

we're
short for *we are*

werewolf noun werewolves
in stories, a person who sometimes changes into a wolf

west noun
1 the direction where the sun sets **2** the part of a country or city that is in this direction
west adjective, adverb
1 towards the west or in the west **2** coming from the west *There was a west wind blowing.*

westerly adjective
a westerly wind is one that blows from the west

western adjective
from or to do with the west

western noun westerns
a film or story about the people of western America in the 19th century and early 20th century

westward or
westwards adjective, adverb
towards the west

wet adjective wetter, wettest
1 covered or soaked in water or other liquid 2 not yet set or dry *Watch out for wet paint.* 3 rainy *It's been wet here all day.*
wetness noun

wet verb wets, wetting, wet or wetted
to wet something is to make it wet

wet blanket noun wet blankets
someone who is gloomy and who prevents other people from enjoying themselves

wet suit noun wet suits
a rubber suit that clings to the skin, worn by divers and windsurfers to keep them warm and dry

we've
short for *we have*

whack verb whacks, whacking, whacked
to whack someone or something is to hit them hard

whack noun whacks
a hard hit or blow

whale noun whales
a very large sea animal

whaler noun whalers
a person or ship that hunts whales

whaling noun
whaling is hunting whales

wharf (say worf) noun wharves or wharfs
a quay where ships are loaded or unloaded

what determiner
1 used to ask the amount or kind of something *What kind of bike have you got?*
2 used to say how strange or great a person or thing is *What a fool you are!*

what pronoun
1 what thing or things *What did you say?*
2 the thing that *This is what you must do.*

whatever pronoun
1 anything or everything *Do whatever you like.* 2 no matter what *I'll be there whatever happens.*

whatever determiner
of any kind or amount *Get whatever help you can.*

wheat noun
wheat is a cereal plant from which flour is made

wheel noun wheels
1 a round device that turns on an axle passing through its centre. Wheels are used to move vehicles or work machinery
2 a horizontal revolving disc on which clay is made into a pot

wheel verb wheels, wheeling, wheeled
1 to wheel a bicycle or cart is to push it along on its wheels 2 to wheel is to move in a curve or circle *The line of soldiers wheeled to the right.*

wheelbarrow noun wheelbarrows
a small cart with one wheel at the front and two handles at the back

wheelchair noun wheelchairs
a chair on wheels for a person who cannot walk

wheeze verb wheezes, wheezing, wheezed
to make a whistling or gasping noise as you breathe

whelk noun whelks
a shellfish that looks like a snail

when adverb
at what time *When can you come to tea?*

when conjunction
1 at the time that *The bird flew away when I moved.* 2 because; considering that *Why do you smoke when you know it is dangerous?*

a b c d e f g h i j k l m n o p q r s t u v w x y z

A B C D E F G H I J K L M N O P Q R S T U V

W

X Y Z

whenever conjunction
at any time; every time *Whenever I see him, he's smiling.*

where adverb, conjunction
1 in or to what place *Where have you put the glue?* **2** in or to that place *Leave it where it is.*

whereabouts adverb
roughly where; in what area *Whereabouts is Timbuktu?*

whereabouts noun
the place where something is *Have you any idea of her whereabouts?*

whereas conjunction
but on the other hand *Some people like sailing, whereas others hate it.*

whereupon conjunction
after that; and then

wherever adverb, conjunction
in or to whatever place; no matter where

whether conjunction
used to introduce more than one possibility *I don't know whether they are here or not.*

whey noun
whey is the watery liquid left when milk forms curds

which determiner
what particular *Which way did he go?*

which pronoun
1 what person or thing *Which is your desk?* **2** the person or thing just mentioned *Here's my book, which you asked me to bring.*

whichever pronoun, determiner
that or those which; any which *Take whichever you like. Choose whichever cake you prefer.*

whiff noun whiffs
a slight smell of something *He caught a whiff of perfume as she walked past him.*

while conjunction
1 during the time that; as long as *She was singing while she worked.* **2** but; although *She is fair, while her sister is dark.*

while noun
a period of time *We have waited all this while.*

while verb whiles, whiling, whiled
to while away time is to pass it doing something leisurely *It poured all that afternoon, and the little company in the lighthouse whiled away the time playing cards.* – Enid Blyton, *Five Go to Demon's Rocks*

whilst conjunction
while

whim noun whims
a sudden desire to do or have something

whimper verb whimpers, whimpering, whimpered
to cry with a low trembling sound

whimper noun whimpers
a sound of whimpering

whine verb whines, whining, whined
1 to whine is to make a long high piercing sound **2** to whine is also to complain in an annoying way

whine noun whines
a whining sound

whinny verb whinnies, whinnying, whinnied
a horse whinnies when it neighs gently

whip noun whips
a cord or strip of leather fixed to a handle and used for hitting people or animals

whip verb whips, whipping, whipped
1 to whip a person or animal is to beat them with a whip **2** to whip cream is to beat it until it becomes thick and frothy **to whip something out** (informal) is to take it out quickly or suddenly **to whip something up** is to stir up people's feelings *They quickly whipped up support for the idea.*

whirl verb whirls, whirling, whirled
you whirl something round, or it whirls, when it turns or spins very quickly

whirl noun whirls
when something turns or spins very quickly

whirlpool noun whirlpools
a strong current of water going round in a circle and pulling things towards it

whirlwind noun whirlwinds
a very strong wind that whirls around or blows in a spiral

whirr verb whirrs, whirring, whirred
to make a continuous buzzing sound *The light startled the creatures, and one of them took to the air, its wings whirring heavily through the dust. — Neil Gaiman, Coraline*

whirr noun whirrs
a continuous buzzing sound

whisk verb whisks, whisking, whisked
1 to whisk cream or eggs is to beat them until they are thick or frothy 2 to whisk something somewhere is to move it there very quickly *A waiter whisked away my plate.*

whisk noun whisks
1 a device for whisking eggs or cream 2 a whisking movement

whisker noun whiskers
1 whiskers are the long stiff hairs on the face of a cat or other animal 2 you can refer to the hair growing on a man's face as his whiskers

whisky noun whiskies
a kind of very strong alcoholic drink

whisper verb whispers, whispering, whispered
to speak very softly or secretly

whisper noun whispers
a very soft voice or sound

whist noun
whist is a card game usually for four people

whistle verb whistles, whistling, whistled
1 you whistle when you make a shrill or musical sound by blowing through your lips 2 something whistles when it makes a shrill sound *The wind whistled through the forest.*

whistle noun whistles
1 a whistling sound 2 a device that makes a shrill sound when you blow into it

white adjective whiter, whitest
1 of the very lightest colour, like snow or milk 2 having light-coloured skin 3 white coffee is coffee with milk

white noun whites
1 a white colour 2 the substance round the yolk of an egg, which turns white when it is cooked

white–hot adjective
something is white-hot when it is extremely hot, or so hot that heated metal looks white

whiten verb whitens, whitening, whitened
1 to whiten something is to make it white 2 to whiten is to become white

Whitsun noun
Whitsun is Whit Sunday, or the period around it.

Whit Sunday noun
Whit Sunday is the seventh Sunday after Easter.

whiz verb whizzes, whizzing, whizzed
1 to whiz is to move very quickly 2 to whiz is also to sound like something rushing through the air

who pronoun
1 which person or people *Who threw that?* 2 the person or people spoken about *These are the boys who did it.*

whoever pronoun
any person who *Whoever comes is welcome.*

whole adjective
1 all of something *Could you eat a whole pizza?* 2 not broken or damaged

whole noun wholes
a complete thing; all the parts of something
on the whole considering everything; mainly

wholemeal adjective
wholemeal flour or bread is made from the whole grain of wheat

whole number noun whole numbers
a number without a fraction

a
b
c
d
e
f
g
h
i
j
k
l
m
n
o
p
q
r
s
t
u
v
w
x
y
z

A
B
C
D
E
F
G
H
I
J
K
L
M
N
O
P
Q
R
S
T
U
V
W
X
Y
Z

wholesale adjective, adverb
1 wholesale goods are sold in large quantities to shops that then sell them again to customers **2** on a large scale; including everybody or everything *There has been wholesale destruction.*

wholesome adjective
healthy and good for you *We all need wholesome food.*

wholly adverb
completely or entirely

whom pronoun
a word used for **who** when it is the object of a verb or comes after a preposition, as in *the boy whom I saw* or *the boy to whom I spoke*

whoop (say woop) noun **whoops**
a loud excited cry

whooping cough
(say **hoop**-ing-kof) noun
whooping cough is an illness that makes you cough and gasp

who's
short for *who has* or *who is*

whose adjective, pronoun
1 belonging to what person *Whose bike is that?* **2** of which; of whom *the girl whose party we went to*

why adverb
for what reason or purpose

wick noun **wicks**
1 the string that goes through the middle of a candle and is lit to give a flame **2** the strip of material that you light in a lamp or heater that uses oil

wicked adjective **wickeder, wickedest**
1 very bad or cruel; doing things that are wrong **2** mischievous *He gave a wicked smile.* **3** (informal) very fine or good *That's a wicked goal!* **wickedly** adverb **wickedness** noun

wicker or **wickerwork** noun
wicker or wickerwork is reeds or canes woven together to make baskets and furniture

wicket noun **wickets**
1 in cricket, each set of three stumps with two bails on top of them **2** the part of a cricket ground between or near the wickets

wicketkeeper noun **wicketkeepers**
the fielder in cricket who stands behind the batsman's wicket

wide adjective **wider, widest**
1 measuring a lot from one side to the other *The river was wide.* **2** from one side to the other *The room is 4 metres wide.* **3** covering a large range *She has a wide knowledge of birds.*

wide adverb **wider, widest**
1 you are wide awake when you are completely or fully awake **2** to open or spread something wide is to open or spread it as far as possible **3** far from the target *The shot went wide.* **4** over a large area *She travelled far and wide.*

widely adverb
among many people *They are widely admired.*

widen verb **widens, widening, widened**
1 to widen something is to make it wider **2** to widen is to become wider

widespread adjective
existing or found in many places; common

widow noun **widows**
a woman whose husband has died

widower noun **widowers**
a man whose wife has died

width noun **widths**
the width of something is how much it measures from one side to the other

wield (say weeld) verb **wields, wielding, wielded**
to wield a weapon or tool is to hold it and use it *a picture of a knight wielding a sword*

wife noun **wives**
the woman that a man has married

wig noun **wigs**
a covering of false hair worn on the head

wiggle verb wiggles, wiggling, wiggled
to wiggle something is to move it from side to side

wiggle noun wiggles
a wiggling movement

wigwam noun wigwams
the tent of a Native American

wild adjective wilder, wildest
1 wild animals and plants live or grow in their natural state and are not looked after by people 2 wild land is in its natural state and has not been changed by people 3 not controlled; violent or angry *His behaviour became more and more wild. She went wild when she saw the mess.* 4 very foolish or unreasonable *They do have wild ideas.* **wildly** adverb in a way that is not controlled *My heart was beating wildly.* **wildness** noun

wild noun wilds
1 animals live in the wild when they live in their natural environment 2 the wilds are areas of a country far from towns and cities, where there are few people

wilderness noun wildernesses
an area of wild country; a desert

wildlife noun
wildlife is wild animals in their natural setting

wilful adjective
1 someone is wilful when they are determined to do exactly what they want *What a wilful child.* 2 something is wilful when it is done deliberately *This is wilful disobedience.* **wilfully** adverb **wilfulness** noun

will[1] verb past tense would
used to refer to the future *I will be there at 12 o'clock.*

will[2] noun wills
1 will is the power to use your mind to decide and control what you do 2 someone's will is what they choose or want *He was forced to write the letter against his will.* 3 someone's will to do something is their determination to do it *She has a strong will to succeed.* 4 a will is a legal document saying what is to be done with someone's possessions after they die

willing adjective
ready and happy to do what is wanted *Are you willing to help?* **willingly** adverb **willingness** noun

willow noun willows
a tree with thin flexible branches, often growing near water

wilt verb wilts, wilting, wilted
a plant wilts when it loses freshness and droops *'A fairy flower bracelet doesn't wilt until all the fairy dust wears off,' Flora explained.* — Gwyneth Rees, *Fairy Dust*

wily adjective wilier, wiliest
crafty or cunning **wiliness** noun

wimp noun wimps (informal)
a feeble or timid person

win verb wins, winning, won
1 to win a contest or game or battle is to do better than your opponents 2 to win something is to get it by using effort or in a competition *She won second prize.*

win noun wins
a success or victory

wince verb winces, wincing, winced
to make a slight movement because you are in pain or embarrassed

winch noun winches
a device for lifting or pulling things, using a rope or cable that goes round a wheel or drum

winch verb winches, winching, winched
to winch something is to lift it or pull it with a winch

wind[1] (rhymes with **tinned**) noun winds
1 wind, or a wind, is a current of air 2 wind is gas in the stomach or intestines that makes you uncomfortable 3 wind is also breath used for a purpose, such as running 4 in an orchestra, the wind is the wind instruments

a
b
c
d
e
f
g
h
i
j
k
l
m
n
o
p
q
r
s
t
u
v
w
x
y
z

A
B
C
D
E
F
G
H
I
J
K
L
M
N
O
P
Q
R
S
T
U
V
W
X
Y
Z

wind² (rhymes with **find**) verb **winds, winding, wound**
1 something like a road or river winds when it twists and turns *The river winds down the valley.* **2** to wind something is to wrap or twist it round something else *She wound her scarf round her neck.* **3** to wind, or wind up, a watch or clock is to tighten its spring so that it works **to wind up somewhere** is to end up there *They wound up in prison.*

windfall noun **windfalls**
1 a fruit blown down from a tree **2** a piece of unexpected good luck, especially a sum of money

wind instrument noun **wind instruments**
a musical instrument played by blowing, such as a flute or clarinet

windmill noun **windmills**
a mill with four long arms called *sails* which are turned by the wind

window noun **windows**
1 an opening in a wall or roof to let in light and air, usually filled with glass **2** the glass in a window opening **3** (in computing) an area on a computer screen used for a particular purpose

windpipe noun **windpipes**
the tube through which air reaches your lungs

windscreen noun **windscreens**
the window at the front of a motor vehicle

windsurfing noun
windsurfing is surfing on a board with a sail fixed to it **windsurfer** noun

wind turbine noun **wind turbines**
an upright machine with large vanes that rotate in the wind to generate electricity

windward adjective
facing the wind, especially on a ship

windy adjective **windier, windiest**
with a lot of wind *It's a windy day today.*

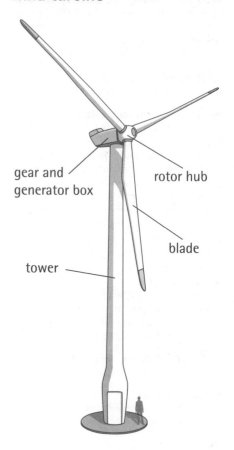

wind turbine

gear and generator box

rotor hub

blade

tower

wine noun **wines**
1 an alcoholic drink made from grapes or other plants **2** a dark red colour

wing noun **wings**
1 a bird's or insect's wings are the parts it uses for flying **2** an aircraft's wings are the long flat parts that stick out from its sides and support it in the air **3** a part of a building that extends from the main part **4** each side of a theatre stage, out of sight of the audience **5** the part of a motor vehicle's body above a wheel **6** each of the players in football and other ball games whose place is at the side of the field **7** a section of a political party, having

particular views **on the wing** flying **to take wing** is to fly away

wing verb **wings, winging, winged**
1 to wing someone is to wound them in the side **2** a bird wings its way when it flies a long way

winged adjective
winged insects or other creatures have wings *Pegasus was a mythical winged horse.*

wingless adjective
wingless insects have no wings

wingspan noun **wingspans**
the distance across the wings of a bird or aeroplane

wink verb **winks, winking, winked**
1 you wink when you close and open one of your eyes quickly **2** a light winks when it flickers or twinkles *It looked like Aladdin's cave. Necklaces and bracelets hung winking from the roof of the shelter.* – Clive King, *Stig of the Dump*

wink noun **winks**
1 when you close and open one of your eyes quickly **2** a short period of sleep *I didn't sleep a wink.*

winkle noun **winkles**
a shellfish that is used for food

winkle verb **winkles, winkling, winkled**
to winkle something out is to find it with a lot of effort

winner noun **winners**
1 a person who wins something **2** (informal) something very successful *Her new book is a winner.*

winnings plural noun
the money someone wins in a game or by betting

winter noun **winters**
the coldest season of the year, between autumn and spring

wintry adverb **wintrier, wintriest**
1 wintry weather is cold, like winter
2 a wintry smile is cold and unfriendly

wipe verb **wipes, wiping, wiped**
to wipe something is to rub it gently to dry it or clean it **to wipe something out** is to destroy it or cancel it

wipe noun **wipes**
the action of wiping *Give it a quick wipe.*

wiper noun **wipers**
a device for wiping something, especially on a vehicle's windscreen

wire noun **wires**
a thin length of metal used to carry electric current or for making fences

wire verb **wires, wiring, wired**
to wire something, or wire it up, is to connect it with wires to carry electricity

wireless noun **wirelesses** (old use)
a radio set

wireless adjective
something that is wireless can send and receive signals without using wires *You can get a wireless Internet connection for your computer.*

wiring noun
wiring is the system of wires carrying electricity in a building or in a device

wiry adjective **wirier, wiriest**
1 a wiry person is lean and strong **2** wiry hair is tough and stiff

wisdom noun
1 wisdom is being wise **2** wisdom is also wise sayings or writings

wisdom tooth noun **wisdom teeth**
a molar tooth that may grow at the back of your jaw much later than the other teeth

wise adjective **wiser, wisest**
knowing or understanding many things and so able to make sensible decisions **wisely** adverb sensibly *He wisely decided to tell the truth.*

wish verb **wishes, wishing, wished**
1 to wish something, or wish to do something, is to think or say that you would like it **2** to wish someone something is to say that you hope they will get it *They wished us luck.*

a
b
c
d
e
f
g
h
i
j
k
l
m
n
o
p
q
r
s
t
u
v
w
x
y
z

A
B
C
D
E
F
G
H
I
J
K
L
M
N
O
P
Q
R
S
T
U
V
W
X
Y
Z

wish noun wishes
1 something you want 2 when you wish for something *Make a wish. We send you our best wishes.*

wishbone noun wishbones
a forked bone from the breast of a chicken or other bird

wisp noun wisps
a thin piece or line of something light or fluffy, such as hair or smoke

wistful adjective
thinking sadly about something you can no longer have *Pollyanna laughed again, but she sighed, too; and in the gathering twilight her face looked thin and wistful.* – Eleanor H. Porter, *Pollyanna* **wistfully** adverb **wistfulness** noun

wit noun wits
1 wit is intelligence 2 wit is also a clever kind of humour 3 a wit is a witty person **to keep your wits about you** is to stay alert

witch noun witches
a woman who is believed to use magic

witchcraft noun
witchcraft is using magic, especially to make bad things happen

witch doctor noun witch doctors
a magician who belongs to a tribe and is thought to heal people

with preposition
there are many meanings, of which the most important are: 1 having *I saw a man with a wooden leg.* 2 in the company of or accompanied by *I came with a friend.* 3 using *Hit it with a hammer.* 4 against *They fought with each other.* 5 because of *He shook with laughter.* 6 towards or concerning *Be careful with that.*

withdraw verb withdraws, withdrawing, withdrew, withdrawn
1 to withdraw something is to take it away or take it back *She withdrew her offer.*
2 to withdraw is to retreat or drop out of something *The troops have withdrawn*

from the frontier. His injury meant he had to withdraw from the race.

withdrawal noun withdrawals
1 withdrawal is when someone withdraws something or withdraws from a place
2 a withdrawal is an amount of money someone takes out of their bank account

wither verb withers, withering, withered
a plant withers when it shrivels or wilts

withhold verb withholds, withholding, withheld
to withhold something is to refuse to give it to someone *He has withheld his permission.*

within preposition, adverb
inside; not beyond something *Is the top shelf within your reach?*

without preposition
not having; free from *It is difficult to live without money.*

withstand verb withstands, withstanding, withstood
to withstand something is to resist it or put up with it successfully *The bridge is designed to withstand high winds.*

witness noun witnesses
1 a person who sees something happen and can describe it *There were no witnesses to the accident.* 2 a person who gives evidence in a law court

witty adjective wittier, wittiest
clever and amusing **wittily** adverb

wizard noun wizards
1 a man who has magic powers 2 a person who is very good at something *He's a wizard on the accordion.* **wizardry** noun the clever and impressive things that a computer or other machine can do

wobble verb wobbles, wobbling, wobbled
to wobble is to move unsteadily from side to side

wobble noun wobbles
a wobbling movement **wobbly** adjective

woe to woolly

woe noun woes
1 someone's woes are their troubles and misfortunes 2 woe is great sorrow

woeful adjective
1 a woeful person is very sad 2 you can say something is woeful when it is very bad or serious **woefully** adverb

wok noun woks
a deep round-bottomed frying pan used in Chinese cookery

woke
past tense of wake[1] Hana woke with a start.

woken
past participle of wake[1] Jack had woken early.

wolf noun wolves
a wild animal like a large fierce dog

woman noun women
a grown-up female human being

womb (say woom) noun wombs
the part of a female's body where babies develop before they are born

won
past tense and past participle of win verb
We won the game easily. He looks as if he has just won the lottery.

wonder verb wonders, wondering, wondered
1 to wonder about something is to be trying to decide about it I wonder what we should do next. 2 to wonder at something is to feel surprise and admiration about it

wonder noun wonders
1 wonder is a feeling of surprise and admiration 2 a wonder is something that makes you feel surprised and admiring **no wonder** it is not surprising

wonderful adjective
marvellous or excellent **wonderfully** adverb

won't
short for will not

wood noun woods
1 wood is the substance that trees

are made of 2 a wood is a lot of trees growing together

wooded adjective
a wooded area is covered with growing trees

wooden adjective
1 made of wood 2 stiff or awkward His movements were wooden.

woodland noun woodlands
land covered with trees

woodlouse noun woodlice
a small crawling creature with seven pairs of legs, living in rotten wood or damp soil. It rolls itself into a ball if it is alarmed

woodpecker noun woodpeckers
a bird that taps tree trunks with its beak to find insects

woodwind noun
in an orchestra, the woodwind is the wind instruments that are usually made of wood or plastic, such as the clarinet and oboe

woodwork noun
1 woodwork is making things with wood 2 woodwork is also things made out of wood

woodworm noun woodworm or woodworms
the larva of a beetle that bores into wood

woody adjective woodier, woodiest
1 like wood or made of wood 2 full of trees

wool noun
1 wool is the thick soft hair of sheep or goats 2 wool is also thread or cloth made from this hair

woollen adjective
made of wool

woollens plural noun
clothes made of wool

woolly adjective woollier, woolliest
1 covered with wool 2 made of wool or like wool 3 vague and not clear He has woolly ideas. **woolliness** noun

a b c d e f g h i j k l m n o p q r s t u v **W** x y z

595

A
B
C
D
E
F
G
H
I
J
K
L
M
N
O
P
Q
R
S
T
U
V
W
X
Y
Z

word noun **words**
1 a set of sounds or letters that has a meaning and is written with a space before and after it 2 a brief talk with someone *Can I have a word with you?* 3 your word is when you promise to do something *He cannot keep his word.* 4 a command or signal to do something *Run when I give the word.* 5 a message or piece of news *We sent word that we had arrived safely.*

word verb **words, wording, worded**
to word something is to express it in words

word class noun **word classes**
each of the groups (also called **parts of speech**) into which words can be divided in grammar: noun, adjective, pronoun, adverb, preposition, determiner, conjunction, interjection, verb

wording noun
the wording of something is the words used to say it

word processing noun
word processing is using a computer for writing and editing letters and documents, and for printing them out
word processor noun

wordy adjective **wordier, wordiest**
using too many words *We heard a wordy speech.*

wore
past tense of **wear** verb *She wore her new dress to the party.*

work verb **works, working, worked**
1 to work is to spend time doing something that needs effort or energy 2 to work is also to have a job or be employed *She works in a bank.* 3 something works when it operates correctly or successfully *Is the lift working?* 4 to work something is to make it act or operate *Can you work the lift?* 5 to work (for example) loose is to become gradually loose *The screw had worked loose.* **to work out** is to succeed or reach the right answer **to work something out** is to find the answer to it

work noun **works**
1 work is something that you have to do that needs effort or energy *Digging is hard work.* 2 a person's work is their job *What work do you do?* 3 at school, your work is something you write or produce *Please get on with your work quietly.* 4 a work is a piece of writing or music or painting *The book has all the works of Shakespeare.* **to be at work** is to be working

worker noun **workers**
1 someone who works 2 a bee or ant that does the work in a hive or colony but does not produce eggs

workforce noun **workforces**
the number of people who work for a business or factory

working class noun or
working classes plural noun
people who do paid manual or industrial work **working-class** adjective

workman noun **workmen**
a man who does manual work

workmanship noun
workmanship is skill in making something

workout noun **workouts**
a session of physical exercise or training

works plural noun
1 the moving parts of a machine 2 a factory or industrial site

worksheet noun **worksheets**
a sheet of paper with a set of questions about a subject for students

workshop noun **workshops**
a place where things are made or mended

world noun **worlds**
1 the world is the earth with all its countries and peoples 2 a world is a planet *The film is about creatures from another world.* 3 everything to do with a particular subject or activity *He knows a lot about the world of sport.*

worldly adjective **worldlier, worldliest**
1 to do with life on earth 2 only interested in money and possessions

world war noun **world wars**
a war involving many countries all over the world

worldwide adjective, adverb
over the whole world

World Wide Web noun
the system for keeping information on computers all over the world so that people can use it by using the Internet

worm noun **worms**
a small thin wriggling animal without legs, especially an earthworm

worm verb **worms, worming, wormed**
to worm your way somewhere is to get there by wriggling or crawling **to worm something out of someone** is to get them to tell you something secret

worn[1]
past participle of **wear** verb *I have never worn those shoes.*

worn[2] adjective
damaged because it has been rubbed or used so much **to be worn out** is to be very tired

worry verb **worries, worrying, worried**
1 to worry is to feel anxious or troubled about something **2** to worry someone is to make them feel anxious or troubled about something **3** an animal worries its prey when it holds it in its teeth and shakes it **worried** adjective

worry noun **worries**
1 worry is worrying or being anxious **2** a worry is something that makes you anxious

worse adjective, adverb
1 comparative of **bad** and **badly 2** more bad or more badly; less good or less well

worsen verb **worsens, worsening, worsened**
1 to worsen is to become worse **2** to worsen something is to make it worse

worship verb **worships, worshipping, worshipped**
to worship God or a god is to give them praise or respect **worshipper** noun

worship noun
worship is worshipping; religious ceremonies or services

worst adjective, adverb
1 superlative of **bad** and **badly 2** most bad or most badly; least good or least well

worth adjective
1 having a certain value *This stamp is worth £100.* **2** deserving something; good or important enough for something *That book is worth reading.*

worth noun
a thing's worth is its value or usefulness

worthless adjective
having no value; useless

worthwhile adjective
important or good enough to be worth doing

worthy adjective **worthier, worthiest**
deserving respect or support *The sale is for a worthy cause.* **worthily** adverb **worthiness** noun

would verb
1 past tense of the verb **will**[1] *We said we would do it. He said he would come if he could.* **2** used in polite questions or requests *Would you like some tea?*

wouldn't
short for *would not*

wound[1] (say woond) noun **wounds**
an injury done to a part of a person's or animal's body, especially one in which the skin is cut

wound verb **wounds, wounding, wounded**
1 to wound a person or animal is to give them a wound **2** to wound someone is to hurt their feelings

wound[2] (say wownd)
past tense and past participle of **wind**[2] *The path wound through the woods. She had wound a handkerchief round the cut finger.*

a
b
c
d
e
f
g
h
i
j
k
l
m
n
o
p
q
r
s
t
u
v
W
x
y
z

wove
past tense of weave *They wove in and out of the parked cars.*

woven
past participle of weave *The wizard had woven his magic.*

wrap verb wraps, wrapping, wrapped
to wrap something is to put paper or some other covering round it
wrap noun wraps
a shawl or cloak worn to keep you warm

wrapper noun wrappers
a piece of paper or plastic that something is wrapped in

wrapping noun wrappings
wrapping is material used to wrap something, especially a present

wrath (rhymes with **cloth**) noun
(old-fashioned use)
anger **wrathful** adjective angry **wrathfully** adverb

wreath (say reeth) noun wreaths
flowers and leaves and branches bound together to make a circle

wreathe (say reeth) verb wreathes, wreathing, wreathed
to be wreathed in something is to be covered in it or decorated with it *Her face was wreathed in smiles.*

wreck verb wrecks, wrecking, wrecked
to wreck something is to damage or ruin it so badly that it cannot be used again
wreck noun wrecks
a badly damaged ship or car

wreckage noun
wreckage is the pieces of something that has been wrecked

wren noun wrens
a very small brown bird

wrench verb wrenches, wrenching, wrenched
to wrench something is to pull or twist it suddenly or violently *He wrenched the door open. But at the Faun's cave a terrible surprise awaited them. The door had been wrenched off its hinges and everything lay smashed on the floor.* — C. S. Lewis, *The Lion, The Witch and the Wardrobe*

wrench noun wrenches
1 a wrenching movement 2 a tool for gripping and turning bolts or nuts

wrestle verb wrestles, wrestling, wrestled
1 to wrestle with someone is to fight them by grasping them and trying to throw them to the ground 2 to wrestle with a problem or difficulty is to struggle to solve it
wrestler noun **wrestling** noun

wretch noun wretches
someone who is unhappy, poor, or disliked

wretched (say **rech**-id) adjective
1 poor and unhappy *a wretched beggar* 2 not satisfactory or pleasant *This wretched car won't start.*

wriggle verb wriggles, wriggling, wriggled
to twist and turn your body
wriggle noun wriggles
a wriggling movement **wriggly** adjective

wring verb wrings, wringing, wrung
1 to wring something wet, or to wring it out, is to squeeze or twist it to get the water out of it 2 to wring something is to squeeze it violently *I'll wring your neck!*
wringing wet very wet; soaked

wrinkle noun wrinkles
1 wrinkles are the small lines and creases that appear in your skin as you get older 2 a small crease or line on the surface of something
wrinkle verb wrinkles, wrinkling, wrinkled
something wrinkles when wrinkles appear in or on it **wrinkled** adjective

wrist noun wrists
the joint that connects your hand to your arm

wristwatch noun wristwatches
a watch that you wear on your wrist

A B C D E F G H I J K L M N O P Q R S T U V **W** X Y Z

write verb writes, writing, wrote, written
1 to write words or signs is to put them on paper or some other surface so that people can read them **2** to write a story or play or a piece of music is to be the author or composer of it **3** to write to someone is to send them a letter **to write something off** is to think it is lost or useless

writer noun writers
a person who writes; an author

writhe (say ryth) verb writhes, writhing, writhed
to twist your body about because you are in pain or discomfort

writing noun writings
1 writing is something you write **2** your writing is the way you write

wrong adjective
1 not fair or morally right *It is wrong to cheat.* **2** incorrect *Your answer is wrong.* **3** not working properly *There's something wrong with the engine.*
wrongly adverb

wrong adverb
wrongly *You guessed wrong.*

wrong noun wrongs
something that is wrong **to be in the wrong** is to have done or said something wrong

wrong verb wrongs, wronging, wronged
to wrong someone is to do wrong to them

wrote
past tense of write *He wrote his name down.*

wrung
past tense and past participle of wring *Gran wrung her hands. Emma had wrung the paper into a ball.*

wry adjective wryer, wryest
slightly mocking or sarcastic *He gave a wry smile.*

Xx

Xmas noun (informal)
Christmas

X–ray noun X-rays
a photograph of the inside of something, especially a part of the body, made by a kind of radiation that can pass through something solid

X–ray verb X-rays, X-raying, X-rayed
to X-ray something is to make an X-ray of it

xylophone (say zy-lo-fohn) noun xylophones
a musical instrument made of wooden bars of different lengths, that you hit with small hammers

Yy

yacht (say yot) noun yachts
1 a sailing boat used for racing or cruising **2** a private ship

yachtsman or **yachtswoman** noun
yachtsmen, yachtswomen
a man or woman who sails in a yacht

yam noun yams
a tropical vegetable that grows underground

yank verb yanks, yanking, yanked
to yank something is to pull it strongly and suddenly

yap verb yaps, yapping, yapped
a small dog yaps when it makes a shrill barking sound

yap noun yaps
a shrill barking sound

a
b
c
d
e
f
g
h
i
j
k
l
m
n
o
p
q
r
s
t
u
v
w
x
y
z

A
B
C
D
E
F
G
H
I
J
K
L
M
N
O
P
Q
R
S
T
U
V
W
X
Y
Z

yard¹ noun yards
a measure of length, 36 inches or about 91 centimetres

yard² noun yards
a piece of ground beside a building, or one used for a special purpose, such as a railway yard

yarn noun yarns
1 yarn is thread spun by twisting fibres together **2** (informal) a yarn is a tale or story

yashmak noun yashmaks
a veil covering most of the face, worn by some Muslim women

yawn verb yawns, yawning, yawned
1 you yawn when you open your mouth wide and breathe in deeply because you are tired or bored **2** to yawn is also to form a wide opening *The chasm yawned in front of them.*
yawn noun yawns
an act of yawning

ye pronoun (old use)
you (referring to more than one person)

year noun years
the time that the earth takes to go right round the sun, about 365¼ days or twelve months

yearly adjective, adverb
every year

yearn verb yearns, yearning, yearned
to yearn for something is to long for it

yeast noun
yeast is a substance used in baking bread and in making beer and wine

yell noun yells
a loud cry or shout
yell verb yells, yelling, yelled
to cry or shout loudly

yellow noun yellows
the colour of ripe lemons and buttercups
yellow adjective yellower, yellowest
1 yellow in colour **2** (informal) cowardly

yelp verb yelps, yelping, yelped
to make a shrill bark or cry, as a dog does when it is hurt
yelp noun yelps
a yelping sound

yes interjection
a word used for agreeing to something

yesterday noun, adverb
the day before today

yet adverb
1 up to now; by this time *Has the postman called yet?* **2** eventually; still *I'll get even with him yet.* **3** in addition; even *She became yet more excited.*
yet conjunction
nevertheless *It is strange, yet it is true.*

yeti (say yet-ee) noun yetis
a very large hairy creature thought to live in the Himalayas

yew noun yews
an evergreen tree with red berries and dark leaves like needles

yield verb yields, yielding, yielded
1 to yield is to surrender or give in *He yielded to persuasion.* **2** to yield a crop or profit is to produce it *These trees yield good apples.*
yield noun yields
an amount produced by something *What is the yield of wheat per acre?*

yippee interjection
a shout of joy

yodel verb yodels, yodelling, yodelled
to sing or shout with your voice going rapidly from low to high notes

yoga noun
yoga is a Hindu system of exercise, meditation, and self-control

yoghurt (say yog-ert) noun yoghurts
yoghurt is milk made thick by the addition of bacteria, giving it a sharp taste

yoke noun yokes
a curved piece of wood put across the necks of animals pulling a cart

yoke verb yokes, yoking, yoked
to yoke animals is to harness them or link them by means of a yoke

yolk (rhymes with **coke**) noun yolks
the yellow part of an egg

Yom Kippur noun
the Day of Atonement, an important Jewish religious festival

yonder adverb, adjective (old use)
over there

Yorkshire pudding noun
Yorkshire puddings
a pudding made of batter and usually eaten with roast beef

you pronoun
1 the person or people someone is speaking to *Who are you?* 2 people; anyone *You can never be too sure.*

you'd
short for *you had* or *you should* or *you would*

you'll
short for *you will*

young adjective younger, youngest
having lived or existed only a short time; not old

young plural noun
an animal's or bird's young are its babies

youngster noun youngsters
a young person or child

your determiner
belonging to you *Is this your pencil?*

you're
short for *you are*

yours pronoun
belonging to you *Is this house yours?* **Yours faithfully, Yours sincerely, Yours truly**
ways of ending a letter before you sign it

yourself pronoun yourselves
you (referring to one person) and nobody else, used to refer back to the subject of a verb *Have you hurt yourself?* **by yourself** or

yourselves on your own *Did you do the work all by yourself?*

youth noun youths
1 youth is being young, or the time when you are young 2 a youth is a young man 3 youth also means young people *What do you think of today's youth?*

youth club noun youth clubs
a club providing leisure activities for young people

youthful adjective
someone is youthful when they are young or seem to be young

youth hostel noun youth hostels
a hostel where young people can stay cheaply when they are on holiday

you've
short for *you have*

yo-yo noun yo-yos
a round wooden or plastic toy that moves up and down on a string which you hold

Zz

zany adjective zanier, zaniest
funny in a crazy kind of way

zap verb zaps, zapping, zapped (informal)
1 to zap something or someone is to attack or destroy them, especially in a computer game 2 to zap is to move very quickly *Ideas zapped through his head.*

zeal noun
zeal is keenness, especially in doing what you believe to be right

zealous (say zel-us) adjective
very enthusiastic **zealously** adverb

zebra noun zebras
an African animal like a horse with black and white stripes

A
B
C
D
E
F
G
H
I
J
K
L
M
N
O
P
Q
R
S
T
U
V
W
X
Y

zebra crossing noun zebra crossings
part of a road marked with broad white stripes for pedestrians to cross

zenith noun
1 the part of the sky directly above you *The south wind began to blow and the June sunset reddened the sky to the zenith.* — Richard Adams, *Watership Down* 2 the highest point of something

zero noun zeros
nought; the figure 0

zest noun
zest is great enjoyment or enthusiasm

zigzag noun zigzags
a line or route full of sharp turns from one side to the other

zigzag verb zigzags, zigzagging, zigzagged
to move in a series of sharp turns from one side to the other *The tunnel veered to the left, zigzagged violently, and came to an end on a ledge overlooking a great void.* — Alan Garner, *The Weirdstone of Brisingamen*

zinc noun
zinc is a white metal

zip noun zips
1 a zip, or zip fastener, is a device with two rows of small teeth that fit together, used to join two pieces of material 2 a zip is also a sharp sound like a bullet going through the air 3 zip is liveliness or energy

zip verb zips, zipping, zipped
1 to zip something, or zip it up, is to fasten it with a zip 2 to zip, or zip along, is to move quickly with a sharp sound

zodiac (say zoh-di-ak) noun
an area of the sky divided into twelve equal parts, called **signs of the zodiac**, each named after a constellation

zombie noun zombies (informal)
someone who seems to be doing things without thinking, often through tiredness

zone noun zones
a district or area set aside for a particular use *This is a no-parking zone.*

zoo noun zoos
a place where wild animals are kept so that people can look at them or study them

zoology (say zoh-ol-o-jee) noun
zoology is the study of animals **zoological** adjective **zoologist** noun

zoom verb zooms, zooming, zoomed
to move very quickly, especially with a buzzing sound

zoom lens noun zoom lenses
a camera lens that can be adjusted continuously to focus on things that are close up or far away

Z

Appendices

Spelling Tips

Watch out for words which are often misspelled

an **abandoned** puppy
your email **address**
an **annual** prize
a day in **autumn**
a hot-air **balloon**
an advent **calendar**
a hairy **caterpillar**
I'm **desperate** for a cold drink!
a jam **doughnut**
a castle **dungeon**
the **eighth** floor
I'm so **embarrassed!**
the first of **February**
a **gnarled** tree trunk
a Greek **goddess**
a prison **guard**
a Girl **Guide**
a fit of **hiccups**
a **jewellery** box

a **length** of the pool
our local **library**
a bolt of **lightning**
a **miniature** doll's house
our next-door **neighbour**
a **queue** to get tickets
a football **referee**
a Chinese **restaurant**
two words which **rhyme**
a catchy **rhythm**
a pair of **scissors**
a **separate** pocket
a forward **somersault**
a plate of **spaghetti**
superhuman **strength**
a great **success**
the day after **tomorrow**
my **twelfth** birthday
next **Wednesday**

Watch out for these pairs of words, which sound the same but are spelled differently

a guitar **chord**

a **cord** of rope

a **desert** island

a scrumptious **dessert**

a **hoard** of Viking silver

hordes of shoppers

a **knight** in shining armour

a dark and stormy **night**

a cat's **paws**

a short **pause**

an amazing **sight**

the **site** of a Roman fort

a **whole** pizza

a **hole** in the road

Spelling Tips

Some tricky plurals

a radio **antenna**	a type of **fungus**
a bee's **antennae**	some poisonous **fungi**
a flowering **cactus**	a giant **octopus**
some potted **cacti**	a pair of **octopuses**
a **cupful** of sugar	a single **passer-by**
two **cupfuls** of flour	a group of **passers-by**
the tracks of a **deer**	a football **stadium**
a herd of wild **deer**	one of the Olympic **stadiums**
a baby **hippopotamus**	half a **teaspoonful**
a family of **hippopotamuses**	two **teaspoonfuls**

Watch out for these plurals of words which end in -o

an ancient **hero**	my favourite **photo**
legendary **heroes**	old family **photos**
a baked **potato**	an extinct **volcano**
roasted **potatoes**	a range of **volcanoes**
a ripe **tomato**	a grand **piano**
sliced **tomatoes**	a shop selling **pianos**

Watch out for these plurals of words which end in -f

one and a **half**	on the top **shelf**
both **halves**	a row of **shelves**
a horse's **hoof**	a tale about a **dwarf**
the sound of horses' **hooves**	Snow White and the Seven **Dwarfs**
a lettuce **leaf**	the **roof** of the cave
autumn **leaves**	a row of thatched **roofs**

Common irregular verbs

begin / began / begun
Let's **begin** again.
Max **began** to sneeze violently.
My ice cream had **begun** to melt.

break / broke / broken
Don't **break** my camera!
You **broke** your promise.
I've **broken** the strap on my watch.

bring / brought / brought
I forgot to **bring** my phone.
We **brought** our own tent.
Have you **brought** any food?

buy / bought / bought
What are you going to **buy**?
We **bought** a large tub of popcorn.
Have you **bought** my present yet?

catch / caught / caught
I didn't **catch** what you said.
Hannah **caught** the ball in one hand.
I've **caught** a nasty cold.

choose / chose / chosen
Please **choose** a seat.
I think I **chose** the wrong answer.
Have they **chosen** a name yet?

draw / drew / drawn
I wish I could **draw** better.
One of the knights **drew** his sword.
I had **drawn** a map of the island.

eat / ate / eaten
Let's **eat** outside.
Ron **ate** a sandwich for lunch.
Have you **eaten** the whole thing?

give / gave / given
Can you **give** me a lift home?
I **gave** him my email address.
You've **given** me an idea!

hide / hid / hidden
Let's **hide** in here.
The stranger **hid** his face.
Where have you **hidden** the key?

know / knew / known
Do you **know** the answer?
I never **knew** her real name.
I wish I had **known** that.

run / ran / run
I'm going to **run** in the relay race.
A fox **ran** right in front of me.
Jake had **run** all the way home.

see / saw / seen
Can you **see** anyone there?
I **saw** it with my own eyes.
I've **seen** that film five times!

sing / sang / sung
Suddenly Lisa began to **sing**.
We all **sang** 'Happy Birthday'.
Have you ever **sung** in a choir?

speak / spoke / spoken
Please **speak** clearly.
No one **spoke**.
Have you **spoken** to her yet?

swim / swam / swum
Sharks can **swim** long distances.
I **swam** ten lengths yesterday.
Have you ever **swum** in the sea?

think / thought / thought
I **think** that's a terrible idea!
I **thought** you were hungry.
I've **thought** of a good plan.

throw / threw / thrown
Throw the ball over here!
Ted **threw** his coat on the floor.
I've **thrown** the box away.

Common prefixes and suffixes

A **prefix** is a group of letters which you can add to the start of a word to change its meaning and so make a new word.
For example, **pre-** + *historic* = *prehistoric* and **re-** + *write* = *rewrite*.

anti-	means 'against', e.g. *anticlockwise*
de-	means 'undo' or 'take away', e.g. *decoding a message*
fore-	means 'before' or 'in advance', e.g. *foretelling the future*
inter-	means 'between' or 'among', e.g. *interplanetary travel*
micro-	means 'very small', e.g. *a microscope magnifies tiny objects*
mis-	means 'wrong' or 'badly', e.g. *misspelling a word*
multi-	means 'many', e.g. *a multicoloured scarf*
over-	means 'too much', e.g. *overdoing it, overeating*
post-	means 'after', e.g. *post-war Europe*
pre-	means 'before', e.g. *a prehistoric skeleton*
re-	means 'again', e.g. *rewriting a story*
semi-	means 'half', e.g. *a semicircle*
sub-	means 'below' or 'under', e.g. *a submarine travels under water*
super-	means 'above' or 'beyond', e.g. *superhuman powers*
trans-	means 'across' or 'through', e.g. *a transatlantic flight*

The following prefixes all mean 'not' and you can add them to some words to make their opposites:

dis-	e.g. *disagree, dishonest*
il-	e.g. *illegal, illogical*
im-	e.g. *imperfect, impossible*
in-	e.g. *informal, invisible*
ir-	e.g. *irregular, irrelevant*
non-	e.g. *non-fiction, nonsense*
un-	e.g. *unfriendly, unhealthy*

A **suffix** is added at the end of a word, for example, *fear* + **-less** = *fearless*.

-able or **-ible**	means 'able to be' or 'easy to', e.g *edible food*
-ess	means 'female', e.g. *goddess, lioness*
-ful	means 'full of', e.g. *a colourful costume, a painful tooth*
-ish	means 'rather like', e.g. *a greenish tinge, a smallish slice*
-less	means 'without' or 'lacking', e.g. *a fearless enemy*
-let	means 'small', e.g. *booklet, piglet*
-wards	means 'in the direction of', e.g. *heading homewards*

astronaut comes from the Greek words *astron* and *nautes*, meaning 'star sailor'

atlas is named after *Atlas*, a character in Greek mythology who was made to carry the universe on his shoulders, and who was often pictured in old books of maps.

cardigan is named after the Earl of *Cardigan*, a commander in the Crimean War whose soldiers wore a kind of woollen jacket

caterpillar comes from the Old French word *chatepelose*, meaning 'hairy cat'

conker comes from an English dialect word meaning 'a snail shell', because the game was first played with snail shells

crocodile comes from the Greek word *krokodilos*, meaning 'worm of the stones'

dandelion comes from the French word *dent-de-lion*, meaning 'lion's tooth', because of the jagged shape of its leaves

dinosaur comes from the Greek words *deinos* and *sauros*, meaning 'terrible lizard'

galaxy comes from the Greek word *galaxias*, meaning 'milky', because it used to refer only to the 'Milky Way'

hippopotamus comes from the Greek words *hippos* and *potamos*, meaning 'river horse'

leotard is named after a French trapeze artist, Jules *Léotard*, who invented it

orang-utan comes from Malay words meaning 'man of the forest'

planet comes from the Greek word *planetes*, meaning 'wanderer', because the planets appear to move among the stars

piano is short for *pianoforte*, an Italian word meaning 'soft (and) loud', because it can be played either quietly or loudly

pyjamas comes from the Persian and Urdu words *pay* and *jamah*, meaning 'leg clothing'

sandwich is named after the Earl of *Sandwich*, who is said to have invented it so that he could eat at the same time as gambling

umbrella comes from the Italian word *ombrella*, meaning 'a little shade'

volcano comes from an Italian word and is named after *Vulcan*, the Roman god of fire

wellingtons are named after the first Duke of *Wellington*, who wore long leather boots

wizard comes from an old meaning of *wise* and originally meant 'a wise person'